Tanzania

Mary Fitzpatrick

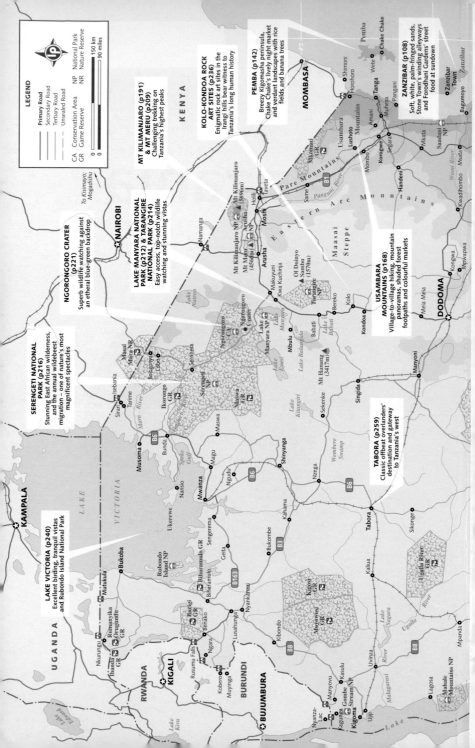

LEGEND

Primary Road
Secondary Road
Tertiary Road
Unsealed Road

CA Conservation Area   NP National Park
GR Game Reserve   NR Nature Reserve

0   150 km
0   90 miles

KOLO-KONDOA ROCK ART SITES (p236)
Enigmatic rock art sites in the Irangi hills bear witness to Tanzania's long human history

PEMBA (p142)
Breezy Kigomasha peninsula, Chake Chake's lively night market and verdant landscapes with rice fields and banana trees

MT KILIMANJARO (p191) & MT MERU (p209)
Challenging trekking on Tanzania's highest peaks

ZANZIBAR (p108)
Soft, white, palm-fringed sands, Stone Town's winding alleyways and Forodhani Gardens' street food at sundown

NGORONGORO CRATER (p221)
Superb wildlife watching against an ethereal blue-green backdrop

LAKE MANYARA NATIONAL PARK (p212) & TARANGIRE NATIONAL PARK (p214)
Easy access, top-notch wildlife watching and stunning vistas

USAMBARA MOUNTAINS (p168)
Village-to-village hiking, mountain panoramas, shaded forest footpaths and colourful markets

SERENGETI NATIONAL PARK (p216)
Stunning East African wilderness, and the annual wildebeest migration – one of nature's most magnificent spectacles

TABORA (p259)
Classic offbeat overlanders' destination and gateway to Tanzania's west

LAKE VICTORIA (p240)
Excellent birding, tranquil vistas and Rubondo Island National Park

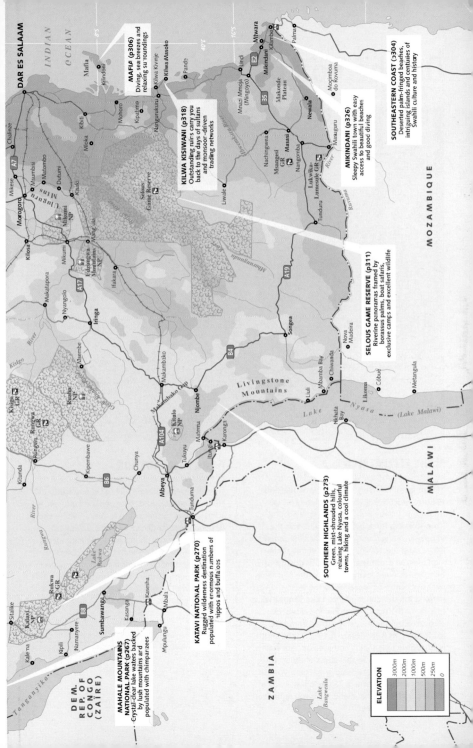

MAFIA (p306)
Diving, sea breezes and relaxing su roundings

KILWA KISIWANI (p318)
Outstanding ruins carry you back to the days of sultans and monsoon-driven trading networks

SOUTHEASTERN COAST (p304)
Deserted palm-fringed beaches, intriguing islands and centuries of Swahili culture and history

MIKINDANI (p326)
Sleepy Swahili town with easy access to beautiful beaches and gooc diving

SELOUS GAME RESERVE (p311)
Riverine panoramas framed by borassus palms, boat safaris, exclusive camps and excellent wildlife

SOUTHERN HIGHLANDS (p273)
Green, mist-shrouded hills, relaxing Lake Nyasa, colourful towns, hiking and a cool climate

KATAVI NATIONAL PARK (p270)
Rugged wilderness destination populated with enormous numbers of hippos and buffa oes

MAHALE MOUNTAINS NATIONAL PARK (p267)
Crystal-clear lake waters backed by lush mountains and populated with chimpanzees

ELEVATION
3000m
2000m
1000m
500m
250m
0

On the Road

MARY FITZPATRICK

It had been a mostly very dusty and bumpy 180km from Makuyuni (where the tarmac ends) to Kolo, which would be a completely undistinguished village but for its proximity to the **Kolo-Kondoa Rock Art Sites** (p236) and the impressive carved door here at the Antiquities Office. And the 180km yet to go before reaching Dodoma promised to be just as dusty and bumpy. Yet, I was loving every minute of it here, near the centre of Tanzania. To the west, the vast hinterlands stretching off into **Lake Tanganyika** (p268). To the north, stampeding wildebeests, elephants, zebras and giraffe, the **Serengeti** (p216) and **Mt Kilimanjaro** (p191). To the south, rolling, green highlands and lively market towns; and to the east the Swahili coast, studded with idyllic beaches and moss-covered ruins. With its diversity and equanimity, Tanzania has a way of getting under your skin, and once you're hooked, it's hard to break free.

ABOUT THE AUTHOR

Originally from Washington, DC, Mary spent several years in Europe after graduate studies. Her fascination with languages and cultures soon led her further south to Africa, where she has spent over a decade living and working all around the continent, including extended periods in Tanzania. She has authored and co-authored many guidebooks on the region, speaks fluent Swahili and is convinced she holds the unofficial record for kilometres-travelled in Tanzania's buses.

Tanzania Highlights

Tanzania lays claim to an astonishing number of Africa's most iconic and alluring places. Narrowing down a selection of the country's highlights was a very tough job, and we've selected an array that ranges from the vast Serengeti, with its great migrations and the wildlife dramas that play out on a daily basis, to the small but intensely memorable moments spent savouring a landscape, catching on to the rhythm of local life, or watching a bird fishing for its lunch. Here are the top picks from Lonely Planet authors and staff.

DENNIS JOHNSON

1 SERENGETI

Time has stood still on the vast plains of the Serengeti (p216). The lions hunt, the wildebeests migrate, the elephants lumber and the leopards race. The people also live as their ancestors did – the same customs and culture. It is a privilege to be allowed to glimpse this vast and wild world that, hopefully, will never change.

Jennifer Garrett, Lonely Planet staff member

CLIMBING KILIMANJARO

On the final night of our ascent up Mt Kilimanjaro (p191) we couldn't get to sleep – partly the effects of altitude, partly knowing that in a few hours we would set off for the final climb. It was raw, cold and damp when we departed, and each step up the scree slope became more laboured. After what seemed like far too long, we reached Gilman's Point and stopped to take in the sunrise over the plains far below. On the final stretch to the peak, we picked our way over rocks and snow. Suddenly, we were at the summit of Africa – an incomparable experience. We took photos and savoured every minute before the fast, sliding descent back to Horombo Hut.

Mary Fitzpatrick, author

DAVID ELSE

SOUTHERN TANZANIA

Don't forget southern Tanzania, especially if you want to leave the crowds behind. Ruaha National Park (p286) is quieter than its better-known northern equivalents and the wildlife is just as stunning. Don't miss the view from Mufindi Escarpment near Iringa – it's quite simply the best view I have ever seen.

Tom Hall, Lonely Planet staff member

ARIADNE VAN ZANDBERGEN

MITCH REARDON

4 NGORONGORO CRATER

While we were driving slowly through the Ngorongoro Crater (p221), a resourceful lion started using our 4WD as cover to stalk a nearby wildebeest. We watched in horror, wondering about our effect on the food chain, when happily the wildebeest got wise and took off. Now that's an effective use of your environment.

Katie Lynch, Lonely Planet staff member

KEITH SHUTTLEWOOD/ALAMY

5 ARRIVING ON ZANZIBAR BY BOAT

Whether it's your first or your 50th time, arriving at Zanzibar (p108) never loses its touch of the exotic. After two wind-buffeted and salt-sprayed hours on the ferry, the waters turn turquoise as Stone Town's skyline slides into view. The spires of St Joseph's Cathedral; Forodhani Gardens; the Old Fort; a jumble of rooftops, and then the harbour – an earthy, timeless and fascinating mix of grime, touts, dockyard workers and ships. After negotiating passport controls and taxis, you're walking through narrow alleyways, past women clad in *bui-bui*, small shops scented with cloves, children playing ball games, men dressed in *kanzu* and *kofia* playing *bao* and chatting. Mainland life seems far away as island rhythms take over and (once again) you're hooked.

Mary Fitzpatrick, author

BWEJUU

Soft white sand at Bwejuu (p136). A view of the Indian ocean. It sparkles in a reassuring, azure kind of way. Looking across the tidal flats, where locals farm seaweed and kids play on the beach. Their voices carry across to where I am lying in the sun. Later I build sandcastles with the kids, and when the tide comes in we catch a ride with a local dhow and go to swim in the lagoon.

Will Gourlay, Lonely Planet staff member

MEDIACOLOR'S/ALAMY

6

7

KHALD KASSEM/ALAMY

ADVENTURE JOURNEY

If you want to get somewhere and don't care how long it takes, try travelling on a local bus (p360). Getting on board and surviving the crush is a major accomplishment. Then there is the mandatory sardine seating, making it impossible not to meet people. The language barriers provide opportunities to break the long-distance tedium – a simple thought can take hours to convey. You relax a little, ignoring the fact that the bus appears to be hurtling out of control. The frenzied pit stops teach you to drink sparingly and tinkle fast. As the miles turn into hours and you gaze upon the villages, you realise the journey is worth far more than the pittance paid.

Jennifer Garrett, Lonely Planet staff member

ARIADNE VAN ZANDBERGEN

8 COASTAL LIFE

At night, almost the entire Tanzanian coast is dotted with the lanterns of small fishing boats anchored off-shore. The fishermen orient themselves by the stars, which carpet the blackness overhead. At dawn, they sail back with their catch. The beachside fish markets (p81) are then at their liveliest, with other dhows setting sail to ferry passengers to nearby villages, brightly clad ladies cooking up *vitambua* (rice cakes) and other delicacies, and vendors setting up their stalls with fruit and other wares.

Mary Fitzpatrick, author

Contents

Regional Map Contents

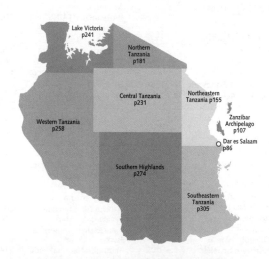

Lake Victoria p241

Northern Tanzania p181

Central Tanzania p231

Northeastern Tanzania p155

Western Tanzania p258

Zanzibar Archipelago p107

Dar es Salaam p86

Southern Highlands p274

Southeastern Tanzania p305

Destination Tanzania

Serengeti, Ngorongoro, Kilimanjaro, Zanzibar… The names roll off the tongue like a roster call of Africa's most alluring destinations, all packed into one country. Resonating with hints of the wild and exotic, these four alone are reason enough to justify packing your bag and heading off to Tanzania. But the list isn't finished. Bagamoyo, Tabora, Ujiji – stops on the 19th-century caravan routes into the heart of what was then an unknown continent. Mafia and Pangani – once famed ports of call for merchant ships from the Orient. Kilwa – linchpin of a far-flung Indian Ocean trading network. Kigoma, Kalema, Kipili, Kasanga – bustling outposts along the remote Lake Tanganyika shoreline. Selous – Africa's largest protected area. Ruaha and Katavi – insider tips for serious safari-goers. Mahale and Gombe – prime destinations for seeing chimpanzees in the wild.

Within the space of several hours, it's possible to go from lazing on idyllic beaches to exploring moss-covered ruins of ancient Swahili city-states; from climbing mist-covered slopes in the Southern Highlands to trekking through the barren landscapes around Ol Doinyo Lengai, guided by a spear-carrying Maasai warrior. Yet, despite its attractions, Tanzania has managed for the most part to remain unassuming and low-key. It has also remained enviably untouched by the tribal rivalries and political upheavals that plague many of its neighbours, and this – combined with a booming tourism industry – makes it an ideal choice for both first-time visitors and Africa old hands.

Throughout, Tanzania offers travellers an array of options, set against the backdrop of a cultural mosaic in which over 100 ethnic groups amicably rub shoulders. While most visitors head straight for the famed northern wildlife-watching circuit, followed by time relaxing on Zanzibar's beaches, Tanzania has much more to offer anyone with the time and inclination to head off the beaten path. Follow the coastline south into a Swahili culture whose rhythms have remained in many ways unchanged over the centuries. Journey through rolling hill country along the Tanzam highway, detouring to Ruaha National Park. Admire ancient rock paintings around Kolo village. Explore the Lake Victoria shoreline, with its small fishing villages and tranquil islands. Experience the seldom-visited wilderness of Katavi, teeming with buffaloes and hippos.

If you're seeking creature comforts, stick to the northern safari circuit and Zanzibar, where there are sealed main roads and many hotels and restaurants. Elsewhere, and especially in the south and west, you'll soon find yourself well off the beaten path, surrounded by a Tanzania that's far removed from Western development.

Wherever you go, take advantage of opportunities to get to know Tanzanians. With their characteristic warmth and politeness, and the dignity and beauty of their cultures, it is they who will inevitably wind up being the highlight of any visit. Chances are that you'll want to come back for more, to which most Tanzanians will say 'karibu tena' (welcome again).

FAST FACTS

Population: 37.6 million

Highest point: Mt Kilimanjaro (5896m)

Lowest point: floor of Lake Tanganyika (358m below sea level)

Inflation: 5%

HIV/AIDS infection rate: 6.5%

Mainland population density: 40 per sq km

Zanzibar Archipelago population density: 400 per sq km

Female cabinet ministers: seven out of 29

Literacy rate: 76%

Elephant population in Ruaha National Park: c 12,000

Getting Started

Tanzania has a fast-growing selection of hotels, safari lodges and restaurants, plus good air connections between major destinations, a wide array of tour operators and a range of amenities for midrange and top-end travellers. However, once away from popular destinations, or if you're travelling anywhere at the budget level, or to really get under the country's skin, you'll need to put in time on rough roads on crowded buses and staying in basic guesthouses.

For more information, see Climate Charts on p335.

Whatever your style, there's plenty to keep you busy – everything from trekking and safaris to lazing on the beach or watching local life. Costs are comparatively high, topping out especially for upmarket safari lodges and the popular northern safari circuit, although it's possible to keep expenses modest if you travel and dine local style.

While there's no problem with sorting out your itinerary once in-country, it's best to prebook safaris and accommodation for popular destinations during the high season. An exception to this is budget safaris and treks, where you can often save a bit by sorting things out on the ground.

WHEN TO GO

Tanzania can be visited during all seasons. The weather is coolest and driest from late June to September, although in July and August, hotels and park lodges, especially in the north, are at their fullest. October and November are very pleasant, with fewer crowds and a slowly greening-up landscape as the short rains begin in many areas. From late December until February, temperatures are high, but not oppressive. Watch out for high-season hotel prices around the Christmas–New Year holidays, as well as during the July-August peak.

For tips on saving money see p341.

During the main rainy season (March to May), you can save substantially on accommodation costs, and enjoy landscapes that are green and full of life. However, some secondary roads may be impassable, and this is the time when many hotels close for a month or so, especially along the coast. Malaria risk, especially in coastal and low-lying areas, also tends to be higher at this time.

COSTS & MONEY

Travelling in Tanzania is relatively expensive, especially for organised tours, safaris and treks. At the budget level, plan on US$20 to US$30 per day for a basic room, local food and public transport, but excluding safaris.

DON'T LEAVE HOME WITHOUT...

You can buy almost anything you'll need in Dar es Salaam or Arusha, except specialist trekking and sporting equipment, and certain toiletries such as contact lens solution. However, choice is limited and prices high. Some things to bring from home:

- binoculars for wildlife watching
- torch (flashlight)
- mosquito repellent and net (p365)
- zoom lens for wildlife shots
- shoes appropriate for beach walking
- sleeping bag and waterproof gear for trekking
- sturdy water bottle
- travel insurance (p339)

Midrange travellers seeking some comforts and Western-style meals should plan on US$40 to US$150 per day, excluding safaris. Top-end luxury lodge travel costs from US$150 to US$500 or more per person per day, with prices at the upper end of this spectrum usually for all-inclusive safari packages.

LANGUAGE

While many Tanzanians, especially in tourist areas, speak English, knowing a few Swahili phrases can go a long way in smoothing your travels and giving you entrée into the culture. While the language may seem daunting at first, its structure is regular and pronunciation is straightforward, and it shouldn't take long to master greetings, numbers (useful for negotiating with market vendors and taxi drivers) and other basics. Greetings in particular are essential, and any efforts you make will be greatly appreciated. For more, see the Language chapter (p371). It's also easy to arrange language courses – see p335.

SUSTAINABLE TRAVEL

As tourism in Tanzania booms, it's increasingly important to give some thought to minimising the impact of your visit, and ensuring that your travels benefit local communities. When choosing a safari or trekking operator, do so with these goals in mind. Choose operators who give more than just lip service to general principles of responsible travel, who view their involvement as part of a long-term, equitable partnership with and investment in local communities and who are committed to protecting local ecosystems. (Also check out Lonely Planet's Greendex, p389.) Whenever possible, try to maximise your 'real' time with locals: take advantage of cultural tourism programmes where they are available, and choose itineraries that are well-integrated with the communities in the areas where you will be travelling. For more tips, see p78.

PREDEPARTURE READING

For an alluring introduction to Tanzania, look for the coffee table–style *Tanzania – Portrait of a Nation* by Paul Joynson-Hicks or *Tanzania – African Eden* by Graham Mercer and Javed Jafferji. *Serengeti – Natural Order on the African Plain*, by Mitsuaki Iwago, is a photographic documentary of the rhythms of nature on the Serengeti plains.

In *The Tree Where Man Was Born*, Peter Matthiessen offers a timeless portrayal of life on the East African plains.

The Worlds of a Maasai Warrior – An Autobiography by Tepilit Ole Saitoti is a fascinating glimpse into Maasai life and culture.

Zanzibari Abdulrazak Gurnah brings WWI-era East Africa to life in his evocative coming-of-age story, *Paradise*.

In *The Gunny Sack*, Tanzanian-bred MG Vassanji explores Tanzania's rich ethnic mix through several generations of an immigrant Indian family. *Into Africa – The Epic Adventures of Stanley and Livingstone* by Martin Dugard is an adventurous and fast-reading account focused around the life and times of the renowned explorer and missionary.

INTERNET RESOURCES

Lonely Planet (www.lonelyplanet.com) Includes summaries on travelling to Tanzania, the Thorn Tree bulletin board, travel news and links to other travel resources.

Tanzania National Parks (www.tanzaniaparks.com) Tanapa's official website, with general information and beautiful photos of the parks.

Tanzania On-Line (www.tzonline.org) An intro to all things official, with links to the government site (www.tanzania.go.tz) and more.

Tanzania Page (www.sas.upenn.edu/African_Studies/Country_Specific/Tanzania.html) Heaps of links.

Tanzania Tourist Board (www.tanzaniatouristboard.com) The TTB's official site.

Zanzibar.Net (www.zanzibar.net) An introduction to Zanzibar.

HOW MUCH?

Midrange safari from US$200/person/day

Plate of *ugali:* Tsh500

Serengeti National Park entry: US$50/person

Papaya: Tsh300

Short taxi ride: Tsh2000

Also see the Lonely Planet Index, inside the front cover.

For a preview of what awaits you in Tanzania, check out www.youtube .com/watch?v=lg8fuc1 _-d8 .

TOP 10

TANZANIA

INDIAN OCEAN

Dar es Salaam

GREAT CULTURAL EXPERIENCES

There's nothing better than immersion for getting to know local life. For starters try:

1 sharing a plate of *ugali* (a staple made from maize or cassava flour, or both) and sauce with Tanzanians (p79)
2 celebrating Eid al-Fitr (p120) on Zanzibar
3 hiking in the Usambara Mountains (p168)
4 participating in a Cultural Tourism Program (p205)
5 spending the morning at a small-town market
6 listening to church singing
7 watching traditional dancing (p33)
8 taking local transport
9 sailing down Lake Tanganyika on the MV *Liemba* (p354)
10 travelling by Tazara train through the northern Selous and then on to Mbeya (p361)

ALLURING PANORAMAS

Tanzania's topography ranges from lushly forested mountains to stunning tropical coastlines, and provides a magnificent backdrop for the country's diverse cultural palette. Some of the most impressive panoramas:

1 the wildebeest migration in the Serengeti (p216)
2 elephants wading into the Rufiji River (p311) against a backdrop of borassus palms
3 sunset over the rooftops of Zanzibar's Stone Town (p109)
4 the stark landscapes around Ol Doinyo Lengai (p227)
5 the patchwork quilt scenery of small farms and villages in the western Usambaras (p170)
6 views down into Ngorongoro Crater from the crater rim (p223)
7 sunset or sunrise from almost anywhere around Lake Victoria (p240), but especially from Lukuba Island (p243), Musoma (p241) or Rubondo Island National Park (p252)
8 impressive lush mountains rising up from the beach along the Lake Tanganyika shoreline near Mahale Mountains National Park (p267)
9 the rolling, open vistas in the highlands around Kitulo National Park (p290) or the countryside around Tukuyu (p297)
10 moonrise over one of the beaches on Zanzibar's east coast (p128)

BEST THINGS TO DO AWAY FROM THE CROWDS

Break away from the trodden trails and discover Tanzania's hidden corners:

1 retrace history in Kilwa (p318), Mikindani (p326), Bagamoyo (p154) and Pangani (p160)
2 go on safari in Mahale Mountains (p267), Katavi (p270) or Ruaha (p286) National Parks or Mkomazi Game Reserve (p179)
3 visit the rock paintings around Kolo (p236)
4 explore the hidden corners of Mafia (p306) or Pemba (p142)
5 discover Zanzibar (p108) in the rainy season
6 bird-watch in Rubondo Island National Park (p252), or around Lake Eyasi (p228) or Lake Manyara (p212)
7 spend a few days in and around Iringa (p282), Mufindi (p289) or Njombe (p289)
8 travel overland between Mikindani and Songea (p301), and on to Mbamba Bay (p300)
9 explore the hills around Mbeya (p291) and Kitulo National Park (p290)
10 enjoy the beaches around Saadani National Park (p158), or around Pangani (p160)

Itineraries
CLASSIC ROUTES

SURF & SAFARI   Two to Three Weeks/Arusha to Zanzibar
From Arusha, explore the northern parks. Good combinations: **Serengeti National Park** (p216) and **Ngorongoro Crater** (p223); Ngorongoro plus **Lake Manyara National Park** (p212) and **Tarangire National Park** (p214); **Arusha National Park** (p207) and a **Mt Meru trek** (p209); and, a **Mt Kilimanjaro trek** (p191), or some hiking and cultural interaction in **Marangu** (p189), **Machame** (p187) or **West Kilimanjaro** (p194).

Head southeast via **Moshi** (p182) to **Lushoto** (p170) for some more hiking. Alternatively, continue straight to **Dar es Salaam** (p84) and the ferry or plane to **Zanzibar** (p109). With more time, travel from Lushoto to **Tanga** (p164), then down the coast via **Pangani** (p160) and **Saadani National Park** (p158) and over to Zanzibar via plane or dhow (from one of the beach lodges near Pangani, or from Saadani).

A less-travelled variant of this itinerary combines **Selous Game Reserve** (p311) with **Mafia** (p306) and Zanzibar's **Stone Town** (p112), although this will involve some flights. Besides Mafia, other post-safari destinations include the beach lodges in Saadani National Park, **Lazy Lagoon** (p158) near Bagamoyo, and the beach lodges near Pangani.

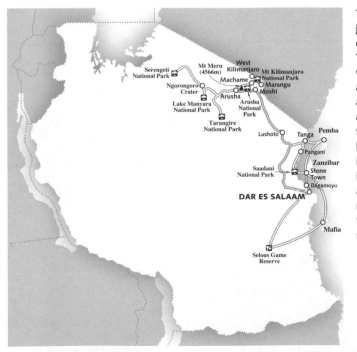

This 1000km journey (more with detours) combines Tanzania's best – wildlife, beaches and culture. Roads are generally good, and there are flights if time is limited. Two weeks is enough for an introduction, but allow three or more to begin to get under the surface.

ROADS LESS TRAVELLED

Away from the Arusha-Zanzibar corridor, most of Tanzania is well off the beaten track. Do a grand circuit, or pick and choose from various smaller loops.

THE GRAND TOUR – 1   At Least Two Months

From **Dar es Salaam** (p84), head north up the coast to **Tanga** (p164), via **Bagamoyo** (p154), **Saadani National Park** (p158) and **Pangani** (p160), before continuing to the **Usambara mountains** (p168) and on to **Moshi** (p182) and **Arusha** (p195). For an off-beat detour, stop at **Mkomazi Game Reserve** (p179) en route. Once in **Arusha** (p195), visit **Ngorongoro Crater** (p223) and some of the northern parks before turning south to **Dodoma** (p231) and **Iringa** (p282) with stops at **Babati** (p235), **Mt Hanang** (p236) and the **Kolo-Kondoa rock art sites** (p236) en route. From Iringa, detour to **Ruaha National Park** (p286) before heading southwest towards **Mbeya** (p291). Time permitting, detour from Mbeya to **Tukuyu** (p297) – an ideal base for some low-key hiking – and to **Kitulo National Park** (p290) and then on to **Lake Nyasa** (p298) and a few days on the beach at **Matema** (p299). Backtracking a bit, make your way via **Njombe** (p289) to **Songea** (p301) and then east via **Tunduru** (p303) to **Mikindani** (p326) and **Mtwara** (p322). Continue north up the coast, with stops at **Lindi** (p320), **Kilwa** (p316) – including the ruins on **Kilwa Kisiwani** (p318) – and **Mafia** (p306). Wind up with time on **Zanzibar** (p108) and **Pemba** (p142) before finishing in Dar es Salaam.

To get into Tanzania's pulse, allow at least two months to follow this 2500km-plus loop – longer including detours or for time out hiking and exploring. Main roads are tarmac. Elsewhere, expect lots of bumps and dust (or mud).

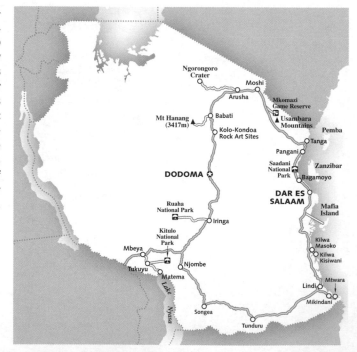

THE GRAND TOUR – 2
Two to Four Months

From **Dar es Salaam** (p84), journey through the Southern Highlands, stopping at **Mikumi National Park** (p278), **Iringa** (p282), **Ruaha National Park** (p286), **Mufindi** (p289) and **Mbeya** (p291). (A good alternative to the bus: take the Tazara line train through the Selous Game Reserve and on to Mbeya.) Continue northwest via **Sumbawanga** (p271) towards **Katavi National Park** (p270), **Mpanda** (p269), **Tabora** (p259), and then north to **Mwanza** (p244) via Nzega and Shinyanga. After exploring the Lake Victoria area, make your way through the western **Serengeti** (p216) to **Arusha** (p195), then southeast to **Zanzibar Archipelago** (p106) and the coast. Alternatively, from Tabora, head west to **Kigoma** (p262) and **Gombe Stream National Park** (p265) – or south via lake steamer to **Mahale Mountains National Park** (p267) before returning east. For a condensed version of this loop, fly from Ruaha National Park to Katavi National Park and/or Mahale Mountains National Park and Lake Tanganyika, then make your way east.

Another option from Dar es Salaam: follow the coast south, stopping at **Mafia** (p306), **Kilwa** (p316), **Lindi** (p320), **Mikindani** (p326) and **Mtwara** (p322) before continuing south to Mozambique, or west to **Songea** (p301). From Songea, travel up to **Mbeya** (p291) or southwest to Mbamba Bay and over to Malawi.

Two alternatives from Arusha: travel via the western Serengeti to Lake Victoria, and **Rubondo Island National Park** (p252), **Ukerewe** (p250) or **Lukuba** (p243) islands. Or, visit **Tarangire National Park** (p214) and **Lake Manyara National Park** (p212) before heading north to **Lake Natron** (p227) then west into the Serengeti. Spend as much time in and around the Serengeti as possible before continuing west to Lake Victoria. Fly back to Arusha or on to Dar es Salaam and the coast.

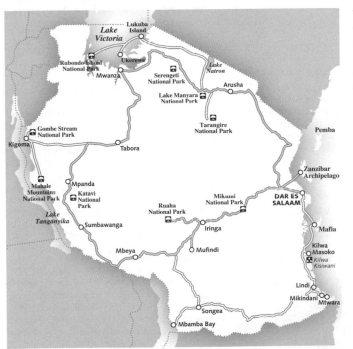

To get in everything mentioned here, plan on at least three to four months and too many kilometres to count. Or, pick and choose from among the shorter alternate loops, each of which is a journey's worth in itself.

TAILORED TRIPS

SWAHILI SAMPLER

Exploring Tanzania's Swahili heritage brings you on a fascinating journey spanning centuries and cultures. A good place to start is **Dar es Salaam** (p84), where modern-day urbanity is only a thin veneer over the area's Swahili roots. Nearby is sleepy **Bagamoyo** (p154), a historical treasure trove. Don't miss the handful of carved doorways, or the chance to watch the day come to life at the town's bustling harbour. Crumbling **Pangani** (p160), once a major port on the Swahili coast, is best explored on a leisurely stroll from a base on one of the lovely beaches running north and south of town. **Zanzibar** (p108) and **Pemba** (p142) are essential stops, although to immerse yourself in things Swahili, you'll need to get away from the resorts and into the villages. The ruins on **Kilwa Kisiwani** (p318) carry you back to the days when this part of the coast was the centre of trading networks stretching to Persia and the Orient. Uncluttered and unfussed, **Mafia** (p306) is easily combined with Kilwa, and makes an optimal stop, with its clear, turquoise waters and plethora of small islands. Further south are pretty, palm-fringed **Lindi** (p320) and tiny **Mikindani** (p326), the epitome of a traditional Swahili village. Use any time remaining to follow old trade caravan routes inland to **Tabora** (p259), and then to **Ujiji** (p265), with its Swahili-style houses and flourishing tradition of dhow building.

HIKER'S PATHS

Tanzania's forested mountains, dramatic peaks and Rift Valley escarpment combine with dozens of colourful tribal groups for wonderful hiking. Head first to **Lushoto** (p170) and the western Usambaras, with its cool climate, winding paths and picturesque villages. The nearby eastern Usambaras around **Amani Nature Reserve** (p169) are ideal for botanists and birders, and have an easy network of short trails, while the less-visited **Pare Mountains** (p176) are intriguing for their opportunities of cultural immersion. For something more vigorous, head to **Mt Hanang** (p236) – a straightforward climb offering views over the plains and an introduction to local Barabaig culture. To the south are the wild, forested slopes of the **Udzungwas** (p280), where you are guaranteed to be walking away from the crowds. For rugged beauty and Rift Valley vistas, it's hard to beat northern Tanzania's **Crater Highlands** (p221) and, for experienced trekkers, a climb up **Ol Doinyo Lengai** (p227). Also in the north is **Mt Meru** (p209), with its stately silhouette, sunrise views and classic trek to the summit. Topping it all off is **Mt Kilimanjaro** (p191), where you can wander through moorlands and heather before ascending to the snowfields capping the continent's highest peak.

History Natalie Folster

IN THE BEGINNING

About 3.6 million years ago, a party of two or three trekked across the plain at Laetoli near Olduvai Gorge (p226) in northern Tanzania, leaving their footprints in a blanket of volcanic ash. The prints were still there when archaeologist Mary Leakey uncovered them in 1978. She pegged them as the steps of our earliest known ancestors – hominids known as *Australopithecines,* whose remains have been found only in East Africa.

About two million years ago, the human family tree split, giving rise to *homo habilis,* a meat-eating creature with a larger brain who used crude stone tools, the remains of whom have been found around Olduvai Gorge. By 1.8 million years ago, *homo erectus* had evolved, leaving bones and axes for archaeologists to find at ancient lakeside sites throughout East Africa and around the world.

What is today Tanzania was peopled by waves of migration. Rock paintings dating back 10,000 years have been found around Kondoa (p236). These are believed to have been made by clans of nomadic hunter-gatherers who spoke a language similar to that of southern Africa's Khoisan. Between 3000 and 5000 years ago, they were joined by small bands of Cushitic-speaking farmers and cattle-herders moving down from what is today Ethiopia. The Iraqw who live around Lake Manyara trace their ancestry to this group of arrivals. The majority of modern Tanzanians are descendants of Bantu-speaking settlers who began a gradual, centuries-long shift eastward from the Niger delta around 1000 BC, arriving in East Africa in the 1st century AD. The most recent influx of migrants occurred between the 15th and 18th centuries when Nilotic-speaking pastoralists from southern Sudan moved into northern Tanzania and the Rift Valley. The modern Maasai trace their roots to this stream.

By the 1st century AD, the outside world had reached the coast of East Africa, known as 'Rhapta' to ancient mariners. Merchant vessels from southern Arabia and the Red Sea were loaded with ivory and slaves. With the traders came Islam, established along the coast between the 8th and 10th centuries AD. By the early 14th century, Kilwa had been transformed by Yemeni settlers from a fishing village into a major centre of commerce. When Moroccan traveller Ibn Battuta visited in 1331, he found a flourishing town of 10,000-20,000 residents, with a grand palace, mosque, inn and slave market.

The first European to set foot in Tanzania was Portuguese sailor Vasco de Gama, who fumbled his way along the coast in 1498 in search of the Orient. Portuguese traders kept to the coast, and were driven out two centuries

DNA lineages found in Tanzania are among the oldest anywhere on Earth, making the country a strong contender for distinction as the 'cradle of humanity'.

The first travel guide to the Tanzanian coast was the *Periplus of the Erythraean Sea,* written for sailors by a Greek merchant around AD 60.

Portuguese influence is still seen in the architecture, customs (eg bull fighting on Pemba, p147) and language. The Swahili *gereza* (jail), from Portuguese *igreja* (church) dates to the days when Portuguese forts contained both edifices in the same compound.

TIMELINE

c 25 million BC	3.6 million BC	10,000–3000 BC
The vast plain of East Africa buckles as tectonic plates collide. A great tear in the Earth's crust forms the Rift Valley. Volcanoes bubble up, creating Kilimanjaro and other peaks.	Our earliest ancestors ambled across the plain at Laetoli in northern Tanzania, leaving their footprints for modern-day archaeologists to find.	Scattered clans of hunter-gatherers followed by farmers and cattle herders settle the plains of the East African plateau, the well-watered highlands and lakeshores of what is modern-day Tanzania.

later by Omani Arabs. The Omanis took control of Kilwa and Zanzibar and set up governors in coastal towns on the mainland. Traders from the coast plied the caravan routes through the interior to the Great Lakes, flying the blood red banner of the Sultan of Zanzibar. They bought ivory and slaves in exchange for cheap cloth and firearms. The traders carried with them virulent strains of small pox and cholera as well as guns. By the late 19th century, when Europe cast a covetous eye on Africa, East Africa was weakened by disease and violence.

Third century AD coins from Persia and North Africa have been found on Zanzibar and along the Tanzanian coast – testaments to a long history of trade links between Africa, Arabia and the Mediterranean.

EUROPEAN CONTROL

The romantic reports of early-19th-century European travellers to East Africa such as Richard Burton, John Speke, David Livingstone and Henry Morton Stanley caught the attention of a young German adventurer in the late 19th century. In 1885, not bothering to obtain his government's endorsement, Carl Peters set up a Company for German Colonization. From Zanzibar, he travelled into the interior on the mainland, shooting his way across the plains and collecting the signatures of African chiefs on a stack of blank treaty forms he had brought with him. In Berlin, Chancellor Bismarck approved the acquisition of African territory after the fact, much to the consternation of the British. They had established informal rule over Zanzibar through control of the Sultan of Zanzibar and had their eye on the rich, fertile lands around Kilimanjaro and the Great Lakes.

On 10 November 1871, journalist and adventurer Henry Morton Stanley 'found' Dr David Livingstone – at home at his base in the village of Ujiji on the shore of Lake Tanganyika.

In late 1886, East Africa was sliced into 'spheres of influence' by agreement between the British and the Germans, formalised in 1890. The frontier ran west from the coast to Lake Victoria along the modern Kenya–Tanzania border. Needless to say, the Africans weren't consulted on the agreement. Nor was the Sultan of Zanzibar. The Germans parked a gunboat in Zanzibar harbour until he signed over his claim to the mainland.

The colonial economy was constructed to draw wealth out of the region and into the coffers of the colonial occupiers. Little investment was made in improving the quality of life or opportunities for local people. Peasants were compelled to grow cash crops for export and many were forcibly moved onto plantations. The Maji Maji Rebellion (p302) against German rule in 1905 was brutally suppressed – villages burned, crops ruined, cattle and grain stolen.

The British took over the administration of the territory of Tanganyika following WWI under the auspices of first the League of Nations then the Trusteeship Council of the UN. To assist in its own post-war economic recovery effort, Britain maintained compulsory cultivation and enforced settlement policies. The development of a manufacturing sector was actively discouraged by Britain, who wanted to maintain the Tanzanian market for its own goods. Likewise, very few Africans were hired into the civil service.

1st century AD	1498	c 1400–1700
Monsoon winds push Arab trading ships to the east coast of Africa. They are followed by Islamic settlers who mix with the local population to create the Swahili language and culture.	Searching for a route to the Orient, Portuguese sailors arrive on the coast of East Africa and set up a coastal trade in slaves and ivory that lasted for 200 years.	In several waves, small bands of nomadic cattle herders migrate south from the Sudan into the Rift Valley, developing Maasai culture.

In 1948, a group of young Africans formed the Tanganyika African Association to protest colonial policies. By 1953, the organisation was renamed the Tanganyika African National Union (TANU), led by a young teacher named Julius Nyerere. Its objective became national liberation. In the end, the British decamped from Tanganyika and Zanzibar rather abruptly in 1961 and 1963 respectively. This was due at least as much to a growing European sentiment that empires were too expensive to maintain as to recognition of the fundamental right of Africans to freedom from subjugation.

INDEPENDENCE

Tanganyikans embraced independence with jubilant optimism for the future. However, Tanganyika embarked on the project of nation-building with few of the resources necessary for the task. The national treasury was depleted. The economy was weak and undeveloped, with virtually no industry. The British trustees had made little effort to prepare the territory for statehood. In 1961, there were a total of 120 African university graduates in the country – including two lawyers, two engineers and 12 medical doctors.

Faced with this set of circumstances, the first autonomous government of Tanganyika, led by the 39-year-old Julius Nyerere, chose continuity over radical transformation of the economic or political structure. TANU accepted the Westminster-style parliament proposed by the British. It committed to investing in education and a gradual Africanization of the civil service. In the meantime, expatriates (often former British colonial officers) would be used to staff the government bureaucracy.

As detailed by political scientist Cranford Pratt, the Nyerere government's early plans were drawn up on the assumption that substantial foreign assistance would be forthcoming, particularly from Britain. This was not the case. Britain pled poverty at the negotiating table. Then Tanzania's relations with all three of its major donors – Britain, USA and West Germany – soured over political issues in the 1960s. These issues were, namely, Nyerere's disgust at Britain's acquiescence to the Unilateral Declaration of Independence of white-ruled Rhodesia, the American role in stoking the civil war in Congo, and West German opposition to the East German embassy on Zanzibar. The new country was left scrambling for funds to stay afloat during the first rocky years of liberation. While grappling with fixing roads, running hospitals and educating the country's youth, the government managed to diffuse an army mutiny over wages in 1964. When Zanzibar erupted in violent revolution in January 1964 just weeks after achieving independence from Britain, Nyerere skilfully co-opted its potentially destabilising forces by giving island politicians a prominent role in a newly proclaimed United Republic of Tanzania, created from the union of Tanganyika with Zanzibar in April 1964.

The Maji Maji Rebellion of 1905 is so-called because the Africans who rose against German domination believed – at first – that magic would turn German bullets to water *(maji)*.

The World of Swahili by John Middleton is an excellent place to start for anyone wanting to learn more about Swahili life and culture.

19th century	1840	1840s–60s
An export slave trade thrived since the 9th century. A thousand years later, notorious Zanzibari slave trader Tippu Tip controlled a commercial empire that stretched from the Congo River to Lake Tanganyika to the coast.	The Sultan of Oman sets up court in a grand palace facing the lagoon on Zanzibar and exerts his authority over coastal mainland Tanganyika.	The first Christian missionaries arrive from Europe. In 1868 the first mainland mission was established at Bagamoyo as a station for ransomed slaves seeking to buy their own freedom.

Nyerere grew dismayed by what he saw as the development of an elite urban class in Tanzania. In 1966, a group of University of Dar es Salaam students marched to the State House in their academic gowns to protest the compulsory National Service the government had introduced. It required all university graduates to spend two years working in rural areas following their graduation. Nyerere was livid.

'I shall take nobody – not a single person – into this National Service whose spirit is not in it… So make your choice. "I'm not going, I'm not going" – *I'm* not going to spend public money to educate anybody who says National Service is a prison… Is this what the citizens of this country worked for?… You are demanding a pound of flesh; everybody is demanding a pound of flesh except the poor peasant. What kind of country are we building?'

He ordered the students home to their rural areas for an indefinite period, which ended up being five months. Before they left, he declared that, as an example to the educated elite, he was going to cut his own salary – and those of all senior government officials – by 20%, which he did.

In his free time, Julius Nyerere translated Shakespeare's Merchant of Venice and Julius Caesar into Swahili, along with portions of Plato's Republic.

UJAMAA – TANZANIA'S GRAND EXPERIMENT

The events of the first few years following independence – the lack of assistance from abroad, rumblings of civil strife at home and the nascent development of a privileged class amid continuing mass poverty – lead Nyerere to re-evaluate the course his government had charted for the nation.

Since his student days, Nyerere had pondered the meaning of democracy for Africa. In 1962, he published an essay entitled *Ujamaa [familyhood]: The Basis of African Socialism*. In it he set out his belief that the personal accumulation of wealth in the face of widespread poverty was anti-social. Africa should strive to create a society based on mutual assistance and economic as well as political equality, such as he claimed had existed for centuries before European colonisation.

In 1967, the TANU leadership met in the northern town of Arusha, where they approved a radical new plan for Tanzania, drafted by Nyerere. What became known as the *Arusha Declaration* outlined the Tanzanian government's commitment to a socialist approach to development, further articulated in a series of subsequent policy papers. The government vowed to reduce its dependence on foreign aid and instead foster an ethos of self-reliance in Tanzanian society. Throughout the country, people turned out to help their neighbours build new schools, repair roads and to plant and harvest food to sell for medical supplies. Nyerere and his ministers made a regular practice of grabbing a shovel and pitching in. To prevent government becoming a trough where bureaucrats and party members could amass personal wealth, Nyerere passed a Leadership Code. Among other things, it prohibited government officials from holding shares in a private company, employing domestic staff or buying real estate to rent out for profit.

For a detailed assessment of Nyerere's policies and leadership, see Beyond Ujamaa in Tanzania by Goran Hyden.

1856	1873	1885
British explorers Richard Francis Burton and John Hanning Speke venture inland from Zanzibar, searching for the source of the Nile and finding Lake Tanganyika and Lake Victoria.	Under pressure from the British Consul, the Sultan of Zanzibar agrees to abolish the Zanzibar Slave Market and the mainland trade in human beings.	German adventurer Carl Peters beats Henry Morton Stanley in a race to win the allegiance of the inland Kingdom of Buganda, claiming the territory of Tanganyika for Germany en route.

JULIUS KAMBARAGE NYERERE – BABA WA TAIFA (FATHER OF THE NATION)

Julius Nyerere was born in 1922 in the village of Butiama on the shore of Lake Victoria. He was one of 26 children of the Zanaki tribal chief. The family was aristocratic but poor. Although his formal education did not begin until he was 12, Nyerere proved a natural scholar. He earned a teaching degree from Makerere University in Kampala and a few years later came home from Scotland with an MA in History and Political Economy from the University of Edinburgh. Like many of his generation, Nyerere resented the continuing British occupation of his homeland. In 1953, he joined with a band of like-minded nationalists to form the Tanganyika African National Union (TANU), which he led to the successful liberation of Tanganyika from Britain and through its first two decades of government.

Nyerere was known affectionately as *Mwalimu* ('Teacher'). In a series of speeches and essays, he instructed the nation on the nature of democracy, racial equality and the need for harmony, and their rights and responsibilities as citizens. Throughout his life, he was revered in Tanzania and respected around the world as a person of unassailable moral integrity who put the welfare of his people above all else.

Nyerere stepped down as president in 1985 (one of only nine African leaders between 1960 and 1989 who relinquished power voluntarily, versus 82 who were either deposed by war, a coup or assassination). He retired to a modest bungalow in the suburbs of Dar es Salaam. In his later years, he assumed the role of sage international statesman, serving as the chief mediator in the Burundi conflict of 1996. He died of leukaemia in a London hospital in 1999 at the age of 77 and was buried in his home village of Butiama, where many of his manuscripts, photos and other memorabilia are on display at the Nyerere Museum (p242).

The *Arusha Declaration* also announced the government takeover of industry and banking. It curtailed foreign direct investment and stated that the government would itself invest in manufacturing enterprises that could produce substitutes for imported goods. All land was henceforth to be common property, managed by the state. The government strove to provide free education for every child. School children were taught to identify themselves as proud Tanzanians with a shared language – Swahili – rather than just members of one of over 200 ethnic groups residing within the country's borders.

Nyerere himself was fascinated by Chinese economic development strategies, but dismissed Western fears that Tanzania was toying with doctrinaire Marxism, either Chinese- or Soviet-style. He argued that Tanzanians 'have no more need of being "converted" to socialism than we have of being "taught" democracy. Both are rooted in our own past – in the traditional society that produced us.' Nyerere's vision was heady stuff in the late 1960s and was enthusiastically embraced not only by the Tanzanian public, but by a body of Western academics and by aid donors from both East and West. Several of his policies nonetheless provoked the

Exhorting his compatriots to work hard, Nyerere quoted a Swahili proverb: 'Treat your guest as a guest for two days; on the third day, give him a hoe!'

1890

Britain trades Heligoland – a strategically placed chunk of rock in the North Sea – to Germany for recognition of British control of Zanzibar. Between them, they divide up East Africa, with Tanganyika allocated to Germany.

1905–7

In the Matumbi Hills, a charismatic mystic called Kinjikitile stirs African labourers to rise up against their German overlords in what became known as the Maji Maji Rebellion.

1919

At the end of WWI, Tanganyika is placed under the 'protection' of the British acting on behalf of the League of Nations and then its successor the UN.

consternation of even his most ardent supporters abroad. In 1965, TANU voted to scrap the multiparty model of democracy bequeathed to it by Britain. As a consequence, Tanzania became a one-party state. Nyerere argued that democracy was not synonymous with multiparty politics and that the new country's challenges were so great that everyone had to work together. He advocated freedom of speech and the discussion of ideas, but banned opposition parties, saying 'The only socially defensible use of "we" is that which includes the whole society.' Voters were given a choice of candidates, but they were all TANU party members. Furthermore, Nyerere authorised the detention of some individuals judged to be agitating against the best interests of the state. His defenders say he did his best to hold together a sometimes unruly cabinet and a country at a time when all over Africa newly independent states were succumbing to civil war and dictatorships. Critics say he turned a blind eye to violations of fundamental civil liberties.

Perhaps the most controversial of all government policies adopted post-Arusha was 'villagisation'. The vast majority of Tanzanians lived in the countryside, and the *Arusha Declaration* envisioned agriculture as the engine of economic growth. A massive increase in production was to be accomplished through communal farming, such as Nyerere argued was the practice in the old days. Beginning in 1967, Tanzanians were encouraged to reorganise themselves into communal villages where they would work the fields together for the good of the nation. Some did, but only a handful of cooperative communities were established voluntarily.

In 1974, the government commenced the forcible relocation of 80% of the population, creating massive disruptions in national agricultural production. The scheme itself, however, suffered from a multiplicity of problems. The new land was often infertile. Necessary equipment was unavailable. People didn't want to work communally; they wanted to provide for their own families first. Government prices for crops were set too low. To paraphrase analyst Goran Hyden, the peasantry responded by retreating into subsistence farming – just growing their own food. National agricultural production and revenue from cash crop exports plummeted.

Summing up the results of the *Arusha Declaration* policies, Nyerere candidly admitted that the government had made some mistakes. However, he also noted progress towards social equality: the ratio between the highest salaries and the lowest paid narrowed from 50:1 in 1961 to around 9:1 in 1976. Despite a meagre colonial inheritance, Tanzania made great strides in education and healthcare. Under Nyerere's leadership, it forged a cohesive national identity. With the exception of occasional isolated eruptions of civil strife on Zanzibar, it has also enjoyed internal peace and stability throughout its existence.

Nyerere's political philosophy is set out in two collections of his major speeches and essays: *Freedom and Unity* (1966) and *Freedom and Socialism* (1968).

1953

A charismatic young school teacher named Julius Nyerere is elected President of the Tanganyika African National Union, an organisation dedicated to the liberation of Tanganyika from colonial rule.

9 Dec 1961

Tanganyika gains independence from British colonial rule with Nyerere elected president. Zanzibar follows suit in December 1963, establishing a constitutional monarchy under the Sultan.

1964

Following a bloody coup on Zanzibar in which several thousand Zanzibaris were killed, Tanganyika and Zanzibar unite to form the United Republic of Tanzania.

AID DARLING TO DELINQUENT & BACK

Post–*Arusha Declaration* Tanzania was the darling of the aid donor community. It was the largest recipient of foreign aid in sub-Saharan Africa throughout the 1970s and was the testing ground for every new-fangled development theory that came along. An army of expatriate advisors oversaw hundreds of development projects.

As the economy spiralled downward in the late 1970s and early '80s, the World Bank, International Monetary Fund (IMF) and a growing chorus of exasperated aid donors called for stringent economic reform – a dramatic structural adjustment of the economic system. Overlooking their own failing projects, they pointed to a bloated civil service and moribund productive sector, preaching that both needed to be exposed to the fresh, cleansing breezes of the open market. Nyerere resisted the IMF cure. As economic conditions continued to deteriorate, dissension grew within the government ranks. In 1985, Nyerere resigned. In 1986, the Tanzanian government submitted to the IMF terms. The grand Tanzanian experiment with African socialism was over.

For everything you ever wanted to know about the Tanzanian Bunge (Parliament), check out www.parliament.co.tz.

As elsewhere on the continent, structural adjustment was a shock treatment that left the nation gasping for air. The civil service was gutted – slashed by over a third. Some of the deadwood was gone, but so were thousands of teachers, healthcare workers and the money for textbooks and chalk and teacher training. 'For sale' signs were hung on inefficient government-owned enterprises – bakeries, a cement factory, state-owned farms – as well as vital public services such as the Tanzania Railways Corporation. Many were bought by foreign owners at fire sale prices. Tariffs put up to protect local producers from cheap imports were flattened in accordance with the free trade mantra of the World Bank. The lead on national development policy passed from the Tanzanian government to the donors, with long lists of conditions attached to aid.

The long-term impact of structural adjustment on Tanzania is still hotly debated. Critics argue that many of Tanzania's ills were due to external factors – the lasting legacy of colonialism, sky-rocketing oil prices in the 1970s and an unfair global economic system. They charge that the IMF's one-size-fits-all approach to economic reform devastated the national economy and social services. Advocates of structural adjustment argue that without these drastic measures, Tanzania would have been even worse off. They put the blame for Tanzania's economic decay on flawed domestic policies.

Tanzania is an ancient land, but a young country – 44% of the current population is under the age of 14.

Economic growth rates slipped into the negative around 1974, where they languished for the next 25 years. In 1967, revenue from Tanzania's exports was sufficient to cover the costs of its necessary imports (oil, machinery, consumer goods). By 1985, earnings from exports covered only a third of its import bill. The government was forced to borrow money to cover the rest, and from the end of the 1970s, Tanzania began to accumulate a

---

1967

At a gathering of the TANU party faithful in the highland town of Arusha, Julius Nyerere garners enthusiastic support for the *Arusha Declaration*, which sets out Tanzania's path to African socialism.

1978–79

The Ugandan army invades Tanzania, burning and looting border towns. The Tanzanian government responds in force, marching all the way to Kampala to topple Ugandan dictator Idi Amin Dada.

1985

Julius Nyerere voluntarily steps down as president after five terms. This paves the way for a peaceful transition to his elected successor.

crippling burden of debt from which it has yet to escape. Part of this debt is comprised of loans for grand but ultimately unsuccessful development projects it was advised to undertake by its multiplicity of aid donors. In 1997, Tanzania was spending four times as much servicing its external debt than on healthcare, a situation that has improved only slightly in the past decade.

Nyerere's proudest accomplishment was progress towards universal primary education on his watch. In 1980, 93% of children were in school. However, by 2000, enrolment had fallen to 57%. Access to education is again improving with massive aid-supported investments in basic education over the past decade. Swallowing its objections, the Tanzanian government dutifully continues to take the IMF cure, and is held up as a model of aid-recipient behaviour.

Part of the structural adjustment aid program was the re-introduction of Western-style multiparty democracy in 1992. In the most recent elections in December 2005, Jakaya Mrisho Kikwete was elected president with 80% of the popular vote. Five opposition parties took 43 of 319 seats in the National Assembly.

> Ninety-seven (30%) of Tanzanian members of the National Assembly are women, making the country one of only 17 in the world to meet the UN target for female political representation set in 1995.

TANZANIA ON THE WORLD STAGE

Throughout the 1960s to 1980s, Nyerere, representing Tanzania, was a voice of moral authority in global forums such as the UN, the Organization of African Unity and the Commonwealth. He asserted the autonomy of 'Third World' states, and pressed for a fairer global economic structure.

Nyerere's government was also a vocal advocate for the liberation of southern Africa from white minority rule. Nyerere told the UN General Assembly in 1961. 'We who are free have absolutely no right to sit comfortably and counsel patience to those who do not yet enjoy their freedom.' From 1963, Tanzania provided a base for the South African, Zimbabwean and Mozambican liberation movements within its territory as well as military support, at great cost – both human and material – to itself.

While gratefully accepting Chinese assistance to build the Tazara Railway from Zambia to Dar es Salaam in the 1970s, throughout the Cold War Tanzania remained staunchly nonaligned, resisting the machinations and blandishments of both East and West.

Tanzania has a long history of internal harmony, but it has troublesome neighbours. In 1978 Ugandan dictator Idi Amin ordered his soldiers to invade Tanzania, looting and burning villages along the Kagera River thought to harbour Ugandan rebels. The Tanzanian government responded with a force of 20,000 Tanzanian soldiers, who joined with Ugandans to topple Amin and restore Milton Obote to power.

Tanzania's lower profile on the world stage in recent years can be attributed to the passing of the charismatic and revered Nyerere as well as

> **SOME FRIENDS YOU COULD DO WITHOUT...**
>
> Idi Amin sent Nyerere a telegram declaring 'I love you very much, and if you had been a woman I would have considered marrying you.' Nyerere did not reply.

1986	**1992**	**7 August 1998**
After resisting for several years but with the economy in a downward spiral, Tanzania accepts stringent IMF terms for a Structural Adjustment Program loan.	Opposition parties are legalised under pressure from the international donor community. The first multiparty elections are held in Tanzania in 1995 with 13 political parties on the ballot.	Within a few minutes of one another, Al Qaeda truck bombs explode at the American embassies in Nairobi and Dar es Salaam. Eleven Tanzanians die in the attack, with dozens more injured.

the circumscribed room to manoeuvre afforded the government because of its economic woes and aid dependency. Nevertheless, Tanzania has always opened its doors to civilians fleeing violence in the countries that surrounds it – Uganda, Burundi, Congo and Mozambique. It still hosts more than half a million refugees – more than any other African country. They are mainly from Burundi and the Democratic Republic of Congo Zaïre, living in camps along Tanzania's western borders.

The International Criminal Tribunal for Rwanda was established in 1994, and got to work in Arusha in 1997, employing a local staff of 415. So far, the Tribunal has dealt with 33 cases relating to the 1994 Rwandan genocide – about half of the detainees. It is due to wrap up its work in 2008.

The reported incidence of HIV/AIDS in Tanzania is 6.5%; 1.6 million people are living with HIV/AIDS.

2000	2005	2007
Contentious elections for the Zanzibari Legislature boil over into street violence and 22 people are shot by police during mass demonstrations protesting the results.	Chama Cha Mapinduzi (CCM) – the national party created from the unison of TANU and the Zanzibari Afro Shirazi Party in 1977 – maintains its unbroken hold on government by winning a majority.	The snows of Kilimanjaro, which have caught the imagination of writer Ernest Hemingway and countless other visitors since the beginning of time, are estimated to disappear completely by 2020 due to global warming.

The Culture

THE NATIONAL PSYCHE

It takes a lot to ruffle a Tanzanian, and the country is notable for its relatively harmonious and understated demeanour. In contrast to the situation in several neighbouring countries, tribal rivalries are almost nonexistent. It's rare for a Tanzanian to identify themselves at the outset according to tribe; primary identification is almost always as a Tanzanian, and the *ujamaa* (familyhood) ideals of Julius Nyerere permeate society. Religious frictions are also minimal, with Christians and Muslims living side by side in a relatively easy coexistence. Although political differences flare up on occasion, especially on the Zanzibar Archipelago, they rarely come to the forefront in interpersonal dealings.

The workings of society are oiled by a subtle but strong social code. Tanzanians place a premium on politeness and courtesy. Greetings in particular are essential, and you'll probably be given a gentle reminder should you forget this and launch straight into a question without first inquiring as to the wellbeing of your listener and their family. Tanzanian children are trained to greet their elders with a respectful *shikamoo* (literally, 'I hold your feet'), often accompanied in rural areas by a slight curtsy, and strangers are frequently addressed as *dada* (sister) or *mama*, in the case of an older woman; *kaka* (brother); or *ndugu* (relative or comrade).

Much of daily life is shaped by the struggle to make ends meet in an economy that is ranked as one of the world's poorest. Yet, behind these realities is the fact that Tanzania is home, and not a bad place at that. Combined with the inevitably warm reception that you'll receive as a visitor is a dignified reserve, and a quiet resolve that things will be done the Tanzanian way.

Especially in rural areas, it's common for a woman to drop her own name, and become known as *Mama* followed by the name of her oldest son (or daughter, if she has no sons).

LIFESTYLE

At one end of the spectrum, the main diet is *ugali* (a staple made from maize or cassava flour, or both) with sauce; women and children work small *shamba* (farm plots); and school fees (from about Tsh90,000 per year at the secondary level) are a constant worry. Home – often in varying stages of completion, waiting for the finances needed to finish construction – is made of cinderblock or mud brick, with roofing of corrugated tin or thatch, a latrine outside and water drawn from a nearby pump or river. At the other end is a small number of elite, often the families of government ministers, who drive 4WDs and live in Western-style houses in posh residential areas of Dar es Salaam. The remainder of Tanzanians fall somewhere in-between these extremes, although many more are closer to the first scenario than to the latter. Women always work – whether outside the home, or tending to the family and *shamba*. Most students don't have the opportunity to finish secondary school, and many of those who do have unemployment to look forward to, especially in rural areas. Tourism provides opportunities, though there aren't enough good positions to go around.

Tanzania has one of the lowest rates of secondary school enrolment in the world, with less than 7% of suitably aged youth enrolled.

Family life is central, with weddings, funerals and other events holding centre stage. Celebrations are generally splashed-out affairs aimed at demonstrating status, and frequently go well beyond the means of the host family. It's expected that family members who have jobs will share what they have, and the extended family (which also encompasses the community) forms an essential support network in the absence of a government social security

---

ETIQUETTE TANZANIAN STYLE

Tanzanians are conservative, and while they are likely to be too polite to tell you so directly, they'll be privately shaking their head about travellers doing things such as not wearing enough clothing, sporting tatty clothes, or indulging in public displays of affection. Especially along the Muslim coast, you should cover up the shoulders and legs, and avoid plunging necklines, skin-tight fits and the like. A few other tips:

- Pleasantries count. Even if just asking for directions, take time to greet the other person. Handshake etiquette is also worth learning, and best picked up by observation. Tanzanians often continue to hold hands for several minutes after meeting, or even throughout an entire conversation, and especially in the south, a handshake may be accompanied by touching the left hand to the right elbow as a sign of respect.

- Don't eat or pass things with the left hand.

- Respect authority. Losing your patience or undermining an official's authority is always counterproductive, while deference and a good-natured demeanour will see you through most situations.

- Want to visit a Tanzanian friend? Before entering their house, call out *hodi* (May I enter?) and then wait for the inevitable *karibu* (welcome).

- Avoid criticising the government.

- Receive gifts with both hands, or with the right hand while touching the left hand to your right elbow. Giving a gift? Don't be surprised if the appreciation isn't expressed verbally.

---

system. Given that the average per capita GDP is only about US$340 (compared with about US$37,600 in the UK), the system works remarkably well, with relatively few destitute on the streets.

Invisible social hierarchies lend life a sense of order. In the family, the man rules the roost, with the children at the bottom and women just above them. In the larger community, it's not much different. Child-raising is the expected occupation for women, and breadwinning for men, although a small cadre of professional women is slowly becoming more visible. Village administrators (*shehe* on Zanzibar) oversee things, and make important decisions in consultation with other senior community members. Tribal structures, however, range from weak to nonexistent – a legacy of Nyerere's abolition of local chieftaincies following independence.

AIDS is not as widespread in Tanzania as in many southern African countries (a 6.5% adult HIV/AIDS infection rate according to Unaids statistics, compared with about 19% in South Africa). However, its spectre looms on the horizon, and has prompted increased efforts at raising public awareness. You'll see AIDS-related billboards throughout major cities, although real public discussion remains limited, and AIDS deaths are still often explained away as 'tuberculosis', or with silence.

See www.tanzania .go.tz/hiv_aids.html for more on Tanzania's national AIDS policy.

ECONOMY

Agriculture, the mainstay of Tanzania's economy, employs about two-thirds of working-age Tanzanians – most of whom are subsistence farmers – and accounts for almost half of the country's gross domestic product. However, tourism is playing an increasingly important role. Over 600,000 visitors arrived in Tanzania in 2006, bringing with them revenues of over US$800 million. The government is hoping to continue this progress by promoting new investment and improving tourism marketing, especially in the south. Mining is also an important sector; Tanzania is now Africa's fourth largest gold producer, behind South Africa, Ghana and Mali.

BACK TO BASICS?

For a country that was founded by a teacher (Julius Nyerere is still referred to as *Mwalimu*, or 'teacher'), Tanzania ranks near the bottom of the heap when it comes to education. It wasn't always like this. Nyerere was convinced that success for his philosophy of socialism and self-reliance depended on having an educated populace. He made primary education compulsory and offered government assistance to villagers to build their own schools. By the late 1980s, the country's literacy rate had become one of the highest in Africa.

Since then, much of the initial momentum has been lost. Although 85% of children enrol at the primary level (thanks in part to the elimination of primary school fees), about 20% of these drop out before finishing, and barely 5% complete secondary school. The reasons are many, with not enough trained teachers, not enough schools and not enough money topping the list. At the secondary level, school fees are a problem, as is language. Primary school instruction is in Swahili, and many students lack sufficient knowledge of English to carry out their secondary level studies.

Although there is still a long way to go, the situation is beginning to look up: the government is giving increased emphasis to education, especially at the primary level, where enrolment levels have been rising in recent years, and the private secondary school network is slowly expanding to fill gaps in the government system.

With annual economic growth at about 7% and inflation steady on the mainland at just under 5% in recent years, most observers are fairly optimistic about the country's midterm economic prospects.

In Tanzania, it's sometimes hard to know where the family ends and the community begins. Doors are always open, helping out others in the *jamaa* (clan, community) is expected and celebrations involve everyone.

Yet, daily life for many Tanzanians remains a struggle. In addition to wide income variations between rural and urban areas, there is a growing gap between the poor and the more well-off. Unemployment averages about 15% and underemployment is widespread. In 2006, Tanzania was ranked 162 out of 177 countries on the UNDP Human Development Index.

POPULATION

Close to 120 tribal groups rub shoulders in Tanzania, together with relatively small but economically significant numbers of Asians and Arabs, and a small European community. Most tribes are very small, with almost 100 of them combined accounting for only one-third of the total population. As a result, none has succeeded in dominating politically or culturally, although groups such as the Chagga and the Haya, who have a long tradition of education, are disproportionately wellrepresented in government and business circles.

The vast majority of Tanzanians (about 95%) are of Bantu origin. These include the Sukuma (who live around Mwanza and southern Lake Victoria, and constitute about 13% of the overall population), the Nyamwezi (around Tabora), the Makonde (southeastern Tanzania), the Haya (around Bukoba) and the Chagga (around Mt Kilimanjaro). The Maasai and several smaller groups including the Arusha and the Samburu (all in northern Tanzania) are of Nilo-Hamitic or Nilotic origin. The Iraqw, around Karatu and northwest of Lake Manyara, are Cushitic, as are the tiny northern-central tribes of Gorowa and Burungi. The Sandawe and, more distantly, the seminomadic Hadzabe (around Lake Eyasi), belong to the Khoisan ethno-linguistic family.

About 3% of Tanzania's total 37.6 million population live on the Zanzibar Archipelago, with about one-third of these on Pemba. Most African Zanzibaris belong to one of three groups: the Hadimu, the Tumbatu and the Pemba. Members of the non-African population are primarily Shirazi and consider themselves descendants of immigrants from Shiraz in Persia (Iran).

Tanzania is relatively unurbanised, although city dwellers now constitute about 37% of the population, and the urban growth rate is increasing at a rate of about 6% per year. Average population density is 40 people per sq km, although this varies radically from one area to the next. Among the most densely populated areas are Dar es Salaam and the surrounding coast; the Usambara and Pare mountains; the slopes of Mt Kilimanjaro; the Mwanza region; and the Zanzibar Archipelago (with about 400 people per sq km).

MEDIA

In keeping with its rural roots, Tanzania still gets most of its news via the radio, with about 42 radios per 100 people (versus only about four televisions per 100 people).

A countrywide illiteracy rate of about 25% to 30% and distribution difficulties in rural areas mean that the influence of newspapers is limited to urban centres. While most of the main dailies are aligned in some degree with the governing Chama Cha Mapinduzi (CCM) party, the mainland local press is lively and relatively independent.

Tanzania is ranked 88th worldwide, well ahead of all of its East African neighbours, in press freedom by Reporters Without Borders (www .rsf.org).

RELIGION

The vibrant spirituality that pervades much of the African continent fills Tanzania as well. All but the smallest villages have a mosque, a church or both; religious festivals are generally celebrated with fervour – at least as far as singing, dancing and family gatherings are concerned; and almost every Tanzanian identifies with some religion.

Muslims, who account for about 35% to 40% of the population, have traditionally been concentrated along the coast, as well as in the inland towns that lined the old caravan routes. There are several sects represented, notably the Sunni (Shafi school). The population of the Zanzibar Archipelago is almost exclusively Sunni Muslim.

About 45% to 50% of Tanzanians are Christians. Major denominations include Roman Catholic, Lutheran and Anglican, with a small percentage of Tanzanians adherents of other Christian denominations, including Baptist and Pentecostal. One of the areas of highest Christian concentration is in the northeast around Moshi, which has been a centre of missionary activity since the mid-19th century.

The remainder of the population follows traditional religions centred on ancestor worship, the land and various ritual objects. There are also small but active communities of Hindus, Sikhs and Ismailis.

Historically, the main area of friction has been between Tanzania's Muslim and Christian populations. Today, tensions – while still simmering – are at a relatively low level, and religion is not a major factor in contemporary Tanzanian politics.

Tanzania is the only African country boasting indigenous inhabitants from all of the continent's main ethnolinguistic families (Bantu, Nilo-Hamitic, Cushitic, Khoisan). They live in closest proximity around lakes Eyasi and Babati.

WOMEN IN TANZANIA

Tanzania's stellar rankings for tourism and safaris fade when it comes to women in government and high profile positions. Although women form the backbone of the economy – with most juggling child-rearing plus work on the family *shamba*, or in an office – they are near the bottom of the social hierarchy, and are frequently marginalised. This is especially so when it comes to education and politics. Only about 5% of girls complete secondary school, and of these, only a handful goes on to complete university. While secondary school enrolment levels are low across the board, girls in particular are frequently kept home due to a lack of finances, to help with chores, or because of pregnancy. It's still rare to find politically prominent women, and women's literacy rates (62% countrywide) lag behind those of men (78%).

On the positive side, the situation is slowly improving. Since 1996 the government has guaranteed 20% of parliamentary seats for women, and there are currently seven female cabinet ministers (of 29 ministers, total, and up from four in the previous government). In education, the 'gender gap' has been essentially eliminated at the primary level.

About 55% of Tanzania's AIDS sufferers are women.

ARTS

Cinema

Tanzania's tiny and long languishing film industry received a major boost with the opening of the first annual Zanzibar International Film Festival (ZIFF; see p338) in 1998. Today, this festival is one of the best measures of the country's artistic pulse, and one of the region's premier cultural events. The festival, which is held annually on Zanzibar, serves as a venue for artists from the Indian Ocean basin and beyond. Tanzanian prize winners have included *Maangamizi – The Ancient One,* shot in Tanzania and co-directed by Martin M'hando, who is also known for his film, *Mama Tumaini* (Women of Hope); and *Makaburi Yatasema* (Only the Stones Are Talking), about AIDS and directed by Chande Omar Omar. In 2005, Tanzania's Beatrix Mugishawe won acclaim (and two prizes) for *Tumaini,* which focuses on AIDS orphans. Another up-and-coming director is Josiah Kabira, whose first film, *Bongoland* (2003) focuses on the realities of life for immigrants to the USA from the fictionalised Bongoland (Tanzania). Kabira followed this with *Tusamehe* (2005), focusing on the impact of AIDS on a family who has emigrated from Tanzania (Bongoland in the film) to the USA. Not locally directed (although the co-director is transplanted-Zanzibari Yusuf Mahmoud), but with great entrée into local life, is *As Old As My Tongue,* a documentary about Zanzibari music legend Bi Kidude.

> For an English-language introduction to Tanzania's national poet, watch for *The Poetry of Shaaban Robert,* translated by Clement Ndulute.

Literature

Tanzania's literary scene is dominated by renowned poet and writer, Shaaban Robert (1909–62). Robert, who was born near Tanga, is considered the country's national poet, and was almost single-handedly responsible for the development of a modern Swahili prose style. Among his best-known works are the autobiographical *Maisha yangu* (My Life), the poem *Utenzi wa Vita vya Uhuru* (An Epic in the War for Freedom) and several collections of folk tales.

Almost as well-known as Robert is Zanzibari Muhammed Said Abdulla, who gained fame with his *Mzimu wa watu wa kale* (Graveyard of the Ancestors) and other detective stories, and is considered the founder of Swahili popular literature. Other notable authors of Swahili-language works include Zanzibari novelist Shafi Adam Shafi, Joseph Mbele (known for his short stories) and Ebrahim Hussein (known primarily for his dramas and theatre pieces).

> *Mr Myombekere and His Wife Bugonoka, Their Son Ntulanalwo and Daughter Bulihwali – The Story of an Ancient African Community* by Aniceti Kitereza (see p251) is a lengthy but fascinating look into traditional life on Ukerewe island.

One of Tanzania's most widely acclaimed contemporary writers is Abdulrazak Gurnah, who was born on Zanzibar in 1948. Among his best known works are the novel *Paradise,* which is set in East Africa during WWI, and made the short list for the UK's Booker Prize in 1994, *By the Sea* (2001) and *Desertion,* short-listed for the Commonwealth Writers Prize in 2006.

Joining Gurnah among the ranks of English-language writers are Peter Palangyo, William Kamera and Tolowa Marti Mollel. Palangyo's novel *Dying in the Sun* tells the story of a young Tanzanian who, after questioning his existence, comes to terms with his family and his heritage in rural Tanzania. Kamera penned several collections of poetry, as well as *Tales of the Wairaqw of Tanzania.* The prolific Mollel has authored numerous short stories, and is particularly known for his folk tales, including the collection *Waters of the Vultures and Other Stories.*

Complementing this formal literary tradition are proverbs, for which Tanzanians are famous. They're used for everything from instructing children to letting one's spouse know that you are annoyed with them. For a sampling see www.mwambao.com/methali.htm (featuring Swahili proverbs) or look for *Folk Tales from Buhaya* by R Mwombeki & G Kamanzi (Haya proverbs and stories).

Music & Dance
TRADITIONAL
Subtle rhythms and smooth dynamism in movement characterise Tanzanian traditional dance, or *ngoma*, as it's known locally. By creating a living picture and encompassing the entire community in its message, it serves as a channel for expressing sentiments such as thanks and praise, and of communicating with the ancestors. Institutions at the forefront of promoting and preserving Tanzanian dance include the College of Arts (Chuo cha Sanaa; p157) in Bagamoyo, and Bujora Cultural Centre (p250) near Mwanza.

While *marimbas* (percussion instruments with metal strips of varying lengths that are plucked with the thumb) and other instruments are sometimes used to accompany dancing, the drum is the most essential element. The same word *(ngoma)* is used for both dance and drumming, illustrating the intimate relationship between the two, and many dances can only be performed to the beat of a particular type of drum. Some dances, notably those of the Sukuma, also make use of other accessories, including live snakes and other animals. The Maasai leave everything behind in their famous dancing, which is accompanied only by chants and often also by vigorous leaping.

Other traditional musical instruments include the *kayamba* (shakers made with grain kernels); rattles and bells made of wood or iron; xylophones (also sometimes referred to as *marimbas*); *siwa* (horns); and *tari* (tambourines).

The main place for masked dance is in the southeast, where it plays an important role in the initiation ceremonies of the Makonde (who are famous for their *mapiko* masks) and the Makua.

MODERN
The greatest influence on Tanzania's modern music scene has been the Congolese bands that began playing in Dar es Salaam in the early 1960s, which brought the styles of rumba and soukous (*lingala* music) into the East African context. Among the best known is Orchestre Super Matimila, which was propelled to fame by the renowned Dar es Salaam–based Remmy Ongala ('Dr Remmy'), who was born in the Democratic Republic of Congo (Zaïre). Many of his songs (most are in Swahili) are commentaries on contemporary themes such as AIDS, poverty and hunger, and Ongala has been a major force in popularising music from the region beyond Africa's borders. Other groups to watch for – primarily in Dar es Salaam – include Mlimani Park Orchestra and Vijana Jazz.

In the shadow of the dance bands, but thriving nevertheless, are Swahili rap artists (Kwanza Unit, now disbanded, was the pioneering group), a vibrant hip-hop scene and the hip-hop influenced and hugely popular Bongo Flava. Names to watch for include X Plastaz, Sista P, Professor Jay and Juma Nature ('Sir'). The easiest cassettes to find – watch for vendors pushing around small street carts with blaring speakers – are of church choir music *(kwaya)*.

During the colonial days, German and British military brass bands spurred the development of *beni ngoma* (brass *ngoma*) – dance and music societies combining Western-style brass instruments with African drums and other traditional instruments. Variants of these are still *de rigueur* at weddings. Stand at the junction of Moshi and Old Moshi Rds in Arusha on any weekend afternoon, and watch the wedding processions

---

Swahili prose got a relatively late start, but Swahili oral poetry traditions have long roots. See www.humnet.ucla.edu/humnet/aflang/swahili/SwahiliPoetry/index.htm for an excellent overview and anthology.

Want to let someone know how you feel? Tanzanians say it with *kangas* – the writings around the edges of these wraparound skirts range from amorous outpourings to pointed humour. For a sampling of what's being said around you, see www.glcom.com/hassan/kanga.html.

Two good places to get acquainted with Tanzania's contemporary music scene are www.afropop.org and www.bongoflava.com.

MWALIMU'S LEGACY

Although over two decades have passed since Julius Nyerere stepped down from the helm, his portrait still graces the walls of office buildings throughout the mainland. If anything, the late leader is now held in even higher regard on the Tanzanian mainland than during his time in office. Impelled by an egalitarian social vision, the fatherly Nyerere introduced Swahili as a unifying national language, managed to instil ideals of *ujamaa* (familyhood) among the majority of his people and initiated a long and respected tradition of regional political engagement. Thanks to this vision, Tanzania today is one of Africa's most stable countries, and religious and ethnic conflicts are close to nonexistent.

On the economic front, the situation is less rosy, although Nyerere himself would have been one of the first to acknowledge this. When Nyerere left office, the country was close to bankruptcy, with a moribund socialist economy and a network of ailing parastatals. Today Tanzania continues to be ranked near the bottom worldwide in development rankings, and illiteracy and infant mortality rates are high. Yet, the outlook is not all grim: privatisation is proceeding apace, the economy is steadily strengthening – helped along in part by a booming tourism industry – and the country is routinely lauded for its progress by the international donor community.

Corruption – which the upstanding Nyerere managed to rise above completely – is another problem, and entrenched. However, efforts are being made to combat it, and there are signs in banks, immigration offices and elsewhere advertising that you're in a corruption-free zone.

While an amicable path for coexistence has been found, keeping family ties happy between the mainland and proudly independent Zanzibar also requires ongoing attention. The task is made more challenging by the continued overwhelming dominance of Nyerere's Chama Cha Mapinduzi (CCM) party in the national government.

As Tanzania moves into its second half-century and addresses these issues, it will need to hold another element of Nyerere's vision firmly in sight: education. Although Nyerere's goal of universal primary education still hasn't been realised, it is slowly coming closer to fulfilment. The key over the coming decades will be finding a way to ensure that more than 5% of youth (the current figure) can finish secondary school, and go on to university or find employment. If Tanzania manages to do this, it's something that would have been likely to cause *Mwalimu* (or 'Teacher', as Nyerere is universally known) to beam.

---

come by, all accompanied by a small band riding in the back of a pickup truck. For a comprehensive overview of Tanzanian music, check out http://members.aol.com/dpaterson/index.htm.

On Zanzibar, the music scene has long been dominated by *taarab* (see p126), which has experienced a major resurgence in recent years. Rivalling *taarab* for attention, especially among younger generations is the similar *kidumbak*, distinguished by its defined rhythms and drumming, and its often hard-hitting lyrics. For more on music on the Zanzibar Archipelago contact the **Dhow Countries Music Academy** (www.zanzibarmusic.org).

Stop by Mawazo Gallery (www.mawazo-gallery .com) in Dar es Salaam (p97) or check out its website for an introduction to contemporary Tanzanian art and artists.

Visual Arts
PAINTING

In comparison with woodworking, painting has a fairly low profile in Tanzania. The most popular style by far is Tingatinga, which takes its name from painter Edward Saidi Tingatinga, who began it in the 1960s in response to demands from the European market. Tingatinga paintings are traditionally composed in a square, with brightly coloured animal motifs set against a monochrome background, and use diluted and often unmixed enamel paints for a characteristic glossy appearance.

The best place to buy Tingatinga paintings is at the Tingatinga Centre near Morogoro Stores in Dar es Salaam (p97). Other good spots include Msasani Slipway (p97), and the vendors along Hurumzi St in Zanzibar's Stone Town.

Wasanii Art Centre, at the Msasani Slipway, is one of the best first stops for paintings and artwork in general. Also try Dar es Salaam's cultural centres and Nyumba ya Sanaa (p97), all of which host occasional painting exhibitions by contemporary Tanzanian artists.

SCULPTURE & WOODCARVING
Tanzania's Makonde, together with their Mozambican cousins, are renowned throughout East Africa for their original and highly fanciful carvings. Although originally from the southeast around the Makonde Plateau, commercial realities lured many Makonde north. Today, the country's main carving centre is at Mwenge in Dar es Salaam (p98), where blocks of hard African blackwood (*Dalbergia melanoxylon* or, in Swahili, *mpingo*) come to life under the hands of skilled artists.

Among the most common carvings are those with *ujamaa* motifs, and those known as *shetani*, which embody images from the spirit world. *Ujamaa* carvings are designed as a totem pole or 'tree of life' containing interlaced human and animal figures around a common ancestor. Each generation is connected to those that preceded it, and gives support to those that follow. Tree of life carvings often reach several metres in height, and are almost always made from a single piece of wood. *Shetani* carvings are more abstract, and even grotesque, with the emphasis on challenging viewers to new interpretations while giving the carver's imagination free reign.

Safaris

Watching wildlife is at the top of almost everyone's 'must do' list in Tanzania, and little wonder. With its showpiece attractions – Serengeti National Park and Ngorongoro Crater – complemented by a stellar array of other parks and protected areas, the country offers some of the most diverse and rewarding wildlife watching to be found anywhere.

Thanks in part to the number, variety and accessibility of its wildlife, Tanzania's safari industry has become highly competitive. At the budget end there's often only a fine line between operators running no-frills but reliable safaris, and those that are either dishonest, or have cut things so close that problems are bound to arise. At the higher end of the price spectrum, ambience, safari style and the operator's overall focus are important considerations. This chapter provides an overview of factors to consider when planning a safari.

PLANNING A SAFARI
Booking

The best place to organise a visit to the northern parks is in Arusha. For the southern parks, there's no comparable hub, although most southern-focused operators are based in Dar es Salaam. For the far west (Gombe and Mahale Mountains), Kigoma is the main base for independent and budget travellers, while almost all upper-end safaris to these parks, and to Katavi, are organised out of Arusha as fly-in packages or – for Mahale, as well as Katavi – as fly-in add-ons to a Ruaha safari. Mwanza is the best place to organise visits to Rubondo Island National Park, and there is a handful of Mwanza-based operators who also organise safaris into the western Serengeti.

ResponsibleTravel.com (www.responsibletravel.com) is a good place to start planning a culturally and environmentally responsible safari.

Booking (and paying for) a safari before arriving in Tanzania is common, and is also advisable, especially if you'll be travelling in popular areas during high seasons, when lodges tend to fill up completely months in advance. However, only book with operators that you have thoroughly checked out, and are sure are reputable, and take particular care at the budget level. Confirm that the operator you're considering is registered with TATO (see p45 – its website has an updated list, or you can contact the Tanzania Tourist Board [TTB] in Arusha), and try to get as much feedback on the operators you're considering as possible. While overall costs are likely to be about 5% to 10% higher at the budget level for pre-booked safaris, booking in advance will enable you to minimise dealings with safari touts. They're not all bad guys, but many are quite aggressive and the whole experience can be somewhat intimidating. It will also enable you to minimise the amount of cash or travellers cheques that you'll need to carry.

If you wait to book a safari once in Tanzania, allow at least a day to shop around, don't rush into any deals, and steer clear of any attempts of

---

POLE POLE (SLOWLY, SLOWLY)

When planning your safari, don't be tempted to try to fit too much in to your itinerary. Distances in Tanzania are long, and hopping too quickly from park to park is likely to leave you at the end tired, unsatisfied and feeling that you haven't even scratched the surface. Try instead to plan longer periods at just one or two parks – exploring in depth what each has to offer, and taking advantage of cultural and walking opportunities in park border areas.

PRICE CHANGES

As this book was being researched, significant increases in park and reserve concession fees were being discussed. If implemented, the actual amount will vary (from zero to US$50 per person per night in some cases), depending on the particular park and particular lodge in question. So don't be surprised if you receive price quotes from some lodges reflecting this new change.

---

intimidation by touts or dodgy operators to get you to pay immediately or risk losing your seat. In addition to being a reasonably reliable resource for checking on blacklisted operators, the TTB in Arusha also has a bulletin board that's a good spot to find safari companions if you're looking to form a group.

Costs

Most safari operator quotes include park entrance fees, the costs of accommodation or tent rental, transport costs from the starting base to the park, and the costs of fuel plus a driver/guide for wildlife drives. However, this varies enough that it's essential to clarify before paying. Drinks (whether alcoholic or not) are generally excluded (although many operators do provide one bottle of bottled water per day), and budget camping safari prices usually exclude sleeping bag rental (which costs anywhere from US$5 per day to US$10 per trip). Prices quoted by agencies or operators usually assume shared (double) room/tent occupancy, with supplements for single occupancy ranging from 20% to 50% of the shared-occupancy rate.

Check out Tanapa's website – www.tanza niaparks.com – for help in deciding which parks to visit.

If you are dealing directly with lodges and tented camps rather than going through a safari operator, you may be quoted 'all-inclusive' prices. In addition to accommodation, full board and sometimes park fees, these usually include two 'activities' (usually wildlife drives, or sometimes one wildlife drive and one walk) per day, each lasting about two to three hours. They generally exclude transport costs to the park. Whenever accommodation-only prices apply, you'll need to pay extra to actually go out looking for wildlife. Costs for this vary considerably, and can range from about US$30 per person per day per 'activity' to US$200 per day per vehicle for a wildlife drive.

There isn't necessarily a relationship between the price paid and the likelihood of the local community benefiting from your visit. Find out as much as you can about an operators' social and cultural commitment before booking, and check out our Greendex (p389), which highlights operators and establishments with positive community links.

Although obvious, it's worth noting that while booking through an agency abroad may be convenient, it will always be more expensive, as the actual in-country itinerary will be subcontracted to a Tanzania-based operator.

Tsetse flies are present in almost all of Tanzania's parks to varying degrees, depending on location and time of year. With their painful bites they can be unwelcome safari companions. To minimise the nuisance, wear thick, long-sleeved shirts and trousers in khaki or other drab shades, and avoid bright, contrasting and very dark clothing.

BUDGET SAFARIS

Most safaris at the lower end of the price range are camping safaris. In order to keep costs to a minimum, groups often camp outside national park areas (thereby saving park admission and camping fees) or, alternatively, stay in budget guesthouses outside the park. Budget operators also save costs by working with larger groups to minimise per-person transport costs, and by keeping to a no-frills setup with basic meals and a minimum number of staff. For most safaris at the budget level, as well as for many midrange safaris, daily kilometre limits are placed on the vehicles.

For any budget safari, the bare minimum cost for a registered company is about US$90 per person per day (camping), but most reliable operators charge closer to US$100 or US$110. Be wary of anyone offering you prices much below this, as there are bound to be problems. To save money, bring drinks with you, especially bottled water, as it's expensive in and near the parks. During the low season, it's often possible to find a lodge safari for close to the price of a camping safari.

MIDRANGE SAFARIS

The Serengeti is Tanzania's largest park (14,763 sq km) and home to the greatest concentration of large mammals in the world.

Most midrange safaris use lodges, where you'll have a comfortable room and eat in a restaurant. Overall, safaris in this category are comfortable, reliable and reasonably good value. A disadvantage is that they may have somewhat of a packaged-tour or production line feel, although this can be minimised by selecting a safari company and accommodation carefully, by giving attention to who and how many other people you travel with, and by avoiding the large, popular lodges during the high season. Expect to pay from about US$120 to US$200 per person per day for a midrange lodge safari.

TOP-END SAFARIS

Private lodges, luxury tented camps and sometimes private fly camps are used in top-end safaris, all with the aim of providing guests with as authentic and personal a bush experience as possible, while not foregoing the comforts. For the price you pay (from US$200 up to US$600 or more per person per day), expect a full range of amenities, as well as top-quality guiding. Even in remote settings without running water you will be able to enjoy hot, bush-style showers, comfortable beds and fine dining. Also expect a high level of personalised attention, and an often intimate atmosphere (many places at this level have fewer than 20 beds).

When to Go

See www.tourismconcern.org.uk for more on fair trade in tourism, travellers' guidelines and the Kilimanjaro porters' rights campaign.

When you choose to go on safari depends in part on what your interests are. For birding, any time of year is good, with the rainy season months from November/December through to April being particularly rewarding. For walking in wildlife areas, the dry season is generally best. For general wildlife viewing, it's also worth tailoring your choice of park destination according to the season. Large sections of Katavi, for example, are only accessible during the dry season, when vast herds of buffaloes, elephants and others jostle for space at scarce water sources, and almost all of the camps close during the rains. Tarangire National Park, although accessible year-round, is another park best visited during the dry season, when wildlife concentrations are significantly higher than at other times of the

---

TIPPING

Assuming service has been satisfactory, tipping is an important part of the safari experience (especially to the driver/guides, cooks and others whose livelihoods depend on tips), and this will always be in addition to the price quoted by the operator. Many operators have tipping guidelines; in general expect to tip about US$10 to US$15 per group per day to the driver and/or guide, and about US$8 to US$10 per group per day to the cook – more for top-end safaris groups with more people or if an especially good job has been done. It's never a mistake to err on the side of generosity while tipping those who have worked to make your safari experience memorable. Whenever possible, give your tips directly to the staff you want to thank.

SAFARI STYLE

While price can be a major determining factor in safari planning, there are other considerations that are just as important:

- **Ambience** Will you be staying in or near the park? (If you stay well outside the park, you'll miss the good early morning and evening wildlife-viewing hours.) Are the surroundings atmospheric? Will you be in a large lodge or an intimate private camp?

- **Equipment** Mediocre vehicles and equipment can significantly detract from the overall experience, and in remote areas, lack of quality equipment or vehicles and appropriate back-up arrangements can be a safety risk.

- **Access and activities** If you don't relish the idea of hours in a 4WD on bumpy roads, consider parks and lodges where you can fly in. Areas offering walking and boat safaris are best for getting out of the vehicle and into the bush.

- **Guides** A good driver/guide can make or break your safari. Staff at reputable companies are usually knowledgeable and competent. With operators trying to cut corners, chances are that staff are unfairly paid, and are not likely to be knowledgeable or motivated.

- **Community commitment** Look for operators that do more than just give lip-service to 'eco-tourism' principles, and that have a genuine, long-standing commitment to the communities where they work. In addition to being more culturally responsible, they'll also be able to give you a more authentic and enjoyable experience.

- **Setting the agenda** Some drivers feel that they have to whisk you from one good 'sighting' to the next. If you prefer to stay in one strategic place for a while to experience the environment and see what comes by, discuss this with your driver. Going off in wild pursuit of the 'Big Five' means you'll miss the more subtle aspects of your surroundings.

- **Extracurriculars** On the northern circuit, it's common for drivers to stop at souvenir shops en route. While this gives the driver an often much-needed break from the wheel, most shops pay drivers commissions to bring clients, which means you may find yourself spending more time souvenir shopping than you'd bargained for. If you're not interested, discuss this with your driver at the outset, ideally while in one of the operator's offices.

- **Less is more** If you'll be teaming up with others to make a group, find out how many people will be in your vehicle, and try to meet your travelling companions before setting off.

- **Special interests** If bird-watching or other special interests are important, arrange a private safari with a specialised operator.

year. In the Serengeti, by contrast, wildlife concentrations are comparatively low during the dry season; it's during the wet season that you'll see the enormous herds of wildebeests in the park's southeastern section, although the dry season is best for lions and other predators. If you are timing your safari around specific events such as the Serengeti wildebeest migration, remember that seasons vary from year to year and are difficult to accurately predict in advance. See the individual park sections for more details on when to visit.

Other general considerations to keep in mind are that getting around is easier throughout the country in the dry season (late June to October), and in many parks this is when animals are easier to find around water holes and rivers. Foliage is also less dense, making it easier to spot wildlife. However, as the dry season corresponds in part with the high-travel season, lodges and camps become crowded and accommodation prices are at a premium. Also note that a number of lodges and camps, mainly in Selous Game Reserve and in the western parks, close for a month or so around April and May.

Tarangire National Park is home to northern Tanzania's largest elephant population. For more see www.wcs.org/tarangire.

WHAT TO BRING

Useful items to bring along:

- binoculars

- field guides

- good-quality sleeping bag (for camping safaris)

- mosquito repellent

- rain gear and waterproofs for wet-season travel – especially for camping safaris

- sunglasses

- camera (and film or large memory card)

- extra contact lens solution and your prescription glasses (as the dust can be irritating)

- mosquito net (top-end lodges and tented camps usually have nets, but it doesn't hurt to bring one along, and you'll often need one for budget guesthouses)

Additional items for walking safaris include lightweight, long-sleeved/-legged clothing in subdued colours, a head covering and sturdy, comfortable shoes.

For budget safaris, it's a good idea to bring extra food and snacks and a roll of toilet paper. In and near the parks, there's little available, except hotel meals and perhaps a few basics, so if you're on a tight budget, stock up on bottled water and supplies in the nearest major centre.

ACCESS

Although weighty, The Safari Companion – A Guide to Watching African Mammals, by Richard Estes, is an excellent and indispensable guide to many of the animals you'll see on safari.

Most of the northern circuit is readily accessible by road, and there is now a tarmac access road all the way to Ngorongoro Crater. However, distances are long, especially if you head beyond Ngorongoro to explore the Serengeti, so it's worth considering flying at least one way. This is particularly true if you're averse to bumping around on dusty (or muddy) roads. Alternatively, consider planning routes that avoid straight out-and-back drives (such as Arusha–Ngorongoro–Serengeti–Mwanza). For road access, travelling in a group (three to four is optimal) can help you save significantly by splitting vehicle costs.

In the south of Tanzania, Ruaha and Mikumi National Parks are readily accessed via road (here, too, being in a group will save costs) or flight, while most visitors to the Selous Game Reserve arrive via small plane, although road access is perfectly feasible, including by public bus. Unless you happen to be travelling around Sumbawanga, Mpanda or elsewhere in the region, reaching Katavi National Park via road is rough and time-consuming although eminently doable. For those with enough cash, there are also regular charter flights – most from either Arusha or Ruaha. Mahale Mountains National Park is reached via charter flight from Arusha or Ruaha via Katavi, or a long and rather adventurous ferry ride down Lake Tanganyika, while Gombe Stream National Park is accessed via boat from Kigoma. Both Mahale and Gombe are good bets for folk travelling solo, as neither requires vehicles for getting around once in the park (thus there's no need to hunt up a group to minimise transport costs). The same applies also to Kitulo and Udzungwa Mountains National Parks. If you're travelling independently, it's always worth checking for spare seats on charter flights if you're trying to get yourself somewhere, or simply asking the lodge where you'll be staying if it happens to have transport heading your way.

TYPES OF SAFARIS

Traditionally, the main and often the only way to visit most of Tanzania's wildlife-viewing parks has been in a vehicle. Fortunately, this is changing, with walking, cycling and cultural activities in park border areas increasingly available.

Vehicle Safaris

Vehicle safaris are by far the most common type of safari in Tanzania, and, in many parks, due to park regulations, they are still the only option. In the northern parks, vehicle safaris must be done in a 'closed' vehicle, which means a vehicle with closed sides, although there is almost always an opening in the roof, which allows you to stand up, get a better view and take photographs. These openings are sometimes just a simple hatch that flips open or comes off, or (better, as it affords some shade) a pop-up style roof. In wildlife reserves such as Selous and Mkomazi Game Reserves, some of the southern parks and Katavi National Park, safaris in open vehicles are permitted. These are usually high vehicles with two or three seats at staggered levels and a covering over the roof, but completely open on the sides and back. If you have the choice, open vehicles are far better as they are roomier, give you a full viewing range and minimise barriers. The least-preferable option is minibuses, which are sometimes used, especially in the north. They accommodate too many people for a good experience, the rooftop opening is usually only large enough for a few passengers to use at a time and at least some passengers will get stuck in middle seats with poor views.

Whatever type of vehicle you are in, try to avoid overcrowding. Sitting uncomfortably scrunched together for several hours over bumpy roads puts a definite damper on the safari experience. Most safari quotes are based on groups of three to four passengers, which is about the maximum for comfort in most vehicles. Some companies put five or six passengers in a standard 4WD, but the minimal savings don't compensate for the extra discomfort. Also helpful to maximising a good experience on a vehicle safari is abandoning at least to some extent a 'Big Five' mentality, and instead of chasing around from sighting to sighting, staying put for a while in one location, turning the motor off and letting the surrounding environment begin to settle in to your senses. A quality driver/guide will have a good sense of balance between knowing when to do some driving around and searching and when to turn the motor off and sit for a while.

Night drives are currently not permitted in any of Tanzania's parks and reserves except for Lake Manyara, although they're possible in adjacent wildlife areas.

Walking Safaris

Most parks with large wildlife place tight limits on the amount of walking that can be done within their boundaries, and most walking safaris offered are for relatively short walks of two to three hours, usually done in the early morning or late afternoon. At the end of the walk, you'll then return to the main camp or lodge or alternatively to a fly camp, although sometimes it's possible to organise longer walks. Not much distance is covered in comparison to a straight walk for the same time period; the pace is measured and there will be stops en route for observation, or for your guide to pick up an animal's track. Some walking safaris are done within the park and reserve boundaries, while others are in adjacent areas that are part of the park or reserve ecosystem, with similar habitats and wildlife, where longer walks are also possible.

For more about ongoing studies of lions in Serengeti and Ngorongoro Crater, see www .lionresearch.org.

The Kingdon Field Guide to African Mammals by Jonathan Kingdon makes a fine safari companion, with a wealth of information on Tanzania's wildlife.

In the widely acclaimed *Sand Rivers*, Peter Matthiessen takes you on a hauntingly beautiful safari into the heart of Selous Game Reserve – essential reading for anyone planning a visit.

Whatever the length and location, if you have the chance and inclination to do a walking safari, it's highly worthwhile. Although you may not see the numbers of animals that you would in a vehicle (since you won't cover as much ground), you'll experience the bush at a completely different level. There's nothing that quite conveys the vastness of the African plains, or the power and rawness of nature, as having your feet on the ground with nothing between you and the sounds, the breeze, the smells and the grasses. Places where you can walk in 'big game' areas include Selous Game Reserve, Ruaha, Mikumi, Katavi and Arusha National Parks, and in wildlife areas bordering Tarangire National Park. There are also several parks – notably the Kilimanjaro, Udzungwa Mountains and Kitulo parks – that can only be explored on foot. You'll be on foot in Gombe Stream and Mahale Mountains National Parks, and walks are easily arranged in Rubondo Island National Park.

In addition to the 'Big Five' (elephants, lions, leopards, buffaloes and rhinos), there's also the 'Little Five' (elephant shrews, ant lions, leopard tortoises, buffalo weavers and rhino beetles).

Walks are always accompanied by a guide, who is usually armed, and with whom you will need to walk in close proximity.

Boat & Canoe Safaris

Like walking safaris, boat safaris are an excellent way to experience the East African wilderness, and a welcome break from dusty, bumpy roads. They are also the only way to fully explore riverine environments and they'll give you a new perspective on the terrestrial scene as you approach hippos or crocodiles at close range, float by a sandbank covered with birds or observe animals on shore from a river vantage point. With a few possible exceptions along the Rufiji River, where several operators can organise upmarket multinight journeys exploring the delta area, boat safaris are almost always limited to a few hours' duration, and a similarly priced alternative to a vehicle safari for the same period.

The best place by far for boat safaris is along the Rufiji River in Selous Game Reserve (p311), where it is one of the reserve's main draws. They're also possible on the Wami River bordering Saadani National Park (p158), although neither the scenery, the wildlife nor the river can compare with those in the Selous. In Arusha National Park, you can take short (two-hour) canoe safaris on the Momela Lakes (p207).

ITINERARIES

For safaris, the general rule is the longer spent in one park, the better, particularly in large areas such as the Serengeti, Ruaha National Park and Selous Game Reserve. Much of the safari market focusing on the northern circuit has degenerated into quick in-and-out trips that that – apart from the deleterious environmental effects – often wind up as rather unsatisfying, with a disproportionate amount of time spent travelling to and from the parks. While it is possible to see plenty of wildlife on a day trip or an overnight excursion, the more time you take, the better you'll be able to experience the more subtle attractions of Tanzania's magnificent wilderness areas.

Lake Manyara has been declared a Unesco Biosphere Reserve in recognition of its habitat and species diversity, including almost 400 types of birds.

If you're serious about a safari, allow a minimum of five days from Arusha to get off the main roads and explore. In the south and west, or anywhere if you fly in and out, a minimum of three to four days, focused on one park or reserve, is recommended. Several suggestions for itineraries are outlined following.

Northern Parks

Arusha National Park is the best bet for a day trip, while Tarangire and Lake Manyara parks are each easily accessed as overnight trips from Arusha, although all these parks deserve more time to do them justice. For a half-week itinerary, try any of the northern parks alone (although for the Serengeti, it's worth flying at least one way, since it's a full day's drive from Arusha), or Ngorongoro Crater together with either Lake Manyara or Tarangire. With

---

KEEPING THINGS GREEN

Organisations working for environmental conservation include the following:

Lawyers Environmental Action Team (www.leat.or.tz) An environmental law team working to ensure equitable natural resource management.

Sea Sense (www.seasense.org) A local NGO collaborating with local communities to protect dugong (sea cow) and marine turtle populations and their habitats.

Wildlife Conservation Society of Tanzania (WCST; Map p90; ☎ 022-211 2518; www.wcstonline .org; Garden Ave, Dar es Salaam) The best local contact for information on environmental issues; also publishes the informative environmental newsletter *Miombo*.

World Wide Fund for Nature (www.panda.org) Various initiatives in Tanzania, including in the Udzungwa Mountains.

---

a week, you will have just enough time for the classic combination of Lake Manyara, Tarangire, Ngorongoro and the Serengeti, but it's better to focus on just two or three of these. And the Serengeti alone, or in combination with Ngorongoro Crater, could easily keep you happy for a week. Many operators offer a standard three-day tour of Lake Manyara, Tarangire and Ngorongoro (or a four- to five-day version including the Serengeti). However, distances to Ngorongoro and the Serengeti are long, and the trip is likely to leave you feeling that you've spent too much time rushing from park to park and not enough time settling in and experiencing the actual environments.

In addition to these more conventional itineraries, there are countless other possibilities combining wildlife viewing with visits to other areas. For example, you might begin with a vehicle safari in the Ngorongoro Crater followed by a climb of Ol Doinyo Lengai, trekking elsewhere in Ngorongoro Conservation Area, relaxing at one of the lodges around Karatu or visiting Lake Eyasi, or alternatively, combine travel around Lake Victoria and a visit to Rubondo Island National Park with the Serengeti.

> Bernhard Grzimek's 1959 film *The Serengeti Shall Not Die* was one of the most influential wildlife films ever made, drawing world attention to the Serengeti and conservation in Africa.

Southern Parks

Mikumi and Saadani National Parks are good destinations from Dar es Salaam if you only have a couple of nights. Three to four days would be ideal for Selous Game Reserve, or for Ruaha National Park, if you fly. Saadani and Selous also make a possible four- to five-day option, although with Saadani more intended as a beach holiday following Selous, rather than for the wildlife, and Mikumi and Udzungwa Mountains National Parks make a potential safari-hiking combination. Recommended week-long combination itineraries include Selous and Ruaha, and Ruaha and Katavi, in the west, both of which allow you to sample markedly different terrain and wildlife populations. The Ruaha-Katavi combination is increasingly popular given the availability of flights between the two parks. The expanded flight network linking the southern and western parks with the coast has opened up the possibility for longer itineraries combining time on the coast or islands with safaris in Ruaha, Mahale and/or Katavi. Selous and Mafia or Zanzibar is also a recommended safari-beach combination.

> Friends of Ruaha Society (www.friendsofruaha .org) is working for the conservation of the Ruaha ecosystem, and ensuring that tourism benefits from wildlife also reach local communities.

Western Parks

Katavi, Mahale Mountains and Gombe Stream can be visited adventurously and rewardingly via public transport (combining train, bus and ferry), but you will need plenty of time, and most upmarket itineraries use flights. For Katavi alone, however you arrive, plan on a minimum of three days in the park. For a six- to seven-day itinerary, Katavi and Mahale make a fine combination, and many fly-in safari schedules are built around this itinerary. Katavi is also easily and rewardingly combined with Ruaha, and a

Ruaha–Katavi–Mahale grouping is also quite feasible, although at least nine or 10 days should be allotted. At the top end, consider rounding out the Mahale-Katavi combination with a few days relaxing on Lake Tanganyika at the high-end Lupita Island Resort. For Gombe Stream, budget two to three days.

Other Areas

Mkomazi Game Reserve is an intriguing, off-beat stop on any itinerary linking Dar es Salaam or the northeastern coast with Arusha and the northern circuit, or even as a stand-alone bush experience in combination with coastal destinations or hiking in the Usambara Mountains. Kitulo National Park can be worked in to itineraries in the Mbeya-Tukuyu area, while Lukwika-Lumesule Game Reserve is only really feasible for travellers already in the Masasi area. Also in the southeast is Mnazi Bay-Ruvuma Estuary National Marine Park, which is best done as a stand-alone excursion from either Mtwara or Mikindani. Diving in Mafia Island Marine Park is easily incorporated into a stay – whether budget or upmarket – on Mafia island.

OPERATORS

A good operator is the single most important variable for your safari, and it's worth spending time thoroughly researching those you're considering. The following are recommended companies, although the lists are by no means exclusive. Many northern circuit operators also organise trekking, and vice versa; see p54 for trekking operators. An increasing number of private (ie non-chain) lodges also have in-house operators and if you'll be combining several parks in the same area, this is a good alternative. If you plan on organising your safari through your hotel or lodge, confirm in advance that it will have a vehicle and guide available for wildlife drives.

Birds of Kenya and Northern Tanzania, by Dale Zimmerman, Donald Turner & David Pearson, is an essential field guide for birders.

Arusha

Also see the Trekking operators listed on p54, most of whom also organise safaris.

Access2Tanzania (☎ 027-250 4715; www.access2tanzania.com; budget & midrange) A small operator focusing on customised, community-focused itineraries in various areas of the country.

Africa Travel Resource (ATR; ☎ in UK 44-01306-880770; www.africatravelresrouce.com; midrange to top end) A web-based safari broker that matches your safari ideas with an operator, and helps you plan and book customised itineraries. Its website contains heaps of background information on Tanzania, the safari circuits and lodges, and its quotes are extremely detailed, including full descriptions and line-by-line pricing.

In the Shadow of Man, by Jane Goodall, details the author's early years in Gombe Stream National Park, and is excellent background reading for anyone planning a visit.

Duma Explorer (☎ 0787-079127; www.dumaexplorer.com; Njiro Hill; budget to midrange) Northern Tanzania safaris, Kilimanjaro and Meru treks, northern Tanzania cultural tours and safari-coast combinations.

Firelight Expeditions (☎ 027-250 8773; www.firelightexpeditions.com; top end) A high-end outfit with a handful of luxury and mobile camps, including in the Serengeti, Katavi and on Lake Tanganyika. Superb if you have the money and are interested in nontraditional itineraries and locations.

George Mavroudis Safaris (☎ 027-254 8840; www.gmsafaris.com; top end) An upmarket operator, highly respected in industry circles and specialising in exclusive, customised mobile safaris in the northern circuit done in vintage style. It also runs a wonderful, classic bush camp in Mkomazi Game Reserve, and a getaway on Lukuba Island in Lake Victoria – the latter is a fine combination with a Serengeti safari.

Hoopoe Safaris (Map pp196-7; ☎ 027-250 7011; www.hoopoe.com; India St; upper midrange) An excellent, culturally responsible company offering personalised luxury camping and lodge safaris in the northern circuit with an emphasis on individualised itineraries and service. Hoopoe has its own tented camps in the Lake Manyara and West Kilimanjaro areas, and mobile camps in the Serengeti, and in other parts of the northern circuit, where it has formed partnerships with and made investments in the surrounding communities. Staff and guides are highly professional and prices, while not inexpensive, are good value. Combination itineraries with Kenya, Uganda, Rwanda

CHOOSING AN OPERATOR

Following are some things to keep in mind when choosing a safari or trekking operator, particularly if you're planning to book a budget safari on arrival in Tanzania.

■ Get personal recommendations, and talk with as many people as you can who have recently returned from a safari or trek and who have used the company you're considering.

■ Be sceptical of quotes that sound too good to be true, and don't rush into any deals, no matter how good they sound.

■ Don't fall for it if a tout tries to convince you that a safari or trek is leaving 'tomorrow' and that you can be the final person in the group. Take the time to shop around at reliable outfits to get a feel for what's on offer and, if others have supposedly registered, ask to speak with them.

■ Check the blacklist of the **Tanzania Tourist Board's Tourist Information Centre** (TTB; ☎ 027-250 3843; www.tanzania-web.com) in Arusha – although keep in mind that this isn't necessarily the final word. The TTB, as well as the **Tanzanian Association of Tour Operators** (TATO; ☎ 027-250 4188; www.tatotz.org) also maintains lists of licenced operators. While TATO isn't the most powerful of entities, going on safari with one of its members will at least give you some recourse to appeal in case of problems. Legitimate operators should also be able to show you their valid original TALA (Tourist Agents Licensing Authority) licence – a government-issued document without which a company isn't authorised to bring tourists into national parks. (For wildlife parks, a tour or safari operator designation on the licence suffices; for Kilimanjaro treks, a TALA mountaineering licence is required.) Be sceptical of claims that the original is with the 'head office' in Dar es Salaam or elsewhere in the country.

■ Don't give money to anyone who doesn't work out of an office, and don't arrange any safari deals at the bus stand or with touts who follow you to your hotel room.

■ Go with a company that has its own vehicles and equipment. If you have any doubts, don't pay a deposit until you've seen the vehicle that you'll be using. Be aware that it's not unknown for an operator to show you one vehicle, but then arrive in an inferior one on the day.

■ Unless you speak Swahili, be sure your driver-guide can speak English.

■ Go through the itinerary in detail and confirm what is expected and planned for each stage of the trip. Check that the number of wildlife drives per day and all other specifics appear in the contract, as well as the starting and ending dates, and approximate times, and keep in mind that while two competing safari company itineraries may look the same, service can be very different. Normally, major problems such as vehicle breakdown are compensated for by adding additional time to your safari. If this isn't possible (eg if you have an onward flight), reliable operators may compensate you for a portion of the time lost. However, don't expect a refund for 'minor' problems such as punctured tyres and so on. Also note that park fees are non-refundable.

■ If you have any doubts about an operator, only organise local bookings with them. For example, don't book a Kilimanjaro trek from Dar es Salaam; if something goes wrong you'll be far away and without recourse.

■ Beware of client swapping between companies; you can end up in the hands of a company you were trying to avoid.

and Sudan are also possible. Several years ago, distinguished as Best Eco-Tourism Operator in the World by *Condé Nast Traveler*.

IntoAfrica (☎ in UK 44-114-255 5610; www.intoafrica.co.uk; midrange) A small operator specialising in fair-traded cultural safaris and treks in northern Tanzania. It directly supports local communities in the areas where it works, consistently garners positive reviews from travellers and is an ideal choice if your interest is more in gaining insight into local life and culture, than in experiencing the luxury lodge atmosphere. One of its most popular itineraries is a seven-day wildlife-cultural safari in Maasai areas.

SAFARI SCAMS & SCHEMES

When it comes to booking safaris and treks, especially at the budget level, the need for caution can't be overemphasised. If you stick with reliable safari or trekking operators, including the ones recommended in this chapter, you shouldn't have major problems. Most difficulties arise when trying to book budget safaris on arrival. Remember that once your money is paid, it's as good as gone. Also, watch out for the following:

■ Touts who promise you a bargain safari or trek deal, but in order to seal it, payment must be made on the spot – of course with a receipt. The next day, the promised transport doesn't show up, the receipt turns out to be for a bogus company, and the tout is never seen again.

■ Sham operators trading under the same names as companies listed in this or other guidebooks. Don't let business cards fool you; they're easy to print up, and are no proof of legitimacy.

If you do get taken for a ride, the main avenue of recourse is to file a complaint with both the TTB and TATO. The police will be of little help, and it's unlikely that you will see your money again.

Kahembe's Trekking & Cultural Safaris (☎ 027-253 1088, 0784-397477; kahembeculture@hotmail.com, kahembeculture@yahoo.com; budget) A small operator offering Mt Hanang treks and a range of no-frills cultural safaris around Babati. A good choice if you want to experience Tanzania from a local perspective. It can sometimes help arrange volunteer opportunities around Babati, and also can be booked through Responsible Travel (p36).

Maasai Wanderings (☎ 0755-984925; www.maasaiwanderings.com; midrange) A small company offering northern Tanzania safaris and treks, including safaris for families and seniors, plus Zanzibar packages; profits are channelled into various community projects.

Nature Beauties (Map pp196-7; ☎ 027-254 8224, 0732-971859; www.naturebeauties.com; Old Moshi Rd; budget) A low-key outfit offering Kilimanjaro treks and northern circuit safaris, and Tanzania-Kenya combination itineraries.

Nature Discovery (☎ 0732-971859; www.naturediscovery.com; midrange) Individualised, environmentally responsible northern-circuit safaris, and treks on Kilimanjaro, Meru and in the Crater Highlands.

Roy Safaris (Map pp196-7; ☎ 027-250 2115; www.roysafaris.com; Serengeti Rd; all budgets) A highly regarded company offering budget and semiluxury camping safaris in the northern circuit, as well as competitively priced luxury lodge safaris and Kilimanjaro and Meru treks. Known for its high-quality vehicles and value for money.

Safari Makers (☎ 027-254 4446; www.safarimakers.com; budget) A reliable outfit running no-frills northern circuit camping and lodge safaris and treks at surprisingly reasonable prices; some safaris and treks also incorporate Cultural Tourism Program tours.

SOK (☎ 0784-694624; www.sokadventures.com; upper midrange & top end) A small, environmentally responsible operator based in Usa River, and offering tailor-made northern circuit safaris with the chance for cultural interaction.

Sunny Safaris (Map pp196-7; ☎ 027-250 8184, 027-250 7145; www.sunnysafaris.com; Colonel Middleton Rd; budget) A reliable budget operator with a range of no-frills camping and lodge safaris, as well as Kilimanjaro and Meru treks and day walks in the area around Arusha.

Tropical Trails (off Map pp196-7; ☎ 027-250 0358, 027-250 5578; www.tropicaltrails.com; Masai Camp, Old Moshi Rd; upper midrange) In addition to trekking (see listing on p55), this recommended operator also offers northern circuit camping and lodge safaris, and several cultural tours in the Arusha area.

Wild Spirit Safari (☎ 027-254 8961; www.wild-spirit-safari.com) Safaris and treks in northern Tanzania, including trekking in the Crater Highlands, as well as extensions to Zanzibar, Mafia and Pemba.

Dar es Salaam

The following agencies can help you book southern-circuit safaris, or combination itineraries involving Mikumi, Ruaha and Katavi National Parks, Selous Game Reserve, and Zanzibar and Mafia islands.

Iain and Oria Douglas-Hamilton put Lake Manyara on the map with Life Among the Elephants.

Afriroots (☎ 0732-926350; www.afriroots.co.tz; budget) This laid-back group has garnered positive feedback doing backpacker-oriented village-based biking, hiking and other tours around Dar es Salaam, in the Uluguru, Usambara and Udzungwa Mountains and in the southern highlands, plus itineraries to the Selous Game Reserve and other areas.

Authentic Tanzania (☎ 022-276 2093; www.authentictanzania.com; midrange) A flexible, knowledgeable operator offering a variety of good-value itineraries throughout the south and along the coast, as well as to Katavi. Set departure destinations from Dar es Salaam include Udzungwa Mountains, Mikumi, Selous, Kilwa and Ruaha, and customised itineraries are also available. It's also recommended if you're interested in an adventurous Katavi road trip, taking in Ruaha and other stops en route.

Coastal Travels (Map p90; ☎ 022-211 7959, 022-211 7960; safari@coastal.cc; Upanga Rd; midrange) A long-established and recommended outfit with its own fleet of planes, and safari camps and lodges in Ruaha park, the Selous and on Mafia island. It has frequent 'last-minute' flight-and-accommodation deals, and is a good contact for putting together itineraries taking in different parts of the country, or combining safaris with nonsafari touring. Offerings include competitively priced Ruaha packages, day trips to Zanzibar and Selous-Mafia combinations.

Foxes African Safaris (☎ in UK 44-01452-862288, in Tanzania 0744-237422; www.tanzania safaris.info; midrange to top end) A highly regarded family-run company with lodges and camps in Mikumi, Ruaha and Katavi National Parks, on the coast near Bagamoyo and in the Southern Highlands. It's a good choice for personalised combination itineraries to these destinations using plane and road.

Hippotours & Safaris (Map p90; ☎ 022-212 8662/3; www.hippotours.com; Nyumba ya Sanaa, Ohio St; midrange to top end) A specialist agency focusing on itineraries in the south and west and along the coast, including Selous Game Reserve and Mafia island.

Tent with a View (☎ 022-211 0507, 0741-323318; www.saadani.com; upper midrange) This helpful, reliable and recommended group runs lovely lodges in Selous Game Reserve and Saadani National Park and organises good-value midrange and upmarket combination itineraries involving these and other areas, including special honeymoon packages.

Mwanza

For Mwanza-based safari operators, see p246.

Kigoma

For Kigoma-based operators, see p263.

Elsewhere in Tanzania

Gazelle Safaris (Mbeya) – see p292.

Hatari! (1962, John Wayne/Hardy Kruger) was filmed in Arusha National Park and Ngorongoro Crater. While it has little to do with safaris (the stars are capturing animals for zoos), it has great footage of local wildlife and scenery.

TIPS FOR WILDLIFE WATCHING *David Lukas*

- Your best bet for seeing black rhino is Ngorongoro Crater, where about 20 remain. Here they are used to vehicles, while elsewhere in Tanzania they are secretive and occur in remote locations.

- Let the vervet monkeys tell you if there's a predator in the neighbourhood. Listen for their screeching alarm calls and look in the direction they're facing.

- During the July to October dry season, Tarangire National Park provides the best wildlife viewing in Tanzania. Over 3000 elephants and many other migratory animals come here to drink from the Tarangire River.

- Hundreds of thousands of flamingos may be seen at Lake Manyara National Park, though they move from lake to lake as water levels change and their presence is never predictable.

- Without a doubt your best wildlife viewing tool will be a high-quality pair of binoculars. Practics using them at home before departing because some animals, especially birds, don't wait around for you to learn how to aim and focus in the field.

DO-IT-YOURSELF SAFARIS

It is quite possible to visit the parks with your own vehicle, without going through a safari operator, though it's much less commonly done than in some southern African safari destinations. Unless you're already based in Tanzania or are familiar with the country, experienced at driving in the bush and self-sufficient as far as repairs and mechanical issues go, the modest (if any) cost savings are generally offset by the comparative ease of having someone else handle the logistics for you.

For almost all parks and reserves, you'll need a 4WD. In addition to park admission fees, there's a US$40 per day vehicle fee for foreign-registered vehicles (Tsh10,000 for locally registered vehicles). Guides are not required for most of the main parks, except as noted in the individual park entries. However, it's recommended to take one along to help you find your way through the bush, as well as for showing you the best wildlife areas. Guide fees are given on p77.

You'll also need to carry extra petrol, as it's not available in any of the parks, except at Seronera in the Serengeti and at Ngorongoro Crater, where it's expensive; the lodges and hotels will not be able to provide you with petrol. It's also essential to carry spares, and have good mechanical knowledge.

You can rent safari vehicles in Dar es Salaam, Arusha, Mwanza, Karatu and Mto wa Mbu, as well as at Ngorongoro Crater (where you can hire a park vehicle with driver from the NCAA headquarters; advance notice required). It's also sometimes possible to arrange vehicle hire at park headquarters in Katavi National Park. Otherwise, there's no vehicle rental at any of the parks or reserves. Unless you are in a group, renting a car specifically for safari is usually at least as expensive as going through a tour operator, especially for the northern parks.

Camping will give you the most flexibility, as you can always find a spot. If you plan on staying in lodges, book well in advance, especially during the high season.

Cultural Tourism Programs also make a possible DIY safari alternative; see p205.

Trekking

Tanzania is gaining increasing popularity as a trekking destination, offering rugged, varied terrain and a fine collection of peaks and rolling mountain ranges. Landscapes range from the lushly forested slopes of the eastern Udzungwa Mountains to the sheer volcanic cliffs of the inner wall of Mt Meru's crater and the final scree-slope ascent of Mt Kilimanjaro, and the types of treks range from village-to-village walks to isolated wilderness hikes. With the possible exception of Kilimanjaro, trekking and hiking here is generally done as part of a larger itinerary. Throughout the country, almost all trekking can be done without technical equipment, by anyone who is reasonably fit. However, any trekking or hiking in national parks and wildlife areas requires being accompanied by a guide or ranger, which usually also entails adhering to set daily stages. Mt Kilimanjaro and the Ngorongoro Conservation Area are expensive. Otherwise, most trekking can be done at reasonable cost.

Liz de Leyser's excellent *A Guide to the Southern Highlands of Tanzania* is an essential read for anyone planning on hiking in this region. For more about the Southern Highlands region, see www.southernhighland stz.org.

PLANNING
Booking
General booking considerations for treks are similar to those for safaris; see p36. Kilimanjaro treks should be organised through a trekking company (see p54) or through a safari company that also has a TALA mountaineering licence (see p45 for more on TALA licences). Treks in the Ngorongoro Conservation Area should also be organised through a trekking company, while treks on Mt Meru can be organised through a company or independently with park staff. Treks in other destinations are best arranged locally and on the spot, working with local guide associations, cultural tourism programmes or (in the case of national parks) park staff.

The best places for booking Kilimanjaro treks are Moshi and Marangu, followed by Arusha. Meru treks are best booked in Arusha if you'll be going through a trekking operator, as are treks in the Crater Highlands and climbs up Ol Doinyo Lengai.

The 3 Peaks 3 Weeks Challenge (www.3peaks3weeks .org): 10 women trekked Kili, Meru and Mt Kenya to raise money and awareness for education, HIV/AIDS and environmental issues in Africa.

Costs
Trekking in Tanzania has the well-deserved reputation of being expensive, especially for treks on Kilimanjaro and in the Crater Highlands, which are among the most expensive trekking destinations in East Africa. Yet, most other treks can be done on a reasonable budget with a bit of effort, and a few are cheap. Among the least expensive trekking areas – all of which are easily accessed via public transport – are Udzungwa Mountains National Park, where your main costs will be for entry fees and a guide; the Usambara, Pare and Uluguru Mountains, all of which can be done independently (although a guide is recommended) or as part of local cultural tourism programmes; Mt Hanang and Mt Longido (near Arusha), both of which also can be climbed

---

TREKKING SAFETY GUIDELINES

- Pay all fees required by local authorities.
- Be sure you are healthy and prepared for local weather conditions.
- Inform yourself about conditions along your route and about local wildlife regulations.
- Know your own limits.

as part of local cultural tourism programmes; and Kitulo National Park, which can be hiked independently by well-equipped experienced hikers or with a guide.

To minimise costs, trek or hike outside national parks, carry your own camping equipment (to cut down on rental costs), avoid treks that necessitate vehicle rentals for access and consider trekking out of season when you may be able to negotiate discounted rates. However, it's not worth cutting corners where reliability is essential, such as on Kilimanjaro.

The Wildlife Conservation Society's Tanzania page (www.wcs.org/international/Africa/Tanzania) has excellent links detailing conservation projects in trekking and wildlife areas.

When to Go

Throughout most of the country, the best times for trekking are during the dry, warmer season from mid-December to February, and the dry, cooler season from June to October. The least favourable time is from mid-March to mid-May, when the heaviest rains fall. That said, trekking is possible in most areas year-round, with the exception of the Udzungwa, Usambara, Pare and Uluguru Mountains, where conditions become extremely muddy during the March to May rains.

ACCESS

Almost all trekking areas can be accessed via public transport. Exceptions to this include the Crater Highlands, which are generally only trekked as part of a package including transport, and Kilimanjaro, where transport to the trailhead is almost always included in trekking operator quotes (although major trailheads are also readily accessible via public transport).

The Shadow of Kilimanjaro: On Foot Across East Africa by Rick Ridgeway is ideal reading before setting off to explore Tanzania on foot.

TYPES OF TREKS

Stage-by-stage fully-equipped trekking accompanied by guides and porters is the norm for treks on Mt Kilimanjaro and Mt Meru (although climbing Meru doesn't require porters), while the Usambaras, and to a lesser extent the Pares, involve easy village-to-village walks where you can stock up on basic food items as you go along. Ol Doinyo Lengai is also a relatively structured and generally fully-equipped venture, given the rugged conditions and difficulties of access, as is most trekking in the Crater Highlands. Most other areas are somewhere in between, requiring that you stock up in advance on basics and have a guide (or a GPS and some basic Swahili), but with flexibility as to routes and guiding.

GUIDES & PORTERS

Guides are required for treks on Mt Kilimanjaro, Mt Meru, in the Crater Highlands and in Udzungwa Mountains National Park. Elsewhere, although not strictly essential, a local guide is recommended to show you the way, to provide introductions in remote places and to guard against occasional instances of hassling and robberies in some areas. If you decide to hike without a guide, you'll need to know some basic Swahili. Wherever you trek, always

---

TIPPING

Tipping guidelines for guides and porters on Mt Kilimanjaro and Mt Meru are covered separately in the Trekking Mt Kilimanjaro (p191) and Trekking Mt Meru (p209) sections. In other areas, and assuming service has been satisfactory, guides will expect a modest but fair tip for their services. In the case of national parks (such as Udzungwa Mountains National Park), daily rates are predetermined by the park, and noted in the relevant sections of this book. Elsewhere, check with the local Cultural Tourism Program to get an idea of the going rates - which are generally well below those on Mts Kilimanjaro and Meru.

WHAT TO BRING

The list of what to bring varies depending on where you'll be trekking. Some things to consider:

- Good-quality sleeping bag (essential for Mt Kilimanjaro and Mt Meru treks, and available to rent through trekking operators)
- Birding guides and checklists
- Mosquito repellent
- Rain gear and waterproofs
- Sunglasses and sunscreen
- Camera (and film or adequate memory)
- Extra contact-lens solution and prescription glasses
- Mosquito net
- Tent
- Extra water bottles

For Mt Kilimanjaro and Mt Meru, you'll need a full range of waterproof cold-weather clothing and gear. In all of Tanzania's mountain areas, expect rain at any time of year and considerably cooler weather than along the coast. Nights especially can be very chilly, and a water- and windproof jacket and warm pullover are essential. Particularly on Kilimanjaro, waterproof everything, especially your sleeping bag, as things rarely dry on the mountain.

---

be sure your guide is accredited. On Kilimanjaro, this should be taken care of by your trekking company, and on Mt Meru and in Udzungwa Mountains National Park, guides are park rangers. The Ngorongoro Conservation Area also has its own guides. In other areas, check with the local tourist office or guide association before finalising your arrangements.

Porters are commonly used on Mt Kilimanjaro, and sometimes on Mt Meru, though not elsewhere. In some areas, notably the Crater Highlands, donkeys may be used to carry gear.

TREKKING AREAS

The following are pocket summaries of Tanzania's main trekking and hiking areas. For more on each, see the destination chapters. For more information on treks, see Lonely Planet's *Trekking in East Africa*.

Mt Kilimanjaro

This is Africa's highest mountain (5869m) and Tanzania's most famous trek, with a choice of routes, all making their way from the forested lower slopes to moorland and alpine zones to the snow- and glacier-covered summit. There are also many walks on Kilimanjaro's lower slopes, of interest for their lush vegetation, waterfalls and cultural opportunities centred on local Chagga villages. Marangu and Machame make good bases. See p191.

Mt Meru

Although languishing in the shadow of nearby Kilimanjaro, Mt Meru (4566m) is a fine destination in its own right, and considerably less costly than its famous neighbour. It's also worth considering as a preparatory trek for the higher peak and, as part of Arusha National Park, is well suited for safari-trek combination itineraries. The climbing is nontechnical and straightforward, although there's a challenging ridge walk as you approach the summit. See p209.

Kilimanjaro: To the Roof of Africa by Audrey Salkeld is a dramatic recounting of the climb up Africa's highest mountain – highly inspirational if you're planning a trek.

An essential pre-trek read: the porter guidelines at www.hec .org/club/properporter .htm#guidelines.

Mt Hanang

Tanzania's fourth-highest peak (3417m) offers a rewarding and comparatively easy trek along well-worn footpaths to the summit. It's also relatively inexpensive to organise, and makes an intriguing destination if you're interested in combining trekking with an introduction to local cultures. See p236.

Mt Hanang is the south-ernmost of Tanzania's Rift Valley volcanoes. The surrounding area is home to the seminomadic Barabaig. For insights into Barabaig culture, read George Klima's dated but intriguing The Barabaig: East African Cattle Herders.

Crater Highlands & Ngorongoro Conservation Area

Together with adjoining parts of the Ngorongoro Conservation Area, the Crater Highlands offer rugged and rewarding and generally expensive trekking, best organised through a specialist operator. The terrain includes steep escarpments, crater lakes, dense forests and grassy ridges, streams and waterfalls, plus the still-active volcano of Ol Doinyo Lengai, just north of the Ngorongoro Conservation Area boundaries and best accessed from Lake Natron. Apart from the Maasai people who live here, you'll likely have most areas to yourself. See p221.

Usambara Mountains

The western Usambaras offer village-to-village walks along well-worn local footpaths, ranging from a few hours to a week or more. There are enough local guesthouses to make carrying a tent necessary. The main centre for hikes in the eastern Usambaras is Amani Nature Reserve, where there is a network of short forest footpaths – ideal for a weekend ramble or for anyone interested in botany. Hikes combining the two regions (allow five to six days) are best organised in Lushoto. See p168.

Pare Mountains

Ol Doinyo Lengai is the only active volcano in the world that spews natrocarbonatite lava.

Hiking in the Pares is comparable to hiking in the Usambaras, along a network of well-trodden mountain footpaths. However, the Pares are much less developed for tourism and walks tend to be shorter – generally undertaken as part of the local cultural tourism programme – with accommodation in local guesthouses. See p176.

RESPONSIBLE TREKKING

- Carry out all your rubbish, including sanitary napkins, tampons, condoms and toilet paper (these burn and decompose poorly).
- Take minimal packaging and reusable containers or stuff sacks.
- Use toilets where available. Otherwise, bury your waste in a small hole 15cm (6in) deep and at least 100m (320ft) from any watercourse, and cover the waste with soil and a rock.
- Don't use detergents or toothpaste in or near watercourses, even if they are biodegradable.
- For washing, use biodegradable soap and a water container at least 50m (160ft) away from the watercourse. Disperse the waste water widely to allow the soil to filter it fully.
- Wash cooking utensils 50m (160ft) from watercourses using a scourer instead of detergent.
- Stick to existing trails and avoid short cuts, and avoid removing the plant life that keeps topsoils in place.
- Don't depend on open fires for cooking. Cutting firewood in popular trekking areas can cause rapid deforestation. Cook on a lightweight kerosene, alcohol or Shellite (white gas) stove and avoid those powered by disposable butane gas canisters.
- If trekking with a guide and porters, supply stoves for the whole team. In cold areas, see that all members have sufficient clothing so that fires aren't necessary for warmth.
- Don't buy items made from endangered species.

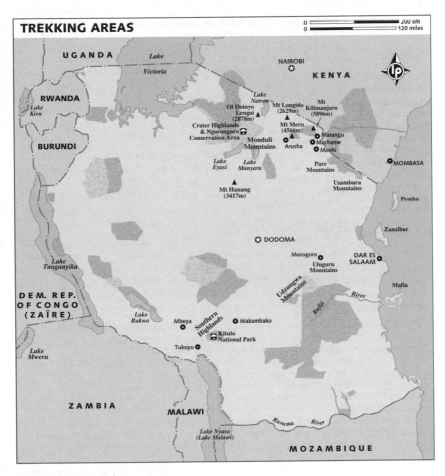

Udzungwa Mountains

The lush Udzungwas lack the ease and picturesque scenery of the Usambaras and the cultural tourism of the Pares, but they are fascinating from a botanical perspective, with more unique plant species than almost anywhere else in the region. They are also a prime destination for birders and – with their appealingly wild feel – anyone seeking something well off the main track. There is only a handful of fully established trails, ranging from a half-hour walk to multiday mountain hikes (for which you'll need a tent and will have to be self-sufficient with food). See p280.

Check out www.african conservation.com/ulu guru for information on the Uluguru Mountains.

Uluguru Mountains

If you happen to be in Morogoro, it's worth setting aside some time for hiking in the densely populated Ulugurus – of interest both culturally and botanically. Hikes (most half-day or day) range from easy to moderately stiff excursions. Guides are easily organised in Morogoro, and costs are very reasonable. See p277.

Southern Highlands & Kitulo National Park

Until recently, the beautiful rolling hill country in southwestern Tanzania, stretching southwards roughly between Makambako and Mbeya, had essentially no tourist infrastructure. With the recent gazetting of Kitulo National Park and a slowly expanding network of basic accommodation, this is beginning to change. Short day hikes and excursions can be organised from Mbeya or, better, Tukuyu. For anything longer and for overnight hiking in Kitulo, you'll still need to be self-sufficient and carry a tent and all your supplies. See p290.

Other Areas

The Monduli Mountains (p207), northwest of Arusha, offer some walks and views down into the Rift Valley from their northern side. Northeast of Arusha, and just east of the Arusha–Namanga road, is Mt Longido (2629m), which can be climbed as part of a local cultural tourism programme (see p204).

Eastern Arc Mountains Information Source (www.easternarc.org) is an information clearinghouse for the many environmental projects being undertaken in the Usambaras, Udzungwas and other Eastern Arc ranges.

OPERATORS

When organising a Kilimanjaro trek, look for companies that have their own mountain-climbing licence (as opposed to the tour-operator licence required for safaris). Many of the safari operators listed on p44 also organise treks. For trekking companies abroad, see p355.

KILIMANJARO'S PORTERS

Mt Kilimanjaro guides and porters have a reputation for being aggressive and demanding when it comes to tips, and higher tips are expected here than elsewhere in the region. But there's another side too, with porter abuse and exploitation a serious concern.

Most of the porters who work on the slopes of Mt Kilimanjaro are local residents who work freelance, usually with no guarantees of a salary beyond the present job. The work is physically hard, rates are low and it's safe to say that even the best-paid porters earn only a pittance in comparison with the salaries of many of the trekkers whose bags they are carrying. Because of the stiff job competition, it's common for porters to agree to back-to-back treks without sufficient rest in between. It's also common for porters to work without proper shoes or equipment, and without adequate protection at night from the mountain's often cold and wet conditions. Equally concerning are cases where unscrupulous guides – perhaps interested in keeping an extra porter's salary for themselves – bribe the rangers who weigh porters' loads. This leaves the porter with the unenviable choice of carrying an overly heavy load or not getting the job at all.

Porters depend on tourism on the mountain for their livelihood, but as a trekker you can help ensure that they aren't exploited and that working conditions are fair. When selecting a trekking operator, tell them this is a concern. Be aware of what goes on around you during your trek. If you see exploitative treatment, tell the tour operator when you get back. Also get in touch with the UK-based **Tourism Concern** (www.tourismconcern.org.uk), which has mounted a worldwide campaign to improve the conditions of porters. Another clued-up group is the **International Mountain Explorers Connection** (IMEC; www.mountainexplorers.org), which runs the **Kilimanjaro Porter Assistance Project** (KPAP; Map p183; ☎ 0754-817615; www .kiliporters.org; Kilimanjaro Backpackers Hotel, Mawenzi Rd, Moshi), a not-for-profit group that's channelling trekking-clothing donations to porters (trekkers coming from the USA are invited to ferry bags of surplus clothes – contact IMEC directly about this), arranging informal English-language training opportunities and lobbying local tour operators to establish a code of conduct on porter pay and conditions. IMEC has guidelines at www.hec.org/club/properporter .htm#guidelines. Both KPAP and Tourism Concern keep lists of trek operators who promote fair treatment of their staff.

KILI'S TOPOGRAPHY

The Kilimanjaro massif has an oval base about 40km to 60km across, and rises almost 5000m above the surrounding plains. The two main peak areas are Kibo, the dome at the centre of the massif, which dips inwards to form a crater that can't be seen from below, and Mawenzi, a group of jagged pinnacles on the eastern side. A third peak, Shira, on the western end of the massif, is lower and less distinct than Kibo and Mawenzi. The highest point on Kibo is Uhuru Peak (5896m), the goal for most trekkers. The highest point on Mawenzi, Hans Meyer Point (5149m), cannot be reached by trekkers and is only rarely visited by mountaineers.

Kilimanjaro is considered an extinct volcano, although it still releases steam and sulphur from vents in the crater centre.

Arusha

If you're organising a Kilimanjaro trek in Arusha, look for operators that organise treks themselves rather than subcontracting to a Moshi- or Marangu-based operator. Arusha-based safari operators that are also recommended for trekking on Kilimanjaro, Meru and in the Crater Highlands include Duma Explorer, Hoopoe Safaris, IntoAfrica, Nature Discovery, Roy Safaris, SOK and Wild Spirit Safari. For Mt Hanang treks, the best contact is Kahembe's Trekking & Cultural Safaris. Contacts for all of these are listed on p44.

Dorobo Safaris (☎ 027-250 9685, ☎ /fax 027-254 8336; dorobo@habari.co.tz; midrange) A down-to-earth outfit that's highly knowledgeable for customised culturally oriented treks in and around the Ngorongoro Conservation Area. It also organises wilderness treks in the areas bordering Ruaha and Serengeti National Parks. All work is done in partnership with local communities, with the emphasis on exploring remote areas in a way that sustainably benefits these communities and the environment.

Kiliwarrior Expeditions (www.kiliwarriors.com; top end) Ethical, upmarket Kilimanjaro climbs, treks in the Ngorongoro Conservation Area, a full range of safaris and a great website.

Summits Africa (www.summits-africa.com; upper midrange & top end) A dynamic, ethical and experienced company offering upmarket adventure safaris with expert guiding, including treks in the Ngorongoro Conservation Area and to Lake Natron with the option to climb Ol Doinyo Lengai, West Kilimanjaro walking safaris, multiday fully-equipped bike safaris and combination bike-safari trips, plus any sort of mountain trekking and trekking-safari combinations that you'd like. Also organises the 3 Peaks 3 Weeks challenge.

Tropical Trails (off Map pp196-7; ☎ 027-250 0358/5578; www.tropicaltrails.com; Maasai Camp, Old Moshi Rd; midrange) A long-standing company offering high-quality treks and walking safaris on Kilimanjaro, Meru, in the Crater Highlands and in the Monduli Mountains. Kosher treks, photographic camping safaris and other special interest tours can be arranged, and a portion of the company's profits goes towards supporting education projects in Maasai schools.

Marangu

Almost all Marangu hotels organise Kilimanjaro treks; see p189. Also worth noting is Marangu Hotel's 'hard way' option that's one of the cheapest deals available for a reliable trek. For about US$200 plus park fees for a five-day Marangu climb, the hotel will take care of hut reservations and provide a guide with porter, while you provide all food and equipment.

Moshi

The following Moshi-based companies focus on Kilimanjaro treks, although most can also organise day hikes on the mountain's lower slopes.

Akaro Tours Tanzania (Map p183; ☎ 027-275 2986; www.akarotours.com; ground fl, NSFF Bldg, Old Moshi Rd; budget) A small outfit offering good, no-frills Kilimanjaro treks, day hikes on Kilimanjaro's lower slopes and a range of other tours, including to the Usambaras.

Since they were first measured in the early 20th century, Kilimanjaro's glaciers have lost over 80% of their ice and they may disappear completely by 2020. For more see p192.

The Highland Mangabey, Africa's first new monkey species in over two decades, was recently discovered around Kitulo National Park and in the Udzungwa Mountains.

CHOOSING A TREKKING OPERATOR

Organised-trek costs vary considerably and depend on the length of the trek, the size of the group, the standard of accommodation before and after the trek, the quality of bunkhouses or tents, plus the knowledge and experience of guides and trek leaders. Many of the points mentioned in the Choosing An Operator boxed text in the Safaris chapter (p45) apply in equal measure to treks. Some other things to consider when choosing a trekking company:

■ Choose operators treating local communities and employees as equal partners and who have conscientious environmental attitudes. Always comment on bad practice and if the goals of ecotourism are not being met as promised.

■ Before you sign up ask for an itinerary in writing and double-check the number of days spent actually trekking and how many nights accommodation are included. Check confirmed hut and bunkhouse reservations.

■ Make sure there are enough porters, a cook and an assistant guide or two (in case the group splits or somebody has to return due to illness).

■ Beware of unscrupulous budget companies charging you for, say, a five-day trek but only paying mountain and hut fees for four days.

■ Be wary of tales about 'running out of money' as promises of refunds are usually forgotten or denied when you get back to base.

Mt Meru's most recent eruption was in 1910. Its famous crater was formed about 7800 years ago when the volcano's summit collapsed.

Key's Hotel (off Map p183; ☎ 027-275 2250; www.keys-hotels.com; Uru Rd; midrange) A long-established place offering standard Kilimanjaro packages.
Moshi Expeditions & Mountaineering (Map p183; ☎ 027-275 4234; www.memtours.com; Kaunda St; budget to midrange) Kilimanjaro treks at competitive prices.
Shah Tours (Map p183; ☎ 027-275 2370/2998; www.kilimanjaro-shah.com; Sekou Toure Rd; midrange) A reliable and long-established operator offering quality Kilimanjaro and Meru treks at reasonable prices, as well as treks in the Ngorongoro highlands and on Ol Doinyo Lengai.
Zara Tanzania Adventures (Map p183; www.zaratravel.com; budget to midrange) Kilimanjaro treks.

WILDLIFE & HABITAT David Lukas

Think of East Africa and the word 'safari' comes to mind – and Tanzania offers the finest safari experiences and wildlife spectacles found anywhere on the planet. You will never forget the shimmering carpets of zebras and wildebeests, the explosion of cheetahs springing from cover, or the spine-tingling roars of lions at night when you visit the Serengeti or Ngorongoro Crater. But with over 40 national parks and game reserves to choose from there is plenty of room to get off the beaten path and craft your own safari.

Cats

In terms of behaviour, the six cats of Tanzania are little more than souped-up housecats; it's just that some weigh half as much as a horse and others jet along as fast as a speeding car. With their excellent vision and keen hearing, cats are superb hunters. And some of the most powerful scenes in Africa are the images of big cats making their kills. If you happen across one of these events you won't easily forget the energy and ferocity of these life-and-death struggles.

1 Leopard

Weight 30-60kg (female), 40-90kg (male); length 170-300cm More common than you realise, the leopard relies on expert camouflage to stay hidden. During the day you might only spot one reclining in a tree after it twitches its tail, but at night there is no mistaking their bone-chilling groans that sound like wood being sawn at high volume.

2 Lion

Weight 120-150kg (female), 150-225kg (male); length 210-275cm (female), 240-350cm (male) Those lions sprawled out lazily in the shade are actually Africa's most feared predators. Equipped with teeth that tear effortlessly through bone and tendon they can take down an animal as large as a bull giraffe. Each group of adults (a pride) is based around generations of females that do all the hunting; swaggering males fight amongst themselves and eat what the females catch.

3 Serval

Weight 6-18kg; length 90-130cm Twice as large as a housecat, but with towering legs and very large ears, the beautifully spotted serval is highly adapted for walking in tall grass and making prodigious leaps to catch rodents and birds. More diurnal than most cats, it may be seen tossing food in the air and playing with it.

4 Cheetah

Weight 40-60kg; length 200-220cm Less cat than greyhound, the cheetah is a world-class sprinter. Although it reaches 112km/h, the cheetah runs out of steam after 300m and must cool down for 30 minutes before hunting again. This speed comes at another cost – the cheetah is so well adapted for running that it lacks the strength and teeth to defend its food or cubs from attack by other large predators.

5 Wildcat

Weight 3-6.5kg; length 65-100cm If you see what looks like a tabby wandering the plains of Tanzania you're likely seeing a wildcat, the direct ancestor of our domesticated house cats. Occurring wherever there are abundant mice and rats, the wildcat is readily found on the outskirts of villages, where it can be identified by its unmarked rufous ears and longish legs.

6 Caracal

Weight 8-19kg; length 80-120cm The caracal is a gorgeous tawny cat with extremely long, pointy ears. This African version of the northern lynx has jacked-up hind legs like a feline dragster. These beanpole kickers enable this slender cat to make vertical leaps of 3m and swat birds out of the air.

Primates

East Africa is the evolutionary cradle of primate diversity, giving rise to over 30 species of monkeys, apes, and prosimians (the 'primitive' ancestors of modern primates). Somewhere along the way, one branch of the family tree apparently tottered onto the path that gave rise to humans – a controversial hypothesis supported by Leakey's famous excavations at Olduvai Gorge. No matter what you believe, it is possible to see hints of human society in the complex social lives of Tanzania's many primates.

❶ Olive Baboon

Weight 11-30kg (female), 22-50kg (male); length 95-180cm Although the formidable olive baboon has 5cm-long fangs and can kill a leopard, its best defence may consist of running up trees and showering intruders with liquid excrement. Either way, you won't want to alarm this animal. Intelligent and opportunistic, troops of these greenish baboons are becoming increasingly abundant over northern Tanzania, while the much paler yellow baboon ranges over the rest of the country.

❷ Black-and-White Colobus

Weight 10-23kg; length 115-165cm Also known as the guereza, the black-and-white colobus is one of about seven colobus species found in Tanzania, but it gets the lion's share of attention due to its flowing white frills. Like all colobus, this agile primate has a hook shaped hand so it can swing through the trees with the greatest of ease. When two troops run into each other, expect to see a real show.

❸ Chimpanzee

Weight 25-40kg; length 60-90cm Travelling to Tanzania's western border for chimpanzees may be off the beaten path, but it's hard to deny the allure of these uncannily human-like primates. It doesn't take a brain surgeon to perceive the deep intelligence and emotion lurking behind such eerily familiar deep-set eyes, and researchers at Gombe Streams and Mahale Mountains National Parks are making startling discoveries about chimp behaviour – you deserve to see for yourself.

❹ Vervet Monkey

Weight 4-8kg; length 90-140cm If any monkey epitomised East Africa, it would be the widespread and adaptable vervet monkey. Each troop of vervets is composed of females that defend a home range passed down from generation to generation, while males fight each other for bragging rights and access to females. If you think their appearance too drab, check out their extraordinary blue and scarlet colours when they get excited.

❺ Greater Galago

Weight 550-2000g; length 55-100cm A cat-sized nocturnal creature with dog-like face, the greater galago belongs to a group of prosimians that have changed little in 60 million years. Best known for its frequent bawling cries (hence the common name 'bushbaby'), the galago would be rarely seen except that it readily visits feeding stations at many popular safari lodges. Living in a world of darkness, galagos communicate with each other through scent and sound.

Cud-chewing Mammals

Africa is arguably most famous for its astounding variety of ungulates – hoofed mammals that include everything from buffalos to giraffes and rhinos. Many of these animals live in herds to protect themselves from the continent's formidable predators, with some herds numbering in the millions. Ungulates that ruminate (chew their cud) and have horns are called bovines. Among this family, antelopes are particularly numerous, with about 40 amazingly different species in East Africa alone.

① Wildebeest

Weight 140-290kg; length 230-340cm Few animals evoke the spirit of the African plain as much as the wildebeest. Over a million gather on the Serengeti alone, where they form vast, constantly moving herds accompanied by a host of predators and gaggles of wide-eyed spectators.

② Greater Kudu

Weight 120-315kg; length 215-300cm The oxen-sized greater kudu is a study in elegance. One of the tallest antelopes, it relies on white pinstripes to conceal it in brushy thickets. The very long spiralling horns of the male are used in ritualised combat.

③ Gerenuk

Weight 30-50kg; length 160-200cm The gerenuk is one of the strangest creatures you'll ever see – a tall slender gazelle with a giraffe-like neck. Adapted for life in the semi-arid brush of northeastern Tanzania, the gerenuk stands on its hind legs to reach 2m-high branches.

④ African Buffalo

Weight 250-850kg; length 220-420cm Imagine a cow on steroids, then add a particularly fearsome set of curling horns, and you get the massive African buffalo. Thank goodness they're usually docile, because an angry or injured buffalo is an extremely dangerous animal.

⑤ Bush Duiker

Weight 12-25kg; length 80-130cm When you're a tiny antelope on every predator's menu, you need some clever ways to protect yourself. The bush duiker lives in dense thickets and marks out escape routes with scent glands on its face.

⑥ Waterbuck

Weight 160-300kg; length 210-275cm If you're going to see any antelope on safari, it's likely to be the big, shaggy, and some say smelly, waterbuck. Dependent on waterside vegetation, waterbuck numbers fluctuate dramatically between wet and dry years.

⑦ Thomson's Gazelle

Weight 15-35kg; length 95-150cm Lanky and exceptionally alert, Thomson's gazelle is one of several long-legged antelopes built for speed. The 400,000 on the Serengeti plains migrate in great herds, along with zebras and wildebeest. Look for their attractive black flank stripes.

⑧ Hartebeest

Weight 120-220kg; length 190-285cm Yes, the long face of the hartebeest (kongoni) is an odd sight, but it helps this short-necked antelope reach grass to graze on. Commonly seen on open plains, the hartebeest is easily recognised by its set of backward twisted horns.

⑨ Sable

Weight 200-270kg; length 230-330cm Looking like a colourful horse with huge soaring horns, the sable ranks as one of Africa's most visually stunning mammals. Breeding males turn black to signal their readiness to fight, and given their fearsome horns it's a signal not to be taken lightly.

Hoofed Mammals

A full stable of Africa's charismatic animals can be found in this group of ungulates. Other than the giraffe, these ungulates are not ruminants and are seen over a much broader range of habitats than bovines. They have been at home in Africa for millions of years and are among the most successful mammals to have ever wandered the continent. Without human intervention, Africa would be ruled by elephants, zebras, hippos and warthogs.

2

❶ Plains Zebra
Weight 175-320kg; length 260-300cm My oh my, those plains zebras sure have some wicked stripes. Although each animal is as distinctly marked as a fingerprint, scientists still aren't sure what function these patterns serve. Do they help zebras recognise each other?

❷ Hippopotamus
Weight 510-3200kg; length 320-400cm The hippopotamus is one strange creature. Designed like a floating beanbag with tiny legs, the 3000kg hippo spends its time in or very near water chowing down on aquatic plants. Placid? No way! Hippos have tremendous ferocity and strength when provoked.

❸ African Elephant
Weight 2200-3500kg (female), 4000-6300kg (male); height 2.4-3.4m (female), 3-4m (male) No one, not even a human or lion, stands around to argue when a towering bull elephant rumbles out of the brush. Commonly referred to as 'the king of beasts', elephant society is actually ruled by a lineage of elder females.

❹ Rock Hyrax
Weight 1.8-5.5kg; length 40-60cm It doesn't seem like it, but those funny tailless squirrels you see lounging around on rocks are actually an ancient cousin to the elephant. You won't see some of the features that rock hyraxes share with their larger kin, but look for tusks when one yawns.

❺ Black Rhinoceros
Weight 700-1400kg; length 350-450cm Pity the black rhinoceros for having a horn that is worth more than gold. Once widespread and abundant south of the Sahara, the rhino has been poached to the brink of extinction. Unfortunately, females may only give birth every five years.

❻ Warthog
Weight 45-75kg (female), 60-150kg (male); length 140-200cm Despite their fearsome appearance and sinister tusks, only the big males are safe from lions, cheetahs, and hyenas. To protect themselves when attacked, warthogs run for burrows and reverse in while slashing wildly with their tusks.

❼ Giraffe
Weight 450-1200kg (female), 1800-2000kg (male) The 5m-tall giraffe does such a good job with upward activity – reaching up to grab high branches, towering above the competition – that stretching down to get a simple drink of water is difficult. Though they stroll along casually, they can outrun any predator.

Carnivores

It is a sign of Africa's ecological richness that the continent supports a remarkable variety of predators. In addition to six types of cats, Tanzania's other two dozen carnivores range from slinky mongooses to highly social hunting dogs. All are linked in having 'carnassial' (slicing) teeth, but visitors may be more interested in witnessing the superb hunting prowess of these highly efficient hunters. When it comes to predators, expect the unexpected and you'll return home with a lifetime of memories!

① Hunting Dog
Weight 20-35kg; length 100-150cm Fabulously and uniquely patterned so that individuals recognise each other, hunting dogs run in packs of 20 to 60 that ruthlessly chase down antelopes and other animals. Organised in complex hierarchies maintained by rules of conduct, these highly social canines are incredibly efficient hunters. At the same time, disease and persecution has pushed them into near extinction and they now rank as one of Africa's foremost must-see animals.

② Golden Jackal
Weight 6-15kg; length 85-130cm It barks and yelps like a dog and looks like a mangy mutt, but the golden jackal is one of Africa's scrappiest critters. Despite its trim, diminutive form, the jackal fearlessly stakes a claim at the dining table of the African plain. If not through sheer fierceness and bluff, then through tact and trickery, a jackal manages to fill its belly while holding hungry vultures and much stronger hyenas at bay.

③ Banded Mongoose
Weight 1.5-2kg; length 45-75cm Tanzania's eight species of mongoose may be difficult to separate, but the commonly observed banded mongoose is easily recognised by its finely barred pattern and social nature. Bounding across the savanna on their morning foraging excursions, family groups are a delightful sight when they stand up on their hind legs for a better view of the world. Not particularly speedy, they find delicious snacks in toads, scorpions, and slugs.

④ Spotted Hyena
Weight 40-90kg; length 125 215cm The spotted hyena is one of Tanzania's most unusual animals. Living in packs ruled by females that grow penis-like sexual organs, these savage fighters use their bone-crushing jaws to disembowel terrified prey on the run or to do battle with lions. The sight of maniacally giggling hyenas at a kill, piling on top of each other in their eagerness to devour hide, bone, and internal organs, is unsettling.

⑤ Ratel
Weight 7-16kg; length 75-100cm Don't be mislead by the small size and skunk-like appearance of the ratel – it may be the fiercest of all African animals. Some Africans say they would rather face a lion than a ratel, and even lions relinquish their kill when a ratel shows up. Also known as 'honey badger', the ratel finds its favourite food by following honey guides, birds that lead the badger to bee hives.

1

Birds of Prey

Tanzania has nearly 100 species of hawks, eagles, vultures and owls. Over 40 types have been seen at Lake Manyara National Park alone, making this one of the best places in the world to see an incredible variety of birds of prey. Look for them perching on trees, soaring high overhead, or gathered around a carcass; and pay particular attention for the scolding cries of small birds harassing one of these feared hunters.

4

❶ African Fish Eagle

Length 75cm Given its name, it's not surprising that you'll see the African fish eagle hunting for fish around water. With a wingspan of over 2m, this replica of the American bald eagle presents an imposing appearance, but it is most familiar for its loud, ringing vocalizations that have become known as 'the voice of Africa'.

❷ Augur Buzzard

Length 55cm Perhaps Tanzania's commonest raptor, the augur buzzard occupies a wide range of wild and cultivated habitats. Virtually identical to the red-tailed hawk of the Americas, this buzzard is sometimes called the African red-tailed hawk. One of their most successful hunting strategies is to float motionlessly in the air by riding the wind, then stooping down quickly to catch unwary critters.

❸ White-Backed Vulture

Length 80cm All eight of Tanzania's vultures can be seen mingling with lions, hyenas and jackals around carcasses. Here, through sheer numbers, they compete – often successfully – for scraps of flesh and bone. It's not a pretty sight when gore-encrusted vultures take over a carcass that no other scavenger wants, but it's the way nature works. The white-backed vulture, with its fuzzy neck and head and white back, is the most common vulture.

❹ Bateleur

Length 60cm The bateleur is an attractive serpent-eagle with a funny name. French for 'tightrope-walker', the name refers to its distinctive low-flying aerial acrobatics. In flight, look for this eagle's white wings and odd tailless appearance; close up, look for the bold colour pattern and scarlet face.

❺ Secretary Bird

Length 100cm In a country full of unique birds, the secretary bird literally stands head and shoulders above the masses. With the body of an eagle and the legs of a crane, the secretary bird towers 1.3m-tall and walks up to 20km a day in search of vipers, cobras and other snakes, which it kills with lightning speed and agility. This idiosyncratic, grey-bodied raptor is commonly seen striding across the savanna.

1

Birds

Bird-watchers from all over the world travel to Tanzania in search of the country's 1100 species of birds – an astounding number by any measure – including birds of every shape and in every colour imaginable. No matter where you travel in the country you will be enchanted and amazed by an ever-changing kaleidoscope of birds.

4

❺ Gray-Crowned Crane
Length 100cm The grey-crowned crane is, simply put, an extremely elegant bird. Topped with a frilly yellow bonnet, this blue-grey crane dances wildly and shows off its red throat pouch during the breeding season.

❶ Superb Starling
Length 18cm The superb starling is a stellar example of the many birds in Tanzania that slap together bright colours and call it a day. With black face, yellow eye, and metallic blue-green upperparts that contrast sharply with their red-orange belly, they seem like a rare find, but are actually surprisingly abundant.

❷ Saddle-Billed Stork
Height 150cm; wingspan 270cm Not only is the saddle-billed stork the most stunning of Tanzania's eight stork species, it is also one of the more remarkably coloured of all the country's birds. As if its 2.7m wingspan wasn't impressive enough, check out its brilliant-red kneecaps and bill.

❸ Speckled Mousebird
Length 35cm Not every bird in Tanzania is the biggest, best, or most colourful. The highly gregarious speckled mousebird is none of those things, but it does attract attention due to its comical habit of hanging from branches and wires while resting or sleeping.

❹ Lesser Flamingo
Length 100cm Coloured a deep rose-pink, and gathering by the hundreds of thousands on shimmering salt lakes, the lesser flamingo creates some of the most dramatic wildlife spectacles found in Africa, especially when they all fly at once or perform synchronised courtship displays.

❻ Hamerkop
Length 60cm The hamerkop is a stork relative with an oddly crested, cartoonish, woodpecker-like head. Nicknamed the 'hammerhead', it is frequently observed hunting frogs and fish at the water's edge. Look for its massive 2m-wide nests in nearby trees.

❼ Ostrich
Height 200-270cm If you think the ostrich looks prehistoric, you aren't far off. Standing 2.7m high and weighing upwards of 130kg, these ancient flightless birds escape predators by running away at 70km per hour or lying flat on the ground to resemble a pile of dirt.

❽ Lilac-Breasted Roller
Length 40cm Nearly everyone on safari gets to know the gorgeously coloured lilac-breasted roller. Related to kingfishers, rollers get their name from the tendency to 'roll' from side to side in flight as a way of showing off their iridescent blues, purples and greens.

❾ Red-Billed Oxpecker
Length 18cm The unique red-billed oxpecker is a starling that sits on the backs of large mammals, eating 100 ticks a day. Any benefit they do the animal is cancelled out because they also keep old wounds open to drink blood and pus.

Habitats

Nearly all of Tanzania's wildlife occupies a specific type of habitat, and you will hear rangers and fellow travellers refer to these habitats repeatedly as if they were code words. Your wildlife viewing experience will be greatly enhanced if you learn how to recognise these habitats and the animals you might expect in each one.

② Savanna

Savanna is the classic East African landscape – broad rolling grasslands dotted with lone acacia trees. The openness of this landscape makes it a perfect home for large herds of grazing zebras and wildebeest, in addition to fast-sprinting predators like cheetahs. Shaped by fire and grazing animals, savanna is a dynamic habitat in constant flux with its adjacent woodlands.

① Woodland

Tanzania is the only place in East Africa to find woodland, locally known as miombo. This important habitat provides homes for many birds, small mammals and insects. Here the trees form a continuous canopy cover that offers shelter from predators and harsh sunlight. Where fingers of woodland mingle with savanna, animals like leopards and antelope find shade and places to rest during the day.

③ Semi-arid desert

Parts of northeastern Tanzania see so little rainfall that shrubs and hardy grasses, rather than trees, are the dominant vegetation. Lack of water limits larger animals such as zebras, gazelles and antelopes to waterholes, but when it rains this habitat explodes with plant and animal life. During the dry season, many plants shed their leaves to conserve water, and grazing animals move on in search of food and water.

Environment

THE LAND

At over 943,000 sq km (almost four times the size of the UK), Tanzania is East Africa's largest country. To the east it's bordered by the Indian Ocean and to the west by the deep lakes of the Western Rift Valley. The narrow coastline consists of long, sandy stretches punctuated by dense stands of mangroves, especially around river deltas.

Inland, the terrain rises abruptly into mountains, before levelling out onto an arid highland plateau averaging 900m to 1800m in altitude and nestled between the eastern and western branches of the Great Rift Valley.

Tanzania's mountain ranges are grouped into a sharply rising northeastern section (the Eastern Arc) and an open, rolling central and southern section (the Southern Highlands or Southern Arc). There is also a range of volcanoes, known as the Crater Highlands, rising from the side of the Great Rift Valley in northern Tanzania.

The largest river is the Rufiji, which drains the Southern Highlands en route to the coast. Other major rivers include the Ruvu, Wami, Pangani and Ruvuma (the border with Mozambique).

About 6% (59,000 sq km) of mainland Tanzania is covered by inland lakes.

WILDLIFE
Animals

Tanzania's fauna is notable both for sheer numbers and variety, with representatives of 430 species and subspecies among the country's more than four million wild animals. These include zebras, elephants, wildebeests, buffaloes, hippos, giraffes, antelopes, dik-diks, gazelles, elands and kudus. Tanzania is also known for its predators, with Serengeti National Park one of the best places for spotting lions, cheetahs and leopards. There are also populations of hyenas and wild dogs and, in Gombe Stream and Mahale Mountains National Parks, bands of chimpanzees.

In *Battle for the Elephants*, Ian and Oria Douglas-Hamilton describe the ongoing political battles over the ivory trade in Africa.

THE GREAT RIFT VALLEY

The Great Rift Valley is part of the East African rift system – a massive geological fault stretching 6500km across the African continent, from the Dead Sea in the north to Beira (Mozambique) in the south. The rift system was formed over 30 million years ago when the tectonic plates comprising the African and Eurasian landmasses collided and then diverged. As the plates separated, large chunks of the earth's crust dropped down between them, resulting over millennia in the escarpments, ravines, flatlands and lakes that characterise East Africa's topography today.

The rift system is notable for its calderas and volcanoes (including Mt Kilimanjaro, Mt Meru and the calderas of the Crater Highlands) and for its lakes, which are often very deep, with floors well below sea level although their surfaces may be several hundred metres above sea level.

The Tanzanian Rift Valley consists of two branches formed where the main rift system divides north of Kenya's Lake Turkana. The Western Rift Valley extends past Lake Albert (Uganda) through Rwanda and Burundi to Lakes Tanganyika and Nyasa, while the eastern branch (Eastern or Gregory Rift) runs south from Lake Turkana, past Lakes Natron and Manyara, before joining again with the Western Rift by Lake Nyasa. The lakes of the Eastern Rift are smaller than those in the western branch, with some only waterless salt beds. The largest are Lakes Natron and Manyara. Lake Eyasi is in a side branch off the main rift.

The escarpments of Tanzania's portion of the Rift Valley are most impressive in and around the Ngorongoro Conservation Area and Lake Manyara National Park.

THE EASTERN ARC MOUNTAINS

The ancient Eastern Arc mountains – which include the Usambara, Pare, Udzungwa and Uluguru ranges – stretch in a broken crescent from southern Kenya's Taita Hills down to Morogoro and the Southern Highlands. They are estimated to be at least 100 million years old, with the stones forming them as much as 600 million years old. Their climatic isolation and stability has offered plant species a chance to develop, and today these mountains are highly biodiverse and home to an exceptional assortment of plants and birds. Plant and bird numbers in the mountain ranges total about one-third of Tanzania's flora and fauna species, and include many unique species plus a wealth of medicinal plants.

In the late 19th century, population growth and expansion of the local logging industry began to cause depletion of the Eastern Arc's original forest cover, and erosion became a serious problem. It became so bad in parts of the western Usambaras that in the early 1990s entire villages had to be shifted to lower areas. It has now somewhat stabilised.

See the Wildlife Guide (p57) for descriptions of some of these animals. In addition, Tanzania has over 60,000 insect species, about 25 types of reptiles or amphibians, 100 species of snakes and numerous fish species.

Complementing this are over 1000 species of birds, including various types of kingfisher, hornbills (around Amani in the eastern Usambaras), bee-eaters (along the Rufiji and Wami Rivers), fish eagles (Lake Victoria) and flamingos (Lakes Manyara and Natron, among other places). There are also many birds that are unique to Tanzania, including the Udzungwa forest partridge, the Pemba green pigeon, the Usambara weaver and the Usambara eagle owl.

Birders: watch for a copy of Field Guide to the Birds of East Africa by Terry Stevenson and John Fanshawe.

ENDANGERED SPECIES

Endangered species include the black rhino (best spotted in Ngorongoro Crater, p223); Uluguru bush shrikes (spotted in Uluguru Mountains, p277, southeast of Morogoro); hawksbill, green, olive ridley and leatherback turtles; red colobus monkeys (in Zanzibar's Jozani Forest, p139); wild dogs (most likely spotted in Selous Game Reserve, p311, followed by Ruaha National Park, p286); and Pemba flying foxes (best seen in Pemba's Ngezi Forest, p151).

Plants

Small patches of tropical rainforest in Tanzania's Eastern Arc range provide home to a rich assortment of plants, many of which are found nowhere else in the world. These include the Usambara or African violet (*Saintpaulia*) and *Impatiens,* which are sold as house plants in grocery stores throughout the West. Similar forest patches – remnants of the much larger tropical forest that once extended across the continent – are also found in the Udzungwas, Ulugurus and several other areas. South and west of the Eastern Arc range are stands of baobab, with some particularly striking baobab-studded landscapes in Tarangire National Park (p214).

Tanzania's montane forests contain 7% of Africa's endemic plant species on only 0.05% of the continent's total area.

Away from the mountain ranges, much of the country is covered by miombo ('moist' woodland), where the main vegetation is various types of *Brachystegia* tree. Much of the dry central plateau is covered with savanna, bushland and thickets, while grasslands cover the Serengeti plain and other areas that lack good drainage.

Amani Nature Reserve (p169) and Kitulo National Park (p290) are among the country's botanical highlights, and Kitulo is one of the few parks in Africa with wildflowers as its focal point.

NATIONAL PARKS & RESERVES

Tanzania's unrivalled collection of parks and reserves includes 14 mainland national parks (with one more – Mkomazi Game Reserve – on the way), 14 wildlife reserves, the Ngorongoro Conservation Area, two marine parks and several protected marine reserves.

Until relatively recently, development and tourism have focused almost exclusively on the northern parks – Serengeti, Lake Manyara, Tarangire and Arusha National Parks, as well as Kilimanjaro National Park for trekkers, and the Ngorongoro Conservation Area. All of these places are easily reached by road or air, and heavily visited, with a range of facilities. Apart from the evocative landscapes, the main attractions in the north are the high concentrations, diversity and accessibility of the wildlife.

The southern protected areas – primarily Ruaha National Park and the Selous Game Reserve, as well as Mikumi and Udzungwa Mountains National Parks – are receiving increasing attention, but still don't see close to the number of visitors that the north does and most areas tend to have more of a wilderness feel. They also tend to be more time consuming to reach by

The Tanzania Forest Conservation Group website (www.tfcg.org) is an excellent introduction to Tanzania's forests and the conservation of their exceptional biodiversity.

MAJOR NATIONAL PARKS & RESERVES

Park	Features	Activities	Best time to visit	Page
Arusha NP	Mt Meru, lakes, crater: zebras, giraffes, elephants	trekking, canoe & vehicle safaris; cultural activities nearby	year-round	p207
Gombe Stream NP	lake shore, forest: chimpanzees	chimp-tracking	year-round	p265
Katavi NP	flood plains, lakes, woodland: buffaloes, hippos, antelopes	vehicle & walking safaris	Jun-Oct	p270
Kilimanjaro NP	Mt Kilimanjaro	trekking; cultural activities on lower slopes	Jun-Oct, Dec-Feb	p191
Kitulo NP	highland plateau: wildflowers, wilderness	hiking	Dec-Apr (for wildflowers), Sep-Nov (for hiking)	p290
Lake Manyara NP	Lake Manyara: hippos, water birds, elephants	vehicle safaris, walking, cycling; cultural activities in border areas	Jun-Feb (Dec-Apr for birding)	p212
Mahale Mountains NP	remote lake shore, mountains: chimpanzees	chimp-tracking	Jun-Oct, Dec-Feb	p267
Mikumi NP	Mkata flood plains: lions, buffaloes, giraffes, elephants	vehicle safaris, short walks	year-round	p278
Mkomazi GR	dry savanna bushlands: rhinos, wild dogs	vehicle & walking safaris	year-round	p179
Ngorongoro CA	Ngorongoro Crater: black rhinos, lions, elephants, zebras, flamingos	vehicle safaris, hiking	Jun-Feb	p221
Ruaha NP	Ruaha River, sand rivers: elephants, hippos, kudus, antelopes, birds	vehicle & walking safaris	year-round	p286
Rubondo Island NP	Lake Victoria: birds, sitatungas, chimps	short walks, chimp-tracking, boating, fishing	Jun-Feb	p252
Saadani NP	Wami River, beach: birds, hippos, crocodiles, elephants	vehicle safaris, short boat trips, short walks	Jun-Feb	p158
Selous GR	Rufiji River, lakes, woodland: elephants, hippos, wild dogs, black rhinos, birds	boat, walking, vehicle & balloon safaris	Jun-Oct, Jan & Feb	p311
Serengeti NP	plains, grasslands, Grumeti River: wildebeests, zebras, lions, cheetahs, giraffes	vehicle & balloon safaris; walks & cultural activities in border areas	year-round	p216
Tarangire NP	Tarangire River, woodland, baobabs: elephants, zebras, wildebeests, birds	vehicle safaris; walks & cultural activities in border areas	Jun-Oct	p214
Udzungwa Mountains NP	Udzungwa Mountains, forest: primates, birds	hiking	Jun-Oct	p280

road. The wildlife, however, is just as impressive, although it's often spread out over larger areas.

In the far west are Mahale Mountains and Gombe Stream National Parks, where the main draws are the chimpanzees and – for Mahale – the remoteness. Katavi is also remote, and probably the closest you can come to experiencing the pristine face of the wild. Rubondo Island National Park is set on its own in Lake Victoria, and is of particular interest to bird-watchers. Saadani National Park, just north of Dar es Salaam, is the only national park along the coast.

TANZANIA'S UNESCO WORLD HERITAGE SITES

- Kilimanjaro National Park (p191)
- Kolo-Kondoa Rock Art Sites (p236)
- Ngorongoro Conservation Area (p221)
- Ruins of Kilwa Kisiwani (p318) and Songo Mnara (p319)
- Serengeti National Park (p216)
- Selous Game Reserve (p311)
- Zanzibar's Stone Town (p109)

National Parks

Tanzania's national parks are managed by the **Tanzania National Parks Authority** (Tanapa; off Map pp196-7; ☎ 027-250 3471/4082/8216; www.tanzaniaparks.com; Dodoma road, Arusha). Entry fees must be paid in hard currency, preferably US dollars cash, although a 'smart card' system is scheduled to be introduced imminently, starting in the northern circuit. For information on national park accommodation and guide fees, see the table following; for park entry fees see the individual listings. Note that all park fees are scheduled to increase again during 2008. For general information on park accommodation, see p331.

Jane Goodall's pioneering chimpanzee research at Gombe Stream National Park has grown into a worldwide organisation for promoting environmental conservation. See www.janegoodall.org and www.rootsandshoots.org.

NATIONAL PARK FEES

Accommodation	US$ (16yr +)	US$ (5-15yr)
Public camp site	30 (Mt Kilimanjaro 50)	5
Special camp site	50	10
Hostel	10	-
Resthouse (Serengeti, Arusha, Ruaha, Katavi)	30 (Gombe Stream 20)	-
Banda or hut	20 (Mt Kilimanjaro 50)	-

Note: not all national parks have a separate price structure for children.

Other costs include guide fees of US$10/15/20 per group per day/overnight/walking safari, plus vehicle fees (US$40/Tsh10,000 per foreign-/Tanzanian-registered car). Park concession fees – fees per visitor paid to Tanapa by hotels and lodges within the parks – have been recently increased, and now many operators are also passing these on to clients; the average is US$30 per person per day, although this figure is currently under review.

Wildlife Reserves

Wildlife reserves are administered by the **Wildlife Division of the Ministry of Natural Resources & Tourism** (off Map p86; ☎ 022-286 6064/6376; scp@africaonline.co.tz; cnr Nyerere & Changombe Rds, Dar es Salaam). Fees should be paid in US dollars cash. Selous and Mkomazi are the only reserves with tourist infrastructure. Large areas of most others have been leased as hunting concessions, as have the southerly parts of the Selous.

Check www.sailvega .com/NGO%20projects /pdf/guide.pdf for a downloadable guide to Zanzibar's Menai Bay Conservation Area.

Marine Parks & Reserves

Mafia Island Marine Park (p309) and Mnazi Bay-Ruvuma Estuary Marine Park (p327) – together with Maziwe Marine Reserve (p162) and the Dar es Salaam Marine Reserves (Mbudya, Bongoyo, Pangavini and Fungu Yasini islands; p101) – are under the jurisdiction of the Ministry of Natural Resources

---

RESPONSIBLE TRAVEL

Tourism is big business in Tanzania. Here are a few guidelines for minimising strain on the local environment:

■ Support local enterprise.

■ Buy souvenirs directly from those who make them.

■ Choose safari or trek operators that treat local communities as equal partners and that are committed to protecting local ecosystems.

■ For cultural attractions, try to pay fees directly to the locals involved, rather than to tour-company guides or other intermediaries.

■ Ask permission before photographing people.

■ Avoid indiscriminate gift-giving; donations to recognised projects are more sustainable and have a better chance of reaching those who need them most.

■ Don't buy items made from ivory, skin, shells etc.

■ Save natural resources.

■ Respect local culture and customs.

The Mpingo Conservation Project (www.mpingo conservation.org) and the African Blackwood Conservation Project (www.blackwoodconservation.org) are working to conserve *mpingo* (East African Blackwood) – Tanzania's national tree, and one of the main woods used in carvings.

& Tourism's **Marine Parks & Reserves Unit** (Map p90; ☎ 022-215 0420/0621; www .marineparktz.com; Olympio St, Upanga, Dar es Salaam).

Ngorongoro Conservation Area

The Ngorongoro Conservation Area was established as a multiple-use area to protect both wildlife and the pastoralist lifestyle of the Maasai, who had lost other large areas of their traditional territory with the formation of Serengeti National Park. It is administered by the **Ngorongoro Conservation Area Authority** (www.ngorongorocrater.org). For information and fees, see p221.

ENVIRONMENTAL ISSUES

Although Tanzania has one of the highest proportions of protected land of any African country (about 39% is protected in some form), limited resources hamper conservation efforts, and erosion, soil degradation, desertification and deforestation whittle away at the natural wealth. According to some estimates, Tanzania loses 3500 sq km of forest land annually as a result of agricultural and commercial clearing. In the national parks, poaching and inappropriate visitor use – especially in the northern circuit – threaten wildlife and ecosystems. Deforestation is also a problem on the offshore islands, with about 95% of the tropical high forest that once covered Zanzibar and Pemba now gone. Both on the archipelago and in mainland coastal areas, dynamite fishing has been a serious threat, although significant progress has been made in halting this practice.

The African Conservation Foundation's website (www.africanconservation.org) has a wealth of links to conservation projects in Tanzania.

On the positive side, great progress has been made in recent years to involve communities directly in conservation, and local communities are now stakeholders in several lodges and other tourist developments. 000

Food & Drink

It's easy to travel through Tanzania thinking that the country subsists on *ugali* – the main staple made from maize or cassava flour, or both– and sauce. But if you hunt around, there are some treats to be found. Enjoy freshly grilled fish in the shade of a palm tree. Let the scents of coriander and coconut transport you to the days when the East African coast was a port of call on the spice route from the Orient. Or, relish five-star cuisine cooked at a luxury safari camp, surrounded by the sounds of the bush.

The Zanzibar Archipelago is one of East Africa's culinary highlights. Elsewhere, lively local atmosphere and Tanzanian hospitality compensate for what can otherwise be a rather bland diet.

One of Zanzibar's great early morning sights is the coffee vendors who carry around a stack of coffee cups and a piping hot kettle on a long handle with coals fastened underneath.

STAPLES & SPECIALITIES

Ugali is the Tanzanian national dish. This thick, dough-like mass – which is somewhat of an acquired taste for many foreigners – varies in flavour and consistency depending on the flours used and the cooking. In general, good *ugali* should be neither too dry nor too sticky. It's usually served with a sauce containing meat, fish, beans or greens. Rice and *matoke* (cooked plantains) are other staples, and chips are ubiquitous.

Mishikaki (marinated, grilled meat kebabs) and *nyama choma* (seasoned roasted meat) are widely available. Along the coast and near lakes, there's plenty of seafood, often grilled or (along the coast) cooked in coconut milk or curry-style.

Check out www.zanzinet.org/recipes/index.html for a sampling of recipes from Zanzibar.

THE GOURMET TRAIL

Staying at upmarket safari camps and hotels, you'll dine well. But for independent travellers or those on a limited budget, a diet of *ugali* (a staple made from maize or cassava flour, or both)and sauce quickly gets tiresome. Following are places to break your trip if you're craving something tasty and wholesome:

- Lushoto – Homemade jam, wholegrain bread and cheese from Irente Farm (p171) and the Montessori sisters at St Eugene's Hostel (p173)
- Njombe – Delicious homemade cheeses at the Duka la Maziwa (p290)
- Iringa to Makambako – Well-prepared farm-fresh cuisine, plus a farm produce shop at Kisolanza – The Old Farmhouse (p288)
- Iringa – Banana milkshakes, pancakes, homemade yogurt and other treats at Hasty Tasty Too (p284)
- Moshi – Wholegrain breads and cheeses from Lushoto's Irente Farm, plus salads, homemade cakes and cookies at The Coffee Shop (p186)
- Pangani – Clarence, the Canadian owner at Capricorn Beach Cottages (p162), prepares smoked fish, dill butter, freshly baked bread and other gourmet delicacies, sometimes available for sale at the small shop
- Arusha – Quality meat and imported items at Meat King (Goliondoi Rd), and well-prepared local and Western cuisine and baked goods at Via Via (p201)
- Pemba – Fresh, warm bread loaves from street vendors mornings and evenings in Chake Chake (p143), plus Pemba honey (*asali*) from the market to spread on top
- Tanga – Fresh yogurt and cheeses at Tanga Fresh (p166)
- Tanzanian coast – Excellent fish everywhere

GREAT CUPS OF COFFEE

Despite Tanzania's many coffee plantations, it can be difficult to find a cup of the real stuff. Here are our picks for some of the best cups of locally produced *kahawa*, or coffee; let us know of others.

- Jambo's Coffee House, Arusha (p201)
- Stone Town Café, Zanzibar Town (p125)
- Msumbi, Zanzibar Town (p125; branches at Seacliff Village in Dar es Salaam and at the TFA/Shoprite Centre in Arusha)
- Utengule Country Hotel, Mbeya (p293)
- Zanzibar Coffee House, Zanzibar Town (p125)
- Coffee Shop, Moshi (p186)
- Tanzania Coffee Lounge, Moshi (p186)

Tap water is best avoided. Bottled water is widely available, except in remote areas, where you should carry a filter or purification tablets. Always boil or purify water and be wary of ice and fruit juices diluted with unpurified water. With fruits and vegetables, it's best to follow the adage: 'Cook it, peel it, boil it or forget it.'

Some Tanzanians start their day with *uji*, a thin, sweet porridge made from bean, millet or other flour. Watch for ladies stirring bubbling pots of it on street corners in the early morning. *Vitambua* – small rice cakes resembling tiny, thick pancakes – are another morning treat, especially in the southeast. On Zanzibar, try *mkate wa kumimina*, a bread made from a batter similar to that used for making *vitambua*.

Three meals a day is usual, although breakfast is frequently nothing more than *kahawa* (coffee) or chai (tea) and *mkate* (bread). The main meal is eaten at midday.

DRINKS

Apart from the ubiquitous Fanta and Coca-Cola, the main soft drink is Tangawizi, a local version of ginger ale. Fresh juices are widely available, although check first to see whether they have been mixed with unsafe water.

In the Tanga area and around Lake Victoria watch for *mtindi* and *mgando*, cultured milk products similar to yogurt, and usually drunk with a straw out of plastic bags

Tanzania's array of beers includes the local Safari and Kilimanjaro labels, plus Castle Lager and various Kenyan and German beers. Finding a beer is usually no problem, but finding a cold one can be a challenge.

Local brews fall under the catch-all term *konyagi*. Around Kilimanjaro, watch for *mbege* (banana beer). *Gongo* (also called *nipa*) is an illegal distilled cashew drink, but the brewed version, *uraka*, is legal. Local brews made from papaw are also common.

Tanzania has a small wine industry based in Dodoma (p231), although it's unlikely to give other vintners much competition.

In restaurants catering to tourists, tip about 10%, assuming service warrants it. Tipping isn't expected in small, local establishments, though rounding up the bill is always appreciated.

WHERE TO EAT & DRINK

For dining local style, sit down in a small *hoteli* – a small, informal restaurant – and watch life pass by. Many have the day's menu written on a blackboard, and a TV in the corner. Rivalling *hoteli* for local atmosphere are the bustling night markets found in many towns, where vendors set up grills along the road side and sell *nyama choma*, grilled *pweza* (octopus) and other street food.

For Western-style meals, stick to cities or main towns, where there's a reasonable to good array of restaurants, most moderately priced compared with their European equivalents.

Lunch is served between about noon and 2.30pm, and dinner from about 7pm to 10pm. The smaller the town, the earlier its restaurants are likely to close; after about 7pm in rural areas it can be difficult to find anything other than street food.

Most main towns have at least one supermarket selling various imported products such as canned meat, fish and cheese (but not speciality items such as trail food or energy bars). In coastal areas, you can always find a fresh catch of fish and someone to prepare it for you; the best time to look is early morning.

Quick Eats

Fast food Tanzanian-style is whatever the dish of the day is at the local *hoteli* – rice or *ugali* with chicken, fish or beans. At lunch time, you'll be served a plate of local fare within a few minutes for about Tsh1000. Outside of regular meal times, ask what is ready, as it can take hours if the cook needs to start from scratch.

VEGETARIANS & VEGANS

There isn't much in Tanzania that is specifically billed as 'vegetarian', but there are many veggie options and you can find *wali* (cooked rice) and *maharagwe* (beans) everywhere. The main challenges are keeping variety and balance in your diet, and getting enough protein, especially if you don't eat eggs or seafood. In larger towns, Indian restaurants are the best places to try for vegetarian meals. Elsewhere, ask Indian shop owners if they have any suggestions; many will also be able to help you find fresh yogurt. Peanuts *(karanga)* and cashews *(korosho)* are widely available, as are fresh fruits and vegetables.

Most tour operators are willing to cater to special dietary requests, such as vegetarian, kosher or halal, with advance notice.

EATING WITH KIDS

Tanzanians are family-friendly, and dining out with children is no problem. Hotel restaurants occasionally have high chairs, and while special children's meals aren't common, it's easy enough to find items that are suitable for young diners. Avoid curries and other spicy dishes, uncooked, unpeeled fruits and vegetables, meat from street vendors (as it's sometimes undercooked) and unpurified water. Supermarkets stock child-size boxes of fresh juice, and fresh fruits (tangerines, bananas and more) are widely available. Also see p334.

A Taste of Zanzibar – Chakula Kizuri, by Zarina Jafferji, is a mouth-watering introduction to cuisine on the island while Modern Zanzibar Cuisine, by Benn Haidari, is a good book of Zanzibari recipes, together with intriguing historical information.

The best fast food is at night markets, such as Zanzibar's Forodhani Gardens (p117), where you can wander around filling up on mishikaki, grilled pweza and other titbits for less than Tsh2000.

DOS & DON'TS

For Tanzanians, a shared meal and eating out of a communal dish are expressions of solidarity between hosts and guests.

- If you're invited to eat and aren't hungry, it's OK to say that you've just eaten, but try to share a few bites of the meal in recognition of the bond with your hosts.
- Leave a small amount on your plate to show your hosts that you've been satisfied.
- Don't take the last bit of food from the communal bowl, as your hosts may worry that they haven't provided enough.
- Never handle food with the left hand.
- If others are eating with their hands, do the same, even if cutlery is provided.
- Defer to your host for customs that you aren't sure about.

HABITS & CUSTOMS

Tanzanian style is to eat with the hand from communal dishes in the centre of the table. There will always be somewhere to wash your hands – either a bowl and jug of water that are passed around, or a sink in the corner. Although food is shared, it's not customary to share drinks. Sodas are the usual accompaniment, and there will also usually be a pitcher of water, though this may be unpurified. Children generally eat separately. If there's a toast, the common salutation is *afya!* – (to your) health!

Street snacks and meals on the run are common. European-style restaurant dining, while readily available in major cities, is not part of local culture. More common are large gatherings at home, or at a rented hall, to celebrate special occasions, with the meal as the focal point.

> Meals connected with any sort of social occasion are usually drawn-out affairs for which the women of the household will have spent several days preparing.

EAT YOUR WORDS

For pronunciation guidelines, see p371.

Useful Phrases

I'm a vegetarian.	*Mimi ni mlaji wa mboga za majani tu.*
I don't eat meat.	*Mimi sili nyama.*
Do you serve food here?	*Mnauza chakula hapa?*
I'd like…	*Ninaomba…*
Without chilli pepper, please.	*Bila pilipili, tafadhali.*
Please bring the bill.	*Lete bili tafadhali.*

Menu Decoder

mchuzi – sauce, sometimes with bits of beef and vegetables
mishikaki – marinated, grilled meat kebabs
nyama choma – seasoned roasted meat
pilau – spiced rice cooked in broth with seafood or meat and vegetables
supu – soup; usually somewhat greasy, and served with a piece of beef, pork or meat fat in it
ugali – thick, porridge-like maize- or cassava-based staple
wali na kuku/samaki/nyama/maharagwe – cooked white rice with chicken/fish/meat/beans

Food Glossary

BASICS

cold	*baridi*
cup	*kikombe*
fork	*uma*
hot	*joto*
knife	*kisu*
plate	*sahani*
spoon	*kijiko*

STAPLES

beans	*maharagwe*
bread	*mkate*
chips	*chipsi*
plantains	*ndizi ya kupika* or (when cooked and mashed) *matoke*
potatoes	*viazi*
rice (cooked)	*wali*

OTHER DISHES & CONDIMENTS

eggs (boiled)	*mayai (yaliyochemshwa)*
salt	*chumvi*
sugar	*sukari*

KARIBU CHAKULA

If you're invited to join in a meal – *karibu chakula* – the first step is hand washing. Your host will bring around a bowl and water jug; hold your hands over the bowl while your host pours water over them. Sometimes soap is provided, and a towel for drying off.

The meal itself inevitably centres around *ugali*. Take some with the right hand from the communal pot, roll it into a small ball with the fingers, making an indentation with your thumb, and dip it into the accompanying sauce. Eating with your hand is a bit of an art, but after a few tries starts to feel natural. Don't soak the *ugali* too long (to avoid it breaking up in the sauce), and keep your hand lower than your elbow (except when actually eating) so the sauce doesn't drip down your forearm.

Except for fruit, desserts are rarely served; meals conclude with another round of hand washing. Thank your host by saying *chakula kizuri* or *chakula kitamu*.

MEAT & SEAFOOD

beef	*nyama ng'ombe*
chicken	*kuku*
fish	*samaki*
goat	*nyama mbuzi*
pork	*nyama nguruwe*
octopus	*pweza*

FRUITS & VEGETABLES

banana	*ndizi*
coconut (green)	*dafu*
coconut (ripe)	*nazi*
fruit	*matunda*
mango	*embe*
orange	*chungwa*
papaya	*papai*
pineapple	*nanasi*
potatoes	*viazisukuma wiki*
spinach (boiled)	*sukuma wiki*
tomatoes	*nyanya*
vegetables	*mboga*

DRINKS

beer (cold/warm)	*bia (baridi/yamoto)*
orange juice	*maji ya machungwa*
soda	*soda*
water (boiled/drinking/mineral)	*maji (ya kuchemsha/ya kunywa/ya madini)*

Dar es Salaam

With a population of almost three million and East Africa's second-largest port, Dar es Salaam is Tanzania's major centre and capital in everything but name (Dodoma is the parliamentary capital). Yet under its veneer of urban bustle, the city remains a down-to-earth, manageable place, with a picturesque seaport, a fascinating mixture of African, Arabic and Indian influences and close ties to its Swahili roots. While there aren't many 'sights' as such, there are craft markets, shops and restaurants enough to keep most visitors busy. The streets, too, are full of colour and activity, as men weave through traffic on large Chinese-made single-speed bicycles, while women clad in brightly hued *kangas* (printed cotton wraparounds worn by many Tanzanian women) stand in the shade of government office blocks balancing trays of bananas and mangoes on their heads. Along the waterfront, colonial-era buildings with their red-tiled roofs jostle for space with sleek, modern high-rises, massive ocean liners chug into the harbour and peacocks stroll across the leafy, manicured State House grounds.

An increasing number of travellers bypass 'Dar' completely, by taking advantage of one of the many international flights into Kilimanjaro International Airport (between Arusha and Moshi). Yet the city merits a visit in its own right as Tanzania's political and economic hub. It's also an agreeable place to break your travels elsewhere in the country, with an array of services and well-stocked shops. For a break from the bustle, there are easily accessed beaches and islands just north and south of town, and Zanzibar is only a short ferry or plane ride away.

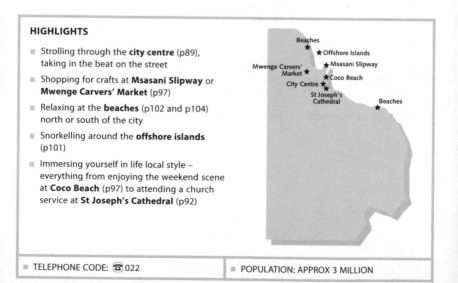

HIGHLIGHTS

- Strolling through the **city centre** (p89), taking in the beat on the street
- Shopping for crafts at **Msasani Slipway** or **Mwenge Carvers' Market** (p97)
- Relaxing at the **beaches** (p102 and p104) north or south of the city
- Snorkelling around the **offshore islands** (p101)
- Immersing yourself in life local style – everything from enjoying the weekend scene at **Coco Beach** (p97) to attending a church service at **St Joseph's Cathedral** (p92)

Beaches
★ Offshore Islands
Mwenge Carvers' Market ★ ★ Msasani Slipway
City Centre ★ ★ Coco Beach
★ St Joseph's Cathedral
Beaches ★

- TELEPHONE CODE: ☎ 022
- POPULATION: APPROX 3 MILLION

HISTORY

Until the mid-19th century, what is now Dar es Salaam was just one of many small fishing villages along the East African coast. In the 1860s Sultan Seyyid Majid of Zanzibar decided to develop the area's inland harbour into a port and trading centre, and named the site Dar es Salaam ('Haven of Peace'). No sooner had development of the harbour begun, however, than the sultan died and the town again sank into anonymity, overshadowed by Bagamoyo, an important dhow port to the north. It wasn't until the 1880s that Dar es Salaam assumed new significance, first as a way-station for Christian missionaries making their way from Zanzibar to the interior, and then as a seat for the German colonial government, which viewed Dar es Salaam's protected harbour as a better alternative for steamships than the dhow port in Bagamoyo. In 1891 the colonial administration was moved from Bagamoyo to Dar es Salaam. Since then the city has remained Tanzania's undisputed political and economic capital, even though the legislature and official seat of government were transferred to Dodoma in 1973.

ORIENTATION

The city centre runs along Samora Ave from the clock tower to the Askari monument, with banks, foreign-exchange bureaus, vendors and shops. Northwest of Samora Ave, around India and Jamhuri Sts, is the Asian quarter, with its warren of narrow streets lined with Indian merchants and traders.

On the other side of town, northeast of Askari monument, is a quiet area of tree-lined streets with the National Museum, Botanical Gardens and State House. Proceeding north from here along the coast are, first, the upper-middle class area of Upanga and then, after crossing Selander Bridge, the fast-developing diplomatic and upmarket residential areas of Oyster Bay and Msasani. The city's only real stretch of sand is at Coco Beach, near Oyster Bay, but better beaches to the north (p102) and south (p104) are only a short ride away.

Maps

The tourist information centre has free photocopied city maps. The unwieldy *Dar es Salaam City Map & Guide* (1:20,000; Tsh5000) is available from the **Surveys & Mapping Division Map Sales Office** (Map p90; cnr Kivukoni Front & Luthuli St; ☺ 8am-2pm Mon-Fri).

Otherwise, there's a good selection of smaller city maps for sale at hotel bookshops.

INFORMATION

Bookshops

A Novel Idea Msasani Slipway (Map p86; ☎ 022-260 1088; Msasani Slipway, Msasani Peninsula); Sea Cliff Village (Map p86; Sea Cliff Village, Toure Dr); Steers (Map p90; cnr Ohio St & Samora Ave) Dar es Salaam's best bookshop, with classics, modern fiction, travel guides, Africa titles, maps and more.

Second-hand Bookstalls (Map p90; Sokoine Dr) Between Pamba Rd and Ohio St. A good bet for older books, especially on colonial-era history; bargaining is required.

Cultural Centres

Alliance Française (Map p86; ☎ 022-213 1406/2; afdar@africaonline.co.tz; Ali Hassan Mwinyi Rd)

British Council (Map p90; ☎ 022-211 6574/5/6; info@britishcouncil.or.tz; cnr Ohio St & Samora Ave)

Nyumba ya Sanaa (Map p90; Mwalimu Julius K Nyerere Cultural Centre, Ohio St)

Russian Cultural Centre (Map p86; ☎ 022-213 6578; cnr Ufukoni & Ocean Rds)

Emergency

Central police station (Map p90; ☎ 022-211 5507; Sokoine Dr) Near the Central Line Train Station.

First Air Responder (☎ 022-276 0087, 0754-777100, 0754-777073; www.knightsupport.com) For emergency evacuations; see p339 for membership details.

Flying Doctors & Amref (Map p90; ☎ in Nairobi emergency 254-20-315454/5, 254-20-600090; www.amref.org; Ali Hassan Mwinyi Rd) For emergency evacuations; see p339 for membership details.

IST Clinic (Map p86; ☎ 022-260 1307/8, 0784-783393, 24hr emergency 0754-783393; www.istclinic.com; Ruvu Rd; ☺ 8am-6pm Mon-Fri, to noon Sat) A Western-run fully equipped clinic. It's the best bet for travellers, with a doctor on call 24 hours. From Chole Rd, look for the small Ruvu Rd signpost just south of and diagonally opposite the Slipway turn-off.

Oyster Bay police station (Map p86; ☎ 022-266 7332; Toure Dr) North of Coco Beach.

Premier Care Clinic (Map p86; ☎ 022-266 8385, 022-266 8320; pcc@ihu.edu; New Bagamoyo Rd) Western standards and facilities; next to Big Bite restaurant.

Traffic police headquarters (Map p90; ☎ 022-211 1747; Sokoine Dr) Near the Central Line Train Station.

Immigration Office

Wizara ya mambo ya ndani (Map p90; ☎ 022-211 8640/3; www.tanzania.go.tz/immigrationf.html; cnr Ghana Ave & Ohio St; ☺ visa applications 8am-noon Mon-Fri, visa collections until 2pm)

DAR ES SALAAM

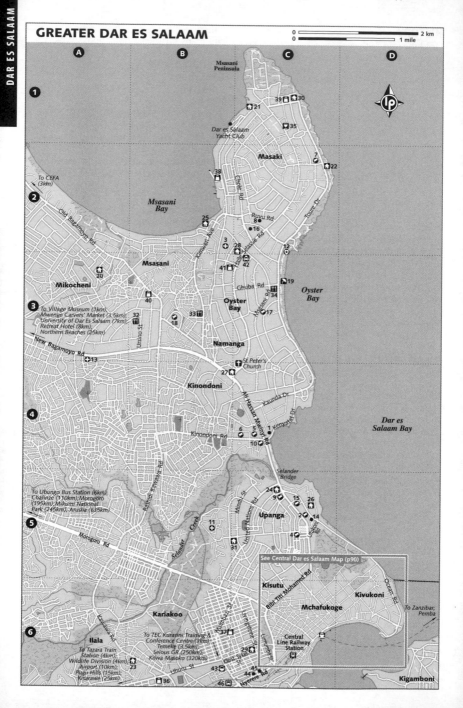

GREATER DAR ES SALAAM

0 ————— 2 km
0 ————— 1 mile

Msasani Peninsula

Dar es Salaam Yacht Club

Masaki

Msasani Bay

To CEFA (3km)

Old Bagamoyo Rd

Msasani

Mikocheni

Ruvu Rd

Chole Rd

Toure Dr

Kenyatta Dr

Haile Selassie Rd

Kinondoni Rd

To Village Museum (1km); Mwenge Carvers' Market (3.5km); University of Dar Es Salaam (7km); Retreat Hotel (8km); Northern Beaches (25km)

New Bagamoyo Rd

Ghuba Rd

Oyster Bay

Msasani Rd

Namanga

St Peter's Church

Kinondoni

Ali Hassan Mwinyi Rd

Kaunda Dr

Oyster Bay

Dar es Salaam Bay

Selander Bridge

To Ubungo Bus Station (6km); Chalinze (310km); Morogoro (195km); Mikumi National Park (245km); Arusha (635km)

Morogoro Rd

Selander Creek

Mindu St

United Nations Rd

Upanga

Lugalo Rd

Rashidi Kawawa Rd

Ursino St

Kawawa Rd

See Central Dar es Salaam Map (p90)

Kisutu

Bibi Titi Mohamed Rd

Kivukoni

Ocean Rd

Mchafukoge

To Zanzibar; Pemba

Kariakoo

Uhuru St

Lumumba St

Livingstone St

Nkrumah St

Msimbazi St

To TEC Kurasini Training & Conference Centre (3km); Temeke (3.5km); Selous GR (250km); Kilwa Masoko (320km)

Central Line Railway Station

Ilala

To Tazara Train Station (4km); Wildlife Division (4km); Airport (10km); Pugu Hills (15km); Kisarawe (25km)

Nyerere Rd

Kigamboni

Internet Access

Alpha Internet Café (Map p90; Garden Ave; per hr Tsh1000; 8.30am-6pm Mon-Fri, to 2pm Sat)

CSS Internet Café (Map p86; 1st fl, Sea Cliff Village; per hr Tsh5000; 7am-9pm Mon-Fri, 9am-6pm Sat, 2-6pm Sun)

Cyberspot (Map p90; Jamhuri St; per hr Tsh1000; 9am-10pm Mon-Sat, 10am-9pm Sun)

Mealz Internet Café (Map p90; cnr Pamba Rd & Sokoine Dr; per hr Tsh1000; 8am-8pm Mon-Sat, 10am-2pm Sun)

Post Office Internet Café (Map p90; Main Post Office, Maktaba St; per hr Tsh1200; 8am-7pm Mon-Fri, 9am-3pm Sat)

Royal Palm Business Centre (Map p90; Mövenpick Royal Palm, Ohio St; per 10min Tsh1000; 7am-8pm Mon-Fri, 8.30am-4pm Sat, 9am-1pm Sun)

Media

Advertising Dar (www.advertisingdar.com) Free weekly with restaurant, club and event listings.

Dar es Salaam Guide Free monthly with restaurant and club listings, embassy listings, airline schedules etc; available from hotels, travel agencies and the tourist information centre.

What's Happening in Dar es Salaam Similar to Dar es Salaam Guide.

Medical Services

CCBRT Disability Hospital (Map p86; 022-260 1543, 022-260 2192; www.ccbrt.or.tz; off Haile Selassie Rd)

IST Clinic (Map p86; 022-260 1307/8, 0784-783393, 24hr emergency 0754-783393; istclinic@istclinic.com; Ruvu Rd; 8am-6pm Mon-Fri, to noon Sat) See listing under Emergency (p85).

Muhimbili Medical Centre (Map p86; 022-215 1351; United Nations Rd) Tanzania's main teaching hospital, with well-qualified staff, but often lacking medicines and supplies.

Money

Forex bureaus give faster service and marginally better exchange rates. There are many scattered around the city centre on or near Samora Ave (all open standard business hours), or try the following:

American Express (Map p90; 022-211 0960, 022-211 4094; www.rickshawtz.com; Upanga Rd) At Rickshaw Travels, next to Citibank; no cash advances, but sometimes offers (slow) help with replacing stolen cheques. Also issues US-dollar travellers cheques up to US$1500 against an Amex card.

Forex Bureau (International Arrivals Area, Julius Nyerere International Airport; for all flights) Straight ahead when exiting customs; cash only.

Galaxy Forex Bureau (International Arrivals Area, Julius Nyerere International Airport; 6am-11pm) Cash and travellers cheques; to the right as you exit customs.

Mövenpick Royal Palm Forex Bureau (Map p90; Mövenpick Royal Palm, Ohio St; 8am-8pm Mon-Sat, 10am-1pm Sun & public holidays) Cash and travellers cheques (receipts required).

NBC (Map p90; cnr Azikiwe St & Sokoine Dr) Changes cash and travellers cheques.

DAR ES SALAAM (side tab)

Sea Cliff Forex Bureau (Map p86; Sea Cliff Village, Toure Dr; 11am-7pm) Cash only.

ATMs are available at the following locations:
Barclays Bank Mövenpick Royal Palm (Map p90; opposite Mövenpick Royal Palm, Ohio St); Msasani Slipway (Map p86; Msasani Slipway Apartments) Accepts Visa and MasterCard.
FBME TanPay/SpeedCash (Map p90; Samora Ave) Just west of Askari Monument, with another ATM diagonally across the intersection; accepts MasterCard.
Kilimanjaro Kempinski (Kilimanjaro Kempinski hotel, Kivukoni Front) Accepts Visa, MasterCard, Cirrus and Maestro.
National Bank of Commerce (Map p90; cnr Azikiwe St & Sokoine Dr) Has an ATM at its headquarters, as well as at all branches; accepts Visa only.
Stanbic Bank (Map p90; Sukari House, cnr Ohio St & Sokoine Dr) Accepts Visa, MasterCard, Cirrus and Maestro.
Standard Chartered Holiday Inn (Map p90; Garden Ave); JM Mall (Map p90; Samora Ave); NIC Life House (Map p90; cnr Ohio St & Sokoine Dr); Shopper's Plaza (Map p86)) Accepts Visa only.

Post
Main post office (Map p90; Maktaba St; 8am-4.30pm Mon-Fri, 9am-noon Sat)

Telephone
Card phones are scattered around town, including in front of Extelecoms House and the main post office. For operator-placed international calls (from US$1.50 per minute), try the **Telecom Office** (cnr Bridge St & Samora Ave; 7.30am-6pm Mon-Fri, 9am-3pm Sat) behind the Extelecoms House.

Tourist Information
Tanzania Tourist Board Information Centre (Map p90; 022-212 0373, 022-213 1555; www.tanzania touristboard.com; Samora Ave; 8am-4pm Mon-Fri,

8.30am-12.30pm Sat) Just west of Zanaki St, with free tourist maps and brochures and city information.
See also the listings under Media (p87).

Travel Agencies
For safari and trek operators, also see p44 and p54. For flight and hotel bookings, try the following:
Coastal Travels (Map p90; 022-211 7959/60; www.coastal.cc; Upanga Rd) A long-established and recommended agency with its own airline. It offers flights to many areas of the country; especially good for travel to Zanzibar, and for flights linking northern and southern safari circuit destinations. Also offers reasonably priced city tours, day trips to Zanzibar and Mikumi park excursions.
Lions of Tanzania Tours & Safari (Map p90; 022-212 8161; www.lions.co.tz; Upanga Rd) City tours from US$25 per person. Next to Citibank.
Kearsley Travel (www.kearsleys.com) Holiday Inn (Map p90; 022-213 1652/3; Garden Ave); Sea Cliff Village (Map p86; 022-260 0467; Toure Dr)
Rickshaw Travels Mövenpick Royal Palm (Map p90; Ohio St); Upanga Rd (Map p90; 022-211 0960, 022-211 4094; www.rickshawtz.com; Upagna Rd) Amex agent.
Skylink (022-211 5381, 022-211 2786; www.skylink tanzania.com) Next to Barclay's Bank (Map p90; opposite Mövenpick Royal Palm, Ohio St); Kilimanjaro Kempinski (Map p90; Kilimanjaro Kempinski hotel, Kivukoni Front)
Travel Mate (Map p86; 022-260 0573; info@travel mate.co.tz; Chole Rd) Near the Slipway turn-off.

DANGERS & ANNOYANCES
Dar es Salaam is safer than many other big cities in the region, notably Nairobi, though it has its share of muggings and thefts and the usual urban-area precautions need to be taken. Watch out for pickpocketing, particularly at crowded markets and bus and train stations, and for bag snatching through

---

DAR ES SALAAM IN THE LATE 1930S

This was my first glimpse of Dar es Salaam...a vast rippling blue-black lagoon and all around the rim of the lagoon there were pale-yellow sandy beaches, almost white, and breakers were running up on to the sand, and coconut palms with their little green leafy hats were growing on the beaches, and there were casuarina trees, immensely tall and breathtakingly beautiful... And then behind the casuarinas was what seemed to me like a jungle, a great tangle of tremendous dark-green trees that were full of shadows and almost certainly teeming...with rhinos and lions and all manner of vicious beasts. Over to one side lay the tiny town of Dar es Salaam, the houses white and yellow and pink, and among the houses I could see a narrow church steeple and a domed mosque and along the waterfront there was a line of acacia trees splashed with scarlet flowers...

Roald Dahl, Going Solo

THE MANY FACES OF DAR

Dar es Salaam is at its most exotic around Mosque St in the busy central area. Here, vendors hawk their wares along narrow, congested streets lined with colonial-era buildings, small *dukas* (shops) sell everything from lighting fixtures to textiles, and Indian-style tea rooms serve up spicy samosas and other snacks for a pittance.

Stretching west and southwest of the city is a jumble of vibrant, earthy neighbourhoods, including Kariakoo, Temeke and Ilala. In these areas – seldom reached by travellers – sandy streets wind past small, square, densely packed houses with corrugated roofs, and bustling night markets do business to the light of dozens of small kerosene lanterns. For something more placid, head out to Msasani Peninsula, following Ocean Rd and Toure Dr along the coast, past the clipped lawns and stately residences of various foreign dignitaries to the peninsula's tip. Here – especially at Msasani Slipway and the nearby Sea Cliff Village – you can enjoy fresh sea breezes and air scented with frangipani blossoms, and immerse yourself in things Western. Southeast of town is Kigamboni Ferry, which takes you five minutes across the bay to laid-back villages and a string of relaxing beaches.

vehicle windows. Stay aware of your surroundings, minimise carrying conspicuous bags or cameras and, if possible, leave your valuables in a reliable hotel safe. At night take a taxi rather than taking a *dalla-dalla* (minibus) or walking, and avoid walking alone along the path paralleling Ocean Rd, and on Coco Beach (which is only safe on weekend afternoons, when it's packed with people).

SIGHTS & ACTIVITIES

Sampling the city's vibrant markets and its craft shops is a fine way to while away a morning. For more options, see Shopping (p97).

National Museum

The **National Museum** (Map p90; ☎ 022-211 7508; www.houseofculture.or.tz; Shaaban Robert St; adult/student US$5/2; 🕙 9.30am-6pm) houses the famous fossil discoveries of *zinjanthropus* (nutcracker man) from Olduvai Gorge (see p223), plus some scattered but intriguing displays on numerous other topics, including the Shirazi civilisation of Kilwa, the Zanzibar slave trade, and the German and British colonial periods. For aficionados of vintage autos, there's a small special collection in the plaza between the main buildings, including the Rolls Royce used first by the British colonial government and later by Julius Nyerere, and the original East African Community Mercedes Benz. In the back building are a couple of old wooden bicycles – one of which uses no metal at all. The museum is near the Botanical Gardens, between Samora Ave and Sokoine Dr.

Village Museum

The centrepiece of the open-air **Village Museum** (Map p102; ☎ 022-270 0437; www.museum.or.tz; cnr New Bagamoyo Rd & Makaburi St; adult/child/student US$3/1/2, camera/video US$3/20; 🕙 9.30am-6pm) is a collection of authentically constructed dwellings illustrating traditional life in various parts of Tanzania. There are sometimes traditional music and dance performances held on afternoons.

The museum is 10km north of the city centre – the Mwenge *dalla-dalla* runs there from New Posta transport stand (Tsh200, 30 minutes).

Msasani Peninsula

At **Golden Tulip** (Map p86; Tour Dr; adult/child Tsh10,000/5000; 🕙 7am-6pm) hotel just south of Sea Cliff Village you can **swim** at the large, beautiful pool – one of the few hotel pools in the city open to nonguests.

Bird Walks

The **Wildlife Conservation Society of Tanzania** (WCST; Map p90; ☎ 022-211 2518; www.wcstonline.org; Garden Ave) has twice-monthly bird walks (admission free, two to three hours), departing from its office at 7.15am on the first and last Saturday of each month. See also the boxed text, p43.

DAR ES SALAAM FOR CHILDREN

Diversions include the **beaches** and **water parks** north of the city (p102); the supervised **play area** at Sea Cliff Village (p95), next to Sea Cliff Hotel, where you can leave your child with a nanny while you go shopping;

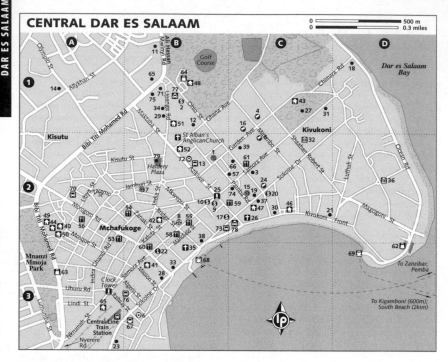

CENTRAL DAR ES SALAAM

Msasani Slipway (p96), with ice-cream cones, movies and a small playground; and the **swimming pool** (p89) at Golden Tulip hotel. On Sunday there's a family brunch at Kilimanjaro Kempinski hotel (per person Tsh29,000; p94), with a children's corner. The Russian Cultural Centre (p85) sponsors frequent cultural activities for children, and there are **children's reading corners** at the Novel Idea bookshop branches (p85) at Msasani Peninsula and Sea Cliff Village.w

SLEEPING

If you're relying on public transport, it's cheaper and more convenient to stay in the city centre, which is also where most budget lodging is located. If you don't mind paying for taxis, or travelling the distance from the airport (about 20km), the hotels on Msasani Peninsula can be a break from the urban scene. To avoid the city entirely, head for the beaches north (p102) or south (p104) of Dar es Salaam. The closest places for camping are at Pugu Hills (p100), and at the beaches north and south of town.

All top-end hotels accept credit cards.

City Centre

BUDGET

Most budget lodging is in the busy, central area around the main post office, or the equally busy Kisutu area, within easy walking distance of the Kisutu bus stand.

YMCA (Map p90; ☎ 022-213 5457; Upanga Rd; s/d without bathroom US$10/13) Around the corner from the YWCA, and marginally quieter (though the step up in price from the YWCA isn't justified). Rooms have mosquito nets, and there's a canteen. Men and women are accepted.

Safari Inn (Map p90; ☎ 022-213 8101; safari-inn@lycos .com; s/d US$10/20, d with air-con US$25; ✷ ☐) A popular travellers haunt in Kisutu, on the western edge of the city centre. Rooms are fan cooled and are sprayed with insect repellant each evening.

Kibodya Hotel (Map p90; ☎ 022-211 7856; cnr Nkrumah & Lindi Sts; tw with fan from Tsh12,000, d with air-con Tsh24,000; ✷) Large, no-frills rooms with fans, and some with local TV. It's in a busy area off the southwestern end of Samora Ave near the clock tower, and about 10 minutes' walk from the Kisutu St bus stand. Meals aren't available.

YWCA (Map p90; ☎ 0713-622707; ywca.tanzania@ africaonline.co.tz; Maktaba St; d Tsh20,000, s/d without bathroom Tsh10,000/15,000) Just up from the post office, this is a good budget deal. Rooms have mosquito net, fan and sink, the clean shared bathrooms smell of disinfectant, and the convenient location makes up for the street noise. Rooms around the inner courtyard are quieter. Men and women are accepted, and the attached restaurant serves inexpensive local-style meals.

Econolodge (Map p90; ☎ 022-211-6048/9; econo lodge@raha.com; s/d/tr US$18/24/30, with air-con US$30/35/40; ⚇) Clean, good, no-frills rooms hidden away in an aesthetically unappealing high-rise near the Kisutu bus stand booking offices and around the corner from Safari Inn and Jambo Inn. Continental breakfast is included; otherwise there's no food available.

Jambo Inn (Map p90; ☎ 022-211 4293; jamboinn hotel@yahoo.com; Libya St; s/d US$20/25) Around the

---

DISCOVERING DAR ES SALAAM'S HIDDEN SIGHTS

Central Dar es Salaam may be lacking in 'sights', but it's full of historical buildings, interesting architecture and atmosphere, and is easily manageable on foot. Leave your daypack, valuables and camera at your hotel, wear low-key clothing that lets you blend in and set off.

As you walk, watch the street names for a mini-overview of Tanzanian history. Luthuli St, for example, is named after Albert Luthuli, the former South African-born African National Congress (ANC) president. Shaaban Robert St honours one of Tanzania's most famous writers, while Sokoine Dr is named after Edward Moringe Sokoine, one-time prime minister and Julius Nyerere's most likely successor until he was killed in a car crash in 1984. *Dar es Salaam: A Dozen Drives Around the City* by Laura Sykes and Uma Waide includes walking tours of the city with extensive historical background.

For views over the harbour and the city centre, or to cool off with a cold drink, head to the outside terrace of the rooftop bar at Kilimanjaro Kempinski hotel (p94). Alternatively, treat yourself to a taxi ride along the coastal Toure Dr, and then head west over to Msasani Slipway (p96) or O'Willie's (p97) for sundowners overlooking Msasani Bay.

Some highlights are described following.

■ **Karimjee Hall** (Map p90; Samora Ave, north of Shaaban Robert St) Now closed to the public, this stately white building was the former house of parliament before the legislature was relocated to Dodoma, and is where Julius Nyerere was sworn in as president. Today it is used for parliamentary committee meetings and political functions.

■ **Botanical gardens** (Map p90; Samora Ave) Opposite Karimjee Hall, Dar es Salaam's languishing botanical gardens date from the German colonial era. They are now just a fraction of their original size.

■ **Ocean Rd Hospital** (Map p90; Ocean Rd) Built in 1897 and no longer operational, but appealing architecturally, with its Moorish influences. The small, white, domed building just before the hospital is where Robert Koch carried out his pioneering research on malaria and tuberculosis around the turn of the 20th century.

■ **State House** (Map p90; Luthuli St) An imposing complex set amid large grounds, the State House was originally built by the Germans and rebuilt after WWI by the British.

---

corner from Safari Inn, and also popular, with a mix of twin and double-bedded rooms with fan, flyscreens in the windows, erratic hot-water supplies, and a good, cheap restaurant with Indian dishes, plus burgers and other standards.

Luther House Centre Hostel (Map p90; ☎ 022-212 6247, 022-212 0734; luther@simbanet.net; Sokoine Dr; s/tw US$25/30; ✖) Centrally located, about two blocks southeast of the post office and just back from the waterfront. Rooms have fan, mosquito nets and air-con, and breakfast is available (at extra charge) at the restaurant downstairs.

Riki Hill Hotel (Map p86; ☎ 022-218 1820; www .rikihotel.com; Kleist Sykes St; s with fan US$36, s/d/tw with air-con US$48/54/66; ✖) This upper-budget/lower-midrange place offers decent value, with clean rooms with TV, as well as a restaurant, local ambience and a bar. It's near the junction of Uhuru and Livingstone Sts.

Out of the city centre are several church-affiliated places – most decent value if you're looking for something clean, quiet and reasonably priced.

Msimbazi Centre Hostel (Map p86; ☎ 022-286 3508, 022-286 3204; Kawawa Rd; s/d/tw Tsh10,000/20,000/50,000) Tiny, stuffy rooms with fan and mosquito net, breezier twins with two rooms sharing bathroom facilities, and an inexpensive canteen. It's noisy, especially on weekends, but otherwise is reasonable value. Take the Buguruni *dalla-dalla* from the Old Posta transport stand (Tsh4000 by taxi) and ask to be dropped off here.

TEC Kurasini Training & Conference Centre (off Map p86; ☎ 022-285 1077; tec@cats-net.com; Nelson Mandela Rd; s/d/tr Tsh12,000/24,000/36,000, s in new wing Tsh15,000) Simple, quiet rooms with fan and mosquito nets, and a canteen for meals. A taxi ride from the city centre costs from Tsh3000.

CEFA (off Map p86; ☎ 022-278 0425, 022-278 0685; cefahostel@gmail.com; Old Bagamoyo Rd, Mikocheni B; s/d/tr

■ **Kivukoni Front** (Map p90) The city's waterfront, sometimes also called Azania Front, is lined with government buildings, all dating to the German era. Opposite is a colourful assortment of street-side vendors and ageing boats.

■ **Forodhani Hotel Training Institute building** (Map p90; Kivukoni Front) Just up from the old Kilimanjaro Hotel (now the Kilimanjaro Kempinski) is the old Forodhani Hotel Training Institute building. It currently houses the Appeals Court, but enjoyed its heyday during the British era as the Dar es Salaam Club, when Evelyn Waugh would stop in on occasion for a drink.

■ **Askari monument** (Map p90; cnr Samora Ave & Azikiwe St) This bronze statue, dedicated to Africans killed in WWI, is now a favourite haunt of street touts and dubious moneychangers.

■ **Azania Front Lutheran Church** (Map p90; cnr Sokoine Dr & Azikiwe St) A striking edifice, with a red-roofed belfry overlooking the water and a rather stern Gothic interior, this is one of the city's major landmarks. The church was built at the turn of the 20th century by German missionaries and is still in active use for services and for choir rehearsals (beautiful – you can sometimes hear the singing from the street).

■ **St Joseph's Cathedral** (Map p90; cnr Sokoine Dr & Bridge St) Just down the road from the Azania Front Lutheran Church is another landmark. The spired cathedral, which is still in use – stop by any Sunday morning to see the standing-room only overflow from the services and hear the singing – was built at the same time as the Lutheran church, also by German missionaries. In addition to the striking stained-glass windows behind the main altar (best viewed late in the afternoon), it still contains many of the original German inscriptions and artwork, including the carved relief above the main altar.

■ **White Fathers' Mission House** (Map p90; Sokoine Dr) Just northeast of St Joseph's Cathedral, this is one of the oldest buildings in the city, reportedly originally used to house Sultan Majid's harem.

■ **Old Boma** (Map p90; Sokoine Dr) Dating to the era of Sultan Majid, and later expanded by the Germans, the Old Boma now houses various offices.

■ **City Hall** (Map p90; Sokoine Dr) Opposite the Old Boma is the German-built City Hall.

Tsh30,000/40,000/50,000) Simple, clean rooms in a private guesthouse, with meals available; popular with volunteers.

MIDRANGE

Heritage Motel (Map p90; ☎ 022-211 7471; www.heritage motel.co.tz; cnr Kaluta & Bridge Sts; s/d from US$60/72; ▒) This place in the Asian quarter of town has various-sized rooms – the doubles come with either one double bed, or one double plus one single and most are reasonably spacious, while the single rooms are very small. All have mini-fridge and mosquito netting in the windows. While it's rather overpriced compared with other centrally located options, and not set up for business travellers, it's worth a look if you're looking for something more upmarket than the budget listings in the city centre. There's also a restaurant.

Peacock Hotel (Map p90; ☎ 022-211 4126; www.pea cock-hotel.co.tz; Bibi Titi Mohamed Rd; s/d/tr US$75/85/110; ▒ 💻) A busy, central location, rooms with TV, a good restaurant and a bar. Caters primarily to a local business clientele, and is often full.

Harbour View Suites (Map p90; ☎ 022-212 4040; www .harbourview-ste.com; Samora Ave; s US$110-200, d US$120-210, breakfast US$7; ▒ 💻) Well-equipped, centrally located business travellers' studio apartments with views over the city or the harbour. Some rooms have mosquito nets, and all have modern furnishings, wi-fi and a kitchenette. A pool and fitness centre are planned, and there's a business centre. Definitely the best value and most upmarket choice in this category. Underneath is JM Mall shopping centre, with an ATM, supermarket and forex bureau.

TOP END

All top-end listings have wi-fi access.

Holiday Inn (Map p90; ☎ 022-213 7575; www.holiday-inn .com/daressalaam; Garden Ave; r from US$210; ▒ 💻) This is a pleasant, popular and solid-value place, with modern rooms and the standard amenities, including TV, telephone and a business centre that's open until 10pm. It's on a quiet, leafy side street near the National Museum and next to Standard Chartered Bank.

Mövenpick Royal Palm (Map p90; ☎ 022-211 2416; www.moevenpick-daressalaam.com; Ohio St; r from US$235; 🛇 🖳 🖃) Spacious, recently refurbished rooms, plus a beautiful pool (25m at its longest expanse) and a fitness centre (both for hotel guests only). Executive level guests have their own business centre and breakfast area. It's in lush gardens overlooking the Gymkhana Club golf greens.

Kilimanjaro Kempinski (Map p90; ☎ 022-213 1111; www.kempinski-daressalaam.com; Kivukoni Front; r from US$250; 🛇 🖳 🖃) This once-classic waterfront hotel has been completely refurbished by the Kempinski chain. The ultramodern rooms are arguably the best in the city – especially those with views over the harbour – with sleek, modern bathrooms and attractive décor. The lobby is rather lacking in character, but the Level 8 rooftop bar is an ideal spot to appreciate the city's port and harbour setting.

Msasani Peninsula & Upanga
BUDGET & MIDRANGE
Q Bar & Guest House (Map p86; ☎ 022-260 2150, 0754-282474; qbar@cats-net.com; cnr Haile Selassie & Msasani Rds; dm US$12, s/d US$45/55, d without bathroom US$45, executive s/d from US$50/65; 🛇) Spotless, good-value rooms – the executive rooms on the upper floors are huge – all with satellite TV, minifridge and bathroom, plus a four-bed backpackers' dorm room and a standard double, both sharing bathrooms. Laundry service is included in room prices, and breakfast is included with all rooms except the dorm. Food is served downstairs, and there's also a bar with live music on Friday evenings.

Akana Lodge (Map p86; ☎ 022-270 0122, 022-277 5261; www.akanalodge.com; s/d US$50/70; 🛇) Rooms are in a private house, with a few smaller rooms next door in an annexe. Local-style meals are available. It's about 7km north of the city centre: take Old Bagamoyo Rd north past Shoppers' Plaza, and watch for a tiny bridge, after which the lodge is signposted to the left.

Swiss Garden Hotel (Map p86; ☎ 022-215 3219; www.swisshostel.net; Mindu St; s/d from US$60/80; 🛇 🖳) A cosy B&B in a quiet, leafy neighbourhood, with helpful hosts and small, spotless rooms with internet connections. Breakfast is included; other meals can be arranged. It's in Upanga, just off United Nations Rd.

Palm Beach Hotel (Map p86; ☎ 022-212 2931, 022-213 0985; www.pbhtz.com; Ali Hassan Mwinyi Rd; s/d/tr US$65/90/100; 🛇 🖳) This Dar es Salaam institution has been completely renovated – look for the bright-blue Art Deco architecture – with spartan but spacious and good-value rooms with TV, wi-fi and a restaurant.

Msasani Slipway Apartments (Map p86; ☎ 022-260 0893; slipway@coastal.cc; Msasani Slipway; r/apt US$70/90; 🛇) Furnished, modern apartments in a good location at the Msasani Slipway (reception is just next to Barclays Bank). All have a hot-plate, sink and refrigerator, and some have views over the bay. Discounted weekly and monthly rates are available.

Souk (Map p86; ☎ 022-260 0893; slipway@coastal .cc; r US$80, day r US$60; 🛇) In the centre of the Msasani shopping area, with simple but pleasant double-bedded hotel-style rooms, including some with views over the water. For meals, you have all the Slipway restaurants at your doorstep. The reception office is near Barclays Bank (to the right before entering the shopping area).

Protea Courtyard (Map p86; ☎ 022-213 0130; www .proteahotels.com/courtyard; Ocean Rd; s/d from US$120/140; 🛇 🖳 🖃) Comfortable, modern rooms around a small courtyard, with the better (brighter) ones on the upper level. There's a restaurant, a business centre, wi-fi and efficient staff. It's 1km south of Selander Bridge. If you don't like air-con, note that the windows don't have flyscreens.

Protea Dar es Salaam Apartments (Map p86; ☎ 022-266 6665; www.proteahotels.com/oysterbay; cnr Haile Selassie & Ali Hassan Mwinyi Rds; apt from US$145; 🛇 🖳 🖃) Modern fully serviced apartments in a secure compound just north of Selander Bridge. All come with kitchenette, TV and access to the fitness and business centres.

TOP END
Peninsula Seaview Hotel (Map p86; ☎ 022-260 1273; www.peninsulaseaviewhotel.com; Chui Bay Rd; r without/with sea view from US$90/145; 🛇 🖳) A 10-room business travellers' hotel on the water, with well-appointed rooms with wi-fi and O'Willie's pub (p97) downstairs. Airport pick-ups are included in the room prices.

Golden Tulip (Map p86; ☎ 022-260 0288; www .goldentuliptanzania.com; Toure Dr; s/d from US$135/150; 🛇 🖳 🖃) Overlooking the ocean in a beautiful setting on a low cliff, this laid-back place – a favourite with conference groups – is just south of Sea Cliff Hotel. Rooms don't quite live up to potential, but the grounds go a long way to compensate, with a beautiful seaside pool and a usually deserted restaurant-bar area. All rooms have small balconies, and suites have full sea views.

Coral Beach (Map p86; ☎ 022-260 1928, 0784-783858; www.coralbeach-tz.com; s/d/f US$135/155/175; 🗙 🖵 🖨) A quiet, often overlooked boutique hotel catering to business travellers, with large and comfortable rooms – though many don't have views – in a secluded location near the northern end of Msasani Peninsula. The family rooms have two large beds, and there's a restaurant.

Retreat (off Map p86; ☎ 022-261 7496; www.retreat safaris.co.tz; d about US$170; 🗙 🖵 🖨) A lovely, intimate six-room place on the beach about 10km north of town off New Bagamoyo Rd, set in tropical gardens and notable also for its cuisine. Very good value.

Sea Cliff Hotel (Map p86; ☎ 022-260 0380/7; www .hotelseacliff.com; Toure Dr; s/d without/with sea view from US$190/220; 🗙 🖵 🖨) Sea Cliff has an excellent, breezy setting overlooking the ocean at the northern tip of Msasani Peninsula, although the standard rooms don't always live up to expectations. On the grounds are a small fitness centre, a resident masseur and a restaurant. Avoid the less expensive but less appealing and viewless rooms in an annexe next door.

EATING

Most restaurants in the city centre are closed on Sunday.

City Centre
BUDGET

For street food, try the stalls near the corner of Garden Ave and Pamba Rd, and along Kivukoni Front, all busiest around midday, dishing up plates of rice or *ugali* (a staple made from maize or cassava flour, or both) with sauce. For inexpensive Indian food and takeaways, head to the area around Zanaki and Jamhuri Sts.

Al-Qayam (Map p90; Zanaki St; snacks from Tsh200; 🕑 8am-8pm Mon-Fri, to 2pm Sat) A tiny Indian place oozing local flavour.

Chef's Pride (Map p90; Chagga St; meals from Tsh1500; 🕑 lunch & dinner, closed during Ramadan) This long-standing and popular local eatery is within easy walking distance of the Kisutu budget hotels, and a Dar es Salaam classic, offering a slice of local life. The large menu fea-

tures standard fare, plus pizza, Indian and vegetarian dishes, and even some Chinese cuisine.

Épi d'Or (Map p90; ☎ 022-213 6006; Samora Ave; light meals from Tsh1500; 🕑 7am-7pm Mon-Sat) A French-run bakery-café with a mouth-watering selection of freshly baked breads (supplies usually run out by midday), pastries and light lunches, plus hummus and other Middle Eastern dishes.

Al Basha (Map p90; ☎ 022-212 6888, 0787-909000; Indira Gandhi St; snacks from Tsh1500, meals Tsh6000; 🕑 breakfast, lunch & dinner) A no-frills eatery with hummus and other Lebanese dishes, plus burgers and subs. It's just off Morogoro Rd, and a few blocks northwest of Samora Ave.

Nyumba ya Sanaa (Map p90; Mwalimu Julius K Nyerere Cultural Centre, Ohio St; meals from Tsh2000; 🕑 lunch & dinner) A small, informal eatery located in the Nyumba ya Sanaa crafts centre, serving plates of chicken and chips and other local fare.

City Garden (Map p90; cnr Pamba Rd & Garden St; meals from Tsh4000; 🕑 lunch & dinner) A lunch buffet (Tsh8500; Monday to Friday) and à la carte dining, featuring standards such as grilled fish/chicken and rice. There's a shady outdoor seating area, and it's one of the few places in the city centre open on Sunday.

Alcove (Map p90; ☎ 022-213 7444; Samora Ave; meals from Tsh4500; 🕑 lunch & dinner, closed lunch Sun) Dark, heavy décor and tasty Indian and Chinese cuisine, including vegetarian dishes.

Also recommended:

Steers (Map p90; cnr Samora Ave & Ohio St; meals from Tsh2000; 🕑 8am-11pm) Burgers and fast food.

Rendezvous Restaurant (Map p90; Samora Ave; meals Tsh4000) Local fare in the central business district.

Debonairs Pizza (Map p90; cnr Samora Ave & Ohio St; pizzas from Tsh5500; 🕑 8am-11pm) Fast-food pizzas, and indoor or outdoor seating.

City Supermarket (Map p90; JM Mall, cnr Samora Ave & Mission St) For self-catering.

MIDRANGE & TOP END

Tausi (Map p90; ☎ 022-211 4126; Peacock Hotel, Bibi Titi Mohamed Rd; meals from Tsh7000; 🕑 lunch & dinner) This restaurant has a mix of local and Western fare, and is as good a place as any to try *ugali* and sauce, if you haven't already.

Baraza (Map p90; ☎ 022-213 7575; Holiday Inn, Garden Ave; meals from Tsh8000; 🕑 breakfast, lunch & dinner) Good à la carte dining featuring seafood grills and Swahili cuisine.

Kibo Bar (Map p90; ☎ 022-211 2416; Mövenpick Royal Palm, Ohio St; meals Tsh11,000-15,000; ☺ lunch-11.30pm) Design-your-own pasta, sandwich, omelette and salad stations at lunchtime on weekdays, and pub fare at all hours.

L'Oliveto (Map p90; Mövenpick Royal Palm, Ohio St; meals from Tsh15,000; ☺ lunch & dinner Tue-Fri, dinner Sat & Sun) Next door to Kibo Bar is this ultramodern eatery, with delicious Italian cuisine on the plates and a constantly changing colour scheme on the walls.

Oriental (☎ 022-213 1111; www.kempinski-dares salaam.com; Kilimanjaro Kempinski Hotel, Kivukoni Front; meals from US$20; ☺ lunch & dinner Tue-Sun) Considered by some connoisseurs to be the best restaurant in town, with excellent sushi and Asian fusion cuisine, and an ambience that's as optimal for business lunches as it is for a romantic evening out.

BUFFETS
Lunchtime buffet fans have a choice, including those at the **Mövenpick Royal Palm** (Map p90; ☎ 022-211 2416; Ohio St; buffet Tsh 21,000), **Kilimanjaro Kempinski** (Map p90; ☎ 022-213 1111; Kivukoni Front; buffet Tsh25,000), **Holiday Inn** (Map p90; ☎ 022-213 7575; Garden Ave; buffet Tsh16,000), **New Africa Hotel's Bandari Grill** (Map p90; Azikiwe St; buffet Tsh15,000) and (the budget winner) **Heritage Motel** (Map p90; ☎ 022-211 7471; www.heritagemotel .co.tz; cnr Kaluta & Bridge Sts; buffet Tsh5000). All are Monday to Friday only. The Kilimanjaro Kempinski also has a Sunday brunch family buffet (Tsh29,000), and all of these places except Heritage Motel also have evening buffets most nights.

Msasani Peninsula
Sea Cliff Village (Map p86; Toure Dr; ☺ all day) A small and frequently changing selection of eateries, including Épi d'Or bakery, a pizzeria, a juice bar and Msumbi Coffee House (opposite), with great coffees.

Addis in Dar (Map p86; ☎ 0713-266299; 35 Ursino St; meals from Tsh5000; ☺ lunch & dinner Mon-Sat) Offers a mouth-watering selection of Ethiopian dishes, including a range of vegetarian selections. It's signposted off Mgombani St.

La Trattoria Jan (Map p86; ☎ 022-255 7640; Kimweri Ave; meals from Tsh5500; ☺ lunch & dinner) A homy, long-standing place that attracts a loyal group of regulars with its good pizza and Italian dishes.

Sweet Eazy Restaurant & Lounge (Map p86; ☎ 0755-754074; Oyster Bay Shopping Centre; meals from Tsh7000)

Thai and seafood specialities, and live music Thursday and Saturday.

Chongqing Chinese Restaurant (Map p86; ☎ 022-260 0678; Toure Dr; meals from Tsh8000; ☺ 11am-11pm Fri-Wed, 3-11pm Thu) Well-prepared Chinese food next door to Golden Tulip hotel, with views over the water.

81 Steps (Map p86; ☎ 022-260 1273; Peninsula Seaview Hotel, Chui Bay Rd; set menu US$25; ☺ dinner) A new rooftop place at the Peninsula Seaview Hotel with sunset views over the water, cushions and throw pillows on the floor, and a set five-course menu (for maximum 16 guests) featuring Tanzanian-Arabian-Moroccan fusion cuisine (no forks – everything's eaten African or Middle Eastern style). Advance bookings are highly recommended. Seating and traditional-style hand washing starts at 7.30pm and the meal itself commences at 8pm.

The eateries at **Msasani Slipway** (Map p86; ☎ 022-260 0893; Msasani Slipway; ☺ all day) serve everything from burgers to sushi. Eating places include **Fairy Delights Ice Cream Shop** (cones from Tsh2000), **Melela Bustani** (breads from Tsh1000) for sustainably produced bakery and gourmet cheese and sausage products, and the good **Terrace Restaurant** (meals Tsh8500-30,000; ☺ dinner Mon-Fri, lunch & dinner Sat), with terrace seating, including some tables overlooking the water, and a selection of well-prepared Italian and seafood dishes. Located upstairs is **Azuma** (meals from Tsh9000), with Japanese cuisine and discounted meals on Wednesday night for ladies dining with ladies, while directly on the water is the **Mashua Waterfront Bar & Grill** (meals from Tsh6500), with grilled fish and pub-style fare. **Garden Bistro** (Map p86; ☎ 022-260 0800; Haile Selassie Rd) is a relaxed restaurant-nightclub featuring Indian dishes and grills downstairs, continental cuisine upstairs, a *sheesha* (waterpipe) lounge and sports bar.

For self-catering:
Shoprite (Map p86; Msasani Slipway)
Village Supermarket (Map p86; Sea Cliff Village, Toure Dr) Pricey but wide selection of Western foods and imported products.

DRINKING
Neither the café nor the pub scene have made their way into local Dar es Salaam life with the intensity they have in other cities, but there are a few good spots.

Slipway Pub (Map p86; ☎ 022-260 0893; Msasani Slipway; ☺ noon–11pm) A cosy British pub near the water, with drinks and meals, and sports TV.

Garden Bistro (Map p86; ☎ 022-260 0800; Haile Selassie Rd) Happy hours Sunday through to Thursday and live music on weekends.

Q Bar (Map p86; ☎ 022-260 2150, 0754-282474; cnr Haile Selassie & Msasani Rds) Happy hours (5pm to 7pm Monday to Friday), live music on Fridays and big-screen sports TV.

Level 8 (Map p90; 8th fl, Kilimanjaro Kempinski, Kivukoni Front) A rooftop bar with views over the harbour, lounge seating and live music some evenings.

O'Willie's Irish Whiskey Tavern (Map p86; www .owillies.com; Peninsula Seaview Hotel, Chui Bay Rd) A classic Irish pub, and popular with the expat crowd, with live music (check its website for the programme), pub food, pizza and seafood grills.

Also recommended:

Épi d'Or (Map p90; ☎ 213 6006; Samora Ave; ☺ 7am–7pm Mon-Sat) Good coffee and juices.

Msumbi Coffee House (Map p86; Sea Cliff Village) A range of good coffees, and roasted beans for sale. **Kibo Bar** (Map p90; ☎ 022-211 2416; Mövenpick Royal Palm, Ohio St; ☺ noon to 11.30pm) Upmarket sports bar at the Mövenpick Royal Palm hotel.

Coco Beach (Map p86; ☺ Sat & Sun) Packed with locals on weekends, and an amenable seaside setting for an inexpensive beer.

ENTERTAINMENT

For the latest on what's on around town, check the listings magazines (p87), the bulletin board at Nyumba ya Sanaa (right) and www.naomba.com.

Cinemas

The **British Council** (Map p90; ☎ 022-211 6574/5/6; info@britishcouncil.or.tz; cnr Ohio St & Samora Ave) shows occasional free cultural films. Movies are also shown at the **Msasani Slipway** (Map p86; ☎ 022-260 0893; Msasani Slipway) on Friday, Saturday and Sunday evenings.

Traditional Music & Dance

Mwalimu Julius K Nyerere Cultural Centre (Map p90; Nyumba ya Sanaa, Ohio St) Traditional dance performances at 7pm on Friday, and the best place to find out about traditional dance events around the city.

Village Museum (Map p102; ☎ 022-270 0437; www.museum.or.tz; cnr New Bagamoyo Rd & Makaburi St) *Ngoma* (drumming and dancing) performances from 4pm to 6pm on Saturday and

Sunday, plus occasional special afternoon programmes highlighting the dances of individual tribes.

SHOPPING
Handicrafts & Paintings

Nyumba ya Sanaa (Map p90; Mwalimu Julius K Nyerere Cultural Centre, Ohio St) This local artists cooperative sells textiles and crafts daily from around the country; you can also watch some of the artists at work.

Msasani Slipway Weekend Craft Market (Map p86; Msasani Slipway, Msasani Peninsula; ☺ Sat & Sun) Prices are slightly higher here than elsewhere in town, but quality is good and the atmosphere calm. In addition to crafts, there's a large selection of Tingatinga-style paintings.

Mawazo Gallery & Art Café (Map p90; ☎ 0784-782770; Upanga Rd; ☺ 10am-5.30pm Mon-Fri, to 2pm Sat) High-quality paintings, woodcarvings and crafts.

Tingatinga Centre (Map p86; Morogoro Stores, Haile Selassie Rd, Oyster Bay; ☺ 8.30am-5pm) This centre is at the spot where Edward Saidi Tingatinga (p34) originally marketed his designs, and it's still one of the best places to buy Tingatinga paintings and watch the artists at work.

Wasanii Art Gallery (Map p86; wasaniicentre@yahoo .co.uk; Msasani Slipway, Msasani Peninsula; ☺ 1-8pm Mon-Fri, to 6pm Sat) A showcase for up-and-coming Tanzanian artists.

For last-minute craft shopping, **Out of Africa** (Julius Nyerere International Airport) and several other shops in the airport departure lounge have good selections.

Curio shops with batiks, woodcarvings and other crafts are scattered throughout the city centre around Samora Ave near the

---

COMMUNITY TOURISM SPOTLIGHT: MAWAZO GALLERY

Together with friends and colleagues, Mawazo Gallery founder Rachel Kessi has made a significant step in revitalising the local Dar es Salaam art scene. Mawazo (meaning 'ideas' or 'thoughts') was established in 2003 to give local artists a forum for exhibiting their work and promote artistic development. Since then it has quietly established a foothold in the local cultural scene as an artist's meeting point, and as the force behind the semi-annual Makutano arts and crafts fair (see p98).

DAR'S MARKETS

For a gentle initiation into Dar es Salaam's markets, head to the **fish market** (Map p90; Ocean Rd), near Kivukoni Front. It's fairly calm as urban markets go, and you can watch fish auctions. For more excitement, get a reliable taxi driver or Tanzanian friend to take you to **Ilala Market** (Map p86; Uhuru St), near Shaurimoyo Rd, or to the huge, sprawling **Kariakoo Market** (Map p86; Msimbazi & Mkunguni Sts), Tanzania's largest; don't bring valuables and watch out for pickpockets. For Western-style shopping, try **Msasani Slipway** (Map p86; Msasani Peninsula) or **Sea Cliff Village** (Map p86; Toure Dr), both at the northern end of Msasani Peninsula, and the less glitzy **Shoppers' Plaza** (Map p86; Old Bagamoyo Rd). For *kangas* (printed cotton wraparounds worn by many Tanzanian women) and other textiles, try the vendors and wholesale shops at **Mnazi Mmoja** (Map p90; Bibi Titi Mohamed Rd).

Askari monument. Most top-end hotels have boutiques with high-quality crafts. Also watch for the semi-annual arts and crafts fair held at the Police Officers' Mess on Toure Dr and organised each May and November by **Makutano – The Centre for Tanzanian Art** (makutanotz@yahoo.com).

Woodcarvings

Mwenge Carvers' Market (Map p102; Sam Nujoma Rd; ⏲ 8am-6pm) This market, opposite the Village Museum, and just off New Bagamoyo Rd, is packed with vendors, and you can watch carvers at work. Take the Mwenge *dalla-dalla* from New Posta transport stand to the end of the route, from where it's five minutes on foot down the small street to the left.

GETTING THERE & AWAY
Air

Julius Nyerere International Airport is the major arrival point for overseas flights and the hub for domestic services. For more information, including international flight connections, see p346. For flights to Zanzibar, the best contacts are Coastal Aviation and ZanAir (see p127). Airline offices in Dar es Salaam include the following:

Air India (Map p90; ☎ 022-215 2642; cnr Ali Hassan Mwinyi & Bibi Titi Mohamed Rds)

Air Tanzania (Map p90; ☎ 022-211 7500, 022-284 4239; Ohio St) Also at Terminal Two, Julius Nyerere International Airport (open 4am to 9pm).

British Airways (Map p90; ☎ 022-211 3820, 022-284 4082; Mövenpick Royal Palm, Ohio St)

Coastal Aviation (Map p90; ☎ 022-211 7959/60, 022-284 3293; aviation@coastal.cc; Upanga Rd) Also at Terminal One, Julius Nyerere International Airport.

Emirates Airlines (Map p90; ☎ 022-211 6100; Haidery Plaza, cnr Kisutu & India Sts)

Ethiopian Airlines (Map p90; ☎ 022-211 7063; Ohio St) Opposite Mövenpick Royal Palm hotel.

Jet Airways (Map p90; ☎ 022-212 7734; jetairway stz@akshar.co.ke; Kilimanjaro Kempinski Hotel, Kivukoni Front)

Kenya Airways (Map p90; ☎ 022-211 9376/7; Upanga Rd) Located with KLM.

KLM (Map p90; ☎ 022-213 9790/1; Upanga Rd) Located with Kenya Airways.

Linhas Aéreas de Moçambique (Map p90; ☎ 022-213 4600; 1st fl, JM Mall, Samora Ave) At Fast-Track Travel (www.fasttracktanzania.com).

Precision Air (Map p90; ☎ 022-216 8000, 022-284 3547, 0787-888407; cnr Samora Ave & Pamba Rd) Also at Terminal Two, Julius Nyerere International Airport (open 5am to 10pm).

South African Airways (SAA; Map p90; ☎ 022-211 7044; Raha Towers, cnr Bibi Titi Mohamed & Ali Hassan Mwinyi Rds)

Swiss International Airlines (Map p90; ☎ 022-211 8870; Luther House Centre Hostel, Sokoine Dr)

Yemenia Yemen Airways (Map p90; ☎ 022-212 6036; Ohio St) Opposite Mövenpick Royal Palm hotel.

Zambian Airways (Map p90; ☎ 022-212 8885/6; Ground fl, Haidery Plaza, cnr Kisutu & India Sts)

ZanAir (☎ 022-284 3297; Terminal One, Julius Nyerere International Airport)

The airport has two terminals. Most regularly scheduled domestic flights and all international flights depart from Terminal Two (the 'new' terminal, and the first one you reach coming from town), while many flights on small planes and most charters depart from Terminal One (the 'old' terminal), about 700m further down the road. Verify the departure terminal when purchasing your ticket.

Boat

The main passenger routes are between Dar es Salaam, Zanzibar and Pemba.

TO/FROM ZANZIBAR & PEMBA

There are several 'fast' ferry trips (on *Sea Star, Sea Express* or *Seabus*) daily between Dar es Salaam and Zanzibar, departing at 7.30am (*Sea Express*), 10.30am (*Sea Star*), 2pm (*Seabus*) and 4pm (*Seabus*). All take 1½ hours and cost US$35/40 regular/VIP (VIP gets you a seat in the air-con hold). There are also several slow ferries. The main one is *Flying Horse*, which departs daily at 12.30pm (one way US$25) and takes almost four hours. *New Happy* and *Aziza* each depart several times weekly at noon (one way US$25, three hours).

Ferry departures from Zanzibar (Map p86) are daily at 7am (*Sea Star*), 10am (*Seabus*), 1pm (*Seabus*), 4pm (*Sea Express*) and 10pm (*Flying Horse*, arriving before dawn the next day).

The MS *Sepideh* also runs daily between Dar and Zanzibar, departing from Dar at 7.30am and Zanzibar at 4pm (one way US$35). Vehicles can be transported on the *New Happy*.

Only buy your tickets at the ticket windows – each company has its own, all lined up on Kivukoni Front opposite St Joseph's Cathedral – and don't fall for touts at the harbour trying to collect extra fees for 'doctors' certificates', departure taxes and the like. The only fee is the ticket price (which includes the US$5 port tax). Also, avoid touts who want to take you into town to buy 'cheaper' ferry tickets, or who offer to purchase ferry tickets for you at less expensive resident rates; although it's easy enough to get resident-rate tickets and get on the boat with them, you're likely to have problems later when the tout or his buddies come around to collect payment for the favour.

For ferry connections to Pemba, see p148.

TO/FROM MTWARA

There are currently no boats running between Dar es Salaam and Mtwara.

Bus

Except as noted following, all buses depart from and arrive at the main bus station at Ubungo, about 8km west of the city centre on Morogoro Rd. It's a sprawling place with the usual assortment of bus station hustle and touts. Keep an eye on your luggage and your wallet and try to avoid arriving at night. *Dalla-dallas* to Ubungo (Tsh200) leave from the local New Posta and Old Posta transport stands (Map p90), as well as from various other spots in town. Taxis from the city centre cost from about Tsh8000. If you're coming into Dar es Salaam on Scandinavian Express, Dar Express and Royal Coach bus lines, you can usually stay on the bus past Ubungo until the bus line's town office – which is worth doing as it will be less chaotic and you'll have a cheaper taxi fare to your hotel. Except for Scandinavian Express buses (which you can also board at its terminal), it doesn't work out leaving the city, since departures are directly from Ubungo. To book tickets, head to the bus line offices (listed following). As usual, only buy tickets inside the bus office itself.

Dar Express (Map p90; Libya St, Kisutu) Daily buses to Arusha (Tsh17,000) departing at 6am, 7am, 8am, 9am and 10am from Ubungo bus station.

Royal Coach (Map p90; ☎ 022-212 4073; Libya St, Kisutu) Daily departures to Arusha (Tsh22,000) at 9am from Ubungo bus station (7am from its Kisutu office).

Scandinavian Express (Map p86; ☎ 022-218 4833/4; www.scandinaviagroup.com; cnr Msimbazi St & Nyerere Rd) Has its own bus terminal for arrivals and departures (which is also where you book tickets). It's calmer than Ubungo, and closer to the city centre, though all Scandinavian Express buses also pass by Ubungo. There's at least one bus daily to Iringa and Mbeya, another via Iringa to Njombe and Songea, two daily to Dodoma and several daily to Arusha, but many routes were in flux at the time of publication, so contact Scandinavian Express for an update.

The following table lists price and frequency for bus travel from Dar es Salaam to various locations:

Destination	Price (Tsh)	Frequency
Arusha	18,000-24,000	3 daily
Dodoma	10,000-13,000	2 daily
Iringa	15,000	1 daily
Kampala	62,000	1 daily
Mbeya	25,000	1 daily
Mwanza	50,000	1 daily
Nairobi	39,000	1 daily
Songea	27,000	1 daily

Minibuses to Kilwa Masoko depart from Temeke bus stand, located about 5km southwest of the city centre, just off Nelson Mandela Rd.

For information about buses between Dar es Salaam and Kenya, Uganda, Zambia and Malawi, see p349.

Car & Motorcycle

See p100 for car-rental agencies.

Train

For information about the Tazara line between Dar es Salaam, Mbeya and Kapiri Mposhi (Zambia), see p361. The **Tazara train station** (off Map p86; ☎ 022-286 5187, 0713-225292; www.tazara.co.tz; cnr Nyerere & Nelson Mandela Rds; ⊙ ticket office 7.30am-12.30pm & 2-4.30pm Mon-Fri, 9am-12.30pm Sat) is about 6km southwest of the city centre (Tsh6000 in a taxi). *Dalla-dallas* to the train station leave from either New or Old Posta transport stands, and are marked Vigunguti, U/Ndege or Buguruni.

For more on Central Line trains between Dodoma, Kigoma and Mwanza (the Dar to Dodoma section is currently closed), see p361. **Tanzanian Railways Corporation (Central Line) train station** (Map p90; ☎ 022-211 7833; www.trctz.com; cnr Railway St & Sokoine Dr) is in the city centre southwest of the ferry terminal.

GETTING AROUND
To/From the Airport

Julius Nyerere International Airport is about 12km from the city centre. *Dalla-dallas* (marked U/Ndege) go to the airport from New Posta transport stand. In heavy traffic the trip can take over an hour, and there's generally no room for luggage. Taxis to central Dar es Salaam cost Tsh10,000 (to Msasani Peninsula Tsh20,000 to Tsh25,000).

Car & Motorcycle

See p359 for general information. Most rental agencies offer self-drive options in town; none offer unlimited kilometres. Rental agencies include the following:

Avis (☎ 022-211 5381, 022-212 1061/2; www.avisworld .com); Airport (Julius Nyerere International Airport); Kilimanjaro Kempinski (**Map p90**; Kivukoni Front); Skylink Travel & Tours (**Map p90**; Ohio St)

Green Car Rentals (Map p86; ☎ 022-218 2022, 022-218 2107; www.greencars.co.tz; Nyerere Rd) A recommended place, with competitive rates. It's near MD Motors in the Gerezani area.

Hertz (Map p86; ☎ 022-218 2612; hertz@cats-net .com; cnr Nyerere Rd & Swahili St) A Hertz franchise, a block away from Green Car Rentals.

Travel Mate (Map p86; ☎ 022-260 0573; info@travel mate.co.tz; Chole Rd) Near the Slipway turn-off.

Public Transport

Dalla-dallas (minibuses) go almost everywhere in the city for Tsh200. They are invariably packed to overflowing, and are difficult to board with luggage. First and last stops are shown in the front window, but routes vary, so confirm that the driver is going to your destination. Terminals include the following:

New Posta transport stand (Map p90; Maktaba St) At the main post office.

Old Posta transport stand (Map p90; Sokoine Dr) Down from the Azania Front Lutheran Church.

Stesheni transport stand (Map p90; Algeria St) Off Samora Ave near the Central Line Train Station; *Dalla-dallas* to Temeke bus stand also leave from here; ask for 'Temeke mwisho'.

Taxi

Taxis don't have meters. Short rides within the city centre cost Tsh2000. Fares from the city centre to Msasani Peninsula start at Tsh5000 (Tsh8000 to Sea Cliff Village).

Taxi stands include those opposite the Mövenpick Royal Palm hotel (Map p90), on the corner of Azikiwe St and Sokoine Dr (Map p90) and on the Msasani Peninsula on the corner of Msasani and Haile Selassie Rds (Map p86).

Reliable taxi drivers, recommended also for airport pick-ups, include **Jumanne Mastoke** (☎ 0784-339735; mjumanne@yahoo.com), based opposite the Mövenpick Royal Palm hotel, and **Godwin Muganga** (☎ 0713-252459, 0757-080659; godwin.muganga@yahoo.com).

AROUND DAR ES SALAAM

PUGU HILLS

Pugu Hills, which begins about 15km southwest of Dar es Salaam and extends past Kisarawe, is lightly wooded, with several small forest reserves, and offers a change of pace from the urban scene. Despite its proximity to the city, the Pugu area is not urbanised at all, and many communities have remained quite traditional and conservative. Pugu is also interesting from a historical perspective: several mission stations were established here, and it's the site of Pugu Secondary School, where Julius Nyerere taught before entering into politics full-time.

Pugu's roads (most of which are unsealed) are only lightly travelled, and good for biking. There are two short WCST hiking trails, which require a permit (Tsh5000) from the Mali Asili (Natural Resources) office in Kisarawe, just south of the main roundabout. The trailheads

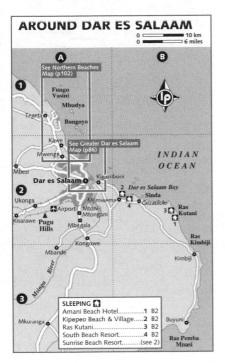

AROUND DAR ES SALAAM

0 — 10 km
0 — 6 miles

See Northern Beaches
Map (p102)

Fungu
Yasini

Mbudya

Tegeta

Bongoyo

Kawe

See Greater Dar es Salaam
Map (p86)

Mwenge

INDIAN
OCEAN

Mbezi

Kiganiboni

Dar es Salaam

Ukonga 2 Dar es Salaam Bay

Mjimwema Sinda
Airport Mtoni- 4 Gezaulole
Kisarawe Pugu Mtongani 3 Ras
Hills Mbagala Kutani
1
Kongowe Ras
Kimbiji
Mbande Kimbiji

SLEEPING
Amani Beach Hotel..............1 B2
Mkuranga Kipepeo Beach & Village.....2 B2 Buyuni
Ras Kutani.........................3 B2
South Beach Resort..............4 B2 Ras Pemba
Sunrise Beach Resort.........(see 2) Mnasi

airport). Continue straight along the unsealed Kisarawe road for about 200m, to the end of a tiny group of shops on your left, where there's a dirt path leading up to Pugu Hills (about 15 minutes further on foot); ask for Bwana Kiki's place. By vehicle, from the old Agip station, follow the sealed road to the left, continue about 1.2km, then turn right at an unmarked dirt path running past a chicken warehouse (the turn-off is about 50m before the railroad tracks). Continue 2km uphill, along a rough road, to Pugu Hills.

OFFSHORE ISLANDS

The uninhabited islands of Bongoyo, Mbudya, Pangavini and Fungu Yasini, just off the coastline north of Dar es Salaam, were gazetted in 1975 as part of the Dar es Salaam Marine Reserve system. Bongoyo and Mbudya – the two most visited islands, and the only ones with tourist facilities – offer attractive beaches backed by dense vegetation, snorkelling and short walking trails, and make an enjoyable getaway from the city. Swimming is possible at any time, unlike the situation on the mainland beaches, where swimming is tide-dependent. Although both attract many visitors on weekends and holidays, there's enough space, especially on Mbudya's long beach, so you can usually find a peaceful spot. The islands are home to populations of coconut crabs, and dolphins can sometimes be spotted in the surrounding waters. There are several nearby dive sites, most off the islands' eastern sides. Fungu Yasini is a large sandbank without vegetation, while Pangavini has only a tiny beach area. Much of its perimeter is low coral outcrops making docking difficult, and it's

are 15 minutes from the office on foot; each trail takes about 30 minutes. There's a military base in Pugu, so don't take pictures anywhere unless you're sure that you're nowhere in its vicinity.

Pugu Hills (☎ 0754-565498, 0754-394875; www.pugu hills.com; entry Tsh2000, camping per person Tsh6000, 4-6 person bandas US$50) is a good, breezy place on a hillside backing onto a forest reserve with spacious, en suite *bandas* (thatched-roof huts with wooden or earthen walls). There's also an area to pitch your tent, along with shower facilities and a restaurant serving vegetarian and other meals. Large groups and overland trucks cannot be accommodated. Nearby are some hiking paths, including a short walk to a lookout with views over Dar es Salaam. Call or SMS in advance, whether for overnight or day visits.

Getting There & Away

Dalla-dallas to Kisarawe leave from Msimbazi St in Kariakoo. You can also get them on Nyerere Rd at the airport turn-off. For Pugu Hills camp site and restaurant, ask the driver to drop you at the old Agip station (about 7km before Kisarawe, and about 7km past the

---

COMMUNITY TOURISM SPOTLIGHT: PUGU HILLS

Pugu Hills makes an ideal destination for anyone interested in local environmental and conservation issues. Walks can be arranged to a nearby charcoal production site to see the rate at which Pugu Forest is disappearing, and ideas and collaboration are welcomed to halt the destruction of the forest. Before going, check out www.puguhills .com/forests for background on the ancient Pugu Forest and on the conservation activities of the Pugu Hills Nature Centre.

DAR ES SALAAM

seldom visited. There's a Tsh6000/4000 per adult/child entry fee to enter the reserve area, including visiting any of the islands. It's usually included in the price of excursions, and collected before departure.

Bongoyo

Bongoyo, about 7km north of Dar es Salaam, is the most popular of the islands, with a small and relatively quiet (except on holiday weekends) stretch of beach offering snorkelling and swimming and some short walking trails. Basic grilled fish meals (about Tsh6000) and sodas are available, and snorkelling equipment can be rented.

A boat goes to the island daily (except during the long rains) from Msasani Slipway at Msasani Peninsula, departing at 9.30am, 11.30am, 1.30pm and 3.30pm, and returning at 10.30am, 12.30pm, 2.30pm and 5pm (Tsh16,000 return, including marine reserve entry fees; minimum four people). The departure and ticketing point is Mashua Waterfront Bar & Grill. It's also possible to organise visits from Sea Breeze Marine (right) and from most of the northern beach hotels (see opposite), although the distance from there to Bongoyo is longer.

Mbudya

Pretty Mbudya, north of Bongoyo, and directly offshore from Kunduchi Beach Hotel & Resort, has several beaches (the best and longest one runs along the island's western edge), short walking trails and snorkelling. Near the island's northern end is an old graveyard. Grilled fish and chips are available for about Tsh6000, as are drinks, and snorkelling equipment can be rented for Tsh10,000 per day. There are thatched *bandas* for shade and **camping** (per person with own tent or under open-sided banda Tsh20,000, per person incl tent rental Tsh30,000). The island is best reached from the beaches north of Dar es Salaam, and all the hotels there, plus Sea Breeze Marine (right) arrange excursions (about Tsh10,000 per person, minimum two people, including entry fees).

NORTHERN BEACHES

The coastline about 25km north of Dar es Salaam and east of New Bagamoyo Rd is lined with resorts and is a popular weekend getaway. While lacking the exotic tropical island ambience of Zanzibar's coastline, the beaches here make a relaxing break from the city and – with a selection of swimming pools

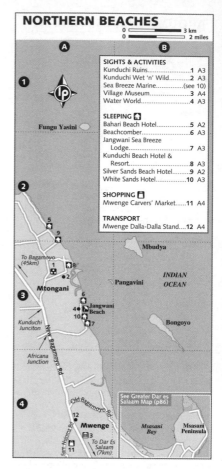

NORTHERN BEACHES

0 — 3 km
0 — 2 miles

SIGHTS & ACTIVITIES
Kunduchi Ruins.....................1 A3
Kunduchi Wet 'n' Wild..........2 A3
Sea Breeze Marine.............(see 10)
Village Museum.....................3 A4
Water World..........................4 A3

SLEEPING
Bahari Beach Hotel.................5 A2
Beachcomber............................6 A3
Jangwani Sea Breeze
   Lodge.................................7 A3
Kunduchi Beach Hotel &
   Resort................................8 A3
Silver Sands Beach Hotel........9 A2
White Sands Hotel................10 A3

SHOPPING
Mwenge Carvers' Market......11 A4

TRANSPORT
Mwenge Dalla-Dalla Stand....12 A4

and two water parks – are a good destination for families. They are close enough to Dar es Salaam that you can visit for the day, or base yourself here. The southern section of coast – Jangwani Beach – is broken by frequent stone jetties, although it offers a wider range of facilities than the more attractive coastline running from Kunduchi north.

Sights & Activities
DIVING & SNORKELLING

Diving around the coral gardens near Bongoyo and Mbudya islands, and diving certification courses (PADI), can be arranged year-round at the long-standing **Sea Breeze Marine** (☎ 0754-783241; www.seabreezemarine.org) next to White Sands Hotel.

RUINS

Just north of Kunduchi Wet 'n' Wild are the overgrown **Kunduchi ruins**, which include the remnants of a late-15th-century mosque as well as Arabic graves from the 18th or 19th centuries, with some well-preserved pillar tombs. Fragments of Chinese pottery found here testify to ancient trading links between this part of Africa and the Orient. Arrange a guide with your hotel – it's not safe to walk on your own to the ruins, as there have been muggings.

WATER PARKS

Kunduchi Wet 'n' Wild (☎ 022-265 0326, 022-265 0332; wetnwild@raha.com; adult/child Tsh4950/4500; ☺ 9am-6pm, women only Tue) This large and crowded place next to Kunduchi Beach Hotel & Resort has several pools, water slides, video arcades, a small playground, an adjoining go-kart track and a restaurant. Although the complex opens at 9am, the slides and pools usually don't get going until closer to 10am. To get here, see Getting There & Away (p104).

Water World (☎ 022-264 7627, 022-264 7620; adult /child Tsh4000/3000; ☺ 10am-5.30pm Tue-Sun, women only Wed) Similar to Kunduchi Wet 'n' Wild, but somewhat smaller and quieter. It's run by White Sands Hotel, and is next door, between White Sands and Beachcomber hotels.

Sleeping & Eating

At all the hotels, it's worth asking about weekend discounts on accommodation. All hotels also charge an entry fee for day visitors on weekends and holidays, averaging Tsh3000 to Tsh5000 per person.

BUDGET

Silver Sands Beach Hotel (☎ 022-265 0428, 0754-850001; www.silversands.netfirms.com; camping per person /vehicle Tsh3000/2000, s/d standard Tsh30,000/32,000, s/d deluxe Tsh45,000/46,000; ☒) This place is set on a quiet stretch of beach and has seen better days, but remains a respectable budget choice. The camping facilities have hot water (usually), and there are basic but adequate rooms set around a grassy square just in from the beach, all with mosquito nets. Meals cost from Tsh4500.

Bahari Beach Hotel (☎ 022-265 0352; baharibeach hotel@yahoo.com; camping per person US$5, d US$65; ☒) The former government hotel, north of Silver Sands, has an attractive beachside setting, although the 1970s-style rooms are well

past their prime. A better-value option – and popular with overlanders – is camping on the surrounding lawns.

MIDRANGE

Jangwani Sea Breeze Lodge (☎ 022-264 7215; www .jangwani.org; s/d US$70/85; ☒ 🖳 🖳) This tidy formerly German-run establishment has changed hands and is now part of the Eclipse Hotels group. The 34 rooms are comfortable and some are spacious, although most are on the inland side of the road and without beach views. Just opposite is a bougainvillea-draped beachside courtyard, and a restaurant with weekend barbecues and buffets (per adult /child about Tsh12,500/6500; open Saturday evening and Sunday lunch).

Beachcomber (☎ 022-264 7772/3; www.beachcomber .co.tz; s/d from US$85/100; ☒ 🖳 🖳) Although in need of a facelift, new paint and lighting in the hallways, rooms are adequate and all have small balconies, though most don't have full beach-facing views. There's also a gym and a pool. Despite the waterside location, the beach in front of the hotel is dirty and unsuitable for swimming – you'll need to use the pool, or go to neighbouring White Sands, about 500m to the south.

White Sands Hotel (☎ 022-264 7620/1; www.hotel whitesands.com; s/d Mon-Fri US$115/132, Sat & Sun US$85/95, deluxe apt from US$140; ☒ 🖳 🖳) This large, somewhat hectic and often full place (with 88 rooms, 28 self-catering apartments and conference facilities) is on the beach between Jangwani Sea Breeze Lodge and Beachcomber. The well-kept rooms are in two-storey rondavels lined up along the waterfront, all with TV, minifridge and sea views. At the northern end of the complex are newer self-catering apartments – some directly overlooking the beach, and the others just behind overlooking a well-tended lawn. There's also a gym and a business centre, and the restaurant has weekend buffets (per adult/child about Tsh16,000/8000). Waterskiing, laser sailing and wind surfing can be arranged. Room prices include free airport transfers (with two days' advance notice) and free entry to Water World. There's a nightclub on most Friday and Saturday nights.

Kunduchi Beach Hotel & Resort (☎ 022-265 0050; www.kunduchiresort.com; s/d US$150/174; ☒ 🖳 🖳) After being closed for many years, this former government hotel has recently reopened. It's set on the best stretch of beach – a large expanse of clean white

THE ZARAMO WORLD VIEW

The original inhabitants of the area around Dar es Salaam are the Zaramo, known for their skilled woodworking and for their creation beliefs. In the beginning, according to the Zaramo, was Nyalutanga, the common mother from whom springs forth all life and knowledge. Nyalutanga herself had no creator and no husband, but rather emerged from the female earth, later bringing forth a line of daughters, from whom all Zaramo are descended. Men fit into the picture as nourishers of the female creative power, and as the source of the cultural qualities that complement women's biological contribution. Thus, while family lines are continued through the mother, Zaramo children take the name of their father's mother's clan and are considered to inherit the cultural qualities of their father.

The Zaramo believe that all life arises from death. Death is seen as part of the natural continuum of life, as a transition rather than a transformation. The rituals marking this transition extend into many areas. For example, Zaramo traditional healers often place newly procured medicinal plants on compost heaps for several days to gain potency. As the plants wither, they take on new powers, and a place connected with death and decay (the compost heap) assumes the symbolism of a place of regeneration.

For more, look for a copy of *Blood, Milk and Death: Body Symbols and the Power of Regeneration Among the Zaramo of Tanzania* by Marja-Liisa Swantz with Salome Mjema and Zenya Wild, on which this text is based.

---

sand, with no jetties to mar the view – with a long row of attractive beach-facing rooms, expansive green grounds and a generally quiet ambience. All the rooms have floor to ceiling windows with balconies and wonderfully firm mattresses, and once the decidedly mediocre restaurant is injected with some life and the occasional hiccups with services sorted out, it promises to be a good option for those seeking a quieter ambience than that found at the hotels along Jangwani Beach to the south. It also has a business centre and a gym.

Getting There & Away

The Jangwani Beach hotels – Jangwani Sea Breeze Lodge, White Sands Hotel and Beachcomber – are all reached via the same signposted turn-off from New Bagamoyo Rd. About 3km further north along New Bagamoyo Rd is the signposted turn-off for Kunduchi Beach, Silver Sands Beach and Bahari Beach hotels.

Via public transport, take a *dalla-dalla* from New Posta transport stand in Dar es Salaam to Mwenge (Tsh200). Once at Mwenge, if you're heading to one of the Jangwani Beach hotels, take a 'Tegeta' *dalla-dalla* to Africana Junction (Tsh200), from where you'll need to take a bicycle taxi (Tsh500), *majaji* (tuk-tuk; Tsh1000) or taxi (Tsh2000) the remaining couple of kilometres to the hotels. It's also possible to get a direct *dalla-dalla* from

Kariakoo to Tegeta (Tsh250). For Kunduchi Beach, Silver Sands and Bahari Beach hotels, stay on the Tegeta *dalla-dalla* until Mtongani (near the Kunduchi junction; Tsh250), where you'll need to take a taxi for the remaining distance (Tsh2500 to Silver Sands Beach Hotel). Don't walk, as there have been several muggings along this stretch of road.

Taxis direct from Dar es Salaam cost Tsh10,000 to Tsh15,000 one way (Tsh20,000 to Tsh25,000 from the airport), depending on your bargaining abilities. All hotels arrange airport pick-ups. If you're driving, the fastest route is via Namanga and Kawe (and not via Mwenge).

SOUTHERN BEACHES

The coastline south of Dar es Salaam gets more attractive, tropical and rural the further south you go, and makes an easily accessible getaway, far removed – in ambience, if not in distance – from the city. The beach begins just south of Kigamboni, which is opposite Kivukoni Front and reached in a few minutes by ferry. About 25km further south are two lovely, exclusive resorts.

Kigamboni

The long, white-sand beach south of Kigamboni, around Mjimwema village, is the closest spot to Dar es Salaam for camping and chilling. It's also an easy and enjoyable day trip if you're staying in the city and want some sand and surf.

SLEEPING & EATING

Sunrise Beach Resort (Map p101; ☎ 022-282 0222; www
.sunrisebeachresort.co.tz; camping US$4, 2-person 'safari'
tent US$12, standard r US$25, s/d with sea view US$50/60,
s/d executive US$65/75) A good place with straight-
forward standard and 'sea view' rooms clustered together in the central hotel area on
a long, good stretch of beach just up from
Kipepeo, plus nicer air-con 'executive' rooms
in two-storey brick rondavels several hundred metres back. Adjoining the main hotel
area in an uncluttered spot on the sand is a
row of clean canvas tents – all with a double
mattress on the sand and small windows,
and hot-water showers close by. There's
a per person day use fee on weekends of
Tsh5000, of which Tsh3000 can be redeemed
at the restaurant.

Kipepeo Beach & Village (Map p101; ☎ 0754-
276178; www.kipepeovillage.com; camping per person US$8,
s/d/tr beach banda US$13/20/28, s/d/tr cottage US$50/65/95)
Raised cottages lined up about 300m back
from a long stretch of beach, all with balconies
and mosquito nets. Closer to the water, but
enclosed behind a fence and a long way from
the nearest bathroom, are makeshift thatched
bandas with mosquito nets but no windows,
and – on the other side of the compound, also
near the beach and also fenced in – a shadeless
camping area. Breakfast is included in cottage
rates. There's a large beachside restaurant-
bar. The place is very popular, especially on
weekends, when there's a Tsh3000 fee for day
use of the beach and facilities (the price can be
redeemed at the bar or restaurant). Kipepeo
is 8km south of the ferry dock.

The midrange South Beach Resort (Map
p101), just south of Kipepeo Beach & Village,
is set to open shortly, with a pool, play area for
children and shaded *bandas* on the beach.

GETTING THERE & AWAY

Making a good excursion in itself – it's a slice
of local life – the Kigamboni (Magogoni) ferry
(per person/vehicle Tsh100/800, five minutes)
runs throughout the day between the eastern
end of Kivukoni Front in Dar es Salaam and
Kigamboni village. Once on the other side,
catch a *dalla-dalla* heading south and ask the
driver to drop you off. Taxis from Kigamboni
charge about Tsh3000 to Kipepeo Beach &
Village and Sunrise Beach Resort.

With your own car, an alternative route back
to the city is to turn right along the tarmac road
just south of Kipepeo, and follow it past stands
of coconut palms and scattered villages to Dar
es Salaam via Kongowe (at the junction with
Kilwa Rd), Mbagala and Mtoni-Mtongani.

Gezaulole

About 13km south of Kigamboni on the
beach, Gezaulole village was previously the
site of a cultural tourism programme focusing on local Zaramo life (see the boxed text,
opposite) and on excursions to nearby Sinda
island. The starting point – Akida's Garden –
is currently closed, as is the affiliated Kim
Beach & Campsite on a palm-lined stretch
of sand nearby, but it's worth asking around
to see if it's started up again. Alternatively,
contact Afriroots (p47), which may be able
to help arrange a visit.

Dalla-dallas to Gezaulole leave from the
Kigamboni ferry dock when full.

Ras Kutani

This secluded cape, about 30km south of
Dar es Salaam, offers tranquil surroundings,
water sports (there's snorkelling but no diving), fishing, beach walking and the chance
for a tropical island–style getaway without
actually leaving the mainland. There are two
places to stay, both accessed via the same signposted turn-off, and both requiring advance
bookings. Nearby is an airstrip for charter
flights. Nesting sea turtles favour this section
of coast, and both resorts are involved in local
conservation projects.

The exclusive **Ras Kutani** (Map p101; www.selous
.com; per person all inclusive US$305, ste per person full board
US$390; ☼ Jun–mid-Mar; ☎), set between the sea
and a small lagoon, has nine lovely, spacious
bungalows made from natural materials, and
all with beach-facing verandas. On a rise away
from the main lodge are four more upmarket suites, each with their own plunge pool.
Bird-watching, forest walks, horse riding,
canoeing in the lagoon and snorkelling can
be arranged.

Just south and around the bend is the wonderfully peaceful and aptly named **Amani Beach
Hotel** (Map p101; ☎ 0754-410033; www.amanibeach.com;
s/d full board US$220/380; ☎ ▢ ☎), with 10 spa-
cious and well-spaced cottages set on a low
cliff directly above the beach and backed by
extensive flowering gardens. There's also a
beachside swimming pool and delicious, well-
prepared cuisine available, as well as bird-
watching, forest and beach walks, horse riding
and windsurfing opportunities.

Zanzibar Archipelago

Step off the boat or plane onto Zanzibar, and you'll be transported through the miles and the centuries – to the ancient kingdom of Persia, to the Oman of bygone days with its caliphs and sultans, to the west coast of India with its sensual rhythms and heavily laden scents. In Stone Town – the heart of the archipelago – narrow, cobbled alleyways wind past Arabic-style houses with brass-studded wooden doors. Elderly men in their *kanzu* (white robes) and *kofia* (caps) chat animatedly over cups of strong coffee while playing a seemingly never-ending game of *bao* (a board game). Nearby, veiled women in their flowing, black *bui-bui* (cover-alls) pause to share the latest gossip, while children chase balls through the streets.

Along the coast, life goes on as it has for centuries, its pace set by the rhythm of the tides and the winds of the monsoon. Just across the deep waters of the Pemba channel lies hilly, verdant Pemba – the archipelago's 'other' island, seldom visited and steeped in mystique. Dense mangrove swamps line its coast, opening occasionally onto stunning white-sand coves, and a patchwork of neat farm plots covers the hillsides.

There is, of course, another side to life on the archipelago: hassles from Zanzibar's ever-present street touts will probably be your first introduction, development threatens to over-whelm some areas of the coast, costs creep constantly skywards and *piki-piki* (motorbikes) career recklessly through Stone Town's streets. However, there are still some quiet, unspoiled spots left and good deals to be found. And, while your reverie on caliphs and sultans may not last, the archipelago's allure will captivate long after you've finished your visit.

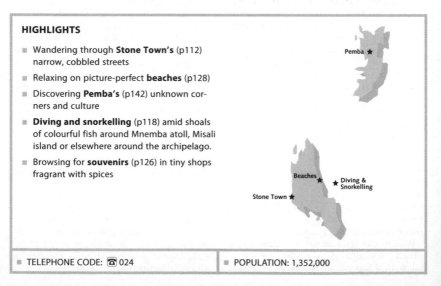

HIGHLIGHTS

- Wandering through **Stone Town's** (p112) narrow, cobbled streets
- Relaxing on picture-perfect **beaches** (p128)
- Discovering **Pemba's** (p142) unknown corners and culture
- **Diving and snorkelling** (p118) amid shoals of colourful fish around Mnemba atoll, Misali island or elsewhere around the archipelago.
- Browsing for **souvenirs** (p126) in tiny shops fragrant with spices

Pemba ★

Beaches ★   ★ Diving & Snorkelling

Stone Town ★

- TELEPHONE CODE: ☎ 024
- POPULATION: 1,352,000

History

The archipelago's history stretches back at least to the start of the first millennium, when Bantu-speaking peoples from the mainland ventured across the Zanzibar and Pemba channels – perhaps in search of bigger fish and better beaches. The islands had probably been visited at an even earlier date by traders and sailors from Arabia. The *Periplus of the Erythraean Sea* (written for sailors by a Greek merchant around AD 60) documents small Arabic trading settlements along the coast that were already well established by the 1st century, and makes reference to the island of Menouthias, which many historians believe to be Zanzibar. From around the 8th century, Shirazi traders from Persia also began to make their way to East Africa, where they established settlements on Pemba, and probably also at Zanzibar's Unguja Ukuu.

Between the 12th and 15th centuries, the archipelago came into its own, as trade links with Arabia and the Persian Gulf blossomed. Zanzibar became a powerful city-state, supplying slaves, gold, ivory and wood to places as distant as India and Asia, while importing spices, glassware and textiles. With the trade from the East also came Islam and the Arabic architecture that still characterises the archipelago today. One of the most important archaeological remnants from this era is the mosque at Kizimkazi (p138), whose mihrab (prayer niche showing the direction to Mecca) dates from the early 12th century.

The arrival of the Portuguese in the early 16th century temporarily interrupted this golden age, as Zanzibar and then Pemba fell under Portuguese control. Yet Portuguese dominance did not last long. It was challenged first by the British, who found Zanzibar an amenable rest stop on the long journey to India, and then by Omani Arabs, who in the mid-16th century gave the Portuguese the routing that they no doubt deserved. By the early 19th century Oman had gained the upper hand on Zanzibar, and trade on the island again flourished, centred on slaves, ivory and cloves. Caravans set out for the interior of the mainland, and trade reached such a high point that in the 1840s the Sultan of Oman relocated his court here from the Persian Gulf.

From the mid-19th century, with increasing European interest in East Africa and

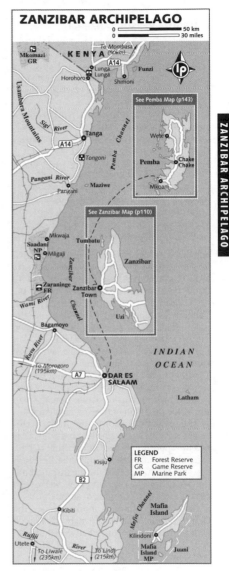

the end of the slave trade, Omani rule over Zanzibar began to weaken, and in 1862 the sultanate was formally partitioned. Zanzibar became independent of Oman, with Omani sultans ruling under a British protectorate. This arrangement lasted until 10 December 1963 when Zanzibar gained its independence. Just one month later, in January 1964, the

---

UNGUJA VERSUS ZANZIBAR

Unguja is the Swahili name for Zanzibar. It's often used locally to distinguish the island from the Zanzibar Archipelago (which also includes Pemba), as well as from Zanzibar Town. In this book, for ease of recognition, we've used Zanzibar.

The word 'Zanzibar' comes from the Arabic Zinj el-Barr or 'Land of the Blacks'. It was used by Arab traders from at least the 8th or 9th century until the arrival of the Portuguese to refer to both the archipelago and the adjacent coast (Zanguebar). Now the name refers just to the archipelago. Azania – the name given by the early Greeks for the East African coast – is perhaps a Hellenised version of the Arabic *zinj*.

---

sultans were overthrown in a bloody revolution instigated by the Afro-Shirazi Party (ASP), which then assumed power. On 12 April 1964 Abeid Karume, president of the ASP, signed a declaration of unity with Tanganyika (mainland Tanzania) and the union, fragile from the outset, became known as the United Republic of Tanzania.

Karume was assassinated in 1972 and Aboud Jumbe assumed the presidency of Zanzibar until he resigned in 1984. A succession of leaders followed, culminating in 2000 with the highly controversial election of Aman Abeid Karume, son of the first president.

Today the two major parties in the archipelago are the Chama Cha Mapinduzi (CCM) and the opposition Civic United Front (CUF), which has its stronghold on Pemba. Tensions between the two peaked during disputed national elections in 1995, and now, well over a decade later, still continue to simmer.

In 1999 negotiations moderated by the Commonwealth secretary general concluded with a brokered agreement between the CCM and CUF. However, the temporary hiatus this created was shattered by highly controversial elections in 2000, and ensuing violence on Pemba in January 2001. Since then renewed efforts at dialogue between the CCM and CUF have restored a fragile calm, and the 2005 elections – albeit somewhat tarnished by accusations of vote rigging – proceeded comparatively smoothly. However, little progress has been made at resolving the underlying issues.

Climate

Zanzibar's climate is shaped by the monsoon, with tropical, sultry conditions year-round, moderated somewhat by sea breezes. The main rains fall from March until May, when many hotels and eateries close. There's also a short rainy season from November into early December, and throughout the year showers can come at any time, especially on Pemba.

Dangers & Annoyances

While Zanzibar remains a relatively safe place, robberies, muggings and the like occur with some frequency, especially in Zanzibar Town and along the beaches.

Follow the normal precautions: avoid isolated areas, especially isolated stretches of beach, and keep your valuables out of view. If you go out at night in Zanzibar Town, take a taxi or walk in a group. Also avoid walking alone in Stone Town during predawn hours. As a rule, it's best to leave valuables in your hotel safe, preferably sealed or locked. Should your passport be stolen, get a written report from the police. Upon presentation of this report, Immigration will issue you a travel document that will get you back to the mainland.

If you've rented a bicycle or motorcycle, avoid isolated stretches of road, and don't stop if you're flagged down in isolated areas.

Given the ongoing history of political tensions on Zanzibar and Pemba, and the overall world political situation, it's a good idea to check for updates on your government's travel advisory site (see the boxed text, p336), especially if you plan on travelling to the archipelago in late 2010, when elections are scheduled.

ZANZIBAR

☎ 024 / pop 990,000

Zanzibar gets the lion's (sultan's?) share of attention on the archipelago, and with good reason. Its old Stone Town, where everyone arrives, is one of Africa's most evocative locations, with a mesmerising mix of influences from the Indian subcontinent, the Arabian peninsula, the African mainland and Europe. An easy drive away are the island's beaches, which are among the finest stretches of sand to be found anywhere. Zanzibar is small enough that you can base yourself either in Stone Town or at one of the beaches to do all your exploring, and tourist infrastructure is highly developed, with hotels and restaurants for every taste and budget.

Getting There & Around

There are daily flights linking Zanzibar and Pemba with Dar es Salaam, Tanga, Arusha and the northern safari circuit airstrips and Selous Game Reserve. Ferries link Zanzibar with Dar es Salaam daily, and with Pemba several times weekly. Once on Zanzibar, taxi and motorbike hire is quite affordable, and networks of cheap, slow and crowded *dalla-dallas* (minibuses) or faster and pricier private minibuses cover the island.

ZANZIBAR TOWN
Orientation

Zanzibar Town, on the western side of the island, is the heart of the archipelago, and the first stop for most travellers. The best-known section by far is the old Stone Town

(Mji Mkongwe), surrounded on three sides by the sea and bordered to the east by Creek Rd. Directly east of Stone Town is the bustling but much less atmospheric section of Ng'ambo, which you'll pass through en route to some of the beaches.

MAPS

Commission for Lands & Environment (Planning Office; Map p113) Sells dated topographical maps of Zanzibar Town and of the archipelago; it's behind the Shangani St tunnel.

MaCo Map The best, with a detailed, hand-drawn map of Stone Town on one side and Zanzibar on the other; it's widely available in Stone Town.

Information
BOOKSHOPS

Gallery Bookshop (Map p113; ☎ 024-223 2721, 0773-150180; 48 Gizenga St; ◷ 9am-6pm Mon-Sat, to 2pm Sun) An excellent selection of books and maps, including travel guides, Africa titles and historical reprint editions.

PAPASI

In Zanzibar Town you will undoubtedly come into contact with street touts. In Swahili they're known as *papasi* (ticks). They are not registered as guides with the Zanzibar Tourist Corporation (ZTC), although they may carry (false) identification cards, and while a few can be helpful, others can be aggressive and irritating. The main places that you'll encounter them are at the ferry dock in Zanzibar Town – where they can be quite overwhelming, especially if it's your first visit to the region – and in the Shangani area around Tembo House Hotel and the post office. Many of the more annoying ones are involved with Zanzibar's drug trade and are desperate for money for their next fix, which means you're just asking for trouble if you arrange anything with them.

If you do decide to use the services of a tout (and they're hard to avoid if you're arriving at the ferry dock for the first time and don't know your way around), tell them where you want to go or what you are looking for, and your price range. You shouldn't have to pay anything additional, as many hotels pay commission. If they tell you your hotel of choice no longer exists or is full, take it with a grain of salt, as it could well be that they just want to take you somewhere where they know they'll get a better commission.

Another strategy is to make your way out of the port arrivals area and head straight for a taxi. This will cost you more, and taxi drivers look for hotel commissions as well, but most are legitimate and once you are 'spoken for', hassles from touts usually diminish.

Most *papasi* are hoping that your stay on the island will mean ongoing work for them as your guide, so if you do use one to help you find a hotel, they'll invariably be outside waiting for you later. If you're not interested in this, explain (politely) once you've arrived at your hotel. If you want a guide to show you around Stone Town, it's better to arrange one with your hotel or a travel agency. For any dealings with the *papasi*, if you're being hassled, a polite but firm approach usually works best – yelling or showing irritation, although quite tempting at times, just makes things worse. Another thing to remember is that you have a better chance of getting a discount on your hotel room if you arrive alone, since the hotel can then give you the discount that would have been paid to the touts as commission.

When arranging tours and excursions, never make payments on the street – be sure you're paying at a legitimate office and get a receipt.

ZANZIBAR ARCHIPELAGO

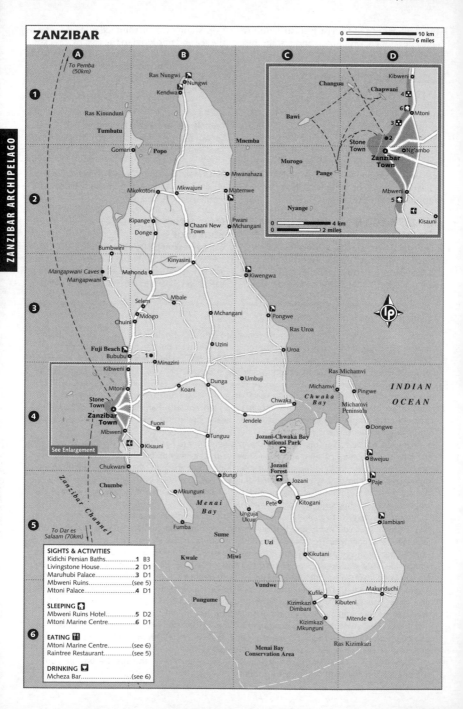

ZANZIBAR

SIGHTS & ACTIVITIES
Kidichi Persian Baths..............**1** B3
Livingstone House..................**2** D1
Maruhubi Palace....................**3** D1
Mbweni Ruins.......................(see 5)
Mtoni Palace........................**4** D1

SLEEPING
Mbweni Ruins Hotel................**5** D2
Mtoni Marine Centre...............**6** D1

EATING
Mtoni Marine Centre...............(see 6)
Raintree Restaurant................(see 5)

DRINKING
Mcheza Bar.........................(see 6)

Zanzibar Gallery (Map p113; ☎ 024-223 2721; gallery@swahilicoast.com; cnr Kenyatta Rd & Gizenga St; ⏰ 9am-6.30pm Mon-Sat, to 1pm Sun) Books are also sold just down the road at this gallery (see p126).

CONSULATES
Mozambique (Map p113; ☎ 024-223 0049; Mapinduzi Rd)
Oman (Map p113; ☎ 024-223 0066/0700; Vuga Rd)

INTERNET ACCESS
Azzurri Internet Café (Map p113; New Mkunazini Rd; per hr Tsh500; ⏰ 8.30am-10.30pm) Around the corner from the Anglican cathedral.
Macrosoft Internet Café (Map p113; Hurumzi St; per hr Tsh500; ⏰ 9am-11pm)
Shangani Internet Café (Map p113; Kenyatta Rd; per hr Tsh2000; ⏰ 9am-10pm)
Shangani Post Office Internet Café (Map p113; Kenyatta Rd; per hr Tsh1000; ⏰ 8am-9pm Mon-Fri, 8.30am-7pm Sat & Sun)
Too Short Internet Café (Map p113; Shangani St; per hr Tsh1000; ⏰ 8.30am-11pm) Diagonally opposite NBC.

MEDICAL SERVICES
Anything serious should be treated in Dar es Salaam or Nairobi (Kenya).
Shamshuddin's Pharmacy (Map p113; ☎ 024-223 1262, 024-223 3814; Market St; ⏰ 9am-8.30pm Mon-Thu & Sat, 9am-noon & 3-8.30pm Fri, 9am-1.30pm Sun) Just behind (west of) the Darajani market.

MONEY
Despite its initial appearance as a backpacker's paradise, Zanzibar is not the place to go looking for rock-bottom prices. While it doesn't need to be expensive, prices are higher than on the mainland and you'll need to make an effort to keep to a tight budget. Plan on spending at least US$10 to US$15 per night for accommodation, and from Tsh7000

ZANZIBAR ETIQUETTE

Zanzibar is a conservative, Muslim society, and many locals take offence at scantily clad Westerners. Women should avoid sleeveless tops and plunging necklines, and stick with pants, skirts or at least knee-length shorts. For men, keep your shirt on when wandering around town, preferably also wearing pants or knee-length shorts. During Ramadan take particular care with dress, and show respect by not eating or drinking in the street or other public places during daylight hours.

---

per day for food (unless you stick to street food only), plus extra for transport, excursions and diving or snorkelling. During the low season, for longer stays or if you're in a group, you'll often be able to negotiate discounts, although even at the cheapest places it won't go much below US$8/16 per night per single/double. Many midrange and top-end hotels charge high-season supplements during August and the Christmas/New Year holiday period.

Prices are higher away from Stone Town, and at the budget beach hotels it can be difficult to find a meal for less than Tsh4000. If you're on a tight budget, consider stocking up on food and drink in Stone Town. Many hotels and restaurants close from March to May.

There are many forex bureaus – most open until about 8pm Monday to Saturday and often also on Sunday – where you can change cash and travellers cheques with a minimum of hassle. Rates vary, so it pays to shop around; rates in Stone Town are better than elsewhere on the island, but slightly lower than those on the mainland, and rates for US dollars are generally better than those for British pounds, euros and other hard currencies. Officially, accommodation on Zanzibar must be paid for in US dollars, and prices are quoted in dollars, but especially at the budget places it's rarely a problem to pay the equivalent in Tanzanian shillings.

Maka T-Shirt Shop (Map p113; Kenyatta Rd) Changes travellers cheques and cash.
NBC (Map p113; Shangani St) Changes cash and travellers cheques and has an ATM (Visa only). There's also an NBC ATM on Creek Rd, near the market, and just down from the Tourist Information Office.
Queens Bureau de Change (Map p113; Kenyatta Rd) Changes cash and travellers cheques.
Speed Cash/TanPay (Map p113; Kenyatta Rd) Has an ATM (accepts Visa, MasterCard, Cirrus, Maestro). Diagonally opposite Mazsons Hotel.

POST
Shangani post office (Map p113; Kenyatta Rd; ⏰ 8am-4.30pm Mon-Fri, to 12.30pm Sat) Has poste restante.

PUBLICATIONS
Recommended in Zanzibar Free quarterly magazine with listings of cultural events, transport schedules, tide tables etc.
Swahili Coast (www.swahilicoast.com) Hotel and restaurant listings, cultural articles.

TELEPHONE

Robin's Collection (Map p113; Kenyatta Rd; ☼ 9am-8pm Mon-Sat) International calls for about US$2 per minute; also good for flash drives and digital camera components.

Shangani post office (Map p113; Kenyatta Rd; ☼ 8am-9pm Mon-Fri, 8.30am-7pm Sat & Sun) Operator-assisted calls from Tsh1300 per minute, and card phones.

TOURIST INFORMATION

Tourist Information Office (Map p113; ☎ 0777-482356; Creek Rd; ☼ 8am-5pm) Just down from Darajani market, with tourist information, ferry bookings and all the standard tours at very reasonable prices.

TRAVEL AGENCIES & TOUR OPERATORS

All the following can help with island excursions, and plane and ferry tickets. Only make bookings and payments inside the offices, and not with anyone outside claiming to be staff. For specific trips, see Tours (p117).

Eco + Culture Tours (Map p113; ☎ 024-223 0366; www.ecoculture-zanzibar.org; Hurumzi St) Opposite 236 Hurumzi hotel; culturally friendly tours and excursions, including to Nungwi and Unguja Ukuu, Jambiani village and Stone Town, plus spice tours, all with a focus on environmental and cultural conservation.

Gallery Tours & Safaris (☎ 024-223 2088; www .gallerytours.net) Top-of-the line tours and excursions throughout the archipelago; it also can help arrange Zanzibar weddings and honeymoon itineraries. It also has an office in Mbweni.

Madeira Tours & Safaris (Map p113; ☎ 024-223 0406; madeira@zanlink.com) All price ranges.

Sama Tours (Map p113; ☎ 024-223 3543; www.sama tours.com; Hurumzi St) Reliable and reasonably priced.

Tabasam (Map p113; ☎ 024-223 0322; www.tabasam zanzibar.com; Kenyatta Rd) Opposite Stone Town Café; midrange and upper-end tours.

Tima Tours (Map p113; ☎ 024-223 1298; www.tima tours.com; Mizingani Rd)

Tropical Tours (Map p113; ☎ 024-223 3695, 0777-413454; http://tropicaltours.villa69.org; Kenyatta Rd) Budget tours.

Zan Tours (Map p113; ☎ 024-223 3042, 024-223 3116; www.zantours.com; Malawi Rd) Offers a wide range of quality upmarket tours on Zanzibar and Pemba and beyond.

Sights

If Zanzibar Town is the archipelago's heart, Stone Town is its soul, with a magical jumble of alleyways where it's easy to spend days wandering around and getting lost – although you can't get lost for long because, sooner or later, you'll end up on either the seafront or Creek Rd. Nevertheless, each twist and turn of the narrow streets brings something new – be it a school full of children chanting verses from the Quran, a beautiful old mansion with overhanging verandas, a coffee vendor with his long-spouted pot fastened over coals, clacking cups to attract custom, or a group of women in *bui-bui* sharing a joke and some local gossip. Along the way, watch the island's rich cultural melange come to life: Arabic-style houses with their recessed inner courtyards rub shoulders with Indian-influenced buildings boasting ornate balconies and latticework, and bustling oriental bazaars alternate with streetside vending stalls.

While the best part of Stone Town is simply letting it unfold before you, it's worth putting in an effort to see and experience some of its major features.

BEIT EL-AJAIB (HOUSE OF WONDERS)

One of the most prominent buildings in the old Stone Town is the elegant Beit el-Ajaib, now home to the **Zanzibar National Museum of History & Culture** (Map p113; Mizingani Rd; adult/child US$3/1; ☼ 9am-6pm). It's also one of the largest structures in Zanzibar. It was built in 1883 by Sultan Barghash (r 1870–88) as a ceremonial palace. In 1896 it was the target of a British naval bombardment, the object of which was to force Khalid bin Barghash, who had tried to seize the throne after the death of Sultan Hamad (r 1893–96), to abdicate in favour of a British nominee. After it was rebuilt, Sultan Hamoud (r 1902–11) used the upper floor as a residential palace until his death. Later it became the local political headquarters of the CCM. Its enormous doors are said to be the largest carved doors in East Africa. Inside it houses exhibits on the dhow culture of the Indian Ocean (ground floor) and on Swahili civilisation and 19th-century Zanzibar (1st floor). Everything is informatively labelled in English and Swahili, and well worth visiting. Just inside the entrance is a life-size *mtepe* – a traditional Swahili sailing vessel made without nails, the planks held together with only coconut fibres and wooden pegs.

BEIT EL-SAHEL (PALACE MUSEUM)

Just north of the Beit el-Ajaib is this palace, **Beit el-Sahel** (Map p113; Mizingani Rd; adult/child US$3/1; ☼ 9am-6pm), which served as the sultan's residence until 1964, when the dynasty was overthrown. Now it is a museum devoted to the era of the Zanzibar sultanate.

The ground floor displays details of the formative period of the sultanate from 1828

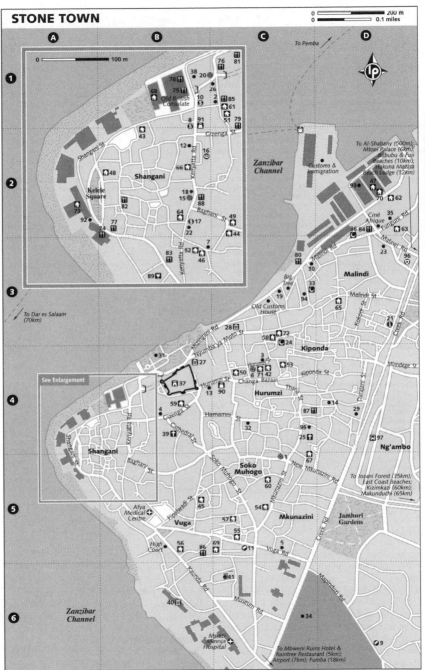

STONE TOWN

ZANZIBAR ARCHIPELAGO

to 1870, during which commercial treaties were signed between Zanzibar and the USA (1833), Britain (1839), France (1844) and the Hanseatic Republics (1859). There is also memorabilia of Princess Salme, a Zanzibari princess who eloped with a German to Europe and later wrote an autobiography. The exhibits on the 2nd floor focus on the period of affluence from 1870 to 1896, during which modern amenities such as piped water and electricity were introduced to Zanzibar under Sultan Barghash. The 3rd floor consists of the modest living quarters of the last sultan, Khalifa bin Haroub (1911-60), and his two wives, each of whom clearly had very different tastes in furniture. Outside is the Makusurani graveyard, where some of the sultans are buried.

OLD FORT
Just south of the Beit el-Ajaib is the Old Fort (Map p113), a massive, bastioned structure originally built around 1700 on the site of a Portuguese chapel by Omani Arabs as a defence against the Portuguese. In recent years it has been partially renovated to house the **Zanzibar Cultural Centre** (Map p113), as well as the offices of the Zanzibar International Film Festival (ZIFF). Inside is an open-air theatre

that hosts music and dance performances. There's also a small information centre that has schedules for performances, and a good restaurant. The tree growing inside the fort, in the area in front of the café, is known in Swahili as *mwarobaini* (the tree of 40) because its leaves, bark and other parts are used to cure up to 40 different ailments.

ANGLICAN CATHEDRAL & OLD SLAVE MARKET

Constructed in the 1870s by the Universities' Mission to Central Africa (UMCA), the **Anglican cathedral** (Map p113; admission Tsh3500; 8am-6pm Mon-Sat, noon-6pm Sun) was the first Anglican cathedral in East Africa (see the boxed text, p130). It was built on the site of the old slave market alongside Creek Rd. Although nothing remains of the slave market today, other than some holding cells under St Monica's Hostel next door, the site remains a sobering reminder of the not-so-distant past. Services are still held at the cathedral on Sunday mornings; the entrance is next to St Monica's Hostel.

ST JOSEPH'S CATHEDRAL

One of the first sights travellers see when arriving at Zanzibar by ferry is the spires of the Roman Catholic **St Joseph's cathedral** (Map p113; Cathedral St). Yet the church is deceptively difficult to find in the narrow confines of the adjacent streets. (The easiest route is to follow Kenyatta Rd to Gizenga St, then take the first right to the back gate of the church, which is usually open, even when the front entrance is closed.) The cathedral, which was designed by French architect Beranger and built by French missionaries, celebrated its centenary in 1998. There's a brief summary of the mission's history just inside the entrance. The church is still in use, with several services on Sunday.

MOSQUES

The oldest of Stone Town's many mosques is the **Msikiti wa Balnara** (Malindi Minaret Mosque; Map p113), originally built in 1831, enlarged in 1841 and extended again by Seyyid Ali bin Said in 1890. Others include the **Aga Khan Mosque** (Map p113) and the impressive **Ijumaa Mosque** (Map p113). It's not permitted to enter many of the mosques, as they're all in use, although exceptions may be made if you're appropriately dressed.

HAMAMNI PERSIAN BATHS

Built by Sultan Barghash in the late 19th century, these were the first public **baths** (Map p113; Hamamni St; admission Tsh500) on Zanzibar. Although they're no longer functioning and there's no water inside, they're still worth a visit, and it doesn't take much imagination to envision them in bygone days. To get in, you'll need to ask the caretaker across the alley to unlock the gate.

STONE TOWN'S ARCHITECTURE

Stone Town's architecture is a fusion of Arabic, Indian, European and African influences. Arabic buildings are often square, with two or three storeys. Rooms line the outer walls, allowing space for an inner courtyard and verandas, and cooling air circulation. Indian buildings, also several storeys high, generally include a shop on the ground floor and living quarters above, with ornate façades and balconies. A common feature is the *baraza*, a stone bench facing onto the street that serves as a focal point around which townspeople meet and chat.

The most famous feature of Zanzibari architecture is the carved wooden door. There are more than 500 remaining today in Stone Town, many of which are older than the houses in which they are set. The door, which was often the first part of a house to be built, served as a symbol of the wealth and status of a household. While older (Arabic) doors have a square frame with a geometrical shape, 'newer' doors – many of which were built towards the end of the 19th century and incorporate Indian influences – often have semicircular tops and intricate floral decorations.

Many doors are decorated with carvings of passages from the Quran. Other commonly seen motifs include images representing items desired in the household, such as a fish (expressing the hope for many children), chains (displaying the owner's wish for security) or the date tree (a symbol of prosperity). The lotus motif signifies regeneration and reproductive power, while the stylised backwards 'S' represents the smoke of frankincense and signifies wealth. Some doors have large brass spikes, which are a tradition from India, where spikes protected doors from being battered down by elephants.

THINGS TO DO IN STONE TOWN

- Enjoy a cup of coffee (p125)
- Stop by Dhow Countries Music Academy and arrange drumming lessons (right)
- Watch the sunset from Forodhani Gardens (opposite)
- Take a walk through Darajani market in the morning, when everything is still fresh (opposite)
- Visit the old slave market (p115)
- Buy a *kanga* (cotton wraps worn by women all over Tanzania) or *kikoi* (the thicker striped or plaid equivalent worn by men on Zanzibar and in other coastal areas) and dress like a local (p126)
- Watch a weekend afternoon football game at Mnazi Mmoja Sporting Grounds (opposite)
- Go diving or snorkelling (opposite)

BEIT EL-AMANI (PEACE MEMORIAL MUSEUM)

The larger of the two buildings that make up this **museum** (cnr Kaunda & Creek Rds) previously contained a poorly presented history of the island from its early days until independence, while the smaller building across the road housed a decaying natural history collection. Both are in the process of being rehabilitated and merged with the Zanzibar National Museum of History & Culture at the Beit el-Ajaib (p112), and are currently closed.

LIVINGSTONE HOUSE

Located about 2km north of town along the Bububu road, Livingstone House (Map p110) was built around 1860 and used as a base by many of the European missionaries and explorers before they started their journeys to the mainland. Today it's mostly remembered as the place where David Livingstone stayed before setting off on his last expedition. Now it houses the office of the Zanzibar Tourist Corporation. You can walk from town, or take a 'B' *dalla-dalla*.

OLD DISPENSARY

Near the port you'll find the **Old Dispensary** (Map p113; Mizingani Rd), built at the turn of the 20th century by a wealthy Indian merchant. It has been impressively renovated by the Aga Khan Charitable Trust, and now houses boutiques and shops, and small displays of local artists' work. Upstairs are the offices of the **Dhow Countries Music Academy** (Map p113; ☎ 024-223 4050; www.zanzibarmusic.org; Mizingani Rd), where you can organise dance and drumming lessons, and buy CDs of local and regional music.

VICTORIA HALL & GARDENS

Diagonally opposite Mnazi Mmoja hospital is the imposing **Victoria Hall** (Map p113; Kaunda Rd), which housed the legislative council during the British era. The hall is not open to the public, but you can walk in the small surrounding gardens. Opposite is the **State House** (Map p113), also closed to the public.

RUINS

There are a number of historical sites around Zanzibar Town. All can be easily reached as short excursions from town, and many are included in spice tours (opposite).

Mbweni (Map p110), located around 5km south of Zanzibar Town, was the site of a 19th-century UMCA mission station that was used as a settlement for freed slaves. In addition to the small and still functioning St John's Anglican church, dating to the 1880s, you can see the atmospheric ruins of the UMCA's St Mary's School for Girls, set amid lush gardens on the grounds of the Mbweni Ruins Hotel (p123).

The once-imposing **Maruhubi Palace** (Map p110), around 4km north of Zanzibar Town, was built by Sultan Barghash in 1882 to house his large harem. In 1899 it was almost totally destroyed by fire, although the remaining ruins – primarily columns that once supported an upper terrace, an overhead aqueduct and small reservoirs covered with water lilies – hint at its previous scale. The ruins are just west of the Bububu road and signposted.

The ruins of **Mtoni Palace** (Map p110), built by Sultan Seyyid Said as his residence in the early 19th century, are located just northeast of Maruhubi Palace. In its heyday, the palace was a beautiful building with a balconied exterior, a large garden courtyard complete with peacocks and gazelles, an observation turret and a mosque. By the mid-1880s the palace had been abandoned, and during WWI parts of the compound were used as a supplies storehouse. Today nothing remains of Mtoni's grandeur other than a few walls, although you can get an idea of how it must have looked once by reading Emily Said-Reute's *Memoirs of an Arabian Princess*. To get here, continue north on the main road past the Maruhubi Palace turn-off for about 2km, from where the ruins are signposted to the west.

The **Kidichi Persian Baths** (Map p110), northeast of Zanzibar Town, are another construction of Sultan Seyyid, built in 1850 for his Persian wife at the island's highest point. Like the other nearby ruins, they're rather unremarkable now, but with a bit of imagination, you can see the sultan's lavishly garbed coterie disrobing to test the waters. The décor, with its stylised birds and flowers, is typically Persian, though it's now in poor condition. To get here, take *dalla-dalla* 502 to the main Bububu junction, from where it's about a 3km walk east down an unsealed road. Look for the bathhouse to your right.

Activities

FORODHANI GARDENS

One of the best ways to ease into life on the island is to stop by **Forodhani Gardens** (Jamituri Gardens; Map p113) in the evening, when the grassy plaza comes alive with dozens of vendors serving up such delicacies as grilled *pweza* (octopus), plates of goat meat, Zanzibari pizza (rolled-up, omelette-filled chapati), a thick, delicious local version of naan, plus piles of chips, samosas and much more. The gardens are also a meeting point, with women sitting on the grass chatting about the events of the day, children playing and men strolling along the waterfront. It's all lit up, first by the setting sun and then by small lanterns, and the ambience is superb. The gardens are along the sea opposite the Old Fort.

SHOPPING AT DARAJANI MARKET

The dark, narrow passageways of the chaotic Darajani market (Map p113) assault the senses, with occasional whiffs of spices mixing with the stench of fish, the clamour of vendors hawking their wares, neat, brightly coloured piles of fruits and vegetables, and dozens of small shops selling everything from plastic tubs to auto spares. It's just off Creek Rd, and at its best in the morning before the heat and the crowds, when everything is still fresh.

WATCHING A LOCAL FOOTBALL GAME

Zanzibaris are passionate football fans, and watching a game is a good introduction to island life. Stroll by Mnazi Mmoja Sporting Grounds any weekend afternoon, and you're likely to catch a match. For early risers, there are also usually informal pick-up games most mornings at daybreak in the fields lining Kaunda Rd, diagonally opposite the Mnazi Mmoja grounds.

DIVING & SNORKELLING

For more on diving around the archipelago, see the boxed text, p118. Recommended dive operators:

Bahari Divers (Map p113; ☎ 0777-415011, 0784-254786; www.zanzibar-diving.com; Shangani St) This small, friendly and professional outfit primarily organises dives around the islands offshore from Stone Town. It offers a range of PADI certification courses, and caters to families (including rental of children's masks and fins). It can also help organise dives around Pemba, and is planning to open a branch at Nungwi.

One Ocean/The Zanzibar Dive Centre (Map p113; ☎ 024-223 8374, 0748-750161; www.zanzibaro neocean.com; just off Shangani St) This highly regarded PADI five-star centre has more than a decade of experience on Zanzibar. In addition to its main office in Stone Town – just down from the tunnel and NBC – it has branches at Matemwe Beach Village (Matemwe) and at various other locations along the east and southwestern coasts, and can organise dives all around the island, for divers of all levels. It also rents underwater cameras, prescription masks and Suunto computers.

Tours

SPICE TOURS

While spices no longer dominate Zanzibar's economy as they once did, plantations still dot the centre of the island. It's possible to visit them on 'spice tours', learning about what cloves, vanilla and other spices look like in the wild. These half-day excursions from Zanzibar Town take in some plantations, as well as some of the ruins described earlier and other sights of historical interest. Along the way you'll be invited to taste many of the spices, herbs and fruits that the island produces, including cloves, black pepper, cardamom, cinnamon, nutmeg, breadfruit, jackfruit, vanilla and lemongrass.

Organise tours through your hotel, a travel agent, the Tourist Information Office (p112) or through the long-standing **Mr Mitu's office** (Map p113; ☎ 024-223 4636; mitusspicetour@hotmail.com;

DIVING THE ZANZIBAR ARCHIPELAGO

The archipelago's turquoise waters are just as amazing below the surface as they are from above, with a magnificent array of hard and soft corals and a diverse collection of sea creatures, including shadowy manta rays, hawksbill and green turtles, barracudas and sharks. Other draws include the possibility for wall dives, especially off Pemba; the fascinating cultural backdrop; and the opportunity to combine wildlife safaris with underwater exploration. On the down side, visibility isn't as reliable as in some other areas of the world, although sometimes you'll be treated to ranges of 25m to 30m. Another thing to consider, if you're a serious diver and coming to the archipelago exclusively for diving, is that unless you do a live-aboard arrangement, you'll need to travel – often for up to an hour – to many of the dive sites. Also, prices are considerably higher than in places such as the Red Sea or Thailand.

Seasons

Diving is possible year-round, although conditions vary dramatically. Late March until mid-June is generally the least favourable time because of erratic weather patterns and frequent storms. However, even during this period you can have some good days, particularly in March when water temperatures are also warmer. July or August to February or March tends to be the best time overall, although again, conditions vary and wind is an important factor. On Pemba, for example, the southeastern seas can be rough around June and July when the wind is blowing from the south, but calm and clear as glass from around November to late February when the monsoon winds blow from the north. On both islands, the calmest time is generally from around September to November during the lull between the annual monsoons.

Water temperatures range from lows of about 22°C in July and August to highs of about 29°C in February and March, with the average about 26°C. Throughout, 3mm wetsuits are standard; 4mm suits are recommended for some areas during the July to September winter months, and 2mm are fine from around December to March or April.

Costs, Courses & Planning

Costs are fairly uniform throughout the archipelago, though somewhat cheaper on Zanzibar than on Pemba. Expect to pay from US$350 for a four-day PADI open water course, from about US$45/75 for a single-/double-dive package, and from about US$50 for a night dive. Most places discount about 10% if you have your own equipment, and for groups. In addition to open water certification, many operators also offer other courses, including Advanced Open Water, Medic First Aid, Rescue Diver and speciality courses, including underwater photography and navigation.

As for deciding where to dive: very generally speaking, Zanzibar is known for the corals and shipwrecks offshore from Stone Town, and for fairly reliable visibility, high fish diversity and the

off Malawi Rd), although the tours are no longer led by Mr Mitu, and don't differ significantly from those organised elsewhere, other than perhaps being more crowded. The office is signposted near Ciné Afrique. Costs for all tours are about US$10 per person in a group of about 15, and include a lunch of local food seasoned with some of the spices you've just seen. They depart about 9.30am and return by about 2.30pm (later, if a stop at Mangapwani beach is included). It's best to book a day in advance (you will be collected from your hotel), though it's usually no trouble to just show up in the morning. If you want your own spice tour – ie not join up with groups from other hotels – you'll need to make this clear when booking, and will probably have to pay US$5 to US$15 more per person, depending on how many are in your group.

COLOBUS MONKEY TOURS

The Zanzibar or Kirk's red colobus is unique to Zanzibar, and is the focal point of excursions to Jozani Forest. All of the listings under Travel Agencies & Tour Operators (p112) can organise excursions. For more details, see Jozani Forest (p139).

DHOW & ISLAND TOURS

All the listings under Travel Agencies & Tour Operators (p112), plus the Tourist Information Office (p112), can arrange exchance to see pelagics to the north and northeast. While some sites are challenging, there are many easily accessed sites for beginning and midrange divers.

Unlike Zanzibar, which is a continental island, Pemba is an oceanic island located in a deep channel with a steeply dropping shelf. Because of this, diving tends to be more challenging, with an emphasis on wall and drift dives, though there are some sheltered areas for beginners, especially around Misali island. Most dives are to the west around Misali, and to the north around the Njao Gap.

Wherever you dive, allow a sufficient surface interval between the conclusion of your final dive and any onward/homeward flights. According to PADI recommendations, this should be at least 12 hours, or more than 12 hours if you have been doing daily multiple dives for several days. Another consideration is insurance, which you should arrange before coming to Tanzania. Many policies exclude diving, so you'll probably need to pay a bit extra, but it's well worth it in comparison to the bills you will need to foot should something go wrong.

Most of the archipelago's dive operators also offer snorkelling. Equipment rental costs US$5 to US$15; when you're selecting it pay particular attention to getting a good mask. Most snorkelling sites are only accessible by boat. Trips average US$20 to US$50 per half-day, often including a snack or lunch.

Dive Operators

When looking to choose a dive operator, quality rather than cost should be the priority. Consider: the operator's experience and qualifications; knowledgeability and competence of staff; and the condition of equipment and frequency of maintenance. Assess whether the overall attitude of the organisation is serious and professional, and ask about safety precautions that are in place – radios, oxygen, emergency evacuation procedures, boat reliability and back-up engines, first aid kits, safety flares and life jackets. On longer dives, do you get an energising meal, or just tea and biscuits? An advantage of operators offering PADI courses is that you'll have the flexibility to go elsewhere in the world and have what you've already done recognised at other PADI dive centres.

There's now a decompression chamber in Matemwe (otherwise the closest ones are in Mombasa, Kenya – an army facility and not necessarily available to the general public – and in Johannesburg, South Africa), and you can check the **Divers Alert Network Southern Africa** (DAN; www.dansa.org) website for a list of Zanzibar and Pemba-based operators that are part of the DAN network. If you choose to dive with an operator that isn't affiliated with DAN, it's highly recommended to take out insurance coverage with DAN.

Dive operators are listed by location elsewhere in this chapter.

cursions to the offshore islands near Stone Town. Sunset dhow cruises can be arranged by the tour operator listings and by many hotels, especially in the midrange and top-end categories. For something different, contact **Safari Blue** (☎ 0777-423162; www.safariblue.net), which organises day excursions on well-equipped dhows around Menai Bay (p140). The excursions, which leave from Fumba, include a seafood and fruit lunch, plus snorkelling equipment and time to relax on a sandbank. The dhows can also be privately chartered, for honeymoons or groups. Before booking, it's worth checking weather conditions, as some months, notably April/May and July/August, can get quite windy or rainy.

FREDDIE MERCURY TOURS

One of Zanzibar's most famous sons is Queen lead vocalist Freddie Mercury, born Faroukh Bulsara in 1946 in Stone Town to Parsee parents. He lived on the island until he was about eight years old, when he was sent off to India to boarding school. His family left Zanzibar in the wake of the 1964 revolution, never to return. There's no agreement as to which house or houses Freddie – he acquired the name while at school in India – and his family actually occupied, and several make the claim. For anyone wanting to make a Mercury pilgrimage, two good places to start are the **Zanzibar Gallery** (Map p113; ☎ 024-223 2721; gallery@swahilicoast.com; cnr Kenyatta Rd & Gizenga St;

🕘 9am-6.30pm Mon-Sat, to 1pm Sun), with a gold plaque on the outside memorialising Mercury, and the popular Mercury's restaurant (p124), which doesn't claim that he lived there, but capitalises on his name. Freddie Mercury died on 24 November 1991 in London of complications from AIDS.

Festivals & Events

Muslim holidays are celebrated in a big way on Zanzibar. **Eid al-Fitr** (p339) especially is a fascinating time to be in Stone Town, with countless lanterns lighting the narrow passageways, families dressed in their best and a generally festive atmosphere. Note that many restaurants close down completely during Ramadan.

Some festivals unique to Zanzibar (see p338 for more details):

Sauti za Busara (Voices of Wisdom; ☎ 024-223 2423; www.busaramusic.com) A celebration of all things Swahili, which got its start at Forodhani Gardens; well worth timing your visit to catch it in February.

Festival of the Dhow Countries and Zanzibar International Film Festival (www.ziff.or.tz) Film screenings, performing arts groups from around the region, village events and a wonderful, festive atmosphere; check the website or with the Zanzibar Cultural Centre at the Old Fort for details. Yearly in July.

Mwaka Kogwa The Shirazi New Year, in July, is at its best in Makunduchi (p138).

Sleeping

BUDGET

Stone Town has a large selection of budget guesthouses, most costing about the same and with similar facilities – mosquito nets and fans, and usually shared bathrooms and cold-water showers. The standard price is US$10 to US$15 per person (US$20 with bathroom), though it's usually easy to negotiate this down in the low season.

The following options are located in the lively Mkunazini area, on the eastern edge of town near the Anglican cathedral.

Flamingo Guest House (Map p113; ☎ 024-223 2850; flamingoguesthouse@hotmail.com; Mkunazini St; s/d US$12/24, without bathroom US$10/20) No frills but cheap and fine, with straightforward rooms – all with mosquito nets and fans – around a courtyard. There is also a common TV and a rooftop sitting/breakfast area.

Haven Guest House (Map p113; ☎ 024-223 5677/8; s/d US$13/25) This old favourite and very backpacker-friendly place has clean, basic

rooms, a travellers' bulletin board, free coffee and tea, and a small kitchenette for self-catering. It's just south of Mkunazini, between Soko Muhogo St and Vuga Rd.

Jambo Guest House (Map p113; ☎ 024-223 3779; jamboguest@hotmail.com; s/d/tr without bathroom US$20/30/45; 🖳) Just around the corner from Flamingo Guest House, and also popular with backpackers, Jambo has free tea and coffee, clean rooms, including some with air-con, decent breakfasts and an internet café opposite. Green Garden Restaurant, with cheap local meals, is just out the front.

St Monica's Hostel (Map p113; ☎ 024-223 0773; monicaszanzibar@hotmail.com; s/d US$28/32, s/d/tr without bathroom US$12/24/36) An old, rambling place next to the Anglican cathedral, with spacious rooms, including some with a small veranda. Breakfast is served next door at St Monica's Restaurant.

The following places are near the southern edge of Stone Town, around Vuga Rd.

Florida Guest House (Map p113; ☎ 0777-421421; floridaznz@yahoo.com; Vuga Rd; r per person US$20) This family-run guesthouse has small, clean rooms (check out a few as they're all different) – many with bathroom – and solicitous proprietors. It's next to Culture Musical Club, and there are discounts for stays of more than two days.

Annex of Coco de Mer Hotel (☎ 024-223 8466; coco demer_znz@yahoo.com; s/d without bathroom US$20/35) Formerly Vuga Guest House, and now under the same management as Coco de Mer Hotel (see p122), this place just off Vuga St has clean, bright, mostly spacious rooms, most of which have shared bathroom.

Garden Lodge (Map p113; ☎ 024-223 3298; garden lodge@zanlink.com; Kaunda Rd; s/d/tr US$30/40/60) Garden Lodge is an efficient, friendly, family-run place in a convenient, quiet location – diagonally opposite the High Court. Rooms are good value, especially the upstairs ones, which are clean, bright and spacious, and have hot water, mosquito nets and ceiling fans. There's a rooftop breakfast terrace.

Victoria House (Map p113; ☎ 024-223 2861; www.victoriahotel-zanzibar.com; s/d/tr US$40/50/70) This place has had a facelift in recent times, and now offers large, airy rooms and an agreeably green and quiet location just off Kaunda Rd. Upstairs is a rooftop breakfast area.

On the northern side of town is a clutch of good-value places. The area isn't as pleasant as Shangani or Mkunazini, especially in the evening, but it's convenient to the port, which is within a five-minute walk away from most of these listings.

Bandari Lodge (Map p113; ☎ 024-223 7969; banda rilodge@hotmail.com; s/d/tw/tr US$15/25/30/35) Good, clean rooms with high ceilings, mosquito nets and fan, plus a common kitchen and a fridge. Turn left as you exit the port – it's just two minutes' walk ahead on the right-hand side.

Malindi Guest House (Map p113; ☎ 024-223 0165; malindi@zanzinet.com; r per person with air-con US$20, without bathroom US$15; ⏂) This long-standing and consistently popular guesthouse has whitewashed walls, attractive, atmospheric and well-maintained rooms with mosquito nets and fan or air-con, as well as a small rooftop restaurant.

Warere Town House (Map p113; ☎ 024-223 3835; www.wareretownhouse.com; s/d/tr US$20/35/45) Warere has good-value rooms – some with small balconies and all with hot water – plus a rooftop terrace. It's just minutes' walk from the port (staff will meet you), and behind Bandari Lodge and Annex of Malindi Lodge.

Malindi Lodge (Map p113; ☎ 024-223 2350/9; sunset bungalows@hotmail.com; s/d US$20/40, r per person without bathroom & with fan US$15; ⏂) Clean, basic rooms – most with air-con – near Ciné Afrique and the port, and diagonally opposite Mr Mitu's spice tours office.

Annex of Malindi Lodge (Map p113; ☎ 024-223 6588; d US$35, s/d without bathroom US$15/25) Confusingly named, as it's currently under different management to Malindi Lodge, this place is just behind Bandari Lodge, with no-frills, somewhat rundown but decent rooms sharing cold-water bathrooms.

The following options are located in and around the Kiponda area, roughly between the Old Fort and Malindi.

Pyramid Hotel (Map p113; ☎ 024-223 3000; pyramidho tel@yahoo.com; s/d US$20/30, d without bathroom US$25) This long-standing place notable for its very steep staircase has a mix of rooms, most with private bathroom and hot water, and all with Zanzibari beds, mosquito nets and fan. Look at a few rooms as standards vary; a few have small balconies, and there's a rooftop terrace.

ZANZIBAR ARCHIPELAGO

RESPONSIBLE DIVING

- Never use anchors on the reef, and take care not to ground boats on coral.
- Avoid touching or standing on living marine organisms or dragging equipment across the reef. If you must hold on to the reef, only touch exposed rock or dead coral.
- Be conscious of your fins. Even without contact, the surge from fin strokes near the reef can damage delicate organisms. Take care not to kick up clouds of sand, which can smother organisms.
- Practise and maintain proper buoyancy control. Major damage can be done by divers descending too fast and colliding with the reef.
- Take care in underwater caves. Spend as little time within them as possible as your air bubbles may be caught within the roof and thereby leave organisms high and dry. Take turns to inspect the interior of a small cave.
- Resist the temptation to collect or buy corals or shells.
- Take home all your rubbish. Plastics in particular are a serious threat to marine life.
- Don't feed fish.
- Never ride on the backs of turtles.

Book your stay at lonelyplanet.com/hotels

ZANZIBAR ARCHIPELAGO

Hotel Kiponda (Map p113; ☎ 024-223 3052; hotel kiponda@email.com; Nyumba ya Moto St; s/d/tr US$25/45/60) This hotel is slightly pricier than others in this category, but rooms are spotless and very good value, the building is atmospheric and the location – tucked away in a small lane near the waterfront – is convenient. All rooms have private bathroom, except two that have a private bathroom outside. There's also a pleasant rooftop restaurant.

The following option is in the Shangani area, at the western tip of Stone Town, and convenient to restaurants and nightlife.

Karibu Inn (Map p113; ☎ 024-223 3058; karibuinnho tel@yahoo.com; dm US$15, s/d/tr US$30/40/60) Karibu has a convenient location in the heart of Shangani, within a five-minute walk of Forodhani Gardens, with dorm beds and quite decent rooms with private bathroom.

MIDRANGE
The following are all in the Shangani area.

Coco de Mer Hotel (Map p113; ☎ 024-223 0852; cocode mer_znz@yahoo.com; s/d/tr US$35/50/60) Conveniently located just off Kenyatta Rd, near the tunnel, and vaguely reminiscent of the Algarve, with white walls and tile work. Avoid the one closet-sized room on the 1st floor, and the downstairs room, many of which have only interior windows; otherwise rooms are pleasant and good value.

Abuso Inn (Map p113; ☎ 024-223 5886; inafaa@hotmail .com; Shangani St; s/d/tr US$50/65/75; 🖭) This family-run place has spotless, mostly quite spacious rooms with large windows, wooden floors and fan or air-con. Some rooms have glimpses of the water.

Shangani Hotel (Map p113; ☎ 024-223 3688, 024-223 6363; www.shanganihotel.com; Kenyatta Rd; s/d/tr US$55/75/85) An unpretentious place opposite Shangani post office, with cluttered but reasonably comfortable rooms, most with TV, fridge and fan, plus a restaurant.

Baghani House Hotel (Map p113; ☎ 024-223 5654; baghani@zanzinet.com; s US$55, d US$70-90, tr US$110) This small, atmospheric hotel is one of the best-value choices in this category, with rooms that are full of character – most on the upper level, reached via a steep staircase – dark wood and Zanzibari furnishings. Advance bookings and reconfirmations are recommended. It's just off Kenyatta Rd.

Mazsons Hotel (Map p113; ☎ 024-223 3694; www .mazsonshotel.net; Kenyatta Rd; s/d US$70/90; 🖭) The long-standing Mazsons has impressively

restored lobby woodwork and a convenient location, which go some way to compensating for its rooms – modern and quite comfortable, though rather pallid. There's also a restaurant.

Chavda Hotel (Map p113; ☎ 024-223 2115; www .chavdahotel.co.tz; Baghani St; s/d from US$80/100; 🖭) Chavda is a quiet, reliable hotel with some period décor and a range of bland, carpeted rooms with TV, telephone and minibar. The rooftop bar and restaurant are open during the high season only. It's just around the corner from Baghani House Hotel.

Outside the Shangani area are several more choices.

Clove Hotel (Map p113; ☎ 0777-484567; www.zanzi barhotel.nl; Hurumzi St; s/d/f from US$38/55/78) Renovated several years ago in shades of lavender and peach, Clove has rather spartan but reasonable-value rooms (check out a few) with mosquito nets and fans. The family rooms also have small balconies with views down onto the small square below. On the rooftop is a terrace for breakfast, drinks and views.

Zanzibar Coffee House Hotel (Map p113; ☎ 024-223 9319; www.riftvalley-zanzibar.com; s/d from US$75/95, without bathroom US$60/75, upstairs US$115/145, family ste US$145) This small, new, good-value boutique-style hotel above the eponymous coffee house in Hurumzi has just eight rooms, most spacious, some with bathroom and all decorated with Zanzibari beds and décor. You get a great rooftop breakfast (both the rooftop area and the breakfast). It's no frills, but in a comfortable, upmarket sort of way, and atmospheric, and gets good reviews.

TOP END
Dhow Palace (Map p113; ☎ 024-223 3012; dhowpalace@ zanlink.com; s/d US$70/90; 🖭 Jun-Mar; 🖭) This is a classic place with old Zanzibari décor, a fountain in the tastefully restored lobby and comfortable, well-appointed rooms. It's just off Kenyatta Rd, and under the same management as Tembo House Hotel.

Beyt al-Chai (Map p113; ☎ 0777-444111; www.stone towninn.com; Kelele Sq; s US$70-230, d US$100-260) This converted tea house is a lovely, atmospheric choice with just six rooms, each individually designed, and all with period décor. For a splurge, try one of the top-floor Sultan suites, with views to the sea in the distance and raised Jacuzzi-style baths. Downstairs is an excellent restaurant (meals from Tsh12,000; open lunch and dinner).

Ahlan Palace Hotel (Map p113; ☎ 024-223 1435; www
.ahlanpalace.com; s/d US$80/110; ☒) A new place,
down-to-earth and welcoming, with simply
furnished but clean and comfortable rooms
and a restaurant (no alcohol). It's diagonally
opposite Chavda Hotel.

Tembo House Hotel (Map p113; ☎ 024-223 3005;
tembo@zitec.org; s/d US$90/100; ☒ ⧠ ⧉) This at-
tractively restored building has a prime waterfront location, including a small patch of
beach (no swimming), efficient management
and comfortable, good-value rooms – some
with sea views – in new and old wings. Most
rooms have a TV and fridge, and there's a
small pool, a restaurant (no alcohol) and a
great buffet breakfast on the seaside terrace.

Zanzibar Palace Hotel (Map p113; ☎ 024-223 2230;
www.zanzibarpalacehotel.com; Kiponda; s US$95-110, d
US$95-225, ste US$285; ☒) A new place – actually
a renovation of an older hotel. Rooms all have
Zanzibari beds and period design, some have
separate sitting areas, some small balconies,
most have large raised or sunken-style bathtubs, and most have air-con. It's not to be
confused with the similarly named restaurant
and internet café around the corner. No credit
cards accepted.

236 Hurumzi (Map p113; ☎ 0777-423266; www
.236hurumzi.com; Hurumzi St; r US$165-200) Formerly
Emerson & Green, but now operating
under a new name and without Emerson,
this Zanzibar institution is in two adjacent
historic buildings that have been completely
restored along the lines of an *Arabian Nights*
fantasy and are full of character. Each room is
unique – one even has its own private rooftop
teahouse – and all are decadently decorated to
give you an idea of what Zanzibar must have
been like in its heyday. It's several winding
blocks east of the Old Fort.

Jafferji's House & Spa (Map p113; ☎ 024-223 2088;
www.gallerytours.net; Gizenga St; r about US$180-250) This
upmarket place, under the same management
as the Zanzibar Gallery and Gallery Tours &
Safaris, is scheduled to open by this book's
publication, with nine top-of-the-line rooms –
all named after famous Zanzibari figures, and
authentically furnished – and a spa.

Emerson Spice (Map p113; www.emersonspice.net;
Tharia St, Kiponda; r about US$200; ⧠) This five-star
hotel in a 200-year-old restored building in
the Kiponda area is the latest project of the
venerable Emerson, of Emerson's House and
Emerson & Green fame, and undoubtedly the
best. It's scheduled to open soon after this

book's publication, with just a dozen impeccably appointed rooms, a butler on each floor,
a pool running throughout the building and
then into a central courtyard, a full-service
health spa, hammam and Jacuzzi, a downstairs
bistro, a rooftop tapas bar – the food promises
to be an experience in itself – and throughout, Emerson's signature *Arabian Nights*
meets Zanzibar style. The project is being
done together with youth training groups
and women's cooperatives and is impressively
community integrated. Check out the excellent
website for an update on the project.

Zanzibar Serena Inn (Map p113; ☎ 024-223 2306,
024-223 3587; www.serenahotels.com; s/d from US$325/475;
☒ ⧠ ⧉) The Zanzibar Serena, in the refurbished Extelecoms House, is Zanzibar Town's
most upmarket accommodation option, with
a beautiful setting on the water, plush rooms
with all the amenities, and a business centre,
although we've had some complaints about
lackadaisical staff.

Just outside Stone Town are a few more
options that make agreeable bases if you want
proximity to the town as well as greenery and
relaxing surroundings. Also see the listings for
Hakuna Matata Beach Lodge and other places
around Bububu (p128).

Mtoni Marine Centre (Map p110; ☎ 024-225
0140; www.mtoni.com; club s/d US$70/90, palm court s/d
US$95/120; ☒ ⧠ ⧉) This long-standing family-
friendly establishment has been completely
refurbished, and now offers spacious and well-
appointed 'club rooms', and more luxurious
'palm court' sea-view rooms with private
balconies. There's a small beach, large, green
grounds and gardens, a popular waterside
bar and top-notch dining in the main restaurant. It's in large grounds overlooking
the water about 3km north of town along
the Bububu road. The hotel is affiliated with
Coastal Aviation (p127), and it has package
deals from Dar es Salaam.

Mbweni Ruins Hotel (Map p110; ☎ 024-223 5478;
www.mbweni.com; s/d US$105/180; ☒ ⧠ ⧉) Mbweni
is a quiet, genteel establishment set in lovely,
expansive and lushly vegetated gardens about
5km from town, and several kilometres off the
airport road. In addition to well-appointed
rooms and a relaxing ambience, it has the
very good Raintree Restaurant and the new
and relaxing Mangrove Bar, overlooking the
water and stands of mangroves and ideal for
bird-spotting. There's also a private jetty, from
which dhow transfers to and from Stone Town

ZANZIBAR ARCHIPELAGO

or elsewhere can be arranged. The property was formerly the site of the UMCA mission school for the children of freed slaves.

Eating

Stone Town has a wide selection of eateries, enough to keep even the most avid gastronomes happily occupied for days. Note that during the low season and Ramadan, many restaurants close or operate reduced hours.

RESTAURANTS

Amore Mio (Map p113; Shangani St; ice cream from Tsh2000, light meals from Tsh4000; ☺ high season) Across the road from La Fenice, Amore Mio has delectable ice cream, as well as pasta dishes and other light meals, good coffees and cappuccinos, and fantastic, quiet views of the water.

Archipelago Café-Restaurant (Map p113; ☎ 024-223 5668; mains Tsh5000-11,000; ☺ lunch & dinner) This popular place has an excellent, breezy location on a 1st-floor terrace overlooking the water just opposite NBC in Shangani, and a menu featuring such delicacies as vegetable coconut curry, orange and ginger snapper, and chicken pilau, topped off by an array of homemade cakes and sweets. There's no bar, but you can bring your own alcohol.

Old Fort Restaurant (Map p113; ☎ 0777-416736; Old Fort; meals from Tsh5500; ☺ 11am-late) The chefs from the former Sweet Eazy on the waterfront have now moved to the Old Fort, and serve up a well-prepared menu featuring grilled seafood and meat, salads, pasta dishes and more. For info on the accompanying traditional dance and drum performances, see p126.

Luis Yoghurt Parlour (Map p113; Gizenga St; meals from Tsh6000; ☺ 10.30am-2pm & 6-8pm Mon-Sat) This old favourite has reopened after a long hiatus, and is once again serving delicious and spicy home-cooked Goan cuisine, plus lassis, yogurt and milkshakes.

Mcheza Bar (Map p110; meals from Tsh6000; ☺ lunch & dinner) Next door to Mtoni Marine Centre is this recently completely refurbished beachside sports bar, with a mix of booth and table seating, two big screens, plus burgers and pub food, seafood, South African steaks and a pizza oven. A sushi bar is set to open soon on the adjoining beach. There's live music on Saturday evenings in season.

Kidude (Map p113; ☎ 0777-423266; 236 Hurumzi, Hurumzi St; meals Tsh6000-25,000; ☺ lunch & dinner; ☒) Downstairs at 236 Hurumzi, Kidude has a dark-wood interior with period décor, sky-

high ceilings, a lunch menu featuring well-prepared sandwiches, salads and cakes, an evening set menu similar to that upstairs at Tower Top Restaurant (also located at this hotel), a bar, and tea or coffee and delicious cakes throughout the day.

Monsoon Restaurant (Map p113; ☎ 0777-410410; meals from Tsh6500; ☺ lunch & dinner) The impeccably decorated and atmospheric Monsoon has traditional-style dining on floor cushions, and well-prepared Swahili and Western cuisine served to a backdrop of live *taarab* (Zanzibari music combining African, Arabic and Indian influences) on Wednesday and Saturday evenings. It's at the southwestern edge of Forodhani Gardens.

Radha Food House (Map p113; ☎ 024-223 4808; thalis Tsh7000) This great little place is tucked away on the small side street just before the Shangani tunnel. The menu – strictly vegetarian – features thalis, lassis, homemade yogurt and other dishes from the subcontinent.

Livingstone Beach Restaurant (Map p113; ☎ 0773-164939; meals from Tsh7000; ☺ lunch & dinner) This justifiably popular place in the old British Consulate building has seating directly on the beach – lovely in the evening, with candlelight – and a good array of well-prepared seafood grills and other dishes, plus a bar.

Mercury's (Map p113; ☎ 024-223 3076; meals Tsh8000-16,000; ☺ 10am-midnight) Named in honour of Queen vocalist Freddie Mercury (see p119), this is Stone Town's main waterside hang-out. On offer are good seafood grills, pasta dishes and pizza, and a well-stocked bar and a terrace that's a prime location for sipping sundowners. There's a beach bonfire nightly, and live music on Wednesday, Friday, Saturday and Sunday evenings.

La Fenice (Map p113; ☎ 0777-411868; Shangani St; meals from Tsh8500; ☺ lunch & dinner) A breezy little patch of Italy on the waterfront, La Fenice has top-notch Italian cuisine and outdoor tables where you can enjoy your pasta while gazing out at the turquoise sea in front of you.

Mtoni Marine Centre (Map p110; ☎ 024-225 0117; mtonirestaurant@zanzibar.cc; meals Tsh10,000-27,000; ☺ dinner) Mtoni Marine's main restaurant has what many connoisseurs consider to be the finest cuisine in Stone Town, with a range of seafood and meat grills, and waterside barbecues several times weekly, with a backdrop of *taarab* or other traditional music.

Sambusa Two Tables Restaurant (Map p113; ☎ 024-223 1979; meals US$10; ☺ dinner) For sampling authentic Zanzibari dishes, it's hard to beat this small, family-run restaurant just off Kaunda Rd, where the proprietors bring out course after course of delicious local delicacies. Advance reservations are required; up to 15 guests can be accommodated.

236 Hurumzi Tower Top Restaurant (Map p113; ☎ 024-223 0171, 0777-423266; www.236hurumzi .com; 236 Hurumzi, Hurumzi St; meals US$25-30; ☽ dinner) Dinner at this rooftop restaurant has long been a Zanzibar tradition, and while it seems to have rather suffered from success somewhat in recent years, it still makes an enjoyable evening out and a fine spot for sundowners. The menu is fixed, and reservations are essential. On Friday, Saturday and Sunday, meals are served to a backdrop of traditional music and dance. The terrace is open from 5pm, drinks start at 6pm and dinner at 7pm.

Also recommended:

Pagoda Chinese Restaurant (Map p113; ☎ 024-223 1758; meals from Tsh6500; ☽ lunch & dinner) Tasty Chinese food near the Africa House Hotel, including a good-value set-menu lunch.

Raintree Restaurant (Map p110; ☎ 024-223 5478; Mbweni Ruins Hotel; meals from Tsh9000) Elegant dining in a lovely setting overlooking the surrounding gardens and the water; delicious seafood grills and salads. Special features include occasional evening beachside barbecues, and a Sunday lunchtime curry buffet (Tsh15,000).

CAFÉS

Msumbi Coffee House (Map p113; off Kelele Sq) Tucked away in a small alleyway near the Zanzibar Serena Inn, this small, informal place has a full array of coffees, cappuccinos and more, and also sells roasted beans (all Tanzanian grown) to take away.

Buni Café (Map p113; Shangani St; snacks & light meals from Tsh2000; ☽ 8.30am-6.30pm) Just before the Shangani tunnel and around the corner from Monsoon restaurant, with a similar menu to Stone Town Café (though no all-day breakfasts) and a nice outdoor porch where you can watch the passing scene.

Zanzibar Coffee House (Map p113; ☎ 024-223 9319; coffeehouse@zanlink.com; snacks from Tsh2000) A great place below the hotel of the same name, with a large coffee menu, plus milkshakes, fruit smoothies and freshly baked cakes. It's affiliated with Utengule Country Lodge in Mbeya, from where much of the coffee is also sourced, and coffee beans are available to take away.

Stone Town Café (Map p113; Kenyatta Rd; breakfast Tsh5000, meals from Tsh2500; ☽ 8am-6pm Mon-Sat) A new, good eatery opposite Shangani Internet Café, with all-day breakfasts, milkshakes, freshly baked cakes, veggie wraps and very good coffee.

QUICK EATS

Forodhani Gardens (Map p113; meals from Tsh1000; ☽ dinner) These waterside gardens (p117) have great-value street food, with piles of grilled fish and meat, chips, snacks and more, all served on a paper plate or rolled into a piece of newspaper and eaten while sitting on benches or on the lawn. Locals advise against eating fish and meat during the height of the low season (when food turnover is slower), but we've never heard of any problems.

For inexpensive meals, try **Passing Show** (Map p113; Malawi Rd; meals from Tsh1000), opposite Ciné Afrique, or **Al-Shabany** (off Malawi Rd; meals from Tsh1000; ☽ 10am-2pm), another local favourite on a small side street just off Malawi Rd and east of Creek Rd. Both serve delicious pilau and biryani, plus chicken and chips.

SELF-CATERING

Shamshuddin's Cash & Carry (Map p113; Soko St) Just behind the Darajani market.

Drinking

Stone Town isn't known for its nightlife, but there are a few popular spots.

Dharma Lounge (Map p113; Vuga Rd; ☽ 7.30pm-late) Zanzibar's first and only cocktail lounge, with big cushions for relaxing, a well-stocked bar, air-con and a good selection of music. It's next to the Culture Musical Club.

Africa House Hotel (Map p113; www.theafricahouse -zanzibar.com; Shangani St) Terrace-level sundowners overlooking the water.

Also recommended:

Mcheza Bar (Map p110; ☎ 024-225 0117; mtonires taurant@zanzibar.cc) A happening sports bar that draws mainly an expat crowd; see also opposite.

Mercury's (Map p113; ☎ 024-223 3076) Waterside sundowners and a beach bonfire nightly plus live music Wednesday, Friday, Saturday and Sunday evenings.

Entertainment

Entertainment Zanzibari-style centres on traditional music and dance performances.

Zanzibar's most famous contribution to the world music scene is *taarab;* for more information and details on where to hear it, see the boxed text, p126.

TAARAB MUSIC

No visit to Zanzibar would be complete without spending an evening listening to the evocative strains of *taarab*, the archipelago's most famous musical export. *Taarab*, from the Arabic *tariba* (roughly, 'to be moved'), fuses African, Arabic and Indian influences, and is considered by many Zanzibaris to be a unifying force among the island's many cultures. A traditional *taarab* orchestra consists of several dozen musicians using both Western and traditional instruments, including the violin, the *kanun* (similar to a zither), the accordion, the *nay* (an Arabic flute) and drums, plus a singer. There's generally no written music, and songs – often with themes centred on love – are full of puns and double meanings.

Taarab-style music was played in Zanzibar as early as the 1820s at the sultan's palace, where it had been introduced from Arabia. However, it wasn't until the 1900s, when Sultan Seyyid Hamoud bin Muhammed encouraged formation of the first *taarab* clubs, that it became more formalised.

One of the first clubs founded was Akhwan Safaa, established in 1905 in Zanzibar Town. Since then numerous other clubs have sprung up, including the well-known Culture Musical Club, based in the building of the same name, and the smaller, more traditional Twinkling Stars, which is an offshoot of Akhwan Safaa. Many of the newer clubs have abandoned the traditional acoustic style in favour of electronic equipment, although older musicians tend to look down on this as an adulterated form of *taarab*. The performances are an event in themselves. In traditional clubs, men and women sit separately, with the women decked out in their finest garb and elaborate hairstyles. Audience participation is key, and listeners frequently go up to the stage to give money to the singer.

For an introduction to *taarab* music, stop by the **Zanzibar Serena Inn** (Map p113; ☎ 024-223 2306, 024-223 3587; www.serenahotels.com), where the Twinkling Stars play on Tuesday and Friday evening on the veranda from about 6pm to 7.30pm. For something much livelier, head to the **Culture Musical Club** (Vuga Rd), with a classic old-style club atmosphere and rehearsals from about 7.30pm to 9.30pm Monday to Friday. Akhwan Safaa has rehearsals several times weekly from about 9.30pm in the area off Creek Rd near the traffic police; locals can point you in the right direction. An excellent time to see *taarab* performances is during the **Festival of the Dhow Countries** (p120) in July.

The best contact for anything related to traditional music and dance is the Dhow Countries Music Academy (p116).

Old Fort (Map p113; admission Tsh4000) On Tuesday, Thursday and Saturday evening from 7pm to 10pm there are traditional *ngoma* (dance and drumming) performances at the Old Fort, although be prepared for rather flat tourist displays.

Shopping

Stone Town has wonderfully atmospheric craft shopping, and – if you can sort your way through some of the kitsch – there are some excellent buys to be found. Items to watch for include finely crafted Zanzibari chests, *kanga* (cotton wraps worn by women all over Tanzania), *kikoi* (the thicker striped or plaid equivalent worn by men on Zanzibar and in other coastal areas), spices and handcrafted silver jewellery.

A good place to start is Gizenga St, which is lined with small shops and craft dealers. At the western end of Forodhani Gardens are vendors selling woodcarvings, Maasai beaded jewellery and other crafts.

Zanzibar Gallery (Map p113; ☎ 024-223 2721; gallery @swahilicoast.com; cnr Kenyatta Rd & Gizenga St; ♡ 9am-6.30pm Mon-Sat, to 1pm Sun) This long-standing gallery has an excellent collection of souvenirs, textiles, woodcarvings, antiques and more, in addition to its books.

Memories of Zanzibar (Map p113; Kenyatta Rd) Offers a large selection of jewellery, textiles and curios.

Moto Handicrafts (Map p113; www.solarafrica.net /moto; Hurumzi St) Sells baskets, mats and other woven products made by local women's co-operatives using environmentally sustainable technologies. The cooperative itself is based in Pete, shortly before Jozani Forest, where it also has a small shop.

Dhow Countries Music Academy (Map p113; ☎ 024-223 4050; www.zanzibarmusic.org; Mizingani Rd) For CDs of *taarab* and other local and regional music. See also its listing on p116.

Getting There & Away

AIR

Coastal Aviation and ZanAir offer daily flights connecting Zanzibar with Dar es Salaam (US$60), Arusha (US$150 to US$200), Pemba (US$80), Selous Game Reserve and the northern parks. Coastal Aviation also goes daily to/from Tanga via Pemba (US$90), and has day excursion packages from Dar es Salaam to Stone Town for US$112, including return flights, lunch and airport transfers. Air Tanzania and Precision Air also fly daily between Zanzibar and Dar es Salaam, with connections to Nairobi (Kenya). Precision Air, in partnership with Kenya Airways, also has a direct flight between Zanzibar and Nairobi. Note that the Nairobi–Zanzibar flight is routinely overbooked, and passengers are frequently bumped (especially if they've booked through Precision Air). Reconfirm your seat many times, and arrive early at the airport.

Airline offices in Zanzibar Town include the following:

Air Tanzania (Map p113; ☎ 023-223 0213; Shangani St) Next to Abuso Hotel.

Coastal Aviation (Map p113; ☎ 024-223 3489, 024-223 3112; www.coastal.cc; Kelele Sq) Next to Zanzibar Serena Inn, and at the airport.

Kenya Airways (Map p113; ☎ 024-223 4520/1; www .kenya-airways.com; Mizingani Rd) Just southeast of the Big Tree.

Precision Air (Map p113; ☎ 024-223 4520/1; www.pre cisionairtz.com; Mizingani Rd) Located with Kenya Airways.

ZanAir (Map p113; ☎ 024-223 3670; www.zanair.com) Just off Malawi Rd, opposite Ciné Afrique.

BOAT

For information on ferry connections between Zanzibar and Dar es Salaam, see p99. For ferry connections between Zanzibar and Pemba, see p148. You can get tickets at the port, through any of the listings under Travel Agencies & Tour Operators (p112), and – most easily – at the Tourist Information Office (p112). If you leave Zanzibar on the *Flying Horse* night ferry, take care with your valuables, especially when the boat docks in Dar es Salaam in the early morning hours.

Dhows link Zanzibar with Dar es Salaam, Tanga, Bagamoyo and Mombasa (Kenya). Foreigners are not permitted on dhows between Dar es Salaam and Zanzibar. For other routes, the best place to ask is at the beach behind Tembo House Hotel. Allow anywhere

from 10 to 48 hours or more to/from the mainland; also see the boxed text, p357.

TRAIN

Riverman Hotel behind the Anglican cathedral can help you make bookings for the Tazara line for a Tsh1000 fee; you pay for the ticket at the Tazara train station in Dar es Salaam.

Getting Around

TO/FROM THE AIRPORT

The airport is about 7km southeast of Zanzibar Town. A taxi to/from the airport costs Tsh8000 to Tsh10,000. *Dalla-dalla* 505 also does this route (Tsh300, 30 minutes), departing from the corner opposite Mnazi Mmoja hospital. Many Stone Town hotels offer free airport pick-ups for confirmed bookings, though some charge. For hotels elsewhere on the island, transfers usually cost about US$25 to US$50, depending on the location.

CAR & MOTORCYCLE

It's easy to arrange car, moped or motorcycle rental and prices are reasonable, although breakdowns are fairly common, as are moped accidents. Considering how small the island is, it's often more straightforward and not that much more expensive just to work out a good deal with a taxi driver.

You'll need either an International Driving Permit (IDP; together with your home licence), a licence from Kenya (Nairobi), Uganda or South Africa, or a Zanzibar driving permit – there are lots of police checkpoints along the roads where you'll be asked to show one or the other. Zanzibar permits can be obtained on the spot from the **traffic police** (Map p113; cnr Malawi & Creek Rds). If you rent through a tour company, they'll sort out the paperwork.

Daily rental rates average from about US$25 for a moped or motorcycle, and US$45 to US$55 for a Suzuki 4WD, with better deals available for longer-term rentals. You can rent through any of the tour companies, through **Asko Tours & Travel** (Map p113; ☎ 024-223 0712; askot our@hotmail.com; Kenyatta Rd), which also organises island excursions, or by asking around in front of Darajani market, near the bus station. If you're not mechanically minded, bring someone along with you who can check that the motorbike or vehicle you're renting is in reasonable condition, and take a test drive. Full payment is usually required at the time of delivery, but don't pay any advance deposits.

ZANZIBAR ARCHIPELAGO

DALLA-DALLAS

Dalla-dallas piled with people and produce link all major towns on the island. They are open-sided and generally more enjoyable than their mainland Tanzanian counterparts. For most destinations, including all the main beaches, there are several vehicles daily, with the last ones back to Stone Town departing by about 3pm or 4pm. None of the routes cost more than Tsh1000, and all take plenty of time (eg about three hours from Zanzibar Town to Jambiani). All have destination signboards and numbers. Commonly used routes include the following:

Route No	Destination
101	Mkokotoni
116	Nungwi
117	Kiwengwa
118	Matemwe
121	Donge
206	Chwaka
214	Uroa
308	Unguja Ukuu
309	Jambiani
310	Makunduchi
324	Bwejuu
326	Kizimkazi
501	Amani
502	Bububu
504	Fuoni
505	Airport (marked 'U/Ndege')
509	Chukwani

PRIVATE MINIBUS

Private minibuses run daily to the north- and east-coast beaches, although stiff competition and lots of hassles with touts mean that a splurge on a taxi isn't a bad idea. Book through any travel agency the day before you want to leave, and the minibus will pick you up at your hotel in Stone Town between 8am and 9am. Travel takes 1½ to two hours to any of the destinations, and costs a negotiable Tsh5000 per person. Don't pay for the return trip in advance as you'll probably see neither the driver nor your money again. Most drivers only go to hotels where they'll get a commission, and will go to every length to talk you out of other places, including telling you that the hotel is closed/full/burned down etc.

TAXI

Taxis don't have meters, so you'll need to agree on a price with the driver before getting into the car. Town trips cost Tsh1500 to Tsh2000, more at night.

AROUND ZANZIBAR
Beaches

Zanzibar has superb beaches, with the best along the island's east coast. Although some have become overcrowded and built-up, all offer a wonderful respite from bumping along dusty roads on the mainland, or from dreary London winters. The east-coast beaches are protected by coral reefs offshore and have fine, white coral sand. Depending on the season, they may also have a lot of seaweed (most abundant from December to February). Locals harvest the seaweed for export, and you'll see it drying in the sun in many villages.

Everyone has their favourites, and which beach you choose is a matter of preference. For meeting other travellers, enjoying some nightlife and staying at relatively inexpensive accommodation, the best choices are central and west Nungwi in the far north (although for a beach, you'll need to go around the corner to Kendwa, which together with east Nungwi is the real treat of the north), followed by Paje on the east coast. Bwejuu and Jambiani on the east coast are also popular – and have some of the finest stretches of palm-fringed sand you'll find anywhere – but everything is more spread out and somewhat quieter here than in the north. For a much quieter atmosphere, try Matemwe, Pongwe or the southern end of Kiwengwa. If you're seeking the large resort scene, the main area is the beach north of Kiwengwa towards Pwani Mchangani. The coast north of Bwejuu near the tip of Ras Michamvi is worth considering if you're looking for top-end standards away from the large resorts. Except for Kendwa and Nungwi, where you can take a dip at any time, swimming at all of the beaches is tide dependent.

BUBUBU (FUJI BEACH)

This modest stretch of sand, 10km north of town in Bububu, is the closest place to Zanzibar Town for swimming, though if you're after a beach holiday, it's better to head further north or east. It's accessed via the dirt track heading west from just north of the Bububu police station.

Sleeping

Bububu Beach Guest House (☎ 024-225 0110; www .bububu-zanzibar.com; s/d from US$15/25) This budget haunt has airy no-frills rooms near the beach, and meals with advance notice. It's at the end of the dirt track heading west from the

---

BEST BEACHES

Almost all of Zanzibar's beaches would be considered superlative if they were located anywhere else, but a few stand out, even here:

- **Matemwe** (p133) For its powdery, white sands and intriguing village life.
- **Kendwa** (p132) Wide, white and swimmable around the clock.
- **Pongwe** (p135) For its crystal waters and lack of crowds.
- **Jambiani** (p137) For the otherworldly turquoise shades of its waters.

Bububu police station and signposted; staff will come and collect you free from the airport or Stone Town, and can organise excursions around the island.

Hakuna Matata Beach Lodge (☎ 0777-454892; www .hakuna-matata-beach-lodge.com; s US$130-165, d US$160-210; ✷ ▣ ⛲) This lovely place, built among the old Chuini Palace ruins and overlooking a pretty little cove, is about 12km north of Stone Town. Accommodation is in spacious, comfortable and well-appointed stone and thatch bungalows set amid gardens dotted with mango and papaya trees, and there's a good restaurant with traditional music some evenings. There's also a spa and a pool.

MANGAPWANI
The small and unremarkable beach at Mangapwani is notable mainly for its nearby caves, and is frequently included as a stop on spice tours.

The caves are located about 20km north of Zanzibar Town along the coast, and are an easy walk from Mangapwani beach. There are actually two locations. The first is a large **natural cave** with a freshwater pool that is rumoured to have been used in connection with the slave trade. North of here is the sobering **slave cave**, a dank, dark cell that was used as a holding pen to hide slaves after the legal trade was abolished in the late 19th century.

There are no facilities at Mangapwani other than the **Mangapwani Seafood Grill** (☎ 024-223 3587; set lunch US$25; ☽ lunch), with a bar and a set, grilled seafood lunch. It's run by Zanzibar Serena Inn.

To get to the beach, follow the main road north from Zanzibar Town past Bububu to Chuini, from where you head left down a dirt road for about 8km towards Mangapwani village and the beach. Zanzibar Serena Inn provides a shuttle twice daily in the high season, departing from the hotel at 10am and 3.30pm and returning at 2.30pm and 6.30pm (not included in the lunch price). *Dalla-dallas* also run between Stone Town and Mangapwani village, from where it's a short walk to the beach. Just before reaching the restaurant area, there's a small sign for the caves, or ask locals to point the way.

NUNGWI
This large village, nestled among the palm groves at Zanzibar's northernmost tip, is a dhow-building centre and one of the island's major tourist destinations – and this, despite now lacking any sort of substantial beach during much of the year, thanks to shifting tidal patterns and development-induced erosion. It's also where traditional and modern knock against each other with full force. Fishers sit in the shade repairing their nets while the morning's catch dries on neat wooden racks nearby, and rough-hewn planks slowly take on new life as skilled boat builders ply their centuries-old trade. Yet you only need to take a few steps back from the waterfront to enter into another world, with blaring music, an internet café, a rather motley collection of guesthouses packed in against each other and a definite party vibe. For some travellers it's the only place to be on the island (and it's one of the few places you can swim without needing to wait for the tides to come in); others will probably want to give it a wide miss. Most hotels and the centre of all the action are just north and west of Nungwi village, where it can get quite crowded. If partying isn't your scene, there are some lovely, quiet patches of sand on Nungwi's eastern side (where swimming is more tidal), and beautiful Kendwa (p132) is only a short walk, boat or taxi-ride away.

Information
There's an internet café and forex bureau at Amaan Bungalows, though exchange rates are significantly lower than in Stone Town or on the mainland.

Because of the large number of tourists in Nungwi, it's easy to overlook the fact that you're in a traditional, conservative environment. Be respectful, especially with your dress and your interactions with locals, and ask

Book your stay at lonelyplanet.com/hotels

THE SLAVE TRADE

Slavery has been practised in Africa throughout recorded history, but its greatest expansion in East Africa came with the rise of Islam, which prohibits the enslavement of Muslims. Demands of European plantation holders on the islands of Réunion and Mauritius were another major catalyst, particularly during the second half of the 18th century.

At the outset, slaves were taken from coastal regions and shipped to Arabia, Persia and the Indian Ocean islands. Kilwa Kisiwani was one of the major export gateways. As demand increased, traders made their way further inland, so that during the 18th and 19th centuries slaves were being brought from as far away as Malawi and the Congo. By the 19th century, with the rise of the Omani Arabs, Zanzibar had eclipsed Kilwa Kisiwani as East Africa's major slave-trading depot. According to some estimates, by the 1860s from 10,000 to as many as 50,000 slaves were passing through Zanzibar's market each year. Overall, close to 600,000 slaves were sold through Zanzibar between 1830 and 1873, when a treaty with Britain finally ended the regional trade.

As well as the human horrors, the slave trade caused major social upheavals on the mainland. In the sparsely populated and politically decentralised south, it fanned up interclan warfare as ruthless entrepreneurs raided neighbouring tribes for slaves. In other areas the slave trade promoted increased social stratification and altered settlement patterns. Some tribes, for example, began to build fortified settlements encircled by trenches, while others – notably the Nyamwezi and other central-Tanzanian peoples – concentrated their populations in towns as self-defence. Another fundamental societal change was the gradual shift in the nature of chieftaincy from a religiously based position to one resting on military power or wealth – both among the 'gains' of trade in slaves and commodities.

The slave trade also served as an impetus for European missionary activity in East Africa – prompting the establishment of the first mission stations, as well as missionary penetration of the interior. After the abolishment of slavery on Zanzibar, the Universities' Mission to Central Africa (UMCA) took over the slave market, and built the Anglican cathedral that still stands on the site today.

---

permission before snapping photos. Also, watch your valuables, and don't walk along the beach alone or with valuables, particularly at night.

Sights & Activities

Other than diving, snorkelling and relaxing on the beach, you can watch the dhow builders, or visit the **Mnarani Aquarium** (admission Tsh2500; 🕙 9am-6pm), home to hawksbill and green turtles that are being nurtured as part of a local conservation initiative. It's near the lighthouse at the northernmost tip of Ras Nungwi. The lighthouse, which dates to 1886, is still in use and not open to the public.

The best diving in the north is around Mnemba, which can be readily arranged from Nungwi, though it's a bit of a ride to get there. Leven Bank is closer and can be quite rewarding, but you'll need previous experience. Otherwise, there are a collection of sites closer in that is good for beginners. For more on diving around Zanzibar, see the boxed text, p118. Locally based operators include the following:

East Africa Diving & Water Sport Centre (☎ 0777-420588; www.diving-zanzibar.com) Next to Jambo Brothers Beach Bungalows.

Ras Nungwi Beach Hotel (☎ 024-223 3767; www .rasnungwi.com) A PADI five-star centre based at Ras Nungwi Beach Hotel.

Spanish Dancer Dive Centre (☎ 024-224 0091, 0777-417717; www.spanishdancerdivers.com) At Nungwi Inn Hotel.

Sleeping & Eating

The main cluster of guesthouses is on the western side of Nungwi, where there's not much ambience and little to distinguish between the various places, but plenty of activity. Just northeast of here are a few other budget options. Further east, around the tip of the cape and past the lighthouse, everything gets much quieter, with a handful of good hotels spread along a low cliff overlooking the water, surrounded by empty tracts of scrub vegetation. Many of Nungwi's hotels have restaurants, and in the village there's a tiny shop with a few basics. For anything more than that, you'll need to shop in Zanzibar Town.

Nungwi Guest House (☎ 0777-494899, 0784-234980; nungwiguest@yahoo.com; Nungwi village; s/d US$10/20) A good budget option in the village centre, with simple, clean en suite rooms around a small garden courtyard, all with mosquito nets and fans, meals on request and discounted long-term rates.

Jambo Brothers Beach Bungalows (jambobunga lows@yahoo.com; central Nungwi; s/d without bathroom US$20/30) This low-key place on the sand has been spruced up a bit, though rooms are still quite basic and a bit tatty. Meals can be arranged with advance notice. East Africa Diving & Water Sport Centre is next door.

Union Beach Bungalows (central Nungwi; s/d without bathroom US$20/30) A step up, although nothing special, with small, two-room cottages near the beach next to Jambo Brothers.

North Nungwi Beach Resort (east Nungwi; d US$35) This is the cheapest place on Nungwi's eastern side, with very basic rooms in quiet and rather neglected but attractive grounds close to the beach, friendly staff and meals available with advance order. It's just south of Tanzanite Beach Resort, and well away from all the action in the town centre.

Nungwi Inn Hotel (☎ 024-224 0091; www.nungwi-inn .com; west Nungwi; d garden view with fan/air-con US$50/60, d sea view with air-con US$70; ⊠) Located towards the southwestern end of the main hotel strip, this hotel has reasonable rooms scattered around rather hotch-potch grounds in small whitewashed cottages, plus a restaurant and a somewhat quieter location near the beach. Note that the garden view rooms are well back from the beach and the rest of the hotel, across a small dirt road.

Amaan Bungalows (☎ 024-224 0024/6; www.amaan bungalows.com; central Nungwi; tw from US$60, with sea view US$120; ⊠ ⌨) This large and efficiently run place is at the centre of the action, with various levels of accommodation, ranging from small garden-view rooms with fan to quite nice and more spacious sea-view rooms with air-con and small balconies. All rooms have hot water. Also in the complex is a waterside restaurant-bar, internet access, moped rental, a travel agency and more. No credit cards accepted.

Smiles Beach Hotel (☎ 024-224 0472; www.smiles beachhotel.com; east-central Nungwi; s/d US$75/100; ⊠) Smiles – on the eastern edge of Nungwi centre – has well-maintained and well-appointed rooms in two-storey tile-roofed cottages overlooking a manicured lawn and a nice patch of beach. They're spotless and good value,

all with small sea-facing balconies, and with more space and quiet than at some of the other central hotels.

Game Fish Lodge (☎ 0753-451919; gamefish@zanlink .com; east Nungwi; r US$100) In a good setting high up on a hill dotted with fig palms and with lovely views overlooking the sea on Nungwi's quiet eastern side, this new place offers four well-equipped rooms (more are planned), fully equipped fishing (including a three-day catered camping trip to Quata island offshore from Pemba) and a restaurant.

Flame Tree Cottages (☎ 024-224 0100; www.flame treecottages.com; east-central Nungwi; d US$105; ⊠) Nice, simply furnished white cottages in a small fenced-in garden just in from the beach in a quieter spot on the northeastern edge of Nungwi. All have fan and air-con, and some have a small kitchenette (US$10 extra) and minifridge. Dinner can be arranged with advance order. A new, promising-looking upmarket place was being built next door.

Baobab Beach Bungalows (☎ 024-223 6315, 0773-907276; www.baobabbeachbungalows.com; west Nungwi; s US$115-165, d US$180-280; ⊠ ⌨) At the far southwestern end of the strip, and quieter, with clean, small bungalows set around the lawn well away from the water, plus several simpler rooms with fan and spacious, air-con deluxe rooms closer to the beach.

Mnarani Beach Cottages (☎ 024-224 0494; www .lighthousezanzibar.com; east Nungwi; s/d US$72/108, q/family cottage US$128/225, deluxe d US$170, honeymoon ste US$200, all prices include half board; ⌨ ⊠) This small owner-managed lodge is the first place you come to on the placid eastern side of Nungwi – just after the lighthouse (the name means 'at the lighthouse' in Swahili), a fine choice and warmly recommended. It's set on a small rise overlooking the sea and with easy access to the beach below – ideal for swimming or for long walks at low tide. Accommodation is in small and spotless cottages, some with sea views, plus a few larger beachfront family cottages with minifridge and a loft. There are also deluxe rooms in the new Zanzibar House, including the Sunset and Sunrise suites on the top level and a rooftop bar with the best views in Nungwi. At the other end of the complex is the Mahaba honeymoon suite, with a loft, throw pillows for relaxing and a private breakfast, and a good restaurant and a deck that juts out over the water at high tide, with hammocks and swings for lounging. The lodge is well suited for both couples and families, and with a surprising feeling of space despite being often booked out. For children or children-at-heart, there is a pair of fantastic swings overlooking the sea directly above the beach. The same management is also building several two- to three-bedroom self-catering flats nearby.

Ras Nungwi Beach Hotel (☎ 024-223 3767; www .rasnungwi.com; east Nungwi; s/d full board US$220/300, with sea view from US$260/380; ⊙ Jun-Mar) This attractive, upmarket place has a low-key ambience, airy sea-view chalets nestled on a hillside overlooking the sea, and less expensive 'garden-view' rooms in the main lodge, plus a huge and very comfortable and well-appointed suite. The hotel can organise fishing and water sports, and there's a dive centre. It's the last (for now) hotel down on Nungwi's eastern side.

Getting There & Away
Bus 116 runs daily between Nungwi and Zanzibar Town (Tsh1300) along a now completely tarmac road, but almost everyone uses one of the private minibuses (p128). If you're driving on your own, it's faster to take the route from Mahonda via Kinyasini (to the east), rather than the somewhat deteriorated road via Donge and Mkokotoni.

KENDWA
About 3km southwest of Nungwi along the coast is Kendwa, a long, wide and wonderful stretch of sand known for its laid-back atmosphere and its full-moon parties. Apart from the full-moon parties, when it's loud until the wee hours, the beach is lovely and tranquil, swimmable at all hours, and refreshingly free from Nungwi's crush of activity and accommodation. Offshore are some reefs for snorkelling. For diving, there's **Scuba Do** (☎ 0777-417157; www.scuba-do-zanzibar.com), who has a full range of PADI courses and certification and is located at Sunset Bungalows.

Sleeping
All the hotels are within about a 700m stretch, so you can easily go from one place to the next on foot, and just about everywhere has sea views.

Les Toits du Palme (☎ 0777-418548; s/d US$25/50, d banda without bathroom US$10) Basic thatched *bandas* (thatched-roof huts or shelters) on the beach with not much more than a mattress, plus some bungalow-style rooms up on the small escarpment behind.

Malaika (☎ 0777-856167; www.malaikabungalows .com; s/d US$30/40) A handful of no-frills rooms at the southern end of Kendwa, and just in from the beach. No one was there to show us around when we passed by – if you stay, let us know how it is.

Sunset Bungalows (☎ 0777-414647, 0777-413818; sunsetbungalows@hotmail.com; s/d US$35/45, s/d with air-con from US$60/75, s/d deluxe beachfront with air-con US$70/95; ⊠) A long-standing place with straightforward but quite nice rooms and cottages on a small cliff overlooking the beach, plus better, cheerily decorated ones lined up in facing rows on the sand, including a few 'deluxe bungalows' closer to the water. There's also a resident dive operator, and a large and popular beachside restaurant-bar with evening bonfires on the beach. You can also book through Malindi Lodge (p121) in Stone Town.

Kendwa Rocks (☎ 0777-415475; www.kendwarocks .com; s/d wooden bandas US$50/70, d banda without bathroom US$30, s/d stone bungalows from US$55/75; ⊠) A Kendwa classic, with straightforward and recently spruced-up wooden bungalows on the sand, some cooler stone and thatch versions nearby, including some with air-con, some simple *bandas* with shared bathroom up on the small cliff, away from the water, and the biggest full-moon parties.

White Sands Beach Hotel (☎ 0777-411326; www .ajvtours.co.tz; d US$50-80) Nice en suite stone cottages on a small cliff above the beach (prices vary according to size), and a great beachside bar and restaurant.

Kendwa Beach Resort (☎ 0777-492552; www.kend wabeachresort.com; d US$69-109) This large place towards the southern end of Kendwa has been completely redone in recent years and now has various types of rooms. These range from small 'hill-view' rooms, set well back from the water on a hill, to well-appointed and larger 'ocean bungalows' closer to the beach. There's also a good waterside restaurant.

Getting There & Away
You can walk to Kendwa from Nungwi at low tide in about 25 to 30 minutes, but take care as there have been some muggings. Alternatively, inexpensive boats go from near Amaan Bungalows (p131) a few times daily depending on demand. Via public transport from Stone Town, have *dalla-dalla* 116 drop you at the sign for Kendwa Rocks (a few kilometres south of Nungwi), from where it's

HONEYMOON HEAVEN

Tanzania has become a hugely popular destination for honeymooners, and many upmarket hotels, both on Zanzibar and on the mainland (especially along the coast and on the northern safari circuit), offer special honeymoon suites, private candlelit dinners and other luxuries to help you ease into betrothed bliss. We've mentioned a few of the suites in the listings in this book, but it's always worth asking. Web-based tour operators who specialise in arranging upmarket honeymoon safari /beach packages in Tanzania include **Africa Travel Resource** (www.allaboutzanzibar.com) and **Encounter Zanzibar** (www.encounterzanzibar.com). Most of the midrange and top-end safari operators listed on p44 also arrange special honeymoon packages.

about a 2km walk to the beach. (If you're driving, this access road is supposed to be rehabilitated soon, but even now it's passable in 2WD, with some care needed over the rocky patches.)

MATEMWE

The long, idyllic beach at Matemwe has some of the finest sand on Zanzibar. It's also the best base for diving and snorkelling around Mnemba, which lies just offshore. In the nearby village, life moves at its own pace, with women making their way across the shallows at low tide to harvest seaweed, strings of fish drying in the sun, and cows and chickens wandering across the road – all thousands of miles from the world of ringing mobile phones, traffic jams and high-rise office buildings that most of Matemwe's visitors have left behind.

As you head south along the coast, the sands of Matemwe slide almost imperceptibly into those of Pwani Mchangani, a large fishing village that acts as a buffer before the string of Italian resorts further south at Kiwengwa.

Sleeping – Budget
Mohammed's Restaurant & Bungalows (☎ 0777-431881; r per person without bathroom US$15) This establishment has four very basic en suite bungalows, each with two large beds, just

back from the beach. Grilled fish and other local meals can be arranged.

Matemwe Minazini (per person US$20) At the far southern end of the beach, this very chilled place has a handful of very basic rooms and meals. The setup is nothing special, but the price is about as good as it gets on Matemwe.

Sele's (☎ 0777 413449; d US$40) This friendly and no-frills place was still being built when we passed by but looked promising. There are a couple of simple, large en suite rooms with more to come, plus a restaurant – all just in from the beach in a dhow-themed garden.

Nyota Beach Bungalows (☎ 0777-484303; www.nyotabeachbungalows.com; d with garden/sea view US$65/80) Straightforward but atmospheric bungalows (including one two-storey bungalow) set amid the palms and papaya trees just back from the beach, and a restaurant.

Sleeping – Midrange & Top End
Matemwe Baharini Villas Beach Resort (☎ 0777-417768; www.matemwevillas.com; villa per room US$75-100, s/d bungalow US$100/110) This quiet and unassuming place is on the beach between Matemwe Beach Village and Matemwe Bungalows. There are two main houses ('villas'), one with two double rooms downstairs and the other with two rooms upstairs and two rooms downstairs, plus a row of simple, beach-facing attached double bungalows. Furnishings and ambience are simple and functional, and meals can be arranged.

Matemwe Beach Village (☎ 0777-417250, 0777-437200; www.matemwebeach.net; s/d US$85/110, with aircon US$95/120, shamba ste US$190, asali ste incl half board US$400; ☐ ☒) This recommended beachfront place has a wonderful setting on a beautiful stretch of coast, a low-key ambience and spacious, airy bungalows with small verandas. Most are on the beach, separated only by a low wall of vegetation, with a few more set back about 100m on a low rise. There's also a plush and very private beachfront honeymoon suite complete with its own plunge pool, outdoor bathroom, chef and separate stretch of sand, plus several appealingly designed two-storey 'shamba suites' and a convivial open lounge area where you can relax on large throw pillows while looking out to sea. One Ocean/The Zanzibar Dive Centre (p117) has a branch here, which means if you start with them in Stone Town, you can get in some good east-coast diving as well.

ZANZIBAR ARCHIPELAGO

Half-board arrangements are available, as are discounts for children. In Stone Town, book through One Ocean, which can also help with transport arrangements.

Zanzibar Retreat Hotel (☎ 0773-079344; www.zanzibarretreat.com; s/d US$135/145; 🗙 🖵 🐙) A small, well-located place on the beach with just seven rooms – all well appointed and with Zanzibari beds – but on the small side and rather on top of each other, although good value considering the location. The main attraction, besides the lovely beachside setting, are the beautiful common areas – all with polished hardwood floors, and including an upstairs bar overlooking the beach. There's also satellite TV.

Matemwe Bungalows (www.asilialodges.com; ste per person full board US$285; 🌣 mid-Jun–Easter; 🖵 🐙) Matemwe Bungalows, about 1km north of Matemwe Beach Village, is a relaxing, upmarket place with a dozen spacious and impeccably decorated seaside bungalow suites. It has a pampered, upmarket atmosphere and receives consistently positive reviews. All the bungalows have their own veranda and hammock, and there are also more luxurious suites, including one for honeymooners with its own beach.

Matemwe Retreat (www.asilialodges.com; villa per person full board US$485) Just north, and directly opposite Mnemba atoll, is this new and very upmarket retreat, with three luxurious villas and the best access on the island to diving Mnemba (except on Mnemba itself).

Getting There & Away

Matemwe village is located about 25km southeast of Nungwi, and is reached via an unsealed road branching east off the main road by Mkwajuni. *Dalla-dallas* travel here daily from Stone Town (Tsh1200). Early in the day, they continue as far as the fish market at the northern end of the beach (and this is where you can catch them as well). Otherwise, the start/terminus of the route is at the main junction near Matemwe Beach Village hotel. The last *dalla-dalla* in both directions departs about 4pm, the first about 6am.

KIWENGWA

Kiwengwa village is spread out along a fine, wide beach, much of which is occupied by large, Italian-run resort hotels, although there are some much quieter stretches to the north and south.

Sleeping

Shooting Star Lodge (☎ 0777-414166; www.shootingstarlodge.com; s/d garden-view US$100/160, s/d sea-view cottages US$145/235) Classy and intimate, this lodge is highly recommended, both for its location on a small cliff overlooking an excellent stretch of beach – well away from the larger resort developments further north and south – and for its impeccable service, top-notch cuisine and lovely décor. There is a mix of rooms, ranging from four simpler and smaller garden-view 'lodge rooms' to 10 impeccably decorated, spacious sea-view cottages. There's also a salt-water infinity pool with stunning views over the sea, and a raised and cosy beachside bar. It's tranquil, the epitome of class and an overall excellent place to unwind.

Bluebay Beach Resort (☎ 024-224 0240/1; www.bluebayzanzibar.com; per person per night incl half board US$135-290; 🗙 🖵 🐙) The nicest of the large resorts along the Kiwengwa coastline, with a more subdued atmosphere than its neighbours. Rooms have two large beds and all the amenities, and the grounds are expansive, green and serene. One Ocean/The Zanzibar Dive Centre (p117) has a base here, and the pool can be used for introductory lessons.

Also recommended:

Ocean Paradise Resort (☎ 0774-440990; www.oceanparadisezanzibar.com; per person half board US$160; 🗙 🖵 🐙) An agreeable choice if you're seeking a resort, with accommodation in spacious, round bungalows, a raised restaurant with commanding views over the water, large, green gardens dotted with palms and sloping down to the beach and a huge swimming pool. Diving here is catered for by One Ocean/The Zanzibar Dive Centre (p117).

Zamani Zanzibar Kempinski (☎ 0774-444477; www.kempinski-zanzibar.com; r from US$500; 🗙 🖵 🐙) Worth a mention simply because of its considerable presence at the luxury end of the market. Rooms and services are upmarket (though it can't compare with the Kilimanjaro Kempinski in Dar es Salaam), and there are several pools, including a 60m infinity pool as well as smaller private infinity pools. For beach swimming, you'll need to go about 1.5km south to the Zamani Beach Club, the hotel's private stretch of sand.

Getting There & Away

Dalla-dalla 117 runs daily between Kiwengwa village and Stone Town. The village itself is divided into three parts: Cairo to the north; Kiwengwa proper in the centre and just east of the main junction; and Kumba Urembo to the south. Public transport will drop you in

Kiwengwa proper unless you pay the driver extra to take you further.

Almost all transport south takes the new road. The old road south of Kiwengwa turns into a rough dirt lane winding through the tropical vegetation and coconut palms to Pongwe, where it then becomes tarmac. Apart from a few rocky patches between Kiwengwa and Pongwe that need to be negotiated with care, 2WD is fine during most times of the year.

PONGWE

This quiet arc of beach, about 5km south of Kiwengwa, is dotted with palm trees and backed by dense vegetation, and is about as close to the quintessential tropical paradise as you can get. Thanks to its position in a semisheltered cove, it also has the advantage of having less seaweed than nearby Chwaka and other parts of the east coast.

Set on a lovely stretch of sand south of Pongwe village, **Santa Maria Coral Park** (www .santamaria-zanzibar.com; s/d/tr US$30/50/75) is a very laid-back budget beach haunt with accommodation in either simple *makuti* (thatch) *bandas* or stone-and-thatch bungalows. There's a no-frills restaurant focusing on the catch of the day, and the chance for snorkelling or excursions in the local fishing boats. The beachside bar has music in the evenings, and sometimes a bonfire.

The intimate and unassuming **Pongwe Beach Hotel** (☎ 0784-336181; www.pongwe.com; s/d from US$85/140) has just 10 bungalows (including one honeymoon bungalow with a large, Zanzibari bed) nestled among the palms on a wonderful arc of beach. All are sea facing, spacious and breezy, the cuisine is very good, and when you tire of the turquoise panoramas at your doorstep, there's fishing, and excursions to Stone Town. It's justifiably hugely popular, very good value and often fully booked.

UROA

This rather centre-less and nondescript village lies on an attractive and seldom-visited stretch of beach, which is better than that at nearby Chwaka but still not up to the level of other east-coast destinations. It's a reasonable choice if you want to enjoy the sea breezes and sand away from the resort crowds. The small, quiet beachfront **Uroa White Villa** (☎ 0713-326874; www.uroawhite villa.net; s/d US$45/70) consists of a four-room house and a nearby two-room bungalow annexe,

both with a few pleasant, spotless rooms – most with bathroom – and a restaurant. There's a 20% discount on room prices if you book direct.

Getting There & Away

Dalla-dalla 214 runs between Stone Town and Uroa several times daily. Sometimes you can get this at Darajani market, but usually you need to take bus 501 (Amani Stadium) to a junction known as Mwembe Radu (just ask the *dalla-dalla* driver), where you can pick up *dalla-dalla* 214. Alternatively, bus 206 (Chwaka) sometimes continues northwards as far as Uroa. The last departure from Uroa back to Stone Town is at about 4pm.

PAJE

Paje is a wide, white beach at the junction where the coastal road north to Bwejuu and south to Jambiani joins with the road from Zanzibar Town. It's quite built-up, with a dense cluster of mostly unremarkable places all within a few minutes' walk of each other, and somewhat of a party atmosphere, though it's quieter and marginally more low-key than Nungwi. For diving, there's the **Paje Dive Centre** (☎ 024-224 0191; www.pajedivecentre.com) on the beach at Arabian Nights hotel.

Sleeping

Kinazi Upepo (☎ 0777-497495; www.kinaziupepo .com; d bandas without bathroom US$28, d bungalows US$45) Good vibes and good value are the main attractions at this place nestled amid the palms and coastal pines on a very nice section of beach. You can sleep in simple thatched *bandas* on low stilts, or in large bungalows with Zanzibari beds – most bungalows have a private bathroom. The food is good, and there's a well-stocked bar with fruit smoothies, among other drinks. There's often music nightly, and Saturday night currently features an all-night East Coast Beach Party with the hugely popular DJ Yusuf (the force behind Sauti za Busara, p120).

Paradise Beach Bungalows (☎ 024-223 1387; saori@cats-net.com; s/d US$30/40) This long-standing Japanese-run place is hidden among the palms on the beach at the northern edge of Paje and slightly removed from the main cluster of hotels. Each room has two large beds, and there's a restaurant serving tasty food, including sushi and other Japanese cuisine if you order in advance, plus local fare.

Kitete Beach Resort (☎ 024-224 0226; www.kitete beach.com; s US$40-70, d US$60-90) This small place on the beach has a dozen large and comfortably furnished rooms, six smaller and simpler rooms in the original building and a three-room family cottage, plus a good restaurant featuring Zanzibari cuisine.

Paje by Night (☎ 0777-460710; www.pajebynight .net; s/d from US$50/60, d/tr jungle bungalows US$75/90) This chilled place, known for its popular bar and good vibe, has a mix of standard and more spacious rooms, plus several double-storey four-person thatched jungle bungalows. Standards are high, staff are friendly and there's a good restaurant with a pizza oven and a full range of excursions available.

Also recommended:

Arabian Nights (☎ 024-224 0190; www.zanziba rarabiannights.com; d US$100-150; 🗶 🖳 🕲) Well-appointed and comfortable albeit very closely spaced rooms in stone cottages just back from the beach, including some with sea view.

Getting There & Away

Bus 324 runs several times daily between Paje and Stone Town en route to/from Bwejuu, with the last departure from Paje at about 4pm.

BWEJUU

The large village of Bwejuu lies about 3km north of Paje on a long, palm-shaded beach. It's quite spread out, and quieter and less crowded than Paje and Nungwi, with a mellow atmosphere and nothing much more to do other than wander along the sand and listen to the breezes rustling the palm trees. The only blot on the scene is the large amount of rubbish that litters the area back away from the beach.

Sleeping & Eating

Miza wa Miza Kiamboni Bungalows (☎ 0777-871757; ibrahim@kunst-gsund.at; s/d without bathroom US$15/25, d with hot shower US$40-55) A chilled backpacker place set inland away from the water, with small, darkish bungalow rooms downstairs and equally small but nicer ones with views upstairs.

Bahari Beach Village (www.bahari-beach-village .com; r without/with bathroom US$15/35, beachfront bungalows US$50) This refreshingly local beachfront place has a few simple but tidy rooms in a small house plus some nice bungalows. All are set on the sand amid the palm trees. Also

available are tasty local meals, and staff can help you organise airport pick-ups and excursions. It's at the northern end of Bwejuu – just keep heading up the sandy track until you see the sign.

Mustapha's Nest (☎ 024-224 0069; www.fatflatfish .co.uk/mustaphas/; dm US$15, r per person US$20-25) This vibey Rasta-run place has a variety of simple, cheery and very creatively decorated rooms, some with their own bathroom and all with their own theme. Meals are taken family style, and staff can assist with bike rental, drumming lessons and other diversions. It's south of Bwejuu village, and just across the road from the beach. Changes are planned here, so call before arriving.

Robinson's Place (☎ 0777-413479; www.robin sonsplace.net; per person US$20-30) This *Robinson Crusoe*-style getaway just south of Bahari Beach Village has a small collection of appealingly designed rooms nestled amid the palms directly on the beach. The two-storey Robinson House has an upstairs tree-house double, open to the sea and the palms. Downstairs is a tidy single, and there are a few more rooms in a separate house. Some have their own bathroom, and the shared bathroom is spotless. Eddy, the Zanzibari owner, cooks great breakfasts and dinners (for guests only). The same management also has a self-catering house up on the hill behind the beach for long-term stays.

Evergreen Bungalows Bwejuu (☎ 024-224 0273; www.evergreen-bungalows.com; d back from beach US$50, d bungalows US$60-70, d upper bungalows without bathroom US$35) North of Bwejuu village, with pricey but spiffy two-storey bungalows, plus three single-storey cottages back from the beach. There are also a few upstairs bungalow rooms that aren't self-contained, with the loo a bit of a walk away.

Palm Beach Inn (☎ 024-224 0221; palmbeach @zanlink.com; s/d from US$50/70, ste US$120; 🗶) This beachside inn has small, rather heavily furnished rooms with hot water and mini-fridge – all quite OK, but nothing special. There are also two newer and nicer sea-view suites, a tree-house lounge-library area overlooking the beach, a good restaurant and helpful staff.

Sunrise Hotel & Restaurant (☎ 024-224 0270; www.sunrise-zanzibar.com; s/tw US$80/90, s/d sea-view bungalows US$100/110; 🕲) The Belgian-run Sunrise has tidy rooms and bungalows set around a small garden area and a highly regarded restaurant. The beach-facing bungalows are worth the extra money, as they're much nicer than the overly dark rooms. It's on the beach about 3km north of Bwejuu village.

Getting There & Away
Bus 324 goes daily between Stone Town and Bwejuu village, and private minibuses come here as well.

MICHAMVI PENINSULA
Beginning about 4km north of Bwejuu, the land begins to taper off into the narrow and comparatively seldom-visited Michamvi Peninsula, where there are several upmarket retreats. In Michamvi village, there are a few simple *bandas* where you can arrange grilled fish or other local fare.

Breezes Beach Club & Spa (☎ 0774-440883; www .breezes-zanzibar.com; per person half board from €117; 🔀 🖳 🏊) is an intimate place that receives consistently good reviews and is often fully booked. There are lovely garden-view rooms plus deluxe rooms and suites closer to the sea, all beautifully appointed and with a full range of amenities, plus diving, a gym and plenty of other activities to balance out time on the beach. Advance bookings only – you won't get by the tight gate security without one. Next door and under the same management is the exclusive **Palms** (www.palms-zanzibar .com; per person full board €455; 🔀 🖳 🏊), with six luxurious villas, each with their own private outdoor spa bath.

Once past Bwejuu, there's no public transport. Local boats cross between Michamvi village (on the northwestern side of the peninsula) to Chwaka, usually departing from Michamvi in the early morning (Tsh1000), or you can arrange to hire one at any time of day (about Tsh15,000 return).

JAMBIANI
Jambiani is a long village on a stunning stretch of coastline. The village itself – a sunbaked and somnolent collection of thatch and coral-rag houses – is stretched out over more than a kilometre. The sea is an ethereal shade of turquoise and is usually dotted with *ngalawa* (outrigger canoes) moored just offshore. It's quieter than Paje and Nungwi, and has a good selection of accommodation in all price ranges. In the village, there's a post office (with bicycle rental nearby) and a shop selling a few basics.

Sleeping & Eating
Kimte Beach Inn (☎ 024-224 0212, 0777-430992; www .kimte.com; dm US$15, d without/with bathroom US$30/35) At the southern end of Jambiani, this chilled Rasta-run place has spotless rooms on the land side of the road (about half a minute's walk from the beach), a good vibe, delicious meals, and a great beach bar with music and evening bonfires.

Red Monkey Bungalows (☎ 024-224 0207, 024-223 5361; standard@zitec.org; s/d/tr US$25/40/50) Located at Jambiani's far southern end, this place has clean, agreeable sea-facing bungalows set along a nice garden on the beach.

Oasis Beach Inn (☎ 0777-858720; oasisbeachinn45 @yahoo.co.uk; s/d US$30/45, without bathroom US$25/35) This straightforward beachside place has simple but quite decent rooms with shared bathroom, and friendly staff. A restaurant is planned to open soon.

Pakachi Beach Hotel (☎ 024-224 0001, 0777-423331; www.pakachi.com; s/d US$30/50) Just a few small and simple stone-and-thatch bungalows (one is a six-person family bungalow) with mosquito nets set in a lush garden somewhat back from the beach, and a good restaurant featuring local cuisine and pizzas.

Dhow Beach Village (www.dhowbeachvillage.com; s/d US$35/50, without bathroom US$20/30) A vibey place with a restaurant area, a handful of straightforward self-contained rooms, and three simpler rooms with fan and shared bathroom just behind the restaurant area, plus beach volleyball, full-moon parties and more.

Coco Beach (☎ 0777-413125; cocobeach@zanlink.com; s/d US$40/50) A small place with just a handful of rooms in an enclosed garden just back from the beach, and a restaurant.

Blue Oyster Hotel (☎ 024-224 0163; www.zanzi bar.de; s/d US$55/60, with sea view US$65/70, without bathroom US$35/40) This German-run place on the beach at the northern end of Jambiani has pleasant, spotless and very good-value rooms, and a breezy terrace restaurant with delicious meals.

Casa Del Mar Hotel Jambiani (☎ 024-224 0401, 0777-455446; www.casa-delmar-zanzibar.com; d downstairs/ upstairs US$65/85) Two double-storey blocks of six rooms each – the upper-storey rooms have lofts – set around a small, lush garden in a small, enclosed beach area. There's also a restaurant with classical music playing in the background, and a terrace bar area.

ZANZIBAR ARCHIPELAGO

Hakuna Majiwe (☎ 0777-454505; www.hakunama jiwe.net; s/d US$145/182; 🛎) A pleasant place in a lovely setting with nicely decorated cottages with shady porches and Zanzibari beds, and décor that's a fusion of mostly Zanzibar with a touch of Italy. The food is good, though readers have complained about the scanty breakfasts. It's at the far northern end of Jambiani, about 4km north of Jambiani village, and on the edge of Paje.

Also recommended:

Coral Rock (☎ 024-224 0154; www.coralrockzanzibar .com; US$55/76; 🛏 🛎) Set on a large coral rock jutting out into the sea at the southern end of Jambiani and just south of Kimte Beach Inn, with the beach to the side. Accommodation is in a dozen whitewashed stone-and-thatch cottages with fan, air-con and small porches, and there's a bar directly overlooking the water.

Villa de Coco (www.villadecoco.com; s/d €47/75) Airy chalets – all with ceiling fans and hot water – in gardens bordering the beach. It's just north of Mt Zion Long Beach.

Sau Inn Hotel (☎ 024-224 0169; sauinn@zanlink.com; s/d/tr from US$70/80/90; 🛏 🖥 🛎) Modern, reasonably well-equipped, attached bungalow-style rooms scattered around manicured green grounds bordering the beach.

Jambiani Guest House (☎ 0773-147812; www .zanzibar-guesthouse.com; per house US$123, per d US$40) A large whitewashed thatched-roofed house on the beach, with the village just behind. It has five rooms (maximum seven people) and a cook available on request.

Getting There & Away

To get to Jambiani, there are private minibuses, or take bus 309 from Darajani market in Stone Town. Public transport from Jambiani back to Stone Town usually departs by 6am. South of Jambiani the coastal road deteriorates to become a sandy track with very rocky patches, and there's no public transport – all vehicles now use the new tarmac road to Makunduchi.

MAKUNDUCHI

The main reason to come to Makunduchi is for the **Mwaka Kogwa festival** (p120), when this small town – otherwise remarkable mainly for its 1950s East German–style high-rise apartment blocks and a seaweed-strewn and generally deserted stretch of coast – is bursting at its seams with revellers. The only accommodation is at the large **Makunduchi Beach Resort** (☎ 024-224 0348; www.lamadrugada-resort.com; per person US$80), with rows of two-storey attached rooms in a large compound just back from the sea, and generally permanently rented

out to Italian tour groups. It's also easily possible to visit as a day trip from Stone Town or Kizimkazi, and it shouldn't be too hard to arrange accommodation with locals during Mwaka Kogwa, as it's considered an unfavourable omen if you don't have at least one guest during the festival days. Bus 310 runs to Makunduchi on no set schedule, with plenty of additional transport from both Zanzibar Town and Kizimkazi during Mwaka Kogwa. The new tarmac road connecting Makunduchi with Jambiani and Paje was just being finished as this book was researched, although there's not yet any regular public transport along this stretch.

KIZIMKAZI

This small village – at its best when the breezes come in and the late afternoon sunlight illuminates the sand – actually consists of two adjoining settlements: Kizimkazi Dimbani to the north and Kizimkazi Mkunguni to the south. It has a small, breezy and in parts quite attractive beach, but the main reason people visit is to see the **dolphins** that favour the nearby waters, or to relax or go **diving** at one of the handful of upscale resorts that have recently opened in the area. Dolphin trips can be organised through tour operators in Stone Town from about US$20 per person, depending on group size, and some of the hotels at Paje and Jambiani also organise tours from Tsh15,000 per person. Most of the places listed under Sleeping & Eating (opposite) also organise tours. Otherwise, Cabs Restaurant in Kizimkazi Dimbani organises dolphin trips for walk-ins for Tsh50,000 per boat plus US$5 per person for snorkelling equipment (it also serves tasty fresh grilled fish meals). While the dolphins are beautiful, the tours, and especially those organised from Stone Town, are often quite unpleasant, due to the hunt-and-chase tactics used by many of the tour boats, and they can't be recommended. If you do go out, the best time is early morning when the water is calmer and the sun not as hot. Late afternoon is also good, although winds may be stronger (and if it's too windy, it's difficult to get in and out of the boats to snorkel).

Kizimkazi is also the site of a Shirazi **mosque** dating from the early 12th century and thought to be one of the oldest Islamic buildings on the East African coast, although much of what is left today is from later restorations. The building isn't impressive from

---

WATCHING THE DOLPHINS

Unfortunately for Kizimkazi's dolphins, things have gotten out of hand these days, and it's not uncommon to see a group of beleaguered dolphins being chased by several boats of tourists. If you want to watch the dolphins, heed the advice posted on the wall of the Worldwide Fund for Nature (WWF) office in Zanzibar Town, which boils down to the following:

- As with other animals, viewing dolphins in their natural environs requires time and patience.
- Shouting and waving your arms around will not encourage dolphins to approach your boat.
- Be satisfied with simply seeing the dolphins; don't force the boat operator to chase the dolphins, cross their path or get too close, especially when they are resting.
- If you decide to get in the water with the dolphins, do so quietly and calmly and avoid splashing.
- No one can guarantee that you will see dolphins on an outing, and swimming with them is a rare and precious occurrence.
- Remember – dolphins are wild and their whereabouts cannot be predicted. It is they who choose to interact with people, not the other way around…

ZANZIBAR ARCHIPELAGO

the outside, apart from a few old tombs at the front. Inside, however, in the mihrab are inscribed verses from the Quran dating to 1107 and considered to be among the oldest known examples of Swahili writing. If you want to take a look, ask for someone to help you with the key. You'll need to take off your shoes, and you should cover up bare shoulders or legs. The mosque is in Kizimkazi Dimbani, just north of the main beach area.

Sleeping & Eating

Kumi na Mbili Centre (www.zanzibar-tourism.org; r per person US$15) For budget accommodation, it's worth checking in at this centre, which is part of an NGO-sponsored village development centre, near the entrance to Kizimkazi Mkunguni. No one was around when we passed by, but it has several simple guest rooms with mosquito nets.

Kizimkazi Coral Reef Village (s/d US$40/50) Just up from Swahili Beach Resort with six rooms (more planned) with fan and mosquito nets, and set rather well back from the beach. There's also a small restaurant. Decent value.

Karamba (☎ 0773-166406; www.karambaresort .com; s/d €68/92) This place (formerly known as Kizidi) is on the northern end of the beach in Kizimkazi Dimbani. It's recently been completely renovated by the new Spanish management, and makes a thoroughly relaxing stop. Accommodation is in 12 spotless detached whitewashed cottages lined up along a small cliff overlooking the sea, all en suite and good value, and some with open-roof show-

ers. There's also a good restaurant serving a mix of dishes – vegetarian, Mediterranean, sushi, sashimi and milkshakes included – and a beachside chill-out bar with throw pillows.

Unguja Resort (☎ 0774-477477; www.ungujaresort .com; per person half board US$200; ☒) A new place with 12 spacious two-storey villas – all impeccably decorated and well appointed, and some with sea views – set amid reasonably mature gardens dotted with baobab trees. Diving in nearby Menai Bay can be arranged with One Ocean (p117). Very relaxing if you can afford it.

Getting There & Away

To reach Kizimkazi from Stone Town take bus 326 (Kizimkazi) direct (Tsh1500), or take bus 310 (Makunduchi) as far as Kufile junction, where you'll need to get out and wait for another vehicle heading towards Kizimkazi, or walk (about 5km). The last vehicle back to Stone Town usually leaves Kizimkazi about 4pm. The mosque is about 2km north of the main section of town in the Dimbani area. As you approach from Stone Town go right at Kufile junction (ie towards Kizimkazi) and then right again at the next fork to Kizimkazi Dimbani. Kizimkazi Mkunguni is to the left at this last fork.

Jozani Forest

This cool and shady patch of green – now protected as part of the Jozani-Chwaka Bay National Park – is the largest area of mature forest left on Zanzibar. Living among Jozani's tangle of vines and branches are populations of the rare red colobus monkey, as well as Sykes monkeys, bushbabies, Ader's duikers (although you won't see many of these), hyraxes, more than 50 species of butterflies, about 40 species of birds and several other animals. There's a nature trail in the forest, which takes about 45 minutes to walk, the tiny Colobus Café with soft drinks, and the small Tutoni Restaurant next door, with a modest and reasonably priced selection of meals.

Jozani Forest (adult/child incl guide US$8/4; ⏱ 7.30am-5.30pm) is about 35km southeast of Zanzibar Town off the road to Paje, and best reached via bus 309 or 310, by chartered taxi, or with an organised tour from Zanzibar Town (often in combination with dolphin tours to Kizimkazi). The best times to see red colobus monkeys are in the early morning and late evening.

When observing the monkeys, take care not to get too close – park staff recommend no closer than 3m – both for your safety and the safety of the animals. In addition to the risk of being bitten by the monkeys, there's considerable concern that if the monkeys were to catch a human illness it could spread and rapidly wipe out the already threatened population.

Along the main road near Pete village, and signposted shortly before the Jozani Forest entrance, is the small Moto Handicrafts workshop and showroom (see p126), where you can buy crafts and watch the artisans at work.

Menai Bay & Unguja Ukuu

Tranquil Menai Bay, fringed by the sleepy villages of Fumba to the west and Unguja Ukuu to the east, is home to an impressive assortment of corals, fish and mangrove forests, some idyllic sandbanks and deserted islets, and a sea-turtle breeding area. Since 1997 it's been protected as part of the **Menai Bay Conservation Area** (admission US$3). The main reasons to visit are to enjoy the placid ambience, to take advantage of some good **sailing** around the islets and sandbanks offshore, and for the chance to see **dolphins**. Unguja Ukuu is notable as the site of what is believed to be the earliest settlement on Zanzibar, dating to at least the 8th century, although there is little remaining today from this era.

The main place to stay is **Menai Bay Beach Bungalows** (☎ 0777-411753; www.menaibay.com; r from US$60; ⏱ Jul-Mar), on the bay at the southern edge of Unguja Ukuu village. It has straightforward, pleasant enough cottages scattered around leafy grounds just in from the beach, a nice stretch of sand and a restaurant, and staff can help organise excursions on the bay or to nearby sandbanks. Call first, as it's sometimes booked out completely to charter groups.

Eco + Culture Tours (Map p113; ☎ 024-223 0366; www.ecoculture-zanzibar.org; Hurumzi St) in Stone Town also organises trips to Unguja Ukuu and the offshore islands (see p112).

Fumba

This village at the end of the Fumba peninsula fringing Menai Bay boasts a lovely, quiet beach and the pleasant **Fumba Beach Lodge** (☎ 0777-860540; www.fumbabeachlodge.com; per person half board from US$172). Accommodation is in about two dozen cottage-style rooms – which are fine and spacious, albeit a bit frayed at the edges and not quite up to expectations at this price level – set in large grounds, plus there's a small spa built around a baobab tree (including a great Jacuzzi up in the tree) and a resident dive operator. It's also the base for Safari Blue (see p119). Fumba makes an enjoyable change from the more crowded destinations to the east and north, although be prepared for a decent amount of coral rock on the beach. It's only about 18km south of Zanzibar Town, but along a rough road that can take 45 minutes or so to traverse.

Offshore Islands

Once you've had your fill of the main island, there are various smaller islands and islets nearby that make enjoyable excursions and offer some good snorkelling.

CHANGUU

Also known as Prison island, Changuu lies about 5km and an easy boat ride northwest of Zanzibar Town. It was originally used to detain 'recalcitrant' slaves and later as a quarantine station. Changuu is also known for its large family of **giant tortoises**, who are believed to have been brought here from Aldabra in the Seychelles around the turn of the 20th century. There's also a small beach and a nearby reef offering some novice **snorkelling**, as well as the former house of the British governor,

General Lloyd Matthews. Today the island is privately owned and open only to guests of the **Changuu Private Island Paradise** (www.private islands-zanzibar.com; per person incl half board & airport transfers US$190-230), although snorkelling is still possible in the surrounding waters. Day trips to visit the tortoises cost US$25 per person including lunch and the US$4 entry fee to the island, but excluding boat transfer costs from Stone Town.

BAWI

Tiny Bawi, about 7km west of Zanzibar Town and several kilometres southwest of Changuu, offers a beautiful beach and **snorkelling**. For years marketed as a day out from Stone Town, it's now privately owned, and while snorkelling in the surrounding waters is still possible, the island itself can only be visited by guests of the very lovely **Bawe Tropical Island Lodge** (www .privateislands-zanzibar.com; per person-full board incl airport transfers US$340).

CHAPWANI

This tiny, privately owned island (also known as Grave Island, thanks to its small cemetery and the tombs of colonial-era British seamen) is about 4km north of Zanzibar Town. It's surrounded by crystal waters, with a postcard-perfect white-sand beach backed by lush vegetation running down one side, and it makes an agreeable getaway from Stone Town, although it can only be visited if you're either staying or dining at the lodge. As it's a waterless island, all fresh water must be pumped in from Zanzibar. The only development is **Chapwani Island Lodge** (www.chapwaniisland .com; s/d full board US$265/340; ☺ Jun-Mar), with five simple and rustic but cosy attached double-room bungalows along the sand. Day visits are also possible (centred on a meal), though advance bookings are required as well as for overnight stays. Unlike the east-coast beaches, swimming at Chapwani isn't tide dependent. The lodge provides transfers from Stone Town for US$10 per person, minimum two people.

TUMBATU

The large and seldom-visited island of Tumbatu, just off Zanzibar's northwest coast, is populated by the Tumbatu people, one of the three original tribal groups on the archipelago. Although Tumbatu's early history is somewhat murky, ruins of a mosque have been found at the island's southern tip that possibly date to the early 11th century, and it's likely the island was settled even earlier. As recently as the last century, there were no water sources on Tumbatu and villagers had

ZANZIBAR ARCHIPELAGO

COMMUNITY TOURISM SPOTLIGHT: CHUMBE

The uninhabited island of Chumbe, about 12km south of Zanzibar Town, has an exceptional shallow-water coral reef along its western shore that is in close to pristine condition and abounding with fish life. Since 1994, when the reef was gazetted as Zanzibar's first marine sanctuary, the island has gained widespread acclaim, including from the UN, as the site of a highly impressive ecotourism initiative centred on an ecolodge and local environmental education programmes. It's now run as **Chumbe Island Coral Park**, a private, nonprofit nature reserve that is doing fantastic work not only in protecting the reef, but also in community outreach with local school children.

The excellent state of Chumbe's reef is due largely to the fact that from the 1960s it was part of a military zone and off limits to locals and visitors. In addition to nearly 200 species of coral, the island's surrounding waters host about 370 species of fish and groups of dolphins who pass by to feed on the abundant fish life. The island also provides a haven for hawksbill turtles, and more than 50 species of birds have been recorded to date, including the endangered roseate tern. There are historical buildings on Chumbe: a lighthouse and a small mosque dating from the early 1900s, and the former warden's house.

Chumbe island can be visited as a day trip, although if you have the money and an interest in conservation, staying overnight in one of the seven **ecobungalows** (☎ 024-223 1040; www .chumbeilsand.com; s/d full board US$250/440) is highly recommended. Each of these intimate structures has its own rainwater collection system and solar power, and a cosy loft sleeping area that opens to the stars. Advance bookings are essential. Day visits (also by advance arrangement only) cost US$80 per person.

to come over to the mainland for supplies. In between Tumbatu and Zanzibar lies the tiny and uninhabited island of **Popo**.

There's no accommodation, but Tumbatu can be easily visited as a day trip from Kendwa or Nungwi, where the hotels can help you organise a boat (US$35 to US$50 per boat). Alternatively, local boats sail throughout the day between Tumbatu and **Mkokotoni** village, which lies just across the channel on Zanzibar, and which is known for its bustling fish market. The trip takes anywhere from 30 minutes to three hours, depending on the winds (or much less with a motor), and costs about Tsh150. Residents of Tumbatu aren't used to tourists – they are actually notorious for their lack of hospitality – so if you're heading over on your own or if you want to try to arrange an overnight stay with locals, it's best to get permission first from the police station in Mkokotoni, or from the *shehe* (village chief) in Nungwi, who will probably request a modest fee. There's at least one bus daily between Mkokotoni and Stone Town. Once on Tumbatu, the main means of transport are bicycle (ask around by the dock) and walking.

MNEMBA

Tiny, idyllic Mnemba, just northeast of Matemwe, is the ultimate tropical paradise for those who have the money to enjoy it, complete with white sands, palm trees, turquoise waters and total isolation. While the island itself is privately owned with access restricted to guests of Mnemba Island Lodge, the surrounding – and stunning – coral reef can be visited by anyone. It's one of Zanzibar's best **diving** and **snorkelling** sites, with a huge array of fish, including tuna, barracuda, moray eels, reef sharks and lots of colourful smaller species.

The very exclusive 'barefoot luxury'–style **Mnemba Island Lodge** (www.ccafrica.com; per person full board US$1055) is a playground for the rich and famous, and is often rented out in its entirety.

OTHER ISLETS

Just offshore from Zanzibar Town are several tiny islets, many of which are ringed by coral reefs. These include **Nyange**, **Pange** and **Murogo**, which are sandbanks that partially disappear at high tide, and which offer snorkelling and diving (arranged through Stone Town dive operators).

PEMBA

☎ 024 / pop 362,000

For much of its history, Pemba has been overshadowed by Zanzibar, its larger, more visible and more politically powerful neighbour to the south. Although the islands are separated by only about 50km of water, relatively few tourists make their way across the channel for a visit. Those who do, however, are seldom disappointed.

Unlike flat, sandy Zanzibar, Pemba's terrain is hilly, fertile and lushly vegetated. In the days of the Arab traders it was even referred to as 'al Khuthera' or 'the Green Island'. Throughout much of the period when the sultans of Zanzibar held sway over the East African coast, it was Pemba, with its extensive clove plantations and agricultural base, that provided the economic foundation for the archipelago's dominance.

Pemba has also been long renowned for its voodoo and traditional healers, and people come from throughout East Africa seeking cures or to learn the skills of the trade.

Much of the island's coast is lined with mangroves and tidal creeks and lagoons, and Pemba is not a beach destination. However, there are a few good stretches of sand and some idyllic offshore islets. In the surrounding waters, coral reefs, the steeply dropping walls of the Pemba channel and an abundance of fish offer some rewarding diving.

The tourism industry on Pemba is small and low-key, and infrastructure is for the most part fairly basic, although this is slowly but steadily changing, with an ever-increasing number of upmarket hotels and more development on the way. It will be a while, however, before tourism here reaches the proportions it's taken on Zanzibar. Much of Pemba is relatively 'undiscovered' and you'll still have things more or less to yourself, which is a big part of the island's charm. The main requirement for travelling around independently is time, as there's little regular transport off the main routes.

History

Pemba is geologically much older than Zanzibar and is believed to have been settled at an earlier date, although little is known about its original inhabitants. According to legend, the island was once peopled by giants known as the Magenge. More certain is that Pemba's

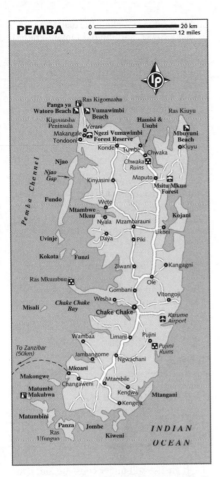

PEMBA

0 — 20 km
0 — 12 miles

Ras Kigomasha
Panga ya Watoro Beach
Kigomasha Peninsula
Vumawimbi Beach
Ras Kiuyu
Makangale
Verani
Ngezi Vumawimbi Forest Reserve
Hamisi & Usubi
Tondooni
Konde
Tumbe
Chwaka
Mbuyuni Beach
Kiuyu
Njao
Chwaka Ruins
Njao Gap
Kinyasini
Maputo
Msitu Mkuu Forest
Fundo
Wete
Pemba Channel
Mtambwe Mkuu
Nyala
Mzambarauni
Kojani
Uvinje
Daya
Piki
Likoni
Kokota
Funzi
Ziwani
Kangagni
Ras Mkumbuu
Gombani
Ole
Vitongoji
Misali
Chake Chake Bay
Wesha
Chake Chake
Karume Airport
Wambaa
Limani
Pujini
To Zanzibar (50km)
Jambangome
Ngwachani
Pujini Ruins
Mkoani
Makongwe
Changaweni
Mtambile
Matumbi Makubwa
Kendwa
Mtangani
Kengeja
Matumbini
Panza
Jombe
Ras Ufungun
Kiweni

INDIAN OCEAN

first inhabitants migrated from the mainland, perhaps as early as several thousand years ago. The Shirazi presence on Pemba is believed to date from at least the 9th or 10th century, with Shirazi ruins at Ras Mkumbuu, northwest of Chake Chake, indicating that settlements were well established on Pemba by that point.

The Portuguese attacked Pemba in the early 16th century and sought to subjugate its inhabitants by ravaging towns and demanding tributes. As a result, many Pembans fled to Mombasa (Kenya). By the late 17th century the Busaidi family of Omani Arabs had taken over the island and driven away the last remaining Portuguese. Before long, however, the Mazrui, a rival group of Omanis based in Mombasa, gained the upper hand

and governed the island until 1822. In 1890 Pemba, together with Zanzibar, became a British protectorate.

Following the Zanzibar revolution in 1964, the archipelago's president, Karume, closed Pemba to foreigners in an effort to contain strong antigovernment sentiment. The island remained closed until the 1980s, although the situation continued to be strained. Tensions peaked during the 1995 elections and relations deteriorated thereafter, with Pembans feeling increasingly marginalised and frustrated. This was hardly surprising, considering that illiteracy rates are as high as 95% in some areas, and roads and other infrastructure are badly neglected. In January 2001 in the wake of the October 2000 elections, tensions again peaked, resulting in at least several dozen deaths and causing many people to flee the island. The 2005 elections proceeded comparatively calmly, and daily life these days is back to normal.

Getting There & Around

Pemba is small, and getting around isn't difficult with a bit of time and patience. A plodding local bus network connects the three main towns and several smaller ones. To reach destinations off these routes, take one of the buses to the nearest intersection, from where you'll either have to walk, rely on sporadic pick-ups, or negotiate an additional fee with the bus driver. There are no regular taxis as there are on Zanzibar or the mainland, but there are plenty of pick-up trucks and 4WDs that you can hire – best arranged in Chake Chake. The main roads connecting Mkoani, Chake Chake and Wete are good tarmac; most secondary routes are unpaved.

Cycling is an excellent way to get around Pemba, although you'll need to bring your own (mountain) bike and spares, unless you're content with one of the single-speed bicycles available locally. Distances are relatively short and roads are only lightly travelled.

CHAKE CHAKE

Lively Chake Chake, set on a ridge overlooking Chake Chake Bay, is Pemba's main town and a good base for diving and for excursions to Misali. Although it has been occupied for centuries, there is little architectural evidence of its past other than the ruins of an 18th-century fort near the hospital, and some ruins at nearby Ras Mkumbuu (p146).

Orientation

Almost everything of interest in Chake Chake is along or within a five-minute walk of the main road.

MAPS

Maps of Chake Chake are a rarity, but the Bureau of Lands & Environment, situated just outside Chake Chake in Machomane, sells a Pemba map. Head north from the town centre for about 1km, take the first right onto the road leading to the Pemba Essential Oil Distillery and continue about 700m to the two-storey white building on the right. The Commission for Lands & Environment in Zanzibar Town (p109) sells topographical maps of Pemba.

Information

INTERNET ACCESS

Adult Computer Centre (Main Rd; per hr Tsh1500; ☼ 8am-8pm) Opposite the telecom building.

MONEY

Speed Cash ATM (Main Rd) Located at the old People's Bank of Zanzibar building on the main road. It currently accepts Visa only, but MasterCard is planned to start soon. This is currently the only place on the island to access cash, so carry some extra, in case it's out of service.

POST

Main post office (Main Rd; ☼ 8am-4pm Mon-Fri, 9am-noon Sat)

TELEPHONE

There are several card telephones around town, including opposite the old fort and at the Telecom building.

Adult Computer Centre (Main Rd; ☼ 8am-8pm) You can place/receive telephone calls here.

TRAVEL AGENCIES & TOUR OPERATORS

Most hotels also organise excursions.

Bachaa Travel & Tours (☎ 0777-423429, 0787-423429; samhamx@yahoo.com; Main Rd) Near ZanAir; ferry ticket bookings and island excursions.

Pemba Island Reasonable Tours & Safaris (☎ 024-245 2023, 0777-435266; Main Rd) Downstairs at Evergreen Hotel; ferry ticket bookings, spice tours and island excursions.

Sights & Activities

Chake Chake's appealingly scruffy main street is lined with small shops and makes for an interesting walk. Apart from the bustling **market**,

buildings of note include the **courthouse**, with its clock tower, and the old Omani-era **fort**, which dates to the 18th century and was probably built on the remains of an earlier structure. Inside is a tiny and dusty **museum** (admission Tsh1000; ☼ 8.30am-4.30pm Mon-Fri, 9am-4pm Sat & Sun), with a few rather forlorn displays of pottery shards and old photos. West of town along the Wesha road are **fairgrounds** (Kiwanja cha Kufurahishia Watoto, or – literally translated – Fairgrounds for Making Children Happy) dating from Pemba's socialist days and now opened only on holidays.

Just out of town to the northeast can be found the sleepy **Pemba Essential Oil Distillery** (admission Tsh1500; ☼ 7.30am-3.30pm Mon-Fri), where you can smell some lemon grass and cloves and see how spices are made into oil. It's best visited in combination with a spice tour, which can be arranged through any of the hotels or the listings under Travel Agencies & Tour Operators (left). About 6km further, reached via an easy bike ride past the oil distillery, are some tiny, baobab-dotted **beaches** near Vitongoji.

Most diving and snorkelling from Chake Chake focuses on Misali island (p146).

Sleeping

Annex of Pemba Island Hotel (☎ 024-245 2215; s/d/tw without bathroom US$10/20/30) Related to Pemba Island Hotel and nearby – in a multi-storey building about 100m down the road to the market in a rather noisier location – rooms here are clean and basic.

Pemba Evergreen Hotel (☎ 024-245 3326; pemba evergreen@hotmail.com; Main Rd; s/d/tw US$20/25/35) A new high-rise still under construction. Four rooms – with TV, window screens (though no mosquito nets) and fan, and a couple with balcony – are finished now, with more planned. Upstairs is the Top Green restaurant, which hadn't yet gotten into full swing when we passed by. It's just up from Le Tavern.

Le Tavern (☎ 024-245 2660; Main Rd; s/d with air-con US$25/30, d without bathroom US$15; ✷) This slightly tatty establishment, opposite the Old Mission Lodge, has clean-ish, no-frills rooms with mosquito nets and is a reasonable budget choice. Included in the price is an early morning wake-up call from the mosque next door.

Pemba Island Hotel (☎ 024-245 2215; pembaisland @yahoo.com; Wesha Rd; s/d/tw US$35/45/55; ✷) Small, clean rooms with mosquito nets, TV, mini-fridge and hot water, plus a rooftop terrace

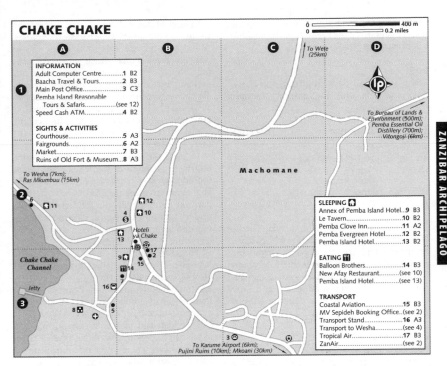

CHAKE CHAKE

0 ————— 400 m
0 ————— 0.2 miles

INFORMATION
Adult Computer Centre............1 B2
Baacha Travel & Tours............2 B3
Main Post Office....................3 C3
Pemba Island Reasonable
 Tours & Safaris...............(see 12)
Speed Cash ATM...................4 B2

SIGHTS & ACTIVITIES
Courthouse..........................5 A3
Fairgrounds..........................6 A2
Market................................7 B3
Ruins of Old Fort & Museum...8 A3

SLEEPING 🛏
Annex of Pemba Island Hotel..9 B3
Le Tavern............................10 B2
Pemba Clove Inn...................11 A2
Pemba Evergreen Hotel.........12 B2
Pemba Island Hotel...............13 B2

EATING 🍴
Balloon Brothers....................14 B3
New Afay Restaurant............(see 10)
Pemba Island Hotel.............(see 13)

TRANSPORT
Coastal Aviation....................15 B3
MV Sepideh Booking Office..(see 2)
Transport Stand.....................16 A3
Transport to Wesha..............(see 4)
Tropical Air..........................17 B3
ZanAir..............................(see 2)

To Wete (25km)

To Bureau of Lands & Environment (500m); Pemba Essential Oil Distillery (700m); Vitongoji (6km)

To Wesha (7km); Ras Mkumbuu (15km)

Machomane

Chake Chake Channel

Jetty

Hoteli ya Chake

To Karume Airport (6km); Pujini Ruins (10km); Mkoani (30km)

ZANZIBAR ARCHIPELAGO

restaurant and a 10% discount for longer stays. It's about 100m downhill from the main junction.

Pemba Clove Inn (☎ 024-245 2794/5; pembacloveinn@zanzinet.com; Wesha Rd; s/d from US$90/120) A new place adjoining the Social Security Administration buildings, about 700m down from the main junction. Rooms are short on ambience, but clean, spacious and well equipped. It's currently the most upmarket accommodation in town.

Eating

Balloon Brothers (Market Rd; snacks & meals from Tsh500) A local haunt with snacks and light meals just up from the market.

New Afay Restaurant (top fl, Le Tavern, Main Rd; meals Tsh2000; ⏱ lunch & dinner) A popular local option with good rice and fish and other standard fare.

Pemba Island Hotel (☎ 024-245 2215; pembaisland@yahoo.com; Wesha Rd; meals Tsh5000) This place has a good rooftop restaurant.

There's also a lively night market in the town centre, where you can get grilled *pweza* (octopus), *maandazi* (doughnuts) and other

local delicacies at rock-bottom prices, and experience a slice of Pemban life. Most shops sell only basic supplies, but there are a few that have more exotic items, such as tinned cheese and peanut butter.

Getting There & Away
AIR
Both **ZanAir** (☎ 024-245 2990, 0777-431143; Main Rd), on the main road uphill from the main post office, and **Coastal Aviation** (☎ 024-245 2162, 0777-418343), diagonally opposite ZanAir, fly daily between Chake Chake and Zanzibar Town (US$80), with direct connections on to Dar es Salaam (US$100). Coastal also goes daily between Pemba and Tanga (US$60).

Tropical Air (☎ 0777-859996; Main Rd) also flies between Dar es Salaam, Zanzibar and Pemba during the high season. Its office is opposite the Adult Computer Centre.

BOAT
See p148 for ferry schedules between Zanzibar and Mkoani (from where you'll need to take a bus or *dalla-dalla* up to Chake Chake). Tickets for the MS *Sepideh* and *Sea Express* ferries are

best arranged through hotels or one of the travel agencies (p144). The *Sepideh* also has a **booking office** (Main Rd) near ZanAir.

BUS

Main routes (all departing from the transport stand behind the market) include the following:

Route No	Destination	Price (Tsh)
603	Mkoani	Tsh1000
306	Wete via the 'old' road	Tsh1200
334	Wete via the 'new' (eastern) road	Tsh1000
335	Konde	Tsh1500
305	Wesha	Tsh500

There's a shuttle bus from Chake Chake (Tsh1000) to Mkoani connecting with *Sepideh* departures and arrivals, departing from the main road in front of Evergreen Hotel about two hours before the *Sepideh's* scheduled departure time. Be sure to book a seat on the bus when buying your boat ticket, as the bus gets very crowded.

Getting Around
TO/FROM THE AIRPORT

Karume airport, about 6km east of town, is Pemba's only airfield. There's no regular bus service to/from the airport, but at least one vehicle meets incoming flights (Tsh8000 to central Chake Chake).

CAR & MOTORCYCLE

Cars and motorbikes can be hired in Chake Chake through hotels and travel agencies, or by negotiating with one of the cars marked with 'Gari ya Abiria' parked at the stand in front of the currently closed Hoteli ya Chake. Prices are fairly standard – US$20 between Mkoani and Chake Chake; US$25 one way between Chake Chake and Wete; and US$35 return between Chake Chake and Ras Kigomasha, including stops at Vumawimbi beach and Ngezi.

AROUND CHAKE CHAKE
Misali

This little patch of paradise lies offshore from Chake Chake, surrounded by crystal waters and stunning coral reefs. Nesting turtles and breeding sea birds favour the beaches on its western side, which have been set aside just for them. Also on the side are some of the best reefs. On the northeast of the island is **Mbuyuni beach**,

with fine, white sands and a small visitors centre, and to the southeast are some mangroves. About a 10-minute walk south of the visitors centre is **Bendera cave**, which is believed to be inhabited by the spirits of ancestors and is used by Pembans from the main island for rituals. To the west are the larger **Mpapaini caves**. Thanks to Misali's lack of fresh water, development of permanent settlements has been limited, but the island is in active use by local fishers, and there are several fishing camps.

In 1998 the island and surrounding coral reef were gazetted as the **Misali Island Marine Conservation Area** (adult/student US$5/3), with the goal of maintaining the island's ecosystems in harmony with usage by local fishers. There are underwater and terrestrial nature trails, and you can arrange guides at the visitors centre. Camping is not permitted.

To get to the island on your own, head to Wesha, northwest of Chake Chake, via bus 305 (Tsh500), which departs from Chake Chake several times daily from in front of the old People's Bank of Zanzibar building. Alternatively, hiring a car costs about Tsh5000. Once in Wesha, you can negotiate with local boat owners to take you to Misali. Expect to pay about Tsh35,000 per person return. There's no food or drink on the island, so bring whatever you'll need with you. It's easier, and only slightly more expensive, to arrange Misali excursions through hotels or travel agencies in Chake Chake, through Sharook Guest House in Wete, or through Jondeni Guest House in Mkoani.

Ras Mkumbuu

Ras Mkumbuu is the long, thin strip of land jutting into the sea northwest of Chake Chake. At its tip are the **ruins** of a settlement known in ancient times as Qanbalu, which is thought to have risen to prominence in the early 10th century, when it may have been one of the major settlements along the East African coast. The main ruins, consisting of a mosque and some tombs and houses, are estimated to date from around the 14th century, and are now quite overgrown.

The best way to visit the area (which is also referred to by locals as Ndagoni, the name of the nearest village, or Makutani) is by boat from Chake Chake, although this can be expensive. If you go via road, you'll have at least an hour's walk at the end; one section of the path often becomes submerged at high tide, so plan accordingly.

COMMUNITY TOURISM SPOTLIGHT: MISALI

When you see Misali, you may wonder why such a paradisical island hasn't been snatched up by developers. The answer in part is that it has been gazetted as a conservation area in order to protect it from this very scenario. However, this conservation status is fragile, and given the right (or wrong) set of factors, it could be reversed.

The idea of Misali as the site of a luxury lodge might be appealing to some. However, there is another side to the picture – namely, the equity issue involved when traditional resource users (ie the indigenous population) are excluded from an area in the name of conservation. The **Misali Island Conservation Project** seeks to empower locals to manage their own natural resources, thereby ensuring promotion of both environmental conservation and also the wellbeing of the at least 8000 people who depend on the island and its waters for their sustenance. An additional benefit of this approach is that the conservation area remains accessible to tourists from various socioeconomic and national backgrounds. Contrast this with a scenario that would exclude not only local fishers, but also any tourist unable to pay several hundred dollars a night to experience their own private and (now) deserted tropical isle.

By visiting Misali you are making an important contribution to a model of ecological conservation that supports community development and 'egalitarian' ecotourism. The more successful the Misali Island Conservation Area is financially, the stronger the argument for resisting developers' attempts to wrest control from the fishers, and the greater the likelihood that it will remain available both to traditional local users and the average tourist, rather than becoming the fenced-off domain of a wealthy few.

AROUND PEMBA

Pemba offers opportunities for some enjoyable and very laid-back exploring. The following places are covered roughly south to north.

KIWENI

Tranquil Kiweni, marked as Shamiani or Shamiani island on some maps, is just off Pemba's southeastern coast. It's a remote backwater area, neglected by the government and overlooked by most visitors, where little seems to have changed for decades. With its undisturbed stretches of sand and quiet waterways, it's also one of the island's more scenic and alluring corners, as well as home to five of Pemba's six endemic bird species and a nesting ground for some sea-turtle colonies. Offshore is some good **snorkelling**.

Near Kiweni, in the area around Kengeja (as well as other spots on Pemba), you'll occasionally come across light-hearted '**bull fights**', said to date back to the days of Portuguese influence on the island. At the moment, there's nowhere around Kiweni to stay. However, the small, midrange **Pemba Lodge** (www.pembalodge.com), under the same management as Mnarani Beach Cottages in Nungwi (p131), is planned to open soon – check its website for an update.

To get here, catch any bus running along the Mkoani–Chake Chake road to Mtambile junction. From Mtambile, you can find pickups or other transport to Kengeja, from where you'll have to walk a few kilometres to the water and then take a boat over to Kiweni (about Tsh2000).

MKOANI & AROUND

Although it's Pemba's major port, Mkoani has managed to fight off all attempts at development and remains a very small and rather boring town. However, its good budget guesthouse goes a long way to redeeming it, and it makes a convenient and recommended base for exploring the sleepy and often overlooked but beautiful southern parts of the island.

Information

For medical emergencies, try the Chinese-run government hospital, although standards leave much to be desired.

The immigration officer usually meets all boat arrivals. Otherwise, if you're coming from anywhere other than Zanzibar, you'll need to go to the immigration office and get stamped in. It's 500m up the main road from the port in a small brown building with a flag.

Sleeping & Eating

IN MKOANI

Jondeni Guest House (☎ 024-245 6042; jondeniguest
@hotmail.com; dm/s/d US$10/20/30, s/d with hot water
US$25/35, without bathroom US$15/25) This friendly
and recommended backpackers' guesthouse,
set up on a hill overlooking the sea in the distance has simple but spotless rooms with mosquito nets, breezes and good meals (Tsh6000).
Staff have lots of information on Pemba, and
can help you arrange snorkelling and excursions, including to Matumbini lighthouse (on
Matumbi Makubwa island), 'Emerald Bay' – a
large, pristine sandbank about 8km away and
good for swimming and snorkelling – and
Ras Ufunguo, with snorkelling around an
old wreck between about October and March
(when it's not too windy). Snorkelling trips
to Misali can also be organised (US$35 per
person). To get here, head left when exiting
the port and walk about 700m up to the top
of the hill.

Apart from Jondeni Guest House, which
has Mkoani's best cuisine, it can be difficult
to find meals, although there is street food
nightly by the port.

OUTSIDE MKOANI

Misale Matumbawe (☎ 024-223 6315; www.misale
matumbawe.com; s/d half board US$200/300) A low-
key place near Jambangome village, about
midway between Mkoani and Wambaa. It's
under the same management as Baobab Beach
Bungalows in Nungwi and accommodation
is of a similar standard, in straightforward,
pleasant beachside bungalows with Zanzibari
beds, mosquito nets and small verandas.
There's also a restaurant, and a full range of
excursions can be organised.

Getting There & Away

BOAT

The MS *Sepideh* sails in theory on Monday
and Wednesday in both directions between
Dar es Salaam and Pemba's Mkoani port via
Zanzibar, departing from Dar es Salaam at
7.30am and Zanzibar around 10am, reaching
Pemba about midday. In the other direction,
the boat departs from Pemba at 1pm, reaching Zanzibar at 3.30pm and then continues
to Dar es Salaam at 4pm. The *Sepideh* is good
when it runs, but service is very sporadic. The
fare is US$40/55 in economy class between
Pemba and Zanzibar/Dar es Salaam, including port tax.

The smaller and less comfortable (especially on rough seas, when it bounces around
like a cork) *Sea Express* does the Pemba
(Mkoani)–Zanzibar–Dar es Salaam route
on Thursday and Saturday, departing from
Dar at 7.30am, Zanzibar at 10am, Pemba at
12.30pm and Zanzibar (back to Dar) at 4pm.
Prices are US$45/60 in economy class between
Pemba and Zanzibar/Dar es Salaam, including port tax.

All boats have their main booking offices
at the port in Mkoani. You can also arrange
tickets through travel agencies in Chake
Chake, and with Sharook Guest House or
travel agents in Wete.

BUS

Bus 603 runs throughout the day between
Mkoani and Chake Chake (Tsh1000, two
hours). The bus station in Mkoani is about
200m east of the port, up the hill and just
off the main road. For Wete, you'll need to
change vehicles in Chake Chake.

WAMBAA

The main reason to come to Wambaa is to
luxuriate in Pemba's only five-star resort.

The exclusive **Fundu Lagoon Resort** (☎ 0774-
438668; www.fundulagoon.com; s/d full board from US$475
/670; ☽ mid-Jun–mid-Apr) is set on a low hillside
overlooking the sea, with luxurious bungalows tucked away amid the vegetation and
an excess of amenities. Particularly notable
are its bar, set over the water on a long jetty,
and its cuisine. In addition to the usual excursions, there's a good dive operator here,
primarily operating around Misali and off
Pemba's southern tip. It's also possible to
arrange private yacht charters and deep-sea
sport fishing.

PUJINI RUINS

About 10km southeast of Chake Chake at
Pujini are the overgrown and atmospheric
ruins of a town dating from about the
14th century and perhaps earlier. It was
here that the infamous Mohammed bin
Abdul Rahman, who ruled Pemba around
the 15th century, prior to the arrival of the
Portuguese, had his seat. Locally, Rahman is
known as Mkame Ndume (Milker of Men)
and for Pembans, his name is synonymous
with cruelty due to the harsh punishments
he meted out to his people. The main area
of interest is framed by what were once the

PEMBA PECULIARITIES

Unlike Zanzibar, where tourist infrastructure is well developed, Pemba is very much a backwater once away from its three main towns. It's also highly picturesque. *Kofia*-clad men ride ageing Chinese-made single-speed bicycles and zebu-drawn carts trundle along, laden with palms for making the *makuti* (thatch) roofing that is interspersed in villages with corrugated tin roofing. Square houses with strong wooden carved doors line the roadsides, and emerald-green rice fields spread out into the distance. Both in its main towns and in the countryside, Pemba offers an authentic experience that's increasingly difficult to find in other parts of the archipelago. A few island-specific tips:

■ Away from the pricier hotels, allow plenty of time for getting around and for meals. At budget places, you'll usually need to put in an order for a meal a few hours in advance. Apart from guesthouses, the main places to eat are at the island's lively night markets. These are found in all the major towns, but are best in Chake Chake. They sell *mishikaki* (skewered meat), *maandazi* (doughnuts), grilled *pweza* (octopus) and other delicacies. Wete has the best selection of vegetables from the mainland.

■ Other than local brews (the most common of which is *nazi*, a fermented coconut wine), there's little alcohol available on the island once away from the hotels. If you try the *nazi*, be sure it's fresh (made within the past 24 hours), otherwise it goes bad.

■ Chake Chake is the only town with banking facilities, so come prepared with enough cash (a mix of US dollars and Tanzanian shillings is best).

■ Most businesses operate from 8am to 4pm, and almost everywhere shuts down for about half an hour for prayers from about 4pm or 4.30pm, and at midday on Friday.

ramparts surrounding Rahman's palace, although several other ruins, including those of a mosque, have been found nearby. While the ramparts are in many places little more than a mound of earth, they show the scale of the residence, and, with some imagination, give an indication of Pujini's power in its heyday.

There's no regular public transport to Pujini. The best way to get here is by bicycle, following the road from Chake Chake southeast past farm plots, small villages and mangroves. Car hire from Chake Chake costs about Tsh12,000 return.

WETE

The lively port and market town of Wete makes an agreeable base from which to explore northern Pemba. The port here is Pemba's second largest after Mkoani, and serves as the export channel for much of the island's clove crop. At the centre of Wete life is the market, which is just off the main road at the eastern end of town.

Information

There's internet access at the Umati office just down from Sharook Guest House. The best place for arranging excursions is

Sharook Guest House, which can also help with booking ferry tickets.

Bachaa Travel & Tours (☎ 0784-423429, 0777-423429; samhamx@yahoo.com) On the main road, and poorly signed; does bookings for *Sea Express* and ZanAir.

Raha Tours & Travel (☎ 024-245 4228) Just off the main road near the post office. Also does MV *Sepideh* bookings.

Sleeping

Wete has a small collection of good budget guesthouses.

Sharook Guest House (☎ 024-245 4386, 0777-431012; sharookguest@yahoo.com; r US$20, without bathroom US$15) There's more competition these days in Wete and rooms may be more modern elsewhere, but for service and a friendly welcome, you can't beat this small guesthouse, just off the main road at the western end of town. Rooms in a private house are basic but clean, all have mosquito net and fan, and there's satellite TV in the living room. The owner is very knowledgeable about Wete and the surrounding area, and is the best contact for organising excursions to Vumawimbi beach, Ngezi Forest, Misali and elsewhere, making ferry bookings, bicycle or motorbike rentals and the like. If all this doesn't persuade you to stay here, you get a free breakfast if you arrive at the guesthouse

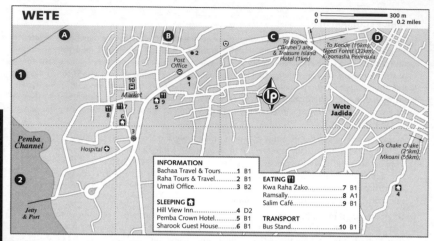

in the morning (lunch and dinner also available). Transfers from the Mkoani port or the airport can be arranged. The same owner is building a new guesthouse near the water that isn't quite finished yet, but it's attractively located and looks very promising – ask for an update when you arrive.

Hill View Inn (☎ 0784-344359; binahmed75@hotmail.com; r per person US$20, without bathroom US$15) A small, friendly establishment with no-frills, clean rooms – the ones upstairs, some with breezes and views to the water in the distance, are nicer. Meals and hot water are available on request. It's at the entrance to town, about two blocks in from the main road, next to a set of apartment blocks in Wete Jadida ('New Wete').

Pemba Crown Hotel (☎ 024-245 4191; www .pembacrown.com; Main Rd; s/d US$20/30; 🔌) Spotless good-value rooms – all with fan and air-con – in a low high-rise diagonally opposite the market. There's no food.

Treasure Island Hotel (☎ 024-245 4171, 0777-454976; treasurehotel@yahoo.co.uk; Gando Rd; s/d US$20/30) This large, new high-rise in the Bopwe (or 'Brunei') area about 2km from the town centre has bland but spacious and comfortable rooms that are quite good value as long as prices stay as they are. There's also a rooftop terrace, and a restaurant is planned.

Eating

The main place to eat in town (order meals ahead) is **Sharook Guest House** (☎ 024-245 4386, 0777-431012; lunch/dinner Tsh4000). Otherwise, try

Ramsally (meals from Tsh500), a local haunt near the market, or **Kwa Raha Zako** (meals Tsh500), diagonally opposite. The quite basic-looking **Salim Café** (meals from Tsh500; Main Rd) just down from Pemba Crown Hotel, has also been recommended for inexpensive local fare.

Getting There & Away
BOAT

The unsteady *Mudasi* – primarily a cargo ship that also takes passengers – sails three times weekly between Wete and Tanga, departing from Wete at 8am on Friday, Saturday and Sunday (three to five hours), and Tanga at 3pm on Saturday, Sunday and Monday.

Wete is also the best place on Pemba to look for a dhow to the mainland, although captains are often unwilling to take foreigners. Inquire at the Wete port; passage costs about Tsh5000 between Wete and Tanga. There are also sporadic dhows between Wete and Mombasa. See also the boxed text, p357.

BUS

A tarmac road (the 'old' road) connects Wete with Chake Chake via Ziwani, winding its way past hills, villages and lots of banana trees en route. East of here, the 'new' road, also tarmac, connects Wete with Chake Chake via Ole. The main bus routes are on bus 306 (Wete to Chake Chake via the 'old' road), bus 334 (Wete to Chake Chake via the 'new' road) and bus 324 (Wete to Konde).

There's also a shuttle bus from Wete to Mkoani (Tsh2500) connecting with MV

Sepideh departures and arrivals, departing from Wete about three hours before the *Sepideh's* scheduled departure time. The main pick-up point is at Raha Tours & Travel; pick-ups at Sharook Guest House can also be arranged.

TUMBE

The large village of Tumbe lies on a sandy cove fringed at each end by dense stands of mangroves. It's the site of Pemba's largest **fish market**, and if you're in the area, it's well worth a stop, especially in the mornings when the catch of the day is brought in and the beach bustles with activity. Just offshore are the two small islands of **Hamisi** and **Usubi**.

About 2km southeast from Tumbe at Chwaka are some overgrown **ruins**, including those of a mosque, an 18th-century fort and some tombs. There are several sites, the best of which is known as the Haruni site, marked by a tiny signpost to the east of the main road. It's named after Harun, who was the son of Mkame Ndume (p148) and, according to local tradition, just as cruel as his father.

There's no accommodation in Tumbe. To get here, take bus 335 and ask the driver to drop you at the junction, from where it's an easy walk.

NGEZI

The small, dense and in parts wonderfully damp and lush forest at Ngezi is part of the much larger natural forest that once covered wide swathes of Pemba. It is notable in that it resembles the highland rainforests of East Africa more than the lowland forests found on Zanzibar. Ngezi is also notable as the home of *Pteropus voeltzkowi*, or the Pemba flying fox, a bat unique to the island and Pemba's only fully endemic mammalian species. The forest is now part of the protected **Ngezi Vumawimbi Forest Reserve** (admission Tsh4000; ☼ 8am–4pm), with a short nature trail that winds its way beneath the shady forest canopy. If you want to see Scops owls and other nocturnal birds, it's possible to arrange evening tours in advance with the caretaker.

Ngezi is along the main road between Konde and Tondooni, which in this section becomes narrow and winding and edged with dense vegetation. To get here via public transport, take the bus to Konde, from where it's a 3km to 4km walk. Bus drivers are sometimes willing to drop you at the information centre

for an additional Tsh1000 to Tsh2000. The best idea is to combine Ngezi with a visit to Vumawimbi beach (below). Despite what the Ngezi caretaker may tell you, you don't need to pay the forest entry fee if you're just passing through en route to the beach.

KIGOMASHA PENINSULA

The main reason to come to the Kigomasha peninsula in Pemba's northwestern corner is to relax on the beautiful, palm- and forest-fringed **Vumawimbi beach** on the peninsula's eastern side, or on **Verani beach** to the west. Until recently, hardly anyone made it up this way, but this is changing fast, with several new hotel developments under way. For now, though, if you want to visit Vumawimbi for the day, bring whatever food and drink you'll need with you.

The **Ras Kigomasha lighthouse** is an easy walk from Manta Reef Lodge. Built in 1904, together with the lighthouse on Chumbe Island, it's still actively maintained by its keeper. Climb up to the top for wonderful views (for a Tsh2000 donation to the lighthouse keeper).

On the northwestern end of the Kigomasha peninsula are Panga ya Watoro Beach, and the relaxing and superbly situated **Manta Reef Lodge** (☎ 0777-423930, in Kenya 41-471771; www.mantareeflodge .com; s/d full board US$150/220; ☼ mid-Jun–mid-Apr), on a breezy escarpment with spectacular views over the ocean. Accommodation is in rustic but comfortable and well-appointed and recently renovated sea-facing cabins – in Europe it would rank as a very nice three-star place – and staff can help you organise diving, including live-aboard arrangements, as well as sea kayaking and fishing charters. There's a bar-restaurant overlooking the water, a pool was being built when we passed by and meanwhile there's swimming at high tide on the beach below. Pick-ups can be arranged with the lodge. Otherwise, there's usually at least one pick-up daily in the morning from Konde to Makangale village, about 4km or 5km south of Manta Reef, from where you'll need to walk or pay the driver extra to bring you all the way up.

Further down to the southwest near Tondooni is the low-key **Verani Beach Hotel** (☎ 0773-321254, 0773-355685, 0777-414408; www.vera nibeach.com; camping per person with own/rented tent US$5/10, s/d bungalows US$25/40), which is not yet complete. For now, it has two no-frills stone-

ZANZIBAR ARCHIPELAGO

and-thatch bungalows, plus a few tents. Meals can be arranged, as can excursions, including a multiday dhow trip over to Saadani National Park on the mainland.

The **Kervan Saray Beach Lodge** (☎ satellite 88-21652-073106; www.kervansaraybeach.com; dm about US$40, bungalows per person about US$120) – an unpretentious and rustic but comfortable diver-oriented lodge and the new base for the well-established Swahili Divers (www .swahilidivers.com) – is set to open soon on the beach near Makangale village, just past Ngezi Forest and about 5km south of Manta Reef Lodge. Accommodation is in either a six-bed divers' bunk dorm or in six double-room, en suite, stone-and-thatch, high-roof bungalows, and there's a restaurant serving daily set menus (lunch/dinner about US$15/30). There's generator-supplied power available nightly for charging cameras and the like, and a satellite internet connection (per hour US$13). Diving, including PADI open-water instruction, is the main activity (per dive US$75 including equipment), but there's also a full range of other excursions around the island, including sunset cruises, overnight sails to Misali island and village walks. Pickups can be arranged from Chake Chake (per vehicle US$70) or Mkoani (US$100), or you

can take a *dalla-dalla* to Konde, from where pick-ups cost US$20.

Other than hiring a vehicle in Chake Chake, the best way to get to all of these places is on bicycle from Konde. The road is sealed until the Ngezi Forest, then dirt, and thereafter loose sand. Alternatively, try to negotiate a lift with one of the Konde bus drivers, although you'll then need to make arrangements for your return. Hitching is usually slow going, as there's little vehicle traffic. See p360 for more information on hitching.

OFFSHORE ISLANDS
There are dozens of tiny islets dotted along Pemba's coastline. Most have nothing on them, but they make enjoyable excursions. If you have any ideas of camping, keep in mind that many of the islands off Pemba's western coast are badly rat infested. Some good destinations include **Hamisi** and **Usubi** (tiny fishing islands offshore from Tumbe village), **Mtambwe Mkuu** (actually a peninsula southwest of Wete) and the large **Kojani** in the northeast, with areas of protected forest. **Ras Kiuyu**, Pemba's far northeastern corner, is also well worth exploring, with forest, villages and beaches, including **Mbuyuni beach**, with some interesting water-sculpted rocks.

Northeastern Tanzania

For at least 2000 years, northeastern Tanzania has been attracting visitors. In the 1st century AD, the author of the mariners' chronicle *Periplus of the Erythraean Sea* mentions the existence of the trading outpost of Rhapta, which is thought to have possibly been somewhere around present-day Pangani. Several centuries later, a string of settlements sprang up along the coast with links to ports in Arabia and the Orient. Today, this long history, plus easy access and lack of crowds, make the northeast's long, tropical, ruin-studded coastline and its lush, mountainous inland areas an appealing region to explore.

Along the coast, visit the medieval, moss-covered ruins at Kaole and Tongoni, step back to the days of Livingstone in Bagamoyo, relax on long stretches of palm-fringed sand around Pangani, or enjoy beach and bush at Saadani, Tanzania's only seaside national park. Inland, hike along shaded forest footpaths around Lushoto while following the cycle of bustling, colourful market days of the local Sambaa people, head to Same and learn about the intriguing burial rituals of the neighbouring Pare, or experience the wild East African bush from the comfort of a wonderful upmarket camp in the seldom-visited Mkomazi Game Reserve.

Most of the region is within an easy half-day's drive or bus ride from both Dar es Salaam and Arusha, and there are good connections between many places in the region and Zanzibar. Main roads are in good to reasonable condition, there's a reasonably wide range of accommodation, and the local transport network reaches many areas of interest.

NORTHEASTERN TANZANIA

HIGHLIGHTS

- Savouring sun and safari at **Saadani National Park** (p158), Tanzania's only coastal national park

- Lazing in a hammock on the beaches around **Pangani** (p160)

- Meandering along winding footpaths in the cool and scenic **Usambara Mountains** (p168)

- Stepping back into history in the former colonial capital of **Bagamoyo** (p154)

- Getting a true bush experience from the comfort of a wonderful upmarket camp in **Mkomazi Game Reserve** (p179)

★ Mkomazi Game Reserve

★ Usambara Mountains

★ Pangani

Saadani National Park ★

★ Bagamoyo

National Parks & Reserves

The northeast is home to Saadani National Park (p158), one of Tanzania's newest national parks and the only one on the coast. Northwest of here, on the Kenya border, is the seldom-visited Mkomazi Game Reserve (p179), soon to be gazetted as a national park and known for its pioneering black rhino conservation project.

Getting There & Around

There are commercial flights to Tanga and, sometimes, to Saadani, and several airstrips for charter flights around Pangani. Otherwise, you'll need to rely on the road network. The major routes are the tarmac roads connecting Dar es Salaam with Tanga and with Arusha. Secondary routes are mostly unpaved but in reasonable condition, except for along the coast, where things are still rough in spots (4WD required). There's no ferry over the Wami River, so it's not yet possible to drive from Dar es Salaam up the coast to Tanga.

Large buses connect towns along the main highways; elsewhere you'll need to rely primarily on *dalla-dallas* (minibuses).

BAGAMOYO

☎ 023

Strolling through Bagamoyo's narrow unpaved streets or sitting at the port watching dhows load up takes you back in time to the early and mid-19th century when the town was one of the most important settlements along the East African coast and the terminus of the trade caravan route linking Lake Tanganyika with the sea. Slaves, ivory, salt and copra were unloaded before being shipped to Zanzibar and elsewhere, and many European explorers, including Richard Burton, Henry Morton Stanley and David Livingstone, began and ended their trips here. In 1868, French missionaries established Freedom Village at Bagamoyo as a shelter for ransomed slaves, and for the remainder of the century the town served as an important way station for missionaries travelling from Zanzibar to the country's interior.

From 1887 to 1891, Bagamoyo was the capital of German East Africa, and in 1888 it was at the centre of the Abushiri revolt (p161), the first major uprising against the colonial government. In 1891 the capital was transferred to Dar es Salaam, sending Bagamoyo into a slow decline from which it has yet to recover. Bagamoyo's unhurried pace, long history and sleepy charm make it an agreeable day or weekend excursion from Dar es Salaam. Once you've had enough of historical explorations, head to the southeastern edge of town, where there are some seaweed-strewn beaches with swimming at high tide.

Information

There's a card phone at the Telecom building at the town entrance. The National Microfinance Bank, next door, changes cash. There's **internet access** (per hr Tsh1000; ⏰ 8.30am-5pm) at the office of the **Bagamoyo Institute of Tourism** (☎ 0784-869652, 0752-712001; bagamoyo2007 @gmail.com; ⏰ 8.30am-5pm Mon-Fri, to 2pm Sat) which can also help with guides and excursions, including town tours (per person per hour US$15), museum tours (per person per half hour US$5) and visits to the Kaole ruins (per person per hour US$20).

Dangers & Annoyances

Bagamoyo has a small coterie of aggressive touts and, at times, a bit of a hard edge. Take the usual precautions, avoid isolated stretches of beach, especially between town and the Kaole ruins, and don't bring valuables with you to the beach. At night, it's best to walk in a group, both in town and along the road to the beachside hotels, and not to carry valuables.

Sights & Activities

BAGAMOYO TOWN

With its cobwebbed portals, crumbling German-era colonial buildings and small alleyways where the sounds of children playing echo together with the footsteps of history, **central Bagamoyo**, or *Mji Mkongwe* (Stone Town) as it's known locally, is well worth a leisurely stroll. The most interesting area is along Ocean Rd. Here, among other buildings, you'll find the imposing remains of the old **German boma** (colonial-era administrative offices), built in 1897; a **school**, which dates to the late 19th century and was the first multiracial school in what is now Tanzania; and **Liku House**, which served as the German administrative headquarters until the capital was moved to Dar es Salaam. Directly on the beach is the **German Customs House** (1895) and Bagamoyo's **port**, where you can while away the time watching boat builders at work. The port is also home to a busy **fish market** (on the site of the old slave market), which has lively

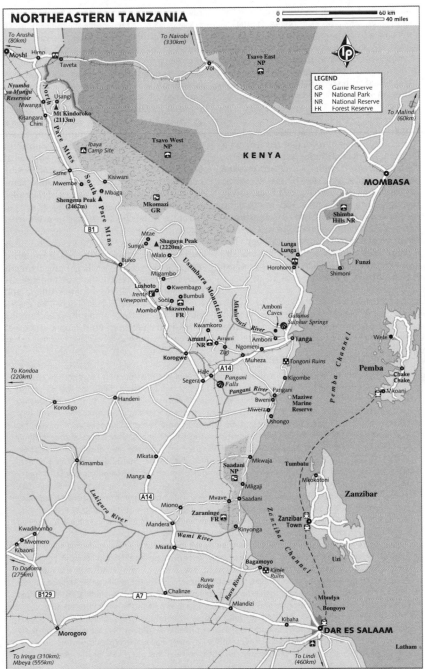

NORTHEASTERN TANZANIA

0 ━━━ 60 km
0 ━━━ 40 miles

LEGEND
GR   Game Reserve
NP   National Park
NR   National Reserve
FR   Forest Reserve

To Arusha (80km)
To Nairobi (330km)
Tsavo East NP
Vol
Moshi
Himo
Taveta
Nyumba ya Mungu Reservoir
Mwanga
Usangi
Mt Kindoroko (2113m)
Kisangara Chini
North Pare Mtns
Ibaya Camp Site
Tsavo West NP
KENYA
To Malindi (60km)
Same
Mwembe
Kisiwani
South Pare Mtns
Mbaga
Shengena Peak (2462m)
Mkomazi GR
MOMBASA
Shimba Hills NR
B1
Mtae
Shagayu Peak (2220m)
Sunga
Mlalo
Buiko
Migambo
Usambara Mountains
Lunga Lunga
Funzi
Horohoro
Shimoni
Lushoto
Irente Viewpoint
Kwembago
Soni
Bumbuli
Mombo
Mazumbai FR
Kwamkoro
Mkuzumuzi River
Amboni Caves
Galanos Sulphur Springs
To Kondoa (220km)
Amani NR
Amani
Zigi
Ngomeni
Amboni
Tanga
Wete
Korogwe
Hale
A14
Muheza
Tongoni Ruins
Pemba
Chake Chake
Mkoani
Segera
Pangani Falls
Pangani River
Kigombe
Pemba Channel
Handeni
Korodigo
Pangani
Bweni
Mwera
Maziwe Marine Reserve
Kimamba
Mkata
Manga
A14
Miono
Mvave
Mandera
Zaraninge FR
Saadani NP
Mkwaja
Mligaji
Saadani
Tumbatu
Mkokotoni
Zanzibar
Lukigura River
Kinyonga
Ushongo
Kwadihombo
Mvomero
Kibaoni
To Dodoma (275km)
Msata
Wami River
Zanzibar Town
Uzi
Zanzibar Channel
B129
A7
Chalinze
Ruvu Bridge
Ruvu River
Bagamoyo
Kaole Ruins
Mbudya
Bongoyo
Mlandizi
Mbweni
Morogoro
Kibaha
Kibaha
DAR ES SALAAM
To Iringa (310km); Mbeya (555km)
To Lindi (460km)
Latham

auctions most afternoons. While you're at the fish market, take a break at one of the makeshift tables by the food vendors and enjoy a peeled orange and some grilled fish or *ugali* (a staple made from maize or cassava flour, or both). Northwest of here are several small streets lined with **carved doors** similar to those found on Zanzibar and elsewhere along the Swahili coast.

HOLY GHOST CATHOLIC MISSION

About 2km north of town and reached via a long mango-shaded avenue is the Holy Ghost Catholic Mission, with its excellent **museum** (☎ 023-244 0010; adult/student Tsh1500/500, camera/video Tsh1000/5000; ⏰ 10am-5pm) – one of Bagamoyo's highlights and an essential stop. In the same compound is the chapel where Livingstone's body was laid before being taken to Zanzibar Town en route to Westminster Abbey. The mission itself dates from the 1868 establishment of Freedom Village and is the oldest in Tanzania.

KAOLE RUINS

Just south of Bagamoyo time slides several centuries further into the past at the **Kaole**

ruins (adult/student Tsh1500/500; ⏰ 8am-4pm Mon-Fri, to 5pm Sat & Sun). At its centre are the remains of a 13th-century mosque, which is one of the oldest in mainland Tanzania and also one of the oldest in East Africa. It was built in the days when the Sultan of Kilwa held sway over coastal trade, and long before Bagamoyo had assumed any significance. Nearby is a second mosque dating to the 15th century, as well as about 22 graves, many of which go back to the same period. Among the graves are several Shirazi pillar-style tombs reminiscent of those at Tongoni (p167), but in somewhat better condition, and a small museum housing Chinese pottery fragments and other remnants found in the area. Just east of the ruins, past a dense stand of mangroves, is the old harbour, now silted, that was in use during Kaole's heyday.

The most direct way to reach the ruins on foot is by following the beach south for about 5km past Kaole village into the mangrove swamps. Where the beach apparently ends, go a few hundred metres inland and look for the stone pillars. There's an easier, slightly longer route along the road running past Chuo cha Sanaa. Both routes, and espe-

---

THIS OPEN SORE OF THE WORLD

David Livingstone – one of Africa's most famous explorers and missionaries – was born in 1813 in Blantyre, Scotland, the second of seven children in a poor family. After a childhood spent working at a local cotton gin, followed by medical studies and ordination, he set off for Africa, arriving in Cape Town (South Africa) in 1841. Over the next two decades, Livingstone penetrated into some of the most inaccessible corners of the continent on a series of expeditions – making his way north into the Kalahari, west to present-day Angola and the Atlantic coast, and east along the Zambezi River and to Victoria Falls. In 1866, he set off from the area around Mikindani for what was to be his final expedition, seeking to conclusively solve the riddle of the Nile's source. He made his way as far as Ujiji, where he was famously 'found' by the American journalist Henry Morton Stanley.

After exploring parts of Lake Tanganyika with Stanley and spending time near Tabora, Livingstone set off again on his quest. He died in 1873 in Chitambo, in present-day Zambia. After cutting out and burying his heart, his porters carried his embalmed body in an epic 1500km journey to Bagamoyo and the sea, where it was then taken to England.

During his travels, Livingstone was tormented by the ravages of the slave trade that surrounded him. On his trips back to Europe, he spoke and wrote ceaselessly against it in an effort to expose its horrors and injustices to the rest of the world. These efforts, combined with the attention attracted by his well-publicised funeral, the establishment of Freedom Village in Bagamoyo and reports from other missionaries, marked a point of no return for the slave trade. British attempts to halt the trade were mobilised, and it finally ground to a halt in the early 20th century.

In 1874, Livingstone was buried with full honours in London's Westminster Abbey. Today a plaque memorialises his efforts to end the horrors of the slave trade with what were purportedly his last written words: 'All I can add in my solitude, is, may heaven's rich blessing come down on every one, American, English or Turk, who will help to heal this open sore of the world.'

COMMUNITY TOURISM SPOTLIGHT: BAGAMOYO LIVING ART & HANDICRAFT DESIGN CENTRE

This little **centre** (www.jamani.nl/site/BLACC .html; 🕙9am-4pm Mon-Sat), just off the main Dar es Salaam road near the entrance to town and the post office, was established with Dutch funding about a decade ago to empower women by training them in business and handicraft design and production, giving them a means to earn their livelihood. Since its founding, several hundred women have been trained, many of whom have gone on to start their own craft-production groups. There's also a small showroom where you can buy crafts and sometimes watch the craftswomen at work.

---

cially the beach route, have a reputation for muggings, so it's best to walk in a group with a guide and not carry valuables. If you want an English-speaking guide, arrange it in advance at either the tourist information office or with your hotel; the going rate is a steep Tsh30,000 per group, though you can probably bargain this way down.

COLLEGE OF ARTS

About 500m south of Bagamoyo along the road to Dar es Salaam is the **College of Arts** (Chuo cha Sanaa; ☎ 023-244 0149, 023-244 0032; www .college-of-arts.org), a renowned theatre and arts college, home of the national dance company and one of the best measure's of Tanzania's artistic pulse. When school is in session there are occasional traditional dancing and drumming performances, and it's possible to arrange drumming or dancing lessons. The annual highlight is the Bagamoyo Arts Festival (p338). For more on the college and arts in Bagamoyo, see the website of the **Bagamoyo Friendship Society** (www.bagamoyo.com).

EXCURSIONS

The coast around Bagamoyo is full of interesting water birds, mangrove ecosystems and a few uncrowded stretches of sand. The tourist information office and most of the hotels can arrange excursions to **Mbegani lagoon**, the **Ruvu River delta** and **Mwambakuni sand bar**, all nearby. Expect to pay from US$20 to US$25 per person with four people.

Sleeping & Eating

BUDGET

Kizota Guest House (r without bathroom Tsh4000) No-frills rooms in a local-style guesthouse along the road leading from the main junction to the beach places, about a 10-minute walk from the *dalla-dalla* (minibus) stand. Buckets of hot water are available on request.

Francesco's Hostel & Camping (camping per person Tsh5000, r Tsh15,000) Basic rooms with cold-water shower, net and fan, just 100m further up the road from Mary Nice Place and reasonable value.

Mary Nice Place (☎ 0754-024015; maryniceplace @yahoo.co.uk; r Tsh25,000) A converted house with a small garden, basic and somewhat overpriced rooms with fan, and meals (Tsh4500) with advance order. Its popularity means that there's also usually a group of touts waiting outside trying to drum up business to go to Kaole ruins and other sites. It's signposted, just in from the road to the left a few minutes on foot after passing the College of Arts.

New Top Life Inn (meals Tsh2000) About 50m back from Kizota Guest House towards the main junction and two blocks northwest of the market, this place has inexpensive local meals.

MIDRANGE

Travellers Lodge (☎ 023-244 0077; www.travellers-lodge .com; camping per person with shower US$5, s/d garden cottages US$40/55, beach cottages US$50/65; ✎) With its relaxed atmosphere and reasonable prices, this is among the best value of the beach places. Accommodation is in clean, pleasant cottages scattered around expansive, lush grounds, including some on the beach, some with two large beds and all with mosquito netting. There's also a restaurant (meals from Tsh5000) and a great children's natural-style play area. It's on the road running parallel to the beach, just south of the entrance to the Catholic mission.

Bagamoyo Beach Resort (☎ 023-244 0083; bbr @baganet.com; bandas per person without bathroom US$10, s/d/tr US$34/42/50; ✎) Fine and friendly, with adequate rooms in two blocks (ask for the one closer to the water), a few no-frills *bandas* (thatched-roof huts) on the beach that have just a bed and net and are good budget value, and a seaside location just north of Travellers Lodge. The cuisine (meals about Tsh6000) is French-influenced and tasty.

In addition to these places, Bagamoyo has a string of bland midrange hotels, most of which

NORTHEASTERN TANZANIA

cater to conferences and groups, and none of which are particularly notable. Among the better ones are the following:

Paradise Holiday Resort (☎ 023-244 0136/40; www .paradiseresort.net; s/d from US$70/85; ☒ ☒) Modern rooms, some with sea views, in a large, apartment-style complex overlooking manicured lawns. Add 6% to these prices if you're paying by credit card. It's along the beach road north of Bagamoyo Beach Resort.

Malaika Beach Resorts (Livingstone Club) (☎ 023-244 0080/0059; www.livingstone.ws; s/d US$90/114; ☒ ☐ ☒) The best of the bunch, with an opulent reception area and comfortable rooms. The pool costs Tsh4000/3000 per adult/child for nonguests.

TOP END

Lazy Lagoon (☎ 0784-237422; www.tanzaniasafaris .info; s/d with full board & boat transfers US$200/280; ☒) A relaxing, upmarket place about 10km south of Bagamoyo on the secluded Lazy Lagoon peninsula. Accommodation is in large *bandas*, and short dhow trips and excursions to Bagamoyo can be arranged. Follow signs from the main highway to the Mbegani Fisheries compound, from where it's just a short boat ride over to the lodge. You can leave your vehicle in the fisheries compound.

Getting There & Away

Bagamoyo is about 70km north of Dar es Salaam and an easy drive along good tarmac. With 4WD it's also possible to reach Bagamoyo from Msata (65km west on the Dar es Salaam–Arusha highway, north of Chalinze).

Via public transport, there are *dalla-dallas* throughout the day from Mwenge (north of Dar es Salaam along the New Bagamoyo road, and accessed via *dalla-dalla* from New Posta) to Bagamoyo (Tsh1200, two hours). The *dalla-dalla* stand in Bagamoyo is about 700m from the town centre just off the road heading to Dar es Salaam. Taxis to the town centre charge Tsh1500 (Tsh500 on a motorbike).

Dhows to Zanzibar cost about Tsh5000, but before jumping aboard, read the boxed text on p357. You'll need to register first with the immigration officer in the old customs building. Departures are usually around 1am, arriving in Zanzibar sometime the next morning if all goes well. There is no regular dhow traffic direct to Saadani or Pangani.

SAADANI NATIONAL PARK

About 70km north of Bagamoyo along a lovely stretch of coastline, and directly opposite Zanzibar, is tiny **Saadani** (www.saadanitanapa.com), a 1000-sq-km patch of coastal wilderness that is one of Tanzania's newest national parks. Unpretentious and relaxing, it bills itself as one of the few spots in the country where you can enjoy the beach and watch wildlife at the same time. It's easily accessed from both Dar es Salaam and Zanzibar as an overnight excursion and is a good choice if you don't have time to explore further afield.

To the south of the reserve is the languidly flowing Wami River, where you'll probably see hippos, crocodiles and many birds, including lesser flamingos (in the delta), fish eagles, hamerkops, kingfishers and bee-eaters. It's interesting to watch the vegetation along the riverbanks change with the decreasing salinity of the water as you move upstream. In some sections, there are also marked variations between the two banks, with areas of date palms and lush foliage on one side, and whistling thorn acacias reminiscent of drier areas of the country on the other.

While terrestrial wildlife-watching can't compare with that in the better-known national parks, animal numbers are slowly but surely increasing now that poaching is being brought under control. In addition to hippos and crocs, it's quite likely that you'll see giraffes, and elephant spottings are increasingly common (we saw a herd of 50-plus on a recent visit, although another group on safari the same day saw none). With more effort, you may see Lichtenstein's hartebeests and even lions, although these are more difficult to spot. The birding is also wonderful.

Away from the wildlife, the lovely and mostly deserted beach stretches as far as you can see in each direction, and because it faces due east, it offers plenty of chances to catch one of the subdued, pastel-toned Indian Ocean sunrises that are so typical of this part of the continent. Just south of the main park area is tiny Saadani village. Although it doesn't look like much today, it was once one of the major ports in the area. Among other things, you can still see the crumbling walls of an Arab-built fort that was used as a holding cell for slaves before they were shipped to Zanzibar. During German colonial times the fort served as the customs house.

Information

Entry to the park costs US$20/5 per day per adult/child aged five to 15 years, and guides cost US$10 per day. Camping costs US$30/10 per adult/child aged five to 15 years. There is also an additional US$20 per person per day fee for river usage that applies to those doing boat safaris. Although the park officially stays open year-round, access during the March to May rainy season is difficult. If you do make it in during this time, you'll probably be limited to the area around the beach and the camps. Saadani is administered by the Tanzania National Parks Authority (Tanapa; see p77), with the **park office** (saadani@saadani tanapa.com; ☯ 8am-4pm) at Mkwaja, at the park's northern edge.

For information on Saadani's history and wildlife, browse through *Saadani: An Introduction to Tanzania's Future 13th National Park* by Dr Rolf Baldus, Doreen Broska and Kirsten Röttcher, available free at http://wildlife-programme.gtz.de/wild life/tourism_saadani.html, or check out the park's informative website, www.saadanita napa.com.

Activities

In addition to relaxing, walking along the beach and observing birdlife, the main activities in Saadani are **boat trips** along the Wami River, **wildlife drives** (in open-sided vehicles, as in Tanzania's southern parks and reserves), **bush walks** and **village tours**.

Sleeping & Eating

Tent With a View Safari Lodge (☎ 022-211 0507, 0713-323318; www.saadani.com; s/d full board US$255/350, s/d all inclusive US$355/550) For a secluded tropical getaway, this wonderful and recommended luxury camp is the place to come, with raised treehouse-style *bandas* tucked away among the coconut groves just outside the park's northern boundary on a lovely stretch of deserted, driftwood-strewn beach. The well-spaced *bandas* – all with verandas and hammocks – are directly on the beach and reached by soft sand paths. In addition to safaris in the park (US$80 per person for a full-day safari, including a boat safari along the Wami River; US$40 for a half-day vehicle safari; US$40 for a walking safari – all prices per person with minimum two people), there are various excursions, including guided walks to a nearby green-turtle nesting site. Park entry fees need

only be paid for days you go into the park on safari. No children under six years old. The same management runs a lodge in Selous Game Reserve, and combination itineraries – also including other destinations in southern Tanzania and special Zanzibar-Saadani combination packages – can be arranged.

Saadani Safari Lodge (☎ /fax 022-277 3294; www .saadanilodge.com; s/d full board US$285/480; ☲) This delightful beachside retreat is the only lodge within the park and a fine base from which to explore the area. Each of the nine cosy and tastefully decorated cottages is set directly on the beach. There's an open, thatched restaurant, also directly on the sand, with a raised sundowner deck, and a treehouse overlooking a small waterhole. The atmosphere is unpretentious and comfortable, and staff are unfailingly friendly and helpful. Safaris – including boat safaris on the Wami River, vehicle safaris, walks and snorkelling excursions to a nearby sandbank – cost US$45/25 per adult/child per excursion, with a minimum of three people. No children under six years old.

There are several park **camp sites** (camping adult /child US$20/5), including on the beach north of Saadani Safari Lodge and along the Wami River at Kinyonga. You'll need to be completely self-sufficient. There's also the faded **Tanapa resthouse** (adult/child US$20/10) near Saadani village, for which you'll also need to be self-sufficient. A new resthouse is planned for the near future.

In Mkwaja village, at the northern edge of the park, is **Mwango Guest House** (r Tsh2000), a very basic but potentially useful option if you're continuing north via bus.

Getting There & Away

AIR

There are airstrips for charter flights near two of the lodges. Contact them, or any of the charter companies listed on p356 to arrange charters or to see if a charter is going with extra seats for sale. Rates average about US$200 one way from Zanzibar (20 minutes) and about US$300 from Dar es Salaam (30 minutes) for a three-passenger plane. Tropical Air is currently the only airline flying regularly between Saadani and Zanzibar (about US$55, daily), though it's also worth checking with ZanAir, which sometimes operates scheduled flights between Zanzibar and the airstrip near Saadani village during the July to September high season.

BOAT

Local fishing boats sail regularly between Saadani and Zanzibar (from behind Tembo House Hotel), but the journey is known for being rough and few travellers do it. Better to arrange a boat charter with one of the lodges in Saadani or with the lodges further up the coast north and south of Pangani.

ROAD

All the lodges provide road transport to /from Dar es Salaam for between US$150 and US$250 per vehicle, one way. Allow 4½ to five hours for the journey.

From Dar es Salaam, the route is via Chalinze on the Morogoro road, and then north to Mandera village (about 50km north of Chalinze on the Arusha highway). At Mandera bear east along a reasonable dirt road (you'll need a 4WD) and continue about 60km to Saadani. Once at the main park gate (Mvave Gate), there's a signposted turn-off to Kisampa (about 30km south along a road through the Zaraninge Forest). Saadani village and Saadani Safari Lodge (about 1km north of the village) are about 17km straight on. For Tent With a View Safari Lodge, continue north from the village turn-off for about 25km. Some parts of this route get quite muddy during the rains and 4WD is essential. Via public transport, there's a daily bus from Dar es Salaam's Ubungo bus station (Tsh5000, five to six hours), departing Dar at 1pm and Saadani at 6am. It's also easy enough to get to Mandera junction by bus (take any bus from Dar heading towards Tanga or Arusha and ask the driver to drop you off), but from the junction to Saadani there is no public transport,

other than what you might be able to arrange with sporadically passing vehicles.

Coming from Pangani, take the ferry across the Pangani River, then continue south along a rough road past stands of cashew, sisal and teak via Mkwaja to the reserve's northern gate at Mligaji. Although much improved in recent years, this route is only possible with 4WD. Transfers can generally be arranged with the lodges for about US$130 per vehicle each way (1½ to two hours). There's also a daily bus between Tanga and Mkwaja (Tsh5000, five hours), on the park's northern edge, from where you could arrange to be collected by the lodges. However, it's prone to frequent breakdowns and the whims of the Pangani River ferry so ask around locally to be sure it's running. Departures from Tanga are around 11am, and from Mkwaja around 5am.

If you've arrived in the park via public transport, there's no vehicle rental in the park for a safari, unless you've arranged something in advance with one of the lodges. However, if you base yourself at the Tanapa resthouse or adjacent camping ground, it's quite enjoyable just walking along the beach or visiting the village, and the park makes a fine low-budget getaway.

Until the ferry over the Wami River is repaired, there's no direct road access to Saadani from Bagamoyo, although you can arrange boat pick-ups with some of the camps.

PANGANI

☎ 027

About 55km south of Tanga is the small and dilapidated Swahili outpost of Pangani. It rose from obscure beginnings as just one of many coastal dhow ports to become a terminus of

---

COMMUNITY TOURISM SPOTLIGHT: KISAMPA

The small, socially conscious **Kisampa** (☎ 0756-316815, 0753-005442; www.sanctuary-tz.com; per person all inclusive US$220), set off on its own in a private nature reserve bordering Saadani park, has made impressive progress since its opening in promoting conservation of the surrounding Zaraninge Forest and supporting local community development. Village fees paid by each visitor go to the local community to support health, school and other initiatives, and a local beekeeping project aimed at poverty alleviation and environmental conservation has been established. There are six 'stargazer' tents, netted on three sides. Each tent has a mattress on the floor and private outside bathroom with hot-water bucket showers. Unlike the other Saadani camps, Kisampa isn't on the beach, although excursions can be arranged to the coast (about an hour's drive away), as well as into the park for wildlife-watching. If you have your own vehicle, you can drive from Bagamoyo as far as the Wami River, where Kisampa has guards to watch your car. There's a canoe to the other side of the river, where Kisampa staff will meet you and take you the remaining short distance to the camp.

THE ABUSHIRI REVOLT

Although the Abushiri revolt, one of East Africa's major colonial rebellions, is usually associated with Bagamoyo, Pangani was its birthplace. The catalyst came in 1884, when a young German, Carl Peters, founded the German East Africa Company (Deutsch-Ostafrikanische Gesellschaft or DOAG). Over the next few years, in an effort to tap into the lucrative inland caravan trade, Peters managed to extract agreement from the Sultan of Zanzibar that the DOAG could take over the administration of customs duties in the sultan's mainland domains. However, neither the sultan's representative in Pangani nor the majority of locals were amenable to the idea. When the DOAG raised its flag next to that of the sultan, simmering tensions exploded. Under the leadership of an Afro-Arab trader named Abushiri bin Salim al-Harth, a loosely organised army, including many of the sultan's own guards, ousted the Germans, igniting a series of fierce power struggles that continued in other port towns along the coast. The Germans only managed to subdue the revolt over a year later after the arrival of reinforcements, the imposition of a naval blockade and the hanging of Abushiri. In the wake of the revolt, the DOAG went bankrupt and the colonial capital was moved from Bagamoyo to Dar es Salaam.

the caravan route from Lake Tanganyika, a major export point for slaves and ivory, and one of the largest ports between Bagamoyo and Mombasa. Sisal and copra plantations were established in the area, and several European missions and exploratory journeys to the interior began from here. By the end of the 19th century, focus had shifted to Tanga and Dar es Salaam and Pangani again faded into anonymity.

Today, the town makes an intriguing step back into history, especially in the area within about three blocks of the river, where you'll see some carved doorways, buildings from the German colonial era and old houses of Indian traders. More of a draw for many travellers are the beaches running north and south of town, which are also the best places to base yourself.

History

Compared with Tongoni, Kaole and other settlements along the coast, Pangani is a relatively modern settlement. It rose to prominence during the mid-19th century, when it was a linchpin between the Zanzibar sultanate and the inland caravan routes, and it was during this era that the riverfront slave depot was built. Pangani's oldest building is the old boma, which dates to 1810 and was originally the private residence of a wealthy Omani trader. More recent is the Customs House, built a decade later. Probably several centuries older is the settlement at Bweni, diagonally opposite Pangani on the southern bank of the river, where a 15th-century grave has been found.

In September 1888, Pangani was the first town to rebel against the German colonial administration in the Abushiri Revolt (above).

Orientation

The centre of Pangani, with the market and bus stand, is on the corner of land where the Pangani River meets the sea. About 2km north of here is the main junction where the road from Muheza joins the coastal road, and where you should get out of the bus if you're arriving from Muheza and staying at the beaches north of town.

Information

The closest banks are in Tanga. The **Pangani Cultural Tourism Program office** (☺ 8am-5pm Mon-Fri, 8am-noon Sat) on the riverfront organises reasonably priced town tours, river cruises and excursions to Maziwe Marine Reserve and other local attractions, as well as to Saadani National Park. All of the hotels also organise Maziwe trips.

Use caution when walking along the beaches close to town.

Sights & Activities

Meandering along the southern edge of town is the **Pangani River**, which attracts many water birds, as well as populations of crocodiles and sometimes other animals. It's best explored on a river cruise via local dhow, which can be arranged by any of the hotels. For views over the river, climb up the bluff on the southern bank to the currently closed Pangani River Hotel.

Shimmering in the sun about 10km offshore is tiny **Maziwe Marine Reserve** (admission Tsh1000), an idyllic sand island with snorkelling in the surrounding crystal-clear waters. Dolphins favour the area and are frequently spotted. Maziwe can only be visited at low tide; there's no food or drink on the island, but a picnic lunch is included in most hotel excursions.

The **beaches** running north and south of town – especially to the north near Peponi Holiday Resort and Capricorn Beach Cottages, and to the south around Ushongo – are generally deserted and lovely. They're long, with stands of coconut palms alternating with dense coastal vegetation and the occasional baobab.

Sleeping & Eating

Almost all visitors to the Pangani area stay at one of the beaches running north or south of town.

TOWN CENTRE

New River View Inn Restaurant & Lodge (Jamhuri St; s/d without bathroom Tsh3000/4500) This is the cheapest recommendable place, with no frills but decent rooms sharing facilities. It's on the waterfront road, just east of the Customs House.

Stopover Guest House (☎ 0784-498458; d with Tsh7000) A better bet, with simple but good doubles with nets, fan and bathroom, and meals. It's near the beach – turn right after the petrol station at the northern end of town.

NORTH OF PANGANI

Peponi Holiday Resort (☎ 0784-202962, 0713-540139; www.peponiresort.com; camping per person US$4, s & d bandas US$50, extra adult beds in family bandas US$20; 🌐) This relaxing, traveller-friendly place is set in expansive bougainvillea-dotted grounds on a long, good beach about 19km north of Pangani. In addition to simple, breezy double *bandas*, there are several larger five-person chalets – all *bandas* and chalets have been recently refurbished – plus a shady camp site, clean ablution blocks and a small beachside pool (for Peponi guests only). A restaurant, a nearby reef for snorkelling (you can rent equipment at Peponi) and mangrove stands rich with birdlife to the north of Peponi complete the picture. The proprietors are very helpful with information about excursions and onward connections, and the camp has its own *mashua*

(motorised dhow) for sailing and a nice curio shop. If you're camping, bring supplies with you, and if you'll be staying in the *bandas*, book in advance during high season. Take any bus running along the Pangani–Tanga coastal route and ask the driver to drop you near Kigombe village at the Peponi turn-off (Tsh500 from Pangani, Tsh800 from Tanga), from where it's a short walk. Taxis from Tanga cost Tsh15,000 to Tsh25,000, depending on road conditions and your bargaining abilities.

Tinga Tinga Lodge (☎ 027-264 6611, 0784-403553; www.tingatingalodge.com; camping per person US$4, d/tr US$60/85) This down-to-earth, recently renovated place has spacious twin-bedded bungalows set slightly inland and just north of the main junction. Five minutes' walk away is a restaurant-bar gazebo overlooking the water, with swimming possible just below. Walking tours and sunset cruises can be organised.

Mkoma Bay (☎ 027-263 0000; www.mkomabay .com; s/d bandas US$30/50, s/d luxury tents from US$70/140; 🖥 🌐) Architecturally eclectic and subdued in ambience, this place has a range of raised tents of the sort you find in upmarket safari camps, set around expansive grounds on a low cliff directly overlooking the water. All are nicely furnished and come with private bathroom. There are also some small stone *bandas* sharing bathroom facilities, a good restaurant, a sundowner deck overlooking the sea, and a range of excursions. It's signposted about 3km north of the main junction.

Capricorn Beach Cottages (☎ 0784-632529; www .capricornbeachcottages.com; s/d US$60/84; 🖥) This classy, low-key self-catering place on the beach just south of Peponi Holiday Resort offers three spacious, well-equipped and spotlessly clean cottages set in large, lush grounds dotted with baobab trees. Each cottage has its own covered porch, internet access for laptops, a kitchen and mosquito netting, and all have plenty of ventilation and a natural, open feel. It's an ideal choice if you're looking to get away from it all for a while. There's a grill area overlooking the water, either for catered BBQs or for cooking yourself, and the hosts go out of their way to be sure you're not lacking for anything and that no detail is overlooked – from a cooler and ice on the BBQ deck to a jar of homemade jam and top-notch local coffee beans in the refrigerator. Also on the grounds is a tiny internet café and a clothing boutique.

Homemade bread, fresh seafood, cheese, wine and other gourmet essentials are available at a small deli on the premises.

SOUTH OF PANGANI

Though rarely featuring on tourist itineraries, the long, palm-fringed beach about 15km south of Pangani around Ushongo makes a wonderful getaway. Swimming isn't tide-dependent, and apart from the area in the immediate vicinity of Ushongo village, it's clean, and you'll have most spots to yourself.

Beach Crab Resort (☎ 0784-543700; www.thebeach crab.com; camping per person US$3; s/d safari tent without bathroom US$15/24, d bandas US$64) This budget and backpacker-friendly place was under construction at the time of research. About 1km south of The Tides, it's set to open soon with camping (including tents for rent) and permanent safari-style tents just in from the beach, and self-contained *bandas* on a hill just behind. There are clean ablution blocks for campers and guests staying in the permanent tents, and a beachside bar-restaurant. Diving (there's a PADI dive instructor on-site), windsurfing, hiking and other activities are planned. For road access, follow signs to The Tides and continue about 1.2km south. Pick-ups can be arranged from Mwera (about 7km away and along the bus route from Tanga to Mkwaja village near Saadani) or from Pangani.

Emayani Beach Lodge (☎ 027-264 0755, 027-250 1741; www.emayanilodge.com; s/d/tr US$60/86/105) Laid-back Emayani, on the beach about 2km north of The Tides, has a row of rustic bungalows strung out along the sand. All are made entirely of *makuti* (palm-thatching), and all are very open (no locks), except for *makuti* shades that you can pull down in the evening. Small kayaks and windsurfing equipment are available to rent, and staff can arrange sails on a *ngalawa* (outrigger canoe), and excursions to Maziwe Marine Reserve, Pangani and elsewhere in the area. Pick-ups from Pangani can be arranged. Meals are available (breakfast/dinner US$5/12).

The Tides (☎ 027-264 0844, 0713-325812; www .thetideslodge.com; s/d half board US$135/220; ▯) This unpretentious and intimate place mixes a prime seaside location with spacious, breezy bungalows and excellent cuisine. The seven bungalows – all lined up amid the coconut palms and vegetation along the beach – are wonderful, with huge beds surrounded by billowing mosquito nets, large bathrooms and stylish, subdued décor. At night, you can step out directly onto the sand to gaze at the star-studded skies or be lulled to sleep by the crashing of the waves on the shore. There are also two beautifully decorated family cottages set away from the main lodge area, one of which has a plunge pool and is ideal for honeymooners. Other attractions include the beachside bar and restaurant areas, and staff can sort out whatever excursions you'd like, including dhows to Maziwe Marine Reserve, Zanzibar or along the Pangani River, and inshore and offshore fishing. For a honeymoon location, beachside retreat or family destination (children under six stay for free), it's ideal and good value, especially in comparison to similar-quality places elsewhere on the coast. The lodge also arranges private honeymooners' snorkelling trips to Maziwe, complete with a waiter, cool box, champagne and all the trimmings. Pick-ups from Pangani and Tanga can be organised, as can transfers to/from Saadani.

Getting There & Away

AIR

There's an airstrip between Ushongo and Pangani for charter flights. ZanAir, Coastal Aviation and Tropical Air are the best lines to check with, as all have scheduled flights to nearby destinations and may be willing to stop in Pangani if demand is sufficient.

BOAT

Dhows sail regularly between Pangani and Mkokotoni, on the northwestern coast of Zanzibar. Better is to check with the lodges near Pangani, several of which also arrange dhow charters to Zanzibar's Stone Town from about US$150; ones to try include Peponi Beach Resort, The Tides and Emayani.

ROAD

The best connections between Pangani and Tanga are via the rehabilitated coastal road, with about five buses daily (Tsh2000, 1½ hours), except during the height of the rainy season. The first departure from Pangani is at about 6.30am, so you can connect with a Tanga–Arusha bus. It's also possible to reach Pangani from Muheza (Tsh1000), from where there are connections to Tanga or Korogwe, but the road is worse and connections sporadic.

For Ushongo and the beaches south of Pangani, all the hotels there do pick-ups from both Pangani and Tanga. There's also a daily bus between Tanga and Mkwaja (at the northern edge of Saadani National Park) that passes Mwera (6km from Ushongo) daily at about 7am going north and 3.30pm going south. It's then easy to arrange a pick-up from Mwera with the lodges.

The vehicle ferry over the Pangani River runs in theory between 6.30am and 6.30pm daily (Tsh100/4000 per person/vehicle), and there are small passenger boats (large enough to take a motorcycle) throughout the day (Tsh200).

TANGA

☎ 027 / pop 250,000

Tanga, a major industrial centre until the collapse of the sisal market, is Tanzania's second-largest seaport and its third-largest town behind Dar es Salaam and Mwanza. Despite its size, it's a pleasant-enough place with a sleepy, semicolonial atmosphere and faded charm. While there's little reason to make a special detour to visit, it makes a convenient stop en route to or from Mombasa, and is a springboard to the beaches around Pangani.

History

Although there has probably been a reasonably sized settlement at Tanga since at least the Shirazi era, the town first came into its own in the early to mid-19th century as a starting point for trade caravans to the interior. Ivory was the main commodity traded, with a turnover of about 70,000lbs annually in the late 1850s, according to explorer Richard Burton, who visited here. The real boom, however, came with the arrival of the Germans in the late 19th century, who built up the town and harbour as part of the construction of a railway line linking Moshi and the Kilimanjaro region with the sea. The Germans also introduced sisal to the area, and Tanzania soon became the world's leading producer and exporter of the crop, with sisal the centre of local economic life. In WWI, Tanga was the site of the ill-fated Battle of Tanga (later memorialised in William Boyd's novel, *An Ice-Cream War*), in which poorly prepared British troops were soundly trounced by the Germans.

As the world sisal market began to collapse in the 1970s, Tanga's economy spiralled downward. Today, much of the town's in-frastructure has been abandoned and the economy is just a shadow of its former self, although you'll still see vast plantations stretching westwards along the plains edging the Usambara Mountains.

Orientation

The town centre is set along the waterfront and is easily covered on foot. About 1.5km south of here (Tsh1500 in a taxi), and south of the railway tracks in the Ngamiani section is the bus station. About 2km east of town, reached by following Hospital Rd (which runs parallel to the water) is the quiet and suburban Ras Kazone section, with a few hotels and some places to eat.

Information

INTERNET ACCESS

Impala Internet Café (Sokoine St; per hr Tsh800; ⊙ 9am-7pm)

Kaributanga.com (Sokoine St; per hr Tsh800; ⊙ 9am-9pm Mon-Thu, 9am-noon & 2-8pm Fri, 9am-2pm & 4-8pm Sat & Sun)

MEDICAL SERVICES

MD Pharmacy (☎ 027-264 4067; cnr Sokoine St & Mkwakwani Rd; ⊙ 8am-12.45pm & 2-6pm Mon-Fri, to 12.45pm Sat & Sun) Opposite the market.

MONEY

CRDB (Tower St) ATM (Visa card only).

NBC (cnr Bank & Sokoine Sts) Just west of the market. Changes cash and travellers cheques; ATM (Visa card only).

POST

Main post office (Independence Ave) Near the southeastern corner of Jamhuri Park, just off Independence Ave.

TOURIST INFORMATION

Tayodea Tourist Information Centre (☎ 027-264 4350; cnr Independence Ave & Usambara St; ⊙ 8.30am-5pm) Information and English-speaking guides for local excursions; look for the small kiosk near the post office.

Dangers & Annoyances

The harbour area is seedy and best avoided. In the evenings, take care around Port Rd and Independence Ave near Jamhuri Park.

Sights & Activities

Despite its size, Tanga has remarkably few 'sights', apart from its atmospheric colonial-era architecture. The most interesting areas for a stroll are around Jamhuri Park overlook-

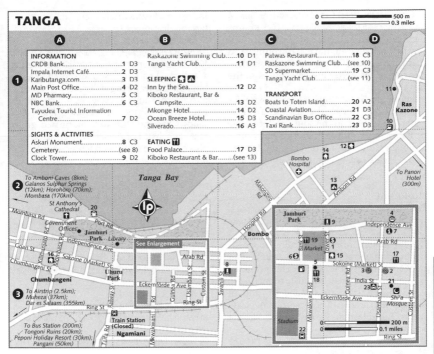

TANGA

0 — 500 m
0 — 0.3 miles

INFORMATION		
CRDB Bank	1	D3
Impala Internet Café	2	D3
Kaributanga.com	3	D3
Main Post Office	4	D2
MD Pharmacy	5	C3
NBC Bank	6	C3
Tayodea Tourist Information Centre	7	D2

SIGHTS & ACTIVITIES		
Askari Monument	8	C3
Cemetery	(see 8)	
Clock Tower	9	D2
Raskazone Swimming Club	10	D1
Tanga Yacht Club	11	D1

SLEEPING 🏠 🛆		
Inn by the Sea	12	D2
Kiboko Restaurant, Bar & Campsite	13	D2
Mkonge Hotel	14	D2
Ocean Breeze Hotel	15	D3
Silverado	16	A3

EATING 🍽		
Food Palace	17	D3
Kiboko Restaurant & Bar	(see 13)	
Palwas Restaurant	18	C3
Raskazone Swimming Club	(see 10)	
SD Supermarket	19	C3
Tanga Yacht Club	(see 11)	

TRANSPORT		
Boats to Toten Island	20	A2
Coastal Aviation	21	D3
Scandinavian Bus Office	22	C3
Taxi Rank	23	D3

ing the harbour, near which you'll find the old German-built **clock tower**, and the park and cemetery surrounding the **Askari monument** at the end of Sokoine St.

Directly offshore is the small, mangrove-ringed **Toten island** (Island of the Dead) with the overgrown ruins of a mosque (dating at least to the 17th century) and some 18th- and 19th-century gravestones. Fifteenth-century pottery fragments have also been found on the island, indicating that it may have been settled during the Shirazi era. The island's apparently long history ended in the late 19th century, when its inhabitants moved to the mainland. Its ruins are less accessible and less atmospheric than those at nearby Tongoni, and it's only worth a look if you have lots of extra time. There are fishing boats on the western side of the harbour that can take you over, although we've only heard unhappy tales from the few travellers we know who have tried this. Better is to organise an excursion through the tourist information office.

Tanga Yacht Club (www.tangayachtclub.com; Hospital Rd, Ras Kazone; day admission Tsh2000) has a small, clean beach, showers and a good restaurant-bar area overlooking the water. It's a pleasant place to relax and, especially on weekend afternoons, it's a great spot to meet resident expats and get the lowdown on what's happening in town. **Raskazone Swimming Club** (Hospital Rd, Ras Kazone; admission Tsh500), about 400m southwest of the yacht club, has a small beach, showers and changing rooms and meals.

Sleeping
BUDGET
Kiboko Restaurant, Bar & Campsite (☎ 027-264 4929, 0784-469292; jda-kiboko@bluemail.ch; Amboni Rd; camping per person US$4) A welcome addition to Tanga's accommodation scene, with secure camping in a large green yard (including tents for rent), spotless hot-water ablution blocks, laundry service, power points, a well-stocked bar and a great garden restaurant. Reasonably priced rooms are planned (about US$40 per double). Management is very helpful and can arrange excursions and provide information on Tanga. It's about 300m in from Hospital Rd; the turn-off is signposted about 500m before Inn by the Sea. Camping is free for children under six years of age.

Ocean Breeze Hotel (☎ 027-264 4445; cnr Tower & Sokoine Sts; r with fan/air-con Tsh7000/12,000) Rooms here are faded and no-frills but quite OK for the price – all have bathrooms and many have nets. It's just east of the market, and one of the better budget choices in the town centre.

Inn by the Sea (☎ 027-264 4614; Hospital Rd; r Tsh12,000; 🖭) Inn by the Sea has a prime waterside setting on the southwestern edge of Ras Kazone, but very run-down rooms, although they're fair enough value for the price. Meals can be arranged; allow about two hours.

MIDRANGE

Panori Hotel (☎ 027-264 6044; panori@africaonline.co.tz; Ras Kazone; s/d old wing Tsh15,000/18,000, old renovated wing Tsh18,000/22,000, new wing Tsh25,000/30,000; 🖭) If you don't mind the location, in a residential area about 3km from the centre (no public transport), this is a decent midrange choice. There are clean, adequate rooms in the new wing, all with nets, fan and TV, and an outdoor restaurant with slow service and tasty meals. Take Hospital Rd east to Ras Kazone and follow the signposts.

Silverado (☎ 027-264 6054, 027-264 5259; cnr Mombasa Rd & Chumbangeni St; r incl breakfast Tsh40,000; 🖭) Clean, generally quiet rooms with minifridge, mosquito netting in the windows (although no bed nets) and TV.

Mkonge Hotel (☎ 027-264 3440; mkongehotel@kaributanga.com; Hospital Rd; s/d US$55/70, with sea view US$60/75; 🖭) The imposing Mkonge Hotel, on a grassy lawn overlooking the sea, has recently had a facelift and now has among the nicest rooms in town (worth the extra money for a sea view). There's also a restaurant.

Eating

Tanga is the home of Tanga Fresh, which produces yogurt and milk that is sold throughout the region – ask locals to point out the way to the Tanga Fresh outlet, where you can get excellent fresh yogurt, milk and cheese.

Patwas Restaurant (Mkwakwani Rd; meals from Tsh1500; 🖭 8am-8pm Mon-Sat) An unassuming, friendly place with very helpful owners who have helped out countless first-time visitors over the years, plus fresh juices and lassis, and tasty, good-value local-style meals. It's just south of the market.

Food Palace (☎ 027-264 6816; Sokoine St; meals from Tsh2000; 🖭 lunch Mon, breakfast, lunch & dinner Tue-Sun)

Indian snacks and meals, including some vegetarian selections.

Kiboko Restaurant & Bar (☎ 027-264 4929, 0784-469292; jda-kiboko@bluemail.ch; Amboni Rd; meals Tsh5000-10,000) A great spot with shady garden seating, a well-stocked bar, a spotless kitchen and a huge menu featuring delicious *kiboko*-sized portions of such delicacies as prawns *kiboko* with green pepper sauce, king fish curry, sandwiches and *mishikaki* (marinated, grilled meat kebabs). For dessert, there's ice cream, plus chocolate truffles and other indulgences on order.

Tanga Yacht Club (☎ 027-264 4246; www.tangayachtclub.com; Hospital Rd, Ras Kazone; admission Tsh2000, meals from Tsh5000; 🖭 10.30am-2.30pm & 6.30-10.30pm Mon-Fri, 11am-3pm & 6-10.30pm Sat, 11am-9pm Sun) The yacht club has a tranquil waterside setting, with a small swimming beach, a sundowner deck and tasty meals, including ice cream. It's a good spot to relax on weekends and evenings, and catch up with Tanga's expat crowd.

Also recommended:

Raskazone Swimming Club (Hospital Rd, Ras Kazone; admission Tsh500; meals Tsh2000-4000; 🖭 dinner) Good, cheap Indian meals.

SD Supermarket (Bank St) For self-caterers; behind the market.

Getting There & Away

AIR

There are daily flights on **Coastal Aviation** (☎ 027-264 6060, 0713-566485; off India St) between Tanga, Dar es Salaam, Zanzibar and Pemba (one-way between Tanga and Pemba /Zanzibar/Dar es Salaam US$70/100/130). Its office is near the mobile-phone tower and the Shi'a mosque. The airstrip is about 3km west of town along the Korogwe road (Tsh2000 in a taxi).

BOAT

The unreliable *Mudasi* – primarily a cargo ship, but also takes passengers – sails three times weekly between Tanga and Wete; see p150.

BUS

To/from Dar es Salaam, the fastest connection is on **Scandinavian** (☎ 027-264 4337), departing at 8am in each direction (Tsh8000, four hours) from its office on Ring St, between the stadium and the railway station, and near the corner of Makwakwani Rd.

Otherwise, Raha Leo departs Tanga every few hours between about 7am and 3pm (Tsh7000, five hours).

To Arusha, there are at least three departures between about 6am and 11am (Tsh12,000, seven hours). To Lushoto (Tsh4000, three to four hours), there are a couple of direct buses departing by 7am, or you can take any Arusha bus and transfer at Mombo.

To Pangani (Tsh2000, 1½ hours), there are small buses throughout the day along the coastal road.

Getting Around

There are taxi ranks at various places around town, including at the bus station, and at the junction of Usambara and India Sts. The tourist information office can help with bicycle rental. Occasional *dalla-dallas* run along Ocean Rd between the town centre and Ras Kazone.

AROUND TANGA
Amboni Caves

Long the subject of local legend, these limestone **caves** (admission Tsh3000) are one of the most extensive subterranean systems in East Africa and an intriguing off-beat excursion for anyone with an interest in spelunking. Now home to thousands of bats, they were traditionally believed to house various spirits, and continue to be a place of worship and ritual. The caves were originally thought to extend up to 200km or more, and are said to have been used by the Kenyan Mau Mau during the 1950s as a hide-out from the British. Although a 1994 survey concluded that their extent was much smaller – with the largest of the caves studied only 900m long – rumours of them reaching all the way to Mombasa persist.

It's possible to visit a small portion of the cave network, which is quite interesting, once you get past the litter at the entrance. Bring along a torch, and wear closed shoes to avoid needing to pick bat droppings off your feet afterwards.

The caves are about 8km northwest of Tanga off the Tanga–Mombasa road, and an easy bicycle ride from town. Otherwise, charter a taxi or take a *dalla-dalla* towards Amboni village and get off at the turn-off for the caves, which is near the forestry office. From here, it's about 2.5km on foot to Kiomoni village; the caves stretch west of Kiomoni along the Mkulumuzi River. Guides can be arranged locally or at the tourist office in Tanga.

Galanos Sulphur Springs

If bending and crawling around the caves has left you feeling stiff in the joints, consider finishing the day with a visit to these green, odoriferous sulphur springs nearby. They take their name from a Greek sisal planter who was the first to recognise their potential for relaxation after the rigours of a long day in the fields. Now, although still in use, they are quite unappealing despite their supposedly therapeutic properties.

The unsignposted turn off for the springs is along the Tanga–Mombasa road, about 2km north of the turn-off for the caves, and just after crossing the Sigi River. From here, it's about 2km further. *Dalla-dallas* from Tanga run as far as Amboni village, from where you'll need to continue on foot.

Tongoni Ruins

Basking in the coastal sun about 20km south of Tanga are the time-ravaged but atmospheric and historically intriguing **Tongoni ruins** (admission Tsh1000; ☺ 8am-5pm). The ruins – which are surrounded by rusted barbed wire and set between baobabs overlooking nearby mangroves and coastline – include

---

PLACE OF RUINS

Together with Mafia, Kilwa and other now sleepy settlements along the coast, Tongoni (Place of Ruins) was once a major port in the network of Swahili trading towns that linked the gold, slave and ivory markets of Africa with the Orient. Its heyday was in the 15th century, when it had its own sultan and was an inadvertent port of call for Vasco da Gama, whose ship ran aground here. By the early 18th century, Tongoni had declined to the point of nonexistence, with the Portuguese disruption of local trade networks and the fall of Mombasa. In the late 18th century, it was resettled by Shirazis fleeing Kilwa (who named it Sitahabu, or 'Better Here than There'), and experienced a brief revival, before declining completely shortly thereafter.

the crumbling remains of a mosque and about 20 overgrown Shirazi pillar-style tombs, the largest collection of such tombs on the East African coast. Both the mosque and the tombs are estimated to date from the 14th or 15th century, when Tongoni was a major coastal trading port (see p167). Although most of the pillars have long since toppled to the ground, you can still see the recessed areas on some where decorative porcelain vases and offering bowls were placed. There are also about two dozen more recent, and largely unremarkable tombs dating from the 18th or 19th century.

To get here, take any vehicle heading towards Pangani along the coastal road and get out at the turn-off (look for a rusty signboard). The ruins are about 1km further east on foot, on the far edge of the village (ask for *'magofu'*). It's worth getting an early start, as finding a lift back in the afternoon can be difficult. Taxis from town charge from about Tsh12,000 for the round trip.

MUHEZA

Muheza is a scrappy junction town where the roads to Amani Nature Reserve and to Pangani branch off the main Tanga highway. Although well inland, it's culturally very much part of the coastal Tanga region, with a humid climate, strong Swahili influences and surrounding landscapes marked by extensive sisal plantations broken by stands of palms. Muheza's main market and trading area, dominated by rows of rickety wooden market stalls and small corrugated metal-roofed houses, is about 1km uphill from the main highway.

Elephant Guest House (r Tsh10,000), just in from the highway near the main junction and a five-minute walk from the bus stand, has self-contained rooms with TV and meals.

Buses to Amani Nature Reserve leave from the main junction along the road leading up towards the market (see opposite for more details). There are direct buses daily in the mornings from Muheza to Lushoto (Tsh2500, three hours), and throughout the day between Muheza and Tanga (Tsh1000, 45 minutes).

KOROGWE

Korogwe is primarily of interest as a transport junction. In the western part of town, known as 'new' Korogwe, are the bus stand and several accommodation options. To the east is 'old' Korogwe with the now defunct train station. Southwest of town, a rough road branches down to **Handeni**, known for its beekeeping and honey production, and its hospital.

Motel White Parrot (☎ 027-264 1068, 027-264 0668; main highway; camping per person Tsh10,000, s/d Tsh30,000/35,000; 🐾) is a large roadside rest stop with surprisingly decent rooms, an adjoining large grassy camp site with hot water showers and a cooking area, and a restaurant (meals from Tsh4000). It also has chilled Ceres fruit juices to go and a nice collection of large plastic animals at the entrance.

USAMBARA MOUNTAINS

With their wide vistas, cool climate, winding paths and picturesque villages, the Usambaras are one of northeastern Tanzania's delights. Rural life here revolves around a cycle of bustling, colourful market days that rotate from one village to the next, and is largely untouched by the booming safari scene and influx of fancy 4WDs in nearby Arusha. It's easily possible to spend at least a week trekking from village to village or relaxing in one spot and doing your exploring as a series of day walks.

The Usambaras, which are part of the ancient Eastern Arc chain (see p74), are divided into two ranges separated by a 4km-wide valley. The western Usambaras, around Lushoto, are the most accessible and have the better road network, while the eastern Usambaras, around Amani, are less developed. Both ranges are densely populated, with an average of more than 300 people per sq km. The main tribes are the Sambaa, Kilindi, Zigua and Mbugu.

MARKET DAYS

Local villages are especially colourful on market days, when traders come on foot from miles around to peddle their wares:
Bumbuli Saturday, with a smaller market on Tuesday
Lushoto Sunday
Mlalo Wednesday
Soni Tuesday and Friday

Although the climate is comfortable year-round, paths get too muddy for trekking during the rainy season. The best time to visit is from July to October, after the rains and when the air is at its clearest.

AMANI NATURE RESERVE

This often overlooked reserve is located west of Tanga in the heart of the eastern Usambara Mountains. It's a peaceful, lushly vegetated patch of montane forest humming with the sounds of rushing water, chirping insects and singing birds, and is exceptionally rich in unique plant and bird species – a highly worthwhile detour if you are ornithologically or botanically inclined. For getting around, there's a network of short, easy walks along shady forest paths that can be done with or without a guide.

History

Although Amani was only gazetted as a nature reserve in 1997, research in the area began about a century earlier when the Germans established a research station and extensive botanical gardens here. Large areas of forest were cleared and numerous new species introduced. Within a few years the gardens were the largest in Africa, totalling 304 hectares and containing between 600 and 1000 different species of plants, including numerous unique species. Soon thereafter, exploitation of the surrounding forest began and the gardens began to decline. A sawmill was set up and a railway link was built connecting Zigi, about 12km below Amani, with the main Tanga–Moshi line in order to facilitate the transport of timber to the coast.

During the British era, research was shifted to Nairobi, and the railway was replaced by a road linking Amani with Muheza. Many of the facilities at Amani were taken over by the nearby government-run malaria research centre and the gardens fell into neglect.

In more recent years, the real work at Amani has been done within the framework of the East Usambara Conservation Area Management Programme, with funding from the Tanzanian and Finnish governments and the EU. In addition to promoting sustainable resource use by local communities, one of the main focuses of the project has been to facilitate visitor access to the forests of the eastern Usambaras through establishing a trail network and training local guides.

Information

At Zigi, there is an **information centre** (⌚ 8am-5pm) at the old Station Master's House with information about the area's history, plants and animals, the traditional uses of medicinal plants and more.

The main office for the **reserve** (☎ /fax 027-264 0313; adult/child US$30/5, Tanzania-registered/foreign vehicle Tsh5000/US$30) is at Amani. The outrageously high entry and guide (per adult/child per day US$20/10) fees can be paid here or at Zigi.

Most trails take between one and three hours. They are detailed in the booklet, *A Guide to Trails and Drive Routes in Amani Nature Reserve,* on sale at the information centre at Zigi and at the reserve office in Amani. Among the unique bird species you may see are Amani and banded green sunbirds, and the green-headed oriole.

Sleeping & Eating

Camping (per person US$5) is possible at both Zigi and Amani with your own tent and supplies.

The **Amani Conservation Centre** (☎ 027-264 0313; anr@twiga.com) runs two guesthouses: the **Amani Conservation Centre Rest House** (r without bathroom Tsh10,000) at Amani and the **Zigi Rest House** (r Tsh10,000) at Zigi. Both are reasonably good, with hot water for bathing and filtered water for drinking. The rooms at Zigi have bathrooms and are large (all with three twin beds) and marginally more comfortable, while the setting and rustic atmosphere are better at Amani. Meals (breakfast/lunch/dinner Tsh1500/3000/3000) are available at both, though it's a good idea to bring fruit and snacks as a supplement. The Zigi Rest House is directly opposite the Zigi information centre. To reach the Amani Conservation Centre Rest House, once in Amani continue straight past the main fork, ignoring the 'resthouse' signpost, to the reserve office. The resthouse is next to the office.

Getting There & Away

Amani is 32km northwest of Muheza along a dirt road which is in fair condition the entire way, except for the last 7km, where the road's are rocky and in bad shape (4WD only). There is at least one truck daily between Muheza and Amani (Tsh2000, two hours), continuing on to Kwamkoro, about 9km beyond Amani.

Departures from Muheza are between about 1pm and 2pm. Going in the other direction, transport usually passes Amani (stopping near the conservation centre office) from about 6am.

In the dry season, you can make it in a 2WD as far as Zigi (25km from Muheza), after which you'll need a 4WD. Allow 1½ to two hours between Muheza and Amani, less in a good car with high clearance. You can also walk from Zigi up to Amani along one of the trails, which takes 2½ to three hours. If you're driving from Muheza, the route is straightforward and signposted until the final junction, where you'll see Bulwa signposted to the right; Amani is about 2km further to the left.

LUSHOTO
☎ 027

Lushoto is a leafy highland town nestled in a fertile valley at about 1200m, surrounded by pines and eucalypts mixed with banana plants and other tropical foliage. It's the centre of the western Usambaras and makes an ideal base for treks – guided or on your own – into the surrounding hills.

Lushoto is also the heartland of the WaSambaa people – the name 'Usambara' is a corruption of WaSambaa or WaShambala, meaning 'scattered' – and local culture is strong. Unlike in Muheza and other parts of the Tanga region closer to the coast, where Swahili is used almost exclusively, the local KiSambaa is the language of choice for most residents.

History

Lushoto's charms were first discovered by outsiders during the German era when the town (then known as Wilhelmstal) was a favoured holiday spot for colonial administrators, a local administrative centre and an important mission station. It was even slated at one point to become the colonial capital. Today, thanks

to a temperate climate, it's best known for its bustling market – overflowing with pears, plums and other produce, and at its liveliest on Sundays – and its superb walking. In addition to a handful of colonial-era buildings – notably the German-built churches, the prison and various old country estates – and the paved road leading up from Mombo, the Germans also left a legacy of homemade bread and cheeses, now produced by several missions in the area.

Due in part to the high population density of the surrounding area and the resulting deforestation, erosion has long been a serious concern. Erosion control efforts were first initiated during the British era and today there are various projects under way, which you're likely to see as you hike in the area.

Information
INTERNET ACCESS
Mount Usambara Communication Centre (per hr Tsh2000; ☯ 7.30am-8pm) On the main road, diagonally opposite the bank.

MEDICAL SERVICES
Afro-Medics Duka la Dawa (☯ 8am-1pm & 2-8pm Mon-Sat, 11am-1pm Sun) On the main road, just before Mount Usambara Communications Centre.

MONEY
There's no ATM in Lushoto that accepts international credit cards.
National Microfinance Bank (☯ 8am-3pm Mon-Fri) On the main road. Changes cash and travellers cheques (minimum US$40 commission for travellers cheques).

TOURIST INFORMATION
Friends of Lushoto Cultural Tourism Centre (☎ 027-264 0132) Just down the small road running next to the bank. In addition to guides and treks, it also arranges bike rentals and cycling excursions in collaboration with the International Bicycle Fund (www.ibike.org).
Tayodea (☎ 0784-861969; youthall2000@yahoo.com) On the small hill behind the bus stand, and next to New Friends Corner guesthouse. Arranges guides and hikes.

Activities
HIKING
The western Usambaras around Lushoto offer some wonderful walking. Routes follow well-worn footpaths that weave among villages, cornfields and banana plantations, and range from a few hours to several days. It's easy to hike on your own, though you'll need to mas-

GREETINGS IN KISAMBAA	
Onga maundo	Good morning
Onga mshee	Good afternoon
Niwedi	I'm fine (in response to Onga maundo or Onga mshee)
Hongea (sana)	Thank you (very much)

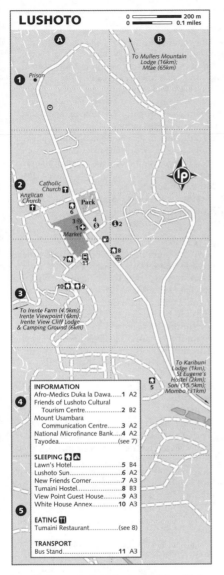

LUSHOTO

0 ————— 200 m
0 ————— 0.1 miles

To Mullers Mountain
Lodge (16km);
Mtae (65km)

Prison

Catholic
Church
Anglican
Church
Park

Market

To Irente Farm (4.5km);
Irente Viewpoint (6km);
Irente View Cliff Lodge
& Camping Ground (6km)

To Karibuni
Lodge (1km);
St Eugene's
Hostel (2km);
Soni (15.5km);
Mombo (31km)

INFORMATION	
Afro-Medics Duka la Dawa......**1** A2	
Friends of Lushoto Cultural	
Tourism Centre.....................**2** B2	
Mount Usambara	
Communication Centre........**3** A2	
National Microfinance Bank....**4** A2	
Tayodea...............................(see 7)	

SLEEPING	
Lawn's Hotel..........................**5** B4	
Lushoto Sun............................**6** A2	
New Friends Corner................**7** A3	
Tumaini Hostel.......................**8** B3	
View Point Guest House.........**9** A3	
White House Annex...............**10** A3	

EATING	
Tumaini Restaurant................(see 8)	

TRANSPORT	
Bus Stand.............................**11** A3	

Several of the establishments listed under Sleeping & Eating (p172)

to go via the handful of villages where local guesthouses are available.

Several of the establishments listed under Sleeping & Eating (p172) can recommend guides and routes, and the two tourist information centres can also help you organise hikes. Don't, however, go with freelancers who aren't associated with an office or reliable hotel. Rates vary depending on the hike, but expect to pay from Tsh8000 per person for a half-day hike to Irente Viewpoint, up to a steep Tsh30,000 to Tsh60,000 per person per day on multiday hikes, including camping or accommodation in very basic guesthouses, guide fees and food. For any hikes that enter forest reserves (which includes most hikes from Lushoto), you'll also need to pay an additional reserve fee of Tsh5000 per person per day (sometimes included in the quoted daily rates). Note that if you're fit and keen on covering some distance, most of the set stages for the popular hikes are quite short and it's easy to do two or even three stages in a day. However, most guides will then want to charge you the full price for the additional days, so you'll need to negotiate an amicable solution. A basic selection of vegetables and fruits is available along most routes and bottled water is sold in several of the larger villages, though if you're hiking on your own, you'll need to carry a filter.

An easy walk to get started is to **Irente Viewpoint** (about 1½ hours return), which begins on the road running southwest from the Anglican church and leads gradually uphill to the viewpoint, with wide views on clear days. It's impressive to see how abruptly the Usambaras rise up from the plains below. En route is **Irente Farm** (⊗ 8am-5pm Mon-Fri, 10am-5pm Sat & Sun), where you can buy fresh cheese (it's in stiff but good-natured competition with the nearby Montessori Centre – buy some cheese at both and judge for yourself), homemade rye bread and granola, and also get accommodation.

Another easy walk to do on your own: head north out of Lushoto along the road running between the Catholic and Anglican churches. After about five minutes, bear sharply left and start climbing, following the road past scattered houses and small farm plots. About 35 minutes further on is the royal village of **Kwembago**, the traditional seat of the local Sambaa chief and notable

ter a few basic Swahili phrases and should also try to get a topographical map of the area from the Surveys & Mapping Division sales office in Dar es Salaam (p85) or carefully study the ones posted on the walls of the two tourist information centres (opposite). Carrying a compass or GPS is a good idea. You should also either carry a tent or plan your route

NORTHEASTERN TANZANIA

NORTHEASTERN TANZANIA

CHIEF KIMWERI

Kimweri, chief of the powerful Kilindi (Shambaa) kingdom during the first half of the 19th century, is one of the Usambara region's most legendary figures. From his capital at Vuga (on the main road between Mombo and Lushoto), he ruled over an area stretching from Kilimanjaro in the north to the Indian Ocean in the east, levying tributes on towns as distant as Pangani. The extent of his dominion in the coastal regions soon brought him into conflict with Sultan Seyyid Said of Zanzibar, who also claimed sovereignty over the same areas. Ultimately, the two leaders reached an agreement for joint governance of the northeastern coast. This arrangement lasted until Kimweri's death in 1869, after which the sultan assumed full authority.

Tradition holds that Kimweri had magical powers, including control of the rain and the ability to call down famines upon his enemies. His kingdom was highly organised, divided into sub-chiefdoms ruled by his sons and districts ruled by governors, prime ministers and local army commanders. It was Kimweri to whom the missionary Johann Ludwig Krapf went to request land to build his first church for the Anglican Church Missionary Society.

Following the death of Kimweri, interclan rivalries caused the kingdom to break up, and fighting over who was to succeed him continued until the Germans arrived in the region.

---

for its large open field and handful of old double-storey, balconied houses. Continue uphill, bear right at the junction, and follow the path around and then down again to the other side of the Lushoto valley, where it joins with the tarmac road heading up to Migambo. For a longer variant, head left at the large junction after Kwembago, and follow footpaths steeply down to the former mission hospital station of **Bumbuli**, where you can find transport back to Lushoto via Soni. From Bumbuli, it's a scenic, gentle climb up and into the cool, lush **Mazumbai Forest Reserve**, which at its higher levels protects some beautiful patches of dense upper montane forest.

There's also a lovely three- to four-day hike that you can do from Lushoto to **Mtae** through stands of pine and past cornfields, villages and patches of wild asters, a five-day walk to Amani Nature Reserve (p169), plus many other possibilities. The tourist information centres have wall maps detailing some of the routes, and several hikes are described in detail in Lonely Planet's *Trekking in East Africa*. Nearby villages where accommodation is available include Bumbuli (with rooms at the old Lutheran mission hospital guesthouse for Tsh10,000), Lukozi (local guesthouse rooms for about Tsh2000), Rangwi (basic rooms in a lovely setting at the local convent), Mtae (local guesthouses) and Mlalo (local guesthouses or the nearby Lutheran mission).

Lushoto can get chilly and wet at any time of year, so bring a waterproof jacket.

CYCLING

Cycling tours in affiliation with **International Bicycle Fund** (www.ibike.org) can be organised at the Friends of Lushoto Cultural Tourism Centre (p170). A seven-day tour from Lushoto to Same via Mkomazi costs US$350 per person (minimum three people) including bicycle and helmet rental, plus extra if a support vehicle is needed. Contact International Bicycle Fund directly or in Lushoto email ymadiwa@yahoo.com.

Sleeping & Eating
IN TOWN
Budget
Karibuni Lodge (☎ 027-264 0104; camping Tsh5000, dm Tsh8000, r Tsh15,000-20,000) Very faded these days and with only a trickle of custom, this private house has a handful of spacious rooms, including some with bathroom, and meals available with a half-day's notice. It's signposted about 1.5km south of the town centre near the district hospital, set back from the main road in a patch of trees; ask the bus driver to drop you at the hospital.

Lushoto Sun (☎ 027-264 0082; s/d Tsh12,000/15,000) Rooms here are a bit cramped, but clean and with hot water. Out front is a restaurant serving *ugali* and other inexpensive dishes. It's on the main road, just south of the Catholic church.

Tumaini Hostel (☎ 027-264 0094; tumaini@elct-ned .org; s/d US$10/17, ste US$25) This hostel offers rather unatmospheric but spotless twin-bedded rooms with nets and hot-water showers in a two-storey compound overlooking small gardens. It's well located in the town centre near the Telecom building and just behind **Tumaini Restaurant** (☎ 027-264 0027; Main Rd; meals from Tsh1200; ✓ breakfast, lunch & dinner), which has great banana milkshakes, plus the usual assortment of standard fare, all well-prepared.

Near the market and bus stand area there are lots of no-frills guesthouses, all with serviceable, undistinguished rooms and hot-water buckets on order. **White House Annex** (d without bathroom Tsh7000, s/d Tsh8000/9500) is cramped and somewhat noisy, though it's arguably the best of the bunch, with hot water and meals on order. Others – all more basic – include **View Point Guest House** (☎ 027-264 0031; r without bathroom Tsh5500), where you should ask for rooms in the annexe, and **New Friends Corner** (s without bathroom Tsh4500, d Tsh6000), next to the Tayodea tourist information centre, with noisy but quite OK rooms. To reach all, head left when coming out of the bus park and go over the small footbridge. New Friends Corner is straight ahead. White House Annex is left and up the hill, and View Point is diagonally opposite White House.

For camping in town, the best bet is Lawn's Hotel (see following).

Midrange

Lawn's Hotel (☎ 027-264 0005, 0784-420252; lawnstony @yahoo.com; camping per person with hot shower US$6, s/d US$40/45; 🖳) This Lushoto institution is full of charm, with vine-covered buildings surrounded by extensive green lawns and gardens, spacious, musty rooms with dark-wood floors, a fireplace, a small library and a bar. If the rooms could be given an airing out and staff given an injection of energy, it would be thoroughly recommendable. As it is though, it's one of the better bets for camping (on the surrounding lawns) and quite a reasonable choice for a double. It's at the entrance to town and signposted – follow the unpaved road up and around to the main entrance. Meals at the restaurant cost about Tsh8000.

St Eugene's Hostel (☎ 027-264 0055, 0784-523710; steugenes_hostel@yahoo.com; s/tw/tr US$20/36/42) This quiet place has spotless, comfortable and spacious rooms, all with good hot showers and balconies with views over the hills. It's run by an order of sisters and profits go to support their work with local children, including a school on the premises. Meals are available, and homemade cheese and jam are available for sale. St Eugene's is along the main road

about 3km before Lushoto, on the left coming from Soni. Ask the bus driver to drop you at the Montessori Centre.

OUTSIDE TOWN
Budget & Midrange

Irente Farm (☎ 027-264 0000, 0784-502935; murless @elct.org; camping per person Tsh3000, r without bathroom Tsh6000, d Tsh18,000-30,000) This rustic place about a 4.5km walk from town has camping, as well as a few tiny rooms sharing ablutions (cold water only). Also at Irente Farm are converted farm buildings that can be rented as a six-bed/two-room self-catering house with a kitchen (bring your own food), plus two simple doubles and a triple room. All are attached and the entire lodge can be rented out for Tsh78,000 (sleeps up to nine people). Irente Farm also prepares picnic lunches for Tsh3000 per person (minimum Tsh5000, order in advance).

Irente View Cliff Lodge (☎ 027-264 0026; www .irenteview.com; s/d from US$50/65) Stunning views over the plains below on clear days from all the rooms compensate for the somewhat over-furnished interior at this new lodge, which is built on the edge of a cliff on the choicest piece of property in the Lushoto area and about 1.5km beyond Irente Farm directly at Irente Viewpoint. Just below is a grassy camping ground (camping per person US$5, with tent rental US$15) with hot-water showers. Transport to/from Lushoto costs US$20 per vehicle for up to six people round-trip.

About 15km outside Lushoto near Migambo village are several more places, all well situated for walking and reasonable options if you have your own transport.

Mullers Mountain Lodge (☎ 026-264 0204; mullers mountainlodge@yahoo.com; camping Tsh5000, s/d/f US$30/40/60) An old family homestead set in sprawling grounds, with rooms in the main house or, for a bit more privacy, in nearby cottages, plus meals (from Tsh6000). There are also a few less appealing cement huts with shared bathroom and a large grassy camping area with a covered cooking area. Transport from Lushoto can be arranged.

Getting There & Away

There are *dalla-dallas* throughout the day between Lushoto and Mombo (Tsh2000, one hour), the junction town on the main highway.

Daily direct buses travel between Lushoto and Tanga (Tsh4000, four hours) on Sashui

NORTHEASTERN TANZANIA

COMMUNITY TOURISM SPOTLIGHT: ST MARY'S MAZINDE JUU

Tucked away in the Usambara Mountains near Lushoto, in the tiny village of Mazinde Juu, is St Mary's Secondary School, an impressive educational success story. The school was founded in 1989 by a Benedictine missionary, based on the idea that Tanzania's long-term development can only be achieved through the education and empowerment of the country's women. The area around Mazinde Juu – long neglected and lagging behind much of the rest of the region economically – was an ideal place to put this belief into practice. Most local families made (and continue to make) their living from small-scale farming, and education for girls, especially secondary education, was traditionally perceived as an unattainable or unnecessary luxury.

Initially, the school had only basic resources and just 42 girls. Today, it has around 350 students and is ranked near the top among the approximately 60 girls' schools and in the top 10 of about 600 secondary schools in the country. Its reputation has also spread well beyond the Usambara Mountains; close to 700 girls from all over Tanzania competed in the most recent entrance exam for places, although true to its original mission, the school reserves 50% of its seats for applicants from the Lushoto–Mazinde Juu area.

While St Mary's is still dependent on outside contributions to make ends meet (write to PO Box 90, Lushoto if you'd like to help), strong emphasis is placed on achieving sustainability. The principal and all of the teachers are Tanzanians, and most are women. Students are taught ecologically sound farming methods and help out on the school farm, which supplies about 80% of the food needs in the compound. The school grows timber, which is used in the construction of new buildings, raises livestock and maintains fruit trees as cash crops.

Although St Mary's is less than two decades old, there is already tangible proof of its success. Several former students are now teaching at the school and at other schools in the area. Others are pursuing further professional training, including nursing and accountancy, and some are studying at university level.

and Tashrif lines, departing at 7am and 9am; Lushoto and Dar es Salaam (Tsh7000, six to seven hours) on Mbaruku and Shambalai lines, departing at 6am, 8am 9am and noon; and Lushoto and Arusha (Tsh9000, six hours) on Fasaha and Chakito lines, departing at 6.30am and 7am. All of these buses stop for a while in Mombo to collect more passengers. If you're going from Lushoto to either Dar es Salaam, Moshi or Arusha, it often works out just as fast to take a *dalla-dalla* or taxi (Tsh25,000) to Mombo, and then get one of the larger express buses to Dar es Salaam. The place to wait is at New Liverpool Hotel, on the main highway about 1km west of the Mombo junction, where all the Dar es Salaam–Arusha buses stop for a rest break. Buses from Dar es Salaam begin arriving at the New Liverpool Hotel from about 10am.

To get to the lodges near Migambo (Mullers Mountain Lodge), take the road heading uphill and northeast of town to Magamba, turn right at the signposted junction and continue for about 7km to Migambo junction. Mullers is about 1km further down the Migambo road and signposted. Via public transport, there's a daily bus between Tanga and Kwamakame that goes to within around 2km of Mullers, departing Tanga at about 9am or 10am and reaching the Migambo area at around 2pm.

AROUND LUSHOTO
Mtae

Tiny Mtae is perched on a cliff about 55km northwest of Lushoto, with fantastic 270-degree views over the Tsavo Plains and down to Mkomazi Game Reserve. It makes a good destination if you only have time to visit one village from Lushoto. Just to the southeast of Mtae is **Shagayu Peak** (2220m), one of the highest peaks in the Usambara Mountains. In addition to its many hiking paths, the area is also known for its traditional healers.

Staff at the Lutheran church will usually allow you to camp on their grounds, or there's the no-frills **Muivano II Guest House** (s/d without bathroom Tsh2500/3500) near the bus stand. Meals are available up the road at Muivano I.

Near Sunga village, 7km southwest of Mtae, there's camping at **Limbe Travellers Camp** (per person Tsh5000) in green grounds about 1km south of the village along the main road.

The road between Lushoto and Mtae is full of turns and hills, and particularly beautiful as it winds its way up the final 7km to Mtae. If travelling by public transport you'll need to spend at least one night in Mtae as buses from Lushoto (Tsh2500, four hours) travel only in the afternoons, departing Lushoto by about 1pm. The return buses from Mtae to Lushoto depart between 4am and 5.30am en route to Dar es Salaam. There are no *dalla-dallas* on the Mtae–Lushoto route.

Mlalo

Set in a valley cut through by the Umba River, Mlalo is an incongruous place with a Wild West feel, a modest selection of basics and a guesthouse. Nearby is **Kitala Hill**, home of one of the Usambara subchiefs. The walk between Mlalo and Mtae (five to six hours, 21km) is beautiful, passing by terraced hillsides, picturesque villages and patches of forest.

Afilfx Guest House (r without bathroom Tsh3000) in the town centre has no-frills rooms with shared bucket showers and meals.

Lutheran Mission (r Tsh4000) sometimes also takes travellers. It's away from the town centre – cross the bridge from the bus stand and head right, asking directions as you go.

Buses run daily between Dar es Salaam and Mlalo via Lushoto, departing Lushoto by about 1pm, and Mlalo by about 5am (Tsh3000 between Mlalo and Lushoto). There are also sporadic *dalla-dallas* between Lushoto and Mlalo.

Soni

Tiny Soni lacks Lushoto's infrastructure, but makes a good change of pace if you'll be staying for a while in the Usambaras. It's known for nearby **Kwa Mungu mountain**, about 30 minutes away on foot, and for the small **Soni Falls**, which you can see to the left along the road coming up from Mombo. Soni is also the starting point for several wonderful walks, including a two- to three-day hike to the Mazumbai Forest Reserve and Bumbuli town (per person per day Tsh50,000), and a short stroll (three to five hours return) to pine-clad **Sakharani**, a Benedictine mission that sells locally produced wine. There's also a lovely, longer walk from Maweni Farm (right) up to Gare Mission and then on to Lushoto. The area around Gare – one of the first missions in the area – was reforested as part of erosion control efforts, and it's

interesting to see the contrast with some of the treeless, more eroded areas surrounding. After Gare, and as a detour en route to Lushoto, stop at the village of **Kwai**, where there's a women's pottery project. Kwai was also an early research post for soil science and erosion control efforts. Guides for all routes from Soni can be arranged at Maweni Farm or in Lushoto.

Budget sleeping options include **Kimalube Guest House** (r Tsh5000), with a few dusty rooms and no food about 1.5km downhill from Soni along the road to Mombo, and **Kwamongo Guest House** (r Ish4000), with basic, grubby rooms – most with two large beds – in a central location five minutes' walk from the main junction (signposted).

No-frills and somewhat dilapidated rooms are available at **Old Soni Falls Hotel** (r Tsh15,000), but the setting is good, overlooking the valley and hills beyond. There's no food, though this may change. It's just uphill from the main junction along the Mombo road and signposted.

Soni Falls Resort (☎ 0784-384603, 0784-510523; d & tr Tsh28,000, f Tsh48,000) offers three enormous, good-value rooms – all with hard-wood flooring and lots of windows – in an old restored colonial-era house perched on a hill overlooking the valley. Apart from continental breakfast, there are no meals, but once a chef is found, food will be available. It's about 100m uphill from the main junction and signposted.

Maweni Farm (☎ 027-264 0426, 0784-279371; www .maweni.com/lodge; s/d safari tent with half board €47/64, s/d without bathroom with half board €30/46, ste with half board €64/78) is an atmospheric old farmhouse is set in lush, rambling grounds about 3km from the main junction, against a backdrop of twittering birds, flowering gardens and a pond covered with water lilies, with Kwa Mungu mountain rising up behind. The recently renovated rooms – some in the main house and some in a separate block – are spacious and quite comfortable. There are also four en suite safari-style tents, plus meals prepared with produce from the organic garden and guides for organising walks. Maweni is 2.9km from the main Soni junction along a rough road and signposted.

Soni is about 12km below Lushoto along the Mombo road, and easy to reach via *dalla-dalla* from either destination (Tsh750 from Lushoto, Tsh1000 from Mombo). Maweni Farm provides free pick-ups if you're staying in its rooms.

Mombo to Same

Mombo is the scruffy junction town at the foot of the Usambara Mountains where the road to Lushoto branches off the main Dar es Salaam–Arusha highway. There's no recommendable accommodation in Mombo, though as most buses from either Arusha or Dar pass at a reasonable hour, you should have no trouble getting a *dalla-dalla* up to Soni or Lushoto to sleep.

Better than staying in Mombo is to head out to **Tembo Lodge & Campsite** (☎ 027-264 1530/9, 0784-663205; tembo.lodges@iwayafrica.com; camping per site US$4, s/d US$14/18; 🖳), at the foot of the mountains about 15km west of town. In addition to camping, it has rooms, food, a bar and a swimming pool, and staff will come to collect you for free in Mombo. There are also numerous hikes in the area. It's about 1km off the main highway and signposted.

Further up, about 45km northwest of Mombo, is **Pangani River Campsite** (camping per person with shower US$5) on the Pangani River, with hot-water showers. It's just off the main road and signposted.

PARE MOUNTAINS

The seldom-visited Pare Mountains – divided into northern and southern ranges – lie southeast of Kilimanjaro and northwest of the Usambara range. Like the Usambaras, they form part of the ancient Eastern Arc chain, and their steep cliffs and forested slopes host an impressive number of unique birds and plants. Also like the Usambaras, the Pares are densely populated, with many small villages linked by a network of paths and tracks. The main ethnic group here is the Pare (also called the Asu). While there are some historical and linguistic differences among various Pare groups, socially they are considered to be a single ethnic entity.

The Pare Mountains are not as accessible or developed for tourism as the Usambaras, and for any exploring you'll be largely on your own. Thanks to the relative isolation, the traditions and folklore of the Pare have remained largely untouched. Also, unlike the Usambaras, there is no major base with developed infrastructure from where a series of hikes can be undertaken. The best way to begin exploration is to head to Mwanga and then up to Usangi (for the north Pares) or

Same and then up to Mbaga (for the south Pares). From both Usangi and Mbaga, there are various hikes, ranging from half a day to three days or more, and English-speaking guides can be arranged.

Information

Lodging and food in the Pares are, for the most part, very basic. With the exception of Hill-Top Tona Lodge in Mbaga, most accommodation is with villagers or camping (for which you'll need your own equipment). Prices for both average Tsh4000 to Tsh7000 per person per night. For all destinations, except Mbaga and Usangi, it's a good idea to bring a portable stove.

There's currently no organised tourism programme in either Same or Mwanga, but one is planned for Same and meanwhile a few enterprising locals are filling in the gap, with routes and hikes modelled on those from a previously existing cultural tourism programme. The best places to arrange guides are Hill-Top Tona Lodge in Mbaga or at local guesthouses in Usangi. Elephant Motel in Same can also put you in touch with guides. For organised hikes, expect to pay from about Tsh8000 per group per day for guide fees, plus about Tsh4000 per person per day for village fees and about Tsh3000 per person per meal. Fees for guides arranged in Same are a bit higher – about Tsh20,000 per person per day including a guide, camping fees and meals. There is a Tsh5000 per visit forest fee for any walks that go into forest reserves, including walks to Shengena Peak. The fees are payable at the Catchment office in Same or through your guide. For any hikes done with guides, the stages are generally quite short – two or three can usually be easily combined for anyone who's reasonably fit – although your guide will still expect you to pay for the same number of days.

The Pares can be visited comfortably at any time of year, except during the March to May long rains, when paths become too muddy.

SAME

Same (*sah*-may) is a lively market town and the largest settlement in the southern Pares. You'll need to pass through here to get to Mbaga, the centre for hikes in this area. Unlike Lushoto in the Usambaras, Same has essentially no tourist infrastructure and the town is more suitable as a starting point for

PARE CULTURE

The Pare (locally, WaPare) hail from the Taita Hills area of southern Kenya, where they were herders, hunters and farmers. It was the Maasai, according to Pare oral traditions, who pursued them into the mountains, capturing and stealing their cattle. Today, many Pare are farmers, cultivating plots of vegetables, maize, bananas, cassava and cardamom. Thanks to significant missionary activity, the Pare also distinguish themselves as being among Tanzania's most educated groups. During the 1940s, leading Pares formed the Wapare Union, which played an important role in the drive for independence.

Traditional Pare society is patrilineal. Fathers are considered to have great authority during their lifetime as well as after death, and all those descended from a single man through male links share a sense of common fate. Once a man dies, his ghost influences all male descendants for as long as the ghost's name is remembered. After this, the dead man's spirit joins a collectively influential body of ancestors. Daughters are also dependent on the goodwill of their father. Yet, since property and status are transmitted through the male line, a father's ghost only has influence over his daughter's descendants until her death.

The Pare believe that deceased persons possess great powers, and thus have developed elaborate rituals centred on the dead. Near most villages are sacred areas where the skulls of tribal chiefs are kept, although you're unlikely to see these unless you spend an extended period in the mountains. When people die, they are believed to inhabit a nether world between the land of the living and the spirit world. If they are allowed to remain in this state, ill fate will befall their descendants. The prescribed rituals allowing the deceased to pass into the world of the ancestors are of great importance.

To learn more about Pare culture, look for copies of *The Shambaa Kingdom* by Steven Feierman (1974), on which some of this section was based, and the intriguing *Lute: The Curse and the Blessing* by Jakob Janssen Dannholz (revised translated edition 1989), who established the first mission station at Mbaga.

NORTHEASTERN TANZANIA

excursions into the Pares rather than as a base. If you do want to stay a few days before heading into the villages, there are several walks into the hills behind town, although for most of the better destinations you will need to take local transport at least part of the way. Sunday is the main market day, when traders from towns all over the Pares come to trade their wares.

The Catchment office (for paying forest reserve fees) is at the end of town, on the main road past the market.

There's currently no reliable internet connection in town. National Microfinance Bank (go left out of the bus stand, up one block, then left again) changes cash.

Amani Lutheran Centre (☎ 027-275 8107; s/d Tsh7000/10,000) offers simple, clean rooms around a quiet compound, and has meals available on order. It's along the main road, just south of the market, and about five minutes' walk from the bus stand.

Same's most 'upmarket' accommodation, **Elephant Motel** (☎ 027-275 8193; www.elephantmotel .com; camping per person US$5, s/tw/tr US$20/25/30) has faded but reasonable rooms, a cavernous res-

taurant serving up decent meals, and a TV. It's on the main highway about 1km southeast of town.

Most buses on the Dar es Salaam–Arusha highway stop at Same on request. Otherwise, *dalla-dallas* travel daily between Same, Dar es Salaam and Moshi, leaving Same in the morning. There is a direct bus between Arusha and Same, departing Arusha at around 8am (Tsh4000, 2½ hours). To Mbaga, there are one or two vehicles daily, departing Same between 11am and 2pm.

MBAGA

Mbaga (also known as Mbaga-Manka), perched in the hills southeast of Same at about 1350m, is a good base for hikes deeper into the surrounding southern Pare mountains. You can also walk from here in two or three days to the top of **Shengena Peak** (2462m), the highest peak in the Pares. Mbaga, an old Lutheran mission station, has long been an influential town because of its location near the centre of the Pare Mountains, and even today, it is in many respects a more important local centre than Same.

A popular three-day circular route is from Mbaga to **Chome** village, where you can spend a night before ascending Shengena Peak on the second day and then returning to Mbaga.

The rustic **Hill-Top Tona Lodge** (☎ 0754-852010; tona_lodge@hotmail.com; camping per person Tsh7000, r per person without bathroom US$10) is the former mission house of Jakob Dannholz (see the boxed text, p177) and one of the best bases in the Pares, with good views, helpful staff, simple cottages and reasonable hiking prices (guides Tsh8000 per group of up to three people; village development fee Tsh3000 per person per day). Traditional dancing performances (about Tsh10,000 per small group) and other activities can also be arranged. Meals are available (Tsh3000).

Kisaka Villa Inn (☎ 027-275 6722; kisakas@yahoo .co.uk; camping per person US$10, r per person with half board US$50) is an amenable although rather overpriced mountain lodge in a good setting in Chome village.

There are one or two vehicles daily around midday between Same and Mbaga, with the last one departing Same by about 2pm (Tsh3000, two to three hours, 40km). If you're coming from Moshi, this means that you'll need to get a bus by 8am in order to get to Mbaga the same day. Coming from Dar es Salaam, you'll probably need to stay overnight in Same. Hiring a vehicle up to Mbaga costs about Tsh40,000 one way; ask Elephant Motel or one of the other Same guesthouses to help you arrange this. From Mbaga back to Same, transport departs by 6am or earlier. It's also possible to catch one of the several daily *dalla-dallas* running from Same to Kisiwani, and then walk about 5km uphill to Mbaga. There's also a daily bus between Same and Chome village, departing Same about 2pm.

If you're driving to Mbaga, there is an alternative route via Mwembe, which can be reached by following the Dar es Salaam–Arusha highway 5km south to the dirt road leading off to the left.

MWANGA & AROUND

This district capital sprawls across the plains at the foot of the Pares about 50km north of Same on the Dar es Salaam–Arusha highway. Once away from the scruffy central junction and old market area, it's a shady, pleasant town with wide, unpaved roads, large swathes of green and stands of palm. The main reason to come here is to change vehicles to get to Usangi, the starting point for excursions in the northern Pares.

For overnight stays, try **Anjela Inn** (☎ 027-275 8381; d Tsh10,000, in newer annexe Tsh15,000), with clean, albeit noisy doubles with nets in the main building and similar but larger and somewhat quieter rooms in a house next door, plus meals. It's about 10 minutes on foot from the highway and bus stand – follow the main road in towards the 'new' market, turn left down a wide, tree-lined lane at the clutch of signboards, and then keep straight on.

About 10km south of Mwanga is **Kisangara Chini**, the site of a cultural tourism programme of sorts that offers the chance to do some walking and to visit a herbal hospital. At the nearby **Nyumba ya Mungu (House of God) Reservoir**, there are Luo fishing communities that originally migrated here from the Lake Victoria area. Take any bus heading south from Mwanga and ask the driver to drop you at Kisangara Chini, from where the tourism programme base is about a 30-minute walk eastwards; ask for the Hasha Project, which also has a camp site and simple rooms. Costs, including guide fees and lunch, total about Tsh22,000 per day, more for overnight and meals, or to hire a vehicle to visit the reservoir.

USANGI

Pretty Usangi, lying in a valley ringed by mountains about 25km east of Mwanga, is the centre of the northern Pares and a possible base for exploring the region.

The main point of interest in town as far as hiking is concerned is **Lomwe Secondary School**, where you can arrange guides. There's a camp site here with water, and the school serves as a **hostel** (camping & dm per person Tsh3000) when classes are not in session. If you can't find anyone at the school, ask for Mr Kangero. Other than Lomwe, accommodation options include homestays in the village (generally in houses near the school) or in **Usangi Guesthouse** (r without bathroom Tsh4000), near the main mosque, with basic rooms and food.

In addition to short jaunts, it's possible to hike in a long day through Kindoroko Forest Reserve (which begins about 7km south of Usangi village) to the top of Mt Kindoroko (2113m), the highest peak in the northern Pares. From the upper slopes of Mt Kindoroko, it's possible to see over the Maasai Steppe to the west and to Lake Jipe and into Kenya to the northeast.

Several small pick ups and *dalla dallas* run daily along the unpaved but decent road between Mwanga and Usangi (Tsh2000, 1½ hours), from around 10am. Hiring a taxi costs Tsh30,000. From Arusha and Moshi there is also a direct bus to Usangi, departing in the morning (four hours from Arusha). Ask the driver to drop you at Lomwe Secondary School. To give yourself time to get here and organise things, allow at least two days for an excursion to Usangi.

MKOMAZI GAME RESERVE

The wild and undeveloped Mkomazi Game Reserve (Mkomazi-Umba Game Reserve) – soon to be gazetted as Mkomazi National Park – spreads along the Kenya border in the shadow of the Pare Mountains, its dry savannah lands contrasting sharply with the moist forests of the Pares. The reserve, which is contiguous with Kenya's Tsavo West National Park, is known for its black rhinos, which were introduced into the area from South Africa for breeding and are part of a pioneering and little-publicised conservation success story (for more, see the highly informative www.wildlifenow.com and www.ifaw.org/ifaw/general/default.aspx?oid=82095). There are currently nine rhinos (up from zero since 1989, when Tony Fitzjohn – the force behind conservation work in Mkomazi – started his work there), including three babies. All are within a heavily protected 45-sq-km enclosure built around Hafino Mountain in the north-central part of the reserve and not viewable as part of general tourism.

In addition to the rhinos, there are wild dogs (also reintroduced and, as part of a special endangered species programme, also not viewable as part of general tourism). Animals that you're more likely to spot include oryx, eland, dik-dik, the rarely seen gerenuk, kudu, Coke's hartebeest and an array of birds. The huge seasonal elephant herds that once crossed regularly between Tsavo and Mkomazi are also beginning to come back, after reaching a low point of just a dozen elephants in the area in 1989, although elephants still are not commonly spotted in Mkomazi. The main reasons for coming to Mkomazi – apart from enjoying the wonderful Babu's Camp – are to appreciate the alluring wilderness area and

evocative nyika bush landscapes studded with baobab and thorn acacia and broken by low, rocky hills. Despite its relative ease of access, Mkomazi is still well away from the beaten track and offers a true wilderness experience. Guided bush walks, including evening walks, are another attraction.

Information

Reserve admission currently costs US$20 per day and camping costs US$20/5 per adult /child, though these fees will almost certainly increase within the lifetime of this book, once Mkomazi's national park status is formalised. The main entrance to the reserve is at Zange Gate, about 5km east of Same, which is also the location of **reserve headquarters** (☎ 027-275 8249; ⏱ 9am-4pm) and the place to arrange an armed ranger for bush walks. Significant sections of Mkomazi's road network were long impassable during the rainy season, although main routes (including the road from Zange Gate to Babu's Camp) are in the process of being made all-weather. Despite this, 4WD is necessary for a visit. Guides for bush walks cost US$20.

Sleeping & Eating

There is a basic camp site (bring everything with you) at Ibaya, about 15km from Zange Gate, and several other cleared areas elsewhere in the reserve without any facilities where camping is permitted.

Babu's Camp (☎ 027-250 3094, 0784-402266; babus camp@bol.co.tz; s/d full board US$248/440) This classic safari-style camp is reason enough to visit Mkomazi. It has just five tents, all well spaced and set amid baobabs and thorn acacias in the northern part of the reserve looking towards the Gulela Hills. The cuisine is wonderful, staff attentive and the entire ambience, together with the evocative surrounding landscapes, recalls quintessential East Africa. Wildlife drives and walks – including to a nearby rock pool and stream, or further afield – can be arranged, as can night drives.

Getting There & Away

Via public transport, *dalla-dallas* between Same and Mbaga can drop you at Zange Gate, from where you can arrange guides and begin a walking safari. Babu's Camp provides transfers for its guests.

Northern Tanzania

With snow-capped Mt Kilimanjaro, the wildlife-packed Ngorongoro Crater and the vast plains of the Serengeti, northern Tanzania embodies what is for many quintessential Africa. While the main attractions are trekking to the top of Africa and wildlife watching on the northern safari circuit, there's much more: haunting calls of water birds fill the air at serene Lake Eyasi; beautiful Mt Meru beckons with unforgettable sunrise panoramas from its summit; the barren landscapes of the Crater Highlands offer rugged but satisfying hiking; and lively rural markets draw traders from miles around to haggle over everything from a head of cattle to a kilo of maize. Enjoy delightful highland lodges amid the coffee plantations around Karatu, take in the Rift Valley vistas around Lake Manyara, experience the subtleties of the Tarangire ecosystem or simply take in all the contrasts, as world-class safari lodges jostle for space with mud-thatch houses, and red-cloaked Maasai warriors follow centuries-old traditions while office workers brush by in Western dress.

Exploring northern Tanzania is relatively easy. Tourist infrastructure is good, with many accommodation and dining options in major towns. There's direct air access from Europe and elsewhere in East Africa via Kilimanjaro International Airport (KIA), a major hub. The main caveat is price – the north is Tanzania's most costly region, especially if you do an organised safari. If you don't mind roughing things a bit, there are some inexpensive alternatives, including an array of Cultural Tourism Programs (p204).

HIGHLIGHTS

- Waking up to the sounds and rhythms of the **Serengeti** (p216)
- Descending into the ethereal blue-green vistas of **Ngorongoro Crater** (p223)
- Trekking on **Mt Kilimanjaro** (p191), or catching the sun's first rays from Mt Meru's **Rhino Point** (p209)
- Watching elephants amid gnarled baobabs in **Tarangire National Park** (p214)
- Taking in the stunning Rift Valley vistas around **Lake Manyara** (p212)

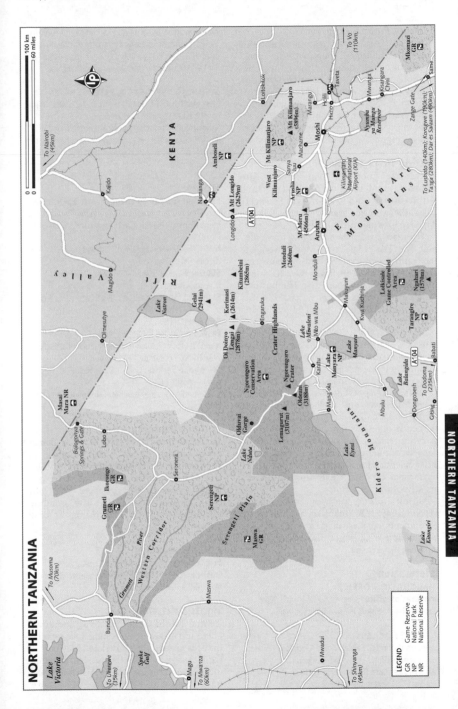

NORTHERN TANZANIA

LEGEND

GR	Game Reserve
NP	National Park
NR	National Reserve

National Parks & Reserves

Northern Tanzania's parks have put this region on the tourist map, with the famed 'northern circuit' taking in the most popular protected areas in the country: Serengeti, Tarangire, Lake Manyara, Arusha and Mt Kilimanjaro National Parks and Ngorongoro Conservation Area. Other protected areas include the extended ecosystems of the Serengeti and Tarangire National Parks.

Getting There & Around

There are good air connections into Kilimanjaro International Airport (KIA) and Arusha airport, and to airstrips in Serengeti, Lake Manyara and Tarangire National Parks. An airstrip is planned soon near Lake Eyasi.

The main road is the tarmac highway running from Dar es Salaam via Moshi through to the Ngorongoro Crater. Heading southwest, the route is tarmac as far as Kwa Kuchinja, near Tarangire National Park. The bus network covers almost all directions.

MOSHI

☎ 027

Moshi, which sits at about 850m at the foot of Mt Kilimanjaro, makes an unassuming introduction to the splendours of the north. It's a low-key place with marabou storks perched in the trees, an appealing blend of African and Asian influences, and a self-sufficient, prosperous feel, due in large part to its status as the centre of one of Tanzania's major coffee-growing regions. It's also the capital of the densely populated Kilimanjaro region and a major educational centre, with one of the highest per-capita concentrations of secondary schools in the country.

Most visitors use Moshi as a starting point for climbing Mt Kilimanjaro, although it's a pleasant enough place in its own right to relax for a couple of days. It's also less expensive than nearby Arusha.

Information

IMMIGRATION OFFICE

Immigration office (Boma Rd; 🕑 7.30am-3.30pm Mon-Fri) Visa extensions handled while you wait.

INTERNET ACCESS

EasyCom (Ground fl, Kahawa House, Clock Tower roundabout; per hr Tsh1000; 🕑 7.30am-8.30pm)
Fahari Cyber Café (Hill St; per hr Tsh1000; 🕑 8.30am-8pm Mon-Sat) Next to the Coffee Shop.

Kicheko.com (Mawenzi Rd; per hr Tsh1000; 🕑 9am-8pm)
Twiga Communications Cybercafé (Old Moshi Rd; per hr Tsh1000; 🕑 8.30am-10pm Mon-Fri, 10am-10pm Sat & Sun) Northeast of the Clock Tower roundabout.

MEDICAL SERVICES & EMERGENCIES

First Health CRCT Hospital (☎ 027-275 4051; Rindi Lane) Next to Standard Chartered Bank.
Kilimanjaro Christian Medical Centre (☎ 027-275 4377/8; Sokoine Rd) Generally considered to have the best medical facilities in Moshi; 3km northwest of town off Kilimanjaro Rd.

MONEY

Executive Bureau de Change (Boma Rd; 🕑 8.30am-6pm Mon-Fri, 9am-5pm Sat) Cash and travellers cheques.
Exim Bank (Boma Rd) ATM (Visa, MasterCard, Maestro, Cirrus).
NBC (Clock Tower roundabout) Cash and travellers cheques; ATM (Visa card).
Stanbic Bank (Boma Rd) ATM (Visa, MasterCard, Maestro, Cirrus).
Standard Chartered Bank (Rindi Lane) ATM (Visa).

TELEPHONE

EasyCom (Ground fl, Kahawa House, Clock Tower roundabout; 🕑 7.30am-8.30pm) International dialling from Tsh200 per minute.
Telephone Service (Clock Tower roundabout; 🕑 8am-6pm) Opposite TTCL.
TTCL (cnr Boma & Mawenzi Rds) Card phones; near the Clock Tower.

TOURIST INFORMATION

The Coffee Shop (☎ 027-275 2707; Hill St), **Tanzania Coffee Lounge** (☎ 027-275 1006; Chagga St) and the rooftop bar at **Kindoroko Hotel** (☎ 027-275 4054; www.kindorokohotel.com; Mawenzi Rd) are good places to meet other travellers. The Coffee Shop sells the *Moshi Guide*, with useful info for longer-term stays. For listings and info, see www.kiliweb.com.

TRAVEL AGENCIES

For trekking operators, see p54.
Emslies (☎ 027-275 2701; emslies.sales@eoltz.com; Old Moshi Rd) Airline bookings.

Sights & Activities

Central Moshi is full of activity and atmosphere and makes an interesting walk, especially the area around the market and Mawenzi Rd, with its vaguely Asian flavour, Hindu temple, mosques and Indian traders. Also fun is catching a glimpse of Kilimanjaro, which hovers

MOSHI

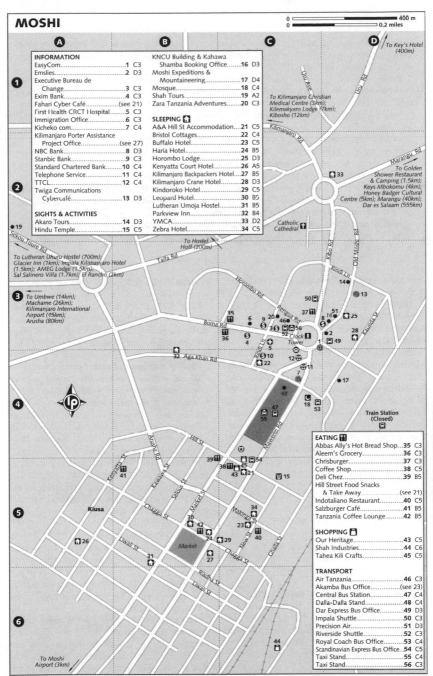

0 _____ 400 m
0 _____ 0.2 miles

INFORMATION
EasyCom.................................1 C3
Emslies...................................2 D3
Executive Bureau de
  Change................................3 C3
Exim Bank..............................4 C3
Fahari Cyber Café...............(see 21)
First Health CRCT Hospital.....5 C3
Immigration Office..................6 C3
Kicheko com...........................7 C4
Kilimanjaro Porter Assistance
  Project Office...................(see 27)
NBC Bank................................8 D3
Stanbic Bank...........................9 C3
Standard Chartered Bank......10 C4
Telephone Service................11 C4
TTCL....................................12 C4
Twiga Communications
  Cybercafé...........................13 D3

SIGHTS & ACTIVITIES
Akaro Tours...........................14 D3
Hindu Temple.......................15 C5

KNCU Building & Kahawa
  Shamba Booking Office.......16 D3
Moshi Expeditions &
  Mountaineering..................17 D4
Mosque................................18 C4
Shah Tours...........................19 A2
Zara Tanzania Adventures.....20 C3

SLEEPING ⌂
A&A Hill St Accommodation...21 C5
Bristol Cottages....................22 C4
Buffalo Hotel........................23 C5
Haria Hotel...........................24 B5
Horombo Lodge....................25 D3
Kenyatta Court Hotel.............26 A5
Kilimanjaro Backpackers Hotel...27 B5
Kilimanjaro Crane Hotel.........28 D3
Kindoroko Hotel....................29 C5
Leopard Hotel.......................30 B5
Lutheran Umoja Hostel..........31 B5
Parkview Inn.........................32 B4
YMCA..................................33 D2
Zebra Hotel..........................34 C5

To Key's Hotel
(400m)

To Kilimanjaro Christian
Medical Centre (3km);
Kilemakyaro Lodge (7km);
Kibosho (12km)

To Golden
Shower Restaurant
Keys Mbokomu (4km);
Honey Badger Cultural
Centre (5km); Marangu (40km);
Dar es Salaam (555km)

Catholic
Cathedral

To Lutheran Uhuru Hostel (700m);
Glacier Inn (1km); Impala Kilimanjaro Hotel
(1.5km); AMEG Lodge (1.5km);
Sal Salinero Villa (1.7km); El Rancho (2km)

To Hostel
Hoff (200m)

To Umbwe (14km);
Machame (26km);
Kilimanjaro International
Airport (15km);
Arusha (80km)

Clock
Tower

Kiusa

Market

To Moshi
Airport (3km)

Train Station
(Closed)

EATING ⌂
Abbas Ally's Hot Bread Shop...35 C3
Aleem's Grocery....................36 C3
Chrisburger..........................37 C3
Coffee Shop..........................38 C5
Deli Chez.............................39 B5
Hill Street Food Snacks
  & Take Away....................(see 21)
Indotaliano Restaurant..........40 C5
Salzburger Café....................41 B5
Tanzania Coffee Lounge........42 B5

SHOPPING ⌂
Our Heritage........................43 C5
Shah Industries.....................44 C6
Tahea Kili Crafts...................45 C5

TRANSPORT
Air Tanzania........................46 C3
Akamba Bus Office.............(see 23)
Central Bus Station...............47 C4
Dalla-Dalla Stand.................48 C4
Dar Express Bus Office..........49 D3
Impala Shuttle......................50 C3
Precision Air........................51 D3
Riverside Shuttle..................52 B5
Royal Coach Bus Office.........53 C4
Scandinavian Express Bus Office...54 C5
Taxi Stand...........................55 C4
Taxi Stand...........................56 C3

NORTHERN TANZANIA

Book your stay at lonelyplanet.com/hotels

TANZANIA & COFFEE

Together with Bukoba, Moshi is one of Tanzania's coffee-growing centres, and it's this aromatic bean that has (together with trekking, in more recent years) kept the town's economy alive for much of the past century.

Coffee, which is said to have originated in southwestern Ethiopia, came to Tanzania around the turn of the 19th century, after being introduced by Jesuit missionaries from Réunion. During the British colonial era, the industry flourished, with the formation of successful coffee-marketing cooperatives among the Chagga in and around Moshi. During the 1960s coffee surpassed sisal as Tanzania's main export crop, and today – despite taking a beating from adverse weather conditions and volatile world prices – is still a linchpin of the national economy.

There are two types of coffee. *Coffea arabica,* which accounts for just under 75% of Tanzanian coffee exports, is used to make higher-quality speciality coffees, and is what you'll see growing around Mt Kilimanjaro, Mt Meru and in the Southern Highlands. *Coffea robusta,* more neutral in taste and used to make less expensive blends and soluble coffees, is grown around western Lake Victoria. More than 90% of Tanzanian coffee is grown on tiny smallholder farms, with the rest coming from cooperatives and private estates.

Many souvenir and coffee shops sell gift-packaged bags of fresh coffee, including the Tanzania Coffee Lounge and the Coffee Shop, both in Moshi. Also see p80 for tips on where to get the best brew.

over the horizon to the north, and is best seen in the evening when the clouds part.

There's a 25m swimming pool (adult/child Tsh3000/1500; 🕙9am-6pm Mon-Sat, to 4.30pm Sun) at the **YMCA** (☎ 027-275 1754; Taifa Rd); no bikinis permitted.

The area outside Moshi is beautiful, and Machame, Umbwe and other towns above Moshi on Kilimanjaro's lower slopes are linked by easy-to-follow footpaths. To explore them, base yourself out of town at Kilemakyaro Lodge (see p186) or in Machame (p187), where all hotels organise hikes for their guests. Another excursion: take a *dalla-dalla* (minibus) from the central bus station to **Kibosho** (Tsh500, 12km), where there's an old German church.

Sleeping

BUDGET

Golden Shower Restaurant (☎ 027-275 1990; Taifa Rd; camping Tsh3000) Conveniently located, with a small, shaded area to pitch a tent, hot-water showers and a restaurant-bar. It's 1.5km northeast of the centre along the Marangu Rd.

Kilimanjaro Backpackers Hotel (☎ 027-275 5159; www.kilimanjarobackpackers.com; Mawenzi Rd; s/d without bathroom US$4/8/15) Formerly the Da Costa Hotel, this backpacker's standby is run by the same management as the nearby Kindoroko Hotel. It has small, clean rooms, a bar and restaurant.

Haria Hotel (☎ 027-275 4054; www.kindorokohotels .com; Mawenzi Rd; d without/with bathroom Tsh6000/10,000) Diagonally opposite Kindoroko Hotel and under the same management, this no-frills establishment has rooms with fans and mosquito nets, and a rooftop patio but no food.

Honey Badger Cultural Centre (☎ 027-275 4608/3365; www.hbcc-campsites.com; camping per person with hot shower US$5; r per person US$25; meals US$5) A family-run place with camping on an enclosed lawn, plus basic rooms in the family house, or in a separate dorm block. Cultural activities can be arranged at extra cost. It's 6km from town off the Marangu road.

Buffalo Hotel (☎ 027-275 0270, 275 2775; New St; s/d Tsh12,000/15,000, d without bathroom Tsh10,000) The long-standing and popular Buffalo Hotel has straightforward rooms with fan and net, and a restaurant. The entrance is on a small street off Mawenzi Rd.

A&A Hill Street Accommodation (☎ 027-275 3455, 0754-299469; sajjad_omar@hotmail.com; Hill St; s/d/tr Tsh12,000/15,000/18,000) Clean, quiet, good-value rooms with fans in a convenient location just one block from the bus stand, with an internet café and inexpensive restaurant just below. There's no breakfast.

Kindoroko Hotel (☎ 027-275 4054; www.kindoroko-hotels.com; Mawenzi Rd; s/d US$15/30, d/tr without bathroom US$15/45; 🖳) Another long-standing and perennially busy place an easy walk from the bus stand, with small but clean and good-value rooms, a rooftop bar, a forex bureau and a restaurant.

Hostel Hoff (☎ 0787-225908; www.foot2afrika.com; dm with half board & laundry US$15) Spotless, good-value hostel-style accommodation that's ideal for longer-term stays. Staff can give tips and assistance for anyone who is seriously interested in longer-term volunteering in Moshi. Check out the website first. It's at the northern end of town – head west along the Arusha road from the YMCA roundabout for about 300m, taking the first right onto a small, unpaved road. The hostel is about 200m further on the right.

Kenyatta Court Hotel (☎ 027-275 4801; kenyatta courthotel@yahoo.com; Kenyatta Rd; s/d US$20/25) Clean rooms with nets and air-con or fan and meals, a few blocks from Salzburger Café in the Kiusa area, away from the main clutch of budget hotels, and about 15 minutes' walk from the central bus station.

Zebra Hotel (☎ 027-275 0611; New St; s/d/tr US$30/35/45) A new-ish high-rise next to Buffalo Hotel with clean, good-value rooms with hot water, and a restaurant.

Other recommendations:

YMCA (☎ 027-275 1754; Taifa Rd; s/d without bathroom US$10/13; ☒) Spartan, noisy rooms, some with views over Kilimanjaro, and a clean 25m swimming pool. It's north of the Clock Tower on the roundabout between Kibo and Taifa Rds.

Lutheran Umoja Hostel (☎ 027-275 0902; uhuru @elct.org; cnr Market & Liwali Sts; s/d Tsh12,000/18,000, without bathroom Tsh6000/10,000) Clean, no-frills rooms around a small courtyard.

Horombo Lodge (☎ 027-275 0134; horombohotel@ yahoo.com; Old Moshi Rd; s/d US$20/30) Diagonally opposite Precision Air, it has sterile rooms with fans and a restaurant.

MIDRANGE

Lutheran Uhuru Hostel (☎ 027-275 4084; www.uhuru-hostel.com; Sekou Toure Rd; s/d US$20/30, newer wing US$40/50, annexe without bathroom US$15/20; ☐) This place has spotless good-value rooms – those in the new wing have balconies – in leafy, expansive grounds, and a good restaurant with meals from Tsh4000. Across the street are some budget rooms in a rustic annexe with shared facilities and kitchen. Rooms are wheelchair-accessible, and the hostel can organise safaris. It's 3km northwest of the town centre on the Arusha road (Tsh2000 in a taxi) and an ideal choice for families.

Leopard Hotel (☎ 027-275 0884; www.leopardhotel .com; Market St; s/d US$35/45; ☒) Bland but well-

appointed rooms in a busy downtown location. Adjoining is the Kili Attik music bar.

Key's Hotel (☎ 027-275 2250; www.keys-hotels .com; Uru Rd; s/d US$30/40, with air-con US$50/60; ☒ ☒) Key's, about 1.5km northeast of the Clock Tower on a quiet side street, has been popular with travellers for years. Accommodation is in spacious, high-ceilinged rooms in the main building, or in small, dark rondavels out back for the same price, and there's a restaurant and a bar. If full, there's Keys Mbokomu (s/d US$25/45, with air-con US$45/65), 4km from town off the Marangu Rd.

Parkview Inn (☎ 027-275 0711; www.pvim.com; Aga Khan Rd; s/d US$40/50; ☒ ☐) This small business travellers hotel has modern rooms with internet access, a quiet, central location and a small restaurant. It's signposted just off the Arusha road.

Kilimanjaro Crane Hotel (☎ 027-275 1114; www .kilimanjarocranehotels.com; Kaunda St; s/d US$40/50; ☒ ☐ ☒) This reliable and recommended midrange establishment has good-value rooms with fans, nets, TV and large beds backing a small garden. Downstairs is a restaurant and souvenir shop and upstairs is a rooftop terrace-bar. It's on a small side street running parallel to and just east of Old Moshi Rd.

Bristol Cottages (☎ 027-275 5083; briscot@kilinet.co.tz; Rindi Lane; s/d/tr cottages US$60/72/90, s/d from US$45/60; ☒) Spotless, modern attached cottages – some with air-con and others with fans – in quiet grounds adjoining Standard Chartered Bank. There are also newer rooms in a two-storey block, and a small restaurant.

TOP END

Sal Salinero Villa (☎ 027-275 2240, 027-275 0420; salinero hotel@yahoo.com; s/d US$65/75, upstairs s/d US$75/85; ☒ ☐ ☒) A private villa with seven spacious, well-equipped rooms, hardwood flooring, a large, winding staircase and an outdoor bar surrounded by green lawns. It's in the Shanty Town area, just off Lema Rd.

AMEG Lodge (☎ 027-275 0175; www.ameglodge.com; s/d from US$69/99; ☒ ☐) Comfortable, spacious rooms in detached cottages – with TV, small porches and fans – set around a grassy compound. There's also a gym, and a restaurant. It's signposted off Lema Rd in Shanty Town.

Impala Kilimanjaro Hotel (☎ 027-275 3443/4; www.impalahotel.com; Lema Rd; s/d US$72/83; ☒) Well-appointed rooms in prim and tranquil grounds, plus a restaurant. It's about 4km northwest of the clock tower roundabout in

Shanty Town, and under the same management as Impala Hotel in Arusha.

Kilemakyaro Lodge (☎ 027-275 4925; www.kilimanjarosafari.com; s/d/tr US$75/125/185) Rooms here – in en suite stone rondavels with TV – are fine, though undistinguished, but the hilltop setting, in a good walking area and with wide views, more than compensates. It's about 7km from the town centre off the Kibosho road (about Tsh6000 in a taxi). There's a restaurant and outdoor tables for sundowners with Kilimanjaro in the distance.

Eating & Drinking

Coffee Shop (☎ 027-275 2707; Hill St; snacks & meals from Tsh1000; ⏰ 8am-5pm Mon, to 8pm Tue-Fri, to 6pm Sat) A laid-back vibe, garden seating, good coffee, and an assortment of homemade breads, cakes, yogurt, breakfast and light meals. Proceeds go to a church project.

Tanzania Coffee Lounge (☎ 027-275 1006; Chagga St; snacks from Tsh1000; ⏰ 8am-7pm Mon-Sat, noon-4pm Sun) Milkshakes, bagels, great coffees and cappuccino, waffles and an internet connection.

Hill Street Food Snacks & Take Away (Hill St; snacks from Tsh1500) Cheap plates of local fast food below A&A Hill Street Accommodation.

Salzburger Café (☎ 027-275 0681; Kenyatta St; meals Tsh3500-5000; ⏰ 8am-11pm) The Alps meet Africa at this classic place, which comes complete with waiters sporting faux-leopard skin vests, Austrian *kneipe* (bar) décor on the walls and a selection of good, cheap dishes (try Chicken Mambo Yote), all with amusing menu descriptions.

Deli Chez (☎ 027-275 1144; Hill St; meals Tsh3500-Tsh7000; ⏰ lunch & dinner) Reasonably priced Indian food – both veg and nonveg – plus continental dishes and burgers.

Indotaliano Restaurant (☎ 027-275 2195; New St; meals about Tsh4000; ⏰ 10am-11pm) The Indo portion of the menu – a range of standards, including some veg dishes – at this small, dark pavement restaurant is better than the Italian part (mediocre pizzas). It's just opposite Buffalo Hotel.

El Rancho (☎ 027-275 5115; meals from Tsh4000; ⏰ closed Monday) Tasty Indian food, including some vegetarian dishes, in a garden setting. It's about 3km northwest of the centre off Lema Rd (no public transport).

For self-catering, try **Aleem's Grocery** (Boma Rd) or **Abbas Ally's Hot Bread Shop** (Boma Rd), situated opposite.

Other recommendations:

Chrisburger (☎ 027-275 0419; Kibo Rd; ⏰ 8am-5pm Mon-Fri, to 2pm Sat) Burgers and snacks.

Glacier Inn (cnr Lema & Kilimanjaro Rds; ⏰ 4pm-late) Drinks and local-style meals in a large garden.

Shopping

Some places to try for crafts:

Our Heritage (Hill St) Carvings, beadwork and other crafts; next to the Coffee Shop.

Shah Industries (☎ 027-275 2414; shahind@kilinet.co.tz) Leatherwork and other crafts, many made by people with disabilities. It's south of town over the railway tracks.

Tahea Kili Crafts (Hill St) Opposite the Coffee Shop, with batiks, basketry, woodcarvings and more; a portion of profits goes to a local women's group.

Getting There & Away

AIR

Most flights to Moshi use Kilimanjaro International Airport (KIA), 50km west of town off the main highway. There's also the small Moshi airport about 3km southwest of town along the extension of Market St, which handles occasional charters. A contact here is www.kiliair.com.

From KIA, there are daily flights to Dar es Salaam (Tsh168,500), Zanzibar (Tsh168,500) and Entebbe (Uganda) on **Air Tanzania** (☎ 027-275 5205; Rengua Rd), near the Clock Tower. **Precision Air** (☎ 027-275 3495; Old Moshi Rd) has daily flights connecting KIA with Dar es Salaam, Mwanza (via Shinyanga, Tsh170,000 to Mwanza) and Nairobi (Kenya; US$227).

BUS

Buses and minibuses run throughout the day to Arusha (Tsh1200, one to 1½ hours) and Marangu (Tsh1000, one hour).

Akamba goes daily to Nairobi en route from Dar es Salaam, departing Moshi about 1.30pm. Alternatively, take one of the shuttle buses, departing Moshi at 6.30am and 11.30am, though you'll need to wait an hour in Arusha in transit; see p350. **Riverside** (1st fl, THB Bldg, Boma Rd) is just off the Clock Tower Roundabout, and **Impala** (☎ 275 3444; Kibo Rd) is just north of the Clock Tower.

To Dar es Salaam, lines include Dar Express (Tsh17,000), with Moshi departures (all originating in Arusha) at 6.30am, 7.15am, 8.30am, 9.30am and 10.30am; Royal Coach (Tsh22,000), originating in Arusha and departing Moshi at 10.15am; and Scandinavian Express, departing Moshi at 9.30am (Tsh17,000) and 12.30pm (Tsh23,000). Akamba also goes to Dar (Tsh20,000), en route from Nairobi. If you're trying to get to Dar es Salaam in time for the afternoon ferry to Zanzibar, Dar Express' 6.30am bus usually arrives in time.

To get to Mwanza, the best lines are Scandinavian and Akamba, both of which should be booked in advance.

Except as noted, all transport leaves from the central bus station in the town centre between Market St and Mawenzi Rd. The station is chaotic and full of touts and disreputable types wanting to take advantage of new arrivals, and it can be quite intimidating getting off the bus (which is a good reason to take one of the lines that let you disembark at their offices). To minimise hassles, look for the area of the station where the taxis are gathered before disembarking and head straight over and hire a driver there, rather than getting caught in the fray by the bus door. Unless you know Moshi, it's worth paying the Tsh1500 to Tsh2000 for a taxi to your hotel, even if it's close enough to walk, just to get away from the station. When leaving Moshi, the best thing is to go to the station the day before without your luggage and book your ticket then, so that the next morning you can just arrive and board.

Bus offices include the following:

Akamba (☎ 027-275 3908; cnr New & Makinga Sts) Around the corner from Buffalo Hotel.

Dar Express (Old Moshi Rd) Opposite KCNU Coffee Tree Hotel, off the Clock Tower roundabout.

Royal Coach (Aga Khan Rd) Opposite the bus stand, and just down from the mosque.

Scandinavian Express (☎ 027-275 1387; Mawenzi Rd) One block south of the bus stand, opposite the Hindu temple.

Getting Around
TO/FROM THE AIRPORT
Both Air Tanzania and Precision Air have free transport to/from KIA for their flights, departing from their offices two hours before flight time. Riverside and Impala (p350) have a shuttle to/from KIA (US$10), departing from their Moshi offices at 6pm daily and coordinated with KLM flight departures. They also meet arriving passengers on KLM.

TAXI & DALLA-DALLA
There are taxi stands near the Clock Tower and at the bus station. *Dalla-dallas* depart from next to the bus station.

MACHAME
☎ 027
The rather ill-defined and spread-out village of Machame lies about 25km northwest of Moshi on Mt Kilimanjaro's lower slopes, surrounded by dense vegetation and stands of banana. Most visitors pass through briefly en route to Machame Gate, but with several good hotels and enjoyable hiking in the area it makes an agreeable alternative for those uninclined to conquer the mountain's higher slopes.

The main budget option for organising hikes and cultural activities in the area is the **Machame Cultural Tourism Program** (☎ 027-275 7033) based in Kyalia village, off the Arusha–Moshi road, somewhat past Machame proper, and about 4km before Kilimanjaro's Machame trail head. Its office is in the centre of Kyalia across the field from the *dalla-dalla* stop and next to the blue building with the Tanzanian flag. It's usually closed, but staff live in the nearby houses, so just ask around for cultural tourism. Everything is very basic, and you'll need to be self-sufficient with food and water, but rates are reasonable (Tsh6000 per group per day for a guide plus Tsh4000 per person per day for village development and administration fees). Take a Machame *dalla-dalla* from the main Moshi transport stand to the end of the line (Kyalia village, Tsh700).

For something more upmarket, Protea Hotel Aishi Machame makes a fine base for hikes, and staff can set you up with guides and a full description of the various routes in the area. Makoa Farm also arranges short cultural walks and horseriding for its guests.

Sleeping & Eating
The only budget option is home stays arranged through the Machame Cultural Tourism Program.

Protea Hotel Aishi Machame (☎ 027-275 6948, 027-275 6941; proteaaishireservations@satconet.net; s/d US$115/145; 🏊) A lovely place, with well-appointed rooms with dark-wood furnishings and beautiful, lush surrounding gardens reminiscent of an old country estate. The hotel is about 6km off the main highway and signposted to the right off the road to the Machame trailhead.

Makoa Farm (☎ 0754-312896; www.makoa-farm.com; d full board US$268) This restored 1930s farmstead

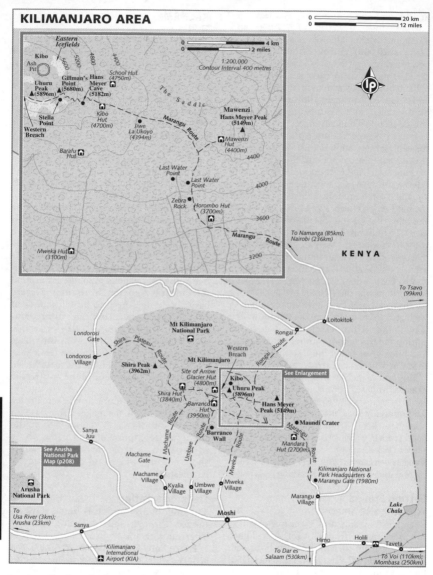

KILIMANJARO AREA

KENYA

is primarily a base for horse-riding safaris, but its guest cottages make a good break for non-riding partners who want to stay behind to relax. Meals are made with farm produce and served family-style together with the owners and an assorted menagerie of pets in the main farmhouse. Animal-lovers and nature enthusiasts only. There's a two-night mini-

mum stay; walking and short rides can be arranged (for guests only). It's about 17km from Moshi, off the Machame road and unsignposted. Most Moshi taxis know the turn-off; otherwise ask for directions when booking. For details on its eight-day West Kilimanjaro safari and other multiday rides, see its website. Previous riding experience is required.

COMMUNITY TOURISM SPOTLIGHT: KAHAWA SHAMBA

Kahawa Shamba (☎ 027-275 0464, 027-275 2785, 0784-517995; www.kirurumu.net/kahawa/index.htm; per person full board US$110/196) is a laudable community-owned and community-run venture that offers insights into the lives of the Chagga coffee farmers who live on Kilimanjaro's lower slopes. It consists of a handful of Chagga huts near Lyamungo village, southeast of Machame and about 27km from Moshi near Umbwe village. While the huts are authentically constructed, they are outfitted with modern amenities such as en suite showers and twin beds, and are clean and comfortable. Meals with local families can be arranged, as can guided walks and horseriding, village and family visits, and learning about local coffee production methods. Book at least two weeks in advance, either via email, or at Kahawa Shamba's Moshi booking office in the KNCU building just off the Clock Tower roundabout. From Moshi, take a *dalla-dalla* to Kibosho-Umbwe (Tsh800, 45 minutes), from where you'll need to walk 20 to 30 minutes to the Lyamungo-Kibera area and Kahawa Shamba.

MARANGU
☎ 027

Nestled on the lower slopes of Mt Kilimanjaro 40km northeast of Moshi, amid dense stands of banana and coffee plants, is the lively, leafy market town of Marangu. The town has an agreeable highland ambience, a cool climate and a good selection of hotels, all of which organise treks. While you'll generally get slightly better budget deals in Moshi, it makes a convenient base for Kili climbs using the Marangu or Rongai routes, and an enjoyable stop in its own right.

Marangu is also the heartland of the Chagga people, and there are possibilities for walks and cultural activities in the surrounding area, including hikes to nearby caves, watching local blacksmiths at work and seeing traditional-style houses. The surrounding area is laced with waterfalls and small streams – *marangu* means 'place of water' – and there are also several nearby waterfalls to visit (most with a small entry charge).

Thanks to the large influx of foreign trekkers, the contrasts between the tourist scene (or the 'developed' world in general) and local life are just as stark in Marangu as in Arusha, although they stand out more in Marangu as it is so much smaller. Well-heeled trekkers come into town outfitted with the latest gear and climbing accessories, and drop from several hundred to several thousand dollars into the coffers of trekking companies, while, nearby, local vendors hawk their wares and struggle to find US$200 per year to pay secondary-school tuition fees for their children.

Information
Marangu Computer Centre (per hr Tsh2000; ☼ 8am-6pm) Behind the post office.

Sights & Activities
Most hotels can arrange **walks and cultural activities** in the area. Good bets for learning more about local culture are Banana Jungle Lodge and Kilimanjaro Mountain Resort, both of which have authentic models of traditional Chagga houses. At Kilimanjaro Mountain Resort, there's also the **Chagga Live Museum** (admission US$2; ☼ 10am-5pm), a small, outdoor museum illustrating traditional Chagga life. Most hotels can also provide English-speaking guides (US$10 to US$15 per person per day) to other attractions in the area, including caves that were used by the Chagga for hiding during the era of Maasai raids about 200 years ago, a sacred tree, local blacksmiths' workshops and waterfalls. About 6km southwest of Marangu is **Ngangu Hill**, with views and the small, old Kilema mission church nearby.

It's possible to do a **day hike** in Mt Kilimanjaro National Park from Marangu Gate as far as Mandara Hut (about two hours up, one hour down; US$60 per person for park fees, plus US$10 per guide, arranged at the park gate).

Sleeping & Eating
BUDGET
Coffee Tree Campsite (☎ 027-275 6513/6604; kilimanjaro@iwayafrica.com; camping US$8, rondavel/chalet per person US$12/15) On the pricey side, but reliable and well-maintained, with expansive, trim grounds, hot-water showers, tents for hire (Tsh10,000 per day) and several four- to six-person rondavels and chalets. It's about 700m

east of the main road, and signposted near Nakara Hotel.

Otherwise, budget options are limited to several places listed under Midrange that also offer camping, and a handful of places with very basic rooms sharing facilities and food on order. These include the no-frills **Bismarck Hut Lodge** (camping per person US$5, r per person without bathroom US$10), along the road to the park gate, shortly before the turn-off to Capricorn Hotel; and the marginally better **Kilimanjaro Parklands Hotel** (r per person US$10), just up from and opposite Marangu Hotel at the entrance to town, which has the advantage of warm-ish showers.

MIDRANGE

Kibo Hotel (☎ 027-275 1308; www.kibohotel.com; camping per person US$5, s/d US$42/66) The Kibo, well over 100 years old, is where Hans Meyer stayed overnight before starting his famous first ascent of Kilimanjaro. (Another prominent guest in more recent times was Jimmy Carter.) Now the hotel is well past its prime, but the wooden flooring, large paned windows and surrounding gardens make it an atmospheric choice, and the rooms – albeit rustic – are quite spacious. It's about 1.5km west of the main junction, and there's a restaurant.

Banana Jungle Lodge (☎ 027-275 6565, 0754-270947; www.yellowpages.co.tz/jungle/index.htm; camping per student/nonstudent US$5/10, s/d/tr US$50/60/75; meals US$4-6) Accommodation at this large family homestead is in standard bungalow-style rooms or modernised Chagga huts, all surrounded by dense plantings of banana and other vegetation on the expansive grounds of the owners' house. It's not luxurious at all, although all the basics are there, but it's a refreshingly genuine and low-key place to learn about Chagga life and culture

and arrange cultural walks. There's also an authentic reproduction of a traditional Chagga house, a small working farm and an English-speaking guide. It's about 5km east of Marangu in Mamba, off the road leading to the Rongai Route trailhead. Head right (east) at Marangu's main junction, go 2km to the Mamba Lutheran church, turn left at the signboard, and then follow the signboards further for another 2.5km.

Marangu Hotel (☎ 027-275 6594; www.maranguhotel .com; camping per person with hot showers US$5, s/d half board US$70/100; ☑) This long-standing place is the first hotel you reach coming from Moshi, with a clipped British ambience, rooms set around expansive grounds and a camp site. Room discounts are available if you join one of the hotel's fully equipped climbs.

Babylon Lodge (www.babylon lodge.net; camping per person US$7, s/d US$25/45) A budget hotel at heart, masquerading behind midrange prices, the efficient Babylon has a row of small, clean twin and double-bedded rooms clustered around a tiny lawn, and is often somewhat more flexible than the other places on negotiating packages for Kili treks. It's about 700m east of the main junction.

Kilimanjaro Mountain Resort (☎ 027-275 8950; www.kilimanjaroresort.com; camping per person US$12, s/d from US$50/90) This stately old-style building is surrounded by gardens and forest 3km west of the main junction, with spacious, well-appointed rooms – some with enormous beds – a restaurant (lunch/dinner US$12/15) and the adjoining Chagga Live Museum.

Nakara Hotel (☎ 027-275 6571; r per person US$50) A reliable if somewhat bland midrange establishment with reasonable twin or double-bedded rooms and a restaurant. It's just off the main road towards the park gate and signposted.

YOHANI KINYALA LAUWO

The first Tanzanian to scale Kilimanjaro was Yohani Kinyala Lauwo, whose memory is still revered in his home town of Marangu. Lauwo was only 18 in 1889 when he was appointed by Chief Marealle I to be the guide for Hans Meyer (the first Westerner to reach Uhuru Peak). In those days the route was not defined, climbing equipment was rudimentary and wages were much lower. During his trek, Lauwo earned just Tsh1 per day.

Following this successful ascent, Lauwo remained in Marangu, where he spent much of the remainder of his life leading foreign trekkers up the mountain and training new guides. In 1989 at the 100th anniversary celebration of the first ascent of Kilimanjaro, Lauwo was the only person present who had been around a century earlier. Lauwo died in 1996, aged 125. His family still lives in Marangu.

THE CHAGGA

Traditional Chagga-style houses are windowless, built in a round beehive form and covered with thick thatching that needs to be changed every few years. Inside, one half of the house is used for cattle, and the other side for parents' and childrens' sleeping areas, with a cooking area in the middle. Unlike in Sukumaland by Lake Victoria, where traditional-style houses are still widely used, Chagga houses these days are all more modern constructions.

The Chagga, who are widely spread around the lower slopes of Kilimanjaro, have absorbed numerous influences over the past two centuries, including blacksmithing skills from the neighbouring Pares. Traditionally, most Chagga have been farmers and also owned cattle, which historically led to conflict with the Maasai, who were notorious for entering Chagga lands and raiding their cattle and, according to the Chagga, their women. The period – dating to about 200 years ago – is referred to by many Chagga as the Chagga-Maasai war.

Getting There & Away

Minibuses run throughout the day between Marangu and Moshi (Tsh1000). In Marangu they'll drop you at the main junction from where there are sporadic pick-ups to the park gate (Tsh500), 5km further. For the Holili border, you'll need to change at Himo junction.

MT KILIMANJARO NATIONAL PARK

Since its official opening in 1977, Kilimanjaro National Park has become one of Tanzania's most visited parks. Unlike the other northern parks, this isn't for the wildlife – although wildlife is there. Rather, it's to gaze in awe at a mountain on the equator capped with snow, and to take advantage of the chance to climb to the top of Africa.

At the heart of the park is the 5896m Mt Kilimanjaro, Africa's highest peak and one of the continent's magnificent sights. It's also one of the highest volcanoes and among the highest freestanding mountains in the world, rising from cultivated farmlands on the lower levels, through lush rainforest to alpine meadows, and finally across a barren lunar landscape to the twin summits of Kibo and Mawenzi. The lower rainforest is home to many animals, including buffaloes, leopards and monkeys, and elands are occasionally seen in the saddle area between Kibo and Mawenzi peaks.

A trek up Kili lures hundreds of trekkers each year, in part because it's possible to walk to the summit without ropes or technical climbing experience. Yet, the climb is a serious (and expensive) undertaking, and only worth doing with the right preparation. There are also plenty of excellent options for exploring the mountain's lower slopes and learning about the Maasai and the Chagga, the main tribes in the area. For some ideas, see the sections on Machame (p187), Marangu (p189) and West Kilimanjaro (p194).

For information on park fees – payable for all activities within the park area – see p192. There are entry gates at Machame: Marangu, which is also the site of park headquarters, Londorosi and several other points. Trekkers using the Rongai Route should pay their fees at Marangu Gate.

TREKKING MT KILIMANJARO

Mt Kilimanjaro can be climbed at any time of year, though weather patterns are notoriously erratic and difficult to predict. During November and March/April, it's more likely that paths through the forest will be slippery, and that routes up to the summit, especially the Western Breach, will be covered by snow. That said, you can also have a streak of beautiful, sunny days during these times, and should come prepared for rain and bitter cold at any time of year. Overall, the best time for climbing the mountain is in the dry season, from late June to October, and from late December to February or early March, just after the short rains and before the long rains.

Don't underestimate the weather on Kilimanjaro. Conditions on the mountain are frequently very cold and wet, and you'll need a full range of waterproof cold-weather clothing and gear, including a good-quality sleeping bag. It's also worth carrying some additional sturdy water bottles. No matter what the time of year, waterproof everything, especially your sleeping bag, as things rarely dry on the mountain. It's often possible to rent sleeping bags and gear from trekking operators, or – for the Marangu Route – from the Kilimanjaro Guides Cooperative Society

NORTHERN TANZANIA

THE (MELTING) SNOWS OF KILIMANJARO

Since 1912, when they were first measured, Kilimanjaro's glaciers have lost over 80% of their ice, which means that they will have disappeared completely by 2020 if things continue at the present rate. Many factors are blamed, one of which is loss of forest cover on the mountain's lower slopes. (Fewer trees means there is less moisture in the air, which in turn means less precipitation, more solar rays getting through to the ice and faster evaporation.)

Various schemes have been dreamed up to halt further disappearance of the glaciers, including spreading huge white sheets over the remaining ice fields, although no one has yet come up with a sure remedy. Meanwhile, speculation is rife about what the disappearance of one of Tanzania's national symbols will mean for the country's tourist industry. For now, perhaps the only certain thing is that if you want to see the top of Kilimanjaro as Ernest Hemingway described it in his classic *The Snows of Kilimanjaro* – 'wide as all the world, great, high, and unbelievably white in the sun' – you shouldn't wait long to book your trek.

stand just inside Marangu Gate. However, especially at the budget level, quality and availability can't be counted on, and it's best to bring your own.

Apart from a small shop at Marangu Gate selling a limited range of chocolate bars and tinned items, there are no shops inside the park. You can buy beer and sodas at high prices at huts on the Marangu Route.

Costs

Kilimanjaro can only be climbed with a licenced guide. Unless you are a Tanzania resident and well-versed in the logistics of Kili climbs, the only realistic way to organise things is through a tour company. For operator listings and some tips see p54. No-frills five-day/four-night treks up the Marangu Route start at about US$850, including park fees, and no-frills budget treks of six to seven days on the Machame Route start at around US$900 to US$1000, although it's highly recommended to budget at least one additional night for the ascent. Better-quality six-day trips on the Marangu and Machame routes start at about US$1000. The Umbwe Route is often sold by budget operators for about the same price as Marangu, and billed as a quick and comparatively inexpensive way to reach the top. Don't fall for this – the route should only be done by experienced trekkers, and should have an extra acclimatisation day built in. For more information, see p194. Prices start at about US$750 on the Rongai Route, and about US$1100 for a seven-day trek on the Shira Plateau Route. As the starting points for these latter routes, particularly Rongai, are much further from Moshi than those for the other routes, transport costs can be significant, so clarify whether they are included in the price.

Whatever you pay for your trek, remember that at least US$525 of this goes to park fees for a five-day Marangu Route climb, and more for longer treks (US$750 for a seven-day Machame-route climb). The rest of the money covers food, tents (if required), guides, porters and transport to and from the start of the trek. Most of the better companies provide dining tents, decent to good cuisine and various other extras to make the experience more enjoyable (as well as to maximise your chances of getting to the top). If you choose a really cheap trip you risk having inadequate meals, mediocre guides, few comforts and problems with hut bookings and park fees. Also remember that an environmentally responsible trek usually costs more. Bringing a stove and fuel, for example, requires additional porters because of the greater weight. (It's not permitted to use firewood on the mountain.)

PARK FEES

Park entry fees – calculated per day, and not per 24-hour period – are US$60/10 per adult/child aged five to 15 years, and must be paid in US dollars, cash or travellers cheques. Huts (Marangu Route) cost US$50 per person per night, and there is a US$20 rescue fee per person per trip for treks on the mountain. Camping costs US$50 per person per night on all routes. Park fees are generally included in price quotes, and paid on your behalf by the trekking operator, but you'll need to confirm this before making any bookings. Guide and porter fees (but not tips) are handled directly by the trekking companies.

Kilimanjaro National Park Headquarters (☎ 027-275 6602/5; kinapa@iwayafrica.com) is at the park gate (open 8am-6pm) in Marangu.

TIPPING

Most guides and porters receive only minimal wages from the trekking companies and depend on tips as their major source of income. As a guideline, plan on tipping about 10% of the total amount you've paid for the trek, divided up among the guides and porters. For the Marangu Route, tips are commonly from US$40 to US$60 for the guide, and from US$15 each for the porters. Plan on more for the longer routes, or if the guide and porters have been particularly good.

Guides & Porters

Guides, and at least one porter (for the guide), are obligatory and are provided by your trekking company. You can carry your own gear on the Marangu Route, although porters are generally used, but one or two porters per trekker are essential on all other routes.

All guides must be registered with the national park authorities. If in doubt, check that your guide's permit is up to date. On Kili, the guide's job is to show you the way and that's it. Only the best guides, working for reputable companies, will be able to tell you about wildlife, flowers or other features on the mountain.

Porters will carry bags weighing up to 15kg (not including their own food and clothing, which they strap to the outside of your bag), and your bags will be weighed before you set off.

The guides and porters provided by some of the cheaper trekking outfits leave a lot to be desired. If you're a hardy traveller you might not worry about basic meals and substandard tents, but you might be more concerned about incompetent guides or dishonest porters. We've heard stories about guides who leave the last hut deliberately late on the summit day, to avoid going all the way to the top. The best way to avoid scenarios like this is by going with a reputable company, familiarising yourself with all aspects of the route, and – should problems arise – being polite but firm with your guide.

Maps

Topographical maps include *Map & Guide to Kilimanjaro* by Andrew Wielochowski and *Kilimanjaro Map & Guide* by Mark Savage. MaCo's *New Map of the Kilimanjaro National Park* has useful gradient profiles, though you'll need to complement it with a topographical map for serious trekking.

SERIOUS BUSINESS

Whatever route you choose, remember that ascending Kilimanjaro is a serious undertaking. While many hundreds of trekkers reach Uhuru Peak without major difficulty, many more don't make it because they ascend too quickly and suffer from altitude sickness. And, every year a few trekkers die on the mountain. Come prepared with appropriate footwear and clothing, and most importantly, allow yourself enough time. If you're interested in reaching the top, seriously consider adding at least one extra day onto the 'standard' climb itinerary, no matter which route you do. Although paying an additional US$150 to US$250 per extra day may seem a lot when you're planning your trip, it will appear as relatively insignificant savings later on if you've gone to the expense and effort to start a trek and then need to come down without having reached the top. Don't feel badly about insisting on an extra day with the trekking companies: standard medical advice is to increase sleeping altitude by only 300m per day once above 3000m – which is about one-third of the daily altitude gains above 3000m on the standard Kili climb routes offered by most operators. Another perspective on it all: Uhuru Peak is several hundred metres higher than Everest Base Camp in the Nepal Himalaya, which trekkers often take at least two weeks to reach from Kathmandu.

It's also worth remembering that it is not essential to reach Uhuru Peak, and you haven't 'failed' if you don't. If time (or money) is limited, you'd be far better off choosing other treks – you could experience several different mountain areas for the price of a single Kili climb. If you really want to sample Kili, instead of just pushing on for the summit, consider trekking up to an area such as the Saddle, the top of the Barranco Wall or the Shira Plateau to appreciate the splendour and magnificence of the mountain before descending.

Trekking Routes

There are at least 10 trekking routes that begin on the lower slopes but only three continue to the summit. Of these, the **Marangu Route** is the easiest and the most popular. A trek on this route is typically sold as a five-day, four-night return package, although at least one extra night is highly recommended to help acclimatisation, especially if you've just flown in to Tanzania or just arrived from the lowlands. Lonely Planet's *Trekking in East Africa* has detailed description of the standard stages of this and other main routes.

Other routes on Kili usually take six days (which costs more, but helps acclimatisation) and pass through a wider range of scenic areas than the Marangu Route, although trekkers must use tents. The increasingly popular **Machame Route** has a gradual ascent, including a spectacular day contouring the southern slopes before approaching the summit via the top section of the Mweka Route. The **Umbwe Route** is much steeper, with a more direct way to the summit – very enjoyable if you can resist the temptation to gain altitude too quickly. Unfortunately, some trekking companies now push attractively priced five-day four-night options on the Umbwe Route in an effort to attract business. Although the route is direct, the top, very steep section up the Western Breach is often covered in ice or snow, which makes it impassable or extremely dangerous. Many trekkers who attempt it without proper acclimatisation are forced to turn back. An indication of its seriousness is that until fairly recently, the Western Breach was considered a technical mountaineering route. It has only gained in popularity recently because of intense competition for business and crowding on other routes. The bottom line is that you should only consider this route if you are experienced and properly equipped, and travelling with a reputable operator. Reliable operators will suggest an extra night for acclimatisation.

Another thing to watch out for is operators who try to sell a 'short' version of the Machame Route, which ascends the Machame Route for the first few stages, but then switches near the top to the final section of the Umbwe Route and summits via the Western Breach. This version is a day shorter (and thus less expensive) than the standard Machame Route, but the same considerations outlined in the preceding paragraph apply here, and you should only consider this combination if you are experienced, acclimatised and properly equipped.

The **Rongai Route**, which has also become increasingly popular in recent years, starts near the Kenyan border and goes up the northern side of the mountain. It's possible to do this in five days, but it's better done in six. The attractive **Shira Plateau Route** (also called the Londorosi Route) is somewhat longer than the others, but good for acclimatisation if you start trekking from Londorosi Gate (rather than driving all the way to the Shira Track road head), or if you take an extra day at Shira Hut.

Trekkers on the Machame and Umbwe routes descend via the Marangu Route or the **Mweka Route**, which is for descent only. Some Marangu treks also descend on the Mweka Route.

Officially a limit of 60 climbers per route per day is in effect on Kilimanjaro. It is currently not being enforced, except on the Marangu Route, which is self-limiting because of maximum hut capacities. If and when this limit is enforced, expect the advance time necessary for booking a climb to increase, with less flexibility for last-minute arrangements.

WEST KILIMANJARO

The West Kilimanjaro area – encompassing the Maasai lands running north of Sanya Juu village up to the Kenyan border and Amboseli National Park and around to Loitokitok – gained attention in recent times when eight local villages were granted permission to form the **Enduimet Wildlife Management Area**, one of just a handful of such community-managed wildlife areas in the country. For visitors, West Kilimanjaro is of interest for its relatively untouched savannah bush lands and its impressive wildlife populations, including, most notably, its elephants, lying as it does along an elephant corridor linking Amboseli with Mt Kilimanjaro National Park. The elephants have regained confidence over the past decade, as wildlife has increasingly become viewed as a local resource and poaching in the area has correspondingly decreased, and can be seen year-round. Among them is an unusually high number of large tuskers who are frequently spotted silhouetted against the backdrop of Mt Kilimanjaro. Other draws include the possibility of arranging visits to Maasai bomas, walks and other cultural activities. West Kilimanjaro also offers easy access to the western/Lemosho routes for mountain treks.

Hoopoe Safaris has a long-standing partnership with the local Maasai, and runs the excellent **Hemingway's Camp** (www.hemingways-camp.com; s/d full board US$540/680), an intimate place with just seven tents and a superb wilderness ambience, plus the chance for wildlife walks and drives and Maasai cultural activities.

Other possible bases include **Kambi ya Tembo** (www.africawilderness.com; s/d full board US$450/636), at Sinya on the Kenyan border, and the 12-tent **Ndarakwai Ranch** (www.ndarakwai.com), just outside the conservation area, plus various small village camp sites.

ARUSHA
☎ 027 / pop 300,000

Cool, lush and green, Arusha is one of Tanzania's most developed and fastest-growing towns. It sprawls near the foot of Mt Meru at about 1300m altitude, and enjoys a cool, temperate climate throughout the year. Arusha is also the gateway to the Serengeti and the other northern parks. As such, it is the safari capital of Tanzania and a major tourism centre. Although further from Kilimanjaro than Moshi and the trailhead towns, it's also the main base for organising Kilimanjaro treks.

Arusha is fringed by coffee, wheat and maize estates tended by the Arusha and Meru people, whom you may see in and around the central market, and who have occupied this area since about the 18th century. Beyond the farmland begin some of East Africa's most alluring landscapes, dominated by the Rift Valley escarpment and the volcanoes of the Crater Highlands.

Present-day Arusha traces its roots to the waning days of the 19th century, when the German boma was constructed. In 1967 Arusha became headquarters of the now defunct original East African Community. Today it is the seat of the new East African Community – a revived attempt at regional collaboration – and the site of the Rwanda genocide tribunal.

Orientation

Arusha is divided by the small Naura River valley. To the west are the bus stations, the market and many budget hotels. To the east are most of the upmarket hotels, the post office, immigration, government buildings, safari companies, airline offices, craft shops and the Arusha International Conference Centre (AICC). In the centre, and about a 10- to 15-minute walk from the bus stand, is the Clock Tower roundabout where the two main roads – Sokoine Rd to the west and Old Moshi Rd to the east – meet.

MAPS
MaCo (www.gtmaps.com) puts out a good map of Arusha, widely available around town. There are small, free photocopied town maps at the tourist information centre.

Information
BOOKSHOPS
Bookmark (☎ 027-250 4053; Jacaranda St) Reasonably well-stocked, including various Africa titles.

IMMIGRATION OFFICE
Immigration office (Simeon Rd; ⏰ 7.30am-3.30pm Mon-Fri) Near the Makongoro Rd junction; visa extensions are usually processed while you wait.

INTERNET ACCESS
Cybernet Café (India St; per hr Tsh1500; ⏰ 9.30am-5pm Mon-Fri, to 1pm Sat)
New Safari Hotel (Boma Rd; per hr Tsh1000; ⏰ 24hr)
Patisserie (Sokoine Rd; per hr Tsh1000; ⏰ 7.30am-6.30pm Mon-Sat, 8.30am-2pm Sun)

MEDICAL SERVICES & EMERGENCIES
Accident Air Rescue (AAR; ☎ 027-50 8020; www.aarhealth.com; Plot 54, Haile Selassie Rd) Off Old Moshi Rd; lab tests and a doctor on call 24 hours.
Moona's Pharmacy (☎ 027-250 9800, 0713-510590; moonas_pharmacy@cybernet.co.tz; Sokoine Rd; ⏰ 8.45am-5.30pm Mon-Fri, to 2pm Sat) Well-stocked pharmacy, west of NBC bank.
Selian Lutheran Hospital (☎ 027-250 9974/5; http://selianlh.habari.co.tz) About 12km north of town in Ngaramtoni and signposted 3km off the main road.

MONEY
In addition to the forex bureaus located at Impala Hotel and other large hotels around town (most open on Sundays and until late on weekdays), there are many forex bureaus clustered around the northern end of Boma Rd, and along Joel Maeda St, near the Clock Tower.
Barclays (Sopa Lodges Bldg, Serengeti Rd) ATM (Visa and MasterCard).
Exim Bank (cnr Sokoine & Goliondoi Rds) ATM (Visa, MasterCard, Cirrus and Maestro).

ARUSHA

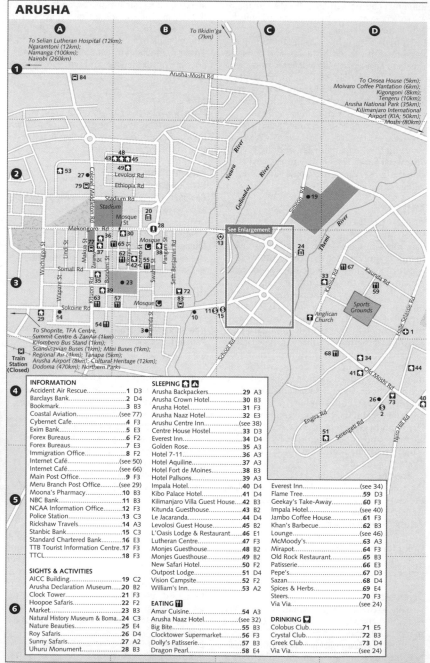

INFORMATION

Accident Air Rescue	1	D3
Barclays Bank	2	D4
Bookmark	3	B3
Coastal Aviation	(see 77)	
Cybernet Cafe	4	F3
Exim Bank	5	E3
Forex Bureaus	6	F2
Forex Bureaus	7	E3
Immigration Office	8	F2
Internet Café	(see 50)	
Internet Café	(see 66)	
Main Post Office	9	F3
Meru Branch Post Office	(see 29)	
Moona's Pharmacy	10	B3
NBC Bank	11	B3
NCAA Information Office	12	F3
Police Station	13	C3
Rickshaw Travels	14	A3
Stanbic Bank	15	C3
Standard Chartered Bank	16	E3
TTB Tourist Information Centre	17	F3
TTCL	18	F3

SIGHTS & ACTIVITIES

AICC Building	19	C2
Arusha Declaration Museum	20	B2
Clock Tower	21	F3
Hoopoe Safaris	22	F2
Market	23	B3
Natural History Museum & Boma	24	C3
Nature Beauties	25	E4
Roy Safaris	26	D4
Sunny Safaris	27	A2
Uhuru Monument	28	B3

SLEEPING

Arusha Backpackers	29	A3
Arusha Crown Hotel	30	B3
Arusha Hotel	31	F3
Arusha Naaz Hotel	32	E3
Arushu Centre Inn	(see 38)	
Centre House Hostel	33	D3
Everest Inn	34	D4
Golden Rose	35	A3
Hotel 7-11	36	A3
Hotel Aquiline	37	A3
Hotel Fort de Moines	38	B3
Hotel Pallsons	39	A3
Impala Hotel	40	D4
Kibo Palace Hotel	41	D4
Kilimanjaro Villa Guest House	42	B3
Kitunda Guesthouse	43	B2
Le Jacaranda	44	D4
Levolosi Guest House	45	B2
L'Oasis Lodge & Restaurant	46	E1
Lutheran Centre	47	F3
Monjes Guesthouse	48	B2
Monjes Guesthouse	49	B2
New Safari Hotel	50	F2
Outpost Lodge	51	F2
Vision Campsite	52	F2
William's Inn	53	A2

EATING

Amar Cuisine	54	A3
Arusha Naaz Hotel	(see 32)	
Big Bite	55	B3
Clocktower Supermarket	56	F3
Dolly's Patisserie	57	B3
Dragon Pearl	58	E4

Everest Inn	(see 34)	
Flame Tree	59	D3
Geekay's Take-Away	60	F3
Impala Hotel	(see 40)	
Jambo Coffee House	61	F3
Khan's Barbecue	62	B3
Lounge	(see 46)	
McMoody's	63	A3
Mirapot	64	F3
Old Rock Restaurant	65	B3
Patisserie	66	E3
Pepe's	67	D3
Sazan	68	D4
Spices & Herbs	69	E4
Steers	70	F3
Via Via	(see 24)	

DRINKING

Colobus Club	71	E5
Crystal Club	72	B3
Greek Club	73	D4
Via Via	(see 24)	

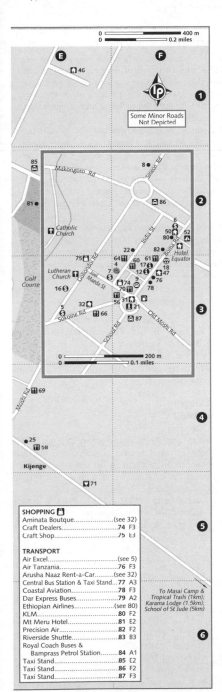

NBC (Sokoine Rd) ATM (Visa); also changes travellers cheques.
Stanbic Bank (Sokoine Rd) ATM (Visa, MasterCard, Cirrus and Maestro).
Standard Chartered (Goliondoi Rd) ATM (Visa).

POST
Main post office (Boma Rd)
Meru branch post office (Sokoine Rd)

TELEPHONE
TTCL (Boma Rd; 🕑 8am-8pm Mon-Sat, 9am-8pm Sun & public holidays) International (from Tsh1000 per minute) and domestic calls; card phones.

TOURIST INFORMATION
The travellers' bulletin board at the Tourist Information Centre is a good spot to find safari mates.
Ngorongoro Conservation Area Authority (NCAA) Information Office (☎ 027-254 4625; www .ngorongoro-crater-africa.org; Boma Rd; 🕑 8am-1pm & 2-5pm Mon-Fri, 8am-1pm Sat) Booklets on Ngorongoro and a relief map of the Ngorongoro Conservation Area.
Tanzania National Parks Headquarters (Tanapa; ☎ 027-250 3471/4082/8216; www.tanzaniaparks.com; Dodoma road) About 5km west of town.
Tanzania Tourist Board (TTB) Tourist Information Centre (☎ 027-250 3842/3; ttb-info@habari.co.tz; Boma Rd; 🕑 8am-4pm Mon-Fri, 8.30am-1pm Sat) Just up from the post office and the Clock Tower roundabout, with helpful staff, information on Arusha, the nearby parks and other attractions, and booking help for Cultural Tourism Program tours. Also has a 'blacklist' of tour operators and a list of registered tour companies.

TRAVEL AGENCIES
For listings of Arusha-based safari and trekking operators – most of which can also arrange itineraries elsewhere in the country – see p44.
Coastal Aviation (☎ 027-250 0087; arusha@coastal .cc; Boma Rd) Northern and southern circuit itineraries, Zanzibar and flight charters.
Rickshaw Travels (☎ 027-250 6655; www.rickshawtz .com; Sokoine Rd) Domestic and international flight bookings.

Dangers & Annoyances
Arusha is the worst place in Tanzania for street touts and slick tour operators who prey on the gullibility of newly arrived travellers by offering them safaris and treks at ridiculously low prices. Their main haunts include Boma Rd and Goliondoi Rd, at the central bus station

---

COMMUNITY TOURISM SPOTLIGHT: SCHOOL OF ST JUDE Tony Wheeler

He's the patron saint of hopeless cases, but St Jude would definitely be smiling at what has been achieved in his name in a school just outside Arusha. To score a place in Australian Gemma Sisia's pioneering establishment you have to meet two very different requirements. First you've got to be extremely bright: only the smartest kids get to even sit the entrance exam and only the best results get a place. Second you've got to be very poor: if you come from a home with more than two rooms or with electricity you're ineligible.

The School of St Jude kicked off in 2002 with a handful of kids and one teacher. By 2007 the school had expanded to 850 children, 60 teachers and 200 staff. A second primary school opens in 2008 and when those first students reach high school graduation age in 2014 the school population will have reached more than 2000. Has Gemma's plan worked, to provide a terrific education opportunity to dirt-poor kids? It's hard to argue with the results: St Jude students' exam scores are outranked only by the most expensive Tanzanian private schools. The huge pride that St Jude parents have in their kids and the fierce competition to get a place underline the school's impact even more effectively.

The school welcomes visitors Monday to Friday during term time, but you will need to email first – schoolofstjude@habari.co.tz – to make an appointment. See the 'Visit Us' page of the school website – www.schoolofstjude.co.tz – for more information. Of course donations are appreciated, US$10 to US$20 is suggested, but lots of visitors are inspired to form a longer term relationship with the project. When you're there ask how they check and double-check to make certain students really do qualify as 'poor'.

---

and near the budget hotels at the northern and western ends of town. Ensure that any tour company you sign up with is properly registered; get recommendations from other travellers and check the current 'blacklist' at the TTB Tourist Information Centre on Boma Rd. Also see the Choosing an Operator and Safari Scams & Schemes boxed texts in the Safaris chapter (p45).

At night, take a taxi if you go out. It's not safe to walk after dusk, especially over the bridge on Old Moshi Rd near the Clock Tower.

Sights & Activities

The small **Arusha Declaration Museum** (☎ 027-250 7800; www.museum.or.tz; Makongoro Rd; adult/student US$5/2; ⏰ 9am-5.30pm) near the Uhuru monument has an interesting display on postcolonial Tanzanian history, while the even smaller **Natural History Museum** (☎ 027-250 7540; www.museum.or.tz; Boma Rd; adult/student US$5/2; ⏰ 9am-5.30pm Mon-Fri, 9.30am-5.30pm Sat & Sun), in the old German boma, has a few fossils and old photos, and is worth a stop if you are in the area. Other diversions include the colourful **market**, which is a good place to buy the tire-tread sandals worn by many Maasai as protection against thorns in the bush, and the many **Cultural Tourism Programs** (p204) in the surrounding countryside.

It's still possible to observe the proceedings of the **UN International Criminal Tribunal for Rwanda** at the AICC building on Simeon Rd, which take place Monday to Thursday; admission is free but you'll need your passport.

Sleeping

BUDGET

Camping

Vision Campsite (off Boma Rd; camping per person Tsh3000) Small, shaded and very basic, this is the only place to pitch a tent in the town centre. Hot water buckets can be arranged. It's next to Equator Hotel.

Masai Camp (☎ 027-250 0358, 0754-829514; masai camp@africamail.com; camping per person US$5, bandas per person without bathroom US$7, r per person without bathroom US$10; 🖳) A long-time favourite, popular with overlanders and on the noisy side, with expansive grounds, hot showers, pool tables, satellite TV, a restaurant with pizzas, burgers and other meals and a happening bar. Tents and sleeping bags are available to be hired, and there are a few no-frills rooms. It's 3km southeast of town off Old Moshi Rd (Tsh2500 in a taxi), and also the base for Tropical Trails (p54).

Meserani Snake Park (☎ 027-253 8282; www .meseranisnakepark.com; camping per person incl admission to snake park US$10) This overlander-oriented place has good facilities, including hot showers, a restaurant (meals US$6) a vehicle repair shop and emergency rooms if you're ill. Short walks and camel rides in the surrounding Maasai area can be organised (per person US$5), and there's a snake park and a small Maasai cultural museum. It's 25km west of Arusha, just off the Dodoma road.

Guesthouses & Hotels – Colonel Middleton Road Area

In the small dusty streets just east of Colonel Middleton Rd and north of the stadium (a 10-minute walk from the bus station) is a clutch of cheap places offering no-frills rooms – most twin-bedded with nets and shared bathrooms (hot water available on request), and most without food. The area isn't great, but many travellers stay here because it's reasonably close to the bus stand, and prices are among the lowest in town. While some of the accommodations are decent value, others let flycatchers onto their premises and should be avoided. Watch out for smooth talkers wanting to sell you safaris or trying to steer you to a hotel other than the one you've picked out.

Levolosi Guest House (s/d without bathroom Tsh4000/5000) Diagonally opposite the main Monjes Guesthouse building, with undistinguished although adequate rooms around an enclosed cement courtyard.

Kitundu Guesthouse (d Tsh12,000, s/d without bathroom Tsh5000/10,000) Another decent, reliable choice, with clean but basic rooms, including a few with bathroom.

Monjes Guesthouse (d Tsh12,000, s without bathroom Tsh9000) This friendly establishment is one of the better ones of the bunch, with clean, no-frills rooms with hot water. It's split between a main building and an annexe diagonally opposite.

William's Inn (☎ 027-250 3578; s/d US$20/25) This reliable place is short on ambience, but the rooms (the doubles have one large bed) are clean and good value. It's on the other side of Colonel Middleton Rd from the previous listings, and somewhat quieter.

Golden Rose (☎ 027-250 7959; Middleton Rd; s/d Tsh25,000/35,000) Functional twin and double-bedded rooms – all with bathroom and hot-water showers – in a convenient location near the Dar Express bus office.

Guesthouses & Hotels – Market Area

These places are all in the busy central market area in the western part of town, marginally closer to the bus stand than the Colonel Middleton Rd area hotels, and generally a few steps up in both price and standard.

Arusha Backpackers (☎ 027-250 4474; www.arusha backpackers.co.tz; Sokoine Rd; s/d/q US$6/12/20) Newish, but already popular, with cheap, clean rooms and clean shared facilities. However, most of the doubles have only interior windows, and a few have no windows at all. Several rooms have fans. There's also a two-bunk quad. It's managed by Kindoroko Hotel in Moshi.

Kilimanjaro Villa Guest House (☎ 027-250 8109; Azimo St; s/d without bathroom Tsh7000/10,000) This low-key place is well past its prime, with tatty but acceptable rooms and warm-ish water in the shared bathrooms. It's on a small side street a few blocks east of the bus stand. There's no food.

Hotel Fort de Moines (☎ 027-250 7406, 027-254 8523; s/d US$20/25) The incongruously named Fort de Moines is a few steps up from the others in this listing in both price and standard, with bland straightforward rooms with fans but no nets. It's good value if you're looking for a 'proper' hotel at budget prices.

Arusha Centre Inn (☎ 027-250 0421; s/d US$20/25) Next door to Hotel Fort de Moines, and nicer, with spotless rooms that are good value for the price, a restaurant and a location within easy walking distance of the bus stand.

Hotel 7-11 (☎ 027-250 1261; s/d/tw US$25/30/35) Directly opposite the central bus station (look for the white multistorey building), with clean, albeit noisy rooms that are decent value for the doubles. The street outside is chaotic enough that it's only worth considering if you have an early morning departure.

Hotel Pallsons (☎ 027-254 8483; hotel_pallsons@ yahoo.com; Market St; s/d US$30/37) This old-timer has faded but functional and relatively spacious rooms in a noisy, central location opposite the market.

Guesthouses & Hotels – Clock Tower Roundabout & Beyond

All of the following places are in the green and leafy and overall quieter eastern part of town. There are also budget rooms at L'Oasis Lodge (see Midrange listings).

Lutheran Centre (☎ 027-50 8856/7; elcthq@elct.or.tz; Boma Rd; s/d without bathroom Tsh8000/15,000) If the drab, institutional atmosphere doesn't put you off, rooms here – all with shared facilities – are quite decent value. There's no food, and unless you've made prior arrangements, check-in and check-out are during regular business hours Monday to Friday only. It's diagonally opposite the post office in a poorly signposted multistorey building above Café Bamboo.

Centre House Hostel (☎ 027-250 2313; Kanisa Rd; r per person without bathroom Tsh10,000) Run by the Catholic diocese, this no-frills place has spacious rooms with shared facilities, and meals (from Tsh3000) on order. Most rooms are doubles, but there's a quad and a triple. The gates shut at 10pm unless you've made previous arrangements. It's about 300m in from Old Moshi Rd.

Outpost Lodge (☎ 027-254 8405; www.outpost tanzania.com; Serengeti Rd; 6-bed dm US$25, s/d/tr US$45/58/75; 🖳 🕿) The Outpost, in a leafy residential area 500m off Old Moshi Rd and about 1km southeast of the Clock Tower roundabout, has a few dorm-style rooms in an old two-storey house, plus small and pleasant detached garden bungalows scattered around the lawns. All have mosquito nets and TV, and there's a restaurant and a tiny gym.

Everest Inn (☎ 027-250 8419; everesttzus@yahoo |.com; Old Moshi Rd; s/d/tr US$30/40/55) Clean, homy rooms behind the Everest Chinese restaurant. There's a triple in the main house, and better, quiet twins and doubles in a small building in the garden behind. All come with mosquito nets and bathroom, and a choice of Western or Chinese breakfast. It's 500m southeast of the Clock Tower roundabout, and signposted along Old Moshi Rd.

Arusha Naaz Hotel (☎ 027-257 2087; www.arusha naaz.net; Sokoine Rd; s/d/tr US$30/45/60; 🖳) Naaz' atmosphere is uninspiring, but the location is convenient and the rooms are decent and spotless, all with TV, fan and hot water. Size and standards vary, so check out a few. Downstairs is a restaurant with inexpensive breakfasts, a lunch buffet (daily except Sunday) and a car rental office.

MIDRANGE
Le Jacaranda (☎ 027-254 4624; jacaranda@tz2000.com; s/d/tr US$40/45/65) Spacious, pleasantly faded rooms in a large house set in pretty gardens, and a restaurant (meals from Tsh5000). It's on a quiet side street about 100m north of Old Moshi Rd at the eastern end of town.

Arusha Crown Hotel (☎ 027-250 8523; www.arusha crownhotel.com; cnr Makongoro Rd & Mosque St; s/d

US$60/80) Well-equipped local business travellers' hotel in a rather scruffy area overlooking the stadium just a few blocks from the bus stand.

L'Oasis Lodge & Restaurant (☎ 027-250 7089; www .loasislodge.com; s/d/tr US$69/85/111, backpackers r per person without bathroom US$18; 🖳 🕿) This popular and clued-in place has a mix of African-style rondavels and airy stilt houses set around pleasant gardens, including several rooms with telephone/internet connection and power-surge protection. Near the main lodge are a dozen clean, twin-bedded backpacker rooms sharing hot-water bathrooms. There's also a restaurant (see Lounge, p201), a sports bar, a tree-house dining/drinking area and a pool. Accommodation prices include full breakfast, and discounts for Peace Corps, VSOs and other volunteers are available for the non-backpacker rooms. Overall, a good balance between proximity to town and relaxing surroundings. It's 2km northwest of the Clock Tower, about 1km off the Moshi–Nairobi road and signposted diagonally opposite the old Mt Meru Hotel.

New Safari Hotel (☎ 027-250 3261; Boma Rd; s/d/tr US$85/105/135; 🔀 🖳) Good-value rooms catering to business travellers in a centrally located high-rise, plus a restaurant, secure parking and 24-hour internet access.

TOP END
City Centre
Impala Hotel (☎ 027-250 8448/51, 027-250 2362; www .impalahotel.com; cnr Moshi & Old Moshi Rds; s/d US$75/95; 🔀 🖳 🕿) Large, reliable and centrally located, this establishment is good value, with a forex bureau, several restaurants, a small garden area and good, hot showers in the rooms in the new wing. The same management is building the soon-to-open high-rise Naura Springs Hotel off the Nairobi–Moshi road.

Kibo Palace Hotel (☎ 027-254 4472; www.kibopalace hotel.com; Old Moshi Rd; s/d from US$145/165; 🖳 🕿) The new Kibo Palace has lovely, well-appointed rooms, a restaurant, and a pool in small, green grounds.

Arusha Hotel (☎ 027-250 7777/8870; Clock Tower roundabout; r from US$200; 🖳 🕿) The Arusha Hotel (formerly the New Arusha Hotel) has been completely renovated and is a recommended central choice in this category. Rooms are of a high standard, there's a restaurant with a daily lunch buffet (US$12), and expansive gardens behind.

Outside the City Centre

Karama Lodge (☎ 0754-475188; www.karama-lodge
.com; s/d US$79/107; 💻) Karama, on a forested
hillside in the Suye Hill area just south of
town, offers proximity to both nature and
the town centre. Accommodation is in about
two dozen rustic and very lovely stilt bungalows, each with a veranda with views to
both Kilimanjaro and Meru on clear days.
There are short walking trails nearby, and a
restaurant, which also caters to vegetarians.
Follow Old Moshi Rd south about 2km from
the edge of town to the signpost; turn left and
continue 1.5km further.

Moivaro Coffee Plantation (☎ 027-255 3242/3;
www.moivaro.com; s/d US$100/136; 💻 🍴) Set amid
the coffee plantations east of Arusha, with
cosy cottages, each with its own fireplace, and
extensive gardens, this place is justifiably popular as a pre- and post-safari overnight respite
for upper-midrange safaris. It's 5km outside
town along the road to Moshi, then about 2km
off the highway along a signposted, unpaved
road. Day rooms are also available.

Onsea House (www.onseahouse.com; s/d US$145/175;
🍴) A new, lovely place self-described with
some accuracy as the 'best luxury bed and
breakfast in Arusha'. Each room has its own
theme, there's a bar and small restaurant, and
gardens. Very tranquil and very classy. The
turn-off is signposted along the Moshi road
about 4km from town, from where it's another
1km or so further.

Kigongoni (☎ 027-255 3087; www.kigongoni.net;
s/d/tr US$155/210; 🍴) Kigongoni has a tranquil
hilltop perch about 8km outside Arusha, a
cosy common area with fireplaces and reading
nooks, a restaurant and spacious cottages, all
with porches, large bathtubs and wide views.
Birding and village walks are possible in
the surrounding area, and a portion of the
lodge's profits go to support a nearby clinic
for children with mental disabilities. Follow
the Moshi road east for 8km to the signposted
turn-off, from where it's another 1km.

Eating

Spices & Herbs (☎ 027-250 2279; Moshi Rd; meals from
Tsh3500; 🕑 lunch & dinner) If you've had your fill
of Tanzanian fare, this is the best spot in town
for Ethiopian cuisine.

Amar Cuisine (☎ 027-250 6911; meals about Tsh4000;
🕑 11am-3pm & 6pm-midnight) Just off Sokoine Rd
at the end of Bondeni St, with tandoori and
other Indian dishes, including some vegetar-

ian selections. Allow 30 to 45 minutes' preparation time for meals.

Via Via (meals Tsh4000-6000; 🕑 9.30am-10pm Fri-
Wed, to midnight Thu, closed Sun) Set in quiet gardens behind the Natural History Museum,
this laid-back place is a popular meeting spot,
with salads, sandwiches, fresh bread, cakes,
yogurt and light meals (a mixture of local and
European fare), plus a bar and live music on
Thursdays from 9pm.

Dragon Pearl (☎ 027-254 4107; Old Moshi Rd; meals
Tsh4000-8000; 🕑 lunch & dinner) A good bet for delicious Chinese food, with a garden setting, fast
service and an attentive host. It's around the
corner from Impala Hotel.

Jambo's Makuti Bar & Restaurant (Boma Rd; meals
from Tsh5000; 🕑 to 10pm) European café vibes in a
Tanzanian setting. There's an à la carte menu
with a mix of Tanzanian and local dishes, and
a plate of the day for about Tsh5500. Jambo's
Coffee House (Boma Rd) next door has cakes,
snacks and good coffee.

Sazan (Old Moshi Rd; meals Tsh5000-6000) This tiny,
incongruous place – directly on the roadside
adjoining a used car lot – has inexpensive
Japanese fast food–style meals.

Khan's Barbecue (Mosque St; mixed grill from Tsh6000;
🕑 from 6.30pm) This Arusha institution –
'Chicken on the Bonnet' – is an auto-spares
store by day and a popular and very earthy
barbecue by night, with a heaping spread of
grilled, skewered meat and salads. Look for
the Zubeda Auto Spares sign.

Everest Inn (☎ 027-250 8419; everesttzus@yahoo.com;
Old Moshi Rd; meals from Tsh6000; 🕑 breakfast, lunch & dinner) Tasty Chinese food served in an outdoor
garden, or indoors in an old, atmospheric
house. The restaurant also runs a small guesthouse (see p200).

Big Bite (cnr Somali Rd & Swahili St; meals from
Tsh6500; 🕑 closed Tue) Delicious Indian food,
including numerous vegetarian dishes, in a
no-frills setting.

Impala Hotel (☎ 027-250 8448/51; www.impalahotel
.com; cnr Moshi & Old Moshi Rds; meals from Tsh6500)
There are several eateries here, with the
open-air Indian restaurant the best of the
bunch, with delicious tandoori and various
veg choices.

Pepe's (Kanisa Rd; pizza from Tsh6000; mains Tsh7000-
15,000; 🕑 lunch & dinner) Outdoor garden seating
or indoors under a large, covered pavilion,
well-prepared Italian and continental food,
and (evenings) good Indian cuisine. It's 500m
off Old Moshi Rd and signposted.

Lounge (☎ 027-250 7089; meals from Tsh8000; ☺ 10am-late) A low-key place with delicious, great-value cuisine, featuring homemade tagliatelle, gourmet wraps, crispy salads, meat and sea-food grills, pizzas and 'Kilimanjaro nachos'. Everything is freshly made and served in generously large portions against a relaxed backdrop of lounge seating and music. It's at L'Oasis Lodge (see p200), on the northern edge of town.

Flame Tree (☎ 0754-370474; trw@cybernet.co.tz; just off Kaunda Rd; set menu about Tsh20,000, mains Tsh8000-17,000; ☺ noon-2pm & 7-10pm Mon-Sat, noon-2pm Sun) This popular place, now in a new location several blocks in from Old Moshi Rd, has cosy seating that's ideal for an intimate dinner or quiet lunch, and well-prepared and well-presented continental cuisine featuring all fresh ingredients.

For inexpensive burgers, pizza, sandwiches and other Western-style fast food try the ever-popular **Patisserie** (Sokoine Rd; snacks & meals from Tsh1500; ☺ 7.30am-6.30pm Mon-Sat, 8.30am-2pm Sun), which also has soup, light meals and an internet café; **McMoody's** (Sokoine Rd; ☺ 11am-10pm Tue-Sun), with mostly burgers; and a branch of the South African chain, **Steers** (Joel Maeda St).

For more local flavour, try **Geekay's Take-Away** (India St; meals from Tsh1000; ☺ 7.30am-6pm Mon-Sat), and **Mirapot** (India St; meals from Tsh1000), diagonally opposite, both with inexpensive plates of rice, *ugali* (a staple made from maize or cassava flour, or both) and sauce. There's a good-value lunch buffet at **Arusha Naaz Hotel** (☎ 027-257 2087; www.arushanaaz.net; Sokoine Rd; lunch buffet US$5; ☺ lunch Mon-Sat), with mostly Indian cuisine, and the clean, no-frills **Old Rock Restaurant** (Mosque St; meals Tsh2000-5000) has burgers and local-style meals near the main market.

Just out of town adjoining Shoprite is the TFA Centre, with gelato and gourmet coffee shops. Most shops at the mall are open from about 9am to 6pm Monday to Saturday, and between around 10am and 2pm on Sunday.

For self-caterers:

Clocktower Supermarket (Clock Tower roundabout)
Shoprite (Dodoma Rd; ☺ 9am-7pm Mon-Fri, 8am-5pm Sat, 9am-1pm Sun) About 2km west of the town centre, with a large selection.

Drinking & Entertainment

Via Via (Boma Rd) A good spot for a drink and one of the best places to find out about upcoming music and traditional dance events; it's in the grounds of the Natural History Museum.

Greek Club (cnr Old Moshi & Serengeti Rds; ☺ closed Mon & Thu) A popular expat hang-out, especially on weekend evenings; it has free movies on Sunday afternoon, good pizza and a lively sports bar.

Colobus Club (Old Moshi Rd; admission Tsh5000; ☺ 9pm-dawn Fri & Sat) Arusha's loudest and brashest nightclub.

Crystal Club (Seth Benjamin Rd; ☺ from 11pm Fri & Sat) Come here for dancing till late.

Shopping

The small alley just off Joel Maeda St is lined with vendors selling woodcarvings, batiks, Maasai jewellery and other crafts. Quality is generally good, but hard bargaining is required. Other places to try include the nearby **Craft Shop** (☎ 027-254 8565; Goliondoi Rd), with mostly carvings, and the large and unmissable **Cultural Heritage** (Dodoma Rd), 12km west of town. Quality and selection here are good, although intermediaries get a fairly large cut of the (high) purchase prices. **Aminata Boutique** (Sokoine Rd), in the covered entry passage to Arusha Naaz Hotel, has textiles.

Colourful local-produce markets in the region include the **Ngaramtoni market**, on Thursday and Sunday, 12km north of town on the Nairobi road, which draws Maasai from miles around; and the **Tengeru market**, on Saturday, with a smaller market on Wednesday. It's 10km east of town along the Moshi road.

Getting There & Away

AIR

There are daily flights to Dar es Salaam and Zanzibar (ZanAir, Coastal Aviation, Precision Air and Air Tanzania), Nairobi (Precision Air), Seronera and other airstrips in Serengeti National Park (Coastal Aviation, Air Excel, Regional Air), Mwanza (Precision Air, via Shinyanga), and Lake Manyara and Tarangire National Parks (Coastal Aviation, Air Excel, Regional Air). Some flights use Kilimanjaro International Airport (KIA), about halfway between Moshi and Arusha off the main highway, while others leave from Arusha airport, 8km west of town along the Dodoma road; verify the departure point when buying your ticket. International airlines flying into KIA include KLM and Ethiopian Air. Some sample prices: Arusha–Dar (Tsh160,000), Arusha–Mwanza (Tsh165,000) and Arusha–Seronera (US$150).

Airline offices include.

Air Excel (☎ 027-254 8429, 027-250 1597; reservations@ airexcelonline.com; 2nd fl, Subzali (Exim Bank) Bldg, Golion-doi Rd) Diagonally opposite Standard Chartered Bank.

Air Tanzania (☎ 027-250 3201, 027-250 3203; www .airtanzania.com; Boma Rd)

Coastal Aviation (☎ 027-250 0087; 0754-317808; arusha@coastal.cc; Boma Rd)

Ethiopian Airlines (☎ 027-250 6167, 027-250 4231; www.ethiopianairlines.com; Boma Rd)

KLM (☎ 027-250 8062/3; reservations.arusha@klm.com; Boma Rd)

Precision Air (☎ 027-250 2818/36; www.precision airtz.com; Boma Rd; ☯ 8am-5pm Mon-Fri, to 2pm Sat & Sun)

Regional Air (☎ 027-250 4477, 027-250 2541; www .airkenya.com; Nairobi Rd)

ZanAir (☎ 024-223 3670, 024-223 3768; Summit Centre, Sokoine Rd)

BUS

Arusha has two main bus stations: the central bus station near the market, for buses to Dar es Salaam, Tanga, Mwanza, Nairobi, Mombasa and other points north and east; and the Kilombero bus station, 2km west of town along the Dodoma road, opposite Shoprite, for buses to Babati, Kondoa and points south. Buses to Singida (via Babati) and other destinations towards Lake Victoria also leave from the central bus station. Both, but especially the central bus station, are chaotic and popular haunts for flycatchers and touts. Watch your luggage, and don't negotiate any safari deals at the stations. If you're arriving for the first time, head straight for a taxi, or – if arriving at the central station – duck into the lobbies of Hotel 7-11 or Hotel Aquiline, both across the street, to get your bearings.

If you're arriving at the central bus station (and unless you're staying in the budget-hotel area downtown, in which case it makes sense to stay on the bus), you can avoid the bus station altogether by asking the driver to drop you off in front of the (currently closed) Mt Meru Hotel. All buses coming from Dar es Salaam and Moshi pass by here. There are taxis just opposite, and the scene is less hectic than at the central station. Fares from here to central hotels shouldn't be more than Tsh2000. When leaving Arusha, the best thing to do is book your ticket the day before, so that in the morning when you arrive with your luggage you can get straight on your bus. For pre-dawn buses, take a taxi to the station and ask the driver to drop you directly at your bus. Despite what you may hear, there are no luggage fees (unless you have an extraordinarily large pack).

To/From Dar es Salaam

The main lines to/from Dar es Salaam (all about nine hours) include the following. All depart from and arrive at their own offices away from the main bus stations.

Dar Express (Colonel Middleton Rd, just down from Sunny Safaris; tickets Tsh17,000) Buses depart Arusha at 5.15am and 6am sharp and, with luck, arrive in Dar es Salaam in time to catch the 4.15pm ferry to Zanzibar (the 5.15am bus is the best bet for this). If you're trying to do this, don't get off at Ubungo bus station in Dar es Salaam, but stay on the bus until it terminates at its offices in the city centre near Kisutu, from where it's Tsh2500 and about 10 minutes in a taxi to the ferry docks. If the bus is running behind schedule from Arusha, it's occasionally faster to get off at Ubungo and get a taxi from there straight to the ferry dock, but only marginally so, and the taxi from Ubungo will cost you several times as much. Other departures from Arusha are at 7am, 8am, 9.15am and 10.30am.

Royal Coach (☎ 0784-851831; royalty2000@hot mail.com; cnr Nairobi & Colonel Middleton Rds; tickets Tsh22,000) Departures at 8.30am from Bamprass petrol station on the Nairobi Rd in Mianzini (Tsh2500 in a taxi from the Clock Tower).

Scandinavian Express (small side street next to Kilombero Bus Stand, & opposite Shoprite; tickets Tsh18,000/24,000 ordinary/luxury) Ordinary and luxury departures at 8.30am and a second luxury bus at 11.30am.

To/From Moshi

Buses and minibuses run throughout the day between Arusha and Moshi (about Tsh1200, one hour). It's pricier but safer and more comfortable to take one of the Arusha-Nairobi shuttles (p350; Tsh5000 between Moshi and Arusha).

To/From Nairobi (Kenya)

For information on this route see p350. Akamba buses to Nairobi en route from Dar es Salaam depart Arusha about 2.30pm from next to Eland Hotel in Mianzini, along the Nairobi road.

To/From Babati, Kolo, Kondoa & Dodoma

Mtei line buses run three to four times daily (from the Mtei booking office next to the Scandinavian Express booking office

NORTHERN TANZANIA

near Shoprite) between Arusha and Babati (Tsh5000, four hours), departing between 6am and 2pm. The 6am bus continues on to Kondoa (Tsh10,000, seven hours). Otherwise, for Kondoa and Dodoma (about 12 hours), you'll need to change vehicles at Babati, as most transport to Dodoma uses the longer tarmac route via Chalinze. This generally involves an overnight in Babati, as most southward transport from Babati departs early in the morning.

To/From Musoma & Mwanza
Falcon and Spider lines go from the central bus stand to Mwanza via Nairobi and Musoma (Tsh38,000 plus US$20 for a Kenyan transit visa, 20 hours), departing Arusha at about 3.30pm.

The other option is to go via Singida and Shinyanga in a rugged southwestern loop (about Tsh30,000), where the road is much better than it was. Check with Coast and Jordan lines at the central bus stand.

To/From Kampala (Uganda)
Scandinavian Express goes daily between Arusha and Kampala (Tsh30,000, 17 hours), departing in each direction about 3pm. For more information on connections to Kampala see p353.

To/From Lushoto
Fasaha and Chikito line buses depart daily at about 6.30am (Tsh9000, six hours). However it often works out just as fast (although more expensively) to take an express bus heading for Dar as far as Mombo, and then get local transport from there to Lushoto.

To/From Tanga
Tashriff departs Arusha daily for Tanga at 8.30am and 11.30am (seven hours). Otherwise, take any Dar es Salaam bus and transfer at Segera junction, though this can entail a rather lengthy wait.

Getting Around
TO/FROM KILIMANJARO INTERNATIONAL AIRPORT
Both Air Tanzania and Precision Air have free shuttles to KIA for their passengers, departing from their offices about two hours before the scheduled flight departure. In the other direction, look for the airlines' buses in the airport arrivals area.

Riverside Shuttle has a daily bus to Kilimanjaro International Airport (KIA) coordinated with KLM departures and arrivals. It costs US$10 and departs at 6pm sharp from its office. It also waits for arriving passengers; look out for the bus in the airport arrivals area.

The starting price for taxis from town to KIA is Tsh50,000, though it's usually possible to almost halve this.

TO/FROM ARUSHA AIRPORT
Any *dalla-dalla* heading out along the Dodoma road can drop you at the junction, from where you'll have to walk about 1.5km to the airstrip. Taxis from town charge from Tsh8000.

CAR & MOTORCYCLE
Arusha Naaz Rent-a-Car (☎ 027-250 2087; www.arusha naaz.net) An efficient, reliable outfit based at Arusha Naaz Hotel (see p200), with a selection of 2WD and 4WD vehicles. Self-drive rentals can sometimes be arranged for Arusha town rentals only. Rates (from US$80 to US$100 per day for 4WD) include 120 free kilometres per day.

TAXI
There are taxi stands around the central bus station, opposite the old Mt Meru Hotel, on the southern side of the Clock Tower roundabout near the Arusha Hotel, and at the eastern end of Makongoro Rd. Town rides cost from Tsh2000.

AROUND ARUSHA
Cultural Tourism Programs
There are many Cultural Tourism Programs in the Arusha area, with the following just a sampling. The TTB information office (p197) is the best place for details. For booking information, see the boxed text, above.

NG'IRESI
This popular tour to Ng'iresi village, about 7km northeast of Arusha on the slopes of Mt Meru, includes visits to local irrigation projects and Maasai homes, plus some walking and a visit to a local farm. There's an overnight option with a hike up a small volcano.

LONGIDO
The 2629m-high Longido lies just to the east of the main road between Arusha and Namanga (the Tanzania–Kenya border), and

---

COMMUNITY TOURISM SPOTLIGHT: CULTURAL TOURISM PROGRAMS

Numerous villages outside Arusha (several of which are described in the text accompanying this box) as well as elsewhere in the country (including Machame, Engaruka, Mto wa Mbu, Kondoa, the Usambara Mountains near Lushoto and Pangani) have organised 'cultural tourism programs' that offer an alternative to the safari scene and an opportunity to experience local culture. They range in length from a few hours to a few days, and usually centre on light hikes and cultural activities.

Although some have now deviated from their initial founding purpose of serving as income generators for community projects – often revolving instead these days around the enterprising individuals who run them – they nevertheless offer an excellent chance to get to know Tanzania at the local level. Most have various 'modules' available, from half a day to several nights, and fees are generally reasonable, starting from Tsh20,000/30,000 per person for a half-/full-day programme with lunch (less for two or more people). Payments should be made on site; always ask for a receipt. For overnight tours, camping or home stays can be arranged, though expect conditions to be very basic and rustic.

All tours in the Arusha area can be booked through the Arusha TTB Tourist Information Centre (p197), which can also tell you the best transport connections. Tours elsewhere should be arranged directly with the local coordinator, although the Arusha TTB may also be able to help. Book a day in advance for the more distant ones; for Ng'iresi and other programmes close to town, guides usually wait at the TTB office on stand-by each morning. Check with the TTB to ensure the one you go with is authorised.

80km north of Arusha. It's not volcanic in origin, but a remnant of much older rock. The lower slopes are covered in dense bush, but Longido's summit is a peak of bare rock, giving views west to the Rift Valley, north into Kenya, south to Mt Meru and east to Kilimanjaro. In addition to the climb itself (eight to 10 hours return from the main road), the area makes an interesting excursion to get an introduction to Maasai life, including a visit to some bomas and to a local cattle market.

OL DOINYO SAMBU

This tour involves short walks in Maasai country, about 35km north of Arusha off the Nairobi road, visits to a Maasai boma and market, and an introduction to Maasai traditions.

ILKIDIN'GA

Walks (ranging from half-day strolls to a three-day 'cultural hike') and the chance to experience the traditional culture of the Arusha people are the main attractions in this well-organised program around Ilkidin'ga, 7km north of Arusha.

MULALA

Set in a region about 30km northeast of Arusha; this is the only tour completely implemented by women. It involves visits to a local women's cooperative and some short walks; an overnight stay is possible if you have camping gear. With an early start, it's no problem to do this tour as a day trip from Arusha.

MKURU

Mkuru, near Arusha National Park's Momela Gate, is the site of a camel camp where you can take camel safaris ranging from a half-day to several days, or climb nearby Ol Doinyo Landaree mountain (about two hours to the summit). This tour is more time-consuming to organise than the others, but you'll have the chance to experience life in a small and relatively isolated Maasai community and you're unlikely to see many other tourists. Bring everything with you, including all food and drinking water, especially for overnight tours. Riding camels entails at least one night in Mkuru or at the nearby Momella Wildlife Lodge (p208) to organise things; there's also a 5km walk from Ngare Nanyuki village (p209) to reach the camel camp. With several days, it's possible to combine the Mkuru programme with the Longido programme on a three-day/two-night camel safari from Mkuru to Longido Mountain, with the final night spent in Longido before returning to Arusha.

AROUND ARUSHA

TENGERU

About 12km east of Arusha and just off the main highway, the Tengeru programme includes visits to a coffee farm, a local school and the Tengeru market, and an introduction to the life of the Meru people. Home stays can also be arranged.

Lake Duluti

This small and tranquil crater lake – part of the Duluti Forest Reserve – lies about 11km east of Arusha, just off the main road near the village of Tengeru. It's a pleasant getaway, although walks around the lake were being discouraged at the time of writing due to a spate of robberies.

The **Lake Duluti Club** (day admission Tsh1000) has a small lawn, a restaurant serving a limited selection of drinks and meals with advance order only and a couple of rowboats (per hour without/with guide Tsh6000/7000). If the security situation improves – ask at the club or in Arusha – walking around the lake is also possible, though you'll need to pay the forest reserve fee (per person US$7) at the reserve office just up from the club.

SLEEPING & EATING

Serena Mountain Village (☎ 027-255 3313, 027-250 8175; www.serenahotels.com; s/d US$180/225) An old British-style manor with a genteel ambience, views over the lake's green waters from the terrace and well-appointed small stone-and-thatch cottages covered with ivy.

It's possible to **camp** (per person US$7) on the lawn behind the forest reserve office, although there's nowhere for bathing or cooking and the site isn't secure. Better is the Lake Duluti Club, with **camping** (per person Tsh5000) inside its small compound, including a small cooking area and meals on order.

GETTING THERE & AWAY

Have any bus or *dalla-dalla* along the Arusha–Moshi Rd drop you at the Tengeru junction, from where it's about a 2km walk in to the lake (signposted for Serena Mountain Village), and go about 2km to the hotel. To reach the forestry office and Lake Duluti Club: continue for about 300m past the hotel entrance to the Institute of Livestock Training. Turn right, follow the road down and then up for about 200m, and go right at the Duluti Forest Reserve sign. The reserve office is ahead to the left, and Lake Duluti Club is about 200m further on to the right.

Usa River

This tiny, nondescript town on the Arusha–Moshi Rd about 20km east of Arusha, is of interest for its proximity to Arusha National Park, and for the handful of atmospheric, upmarket lodges based nearby. All are signposted from the main road.

The **Ngare Sero Mountain Lodge** (☎ 027-255 3638; www.ngare-sero-lodge.com; per person full board garden cottages/main house US$130/170) is a lovely colonial-era lodge with small, attached cottages set around lush gardens or better suites in the main house – itself reminiscent of an old hunting-lodge estate. There are also two family-style cottages, and fishing, walking, canoeing, cultural tours and yoga can be arranged.

Mount Meru Game Lodge & Sanctuary (www.intimate-places.com; s/d from US$140/190) is a cosy place set in its own private wildlife reserve. There are 15 rooms and two suites, and the attractive gardens and adjoining wildlife sanctuary make an amenable backdrop.

Rivertrees Country Inn (☎ 027-255 3894; www.rivertrees.com; s/d from US$145/175; 🖳) has a genteel old-world ambience and excellent cuisine served family-style around a large wooden dining table. Accommodation is in the main building – a renovated colonial-era farmhouse – or in garden rooms, or two private 'river cottages' with fireplaces and one with wheelchair access.

The newer **Arumeru River Lodge** (☎ 027-255 3573; www.arumerulodge.com; s/d US$117/174; 🖵 🐾) lacks the old-style atmosphere of the other places, but is nevertheless attractive, with 10 attached two-room chalets in expansive gardens and a heated swimming pool.

Monduli Mountains

The Monduli range, northwest of Arusha and west of Mt Meru, offers offbeat walking from its northern side, with views over the Rift Valley plains and to the distant cone of Ol Doinyo Lengai. There are no set routes. All walks follow old cattle trails that become overgrown during the rains, and a local guide is essential. The base for trekking is the area of Monduli Juu, near Emairete village (9km from Monduli town), where you can arrange a guide and pay the fees. All walks (about Tsh20,000 per day including guide and lunch, plus Tsh4000 for any walks that enter the forest) need to be arranged either through the cultural tourism representative, who lives along the main road in Emairete, through the village chief or with the TTB in Arusha. They can also help you find a spot to camp (bring everything with you from Arusha) or arrange an overnight stay in a Maasai boma. Tropical Trails (p46) also organises hikes here. Bring plenty of water, sunscreen, a hat and long pants, as many of the trails are overgrown with thick, thorny brush.

ARUSHA NATIONAL PARK
☎ 027

Arusha National Park, although one of Tanzania's smallest parks, is one of its most beautiful and most topographically varied. Its main features include Ngurdoto Crater (often dubbed Little Ngorongoro) and the Momela Lakes to the east. To the west is beautiful Mt Meru. The two areas are joined by a narrow strip, with Momela Gate at its centre. The park's altitude, which varies from 1500m to more than 4500m, has a variety of vegetation zones supporting numerous animal species.

Ngurdoto Crater is surrounded by forest, while the crater floor is a swamp. West of the crater is Serengeti Ndogo (Little Serengeti), an extensive area of open grassland and the only place in the park where herds of Burchell's zebras can be found.

The **Momela Lakes**, like many in the Rift Valley, are shallow and alkaline and attract a wide variety of wader birds, particularly flamingos. The lakes are fed by underground streams; due to their varying mineral content, each lake supports a different type of algal growth, which gives them different colours. Bird life also varies quite distinctly from one lake to another, even where they are only separated by a narrow strip of land. **Mt Meru** (see Trekking Mt Meru, p209) is a mixture of lush forest and bare rock with a spectacular crater.

Animal life in the park is abundant. You can be fairly certain of sighting zebras, giraffes, waterbucks, reedbucks, klipspringers, hippos, buffaloes, elephants, hyenas, mongooses, dik-diks, warthogs, baboons and vervet and colobus monkeys, despite dense vegetation in some areas. You may even catch sight of the occasional leopard. There are no lions, and no rhinos due to poaching.

While tour companies often relegate the park to a day trip, it's better to allow at least a night or two to appreciate the wildlife and do a walking or canoe safari.

Information

Entry fees are US$35/10 per adult/child aged five to 15 years per 24-hour period. For camping fees see p77. There is a US$20 rescue fee per person per trip for treks on Mt Meru. Guides cost US$15 per day (US$20 for walking), and the huts on Mt Meru cost US$20.

The main park entrance is at Ngongongare Gate, about 10km from the main road, while **park headquarters** (☎ 027-255 3995, 0732-971303; ⏰ 6.30am-6.30pm) – the main contact for making camp site or resthouse reservations and for arranging guides and porters to climb Mt Meru – are about 14km further in near Momela Gate. There is another entrance at Ngurdoto Gate, on the southeastern edge of the park. All gates are open from 6am to 6pm. Walking is permitted on the Mt Meru side of the park, and there is also a walking trail along part of the Ngurdoto Crater rim (though it's not permitted to descend either on foot or in a vehicle to the crater floor). **Green Footprint Adventures** (www.greenfootprint.co.tz) does canoe safaris on the Momela Lakes.

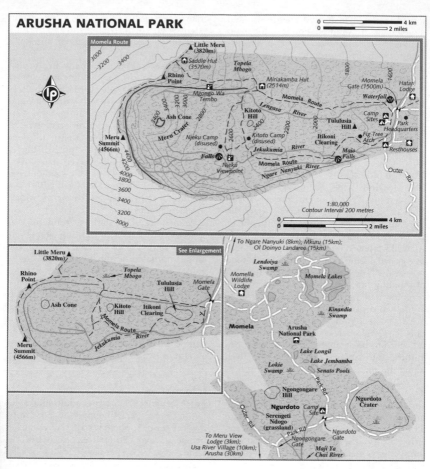

ARUSHA NATIONAL PARK

The best map of the park is the MaCo *Arusha National Park* map, widely available in Arusha.

Sleeping & Eating

The park has four public camp sites, three near Momela Gate (including one with a shower), and one near Ngurdoto Gate. There are also two resthouses with kitchen facilities near the park headquarters.

Momella Wildlife Lodge (☎ 027-250 6423/6; www.lions-safari-intl.com/momella.html; s/d/tr half board US$70/93/115) This long-standing establishment, 1.5km off the road from Momela Gate, has small, serviceable cottages set around modest gardens. Vehicle rental with driver costs US$75/100 per half/full day.

Meru View Lodge (☎ 0784-419232; www.meru -view-lodge.de; s/d US$75/90; 🖳) An unassuming, good-value place with a mix of large and small cottages (all priced the same) set in pleasant grounds on the main park road. A vehicle safari costs from US$90 per day including park fees.

Hatari Lodge (☎ 027-255 3456/7; www.hatarilodge .com; r per person full board US$250) The most atmospheric and upmarket of the park lodges – the property was originally owned by Hardy Kruger, of *Hatari!* film fame – with 'modern retro' room décor, a prime location on large lawns frequented by giraffes, and views of Meru and Kilimanjaro on clear days. Rooms are spacious, with large windows, and there's a fireplace and top-notch cuisine. It's on the edge of the park, about 2km north of Momela Gate.

Getting There & Away

Arusha National Park gate is 35km from Arusha. Take the main road between Arusha and Moshi until you reach the signboard, where you turn left. From here, it's about 10km to Ngongongare Gate, where you pay your fees. This is also where the road divides, with both forks joining up again at Momela Gate.

Transport from Arusha can be arranged with all of the lodges (about US$100 per vehicle for a drop, and up to double this for an all-inclusive one-day safari). If you arrive at the park without your own vehicle, most of the lodges can arrange wildlife-viewing drives for guests from about US$70 per day, transport only. If you arrive with your own vehicle and want to climb Mt Meru, you can leave it at Momela Gate (where you will have to pay standard park fees) or, less expensively, at Momella Wildlife Lodge.

Once in the park, there's a good series of gravel roads and tracks leading to all the main features and viewing points. Most are suitable for all vehicles, though some of the tracks get slippery in the rainy season, and a few areas are accessible only with 4WD. From Hatari Lodge, it's possible to continue via a rough track that joins the main Nairobi highway near Longido.

Via public transport, there's a daily bus between Arusha and Ngare Nanyuki village (10km north of Momela Gate) that departs Arusha at about 1pm and Ngare Nanyuki at 7am, and can drop you at the park gate (Tsh2000, 1½ hours). Otherwise, you could take any bus between Arusha and Moshi, and get off at Usa River village, 1km east of the park junction. From Usa River there are sporadic pick-ups that run most days through the park en route to Ngare Nanyuki. However, unless you've arranged with one of the lodges for pick-up, these options won't do you much good as the park doesn't rent vehicles. If you're planning on trekking Mt Meru, there is no onward park transport from Ngongongare Gate, where you need to pay entry fees, to Momela Gate, 14km further on, where you need to arrange your guide and pay your mountain-climbing fees. Walking along this road isn't permitted, and hitching is normally very slow. For more information on hitching, see p360.

TREKKING MT MERU

At 4566m, Mt Meru is the second-highest mountain found in Tanzania. Although completely overshadowed by Kilimanjaro and frequently overlooked by trekkers, it is a spectacular volcanic cone with one of East Africa's most scenic and rewarding climbs. A trek to the summit takes you through grassland and lush forest on the mountain's lower slopes, followed by a dramatic and exhilarating walk along the knife edge of the crater rim.

Mt Meru has a circular base some 20km across at 2000m, where it rises steeply above the plains as an almost perfect cone with an internal crater surrounded by a steep wall of cliffs. At about 2500m the wall has broken away so the top half of the mountain is shaped like a giant horseshoe. The cliffs of the inner wall below the summit are more than 1500m high – among the tallest in Africa. Inside the crater, more recent volcanic eruptions have created a subsidiary peak called the Ash Cone.

Information

COSTS

Most of the companies listed in the Trekking chapter also organise treks on Mt Meru. Rates for a four-day trip range from about US$400 to US$600.

That said, organised treks are not obligatory, and you can do things quite easily on your own. Costs for an independent trek are mostly park entrance, hut and guide fees. Porters are optional. You'll also need to add in the costs of food (which you should get in Arusha, as there's nowhere to stock up near the park), and of transport to the park (minimal, if you take a *dalla-dalla*).

Park Fees

See p207 for park entry fees, all of which are payable at Ngongongare Gate. After paying your entry fees, continue to Momela Gate to arrange a guide and pay mountain fees. All this can take a couple of hours, so it's worth getting an early start or making arrangements the afternoon before. If you enter the park at Ngurdoto Gate, you can pay your entry fees there.

Tipping

Generally the guides and porters on Mt Meru are hard-working and reliable, and do not expect the huge tips sometimes demanded by their counterparts on Kilimanjaro. However, the guides receive a fixed monthly salary for their work as rangers, and get no additional payment from the park for guiding, which means that tips are much appreciated, particularly for going to the summit. In fact, without tips a guide has little extra incentive to take you to the top, so you should calculate this in as part of your fixed costs. Make it clear to the guide that you will tip, but that payment is conditional on them guiding you at an appropriate pace over the full route. We've heard all-too-frequent reports of poorly motivated guides doing everything possible to avoid going to the summit. One of the most common ploys is to rush clients on the early stages of the climb, with the result that the trekkers themselves are forced to bail out early. As a guideline, for a good guide who has completed the full trek with you, plan on a tip of about Tsh10,000 per day per group. Tips for porters average about Tsh5000 per porter per group per trip.

GUIDES & PORTERS

A guide is mandatory and can be arranged at Momela Gate. The fee of US$20 per day is paid to the national park rather than to the guide themself. Unlike on Kilimanjaro, guides on Meru are armed rangers whose purpose is to assist you in case you meet some of the park's buffaloes or elephants, rather than to show you the way (although they do know the route). It's unlikely that an animal will have to be shot, but you should not underestimate the danger and walk too far away from your guide.

Most trekkers go up Mt Meru with only a guide, but if you want porters they are also available at Momela Gate. They come from one of the nearby villages and are not park employees. The charge is Tsh6000 or US$5 per porter per day. This is paid at Momela Gate and given to the porters by park staff after the trip. You will also need to pay park entrance and hut fees for porters (Tsh1500 per day park fee plus Tsh800 per night hut fee). Porters will carry rucksacks weighing up to 15kg (excluding their own food and clothing). Heavier bags will be carried for a negotiable extra fee.

MAPS

The only map is on the reverse of MaCo's *Arusha National Park* map.

Momela Route

The Momela Route is the only route up Meru. It starts at Momela Gate on the eastern side of the mountain and goes to the summit along the northern arm of the horseshoe crater. The route is steep but can be done comfortably in four days (three nights), although trekkers often do it in three days by combining Stages 3 and 4 of the trek. While Meru appears small compared with Kilimanjaro, don't underestimate it. It's still high enough to make the effects of altitude felt, so don't try to rush up if you are not properly acclimatised.

For information on getting to the Momela Gate trailhead, see p209.

SLEEPING

On Mt Meru, the Momela Route has two blocks of bunkhouses ('huts'), conveniently spaced for a three- or four-day trek. Especially during the July-August and December-January high seasons, they are often full, so it's a good idea to carry a tent (though if you camp, you'll still need to pay hut fees). It's currently not possible for independent trekkers to make bookings for the bunkhouses, which operate on a first-come, first-served basis. Each bunkhouse has a cooking and eating area; bring your own stove and fuel. There's also a separate dorm for guides and porters.

STAGE 1: MOMELA GATE TO MIRIAKAMBA HUT

(10km, 4-5hr, 1000m ascent)

Two routes are available from Momela Gate. The first is a track that goes through the forest towards the crater floor, and then steeply up to Miriakamba Hut (2514m). The second is a path that climbs gradually through the grassland direct to Miriakamba. The first option is more interesting and is described here. The second option is shorter and makes a suitable descent route. Some guides prefer to go up and down the short route, and it may require some persuading to take the forest route.

From Momela Gate, cross the Ngare Nanyuki River and follow the track into the forest. The track winds uphill, to reach **Fig Tree Arch** about one hour from the gate. This parasitic wild fig originally grew around two other trees, eventually strangling them. Now only the fig tree remains, with its distinctive arch big enough to drive a car through.

The track continues to climb, reaching Itikoni clearing on the left side of the track after another 15 minutes. From a small hill on the right, you can often see buffaloes grazing. Half an hour further, the track crosses a large stream, just above Maio Falls. Continue for another hour to reach **Kitoto Camp**, with excellent views over the Momela Lakes and out to Kilimanjaro in the distance.

Continue following the track and you will reach a junction after 30 minutes. Take the right track – the left track leads to the floor of Meru Crater – over flat ground, to cross a rocky stream bed (usually dry) and descend slightly through trees, ignoring the path that comes in from the left, to reach Miriakamba Hut, one hour from Kitoto Camp.

From Miriakamba you can walk to **Meru Crater floor** (a two- to three-hour return trip) either in the afternoon of Stage 1 or before Stage 2. The path across the floor leads to Njeku Camp (an old forest station) and Njeku Viewpoint, on a high cliff overlooking a waterfall, with excellent views of the Ash Cone and the entire extent of the crater.

STAGE 2: MIRIAKAMBA HUT TO SADDLE HUT
(4km, 2–3hr, 1050m ascent)

From Miriakamba the path climbs steeply up through pleasant glades between the trees to reach **Topela Mbogo** (Buffalo Swamp) after 45 minutes and **Mgongo Wa Tembo** (Elephant Ridge) after another 30 minutes. From the top of Mgongo Wa Tembo there are great views down into the crater and up to the main cliffs below the summit. Continue through some open grassy clearings and over several stream beds (usually dry) to **Saddle Hut** (3570m).

From Saddle Hut you can walk up to the summit of **Little Meru** (3820m) in about an hour on a clear path. From the top you'll get impressive views of Meru's summit, the horseshoe crater, the top of the Ash Cone, and the sheer cliffs of the crater's inner wall. In the other direction, across the top of the clouds, you can see the great dome of Kilimanjaro. As the sun sets behind Meru, casting huge jagged shadows across the clouds, the snows on Kili turn orange and then pink, as the light fades. Allow 45 minutes to get back to Saddle Hut.

Alternatively, you can go to **Rhino Point** (about two hours return from Saddle Hut), from where the views of Kili are similarly stunning and you can also see down to the base of the Ash Cone and across the crater floor. You'll pass this point on your way both

to and from the summit, but the views are so impressive it's worth going at least twice.

STAGE 3: SADDLE HUT TO MERU SUMMIT & RETURN
(5km, 4–5hr, 1000m ascent, plus 5km, 2–3hr, 1000m descent)

This stage, along a very narrow ridge between the outer slopes of the mountain and the sheer cliffs of the inner crater, is one of the most dramatic and exhilarating sections of trekking anywhere in East Africa. Some trekkers leave Saddle Hut early in the morning (2am to 3am) to reach the summit in time to see the sun rising from behind Kilimanjaro, and to stand a chance of avoiding the late morning mist, although others find this section too exposed for comfort, especially when done in the dark, or find the altitude makes the going beyond Saddle Hut a bit tough. If the sunrise is your main point of interest, there's no need to go to the top. It's just as impressive from Rhino Point (about an hour from Saddle Hut), and perhaps even more so because you also see the main cliffs of the inner wall of the crater being illuminated by the rising sun. The ideal combination is sunrise at Rhino Point, then up to the summit for the views (depending on the mist). If you spend two nights at Saddle Hut you can still see the sunrise at Rhino Point, then trek up to the summit and back in daylight. Many trekkers combine Stages 3 and 4, but this doesn't leave a margin for delays.

If you decide to go for the summit, take plenty of water. Even though it can be below freezing just before dawn, as soon as the sun rises the going becomes hot and hard. During the rainy season, ice and snow can occur on this section of the route, so take care.

For the ascent take the path from behind Saddle Hut, across a flat area, then steeply up through bushes. After an hour the vegetation gives way to bare rock and ash. Rhino Point is marked by a cairn and a pile of bones (presumably a rhino, but what was it doing up here?).

From Rhino Point the path drops slightly then rises again to climb steeply around the edge of the rim over ash scree and bare rock patches. Continue for three to four hours to reach Mt Meru summit (4566m). The views are spectacular. To the west, if it's clear, you can see towards the Rift Valley and the volcanoes of Kitumbeini and Lengai, while down below you can see the town of Arusha, and the plains of the Maasai Steppe beyond.

To descend from the summit, simply retrace the route around the rim back to Saddle Hut (two to three hours).

STAGE 4: SADDLE HUT TO MOMELA GATE
(9km, 3-5½hr, 2000m descent)
From Saddle Hut, retrace the Stage 2 route to Miriakamba (1½ to 2½ hours). From Miriakamba, you can either return through the forest (2½ to three hours), or take a shorter route down the ridge that leads directly to Momela Gate (1½ to 2½ hours). This direct route goes through forest for some of the way, then through open grassland, where giraffes and zebras are often seen.

LAKE MANYARA NATIONAL PARK
Lake Manyara National Park is one of Tanzania's more underrated parks, and often allocated only a quick stop on a loop including Tarangire National Park and Ngorongoro Crater. Yet, while Manyara doesn't have the raw drama and variety of animals of other northern circuit destinations, it has much to offer and many visitors are surprised by how nice it really is. In addition to a stunning setting spanning the Rift Valley escarpment, Manyara's main attractions are its superb birdlife, its tree-climbing lions (though these aren't often seen) and its hippos, which you can observe at closer range here than at most other places. There are also elephants, although the population has been declining in recent years. The park, which is between 900m and 1800m above sea level, is bordered to the west by the dramatic western escarpment of the Rift Valley. To the east is the alkaline Lake Manyara, which at certain times of year hosts tens of thousands of flamingos, as well as a diversity of other birdlife. Depending on the season, about two-thirds of the park's total 330 sq km area is covered by the lake. Despite the park's small size, its vegetation is diverse, ranging from savanna to marshes and acacia woodland, enabling it to support a remarkable variety of habitats.

Information
Entry fees are US$35/10 per adult/child aged five to 15 years, valid for multiple entries within 24 hours. For camping fees see p77. For booking camp sites contact the **senior park warden** (☎ 027-253 9112/45; manyarapark@africaonline .co.tz). The park gate and park headquarters are at the northern tip of the park near Mto

wa Mbu village, where there is also a helpful tourist information office and a worthwhile visitors centre. MaCo and Harms-ic put out good park maps, available at the park gate, together with a bird checklist.

Hoopoe Safaris (p44) is a recommended contact for upmarket cycling and cycling-safari combination trips in the Lake Manyara area. Green Footprint Adventures (see p207), based at Lake Manyara Serena Lodge, organises village walks, mountain biking and forest hikes around Lake Manyara, as well as full-day 'Manyara active excursions', all upmarket. It also does night drives in the park (Manyara is the only northern park where you can do this). Budget cultural walks and cycling outside the park can be organised through the Mto wa Mbu Cultural Tourism Program.

Binoculars are especially useful for wildlife viewing at Manyara.

Sleeping & Eating
CAMPING
There are two **public camp sites** (per adult/child US$30/5) – Campsite 1, close to park headquarters and the park gate, with toilet and shower, and the shaded Campsite 2 ('Riverside' or 'Endabash' camp site), set amid sausage trees and other vegetation near the Endabash river about an hour's drive from the gate, with new toilet and shower facilities, and tank water for cooking (and – if treated – for drinking). There are also three **special camp sites** (per adult /child US$50/10) – Bagayo A & B, both set in acacia woodland somewhat in from the lake about 15km from the main gate, and Endabash Lake Shore, somewhat further south and with lake views, but with the nuisance of tsetse flies.

The park also has about 10 double en suite **bandas** (per adult/child US$20/10) with hot water, bedding and a cooking area. For park-run accommodation prices, see p77.

Basic foodstuffs are available in Mto wa Mbu. For saving money, it's cheaper to stay in Mto wa Mbu village, 3km east of the park gate on the Arusha road.

LODGES & TENTED CAMPS
Ol Mesera Tented Camp (☎ 0784-428332; www.ol-me sera.com; s/d US$60/120) This small, personalised and good-value place – in a placid setting amid baobab and euphorbia trees – has five straightforward tented *bandas* (thatched-roof huts or shelters) and is an ideal spot to relax for a few days and get a glimpse into local

culture. There are local cultural walks in the area, and staff can also help you organise excursions to Lake Manyara and Ngorongoro Crater. It's in Selela village, 14km north of Mto wa Mbu and signposted off the Engaruka road. Public transport towards Engaruka can drop you at the turn-off, from where it's an easy 1.5km walk.

Kirurumu Luxury Tented Camp (☎ 027-250 7011, 027-250 7541; www.kirurumu.com; s/d half board US$160/250) A genteel, low-key ambience, closeness to the natural surroundings and memorable cuisine are the hallmarks of this highly regarded camp. It's set on the escarpment about 12km from the park gate and 6km from the main road, with views of Lake Manyara in the distance. The 20 well-spaced double tents are hidden away in the vegetation, and there are several larger 'family suite' tents. Maasai-guided ethno-botanical walks, hikes and fly-camping can be organised. Overall excellent value.

E Unoto Retreat (www.maasaivillage.com; s/d half board US$250/400; ☒) This classy lodge with Maasai overtones and spacious luxury bungalows nestles at the base of the Rift Valley escarpment near Lake Miwaleni about 10km north of Mto wa Mbu. There's rewarding birding in the area, as well as the chance for cycling and cultural walks, including one focusing on traditional medicinal plants. E Unoto is about 10km north of Mto wa Mbu, just off the road to Lake Natron.

Lake Manyara Serena Lodge (☎ 027-253 9160/1; www.serenahotels.com; s/d full board US$375/550; ☒) The large Serena complex – in a beautiful location on the escarpment overlooking the Rift Valley – offers comfortable accommodation with all the amenities in appealing two-storey conical thatched bungalows, buffet-style dining and wonderful views from its pool-bar area. It lacks the intimacy and naturalness of Kirurumu, but is nevertheless a justifiably popular choice. It's about 2km from the main road and signposted.

Other recommendations:
Wild Africa Manyara Lodge (☎ 022-211 5104; www .kiutuadventures.com/wildafrica.htm; per person from US$150) Straightforward raised makuti-shaded double tents around a central dining and pool area and a raised sundowner deck with fine views towards the lake. Cultural walks can be arranged.
Lake Manyara Wildlife Lodge (☎ 027-254 4595/4795; www.hotelsandlodges-tanzania.com; r per person full board US$380; ☒) Formerly the government hotel, this place has a prime location on the edge of the

escarpment, which goes quite a ways to compensating for its merely adequate rooms and cuisine.
Lake Manyara Tree Lodge (www.ccafrica.com; per person all-inclusive US$855; ☸ Jun-Mar; ☒) Lake Manyara's most exclusive lodge, and the only one inside the park, with 10 stilted tree-houses with private decks and views, set in a mahogany forest at the southern end of the park.

Mto Wa Mbu
☎ 027

Mto wa Mbu (River of Mosquitoes) is a small village with a hard edge and a large number of aggressive touts, although it's somewhat redeemed by its lively market and its beautiful vegetation – a profusion of palms, baobabs and acacia trees framed by the backdrop of the Rift Valley escarpment. It's just north of Lake Manyara, which is fed by the town's eponymous river, and makes a convenient base for visiting the park.

There are cultural walks in the surrounding area, organised through the **Cultural Tourism Program office** (☎ 027-253 9393; mtoculturalprogramme@ hotmail.com) at the Red Banana Café on the main road, opposite the post office. While most of the guides are quite good and helpful, and the tours overall are generally well-organised, there is a handful of aggressive guides affiliated with this office that resorts to heavy, tout-style harassment of travellers, so that it is difficult at present to give an unqualified recommendation for this programme. Rates average about Tsh22,000 to Tsh33,000 per person per day (less if you're in a group); bike rental can also be arranged.

SLEEPING & EATING
Twiga Campsite & Lodge (☎ 027-253 9101; twigacamp site@hotmail.com; camping per person US$5, new d/tr US$60/63, old d/tr without bathroom US$30/45; ☒) A popular place set in a large compound along the main road, with cooking facilities, restaurant, ablution blocks with hot and cold water and newer rooms in attached blocks. Car hire to visit Lake Manyara and Ngorongoro Conservation Area costs US$140 per day, including petrol and driver, and bike rental can be arranged.

Jambo Lodge & Campsite (☎ 027-253 9170; www .njake.com; camping per person US$7, camping per person with tent & bedding rental US$20, s/d US$75/90; ☒) Signposted along the main road about 200m east of Twiga, this place has undergone a complete overhaul and now gives stiff competition to its neighbour, with a lovely, shaded and well-maintained grassy camping area, plus a dozen or so comfortable, en suite rooms in double-storey chalet blocks and helpful staff. Car hire can be arranged from US$130 per day, including petrol and driver.

Marowiwi Green House (☎ 027-253 9273; marowiwi@yahoo.com; s/d/tr US$30/60/90) On the north side of the road, and just before the park gate, with no-frills but clean and quiet rooms in a dark green house. It's just after the Lutheran Hospital and signposted. Meals can be arranged.

Lake Manyara Tented Camp (☎ 027-255 3242; www.moivaro.com; s/d full board US$120/160) The main attraction of this place – formerly Migunga Forest Camp – is its setting, in a grove of fever trees (*migunga* in Swahili) that echoes with bird calls. The 13 tents – set around large, grassy grounds – are small but quite adequate, and there's a camp site with hot water and a mess tent. It's 2km south of the main road and signposted.

There are several inexpensive guesthouses in town within a few minutes' walk of each other, and most about two blocks back from (south of) the main road. These include **Sayari Lodge** (d without bathroom Tsh5000), behind the market, with no-frills rooms named after the planets (*sayari* means planet in Swahili), and the slightly more upmarket **New Continental Luxury Lodge** (s/d Tsh15,000/20,000), a block away and following the theme, with en suite rooms named after the continents, complete with mosquito net, fan and hot water. The Lutheran Hospital **hostel** (dm Tsh3000) – along the main road towards the park gate – has no-frills twin-bedded rooms that are open to visitors, space permitting.

Getting There & Away
AIR
Coastal Aviation, Air Excel and Regional Air offer scheduled daily, or near-daily, services between Arusha and Lake Manyara for about US$65 one way. The airstrip is at the northwestern edge of the park.

BUS
There are several buses daily to Arusha (Tsh3000) and Karatu (Tsh1000), and at least one bus daily direct to Dar es Salaam (Tsh27,000). Departures are from the transport stand along the main road in the town centre near Red Banana Café.

CAR & MOTORCYCLE
The only road access into the park is from Arusha via Makuyuni and Mto wa Mbu (where petrol is available). There's no vehicle rental at the park, although vehicles can be rented with Jambo and Twiga camp sites and some of the other listings in Mto wa Mbu. Quoted prices usually include Manyara and Ngorongoro Crater, but you should be able to negotiate something better if you will only be visiting Lake Manyara, as much less driving is involved.

TARANGIRE NATIONAL PARK
Beautiful, baobab-studded Tarangire stretches southeast of Lake Manyara around the Tarangire River. Like nearby Lake Manyara National Park, it's often assigned no more than a day visit as part of a larger northern circuit safari, although it is well worth longer exploration. Tarangire is a classic dry-season destination, particularly between August and October, when it has one of the highest concentrations of wildlife of any of the country's parks. Large herds of zebras, wildebeests, hartebeests and – in particular – elephants can be found here until October when the short wet season allows them to move on to new grasslands. Elands, lesser kudus, gazelles, giraffes, waterbucks, impalas and the occasional leopard or rhino can be seen at Tarangire year-round. The park is also good for bird-watching, especially between October and May, with more than 300 different species recorded.

Tarangire is part of an extended ecosystem where animals roam freely. It includes the large Mkungunero Game Controlled Area to the south, and the Lolkisale Game Controlled Area to the northeast. It's possible to do walks and night drives in several of these bordering areas, with local villagers benefiting from tourist revenues.

Information
Entry fees are US$35/10 per adult/child aged five to 15 years, valid for multiple entries within 24 hours. For bookings, contact the **senior park warden** (☎ 027-253 1280/1, 027-250 8642). The entry gate and park headquarters are at the northwestern tip of the park, together with an excellent visitors centre. Within the park, walking accompanied by rangers is only permitted in the Silale area near Oliver's Camp. Otherwise, most of the camps and lodges lo-

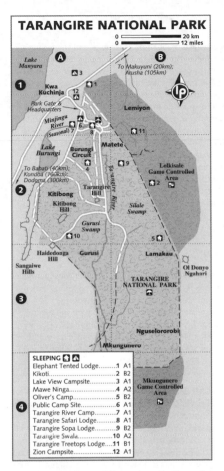

TARANGIRE NATIONAL PARK

SLEEPING 🏠 🛏

Elephant Tented Lodge..........1	A1
Kikoti..................................2	B2
Lake View Campsite............3	A1
Mawe Ninga.......................4	A2
Oliver's Camp.....................5	B2
Public Camp Site.................6	A1
Tarangire River Camp..........7	A1
Tarangire Safari Lodge.........8	A1
Tarangire Sopa Lodge..........9	B2
Tarangire Swala.................10	A2
Tarangire Treetops Lodge....11	B1
Zion Campsite...................12	A1

cated outside the park boundaries offer walking and night drives.

MaCo puts out the best Tarangire map, available in Arusha and at the park gate.

Sleeping
CAMPING

There is a public camp site near park headquarters with basic toilet and shower facilities, and about 12 special camp sites, all in the upper-eastern and upper-western areas, near Matete, Burungi and Kitibong. You'll need to book these in advance, and be completely self-sufficient.

Other options:

Lake View Campsite (☎ 027-254 4057; www.bobby camping.com; camping per person US$7) Several kilometres

northeast of Kwa Kuchinja and west of the Makuyuni road with camping overlooking Lake Manyara in the distance.

Zion Campsite (camping per person Tsh10,000) About 6km before the park gate and bare and scruffy, but it's cheaper than camping inside the park, and the showers are warm. Bring your own food.

LODGES & TENTED CAMPS

Tarangire Safari Lodge (☎ 027-254 4752; www .tarangiresafarilodge.com; s/d from US$89/128; 🏊) A large lodge, notable for its prime location on a bluff overlooking the Tarangire River, about 10km inside the park gate. Accommodation is in closely spaced tents or thatched bungalows. Good overall value.

Mawe Ninga (www.tanganyika.com; per person full board US$175) A newer place about 10km from the park gate, and very bush, with about 10 raised and quite rustic tents perched on an outcrop, each with small porches and views. There are no resident guides (and no vehicles for hire), so you'll need to bring your own. Refreshingly different.

Tarangire River Camp (☎ 022-213 0501, 027-254 7007; www.chimpanzeesafaris.com; s/d full board US$210/320) An 18-tent camp set amid baobabs near the seasonal Minjingu River, and accessed via a signposted turn-off 3km before the park gate. Views – including of elephant and other wildlife in season – are impressive, and the camp is overall reasonable value. Cultural walks can be arranged in the surrounding Maasai areas.

Kikoti (☎ 027-250 8790; www.africanconservancycom pany.com; s/d full board plus bush walks US$265/400) On a rise just east of the park boundaries, this attractive 18-tent camp offers spacious, well-appointed and beautifully decorated luxury tents, good cuisine and the chance for nature walks and night drives.

Tarangire Treetops Lodge (☎ 027-250 0630; www.elewana.com; per person all-inclusive US$710; 🏊) Pampered and upmarket, with 20 spacious suites set on low stilts or built tree-house-style around the baobabs. It's just outside Tarangire's northeastern border, with walking safaris and night drives.

Other recommendations:

Elephant Tented Lodge (☎ 027-275 4925; www .kilimanjarosafari.com; s/d US$70/100) Closely spaced double-bedded tents in a decent location sometimes frequented by elephants.

Tarangire Sopa Lodge (☎ 027-250 0630/39; info@ sopalodges.com; s/d full board US$210/350) Comfortable rooms in a mediocre location about 30km from the gate.

THE MAASAI

Travelling in northern Tanzania, you are almost certain to meet some Maasai, one of the region's most colourful tribes. The Maasai are pastoral nomads who have actively resisted change, and still follow the same lifestyle that they have for centuries. Their culture centres on their cattle, which provide many of their needs – milk, blood and meat for their diet, and hides and skins for clothing – although sheep and goats also play an important dietary role, especially during the dry season. The land, cattle and all elements related to cattle are considered sacred.

Maasai society is patriarchal and highly decentralised. Elders meet to decide on general issues but ultimately it is the well-being of the cattle that determines a course of action. Maasai boys pass through a number of transitions throughout life, the first of which is marked by the circumcision rite. Successive stages include junior warriors, senior warriors, junior elders and senior elders; each level is distinguished by its own unique rights, responsibilities and dress. Junior elders, for example, are expected to marry and settle down – somewhere between the ages of 30 and 40. Senior elders assume the responsibility of making wise and moderate decisions for the community. The most important group is that of the newly initiated warriors, *moran*, who are charged with defending the cattle herds.

Maasai women play a markedly subservient role and have no inheritance rights. Polygyny is widespread and marriages are arranged by the elders, without consulting the bride or her mother. Since most women are significantly younger than men at the time of marriage, they often become widows; remarriage is rare.

In an effort to cope with vastly increased tourist attention in recent years, specially designated cultural villages have been established where you can see Maasai dancing, photograph as much as you want and buy crafts, albeit for a steep $50 fee per vehicle; generally, of course, this is a rather disappointing and contrived experience. For more authentic encounters with the Maasai, visit Maasai areas within the framework of a Cultural Tourism Program (the Longido, Ol Doinyo Sambu and Osotwa programmes – see p204 – are all in Maasai areas), take the chance for guided walks (many camps offer these), or arrange a longer stay or hike at Loliondo, West Kilimanjaro and other areas where partnerships with the Maasai have been established.

Tarangire Swala (☎ 027-250 9816; www.sanctuary lodges.com; s/d full board US$445/640) A premiere-class nine-tent camp, nestled in a grove of acacia trees and overlooking the Gurusi wetlands in the southwestern part of the park.

Oliver's Camp (www.asilialodges.com; per person plus wildlife drives US$480) A 16-bed upmarket camp notable for its fine location near Silale – the only area in the park where walking safaris are permitted – its personalised ambience and its guides.

Nomad Tanzania (www.nomadtarangire.com; s/d all-inclusive US$650/1050; ⌣ Jun-Dec) An exclusive four-tent mobile camp in the central and southern part of the park with wonderful bedouin-style tents, and the chance for walking safaris.

Getting There & Around

AIR
Coastal Aviation, Air Excel and Regional Air all stop at Tarangire on request on their flights between Arusha and Lake Manyara (per seat US$80). The airstrip is in the northern section of the park near Tarangire Safari Lodge.

CAR & MOTORCYCLE
To visit Tarangire you will need to join an organised tour or use your own vehicle, as the park doesn't rent vehicles. The closest petrol is in Makuyuni, 32km from the park gate.

The park is reached via the Makuyuni road from Arusha. At Kwa Kuchinja village, there's a signposted turn-off to the park gate, which is 7km further down a good dirt access road.

SERENGETI NATIONAL PARK
The Serengeti is where Africa's mystery, rawness and power surround you, and where the beauty and synchrony of nature can be experienced as in few other places. On its vast, treeless plains, one of earth's most impressive natural cycles plays itself out again and again, as tens of thousands of hoofed animals, driven by primeval rhythms of survival, move constantly in search of fresh grasslands. The most famous, and the most numerous, are the wildebeests – of which there are more than one million – and their annual migration is the Serengeti's biggest drawcard. During the

rainy season (between December and May), the wildebeests are widely scattered over the southern section of the Serengeti and the Ngorongoro Conservation Area. As these areas have few large rivers and streams, they dry out quickly when the rains cease, nudging the wildebeests to concentrate on the few remaining green areas, and to form thousands-strong herds that migrate north and west in search of food. They then spend the dry season, from about July to October, outside the Serengeti and in the Masai Mara (just over the Kenyan border), before again moving south in anticipation of the rains. Around February, the calving season, more than 8000 wildebeest calves are born per day, although about 40% of these die before they are four months old.

The 14,763 sq km Serengeti is also renowned for its predators, especially its lions, many of which have collars fitted with transmitters so their movements can be studied and their locations tracked. Keeping the lions company are cheetahs, leopards, hyenas, jackals and more. You'll also see zebras (of which there are about 200,000), large herds of giraffes, Thomson's and Grant's gazelles, elands, impalas, klipspringers and warthogs, and fascinating birdlife, including vultures brooding in the trees, haughty secretary birds by the road side and brightly coloured Fisher's lovebirds.

Wildlife concentrations in the park are greatest between about December and June, and comparatively low during the dry season

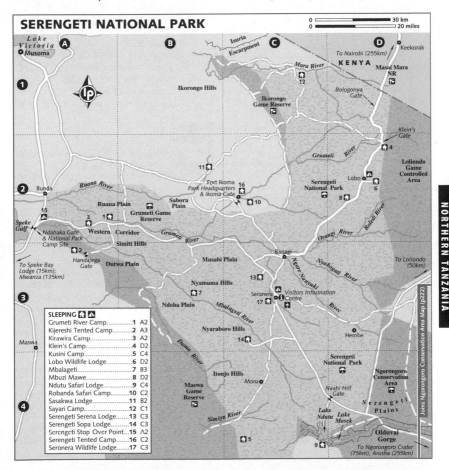

SERENGETI NATIONAL PARK

SLEEPING
Grumeti River Camp.............1 A2
Kijereshi Tented Camp..........2 A3
Kirawira Camp....................3 A2
Klein's Camp......................4 D2
Kusini Camp.......................5 C4
Lobo Wildlife Lodge.............6 D2
Mbalageti..........................7 B3
Mbuzi Mawe.......................8 D2
Ndutu Safari Lodge..............9 C4
Robanda Safari Camp..........10 C2
Sasakwa Camp....................11 B2
Sayari Camp......................12 C1
Serengeti Serena Lodge........13 C3
Serengeti Sopa Lodge..........14 C3
Serengeti Stop Over Point....15 A2
Serengeti Tented Camp.......16 C2
Seronera Wildlife Lodge.......17 C3

NORTHERN TANZANIA

(between about July and October). However, the Serengeti is rewarding to visit at any time. For the wildebeests, the best base from about December to April is at one of the camps near Seronera or in the southeastern part of the park. The famous crossing of the Grumeti River, which runs through the park's Western Corridor, usually takes place somewhere between May and July, although the viewing window can be quite short. In particularly dry years, the herds tend to move northwards sooner, avoiding or only skirting the Western Corridor. There are several camps in or near the Western Corridor, and it's also easily accessed from Seronera. The northern Serengeti, around Lobo and Klein's Gate, is a good base during the dry season, between about August and October. As well as the migrating wildebeests, there are also small resident populations of wildebeests in the park, which you'll see at any time of year.

Almost all shorter safaris, and those done as part of a quick northern circuit loop, use Seronera as a base, although other sections of the park are just as rewarding, if not more so. In the low season, you will see few other vehicles outside of Seronera, although even in the high season the park is large enough that it doesn't feel overrun.

Overall, the opportunities for wildlife viewing are unparalleled and, if you are able to visit, it's a chance not to be missed. Try to schedule as much time here as possible in order to explore the park's varied zones and to appreciate its vastness.

Information

Entry fees are US$50/10 per adult/child aged five to 15 years per 24-hour period, and valid for only one entry. Bookings for camp sites, resthouses and the hostel should be made through the Chief Park Warden or the **Tourism Warden** (☎ 028-262 0091, 028-262 1515, 028-262 1504; www.serengeti.org). Park headquarters are at Fort Ikoma, just outside the park, while the tourism division is at Seronera. It's not mandatory to hire a guide, although having one along is likely to greatly enhance both your wildlife watching and your navigation through the park. Vehicle rentals from both Arusha and Mwanza almost always include a driver-guide.

There is an excellent Visitors Information Centre at Seronera with a self-guided walk through the Serengeti's history and ecosys-tems. Explanations are in English and Swahili, and it's well worth spending time here before exploring the park.

The gift shop at the Seronera Visitors Information Centre sells various booklets and maps, including the excellent MaCo *Serengeti* map.

Activities

Balloon trips – about an hour floating over the plains at dawn, followed by a champagne breakfast in the bush under the acacia trees, complete with linen tablecloths – are offered by **Serengeti Balloon Safaris** (☎ 027-250 8578, 027-254 8967; www.balloonsafaris.com) for US$479 per person. The flight route varies depending on the winds, but often follows a stretch of the Grumeti River. The captains try to stay between 500m and 1000m above ground, weather and wind permitting, which means that if animals are there, you'll be able to see them. Bookings can be made directly, or through any of the central Serengeti lodges.

Short (two- to three-hour) walks outside the park and Maasai cultural activities can be arranged through lodges based in border areas.

Sleeping
CAMPING

There are about nine public camp sites in the Serengeti, including six around Seronera, one at Lobo, one at Kirawira in the Western Corridor and one near Ndabaka Gate in the far west along the Mwanza–Musoma road. There are at least two dozen special camp sites including in the areas around Lake Ndutu, Kirawira Research Station, Seronera, Lobo, Naabi Hill Gate and elsewhere. These should be booked well in advance, especially for groups; a 30% nonrefundable deposit is required one month before your arrival date.

There are also several resthouses at Seronera with running water, blankets and cooking facilities. You'll need to bring your own food, although there's a small shop at Seronera selling soft drinks, water and a few basics.

LODGES & TENTED CAMPS
Central & Southern Serengeti

Central Serengeti is the most visited area of the park, and readily accessed from both Arusha and from Mwanza via the Western Corridor. The main lodge area is at Seronera. Southeast of here near the Ngorongoro Conservation Area (NCA) boundary and Lake Ndutu is a prime base for wildlife watching during the December to April wet season, when it's full of wildebeests. The more rugged southwest, in addition to being well-placed for the wildebeest during the wet season, is also notable for its lion and leopard sightings, especially around the Moru Kopjes area, which has a substantial resident wildlife population year round.

Serengeti Sopa Lodge (☎ 027-250 0630/9; info@sopalodges.com; s/d full board US$210/350; ⊠) Though ponderous and architecturally unappealing, the rooms here – spacious, with small sitting rooms and two double beds – have all the comforts, plus views. It's about 20km south of Seronera as the bird flies, on the edge of the Niaroboro Hills, and well-located for wildlife watching.

Ndutu Safari Lodge (☎ 027-250 6702/2829; www.ndutu.com; s/d full board US$215/326) This good-value place is in a lovely setting just outside the southeastern Serengeti in the far western part of NCA. It's well-placed for wildlife viewing, especially for observing the enormous herds of wildebeests during the wet season, and walking safaris are possible in the surrounding NCA. In addition to NCA fees, you'll need to pay Serengeti fees any time that you cross into the park. Accommodation is in unpretentious but comfortable en suite cottages, and the atmosphere is relaxed and rustic – an overall fine choice, and one of our favourite camps in the Serengeti.

Seronera Wildlife Lodge (☎ 027-254 4595/4795; www.hotelsandlodges-tanzania.com; r per person full board US$400) Good overall value, with a prime location in the heart of the Serengeti and well-situated for wildlife drives, plus modest but pleasant rooms and a lively end-of-the-day safari atmosphere at the evening buffet.

Serengeti Serena Lodge (☎ 027-250 4153/8; www.serenahotels.com; s/d full board US$375/550; ⊠) About 20km northwest of Seronera airstrip, this place is not as favourably located as Seronera Wildlife Lodge but is otherwise a good choice and very comfortable. Accommodation is in well-appointed two-storey Maasai-style bungalows.

Kusini Camp (☎ 027-250 9816; www.sanctuarylodges.com; s/d full board US$765/1030) Laid-back luxury in a prime wet-season setting amid rocky outcrops in the remote southwestern Serengeti, with 12 well-spaced and well-appointed tents. Somewhat unusually for camps of this standard, there are no age restrictions on children.

Northern Serengeti

The hillier and more heavily vegetated northern Serengeti receives relatively few visitors, but makes a fine off the beaten track base, especially between August and October, when the migration passes through. During the rest of the year, things are kept interesting by a substantial permanent wildlife presence, including, most notably, elephants. The Loliondo area, just outside the Serengeti's northeastern boundary, offers the chance for Maasai cultural activities and walking safaris, although almost all accommodation here is upmarket.

Lobo Wildlife Lodge (☎ 027-254 4595/4795; www.hotelsandlodges-tanzania.com; r per person full board US$440) Well located and similar in standard to the Seronera Wildlife Lodge. If your budget is limited, it's the best value in this part of the park.

Klein's Camp (www.ccafrica.com; per person all-inclusive US$855; ⊠) Exclusive and strikingly situated just outside the northeasternmost park boundary, with 10 luxurious stone-and-thatch cottages, and the chance for walks and night wildlife drives.

Watch also for the new 60-bed Kempinski lodge being built near Mbuzi Mawe, and scheduled to open in the near future.

Other recommendations:

Mbuzi Mawe (☎ 027-250 4158, 028-262 2040/2; www.serenahotels.com; s/d full board US$375/550) A 16-tent camp – each tent with two double beds and views – and an excellent location about 45km north of Seronera, convenient also to the central Serengeti wildlife circuits.

Suyan Camp (www.asilialodges.com; per person full board plus wildlife drives US$480) A 10-bed camp under the same management as Sayari that moves between northern and southern Loliondo, and offers walking safaris, night drives and cultural activities.

Sayari Camp (www.asilialodges.com; per person full board plus wildlife drives US$600; ☼ Jun-Apr) This 16-bed previously mobile camp is now permanently based on the south side of the Mara River – well placed for the migration from about July to November.

Western Serengeti

Apart from the park camp sites, the western Serengeti is the only area that has options for budget travellers (all outside the park). In addition to seasonal proximity to the migration (which generally passes through the area from around May/June), it offers the forest-fringed Grumeti River and relatively reliable year-round wildlife watching.

Serengeti Stop-Over Point (☎ 028-262 2273; www.serengetistopover.com; camping per person US$10, s/d US$30/60) This enthusiastic place is directly on the Mwanza–Musoma road about 1km from Ndabaka Gate. There's camping with hot showers and a cooking area, plus 10 simple rondavels, and a restaurant-bar. Local boat trips on Lake Victoria, visits to a traditional healer and other Sukuma cultural excursions can be arranged. Any bus along the Mwanza–Musoma road will drop you nearby. Safari vehicle rental is possible with advance notice.

Kijereshi Tented Camp (☎ 028-262 1231; www.kijereshi.com; s/d tented r half board US$85/125, d bungalows half board US$150; ⊠) A budget place just outside park boundaries, 18km east of the Mwanza–Musoma road and signposted, and about 2km from the Serengeti's Handajega Gate. It's a popular base for overlanders, with functional tented accommodation (you can also pitch your own for US$15) plus a few rooms, a restaurant and cooking facilities.

Serengeti Tented Camp (☎ 027-255 3242; www.moivaro.com; s/d full board US$160/213) A small camp 3km from Ikoma Gate and just outside the park boundary, with 12 no-frills tents with bathrooms and hot water, plus the chance for night drives and guided walks in the border area.

Mbalageti (☎ 028-262 2387, 027-254 8632; www.mbalageti.com; lodge s/d full board US$305/385, tented chalets s/d full board US$315/610; ⊠) One of the newer lodges in this part of the park, although it has already garnered a string of good reviews from guests, with rooms in the main lodge, or spacious tented and stone cottages with large verandas and wonderful views, including from the bathtubs.

Grumeti River Camp (www.ccafrica.com; per person all-inclusive US$855; ⊠) One of the most exclusive camps in the Serengeti. It's in a wild bush location near the Grumeti River that's especially prime around June and July when the wildebeests are often around. Accommodation is in 10 spacious luxury tents with all the amenities.

Kirawira Camp (☎ 027-250 4153/8, 028-262 1518; www.serenahotels.com; s/d all-inclusive US$950/1450; ⊠) Kirawira, set on a small rise about 90km west of Seronera, is more open and somewhat tamer in feel than Grumeti, with luxurious tents done up in what its advertising describes as the epitome of 'colonially styled safari luxury'.

Other recommendations:

Speke Bay Lodge (☎ 028-262 1236; www.spekebay.com; s/d tents without bathroom US$54/90, s/d bungalows US$102/145) On Lake Victoria about 15km southwest of Ndabaka Gate and 125km north of Mwanza, and a good choice if you want to combine the Serengeti with Lake Victoria. There are simple tents with shared facilities, and spotless, if rather soulless, en suite four-person bungalows. The staff can help you organise boat, fishing or birding excursions on the lake, and mountain biking. There's no vehicle hire.

Robanda Safari Camp (☎ 0754-282251; www.robanda-safari-camp.com; s/d full board US$110/150) This 16-tent semipermanent camp near Robanda village just outside Ikoma Gate was about to open when we passed through. Accommodation is in en suite domed tents under thatching, and there's a restaurant. We welcome reports from anyone who stays here once it opens. There's no vehicle rental.

Sasakwa Lodge (www.singita.com; per person all-inclusive US$1500) In the Grumeti Game Reserve north of the Serengeti's Western Corridor with seven stone cottages vaguely reminiscent of a transplanted English country estate. It's one of a trio of exclusive lodges in the area run by Singita. (The other two are Faru Faru Lodge and Sabora Tented Camp.) Wildlife walks and night drives are possible at all three, and horseriding is possible at Sasakwa.

Mobile Camps

There is an increasing number of semipermanent, mostly upmarket camps that move seasonally with the wildlife, with the goal of always being optimally positioned for the migration.

Olakira Camp (www.asilialodges.com; per person full board US$445) This comfortable six-tent camp is based in the Ndutu area with the wildebeests from December until March, and in central Serengeti from June to November.

Simiyu Camp (www.africawilderness.com; s/d full board US$575/860) In the southern Serengeti from December to March, in the Seronera area from May to August and in the north from September to November.

Serengeti Safari Camp (www.nomad-tanzania.com; per person all-inclusive US$590/930) A highly exclusive mobile camp that follows the wildebeest migration, with some of the best guides in the Serengeti.

Getting There & Around

AIR

Coastal Aviation, Air Excel and Regional Air have daily flights from Arusha to various Serengeti airstrips, including Seronera (US$150 per person one way) and Grumeti (US$180). There are also airstrips at Serengeti South, Lobo and most other ranger posts.

Some of Coastal's flights continue on to Mwanza and Rubondo Island National Park on demand.

CAR & MOTORCYCLE

Most travellers visit the Serengeti with an organised safari or in their own vehicle. For shoestring travellers the only other option to try to get a glimpse of the animals is to take a bus travelling between Arusha and Mwanza or Musoma via the Western Corridor route – check with Coastal line at the Arusha central bus station – although you won't be able to stop to observe the wildlife. You will need to pay park fees and, if you disembark at Seronera, you'll have the problem of getting onward transport, as hitching is not permitted in the park.

Access from Arusha is via the heavily used **Naabi Hill Gate** (6am-6pm) at the southeastern edge of the park. From here, it's 75km further to Seronera. **Ndabaka Gate** (6am-4pm) is about 140km northeast of Mwanza along the Mwanza–Musoma road, and gives you direct access to the Western Corridor. The road from Ndabaka to Seronera is in decent to good condition; allow two to three hours. Ikoma Gate is also accessed from the Mwanza–Musoma road, from an unpaved track running east from Bunda. Bologonya Gate, 5km from the Kenyan border, is the route to/from Kenya's Masai Mara National Reserve, but the border is open only to East African residents or citizens. There are other entry points at Handajega (Western Corridor) and in the north near Klein's Camp. Driving is not permitted in the park after 7pm.

Petrol points en route from Arusha include Makuyuni, Mto wa Mbu and Karatu. Petrol is also usually available at Ngorongoro Crater (Park Village) and at the Seronera Wildlife Lodge, although it's expensive. It is not available anywhere else in the park, so if you have your own vehicle come prepared with sufficient supplies. From the west, the most reliable petrol points are Mwanza and Musoma.

NGORONGORO CONSERVATION AREA

The world-renowned Ngorongoro Crater is just one part of a much larger area of interrelated ecosystems consisting of the Crater Highlands (to which the Ngorongoro Crater belongs) together with vast stretches of plains, grasslands, bush and woodland. The entire Ngorongoro Conservation Area

(NCA) – a Unesco World Heritage Site – covers about 8300 sq km. Near its centre is Olduvai Gorge, where many famous fossils have been unearthed. To the west are the alkaline Lakes Ndutu and Masek, although Ndutu is just over the border in the Serengeti. Both lakes are particularly good areas for wildlife viewing between December and April, when they are overrun with wildebeests. In the east of the conservation area is a string of volcanoes and craters (collapsed volcanoes, often referred to as calderas); most, but not all, are inactive. Further east, just outside the NCA's boundaries, is the mysterious archaeological site of Engaruka. Nestled in the barren landscape along the NCA's southern border is Lake Eyasi, while to the northeast of the NCA in the arid expanses near the Kenyan border is the alkaline Lake Natron.

Information

The NCA is under the jurisdiction of the Ngorongoro Conservation Area Authority (NCAA), which has its **headquarters** (027-253 7006, 027-253 9108, 027-253 7019; www.ngorongorocrater .org) at Park Village at Ngorongoro Crater.

Entry fees – which you'll need to pay for all activities within the NCA – are US$50 per person per 24-hour period (US$10 for children five to 16 years old, and free for children under five). Guides, including for walking safaris, cost US$20 per day per group. There is a vehicle fee of US$40 /Tsh10,000 per foreign-/Tanzanian-registered vehicle per entry and an additional, steep crater-service fee of US$200 per vehicle per entry to drive down into Ngorongoro Crater. Camping costs US$30/10 per adult /child in public camp sites (US$50/20 in special camp sites).

The two official entry points to the NCA are **Lodoare Gate** (027-253 7031; 6am-6pm), just south of Ngorongoro Crater, and **Naabi Hill Gate** (027 253 7030; 6am-6pm), on the border with Serengeti National Park.

Both MaCo and Harms-ic put out maps of the NCA, available at the NCA tourist information office in Arusha and at Lodoare Gate.

The Crater Highlands

The ruggedly beautiful Crater Highlands consist of an elevated range of volcanoes and collapsed volcanoes rising up from the side of

NGORONGORO CONSERVATION AREA

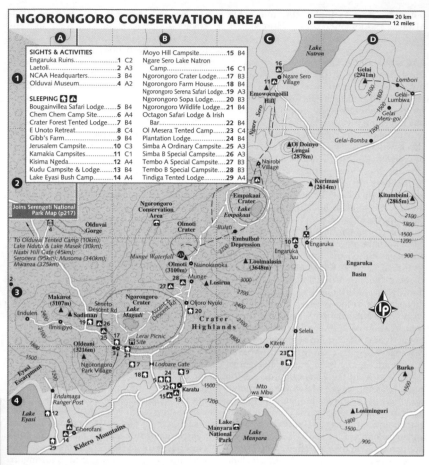

SIGHTS & ACTIVITIES
Engaruka Ruins.........................1 C2
Laetoli....................................2 A3
NCAA Headquarters.................3 B4
Olduvai Museum......................4 A2

SLEEPING
Bougainvillea Safari Lodge.......5 B4
Chem Chem Camp Site...........6 A4
Crater Forest Tented Lodge......7 B4
E Unoto Retreat......................8 C4
Gibb's Farm............................9 B4
Jerusalem Campsite...............10 C3
Kamakia Campsites................11 C1
Kisima Ngeda........................12 A4
Kudu Campsite & Lodge.........13 B4
Lake Eyasi Bush Camp...........14 A4

Moyo Hill Campsite...............15 B4
Ngare Sero Lake Natron
    Camp................................16 C1
Ngorongoro Crater Lodge.....17 B3
Ngorongoro Farm House........18 B4
Ngorongoro Serena Safari Lodge..19 A3
Ngorongoro Sopa Lodge........20 B3
Ngorongoro Wildlife Lodge....21 B4
Octagon Safari Lodge & Irish
    Bar...................................22 B4
Ol Mesera Tented Camp........23 C4
Plantation Lodge....................24 B4
Simba A Ordinary Campsite....25 A3
Simba B Special Campsite......26 A3
Tembo A Special Campsite.....27 B3
Tembo B Special Campsite.....28 B3
Tindiga Tented Lodge............29 A4

the Great Rift Valley and running in a chain along the NCA's eastern edge. The peaks include Oldeani (3216m), Makarot (Lemagurut; 3107m), Olmoti (3100m), Loolmalasin (3648m), Empakaai (also spelled Embagai; 3262m), the still-active Ol Doinyo Lengai ('Mountain of God' in Maasai; 2878m) and Ngorongoro (2200m). The different peaks were created over many millions of years by a series of eruptions connected with the birth of the Great Rift Valley, and the older volcanoes have since collapsed to form the craters that give the range its name. The main residents of the area are the Maasai, who have grazed cattle here for hundreds of years.

Apart from Ngorongoro Crater, much of the Crater Highlands area is remote and

seldom visited, although it offers some of Tanzania's most unusual scenery, as well as good trekking. It can also be visited on a vehicle safari arranged through one of the Arusha-based tour operators. Self-drive visitors will need to be self-sufficient with petrol and water, and to arrange permission and a guide from the NCAA.

TREKKING THE CRATER HIGHLANDS
The best way to explore the Crater Highlands is on foot, although because of the logistics involved, trekking here is expensive. Treks range from short day jaunts to excursions of up to two weeks or more. For all routes, you'll need to be accompanied by a guide, and for anything except day hikes, you will need

donkeys or vehicle support to carry water and supplies.

Nearly all visitors arrange treks through a tour company. A number of Arusha-based companies do treks to Empakaai and to Ol Doinyo Lengai (just outside the NCA boundaries), but for most trekking in this region you'll need to contact a specialist operator. For some recommendations, see p54, and Lonely Planet's *Trekking in East Africa*. Costs vary widely, but expect to pay from about US$200 per person per day in a group of four, including NCA entry fees.

Alternatively, you can contact the NCAA directly and arrange your trek through them. However, this requires at least one month's notice, and usually winds up costing about the same as going through a tour company. You'll need to provide all camping equipment and supplies yourself, including water; you'll also need to hire a vehicle (essential for accessing all treks) and arrange for someone to drive the car to the end of the trek to collect you, as most routes are not circuits. The NCAA will then take care of arranging the camp sites, guides and donkeys. The hikes are usually based at designated Maasai 'cultural bomas', each of which has a Tsh10,000 entry fee.

There are no set routes, and the possibilities are numerous. A popular multiday trek starts just north of Ngorongoro Crater and crosses the highlands to finish at Ngare Sero village near Lake Natron. This normally takes four days, but can be cut to three by starting at Nainokanoka or extended by one day to climb Ol Doinyo Lengai.

To experience the area but still stay within a reasonable budget, there are several good short hikes, including up Makarot or Oldeani, or at Empakaai or Olmoti Craters. All of these can easily be done in a day or less from a base at Ngorongoro Crater, and apart from transport costs, involve only the US$50 NCA entry fee and US$20 guide fee. If you're trying to do things on your own through the NCA, rather than through a tour operator, the least complicated option would probably be Oldeani, which is accessed from Park Village, where you can also arrange a ranger/guide. From Oldeani, it's then possible to continue on down to Lake Eyasi, though for this you'll need an overnight stay or two.

There are no camps or lodges apart from the facilities at Ngorongoro Crater.

Ngorongoro Crater

With its stunning ethereal blue-green vistas, close-range viewing opportunities and unparalleled concentrations of wildlife, the Ngorongoro Crater is one of Tanzania's most visited destinations, and one of Africa's best-known wildlife-viewing areas. At about 20km wide it is also one of the largest calderas in the world. Its steep, unbroken walls provide the setting for an incredible natural drama, as lions, elephants, buffaloes and plains herbivores such as wildebeests, Thomson's gazelles, zebras and reedbucks graze, stalk and otherwise make their way around the grasslands, swamps and forests on the crater floor. Chances are good that you'll also see a black rhino or two, and for many people this is one of the crater's main draws. The birding is also excellent here, including around Lake Magadi, the soda lake at the crater's base, which attracts hundreds of flamingos to its shallows.

Despite the crater's steepness, there is considerable movement of animals in and out, thanks to the permanent water and grassland on the crater floor. Animals and birds share the crater with the local Maasai people, who have grazing rights, and you may come across them tending their cattle. During the German colonial era there were two settlers' farms in the crater; you can still see one of the huts.

Because of the crater's popularity (close to 400,000 visitors in 2007), it can be easy to get sidetracked from the natural magnificence, especially when there are several vehicles crowded around one or two animals, all to a backdrop of clicking cameras and radio static. The NCAA has recently limited the number of vehicles permitted around any particular animal to five, and it's likely that further controls on vehicle access to the crater will be introduced in the near future. Meanwhile, one of the best ways to minimise these distractions is by getting into the crater early (there are relatively few vehicles before about 9am). It also helps to pick one or several strategic spots and then to stay put for a while, letting the nuances and subtleties of the crater's environment gradually come to you rather than joining the dashes across the crater floor when drivers radio each other about particularly good sightings.

INFORMATION

For fee information, see p221. Ngorongoro can be visited at any time of the year, but during April and May it can be wet and difficult to negotiate.

The gates down to the crater floor open at 7am and close (for descent) at 4pm; all vehicles must be out of the crater area before 6pm.

It can get very cold and raw on the crater rim, so bring a jacket and come prepared, especially if you're camping.

SLEEPING
Camping

The only public camp site is Simba A, which has basic but generally clean facilities (latrines and cold showers) and great views over the crater if you're lucky enough to be there when there is no cloud cover. It's along the road from Lodoare Gate, not far from NCAA headquarters.

There are numerous special camp sites (none of which have any facilities), including Simba B, just up the road from Simba A, Tembo A and B north of the Ngorongoro Sopa Lodge; a cluster of sites near Lakes Ndutu and Masek; and one on the southern rim of Lake Empakaai.

Lodges

There are currently four lodges on, or near, the rim of the crater, although new developments are planned.

Ngorongoro Sopa Lodge (☎ 027-250 0630/9; info @sopalodges.com; s/d full board US$210/350) Well located, off on its own on the eastern crater rim, just before the track leading up to Olmoti Crater, and near a crater descent/ascent road. Accommodation is in spacious rooms, each with two double beds, and standards and service are commendable.

Ngorongoro Serena Safari Lodge (☎ 027-250 4153/8; www.serenahotels.com; s/d full board US$375/550) The popular Serena is in a fine location on the southwestern crater rim near the main crater descent route. It's a comfortable, attractive place with standards and facilities at least as good as those at the other Serena hotels, if not better, although during high season its popularity, especially with groups, can detract somewhat from the ambience. Green Footprint Adventures (www.greenfootprint.co.tz) has a base here and organises short hikes from the lodge, including to Olmoti.

Ngorongoro Wildlife Lodge (☎ 027-254 4595/4795, direct 027-253 7058/73; www.hotelsandlodges-tanzania.com; r per person full board US$420) The former government hotel, this old and architecturally unappealing lodge has a prime setting on the southern crater rim. While standards can't compare with those at the other crater rim lodges, they've come up a bit in recent times, and the views go a long way to compensating.

Ngorongoro Crater Lodge (www.ccafrica.com; per person all-inclusive US$1115) This lodge – actually three separate camps – is the most interesting in terms of design, with an eclectic collection of styles and décor. Service and amenities are ultra top end, and prices include your own butler. It's on the southwestern crater rim.

KARATU
☎ 027

This small, scruffy town 20km southeast of Lodoare Gate is surrounded by some beautiful countryside, and makes a convenient base for visiting Ngorongoro. Many camping safaris out of Arusha use Karatu as an overnight stop to economise on entry fees for the crater, but it's also worth considering the town as a base in itself, especially if you're interested in walking in the nearby rolling hills. The seventh day of each month is Karatu's market day (*mnada*) – worth stopping if you happen to be passing through.

There is a post office, and an NBC branch that exchanges cash and travellers cheques and has an ATM. Several hotels have internet access, and there's an internet café at Ngorongoro Safari Resort.

Sleeping & Eating
BUDGET

In addition to the following listings, there are several basic guesthouses in the centre of town, all of about the same standard and all with no-frills rooms for about Tsh3000. A modest selection of supplies is available in Karatu, but if you're on a tight budget, it's cheaper to stock up in Arusha.

ELCT Karatu Lutheran Hostel (☎ 027-253 4230; s/d/tr Tsh22,000/30,000/40,000) The Lutheran Hostel has simple, clean rooms with hot water, and good meals (Tsh6000). It's on the main road at the western end of town.

Moyo Hill Campsite (www.moyohillcamp.com; camping per person US$3, s/d bandas US$30/45) A quiet, no-frills place with a large enclosed lawn for camping, and three basic and somewhat chilly twin-bedded *bandas* with warm-water showers. Meals can be arranged. It's about 1km off the main road, and signposted.

Ngorongoro Camp & Lodge (☎ 027-253 4287; www .ngorongorocampandlodge.com; camping per person US$7, s/d US$79/128; 💻) Good, though crowded, camping with hot showers, a covered dining area and meals from Tsh2000. There are also rooms, which are fine, but pricey for what you get. It's on the main road in the town centre. Car hire to Ngorongoro costs US$120 plus entry and crater fees.

Kudu Campsite & Lodge (☎ 027-253 4055; www .kuducamp.com; camping per person US$10, s/d/tr bungalows US$105/110/132, d/tr rondavels from US$132/176; 💻) Kudu, at Karatu's western end and signposted south of the main road, has quiet gardens, a large lawn to pitch your tent, hot-water showers, clean, comfortable bungalows and a bar-restaurant (meals US$5 to US$8). Vehicle rental can be arranged.

Bytes Pub & Café (☎ 027-253 4488; meals from Tsh6000) Western-style meals with a gourmet touch in the centre of Karatu along the main road behind the Crater Highlands petrol station. A fire greatly reduced operations from what they once were, but the owners are slowly rebuilding.

For self-catering, there are several small supermarkets along the main road, including Olduvai Supermarket and Karatu Mini-Market.

MIDRANGE & TOP END
Bougainvillea Safari Lodge (☎ 027-253 4083; www .bougainvillealodge.net; s/d/tr US$70/125/150) A low-key place signposted off the main road west of Karatu with two dozen spacious attached stone bungalows – all with fireplaces and small verandas – plus a restaurant. Cultural activities can be arranged.

Octagon Safari Lodge & Irish Bar (☎ 027-253 4525; www.octagonlodge.com; s/d half board US$124/208) Cosy, comfortable rooms set amidst beautifully green and lush gardens, good food and an Irish bar. Cultural walks can be arranged, as can Ngorongoro safaris.

Gibb's Farm (☎ 027-253 4397; www.gibbsfarm.net; per person half board US$136-290; 🕙 mid-May–mid-Apr) The long-standing Gibb's Farm has a rustic highland ambience, a wonderful setting with wide views over the nearby coffee plantations, good walking and beautiful, well-appointed cottages – all recently completely refurbished and upgraded – set around the gardens. There's

also a spa and an in-house safari operator (www.amazingtanzania.com). The lodge gets consistently good reviews, as does the cuisine, which is made with home-grown organic produce. It's about 5km north of the main road and signposted.

Crater Forest Tented Lodge (www.craterforest tentedlodge.com; s/d full -board US$160/250) A cosy place with 15 safari-style thatch-and-tent *bandas* in a lovely setting on a coffee farm about 12km off the main road, amenable to walking and relaxing. The turn-off is just before Lodoare Gate – watch for the tiny signpost. Hiking, cultural walks and tours of the coffee plantation can be arranged.

Plantation Lodge (☎ 027-253 4364/5, 027-253 4405; www.plantation-lodge.com; s/d full board from US$193/295; 💻) A genteel place with spacious, well-appointed cottages set in expansive green grounds, large verandas with views over the hills, a crackling fireplace and a cosy, highland ambience. It's west of Karatu and about 2km north of the main road.

Ngorongoro Farm House (☎ 027-250 4093, 0784-207727; www.africawilderness.com; s/d half board US$198/276; 💻) This lovely, atmospheric place is set in the grounds of a 500-acre coffee plantation about 5km from Lodoare Gate. The rooms are exceptionally spacious, and are well-appointed albeit in a rather minimalist style, and the suites have large bathtubs. There's also a large terrace dining area, a pool backed by flame trees and views towards Oldeani. It's a fine base for walking, and guides can be arranged for cultural or farm walks. Other possibilities include croquet, volleyball and coffee demonstrations.

Getting There & Away
There are several buses daily between Arusha and Karatu (Tsh5000, three hours), departing Arusha from the main bus station, with at least one daily (look for Ditto KK and Kulinge lines – both departing about 10am) continuing on to Lodoare Gate (about four hours). Coastal line between Arusha and Mwanza via the Serengeti also stops at Lodoare Gate, departing Arusha by 4am.

Getting Around
Vehicle hire and guides can be arranged at Lodoare Gate. Car hire – which is done informally with private cars belonging to staff, as the NCAA no longer rents vehicles – costs about US$120 per day and is best arranged in

advance. You can also, and more reliably, rent vehicles in Karatu for about the same price (US$120 to US$150 per day). The only petrol between Karatu and Seronera in the Serengeti is at NCAA headquarters.

If self-driving, only 4WDs are allowed down into the crater. All roads into the crater have been recently graded and are in good shape, though all are steep, so be sure your vehicle can handle the conditions. The main route in is the Seneto descent road, which enters the crater on its western side, just west of Lake Magadi. To come out, use the Lerai ascent road, which starts near the Lerai picnic site to the south of Lake Magadi and leads to the rim near Ngorongoro Crater Lodge. There is a third access route on the northeastern edge of the crater near the Ngorongoro Sopa Lodge, which can be used for ascents and descents.

OLDUVAI GORGE

Slicing its way close to 100m down into the plains northwest of Ngorongoro Crater, and through millennia of history, is Olduvai (Oldupai) Gorge – a dusty, 50km-long ravine that has become one of the African continent's best-known archaeological sites. Thanks to its unique geological history, in which layer upon layer of volcanic deposits were laid down in an orderly sequence over a period of almost two million years, it provides remarkable documentation of ancient life, allowing us to begin turning the pages of history back to the days of our earliest ancestors.

The most famous of the fossils yielded by Olduvai has been the 1.8 million-year-old ape-like skull known as *Australopithecus boisei*, which was discovered by Mary Leakey in 1959 and gave rise to a heated debate about human evolution. The skull is also often referred to as 'zinjanthropus', which means 'nutcracker man', referring to its large molars. In 1972, 3.75-million-year-old hominid (human-like) footprints – the oldest known – were discovered at Laetoli, about 45km south of the Olduvai Gorge. Based on these findings as well as other ancient fossils excavated in Kenya and Ethiopia, it has been posited that there were at least three hominid species in the region about two million years ago, including *Australopithecus boisei, Homo habilis* and *Homo erectus*. While *Australopithecus*

boisei and *Homo habilis* appear to have died out (or in the case of *Homo habilis*, been absorbed by or evolved into *Homo erectus*), it is theorised that *Homo erectus* continued and evolved into *Homo sapiens,* or modern man. Other lesser-known but significant fossils excavated from the upper layers of Olduvai provide some of the oldest evidence of *Homo sapiens* in the area.

There is a small and interesting **museum** (☎ 027-253 7037; www.ngorongorocrater.org/oldupai .html; ◷ 8am-4.30pm) here, several kilometres off the road to Serengeti, and an adjoining picnic area. It's also possible at certain times to go down into the gorge, accompanied by a guide, who can be arranged at the museum. As well as the standard fees applying to the NCA, there's an additional US$3 per person per day fee for visiting the museum. Guides into the gorge cost Tsh10,000/20,000 for driving/walking.

The rustic **Olduvai Tented Camp** (www.tangan yika.com; s/d half board US$160/220) is nestled among some kopjes with views over the surrounding area. Standards are quite rudimentary in comparison with other places in this price range, but the setting is good, and if you're into the offbeat, it makes a fine spot to watch wildebeests during the wet season. Maasai-led cultural walks can be arranged. Advance bookings are essential.

ENGARUKA

Engaruka, on the eastern edge of the NCA near the foot of Empakaai, is a small village known for its extensive ruins of a complex irrigation system with terraced stone housing sites estimated to be at least 500 years old. Scientists are unsure of the ruins' origin; some speculate they were built by ancestors of the Iraqw (Mbulu) people, who populate the area today, while others suggest that the site was built by the Sonjo, a Bantu-speaking people. Those interested in Engaruka can read more about the site in the first chapter of Henry Forsbroke's *The Eighth Wonder*. The ruins are best viewed from the air, although archaeology buffs will probably find a ground visit more interesting.

There's a Cultural Tourism Programme of sorts here, which, in addition to tours of the ruins and Maasai cultural tours, offers a two-day hike to Ol Doinyo Lengai or a day climb of nearby Kerimasi (2614m), which is just off the road about halfway between Engaruka

---

OL DOINYO LENGAI

The northernmost mountain in the Crater Highlands, Ol Doinyo Lengai (2878m) – 'Mountain of God' in the Maasai language – is an almost perfect volcanic cone with steep sides rising to a small flat-topped peak. It's the youngest volcano in the Crater Highlands, and still active, although many aspects of its geological activity remain a mystery. There were major eruptions in 1966 and 1993, with the most recent eruptions and major activity in late 2007. At the peak, you can clearly see hot steam vents and growing ash cones in the still-active north crater. A trek from the base village of Ngare Sero is possible in one long day, with a pre-dawn start essential in order to gain as much height as possible in the cool of the morning. Although the number of climbers scaling Ol Doinyo Lengai has exploded in recent years, the north crater poses significant danger to trekkers who approach at too close a range. Before setting off, read the safety overview at www.mtsu.edu/~fbelton/safety.html. For an overview of the mountain, including updated information on eruptions and other activity, see www.mtsu.edu/~fbelton/lengai.html.

---

and Lake Natron. Arrange things through the tourist information office in Arusha, or at Jerusalem Campsite in Engaruka.

There are several camp sites, including one in Engaruka village, and the simple but shaded **Jerusalem Campsite** (camping per person Tsh10,000), about 5km west of the main road in the Engaruka Juu area. It's just after the river and near the Engaruka Juu primary school, and an easy walk from the ruins.

Engaruka is located about 60km north of Mto wa Mbu along an unsealed road, which is in reasonable shape for the first 10km or so, but becomes rough thereafter. There's a daily bus between Arusha and Engaruka via Mto wa Mbu (Tsh6000, four to five hours from Arusha, and Tsh3000 from Mto wa Mbu), departing Arusha by about 10am. At the entry post shortly before reaching Engaruka, you'll need to pay a Tsh5000 per person village fee. Departures from Engaruka are by about 6am. It's also possible to hike in to Engaruka from the Empakaai Crater, but you will need to have a guide from the NCAA.

LAKE NATRON

Shimmering amid the parched, sun-scorched landscapes along the Kenyan border northeast of the NCA is Lake Natron, a 60km-long alkaline lake known for the huge flocks of flamingos that gather here at the end of the rainy season. The surrounding country is remote, with a desolate, otherworldly beauty and an incomparable feeling of space and ancientness, and can be a rewarding – albeit very hot – off the beaten track excursion. The lake also makes a good base for climbing Ol

Doinyo Lengai, 25km to the south. Because the lake has no outlet, its size varies dramatically depending on the time of year.

Sleeping & Eating

There are various camp sites – most budget, and a few more upmarket – all clustered around the southwestern end of the lake.

Kamakia Campsites (camping per person Tsh10,000) These long-standing places – there are actually two camp sites, one near the waterfall and one somewhat downriver near the village – have been spruced up recently and are the best budget places, though facilities are still quite basic. Swimming is possible, and meals are available, as are guides for walks and mountain climbs.

Ngare Sero Lake Natron Camp (☎ 027-255 3638; www.ngare-sero-lodge.com; per person full board per single night US$220, per person full board per night for multinight stays US$170) This upmarket place is the newest and nicest of the various camp sites around Lake Natron, with eight comfortable and well-designed tents situated near a small stream, and comes complete with full meal and bar service. Guides are available for walks, hikes to the nearby waterfalls and climbing Ol Doinyo Lengai.

Getting There & Away

Lake Natron is accessed via the small outpost of Ngare Sero, on the southwestern lake shore and about 60km north of Engaruka. There's no public transport north of Engaruka, but vehicle hire can be arranged in Engaruka through Jerusalem Campsite (about US$120), or in Arusha. The Ngare Sero Lake Natron Camp provides transfers for its guests. There's a US$15 per person district council fee to enter the area, payable at the entrance to Ngare Sero. Self-drivers should carry extra supplies of petrol and water, as there's nothing en route, and no petrol after Engaruka. For upmarket bike safaris to the lake, contact Summits Africa (p55). Once at Natron, the rough road continues northwest to Loliondo and into the Serengeti.

LAKE EYASI

Starkly beautiful Lake Eyasi lies at about 1000m between the Eyasi Escarpment in the north and the Kidero Mountains in the south. It's a hot, dry area, around which live the Hadzabe (also known as Hadzapi or Tindiga) people who are believed to have lived here for nearly 10,000 years and still follow hunting and gathering traditions. Their language is characterised by clicks and may be distantly related to that of Southern Africa's San, although it shows only a few connections to Sandawe, the other click language spoken in Tanzania. Also in the area are the Iraqw (Mbulu), a people of Cushitic origin who arrived about 2000 years ago, as well as Maasai and various Bantu groups. The area is Tanzania's main onion-growing centre, and there are impressive irrigation systems along the Chemchem River near the camp sites. The main village is **Ghorofani**, at the lake's northeastern end, with a weekly *mnada* (auction/market) every Thursday that attracts traders from Arusha and neighbouring villages.

The lake itself varies considerably in size depending on the rains, and in the dry season it is often little more than a parched bed – lending to the rather otherworldly, primeval ambience of the area. However usually a large enough patch of water remains to support a mix of water birds, including populations of flamingos and pelicans.

Eyasi makes a rewarding detour on a Ngorongoro trip for anyone looking for something remote and different, and prepared for the rough road trip from Karatu. English-speaking guides to visit nearby Hadzabe communities can be arranged through Momoya at Lake Eyasi Bush Camp for Tsh40,000 per person (Tsh50,000 including camping at his camp site). Prices decrease if you're in a group (Tsh60,000 for two persons). Staff at Kisima Ngeda can

help those staying at their budget camp site find a non-English-speaking guide for about Tsh5000 per person. Kisima Ngeda also arranges English-speaking guides for guests in its upmarket camp, as does Tindiga Tented Lodge.

Sleeping & Eating

Full board is included in the prices of both upmarket lodges. For campers, you can get basics in Ghorofani, but it's worth stocking up in Karatu before heading to the lake.

Chem Chem Camp Site (camping per person Tsh5000) This village-run camp site – previously located near a spring just outside Ghorofani – recently moved to another not quite as nice site nearby, although there was some discussion of returning to the original site. Ask when you get to the main Ghorofani junction, and follow the signs (it's currently located about 3km from the central area). Facilities are basic, so you will need to bring all that you'll need.

Lake Eyasi Bush Camp (Momoya's Camp; eyasi bush@yahoo.com; camping per person Tsh6000, camping per person plus Hadzabe visit Tsh50,000) This no-frills place is run by the enterprising Momoya. There's a booking office in Karatu at David's Restaurant, behind the petrol station where you catch 4WDs to Ghorofani, and another well-signposted office in Ghorofani itself. Facilities are minimal (cold water only); tents are sometimes available for rent, and meals can be arranged with advance notice.

Tindiga Tented Lodge (www.tindigatentedlodge .com; s/d full board US$160/230) This new and pleasant place is about 4km from Ghorofani, and situated about 2km from the lake in a rustic bush setting. Accommodation is in eight tented bungalows, and a range of excursions is on offer, including birding and cultural walks, and visits to the Hadzabe and Datoga (Tsh60,000 for both, which includes Tsh20,000 to each tribe plus Tsh20,000 for the guide).

Kisima Ngeda (☎ 027-253 4128, 027-254 8715; kisima @habari.co.tz; s/d luxury tented bungalows half board US$205/310) The recommended Kisima Ngeda – in a sublime setting on the lake shore with doum palms in the background – has six tented bungalows along the lake. The emphasis is on bush comfort in a natural environment, rather than luxury, and the cuisine – served by candlelight with the lake bed as a backdrop – is excellent. Nearby is a large hill to climb for sunset views. Away from the main lodge area, the same management also runs three budget camp sites (camping per person US$5) – the only camping on the lake shore – where you can pitch a tent. All have toilet and shower, and for a modest tip the guard can arrange hot water. Kisima Ngeda roughly translates as 'spring surrounded by trees', and there's a natural spring on the property, surrounded by acacia thorns, fever trees and palms. It's about 7km from Ghorofani and signposted.

Getting There & Away

There's public transport several times daily between Karatu and Ghorofani (Tsh4000, two hours), from where you'll need to walk to the camp sites or pay extra to have the driver drop you off. Alternatively, you can hitch a lift with one of the onion trucks. Transport in Karatu leaves around late morning from the 4WD stand behind the petrol station at the western end of town. Returning, transport leaves from the main Ghorofani junction about 3am or 4am, although it's often possible to find something later in the day.

Central Tanzania

Well off most tourist itineraries, central Tanzania has long gotten a bad rap. Its semi-arid climate and lack of permanent rivers discouraged early settlement. More recently, crowds have stayed away due in part to a terrible (albeit now improving) road network. But the region has long historical roots – some of Tanzania's earliest peoples were at home here – and for hardy travellers looking to head off the beaten path, it offers several attractions. Prime among these are the enigmatic Kolo-Kondoa rock art paintings - now a Unesco World Heritage Site. Mt Hanang is another draw, as Tanzania's fourth-highest peak and gateway to the colourful Barabaig and other local tribes. Dodoma – Tanzania's legislative capital and seat of the Bunge (parliament) – makes an amenable stop, with good facilities and a paved road link to Dar es Salaam. Well northwest are Singida, with its pretty lakes, and the gold – and diamond-mining areas around Shinyanga.

Central Tanzania's main appeal, however, is the window it offers on areas little-touched by visitors, and its constantly changing panoramas. South of Lake Victoria, the green, open landscapes of Usukuma (home of the Sukuma people), with small lakes, egrets, long-horned zebu cattle and round, thatched Sukuma-style houses, give way to drier, baobab-studded tracts around Shinyanga and then the countryside around Singida, notable for its massive boulders, lakes and water birds. Dodoma itself is flat, arid and in part treeless, but to the north, the terrain becomes densely wooded and hillier, opening to beautiful vistas around Kondoa. Further north, around Babati, are lush farmlands edged by the soaring wall of the Rift Valley escarpment. If you're prepared to rough things with transport and accommodation, you'll undoubtedly have a memorable time here.

HIGHLIGHTS

- Visiting the enigmatic **Kolo-Kondoa rock art sites** (p236)
- Enjoying the comparative creature comforts of **Dodoma** (opposite), and getting a glimpse of its new parliament building
- Getting to know the Barabaig and other peoples around **Mt Hanang** (p236)
- Experiencing the colourful **mnada** (auction/market; p236) near Katesh
- Relishing travel completely off the beaten path in **Singida** (p239) or **Shinyanga** (p238)

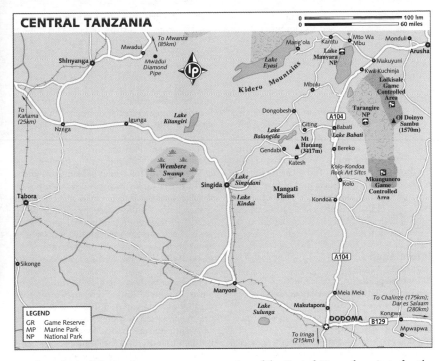

CENTRAL TANZANIA

LEGEND
GR   Game Reserve
MP   Marine Park
NP   National Park

Getting There & Around

There are flights between Dodoma and
Arusha, and sometimes between Dodoma
and Dar es Salaam on Coastal Aviation
,and Precision Air stops in Shinyanga on
some of its flights in and out of Mwanza.
Otherwise, all travel in central Tanzania is
by road – generally rough, although the
network is slowly being improved. The
Dodoma to Arusha trunk road has been
recently graded in part, and paving work
is underway between Nzega, Singida and
Dodoma. From Nzega to Shinyanga and on
to Mwanza is also paved. Buses run on all
major routes; allow plenty of time, and expect the occasional breakdown.

DODOMA

☎ 026 / pop 150,000

Arid Dodoma sits in not-so-splendid isolation in the geographic centre of the country, at a height of about 1100m. Although
the town was located along the old caravan
route that connected Lake Tanganyika and
Central Africa with the sea, it remained little
more than a large village until the construc-

tion of the Central Line railway just after the
turn of the 20th century.

Since 1973 Dodoma has been Tanzania's
official capital and headquarters of the ruling CCM (Chama Cha Mapinduzi) party.
According to the original plan, the entire government was to move to Dodoma by the mid-
1980s and the town was to be expanded to
ultimately encompass more than 300,000 residents, all living in smaller independent communities set up along the lines of the *ujamaa*
(familyhood) village. The plans proved unreal-
istic for a variety of reasons, including a lack of
any sort of viable economic base and an insufficient water supply, and have therefore been
abandoned. Today, although the legislature
meets in Dodoma – hence the periodic profusion of 4WDs along its dusty streets – Dar es
Salaam remains the unrivalled economic and
political centre of the country.

There's little reason to come to Dodoma,
but if you find yourself here it's not a bad
place to spend a day or two. With its grandiose
street layout and the imposing architecture
of many church and government buildings –
all sharply contrasting with the slow-paced

reality of daily life – it's easy to get the feeling that the town is dressed in clothes that are several sizes too big.

Because Dodoma has so many government buildings, photography is prohibited in most areas of town.

Orientation

From the bus stand, the main (Dar es Salaam) road heads west into the centre of town where it meets Kuu St at a large roundabout. Just south of here are the railway tracks, after which everything turns to small dusty lanes. To the north, a warren of small avenues runs off Kuu St into the busiest part of town, with the market and lots of shops. Further north is the airfield, and to the north and east are several large and rather bare residential areas and a few hotels.

Information

INTERNET ACCESS
RAL Internet Café (Kuu St; per hr Tsh1000; ⊗ 8am-9pm Mon-Sat) Just north of the main roundabout.

MONEY
CRDB (Kuu St) ATM (Visa card only).
NBC (Kuu St) Changes cash and has an ATM (Visa card only).
TanPay/Speed Cash (Dar es Salaam Rd) ATM (Visa card and – soon – MasterCard); opposite the Jamatini *dalla-dalla* (minibus) stand.

POST
Main post office (Railway St; ⊗ 8am-6pm) Just west of the train station.

Sights & Activities

The rather forlorn **Museum of Geosciences** (Nyumba ya Mayonyesho ya Madini; Kikuyu St; adult/child Tsh500/100; ⊗ 8am-3.30pm Mon-Fri) contains rock samples and geological information on the entire country, and is worth a stop if you are geologically inclined. It's inside the compound of the Ministry of Energy & Minerals, behind New Dodoma Hotel.

There's a small swimming pool at **Climax Club** (admission Tsh3000; ⊗ 10am-10pm), about 2.5km west of the city centre, and a cleaner, nicer pool at New Dodoma Hotel (Tsh3500 for nonguests).

Lion Rock, which overlooks Dodoma from the northeast, makes a decent hike (about 45 minutes to the top). There have been some muggings there, so don't take any valuables and go in a group. To get to the base, ask any

dalla-dalla driver heading out on the Arusha road to drop you nearby, or take a taxi (about Tsh2500). The enticing-looking hill to the southwest of town near the swimming pool is off limits because of the nearby prison.

If you're intrigued by religious architecture, Dodoma has several places of interest, including the **Anglican church** in the town centre, the large **Lutheran cathedral** opposite, the **Ismaili mosque** nearby and the enormous **Catholic cathedral** just west along the railroad tracks.

The **Bunge** (Parliament) is housed in a beautiful new building on the eastern edge of town just off the Dar es Salaam road and is well worth a look, although it was temporarily closed to the public when this book was researched. If public access resumes, you'll need to bring your passport along; otherwise, check out the informative www.parliament.go.tz for some photos. (Photography of both the exterior and interior is strictly prohibited.)

Dodoma is the centre of Tanzania's tiny wine industry, and there are vineyards throughout the surrounding area that were originally started by Italian missionaries in the early 20th century. Most of what is produced is for church use, and the commercially available vintage won't win awards any time soon. However, it's possible to visit some of the wineries to see the production process. The closest one to Dodoma is **Tanganyika Vineyards Company**, about 2km southeast of town off the Dar es Salaam road.

Dodoma is also a good springboard to Kolo (180km north) and Kondoa, and the area's centuries-old **rock paintings** (p236).

Sleeping

Water supplies are erratic, so expect bucket baths at the cheaper hotels. Also, hotels fill up completely whenever parliament is in session, so don't be surprised if you need to try several before finding a room.

BUDGET
Yarabi Salama (r without bathroom Tsh5000) This cheapest recommended option near the bus stand has very basic twin-bedded rooms with nets. It's about a 10-minute walk west of the bus stand and is often full.

Christian Council of Tanzania (CCT; s/tw/ste Tsh6000 /10,000/12,000) This is the most convenient budget lodging in town, with a central location (at the main roundabout next to the Anglican church,

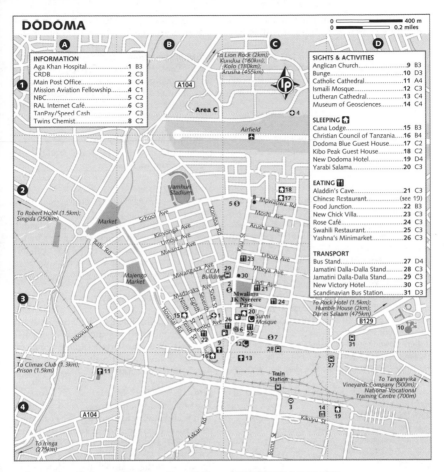

DODOMA

INFORMATION
Aga Khan Hospital...................1	B3
CRDB...............................2	C3
Main Post Office....................3	C4
Mission Aviation Fellowship........4	C1
NBC...............................5	C2
RAL Internet Café..................6	C3
TanPay/Speed Cash................7	C3
Twins Chemist.....................8	C2

SIGHTS & ACTIVITIES
Anglican Church....................9	B3
Bunge.............................10	D3
Catholic Cathedral................11	A4
Ismaili Mosque....................12	C3
Lutheran Cathedral................13	C4
Museum of Geosciences...........14	C4

SLEEPING
Cana Lodge.......................15	B3
Christian Council of Tanzania...16	B4
Dodoma Blue Guest House.......17	C2
Kibo Peak Guest House............18	C2
New Dodoma Hotel................19	D4
Yarabi Salama.....................20	C3

EATING
Aladdin's Cave....................21	C3
Chinese Restaurant..........(see 19)	
Food Junction.....................22	B3
New Chick Villa....................23	C3
Rose Café.........................24	C3
Swahili Restaurant................25	C3
Yashna's Minimarket..............26	C3

TRANSPORT
Bus Stand........................27	D4
Jamatini Dalla-Dalla Stand........28	C3
Jamatini Dalla-Dalla Stand........29	C3
New Victory Hotel.................30	C3
Scandinavian Bus Station........31	D3

and an easy walk from the bus stand), no-frills rooms with mosquito nets, and buckets of hot water on request for bathing. Breakfast costs extra (about Tsh2000); other meals can be arranged with advance notice.

Kibo Peak Guest House (☎ 026-232 2902; d without bathroom Tsh7000, s with/without TV Tsh12,000/10,000) This place has clean, reasonable-value rooms with fan and net, and an almost exclusively male clientele. It's about 1.2km north of the main roundabout off Mpwapwa Rd – about a 20-minute walk from the bus stand.

Dodoma Blue Guest House (☎ 026-232 2085; Mpwapwa Rd; r without bathroom Tsh8000, s Tsh12,000) Just by Kibo Peak, this place has spotless, good-value rooms with fan, most with either twin beds or one larger bed. No food available.

MIDRANGE & TOP END

National Vocational Training Centre (VETA; ☎ 026-232 2181; s without bathroom Tsh8500, s/d Tsh13,000/17,000) A good alternative to the standard hotel scene, with simple, clean rooms, professional staff and a slow restaurant. It's set in pleasant grounds about 2km east of the centre off the Dar es Salaam road, and is frequently full. Meals are available from Tsh4000.

Humble House (☎ 026-235 2261, 0754-093302; Area E; s/d Tsh13,000/15,000; 🖳) This B&B-style place run by the Anglican church offers spotless good-value rooms (some with Western-style sit-down toilets, others with the squat version, and two sharing a bathroom), a small garden, and lunch and dinner on request.

There are also four family apartments available for long-term rentals (one-month minimum, Tsh188,000). It's mainly an option if you have your own transport or don't mind paying for a taxi, as it's buried away in a maze of dirt lanes in Area E (also known as Ipagala), about 2.5km east of town off the Dar es Salaam road.

Cana Lodge (☎ 026-232 1199; Ninth St; s/d from Tsh15,000/22,000, ste Tsh25,000) Spotless and small rooms, plus the inexpensive Galilaya Restaurant and an internet café next door.

New Dodoma Hotel (Dodoma Rock Hotel; ☎ 026-232 1641; reservation_newdodomahotel@yahoo.com; Railway St; s/d with fan Tsh45,000/60,000, with air-con from Tsh65,000/80,000; ✗ ▯ ✦) The former Railway Hotel, now completely renovated and Dodoma's most upmarket option, has a large inner courtyard, pleasant, good-value rooms – the suites face the main street and are noisier than the standard rooms – and a very good Chinese restaurant.

There is a plethora of other midrange hotels, all with clean, bland rooms with mosquito net, TV and bathroom, and all remarkably similar in price and standards. They include the following:

Robert Hotel (☎ 026-230 0306/2252, 0784-335629; s without bathroom from Tsh8000, r with air-con Tsh20,000-40,000) In the Kizota area, about 3km west of town on the Singida road. There's a large poster of Switzerland dominating the reception to remind you of where you aren't.

Rock Hotel (☎ 026-232 0027; rockyhotel2003@yahoo .com; s/d Tsh20,000/25,000) About 2km east of town on the Dar es Salaam road.

Eating

Of the hotel restaurants, the Chinese restaurant at New Dodoma Hotel is well worth a stop, offering delicious food and reasonably prompt service. Meals average about Tsh6000.

Aladdin's Cave (snacks Tsh500-1500; ☯ 9.30am-1pm Mon, 9.30am-1pm & 3.30-8.30pm Tue-Sun) Great milkshakes, soft-serve ice cream, yogurt, apples and other snacks. It's one block east of Kuu St, north of the Ismaili mosque.

Food Junction (Tembo Ave; meals from Tsh1000; ☯ 8.30am-3.30pm & 6.45-10pm Mon-Sat) This popular spot for budget meals serves chicken and rice, and various Indian snacks. It's near the main roundabout, two blocks west of Kuu St.

New Chick Villa (Kuu St; meals from Tsh1000; ☯ 10am-6.30pm) Another local favourite, with the usual assortment of snacks, chicken and chips.

Rose Café (meals from Tsh1500; ☯ breakfast, lunch & dinner Mon-Sat) Good, cheap local meals. It's around the corner from Aladdin's Cave.

Swahili Restaurant (meals from Tsh1500; ☯ lunch & dinner) Another good local-style place, with a wide selection of inexpensive Indian snacks and standard fare, including yogurt and a few vegetarian dishes. It's near the roundabout and one block north of the Dar es Salaam road.

Yashna's Minimarket (Kuu St) For self-catering try this place behind the petrol station near the main roundabout.

Shopping

Dodoma is noted for its crafts, including *marimbas* (musical instruments played with the thumb), *vibuyu* (carved gourds), wooden stools and other items made by the local Gogo people. Sisal crafts are available from the prison to the west of town with an advance order.

Getting There & Away

AIR

Coastal Aviation flies daily between Dodoma and Arusha (US$170), and occasionally has available seats on charters to Dar es Salaam (US$325). The airfield is about 2km north of the main roundabout (Tsh1500 in a taxi).

BUS

The best connection to/from Dar es Salaam is with Scandinavian Express, which has daily departures in each direction at 9.30am (ordinary, Tsh10,000) and 11.15am (luxury, Tsh13,000), both taking six hours. Scandinavian buses depart from the terminal about 1km east of town along the Dar es Salaam road. There are several other daily buses to Dar es Salaam that depart from the main bus stand, with the last departure at about 11am.

To Iringa, there's a daily bus via Makatapora; for details see p284. Going via Chalinze (Urafiki and Shabiby lines) costs Tsh17,000.

To Kondoa (Tsh7000) and Kolo (Tsh10,000) – running along what is actually a section of the old Great North Rd connecting Cape Town and Cairo – Kings Cross and Satellite Coach depart daily at 6am, 10am and noon from the main bus stand. Bookings can be made at the bus stand or at New Victory Hotel, which is off Kuu St at the northern edge of Mwalimu JK Nyerere Park and diagonally opposite the CCM building.

HUKWE ZAWOSE

Hukwe Zawose, a member of central Tanzania's Gogo tribe and one of the country's most famous musicians, was born in the 1930s in Bwigili village outside Dodoma. Although he was known locally for his talents, his star only really began to take off after he was invited to join the national art and dance company that was a predecessor to the College of Arts (Chuo cha Sanaa; p157) in Bagamoyo. In 1980, Zawose relocated to Bagamoyo, where he taught music and further honed his unique style, which features an exceptionally wide vocal range and playing of the *ilimba* (thumb piano), *zeze* (one-stringed violin) and other traditional Gogo instruments. Zawose first appeared at the WOMAD world music festival in 1985, and a long string of international performances and recordings followed, together with his Chibite performing group. Zawose died in 2003 from complications of AIDS, but his legacy is being kept alive through Chibite, which still performs regularly internationally and at the Chuo cha Sanaa, and by the **Zawose Foundation** (www.zawose.org).

To Singida, there are daily direct buses (Tsh15,000, five to six hours), many of which come from Dar es Salaam and are full by the time they reach Dodoma (about noon). On Tuesday, Thursday and Saturday, buses originating in Dodoma depart at 8.30am for Singida.

To Arusha, there are several lines (including Shabiby and Urafiki) going via Chalinze for Tsh18,000 to Tsh22,000.

The *dalla-dalla* stand, known as Jamatini, is on the Dar es Salaam road just east of the Ismaili mosque.

TRAIN
Dodoma lies on the Central Line to Kigoma and Mwanza (it's currently the start and end of both routes until service between Dodoma and Dar es Salaam resumes), and there's also a spur line between Dodoma and Singida; see p361 for more details.

BABATI
☎ 027
The lively market town of Babati is set in fertile countryside along the edge of the Rift Valley escarpment, about 175km southwest of Arusha. It's the main jumping-off point for Mt Hanang climbs and for travel to Singida and beyond along the southern loop via Nzega and Shinyanga to Mwanza and Lake Victoria. Flanking Babati to the southwest is the tranquil **Lake Babati**, fringed by tall reeds and home to hippos and water birds.

Information
There are internet connections at **Rainbow Internet Café** (per hr Tsh2000; ☻ 8am-7pm Mon-Sat), behind Motel Paa Paa, and at **Huddinge** (per hr

Tsh2000; ☻ 9am-6pm Mon-Sat), which is signposted from the main road at the southern end of town. The National Microfinance bank on the main road changes major currencies (cash only).

The **Cultural Tourism Program office** (☎ 027-253 1088, 0784-397477), next to Kahembe's Guest House, can organise Hanang climbs and trips with local fishers on the lake.

Sleeping
Maitsa Executive Guest House (r with/without bathroom Tsh6000/4000, with bathroom & TV Tsh8000) Maitsa offers simple but clean good-value rooms, each with one large bed and net; there's no food available. It's a five-minute walk from the bus stand, and just up from Kahembe's Guest House.

Kahembe's Guest House (☎ 027-253 1088, 0784-397477; kahembeculture@hotmail.com; s/d US$15/25) Just across the large field in front of the bus stand, this good place has twin- and double-bedded rooms (the singles have one large-ish double bed) with reliable hot-water showers and TV. Full breakfast, complete with fruit and eggs, is included in the price.

Just off the main road in the town centre near the market area and bus stand are several no-frills places, including **Motel Paa Paa** (☎ 026-253 1111; r with/without bathroom Tsh5000/3000) and **PM Guest House** (s with/without bathroom Tsh5000/3000, tw without bathroom Tsh4000).

Eating
Abida Best Bites (meals from Tsh2000; ☻ breakfast, lunch & dinner) Abida is on the side street off the main road towards Dodoma that runs directly next to Dodoma Transport Hotel. It has curries, chips, *ugali* (a staple made from maize or

cassava flour, or both) and even a few vegetarian offerings, and is one of the few places open evenings.

Ango Garden Restaurant (Main Rd; meals Tsh4000; 🕑 lunch) Behind the petrol station, this place offers local fare.

Getting There & Away

Mtei line buses run between Arusha and Babati, departing between 6am and 1pm (Tsh5000, 3½ to four hours, three daily). The 6am bus continues on to Kondoa (Tsh4000, about three hours from Babati to Kondoa). The last bus from Babati to Arusha departs at 4pm.

MT HANANG

The volcanic Mt Hanang (3417m) rises steeply above the surrounding plains about 180km southwest of Arusha. It's Tanzania's fourth-highest mountain, with a satisfying trek to the summit, but few visitors know of its existence. The surrounding area is home to a colourful array of ethnic groups, including the Barabaig, who still follow a traditional seminomadic lifestyle and are recognisable by their goatskin garments. Over the past few decades, they have been displaced from some of their lands by large-scale wheat-farming projects.

The most popular route to the top, and the easiest to organise, is the Jorodom Route, which begins in the town of **Katesh** on the mountain's southern side and can be done in one long day (with an additional day necessary for making arrangements). While a guide isn't strictly essential, it's recommended to go with one. This is best arranged through Kahembe's Trekking & Cultural Safaris (p46) in Babati, which is the best contact for doing anything around Hanang or Babati. It costs US$120 per person for a two-day Hanang climb from Arusha, including Hanang forest reserve fees but excluding transport (nominal cost); email or stop at Kahembe's office in Babati first to organise things. If you're trekking independently, you can arrange a guide through the local municipality office (Idara ya Mkuu wa Ilaya) in Katesh for about Tsh5000 per day. However, don't go with any of the freelancers who hang around Katesh and Babati saying they're with Kahembe's or the municipality, as there have been several instances of travellers who have organised things on their own being taken part

way up the mountain and then relieved of their valuables.

For all trekking on the mountain you'll need to pay a US$30 forest reserve fee per person per trip, plus a Tsh2500 village fee per person per trip for climbs on the Jorodom Route. If you're organising things on your own, both fees should be paid prior to the trek at the local municipality office. If you've organised your trek through Kahembe's, staff there will take care of paying the fees for you. The climbing route is described in Lonely Planet's *Trekking in East Africa* guidebook. Allow 10 to 12 hours for the return trek, and get an early start so you have most of the ascent behind you before the sun gets too high. Water supplies up high are unreliable; carry at least 4L with you (even with this you'll probably wish you had more).

Katesh is also known for its large **mnada** (market and auction) held on the 9th and 10th, and again on the 27th of each month. Maasai, Barabaig, Iraqw and other peoples from a wide surrounding area converge at the base of the mountain about a 10-minute walk from town (head out past the bank) to trade their wares. It's a great spot for purchasing everything from *shukas* (blankets) and Barabaig jewellery to cattle and sheep. Bargain hard, and watch out for pickpockets.

There are numerous basic guesthouses in Katesh, the best of which is **Colt** (☎ 027-253 0030; s/d Tsh6000/8000), just past the market, with hot water on request. Others to try include **Tip Top** (r Tsh10,000), near the bus stand, and with cold water only, and the more basic **Hanang View Guesthouse** (s/d Tsh2500/4000), which has nondescript rooms around a cement courtyard and shared bucket baths. None of the guesthouses serve food. For meals, try Kabwogi's, near the Lutheran church.

Mtei line buses from Arusha and Babati pass through Katesh on their way to Singida; the last bus to do this leaves Arusha at 9am. Otherwise, you'll need to spend a night in Babati and catch a bus to Katesh the next morning.

KOLO-KONDOA ROCK ART SITES

The district of Kondoa, especially around the tiny village of Kolo, lies at the centre of one of the most impressive – and most overlooked – collections of ancient rock paintings on the African continent. For anyone with a bent for the offbeat and tolerance for a bit of rugged travel, the rock art sites make an intriguing and worthwhile detour.

The history of most of the paintings remains shrouded in mystery, with little known about either their artists or their age. While some of the paintings date back more than 3000 years, others are much more recent, probably not more than a few hundred years old. One theory maintains they were made by the Sandawe, who are distantly related linguistically to South Africa's San, a group also renowned for its rock art. Others say the paintings, particularly some of the more recent ones, were done by various Bantu-speaking peoples, who moved into the area at a later date.

The paintings, which are spread in a wide radius throughout the Irangi hills around Kondoa and beyond, range in colour from white to shades of red, orange and brown, and were probably done at least in part using hands and fingers, as well as brushes made of reeds or sticks. Some of the colours were probably made by mixing various pigments with animal fat to form crayons. The paintings contain stylised depictions of humans – often hunting, playing musical instruments or pursuing other activities – as well as various animals, notably giraffes and antelopes. Still others are unintelligible forms, perhaps early attempts at abstract art.

To visit, you'll first need to arrange a permit (Tsh2000) and a guide with the Department of Antiquities along the main road in Kolo. There are estimated to be between 150 and 300 sites, of which only a portion have been officially documented, and even fewer of which are realistically accessible to casual visitors. The closest sites – Kolo B1 (Munguni wa Kolo), B2 and B3, which are also among the most interesting – are spread out in the hills rising up near the seasonal and generally dry Kolo (Hembe) River about 9km northeast of Kolo. It's possible to cover most of this distance with a 4WD, except for the final rocky climb up to the sites. With more time and your own 4WD transport, the Fenga-Thawi complex of sites, scattered between 10km and 20km north and west of Kolo and east of the Bubu River, makes a rewarding complement to the Kolo B1–3 sites, though you'll need to allow at least two to three days to organise things and visit both of these areas.

It is possible to hire a vehicle in Kondoa, but it can be difficult to find a 4WD for a reasonable price, so if you're interested in exploring more than the Kolo B1–3 sites (which can be reached with some effort in a 2WD with clearance during the dry season), it's best to arrange vehicle hire in advance.

Despite the recently elevated status of the rock art sites to a World Heritage Site, visitors are not exactly flocking here. Dodoma and Arusha are the logical jumping-off points for independent travellers, but for anything organised it can be difficult to find a safari operator in Arusha willing to sort things out for you. One to try for upmarket tours is **East African Safari & Touring Company** (www.eastafrican safari.info). Budget-level visits can be arranged with Kahembe's Trekking & Cultural Safaris (p46; about US$45 per person per day plus US$120 for transport) or the energetic **Moshi Changai** (☎ 0784-948858; www.tanzaniaculturaltours .com), who runs reasonably priced visits to the main sites as well as a cultural tourism programme focused on the local Irangi people. You can contact Moshi directly or organise your visit through the Tanzania Tourist Board (TTB) Tourist Information Centre in Arusha (p197); ask for the Kondoa-Rangi Cultural Tourism Program.

There's a basic but pleasant **camp site** (camping per person Tsh2000) near the Kolo (Hembe) river bed about 4km from Kolo off the road leading east from the main junction and the Antiquities office, for which you'll need to be fully equipped. Otherwise, the closest overnight base is Kondoa, 20km south, where there are numerous no-frills guesthouses (see p238).

Kolo is about 100km south of Babati and 275km southwest of Arusha. The best connections are from Babati, from where there are several buses daily to Kolo and on to Kondoa, 20km further on (Tsh4000 Babati to Kondoa). Alternatively, there's at least one direct bus daily between Arusha and Kondoa via Kolo, leaving Arusha at 6am (Tsh8000, six hours). Kolo can also be reached from Dodoma, 180km to the south; see p234.

KONDOA
☎ 026

This small, dusty district capital – centre of the Irangi people and a former stop along the old caravan route between the interior and the coast – is of interest nowadays almost exclusively as a springboard to visit the Kolo-Kondoa rock art sites (opposite). There's no internet connection in town, and no ATM, although the local branch of NMB changes dollars and euros cash. Kondoa is about 3km off the main Babati–Dodoma road. En route into town is an old suspension bridge dating to German colonial days and a collection of old German buildings, now mostly used as government buildings.

Sleeping & Eating

New Planet (☎ 026-236 0357; s/d Tsh10,000/12,000, without bathroom Tsh8000/10,000), less than five minutes' walk from the bus stand, is the best place to stay. It has clean rooms with nets, fan and TV, buckets of hot water available on request and good meals at the attached **restaurant** (meals from Tsh3000). Just down the street, and under the same management, is **New Pluto Guest House** (r without bathroom Tsh4000), which has small, clean no-frills rooms.

Should these be booked out, **New Geneva in Africa** (r Tsh12,000) – with an array of large plastic giraffes and other animals out front – and **Sunset Beach Hotel** (r Tsh10,000) both have decent rooms and meals, though rooms at Sunset Beach tend to be on the noisy side on weekends and holidays thanks to a blaring TV in the bar area. Both are well signposted, but inconveniently located from the bus stand – Sunset Beach is at least a 15-minute walk past New Planet.

Getting There & Away

Kings Cross, Satellite and Machame Inv bus lines run daily along the rather rough road between Kondoa and Dodoma, departing Kondoa at 6am, 8am, 10am and 12.30pm (Tsh7000, four to six hours). From Kondoa to Kolo (Tsh3000, one hour) and on to Babati, departures are at 6am, 11am and 1pm. Hiring a taxi to the rock art sites (Kolo B1–3 sites) will cost from Tsh30,000 and can be arranged through New Planet.

SHINYANGA
☎ 028

The large, bustling and sprawling town of Shinyanga lies near the centre of an important mineral mining area and has boomed in recent years with the increase in diamond and gold mining in Tanzania. One of the world's largest diamond pipes, Mwadui, is signposted just a couple of kilometres off the main tarmac road about 30km north of town. After long operating at only a fraction

of capacity, it is once again taking off, with DeBeers having resumed operations here. Further south and west towards Geita are important gold-mining areas. If you have the time, you could investigate the **Minerals Museum** (Makumbusho ya Madini), signposted 3km from town.

The main tarmac road runs along the eastern edge of town, with the market, bus stand and guesthouse areas spreading westwards from here.

NBC (Mwanza Rd), along the main tarmac road just south of Shinyanga Motel, has an ATM. There's an **internet café** (Mwanza Rd; per hr Tsh1000; ⏰ 8am-6pm Mon-Fri, 9am-1pm Sat) next to the post office and just north of Shinyanga Motel.

Sleeping & Eating

Makoa Hotel (r downstairs/upstairs Tsh15,000/20,000) A new place with small, spotless rooms, all with net and TV, and a restaurant. It's diagonally opposite and one block in from the bus stand, and signposted near the Mohammed Trans booking office.

Mwoleka Hotel (☎ 028-276 2249; r Tsh15,000-25,000, ste Tsh40,000) A block up from Makoa Hotel, directly opposite and one block in from the bus stand, the Mwoleka is of similar standard, though rooms are older and not quite as good value.

Shinyanga Motel (☎ 028-276 2458/2369; r Tsh25,000, with air-con from Tsh30,000; ⚒) Opposite the train station, this multistorey orange building has simple but clean and large twin-bedded rooms with nets, window screens, fan, TV and hot water. Food is available on order.

Karena Hotel (☎ 028-276 2205/3031; karenahotel ltd@yahoo.com; s/d from Tsh30,000/35,000, with air-con Tsh35,000/40,000, ste from Tsh45,000; ⚒) Currently the most 'upmarket' place in town, this hotel has small but clean and reasonable tiled rooms and a restaurant. It's somewhat inconveniently located unless you have your own transport – about 1.5km from the bus stand, and off the dusty Old Shinyanga road near Kambarage Stadium.

For local-style meals, take a taxi to 'darajani' (Tsh1500) – the small bridge about 1km up from NBC bank along the main road. Just in from the roadside are small bandas (thatched-roof shelters with wooden or earthen walls) and tables and vendors selling grilled goat meat with chips and drinks. Pick out the cut you'd like, and they'll grill it while you wait.

Getting There & Away

Precision Air stops several times weekly in Shinyanga en route between Mwanza, Arusha and Dar es Salaam. Mohammed Trans goes daily to Tabora (Tsh5500, six hours, departing by 7am; book in advance) and Mwanza (Tsh3000, three hours, several departures between 6am and 8.30am). Departures are from its office, on a side street opposite the bus stand.

There are also daily buses to Kahama (four hours), from where you can get onward transport to Kigoma, or to Rwanda and Burundi via Nyankanazi junction.

NZEGA

☎ 026

This small junction town is where the roads to Kahama (and on to the Rwanda and Burundi borders) and Singida branch off from the Mwanza–Tabora road, which from Nzega southward turns from good tarmac into rough dirt (or mud, depending on the season). It's not a bad place to stop for the night, with a surprisingly decent guesthouse and a bustling market where you'll hear almost exclusively Nyamwezi and other local languages spoken, rather than Swahili.

Note that if you're driving from Shinyanga, there's an earlier turn-off towards Kahama at Tinde junction, north of Nzega. Onward transport has improved greatly in recent times – the road to Singida is now tarmac as far as Igunga and for a stretch from Singida westwards, with only one section in the middle still unpaved.

The best guesthouse is **Forest Guest House** (☎ 026-269 2555; r Tsh10,000-12,000, ste Tsh25,000). It's about 1km from the bus stand (Tsh1500 in a taxi), just off the old (unpaved) Kahama road and signposted. Rooms are clean and self-contained, and prices include breakfast. For inexpensive snacks and light meals, try **Garden Café** (snacks from Tsh250), around the corner from the market.

SINGIDA

☎ 026

It's difficult to think of a compelling reason to visit Singida, other than that it's completely off the beaten track, but if you're travelling between the Lake Victoria area and central Tanzania it makes a convenient stop-over,

and it's the overnight stop of choice for buses travelling between Arusha and Mwanza via the rugged southwestern loop.

The surrounding area is attractive, dotted with huge granite boulders and two lakes – Lake Singidani (just north of town) and the smaller Lake Kindai (to the south) – both of which attract flamingos, pelicans and many other water birds.

Thanks to all the through traffic and Singida's status as regional capital, the town has reasonably good infrastructure, including an **internet café** (per hr Tsh2000), just north of the market, and an NBC bank with an ATM (Visa card only), near the post office, on the northern side of town.

Sleeping & Eating

Stanley Hotel (☎ 026-250 2351; s/d without bathroom Tsh7000/9500, d Tsh16,000) This reliable place near the bus stand has small but quite decent rooms with TV and bathroom. The popular restaurant (meals about Tsh4000) serves up large portions of chicken and chips and other standard dishes.

J-Four (Legho) Motel (☎ 026-250 2526; r Tsh17,000) Quieter than the Stanley and also a reasonable choice, the J-Four has a small garden, a restaurant and rooms with nets and bathrooms. The main disadvantage is the location – it's on the northwestern edge of town, about 10 minutes on foot from the bus stand.

Shana Resort (snacks & meals from Tsh1000), just west of the market, has juices and local dishes, while Florida, nearby, has the usual assortment of snacks, chicken and fries.

Getting There & Away

There are at least two daily buses along the slowly improving route between Singida and Arusha (eight hours), and the trip can feasibly be done in a day, although it's a lot more enjoyable to break the trip at Babati or Katesh (for Mt Hanang). The road on to Nzega and Shinyanga is in the process of being tarmacked and much improved; it is also traversed by daily buses. Daily buses also run between Singida and Dodoma (Tsh15,000, five to six hours), or you can take the train (p361). There's also a daily direct bus between Singida and Dar es Salaam via Dodoma, departing in both directions at about 6am (12 hours).

Lake Victoria

Lake Victoria is Africa's largest lake, and the second-largest freshwater lake in the world. While the Tanzanian portion sees only a trickle of tourists, the region holds many attractions for those who have a bent for the offbeat and who want to immerse themselves in the rhythms of local life. At the Bujora Cultural Centre near Mwanza, you can learn Sukuma dancing and get acquainted with the culture of Tanzania's largest tribal group. Further north at Butiama is the Nyerere museum, an essential stop for anyone interested in the great statesman. Musoma and Bukoba – both with a sleepy, waterside charm – are ideal places for getting a taste of lakeshore life. Bukoba is also notable as the heartland of the Haya people, who had one of the most highly developed early societies on the continent. Mwanza, to the southeast, is Tanzania's second largest city after Dar es Salaam, and an increasingly popular jumping off point for safaris into the Serengeti's Western Corridor. To the southwest is Rubondo Island National Park for bird-watching and relaxing.

The best way to explore the lake region is as part of a larger loop combining Uganda and/or Kenya with Tanzania's northern circuit via the western Serengeti, although you'll need time, and a tolerance for rough roads. While most accommodation is no-frills, there are a few idyllic getaways – notably on Rubondo and Lukuba Islands, and near Mwanza. Most locals you'll meet rely on fishing and small-scale farming for their living, although industry and commercial agriculture – especially coffee and cotton – are increasingly important.

HIGHLIGHTS

- Relaxing and birding in serene **Rubondo Island National Park** (p252)
- Getting into the swing of slow travel, while exploring **Bukoba** (p253) and the surrounding Haya heartland
- Learning about the Sukuma at the **Bujora Cultural Centre** (p250) near Mwanza
- Treating yourself to a night or two at **Lukuba Island Lodge** (p243), offshore from Musoma
- Delving into history at the **Nyerere Museum** (p242) at Butiama

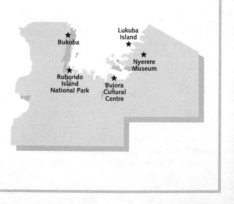

National Parks & Reserves

Rubondo Island National Park, in the south-western corner of Lake Victoria, is the region's only national park. The Serengeti's Western Corridor is covered in the Northern Tanzania chapter (p216). To the west of Lake Victoria are several game reserves, including Rumanyika Orugundu, Ibanda, Burigi and Biharamulo, although none are developed for tourism.

Getting There & Around

Mwanza, Musoma and Bukoba all have airports, and there's an airstrip on Rubondo Island.

Tarmac roads connect Mwanza with Musoma and the Kenyan border; Mwanza with Shinyanga and Nzega; and Biharamulo with Bukoba and on to Mutukula and the Ugandan border. There's also an unsealed but well-maintained road from Bunda through the Serengeti's Western Corridor to Seronera. Otherwise, much of the road network is unsealed and rough, although roadworks are underway at a steady pace. Direct buses run along the main routes, and ferries connect Mwanza with Bukoba and with Ukerewe Island.

LAKE VICTORIA FACTS

Lake Victoria is:

- 68,800 sq km in area, about half of which is in Tanzania
- 100m above sea level
- the world's second largest freshwater lake by surface area after Lake Superior in North America
- infested with bilharzia in many shoreline areas (swimming isn't recommended)
- inhabited by some of the largest Nile perch in the world

MUSOMA
☎ 028

Pretty Musoma – capital of the Mara region – sits serenely on the eastern shore of Lake Victoria, in a lovely setting on a peninsula with both sunrise and sunset views over the water. With its bustling market, colourful fishing port and small-town pace, the town makes

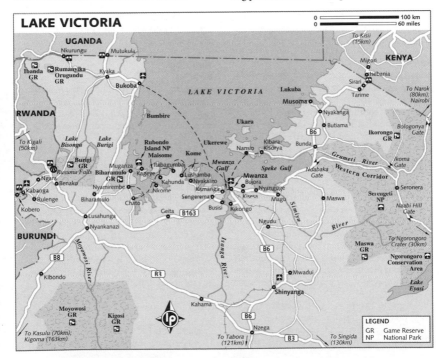

LAKE VICTORIA

an agreeable stop for anyone travelling this way. Its streets, set out in a grid pattern, are lined by small shops and old single-storey Indian trading houses. The surrounding countryside, marked by low, green hills dotted with large boulders, is a melting pot of cultures, with the Kuria, Jita, Luo, Taturu and many more all rubbing shoulders.

About 45km south of Musoma is Butiama, Julius Nyerere's home town. Nyerere attended primary school in the Mwisenge section of Musoma, about 1.5km west of town along the Makoko road.

Information

There are ATMs (both Visa card only) at NBC, four blocks south of the main street, and at CRDB, one block north of the main street. NBC also changes cash and (with difficulty) travellers cheques. There are internet connections at **Musoma Communications Centre** (per hr Tsh1000; ✆ 8.30am-7.30pm), about two blocks east of CRDB on a side street opposite Precision Air, and at **Kokos Internet Café** (per hr Tsh1000; ✆ 8am-7pm), about one block west of CRDB.

There is a large army base in Musoma, and in many areas – particularly around Makoko and along the lake shore – photography is prohibited.

Sights

MWALIMU JULIUS K NYERERE MUSEUM

The **Nyerere Museum** (✆ 028-262 1338; www.museum .or.tz/nyerere.asp; adult/student US$5/2; ✆ 9.30am-6pm), about 45km southeast of Musoma in Butiama, is recommended for anyone interested in the statesman's life and Tanzanian history. It contains memorabilia from the years leading up to Tanzanian independence and from the country's early post-independence days, as well as a large collection of photographs. Boxes of Nyerere's personal effects, including his diaries, a hand-written Swahili translation of part of Plato's *Republic,* and collections of his poetry are also there. Although these are not on display, you may be able to arrange with the curator to view them. A few hundred metres away from the museum is the Nyerere family home, and the graves of Nyerere and his parents.

To get to the museum by public transport, take a minibus to Nyasho (Tsh1200), from where you can get transport to Butiama (Tsh1500). Hiring a taxi will cost about Tsh20,000 return, including waiting time. If you are driving, there are two routes: follow the Mwanza road for approximately 35km to the signposted turn-off, from where it is 11km further down a dirt road; or follow the Mwanza road to Nyakanga, where you bear southeast along a shorter but rougher road to Butiama.

Activities

Not to be missed are the stunning **views** over Mara and Musoma bays at sunrise and sunset (the New Tembo Beach Hotel is ideal for the latter). The lively **fishing port** on the eastern edge of town is at its best in the early morning.

Although local boys plunge daily into the lake – especially from the beaches near New Tembo Beach Hotel, and in Makoko – the waters are infested with bilharzia (*kichocho* in Swahili). To stay on the safe side, try the 25m **swimming pool** (day admission Tsh1500) at Peninsula Beach Hotel (directly opposite Mara Peninsula Hotel). It was closed when we passed through, but supposedly to reopen 'soon'.

Musoma is a good place to learn Swahili, with the well-regarded Makoko Language School (p335) about 5km out of town along the Makoko road.

Sleeping

BUDGET

Anglican Hostel (✆ 0754-671856; r without/with bathroom Tsh3000/5000) The hostel on this large church-run complex has clean, no-frills rooms that are good shoestring value, and meals are available. It's often fully booked. Head out of town along the Mwanza road for about 2km, and watch for the signpost, from where it's about 200m in.

New Tembo Beach Hotel (✆ 028-262 2887; camping per person Tsh5000, r Tsh12,000) This is an amenable choice, and excellent value, with simple, clean rooms – the ones upstairs have a loft bed, those downstairs are all on one level and have a fan – in an ideal setting directly on the lake shore. Also on offer is a nice patch of beach, including space for camping, a restaurant (meals about Tsh3000) and sunset views. It's about 500m from the town centre; take the road out of town past CRDB bank and follow the signs.

Stigma Hotel (✆ 028-262 0088; s/d Tsh10,000/12,000) This is a good value, quiet choice in town, with clean en suite rooms. It's on the same street as NBC bank, about two to three blocks further down.

MIDRANGE

Hotel Matvilla (☎ 028-262 2445; s/d Tsh20,000 /30,000; ✿) Directly opposite Musoma Communications Centre and above the Precision Air office in the town centre, this place caters to local business travellers with small, dark-ish but clean rooms and a restaurant.

Mara Peninsula Hotel (☎ 028-264 2526; marapeninsula@yahoo.com; Makoko road; s/d/ste Tsh25,000/35,000/45,000; ✿ ✿) The long-standing Peninsula, about 1km from the town centre along the Makoko road, has faded but reasonable rooms, hot water, a somewhat quieter setting than the other more central hotels in this category (except on weekends when there's often a disco across the road), and a restaurant.

Eating

Hotel Orange Tree (☎ 028-262 0021; Kawawa St; meals from Tsh3000; ✿ lunch & dinner) serves up plates of grilled fish and rice. **Mara Peninsula Hotel** (☎ 028-264 2526; Makoko road; meals about Tsh5000; ✿ lunch & dinner) has more of the same, plus soups, spaghetti and other standards. **Rama Dishes** (meals from Tsh1000), a local eatery around the corner from NBC bank, is good for plantains or chicken and chips. Further down the same street is a little no-name place selling tasty *nyama choma* (seasoned roasted meat).

For self-catering, try **Flebs Traders** (Main St), or **Kotra's Supermarket** (Mwanza road), about 2.5km from the town centre, which also has a restaurant upstairs. Musoma and the surrounding Mara region is known for its yogurt. To sample some, try the small *mgando* shop just off the main street near the market, and around the corner from Flebs Traders; ask for *maziwa mgando*.

Getting There & Away
AIR

The airfield is about 1km west of the market (Tsh1000 to Tsh2000 to most hotels). Precision Air flies three times weekly from Dar es Salaam (Tsh2,500,000) en route to Mwanza and Shinyanga. The local Precision Air booking agent is **Global Travel** (☎ 028-262 2707, 0713-264294), opposite Musoma Communications Centre.

BOAT

Local boats, including those to villages along the lake shore, depart from the Mwigobero section of town near Afrilux Hotel.

BUS

Frequent buses and minibuses connect Musoma and Mwanza, departing between about 6am and 2pm (Tsh5000, four hours), including the large Mohammed Trans (Tsh5000/10,000 to Mwanza/Shinyanga, departures at 6am, 9am and 1.30pm). Its early bus departs from the main street opposite Flebs Traders; otherwise go to the bus stand. There are minibuses throughout the day to Sirari on the Kenyan border, where you can change to Kenyan transport.

Scandinavian Express (☎ 028-262 0006), with its office just off the CRDB bank road (turn off on the street before Kokos Internet Café and head down towards the port), stops at Musoma on its Mwanza–Nairobi–Dar es Salaam route.

Dalla-dallas (minibuses) run throughout the day between the town centre and the Makoko section of Musoma. The *dalla-dalla* stand is along the road between town and the airfield.

LUKUBA ISLAND

This island (known locally as Rukuba, which means 'place of lightning' in the local Kwaya language) is about 12km offshore northwest of Musoma, and actually consists of two main islands, plus numerous smaller islets. The islands are fringed by lush vegetation and dotted with the massive boulders so characteristic of this part of Lake Victoria. Many of the boulders appear to have huge splits, which has given the island its name – according to local belief, the rock splittings are the result of lightning. In addition to several small villages and seasonal fishing camps, the islands are home to monitor lizards, red monkeys and dozens of bird species – about 70 have been identified thus far. They make an enjoyable excursion from Musoma, especially if you're interested in getting a feel for life on the lake, or in birding. Don't miss climbing one enormous, flat-topped boulder for spectacular sunset views. Staff at Lukuba Island Lodge can show you the way.

The lovely and intimate **Lukuba Island Lodge** (☎ 027-254 8840, 027-250 3094; www.lukubaisland.com; s/d full board US$287/520; ✿), on the smaller of the two main islands, is the only accommodation and a wonderful getaway. There are just five cosy stone-and-thatch bungalows on the lake shore, a pretty beach, and the chance for short walks, birding and boating. Fully equipped fishing can also be arranged. The cuisine is tasty, the ambience laid-back and the lodge comes highly recommended. Advance bookings are required. The same management operates affiliated small lodges in Mkomazi (p179) and near Lake Eyasi (p228), and can arrange upmarket safaris taking you well off the usually trodden trails.

Getting There & Away

There's a public boat between Musoma's Mwigobero port and the main village on the largest of the islands, departing three times daily in each direction, at 7am, 11am and 1pm (Tsh1500, 1½ to two hours). If you time things right, a day trip is quite feasible.

Lukuba Island Lodge has its own speedboat for guests (about one hour, departing from the New Tembo Beach Hotel with advance appointment).

BUNDA
☎ 028

Bunda is a minor transport hub and you'll probably pass through here if you're heading to/from Kenya or Ukerewe Island, or coming from the western Serengeti. The bus stand is along the main Mwanza–Musoma highway; nearby are located a few basic and unappealing guesthouses with rooms for about Tsh6000 or less. A better choice is **CN Motel** (☎ 028-262 1064; small/large s Tsh9000/12,000), with clean singles; the extra Tsh3000 gets you a larger bed and a sit-down loo (versus the squat model in the smaller rooms). It's at the northern edge of town along the road to Musoma.

MWANZA
☎ 028

Booming Mwanza – set on the lake shore and surrounded by hills strewn with enormous boulders – is Tanzania's second-largest city, and the economic heart of the lake region. In addition to being notable for its strong Indian influences, it's a major industrial centre, and its busy port handles much of the cotton, tea and coffee grown in the fertile western part of the country. Yet, despite its size, Mwanza has managed to retain a bit of a village feel, and within just a kilometre or two from the busy

---

> ### SUKUMA GREETINGS
>
> | | |
> |---|---|
> | Mwangaluka | Good morning |
> | Mwadeela | Good afternoon |
> | Wabeyja | Thank you |

central area, you'll be amid crowing roosters, grazing cattle and small farm plots. The main tribe in the surrounding area is the Sukuma, Tanzania's largest ethnic group.

In addition to being the best base for visiting Rubondo Island National Park, Mwanza is also a convenient starting or finishing point for safaris through the western Serengeti.

Orientation

Central Mwanza can easily be covered on foot. Within a 10-minute or less walking radius from the clock tower are the passenger ferry docks (just to the west), ATMs, internet cafés, inexpensive guesthouses and shops, the market and transport stands (both to the east) and the train station (to the southwest). Just beyond the train station is Capri Point, a small peninsula with breezes, lake views and a few upmarket hotels.

Information
IMMIGRATION
Uhamiaji (Station Rd) Just up from and diagonally opposite the train station.

INTERNET ACCESS
Barmedas.com (Nkrumah St; per hr Tsh1000; ⌚ 8am-7pm) One block north of Nyerere Rd.
Karibu Corner Internet Café (cnr Post St & Kenyatta Rd; per hr Tsh1000; ⌚ 8am-8.30pm Mon-Fri, 8am-7pm Sat, 9am-7pm Sun)
MEDICAL SERVICES
Aga Khan Medical Centre (☎ 028-250 2474/0036; Miti Mrefu St; ⌚ 24hr) Southeast of the bus station.
FDS Pharmacy (☎ 028-250 3284; Post St; ⌚ 8am-9pm Mon-Sat, 9am-5pm Sun) At New Mwanza Hotel.

MONEY
DBK Bureau de Change (Post St) At Serengeti Services & Tours; the easiest place to change cash and travellers cheques.
Exim Bank (Kenyatta Rd) ATM (Visa, MasterCard, Cirrus, Maestro all should be accepted by the time this book is printed).
NBC (Liberty St) ATM (Visa only); also changes travellers cheques.
Standard Chartered (Makongoro Rd) ATM (Visa only); near the clock tower.

MWANZA

0 ——— 300 m
0 ——— 0.2 miles

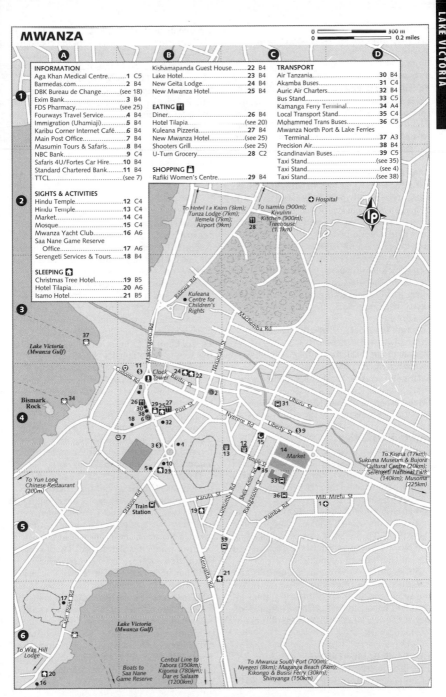

INFORMATION
Aga Khan Medical Centre..........**1** C5
Barmedas.com............................**2** B4
DBK Bureau de Change............(see 18)
Exim Bank.................................**3** B4
FDS Pharmacy.........................(see 25)
Fourways Travel Service............**4** B4
Immigration (Uhamiaji)............**5** B4
Karibu Corner Internet Café......**6** B4
Main Post Office.......................**7** B4
Masumin Tours & Safaris..........**8** B4
NBC Bank................................**9** C4
Safaris 4U/Fortes Car Hire.......**10** B4
Standard Chartered Bank.........**11** B4
TTCL.......................................(see 7)

SIGHTS & ACTIVITIES
Hindu Temple..........................**12** C4
Hindu Temple..........................**13** C4
Market....................................**14** C4
Mosque...................................**15** C4
Mwanza Yacht Club..................**16** A6
Saa Nane Game Reserve
    Office..................................**17** A6
Serengeti Services & Tours.......**18** B4

SLEEPING
Christmas Tree Hotel................**19** B5
Hotel Tilapia...........................**20** A6
Isamo Hotel.............................**21** B5

Kishamapanda Guest House........**22** B4
Lake Hotel...............................**23** B4
New Geita Lodge......................**24** B4
New Mwanza Hotel...................**25** B4

EATING
Diner.......................................**26** B4
Hotel Tilapia...........................(see 20)
Kuleana Pizzeria.......................**27** B4
New Mwanza Hotel...................(see 25)
Shooters Grill..........................(see 25)
U-Turn Grocery.........................**28** C2

SHOPPING
Rafiki Women's Centre..............**29** B4

TRANSPORT
Air Tanzania............................**30** B4
Akamba Buses..........................**31** C4
Auric Air Charters.....................**32** B4
Bus Stand................................**33** C5
Kamanga Ferry Terminal............**34** A4
Local Transport Stand...............**35** C4
Mohammed Trans Buses............**36** C5
Mwanza North Port & Lake Ferries
    Terminal.............................**37** A3
Precision Air............................**38** B4
Scandinavian Buses..................**39** C5
Taxi Stand...............................(see 35)
Taxi Stand...............................(see 4)
Taxi Stand...............................(see 38)

LAKE VICTORIA

POST
Main post office (Post St; 8am-5pm Mon-Fri, 9am-noon Sat)

TELEPHONE
Karibu Corner Internet Café (cnr Post St & Kenyatta Rd; 8am-8.30pm Mon-Fri, 8am-7pm Sat, 9am-7pm Sun) Internet dialling for about Tsh200 per minute internationally.
TTCL (Post St; 8am-6pm Mon-Fri, to 4pm Sat) Operator-assisted calls (Tsh1000 per minute internationally) and card phones.

TRAVEL AGENCIES
All of the following can help with flight bookings, organising trips to Rubondo Island and Serengeti National Parks, and car hire. Prices for 4WD rental start at about US$120 per day plus petrol. For a two-day, one-night return trip to Seronera in Serengeti National Park, transport only, expect to pay from US$350 per vehicle (four to six persons) including petrol. It's not that easy to meet other travellers in Mwanza, so organising a Serengeti safari from here works best if you're already in a group.
Fourways Travel Service (028-250 2620/1853; www.fourwaystravel.net; Station Rd)
Masumin Tours & Safaris (028-250 0192/3295; www.masumintours.com; Kenyatta Rd)
Safaris 4U/Fortes Car Hire (028-250 0561; www.fortescarhire.co.tz; Station Rd)
Serengeti Services & Tours (028-250 0061/0754; www.serengetiservices.com; Post St)

Sights & Activities
Central Mwanza has an Oriental feel due to its many **mosques** and **Hindu temples**, and is well worth a stroll, particularly the area around Temple St. In the area between Temple St west towards Post St, Mwanza's strong Indian influence is particularly evident, with Indian trading houses and pan shops lining the streets. To the southeast is the bustling and chaotic **central market**, where you can find almost anything you could want.

Surrounding Mwanza are many hills and boulders, which offer stunning views over the town and lake. The towering stack of boulders balanced just offshore from Rock Beach Garden Hotel is **Bismarck Rock**, a major local landmark.

SAA NANE GAME RESERVE
This little **reserve** (admission Tsh1000) is on a tiny island just off Capri Point. While it could be a peaceful getaway from the dust of town, it is sadly marred by a dejected-looking collection of caged animals, and not recommended. A boat departs several times daily from next to Hotel Tilapia (Tsh1000, 15 minutes). There's no food or lodging on the island. The reserve's office is on Capri Point Rd, about 200m north of Hotel Tilapia.

Sleeping
For information on accommodation northeast of Mwanza near Serengeti National Park's Ndabaka Gate, see under Serengeti National Park (p219).

BUDGET
It's sometimes possible to arrange camping on the grounds of the Mwanza Yacht Club, next to Hotel Tilapia on Capri Point. Camping is also possible at **Maganga Beach** (camping per person Tsh3000), on a pretty stretch of lake shore in Nyegezi, about 8km from town. There are no facilities, and no food or drink available, and you'll need a vehicle to get there. The road is sometimes inaccessible during the heavy rains. Otherwise, the closest places for camping are Bujora Cultural Centre (p250), or near the Serengeti's Ndabaka Gate (p219).

Lake Hotel (028-250 0658; Station Rd; ground fl s/d Tsh7200/8400, upstairs d Tsh15,000) This hotel is ageing and very tatty, but its shortcomings are easy to overlook if you've just disembarked from a 24-hour-plus haul on the Central Line train. Upstairs rooms – complete with trickling hot-water shower, fan and mosquito net – are better, and management lets three people sleep in a double for no additional charge.

Christmas Tree Hotel (028-250 2001; off Karuta St; r Tsh15,000) Clean, serviceable rooms with a small double bed – just barely big enough for two – plus hot water and TV. Some have nets, and there's a restaurant. The hotel is tucked away in the town centre just off busy Karuta St, from where it is signposted. There's also a signposted entrance from Kenyatta Rd.

St Dominic's Pastoral Centre (Nyakahoja Hostel; 028-250 0830; off Balewa Rd; s/d Tsh13,000/18,000, without bathroom in old wing Tsh6000/9000) A centrally located church-run hostel offering spartan rooms with shared bathroom (no hot water), plus nicer, newer en suite ones with hot water and a canteen (breakfast Tsh1000, lunch/dinner Tsh2000). It's about five minutes' walk north of the Clock Tower roundabout, and good value.

COMMUNITY TOURISM SPOTLIGHT: THE TREEHOUSE

The Treehouse (☎ 028-254 1160; treehouse@streetwise-africa.org; s/d from US$45/55, s without bathroom US$35, 5-person family banda US$65, volunteer discounts; 🖳) is a lovely B&B-style place that's ideal for anyone who wants to get insights into local life, and for socially conscious travellers. About 70% of earnings go to support the affiliated Streetwise Africa charity, and by staying here, you're making a direct contribution to improving the lot of Mwanza's many street children. Besides spotless, comfortable rooms – a large double with a bathtub, a smaller double with a shower, and a single sharing facilities – there's a balcony with breezes and views of the lake in the distance, plus a family *banda* (thatched-roof hut or shelter; also with views towards the lake), and an internet connection point in the evenings. It's in the Isamilo area about 2km northeast of town and Tsh2000 in a taxi. Visitors who are interested in doing more can speak with staff about sponsoring a child or supporting the translation of books into Swahili for use in the reading programmes.

Tema Hotel (r about Tsh18,000) If you need a hotel near the Nyegezi bus stand, try this place. It's located about 10km south of town and about 700m north of the bus stand.

Isamo Hotel (☎ 028-254 1616; Rwegasore St; r with fan/air-con Tsh20,000/30,000; 🛠) Clean rooms within easy walking distance from the bus stand.

There are lots of inexpensive guesthouses in the busy central area of town. Many offer unappealing albeit serviceable singles/doubles, most with mosquito nets and some with fan, for about Tsh3500/4500 with shared facilities, though a good number make their living from business by the hour and none are recommended.

Among the marginally better ones:
Kishamapanda Guest House (cnr Uhuru & Kishamapanda Sts)
New Geita Lodge (Uhuru St)

MIDRANGE & TOP END

Hotel La Kairo (☎ 028-250 0343/5/6; la-kairo@tanzania-online.com; s/d old wing Tsh30,000/35,000, r new wing from Tsh40,000) This once cosy family-run place has expanded massively in recent years. Rooms in the original wing are clean, with fan, and there's a restaurant with good local meals. The adjoining and just-opened high-rise new wing has doubles only, including a few with air-con. It's in the Kirumba area, about 4km north of town, just off the airport road and signposted.

Tunza Lodge (☎ 028-256 2215, 0786-788180; janinebronk@webmail.co.za; s/d Tsh45,000/60,000) An amenable anglers' lodge, with cosy cottages scattered over an expansive lawn sloping down to the lake, a beachside bar and a restaurant. There are great sunset views, weekend beach volleyball games and boat excursions are planned. It's about 8km from town and 2km from the airport: from town, follow the airport road to the Ilemela *dalla-dalla* station; turn left, and continue down a dirt road about 2.5km to the lake, staying left at the forks and following the signs. Public transport goes as far as Ilemela, from where it's a 20-minute walk, or you can arrange transfers with the lodge. On Saturdays, Sundays and holidays there's a free shuttle service several times daily to the lodge from Kuleana Pizzeria.

New Mwanza Hotel (☎ 028-250 1070/1; www.newmwanzahotel.com; cnr Post St & Kenyatta Rd; s/d from Tsh60,000/75,000; 🛠) This barely three-star place with five-star aspirations is the only 'proper' hotel in the central business area. The bland rooms have TV, and there's a restaurant.

Hotel Tilapia (☎ 028-250 0517, 028-250 0617; www.hoteltilapia.com; Capri Point; d/ste from US$90/110; 🛠 🖳 🐟) The efficiently run Tilapia – overlooking the water on the eastern side of Capri Point – is the hotel of choice for most foreign business and upmarket travellers in the area, and is frequently fully booked. There's a popular lakeside bar and sundowners deck, a tiny business centre, a restaurant and a choice of either standard rooms or bungalow-style suites, some quite spacious, all well-equipped and most with internet access in the rooms. Buffet breakfast is included in the price, and credit cards are accepted (5% surcharge).

Wag Hill Lodge (☎ 028-250 2445, 0754-917974; www.waghill.com; per person all-inclusive US$275; 🐟) For a delightful getaway, especially for anyone interested in getting to know Lake Victoria's ecosystems, or in angling, try the intimate and beautiful Wag Hill. It has just three double bungalows nestled into a forested hillside surrounded by the lake, and is completely tranquil, with only birds, monkeys and other local wildlife to keep you company. It's on a small peninsula outside of Mwanza, and staff will come and collect you from the Mwanza Yacht Club by boat. Fully equipped fishing and boat transfers to/from Mwanza are included in the price.

Eating & Drinking

Kuleana Pizzeria (☎ 028-256 0566; Post St; meals from Tsh2500; ⏰ 7am-9pm) Simple good meals – pizzas, omelettes, sandwiches, fruit and fresh-squeezed juices – and a good mix of locals and expats. It's just down from New Mwanza Hotel.

Tunza Lodge (☎ 028-256 2215; meals from Tsh4000, buffet Tsh8500; ⏰ lunch & dinner) Tunza Lodge's large, popular restaurant has beef, fish, pasta and Indian dishes. On weekends, there's beach volleyball on the sand out front.

Kivulini Kitchen (☎ 0784-558869; meals from Tsh5000; ⏰ 9am-11pm) This is a simple one-room place, run by a local women's group, with profits going to a local women's rights organisation. There's an extensive menu, although not everything is available. Best is to ask what the day's special is, and then enjoy the lovely garden area – also with a small children's play area – behind while it's being prepared. Or, to avoid a long wait, order in advance. It's about 2km from town in the Isamilo section of town (Tsh1500 in a taxi, or a 20-minute walk).

Shooters Grill (Post St; meals from Tsh5000; ⏰ 4pm-midnight Tues-Sun) Under the same management as Shooters Grill in Dar es Salaam, with good meat grills, plus a casino and internet café. It's next to New Mwanza Hotel.

New Mwanza Hotel (☎ 028-250 1070/1; www.new mwanzahotel.com; cnr Post St & Kenyatta Rd; meals from Tsh5000; ⏰ lunch & dinner) Good Indian cuisine, although dinner doesn't start until 7.30pm.

Diner (Kenyatta Rd; meals from Tsh6000; ⏰ dinner) Despite the drab exterior and sometimes spotty service, the food here – an extensive selection of Indian dishes, plus some Chinese fare as well – is usually delicious. It's just down from the Air Tanzania office.

Hotel Tilapia (☎ 028-250 0517/0617; www.hotel tilapia.com; Capri Point; meals from Tsh6000; ⏰ lunch & dinner) Pizzas, Indian cuisine and continental fare served on a breezy terrace overlooking the lake, plus a bar.

Yun Long Chinese Restaurant (meals Tsh6000-12,000; ⏰ lunch & dinner) Good Chinese food and sundowners overlooking Bismarck Rock and the lake. Turn left one block west of the post office and continue along the dirt road running parallel to the water for about 500m, crossing the railroad tracks.

For self-catering, try **U-Turn Grocery** (Balewa Rd; ⏰ 8am-8pm Mon-Fri, 8am-2pm & 6-8pm Sat, 10am-2pm Sun).

Shopping

Rafiki Women's Centre (Kenyatta Rd; ⏰ 8.30am-6pm Mon-Sat) This unsigned place diagonally opposite Precision Air has a small but good array of crafts from Tanzania and Kenya. On Sundays, staff set up a display of crafts inside the New Mwanza Hotel between 9am and 1pm.

Getting There & Away

AIR

Mwanza's airport is in the process of being upgraded, so expect changes here.

There are daily flights to/from Dar es Salaam (Tsh170,000) and to/from Bukoba (Tsh120,000) on **Air Tanzania** (☎ 028-250 1059, 028-250 0046; Kenyatta Rd) and **Precision Air** (☎ 028-250 0819; pwmwz@africaonline.co.tz; Kenyatta Rd), with many of the Precision Air flights between Dar es Salaam and Mwanza going via Shinyanga and/or Musoma. Precision also flies several times weekly between Kilimanjaro International Airport (KIA) and Mwanza (Tsh160,000).

Coastal Aviation (☎ 028-256 0441, 0784-520949; mwanza@coastal.cc; at the airport) flies daily in the high season between Arusha and Mwanza via Seronera, and sometimes also has flights between Mwanza and Rubondo.

For air charters to Rubondo Island or elsewhere, contact **Auric Air Charters** (☎ 028-256 1286, 028-256 0524; www.auricair.com; cnr Post St & Kenyatta Rd), **RenAir** (☎ 028-256 2069, 028-256 1158; www.renair.com) at the airport, or Coastal Aviation.

BOAT

Passenger ferries connect Mwanza with Bukoba and with several islands in Lake Victoria, including Ukerewe and Maisome (for Rubondo Island). For schedule and fare information, see p358.

Ferries to Bukoba use Mwanza's North Port, near the Clock Tower. For Ukerewe, departures are also from North Port. Cargo boats to Port Bell (Uganda) and Kenya depart from Mwanza South Port, about 1.5km southeast of the centre.

For information on the ferries crossing the Mwanza Gulf, see the Mwanza to Bukoba section (p251).

BUS

Except as noted following, departures for Shinyanga and other points south are currently from the main bus stand near the market. A new bus stand for the southern routes is soon to open at Nyegezi, about 10km south of town along the Shinyanga road. Once operational, this will be the main departure and arrival point, although some lines may still start/finish at the city bus stand. Buses for Musoma, Nairobi and other points north depart from Nyakato, about 6km north of town along the Musoma road (Tsh250 in a *dalla-dalla* and about Tsh5000 in a taxi).

All Scandinavian Express buses depart at the **Scandinavian office** (☎ 028-250 3315; Rwegasore St) south of the market. Akamba buses start from the **Akamba office** (☎ 028-250 0272), off Mtakuja St, and just north of the small footbridge near Majukano Hotel. Mohammed Trans buses depart from the Mohammed Trans office (just off Miti Mrefu St) diagonally up from the main town bus stand.

To Musoma, Mohammed Trans and other lines go regularly from 6am until about 2pm (Tsh5000, three hours); some buses continue to the Kenyan border. Mohammed Trans departures are at 6.30am, 8.30am, noon and 2.30pm.

To Tabora (Tsh10,000, seven hours), Mohammed Trans goes daily via Shinyanga, departing in each direction at 6am and 1pm. Mohammed Trans also runs almost hourly buses to Shinyanga (Tsh4000, three hours).

To Bukoba, it's best to do the trip in stages via Biharamulo. The road journey is rough (until you get to Biharamulo, where it gets smoother); most travellers take the ferry or fly.

To Geita, there's a daily bus, usually continuing to Biharamulo (Tsh5500), from where there are connections to Bukoba, Lusahunga and on to Benako and Ngara for the Rwanda and Burundi borders. However, to Benako and Ngara it's faster – albeit a considerably longer distance – to go along the paved route via Shinyanga and Kahama (eight hours between Kahama and Benako).

To Muganza (for Rubondo Island), there are sporadic direct buses (Tsh6500, eight hours). It is better to go to Biharamulo and then from there get transport to Nyamirembe and on to Muganza.

To Arusha/Moshi and Dar es Salaam, the best route is via Nairobi (Tsh50,000 plus US$20 for a Kenyan transit visa, about 30 hours to Dar es Salaam; Tsh20,000, about 15 hours to Nairobi). Both Scandinavian and Akamba do the route; for Akamba, you'll need to change buses in Nairobi. Alternatively, you can try the long loop via Singida, which has improved considerably in recent times with the paving of sections of the Nzega–Singida road.

To Kigoma (Tsh15,000, 15 hours), there are two buses daily, going via Biharamulo and Lusahunga, and departing Mwanza at 4.30am. The no-frills Shinyanga Motel next to the Mwanza bus stand is a local favourite and a convenient overnight spot for passengers departing on this route.

See p349 for details of buses to Kenya and Uganda.

TRAIN

Mwanza is the terminus of a branch of the Central Line. See p361 for routes, schedules and fares.

Getting Around

TO/FROM THE AIRPORT

Mwanza's airport is 10km north of town (Tsh6000 in a taxi). *Dalla-dallas* (Tsh200) leave from near the Clock Tower.

BUS & TAXI

Dalla-dallas for destinations along the Musoma road, including Kisesa and Igoma (for Bujora) depart from the Bugando Hill stand, southeast of the market, while those running along the airport road depart from near the Clock Tower. *Dalla-dallas* to Nyegezi depart from Nyerere Rd.

There are taxi stands near the market, at the intersection of Station and Kenyatta Rds in front of Fourways Travel, and in front of the Precision Air office.

CAR & MOTORCYCLE

All the companies listed under Travel Agencies (p246) arrange car rental.

SUKUMA DANCING

The Sukuma – Tanzania's largest tribal group, with about 15% of the country's population – are renowned throughout the region for their pulsating dancing. Dancers are divided into two competing dance societies, the Bagika and the Bagulu, that travel throughout Sukumaland (the Sukuma heartland around Mwanza and southern Lake Victoria), competing. The culmination is at the annual Bulabo dance festival in Bujora, which begins each year on the religious feast of Corpus Christi (about 60 days after Easter) and lasts for about two weeks. The most famous dances are those using animals, including the Bagulu *banungule* (hyena dance) and the Bagika *bazwilili bayeye* (snake and porcupine dance). Before beginning, the dancers are treated with traditional medicaments to protect themselves from injury. (And it's not unheard of for the animals, too, to be given a spot of something to calm their tempers.)

AROUND MWANZA
Sukuma Museum & Bujora Cultural Centre

If you're interested in learning about Sukuma culture, the **Sukuma Museum & Bujora Cultural Centre** (http://photo.net/sukuma; admission Tsh3000; ☾ 8am-6pm Mon-Sat, 1-6pm Sun) makes a worthwhile day trip from Mwanza. The centrepiece is an open-air museum where, among other things, you'll see traditional Sukuma dwellings, the house of a traditional healer, a wooden trough used for rainmaking potions and a blacksmith's house and tools. There is also a large map showing the old Sukuma kingdoms, and nearby a rotating cylinder illustrating different Sukuma systems for counting from one to 10. Traditionally, these systems were used by various Sukuma age-based groups as a sort of secret language or symbol of initiation. Each group – girls, boys, women, men – had its own counting system, which would be used within the group, but which would not be understood by members of any other group.

Also on the grounds is the **royal drum pavilion**, built in the shape of the stool used by Sukuma kings. On the pavilion's upper level is a collection of royal drums that are still played on church feast days, official government visits and at other special events. Traditionally, each Sukuma kingdom had a special place such as this one – though not on the same scale – for preserving its royal drums.

The **round church** in the centre of the museum was built in 1969 by David Fumbuka Clement, the Québecois missionary priest who founded the museum. Inside are some traditionally styled altar pieces. Although services (10am Sunday) are in Swahili, much of the singing is in Sukuma.

On request, the museum can organise performances of **traditional drumming and dancing** for a flat fee of Tsh60,000 per performance, for up to 10 persons. It's best to arrange this in advance, although sometimes you can organise things on the spot. It's also possible to arrange **Sukuma drumming lessons**. There are no set fees; you'll need to negotiate with the instructors, but don't expect it to be cheap. An English-speaking guide is available at the museum.

SLEEPING & EATING

There's **camping** (per person Tsh4000) on the grounds of the centre, and no-frills **rooms** (s/d without bathroom Tsh3000/6000) with mosquito nets and tiny windows. Bucket showers can be arranged, as can meals, with advance notice. Otherwise, you can bring your own food and cook it yourself, or make arrangements for staff to cook it. The closest market is in Kisesa, about 3km away.

GETTING THERE & AWAY

Bujora is about 20km east of Mwanza off the Musoma road. Take a *dalla-dalla* to Igoma, from where you can get a 4WD or pick-up on to Kisesa. Once in Kisesa, walk a short way along the main road until you see the sign for Bujora Primary School (Shule ya Msingi Bujora). Turn left at the sign and follow the small dirt road for about 2km to 3km to the cultural centre. There is no public transport along this road.

En route from Mwanza, around 2km past Igoma on the western side of the main road, is a graveyard for victims of the 1996 sinking of the Lake Victoria ferry MV *Bukoba*.

Ukerewe

The large and densely populated Ukerewe Island is in the southeastern corner of Lake Victoria, and north of Mwanza. It is well off the beaten track, with no paved roads and – outside Nansio, the major town – no electricity. While there isn't much to 'do' here, the island makes an intriguing, offbeat diversion and, with its friendly people and rocky terrain broken by lake vistas and tiny patches of forest, it's an ideal place for getting acquainted with local life. Staff at Gallu Beach Hotel are the best connections for arranging walking and bicycle tours of the island.

SLEEPING & EATING

There's no running water at either place here, but buckets are provided.

Gallu Beach Hotel (☎ 0784-682488; www.gallu.net; s/d/tr with shared bathroom Tsh6000/7000/10,000) This unassuming local guesthouse in Nansio town has clean but very basic rooms and arguably the best meals – all local style – in Nansio. The website is also a good general source of information on the island.

Monarch Hotel (s/d Tsh15,000/25,000/32,000) Just a few minutes' walk from the ferry on the lake shore, this is Nansio's only proper hotel, with self-contained rooms and a small restaurant.

GETTING THERE & AWAY

The MV *Butiama* and MV *Clarius* sail on alternate days between Mwanza's North Port and Nansio, departing Mwanza at 9am and 2pm, and departing Nansio at 8am and 1.30pm (Tsh5000/3500 for 2nd/3rd class plus US$5 port tax, two hours).

It's also possible to reach Nansio from Bunda, about 30km north of the Serengeti's Ndabaka Gate on the Mwanza–Musoma road, which means that you can go from Mwanza to Ukerewe and then on towards Musoma or the Serengeti, or vice-versa, without backtracking. Via public transport, take any vehicle between Mwanza and Musoma and disembark at Bunda. From Bunda, you can get transport to Kibara-Kisorya (Tsh3500), from where it's

a short boat ride (Tsh500 to Tsh1000, 30 minutes) to Ukerewe. This route is usually operated by a vehicle ferry, though it was under repair as this book was researched. When operational, it runs every two to three hours, with the first departure from the mainland at about 8am, and the last at 5.30pm. Plan on leaving Bunda by about 3pm at the latest in order to connect with the last ferry to Ukerewe.

There is little public transport on Ukerewe. A few vehicles meet boat arrivals, and there are daily *dalla-dallas* between Nansio and Rugezi for catching the boat over to Kibara-Kisorya (Tsh500). Otherwise, the only option is walking or bargaining for a lift on a bicycle.

MWANZA TO BUKOBA

Travelling by road from Mwanza westwards along the southern part of Lake Victoria entails crossing the Mwanza Gulf between Mwanza and Sengerema. There are two ferries. The northernmost (Kamanga) ferry docks just south of the passenger ferry terminal at Mwanza North Port, and is the more reliable of the two, departing Mwanza at 8.30am, 10.30am, 12.30pm, 2.30pm (except Sunday), 4.30pm and 6.30pm (per person/vehicle Tsh200/3500, 30 minutes). Departures from Kamanga are every two hours from 8am until 6pm, except there's no 2pm ferry on Sunday. If you are continuing from Kamanga to Sengerema or Geita, see if the Geita bus is in the vehicle queue lined up to board the ferry. If it is, it's worth buying your bus ticket before crossing to avoid the rush on the other side. If there's no bus, the only option is the *dalla-dallas*, which wait on the other side.

The more southerly government-run Busisi ferry operates in theory until 10pm but is frequently broken and shouldn't be counted on – although most Mwanza–Kigoma buses use this route. Its eastern terminus is at Kikongo, about 30km south of Mwanza.

CHILDREN OF THE RAIN-MAKER

One of Ukerewe's most famous sons is Aniceti Kitereza (1896–1981), actually born near Mwanza on the mainland, but grandson of a Ukerewe chief. After a career spent as a translator (he read or spoke eight languages, including Greek and Latin), Kitereza set out to write the biography of his grandfather, King Machunda. The two-volume work – currently available only in German as *Die Kinder der Regenmacher* (Children of the Rain-maker) and *Die Schlangentöter* (The Snake-killer) – weaves priceless strands of local mythology, folk tales and traditional customs into the main family chronicle. Kitereza wrote originally in Kikewere, and later translated his work by hand into Swahili, though he did not live to see the book published.

Once across the Mwanza Gulf, the main towns of interest en route to Bukoba are **Geita** and **Biharamulo**.

Geita has gained prominence in recent times as the centre of Tanzania's now booming gold mining industry – gold was first found in the area in the early 20th century. The town itself is nothing much, but has decent infrastructure and an array of inexpensive hotels. For something a bit nicer, try **Hotel Erin** (r Tsh23,000) on the edge of town, with clean rooms with hot water and a garden.

About 120km further on along a still unrehabilitated road is Biharamulo, a small and dusty but oddly appealing old German colonial settlement. The fortified German boma, perched up on a hill just outside town, was renovated some years ago as a simple guest house. It's currently closed, but worth checking out, at least to see if you can camp. Otherwise, it is worth trying the basic **Savannah Guest House** (r without bathroom Tsh4500) or the better **Robert Hotel** (r Tsh6500), both in the town centre.

Biharamulo is a minor transport hub, and it's easy to get onward transport to Lusahunga – another regional transport hub – with onward connections to Nzega, Kigoma, and the Burundi and Rwanda borders. Southeast of Biharamulo, along the road from Geita, is the turn-off to reach Nyamirembe and then Muganza village – a potential jumping off point for Rubondo Island National Park. See opposite.

Heading north from Biharamulo, the road passes by the 1300 sq km **Biharamulo Game Reserve**, and the adjacent (to the west) **Burigi Game Reserve**. Neither reserve has tourist facilities, although it is reported that animal populations, particularly in Burigi, have made somewhat of a comeback after suffering severely with the large refugee influxes in the area during the 1990s. Roan antelopes, topis, impalas, waterbucks and sitatungas are present, as are elephants, giraffes, zebras and more.

RUBONDO ISLAND NATIONAL PARK

If you relish tranquil surroundings away from the crowds, Rubondo Island National Park, in the southwestern corner of Lake Victoria, is one of Tanzania's best kept secrets. In addition to its excellent **birding**, it offers **fishing**, quiet **beaches** and low-key but rewarding **wildlife watching**. Almost 400 bird species have been identified here, including stately fish eagles, herons, storks, ibis, kingfishers and cormorants. Keeping them company is a wealth of butterflies, and populations of chimpanzees, hippos, crocodiles, giraffes and even elephants (the latter were introduced several decades ago). The island is also one of the few places in East Africa where you can observe the sitatunga, an amphibious antelope that likes to hide among the marshes and reeds along the shoreline. If you find yourself in the region, Rubondo is a complete change of pace from Tanzania's other parks, and well worth a detour.

In addition to Rubondo Island, the park encompasses several smaller nearby islands. It was gazetted in 1977 with a total area of 460 sq km, around 240 sq km of which is land.

Information

Park entry fees are US$20/5 per adult/child aged five to 15 years. For camping fees, see p77. There is also a US$50 per week sportfishing fee. The park is open year-round, but the best time to visit is from June to early November, before the rains set in.

For camp site bookings and information contact the senior park warden. From Mwanza, this is best done via radio, arranged through any of the travel agencies listed in that section (p246). Park headquarters are at Kageye on the island's eastern side.

Both the park and Rubondo Island Camp organise chimpanzee tracking. However, if your primary interest is chimps, your chances of sightings and close-up observation are better in Gombe Stream or Mahale Mountains National Parks (see the Western Tanzania chapter, p257).

Sleeping

The park has an ordinary camp site and some nice double *bandas* on the lake shore just south of park headquarters; both should be booked in advance through the park warden. There's a tiny shop selling a few basics, but it's better to bring all essentials with you.

Rubondo Island Camp (☎ 027-250 8790; www.afri canconservancycompany.com; s/d full board plus airstrip transfers US$265/400, s/d all-inclusive US$450/770; ☒) This intimate luxury camp has a wonderful lakeside setting, cosy en suite tents, tasty cuisine and a highly relaxing ambience. Excursions include guided walks, boat trips and fishing. Ask about low season discounts.

Getting There & Away

AIR

Most guests staying at Rubondo Island Camp arrive via a chartered flight arranged through the camp. It costs about US$350/500 one way from Mwanza for a three-/five-seater plane. For charter companies, see p248.

BOAT

The cheapest, most adventurous and most time consuming way to reach the park is to travel by ferry or bus to one of the villages on the lake shore opposite Rubondo Island, from where you can arrange a boat pick-up with park headquarters. The main villages for doing this are Muganza (on the mainland southwest of Rubondo), Nyamirembe (25km south of Muganza), Nkome (southeast of Rubondo) and Maisome (on Maisome Island, just east of Rubondo). For Nyamirembe, where there's a park officer stationed, and Muganza, there are several direct buses weekly from Mwanza along a rough road. If you get stuck for the night, there are a few basic guesthouses in both places with rooms for about Tsh3000. For Nyamirembe as well as Nkome and Maisome, there are occasional ferry connections, although none were running at the time this book was researched; check at Mwanza North Port for an update. Nkome can also be reached by bus via a rough road (allow a full day from Mwanza); if you're driving you can leave your vehicle at the ranger post there, which is also where you can sleep until the boat comes to collect you.

You will need to radio park headquarters in advance to let them know you'll be arriving this way; in Mwanza, travel agencies or the Saa Nane Game Reserve office can help you call, and there's also a radio at the police station in Muganza. Plan on paying from about Tsh40,000 per boat from Muganza, and up to double this from Nyamirembe (US$80 to US$100), Nkome or Maisome, although with some negotiating you may be able to get it for less. Local fishing boats don't generally enter Rubondo, though if you can manage to sort out the permissions in advance with park headquarters, the captains will give you a much better price deal.

BUKOBA
☎ 028

Bukoba is a bustling town with an attractive waterside setting and amenable small-town feel, and makes a convenient stop if you're travelling between Tanzania and Uganda or Rwanda.

The surrounding Kagera region is home of the Haya people, known for their powerful kingdoms (see the boxed text, p255). Prior to the rise of the Haya kingdoms, Kagera was at the heart of a highly advanced early society known for its techniques of steel production. Various artefacts, including remnants of kilns estimated to be close to 2000 years old, indicate that steel production was well developed here long before equivalent techniques were known in Europe. Although there are no traces of this now in Bukoba, there is a small display on Iron Age findings from the region at the National Museum in Dar es Salaam.

The town of Bukoba traces its roots to 1890, when Emin Pasha (Eduard Schnitzer) – a German doctor and inveterate wanderer – arrived on the western shores of Lake Victoria as part of efforts to establish a German foothold in the region. Since then, the town has kept itself alive through a flourishing local coffee industry and a busy regional port (the second largest on the Tanzanian lake shore).

Information

INTERNET ACCESS
Bukoba Cybercafé (cnr Jamhuri & Kashozi Rds; per hr Tsh500; ⏱ 9am-8pm Mon-Sat)
Post Office Internet Café (cnr Barongo & Mosque Sts; per hr Tsh500; ⏱ 8am-7pm Mon-Fri, 9am-5pm Sat, 11am-3pm Sun)

MONEY
NBC (Jamhuri Rd) ATM (Visa); changes cash and travellers cheques.

TELEPHONE
TTCL (⏱ 7.30am-9pm Mon-Fri, 8am-5pm Sat) For operator-assisted calls.

Sights & Activities

Along the lake are some **colonial-era buildings**, now housing the university and some government offices. More intriguing are the scattered traces of the network of powerful Haya kingdoms that once held sway in this area (see the boxed text, p255). Although the legacy of

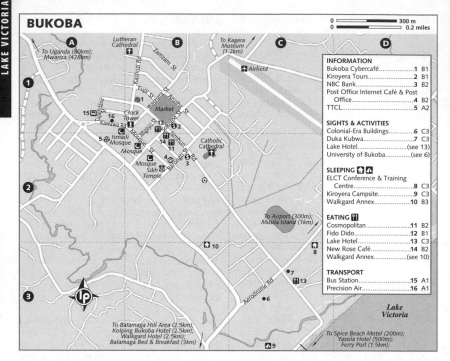

BUKOBA

INFORMATION
Bukoba Cybercafé.....................1 B1
Kiroyera Tours........................2 B1
NBC Bank.............................3 B2
Post Office Internet Café & Post
Office................................4 B2
TTCL.................................5 A2

SIGHTS & ACTIVITIES
Colonial-Era Buildings.............6 C3
Duka Kubwa..........................7 C3
Lake Hotel........................(see 13)
University of Bukoba...............(see 6)

SLEEPING
ELCT Conference & Training
Centre..............................8 C3
Kiroyera Campsite...................9 C3
Walkgard Annex.....................10 B3

EATING
Cosmopolitan.......................11 B2
Fido Dido..........................12 B1
Lake Hotel.........................13 C3
New Rose Café......................14 B2
Walkgard Annex..................(see 10)

TRANSPORT
Bus Station........................15 A1
Precision Air......................16 A1

the kingdoms is preserved today primarily in oral tradition, there are still a few remnants of **royal dwellings** and other spots of interest that can be visited within a half-day's trip from town. Kiroyera Tours (p256) has information leaflets on the various options and can help you organise tours.

At the eastern edge of town near the lake is the old **Lake Hotel** – functioning now in name only – where Ava Gardner and Frank Sinatra reportedly enjoyed a drink or two when filming *Mogambo* in the area northwest of the Kagera River near the Uganda border. Just up the road towards town is the crumbling **Duka Kubwa** ('Big Shop'), which served as the local general store during the German colonial era, and is said to be Bukoba's oldest building.

KAGERA MUSEUM

This **museum** (☎ 028-222 0203; kmuseum@kiroyeratours .com; Nyamukazi area; admission US$2, guided tour per group Tsh2500; ⏱ 9.30am-6pm) houses a collection of top-notch wildlife photographs from the Kagera region by Danish wildlife photographer Dick Persson, as well as an intriguing collection of local tribal items. For a preview, look for

the exhibition of wildlife photography by the same photographer in the National Museum in Dar es Salaam. The museum is on the far side of Bukoba's airstrip. The easiest way to get here is by following the lake shore past the airstrip. However, as you're officially not permitted to walk across the airfield, it's better to take the long way around, heading northeast along Sokoine St past the market, and turning right at the signpost. Kiroyera Tours can sort you out with directions and a guide.

Sleeping

BUDGET

Kiroyera Campsite (www.kiroyeratours.com/campsite.htm; camping per person with own/rented tent US$3/5, bandas per person US$10) A great backpackers' spot on the lake shore, and within easy walking distance of the town and the port, with camping and showers, plus simple *bandas* on the sand, local-style meals and a bar.

Spice Beach Motel (☎ 028-222 0142; s/d Tsh10,000/15,000; ⏱) This small guesthouse is at the southeastern edge of town directly on the water, and not far from the port. There's one single with shared facilities and several small en suite doubles with TV – ask for one facing the lake – and a restaurant.

ELCT Conference & Training Centre (☎ 028-222 3121, 028-222 0027; elct-nwd@africaonline.com; Aerodrome Rd; s/d US$21/30, d without bathroom US$14; 🛰 🖵) A good, long standing place with clean, comfortable rooms and pleasant grounds along the Aerodrome Rd near the lake. Breakfast costs extra.

MIDRANGE

Yassila Hotel (☎ 028-222 1251; s/d Tsh20,000/30,000, d without bathroom Tsh10,000; 🛰) A popular hotel on the lake near Spice Beach Motel and the port. The self-contained rooms have TV and minifridge and some have lake views, and the restaurant serves up good tilapia grills and other dishes.

Balamaga Bed & Breakfast (☎ 0787-757289; www .balamagabb.com; s/d from US$30/40; 🖵) Out of town in the Balamaga Hill area above the port, just past Walkgard and Kolping Bukoba hotels, with four spacious, comfortable rooms (two self-contained and two sharing a bathroom), gardens, cable TV and meals.

Walkgard Hotel (☎ 028-222 0935; www.walkgard.com; s/d US$30/40; 🛰 🖵 🐟) This three-star place is targeted primarily at local business clientele and conferences, with clean, good facilities, a restaurant and a pool (Tsh2500 for non-guests). Check out a few rooms, as size varies; all come with full breakfast and satellite TV. The hotel is on Balamaga Hill about 3km from the town centre in the Kashura area (Tsh2500 in a taxi), with views over the port. The same management runs Walkgard Annex (☎ 028-222 0935; single/double US$20/25) in the town centre, with quite acceptable rooms – all with fan, net and TV, and the best ones upstairs – and a restaurant. It's about 300m southeast of the telecom building on the western side of town.

Kolping Bukoba Hotel (☎ 028-222 0199; s/d/ste Tsh20,000/30,000/40,000) Next to Walkgard Hotel on Balamaga Hill, and giving it stiff competition. Rooms here are pleasant and just as good if not better value than at the Walkgard, and meals can be arranged.

Eating

The unassuming **New Rose Café** (Jamhuri Rd) is a local institution, with inexpensive meals and snacks.

The restaurant at Yassila Hotel (see left) is a popular gathering spot, with lake views and tasty pepper steak, grilled tilapia and other dishes. Spice Beach Motel (see opposite) is also good, with an equally nice setting and

---

THE HAYA

Bukoba is the heartland of the Haya people, and if you spend much time here, you'll undoubtedly make their acquaintance. The Haya, which today is one of Tanzania's largest tribes, also played a prominent role throughout the country's history. It had one of the most highly developed early societies on the continent, and by the 18th or 19th century was organised into eight different states or kingdoms. Each of these was headed by a powerful and often despotic *mukama* who ruled in part by divine right. It was the *mukama* who controlled all trade and who, at least nominally, owned all property, while land usage was shared among small, patrilineal communes. Order was maintained through a system of appointed chiefs and officials, assisted by an age group–based army. With the arrival of the colonial authorities, this political organisation began to erode. The various Haya groups splintered and many chiefs were replaced by persons considered more malleable and sympathetic to colonial interests.

In the 1920s, in the wake of growing resentment towards these propped-up leaders and to the colonial government, the Haya began to regroup and in 1924 founded the Bukoba Bahaya Union. This association was initially directed towards local political reform but soon developed into the more influential and broad-based African Association. Together with similar groups established elsewhere in the country – notably in the Kilimanjaro region and in Dar es Salaam – it constituted one of Tanzania's earliest political movements and was an important force in the drive towards independence.

Now, the Haya receive as much attention for their dancing – characterised by complicated foot rhythms, and traditionally performed by dancers wearing grass skirts and ankle rattles – and for their singing as for their history. Saida Karoli and Maua – popular female singers in the East African music scene – both come from the area around Bukoba.

COMMUNITY TOURISM SPOTLIGHT: KIROYERA TOURS

Kiroyera Tours (☎ 028-222 0203; www .kiroyeratours.com; Sokoine St) is a clued-up agency opposite the market giving new life to tourism in Bukoba and the surrounding Kagera region, and is an essential stop if you're in Bukoba. It has information on nearby attractions, organises cultural and historical outings in and around town, and can help with bus and ferry ticket bookings. In addition to making Haya culture readily accessible to visitors, Kiroyera has also established several community projects, and in 2006, received the Tanzanian Culture Trust Fund's Zeze award for using tourism as a way to enhance local community development. Also check out www.kagera.org for an overview of the region and ideas for excursions.

---

slow service. Up the lake shore a bit, the old **Lake Hotel** (meals from Tsh3500) has decent food, a relaxed ambience, lake views and drinks. In town, try the restaurant at **Walkgard Annex** (meals from Tsh4000). Menus throughout feature grilled fish and local dishes, including the Haya staple *matoke* (cooked plantains).

For self-catering, try **Fido Dido** (Jamhuri Rd) or **Cosmopolitan** (Jamhuri Rd).

Getting There & Away

AIR

There are daily flights to/from Mwanza (Tsh120,000) on **Precision Air** (☎ 028-222 0861, 028-222 0545; Bukoba Machinery Bldg, Kawawa Rd), with connections to Dar es Salaam. Kiroyera Tours (above) also does flight bookings.

BOAT

There is a passenger-ferry service between Bukoba and Mwanza on the MV *Victoria*. For schedules and fares, see p358.

Fishing boats depart for tiny Musila Island, offshore from the airport, from just southwest of Spice Beach Motel.

BUS

Bukoba's roads are getting a facelift – an increasing number of roads in town are now tarmac, and you can go on good tarmac all the way to Kampala (Uganda). Heading south, the road is tarmac as far as Biharamulo. All the bus companies and their ticket offices are based at or near the bus stand at the western end of town. To avoid the hassle, Kiroyera Tours can also help with bus ticket bookings.

Buses go daily to Biharamulo (Tsh4000), from where you can catch onward transport to Lusahunga, and from there on to Ngara or Benako and the Burundi and Rwanda borders.

To Kigoma, there's a bus two or three times weekly, journeying via Biharamulo and Kasulo (Tsh15,000, 12 to 15 hours), though it can work out just as fast to go to Biharamulo and catch onward transport from there.

To Mwanza, you can make your way in stages via Biharamulo, but it's better to take the ferry or fly.

To Dar es Salaam, there are daily connections via Nairobi (Tsh71,500) and three times weekly via Singida and Dodoma (Tsh58,500).

To Uganda and Kenya, several buses go daily from Bukoba to Kampala. See p349 for details.

Western Tanzania

The west is Tanzania's rough, remote frontier land, with few tourists, minimal infrastructure, vast trackless expanses crossed only by the ageing Central Line train and little to draw you here – unless you're interested in chimpanzees. For this, and for watching wildlife in one of Tanzania's most pristine settings, it's a fascinating destination.

Gombe Stream National Park – Jane Goodall's world-renowned chimpanzee research station – and Mahale Mountains National Park offer excellent opportunities to get close to our primate cousins. At Katavi National Park, you'll be just a speck in the surrounding universe of vast floodplains trammelled by thousands of buffaloes, plus zebras, lions and more. Those with a sense of adventure and imagination can visit tiny Ujiji. Now it's a nondescript fishing village, but in its heyday it was the terminus of one of East Africa's most important caravan routes, linking Lake Tanganyika with Bagamoyo and the sea, an important dhow-building centre and a way station for several European expeditions. Lake Tanganyika itself is a scenic and useful transport route if you are heading to or from northern Zambia, and makes a welcome respite from dusty, bumpy roads, with some unforgettable sunset views.

Wherever you go, travel in western Tanzania is rugged, and you will need plenty of time. There are few roads (none of them good), and often the only transport choices are boat, train or truck. Outside of Kigoma, Tabora and the national parks, the region is seldom visited and has few facilities.

HIGHLIGHTS

- Experiencing the primeval rhythms of nature in **Katavi National Park** (p270)
- Visiting **Mahale Mountains National Park** (p267) – the ultimate 'get-away-from-it-all' destination
- Mingling with the chimps at **Gombe Stream National Park** (p265)
- Kicking back on the shores of **Lake Tanganyika** (p262), or sailing towards Zambia on the *Liemba* ferry
- Following the old caravan routes to **Tabora** (p259) or **Ujiji** (p265), or enjoying the modest creature comforts and urban outpost ambience of **Kigoma** (p262)

★ Gombe Stream National Park
★ Kigoma
★ Ujiji
★ Tabora
★ Lake Tanganyika
★ Mahale Mountains National Park
★ Katavi National Park

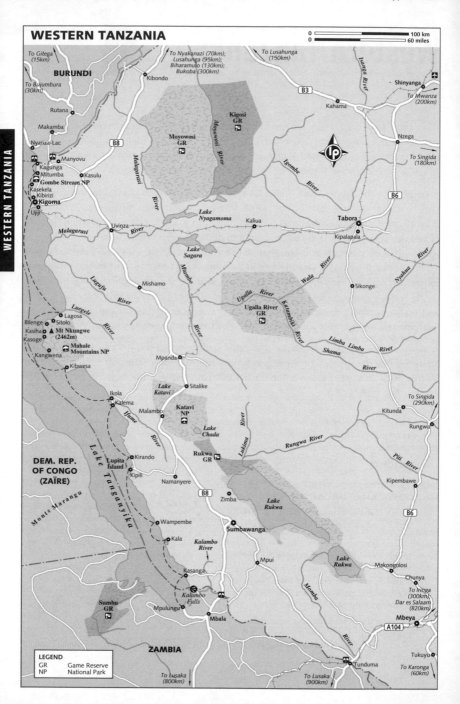

WESTERN TANZANIA

WESTERN TANZANIA

0 ——————— 100 km
0 ——————— 60 miles

To Gitega
(15km)

BURUNDI

To Bujumbura
(30km)

Kibondo

To Nyakanazi (70km);
Lusahunga (95km);
Biharamulo (130km);
Bukoba (300km)

To Lusahunga
(150km)

Isonge River

Shinyanga

To Mwanza
(200km)

B3

Kahama

Nzega

Rutana

Makamba

Nyanza-Lac

B8

Manyovu

Kagunga
Mitumba
Kasulu

Gombe Stream NP

Kasekela
Kibirizi
Kigoma

Ujiji

Malagarasi River

Moyowosi GR

Moyowosi River

Kigosi GR

To Singida
(180km)

B6

Lake
Nyagamoma

Kaliua

Tabora

Igombe River

Nyahua River

Uvinza

Malagarasi River

Lake
Sagara

Kipalapala

Luaufu River

Mishamo

Mlambu River

Ugalla River

Wala River

Sikonge

B6

Luegele River

Lagosa
Sitolo

Bilenge
Kasiha
Kasoge

▲ Mt Nkungwe
(2462m)

**Mahale
Mountains NP**

Kangwena

Kibwesa

River

Ugalla River GR

Katambili River

Limba Limba River

Shama

River

Mpanda

Lake
Katavi

Sitalike

To Singida
(290km)

**DEM. REP.
OF CONGO
(ZAÏRE)**

Ikola
Kalema

Ifume River

Malambo

Katavi NP

Lake
Chada

Lukima River

Rungwa River

Kitunda

Rungwa

Monts Marangu

Lake Tanganyika

Lupita
Island

Kipili

Kirando

Namanyere

B8

Zimba

Rukwa GR

Lake
Rukwa

Kipembawe

B6

Wampembe

Kala

Sumbawanga

Mpui

Lake
Rukwa

Makongolosi

Chunya

To Iringa
(300km);
Dar es Salaam
(820km)

Kalambo
River

Kasanga

Kalambo
Falls

**Sumbu
GR**

Mpulungu

Mbala

Momba River

Mbeya

A104

Tukuyu

ZAMBIA

LEGEND
GR   Game Reserve
NP   National Park

To Lusaka
(800km)

To Lusaka
(900km)

Tunduma

To Karonga
(60km)

National Parks & Reserves

Gombe Stream (p265) and Mahale Mountains (p267) offer the chance to observe chimpanzees at close range, while Katavi (p270) is one of Africa's last great frontier destinations, with top-notch dry season wildlife watching.

Game reserves include Moyowosi, Kigosi, Ugalla River and Rukwa, although none are developed for tourism.

Getting There & Around

There are airports at Kigoma and Tabora, and airstrips in Katavi and Mahale Mountains National Parks.

Roads are in generally poor condition, and self-drivers will need a 4WD, and good supplies of time, spare equipment and mechanical knowledge. Buses run along major routes, although they're prone to breakdowns and journeys can be long and rough. The Central Line train was once a good alternative, but today it's increasingly unreliable, although still worth considering if you have plenty of time. Along Lake Tanganyika, the *Liemba* ferry makes a fine travel alternative for the adventurous.

TABORA

☎ 026

Tabora – a sleepy town basking in the shade of numerous mango and flame trees – was once a major trading centre along the old caravan route connecting Lake Tanganyika with Bagamoyo and the sea. Known in early days as Kazeh, it was the domain of Mirambo, famed king of the Nyamwezi (People of the Moon) tribe, as well as headquarters of infamous slave trader Tippu Tib (see the boxed text, p261). A string of European explorers passed through its portals, most notably Stanley and Livingstone, and Burton and Speke. Stanley, waxing lyrical over the town, noted that it contained 'over a thousand huts and tembes, and one may safely estimate the population…at five thousand people.' After the Central Line railway was constructed, Tabora became the largest town in German East Africa.

By the turn of the 19th century Tabora had also become an important mission station. It soon also gained prominence as a regional educational centre – a reputation that it has somewhat managed to retain even today – and Julius Nyerere attended school here.

Today Tabora is still an important transport junction where the Central Line

branches for Mwanza and Kigoma. It's also the traditional heartland of the Nyamwezi, one of Tanzania's largest tribal groups. If you're travelling by train, you'll probably need to spend at least a day here, and it's worth spending a few more for a glimpse into a Tanzania well away from Zanzibar and the northern safari circuits.

Note that many locals refer to Lumumba St as Kazima Rd (its easterly extension).

Information

CRDB Bank (Jamhuri St) Has an ATM (accepts Visa).
NBC (Market St) Changes cash and travellers cheques; has an ATM (Visa only).
Post Office Internet Café (Jamhuri St; per hr Tsh1000; ☺ 8am-6pm Mon-Fri, 9am-6pm Sat & Sun)
Tabora On-Line (Lumumba St; per hr Tsh1000; ☺ 8am-5.30pm) Next to the library and opposite the Mohammed Trans office.

Sights & Activities

There are a few buildings dating back to the German era, including the **train station** and the old **boma**, at the end of Boma Rd. The main attraction, however, is the deep maroon-coloured and well-maintained **Livingstone's tembe** (admission Tsh2000; ☺ 8am-5pm), a flat-roofed Arabic-style house about 6km southwest of town in Kwihara, off the Kipalapala road. It was here that Livingstone stayed in 1872 after being found by Stanley in Ujiji, and the house – now a small museum – still holds some of his memorabilia, including letters, a diary and other items. To get here, take any *dalla-dalla* (minibus) heading to Kipalapala and have them drop you at the turn-off (to the right, when coming from Tabora), from where it's about 2km further on foot. Taxis from town charge about Tsh6000 return. Once at the tembe, you'll need to find the caretaker to let you in – he lives about 500m away and will probably come bicycling down if he sees visitors. Otherwise, ask anyone in the village for 'Livingstone' and they'll point you in the right direction.

Sleeping

BUDGET

Moravian Hostel (☎ 026-260 4710, 0787-401613; Old Mwanza Rd; s/d in new wing Tsh5000/8000, d without bathroom in old wing Tsh3000) Spartan twin-bed rooms with mosquito nets in a quiet compound about 2km from the train station, and about 10 minutes' walk from the bus station. Follow

WESTERN TANZANIA

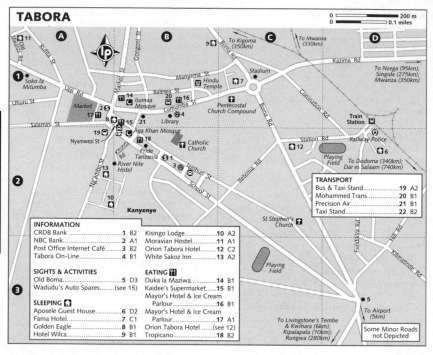

TABORA

the unpaved road past the main entrance to the market. Continue straight, turning right at the Soko la Mitumba onto Old Mwanza Rd. The Moravian Church compound is about 50m further on. Breakfast costs Tsh1000, and meals can be arranged.

Aposele Guest House (☎ 026-260 4510; d in annexe Tsh6000, d without bathroom in main bldg Tsh4000) A reasonable choice if you're travelling by train, with tatty but decent doubles in an annexe, with a mix of 'standing' and 'sitting' toilets, and some doubles sharing bathroom in the main building next door – both within five minutes' walk from the train station. Hot-water buckets can be arranged. Exiting the train station, head right, towards the railway police building. Ignore the road turning right immediately after the police building and follow the next path straight for about 200m.

Golden Eagle (☎ 026-260 4623; Jamhuri St; r 15,000, without bathroom Tsh6000, with TV Tsh25,000) In contrast with the scruffy exterior, rooms at this 1st-storey place are surprisingly decent, with clean sheets, fan and a convenient location just five minutes' walk from the bus stand.

The en suite rooms have one large bed, the rest two twins.

Fama Hotel (☎ 026-260 4657; s/d Tsh7000/8000, d with TV Tsh12,000) Clean and quiet, albeit faded rooms, and a restaurant. It's just off the small side road branching out from Lumumba St opposite the Pentecostal church compound.

Hotel Wilca (☎ 026-260 4105; Boma Rd; r Tsh15,000) Clean and quiet rooms (all with mosquito nets), a restaurant and a small garden. It's at the northeastern edge of town along Boma Rd. From the bus stand, continue straight along Lumumba St past the Pentecostal church compound, turn left on Boma Rd and continue straight on. From the train station, follow Station Rd to the roundabout and go left on Boma Rd.

In the dusty Kanyenye residential area, within a 10-minute walk from the bus stand, are several clean, decent-value budget places, including **White Sakoz Inn** (r Tsh10,000-15,000), in a white building with clean en suite rooms with TV, and the similar and slightly better **Kisingo Lodge** (r Tsh10,000-15,000, ste Tsh25,000). Exit straight from the bus stand, then take the first left and then the first right onto School St. Follow this up past the Aga Khan mosque, take the first major paved right onto Kitunda Rd, go straight for about 300m past the signposted River Nile Hotel – White Sakoz is about half a block to the left. Kisingo Lodge is about one block further on and about two blocks in to the left.

MIDRANGE

Orion Tabora Hotel (☎ 026-260 4369; cnr Boma & Station Rds; camping per person Tsh6000, s/d Tsh36,000/48,000, ste s/d from Tsh60,000/72,000) The old railway hotel has been nicely restored and provides very good value – a lovely and unexpected respite for anyone travelling in the region. All rooms – most spacious and all looking out onto the surrounding gardens – have TV and mosquito net, and there's also a good restaurant and a well-stocked bar. The hotel was originally built by a German baron as a hunting lodge, and still has lots of atmosphere. If you're travelling by train, there is usually someone around to let you in for predawn arrivals.

Eating

Mayor's Hotel & Ice Cream Parlour (snacks from Tsh500, meals Tsh1500; ☯ breakfast, lunch & dinner) Samosas and other snacks and local meals, plus juice and bottles of fresh yogurt and (sometimes) softserve ice cream. The main restaurant is behind NBC bank, with a branch on Lumumba St next to the Mohammed Trans bus office.

TIPPU TIB

Tippu Tib (Hamed bin Mohamed el Murjebi), one of East Africa's most infamous slave traders, was born around 1830 in Zanzibar as the son of a wealthy plantation owner from Tabora. While still young, Tippu Tib began to assist his father with trade and soon came to dominate an extensive area around Lake Tanganyika that stretched well into present-day Democratic Republic of Congo (Zaïre). By the late 19th century he had trading stations strung out across eastern Congo and Tanzania. Tippu Tib assisted Livingstone and Stanley with their expeditions, and in 1887 Stanley persuaded him to become governor of the eastern region of the Congo, although the undertaking was short-lived. In 1890 Tippu Tib left his base in the Congo for Zanzibar, where he died in 1905.

Tropicano (School St; snacks & light meals from Tsh500; ☯ until 7pm) Similar to Mayor's, but quieter. It's next to Pride Tanzania.

Orion Tabora Hotel (☎ 026-260 4369; cnr Boma & Station Rds; meals from Tsh5000; ☯ breakfast, lunch & dinner) Large portions and well-prepared meals – overall excellent value. There's dining in the outside bar-restaurant area and indoors.

For self-caterers:

Kaidee's Supermarket (Jamhuri St) Next Wadudu's Auto Spares.

Duka la Maziwa (Milk Shop) Sells fresh yogurt and milk. It's unsignposted (ask for the Tabora Creamery), to the side of the Ijumaa Mosque and just off Lumumba St.

Getting There & Away

AIR

Flights with **Precision Air** (☎ 026-260 4818; Lumumba St) stop at Tabora daily en route from Dar es Salaam to Kigoma (Tsh152,500 to Kigoma, Tsh329,000 to Dar es Salaam). The airport is about 5km south of town.

BUS

The 'new' Tabora bus stand is along the extension of Market St, past NBC bank. **Mohammed Trans** (Lumumba St) has its own office and departure point, opposite the library.

Mohammed Trans runs between Tabora and Mwanza, departing from Tabora daily at 6am and 10am (Tsh10,000, 7½ hours). If you're heading east, you can disembark at Nzega (which is also serviced daily by 4WDs), and then catch a bus on to Singida, though this means an overnight in Nzega. It's possible to drive between Tabora and Mbeya (4WD only), but it's a long, albeit in part highly scenic, slog; the route is serviced by three to four buses weekly during the dry season.

To Kigoma, the only direct public transport is by train.

TRAIN

Tabora is the main Central Line junction for trains north to Mwanza, west to Kigoma and south to Mpanda. For schedule and fare information, see p361. Trains from Mpanda reach Tabora about 3am, trains from Kigoma and Mwanza arrive by about 5am, and trains from Dar es Salaam reach Tabora by about 9pm. Travelling between Kigoma and Mwanza, you will need to spend the day in Tabora, where you should also reconfirm your onward reservation.

Getting Around

There are taxi stands by the bus station and on the corner of Jamhuri Rd and Nyamwezi St, diagonally opposite Wadudu Auto Spares. Taxis meet all train arrivals (Tsh1500 to the town centre). If arriving in the middle of the night, ask the driver to wait until you're sure that there's someone at your hotel to let you in.

KIGOMA
☎ 028

Kigoma is a scrappy but agreeable lake shore town in a tropical waterside setting with views to the Congo mountains in the distance. In addition to being a regional capital, Kigoma is also the most important Tanzanian port on Lake Tanganyika, the end of the line if you've slogged across the country on the Central Line train and a convenient starting point for visits to Gombe Stream National Park, or Mahale Mountains National Park if you're travelling on by boat. For much of Kigoma's history it was overshadowed by Ujiji to the south, only coming into its own with the building of the Central Line railway terminus. In the wake of the past decades' upheavals in nearby Democratic Republic of Congo (Zaïre), Rwanda and Burundi, the area around Kigoma became a major refugee centre. While many refugees have since returned home, there are still a large number of international aid organisations working in the region.

Information
CONSULATES
See p337 for visa details.
Burundi (☎ 028-280 2865; Kakolwa Ave; ☺ 10am-3pm Mon-Fri)
Congo (Zaïre) (Kaya Rd; ☺ 8.30am-4pm Mon-Fri)

IMMIGRATION OFFICE
An immigration officer is posted at the port on Wednesday to take care of immigration formalities for travellers departing for Zambia on the MV *Liemba*. The immigration office is on the main road towards Ujiji.

INTERNET ACCESS
Baby Come & Call (Lumumba St; per hr Tsh2000; ☺ 8am-7pm Mon-Sat) Just up from the train station.
TCCIA (Chamber of Commerce) Internet Café (Lumumba St; per hr Tsh2000; ☺ 8.30am-7pm Mon-Sat, 10am-1pm Sun)

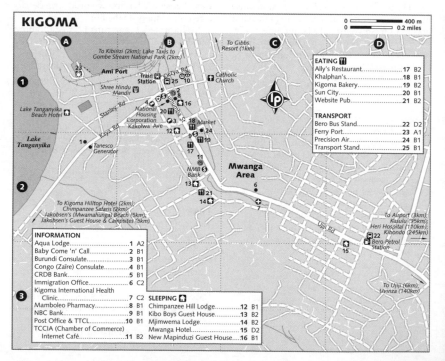

KIGOMA

0 ———— 400 m
0 ———— 0.2 miles

To Kibirizi (2km); Lake Taxis to Gombe Stream National Park (2km)

Ami Port

Train Station

To Gibbs Resort (1km)

Catholic Church

Shree Hindu Mandir

Lake Tanganyika Beach Hotel

National Housing Corporation

Stanley Rd

Kaya Rd

Kakolwa Ave

Lake Tanganyika

Tanesco Generator

Market

Mwanga Area

NMB Bank

To Kigoma Hilltop Hotel (2km); Chimpanzee Safaris (2km); Jakobsen's (Mwamahunga) Beach (5km); Jakobsen's Guest House & Campsites (5km)

Ujiji Rd

To Airport (3km); Kasulu (95km); Heri Hospital (110km); Kibondo (245km)

Bero Petrol Station

To Ujiji (6km); Uvinza (140km)

EATING 🍴
Ally's Restaurant......................17 B2
Khalphan's..............................18 B1
Kigoma Bakery.........................19 B2
Sun City.................................20 B1
Website Pub............................21 B2

TRANSPORT
Bero Bus Stand.........................22 D2
Ferry Port...............................23 A1
Precision Air............................24 B1
Transport Stand........................25 B1

INFORMATION
Aqua Lodge...............................1 A2
Baby Come 'n' Call........................2 B1
Burundi Consulate........................3 B1
Congo (Zaïre) Consulate...............4 B1
CRDB Bank.................................5 B1
Immigration Office.......................6 C2
Kigoma International Health
  Clinic....................................7 C2
Mamboleo Pharmacy....................8 B1
NBC Bank..................................9 B1
Post Office & TTCL.....................10 B1
TCCIA (Chamber of Commerce)
  Internet Café.........................11 B2

SLEEPING 🛏
Chimpanzee Hill Lodge...............12 B1
Kibo Boys Guest House...............13 B2
Mjimwema Lodge........................14 B2
Mwanga Hotel..........................15 D2
New Mapinduzi Guest House....16 B1

MEDICAL SERVICES

Heri Hospital Mission-run hospital about two hours' drive from Kigoma near the Burundi border.

Kigoma International Health Clinic (Ujiji Rd, Mwanga) For minor medical issues.

Mamboleo Pharmacy (Lumumba Rd; ☻ 8am-6pm Mon-Sat, 10am-2pm Sun)

Mission Aviation Fellowship (MAF; ☎ 028-280 4940) May be able to help with emergency medical evacuations.

MONEY

CRDB (Train Station Roundabout) Has an ATM (Visa only).

NBC (Lumumba St) Changes cash; has an ATM (Visa only).

POST & TELEPHONE

Post Office & TTCL (Kiezya Rd) Operator-assisted calls and postal services.

TRAVEL AGENCIES

Both of the following organise boat rentals and visits to Gombe Stream and Mahale Mountains National Parks.

Aqua Lodge (☎ 028-280 2408) On the western edge of town opposite the Tanesco generator.

Chimpanzee Safaris (☎ 028-280 4437; www.mbalimbali.com) At Kigoma Hilltop Hotel.

Sights & Activities

Kigoma's lively **market** is worth a stroll, as is the large and colourful fishing village of **Kibirizi**, which is 2km north of town and best visited in the early morning when the fishing boats pull in. The main fishing activity is at the far end of Kibirizi, downhill from the Tanapa office. In town, there are various buildings dating from the German colonial era, including the **train station** at the base of Lumumba St.

The best place for relaxing is **Jakobsen's (Mwamahunga) Beach** (admission Tsh4000), which is actually two small, beautiful coves reached via steps down a vegetated section of hillside about 5km southwest of town. There are a few *bandas* for shade, the water is bilharzia-free (see p367) and the overall setting – especially if you visit during the week when few people are around – is idyllic. There's no food or drink. Head west from town along the road past Kigoma Hilltop Hotel, keeping right at the small fork until the signpost, from where it's about 3km further uphill and signposted. Via public transport, catch a Katonga *dalla-dalla* at the roundabout near the train station and ask the driver to drop you at the turn-off, from where it's 30 to 40 minutes further on foot.

Sleeping

BUDGET

Mwanga Hotel (Ujiji Rd; r Tsh6000) In the Mwanga area – about 3km north of the train station, but within about 500m of the bus park, and convenient if you have an early bus to Mwanza, Burundi or other points north – try this hotel, about 400m before the Kibondo–Kasulu junction, with no-frills rooms and hot buckets on request.

New Mapinduzi Guest House (☎ 028-280 4978; Lumumba St; s/d Tsh8000/10,000, without bathroom Tsh5000/7000) In a tiny alley just opposite the large white and yellow National Housing Corporation building, and within five minutes' walk of the train and *dalla-dalla* stations. Rooms are basic and without fan, but clean and with mosquito net. The location is convenient and it's one of the better shoestring options. There's no food.

Mjimwema Lodge (☎ 028-280 4500; s/d from Tsh12,000/17,000, s without bathroom Tsh5000) No-frills rooms around a small cement courtyard, all with fan and mosquito net, except for the single with shared bathroom, which has no fan. Follow the dirt road uphill after turning off Lumumba St at NMB bank and before reaching Kibo Boys.

Kibo Boys Guest House (☎ 028-280 2388; s/ste Tsh12,000/20,000) Just off Lumumba St, and about one block in from NMB bank at the northern end of town, this place has noisy but clean single-bed rooms, all with TV and mosquito net. There's no food. The adjoining Kibo Social Hall hosts a disco on Saturday night (free admission if you have a room in the hotel, which is just as well, as you wouldn't get any sleep anyway). Next door is Website Pub (p264).

Jakobsen's Guest House (www.kigomabeach.com; accommodation per family per night Tsh40,000, per additional adult Tsh15,000, electricity per hr Tsh3500) This comfortable private guesthouse is located well out of town on an escarpment above Jakobsen's Beach (left), and is generally rented out in its entirety – three double beds and seven twins divided among several rooms – rather than by room, though space permitting, individual rooms are available as well. There are two well-equipped kitchens, two bathrooms and the quiet, cliff-top perch is lovely. It's overall good value, and a wonderful spot for a respite and for enjoying the lake shore nature. Just five minutes on foot down the hillside, just up from the beach and part of the same guest house complex, are two attractive shaded, grassy camp sites (camping per adult Tsh6000, tent rental per night Tsh10,000) with ablutions, a grill, lanterns and water supply, and just downhill from these is the beach with sunset views. For both camping and the guesthouse, bring all your own food from town.

MIDRANGE

Chimpanzee Hill Lodge (☎ 0754-651319; off Lumumba St; r Tsh12,000-20,000) Reached via the road leading in from NMB bank past Kibo Boys Guest House, with simple rooms in attached rondavels with mosquito netting and TV. A restaurant is planned.

Gibbs Resort (☎ 028-280 4272; r Tsh45,000; ☒) A newish place in the Kieyza area, signposted from the post office road (Tsh2000 in a taxi). The location is peaceful – on a hill overlooking the lake – and rooms (most have twin beds) are reasonable value for the price, though they don't quite live up to expectations. There's a shady porch, and a restaurant (ask for outdoor seating) with meals for about Tsh5000.

Kigoma Hilltop Hotel (☎ 028-280 4437; kht@raha .com; www.chimpanzeesafaris.com; s/d from US$60/80; ☒ ▣ ☎) Kigoma's only hotel approaching upmarket has a prime setting on an escarpment overlooking the lake, with small, slightly faded cottages with small fridge and TV, a not-always-clean pool (nonresidents Tsh5000) and a slow restaurant. The same management also runs camps in Mahale Mountains, Gombe Stream and Katavi National Parks.

Eating & Drinking

For inexpensive *wali maharagwe* (rice and beans) and other local meals, the best places are **Sun City** (Lumumba St; meals Tsh1500-3000), which also has a chicken or fish biryani special on Sundays and fresh juices, or the more no-frills **Ally's Restaurant** (Lumumba St; meals Tsh1000-2500; ☽ until 7pm), with samosas and other snacks in addition to local meals.

Website Pub (off Lumumba St) Cold drinks, light meals and music. Turn left (uphill) just before reaching Kibo Boys Guest House and look for the *makuti* (thatched) roofing.

For self-catering, there are several well-stocked shops near the market, including the following:

Khalphan's (off Lumumba St) Opposite Precision Air.

Kigoma Bakery (Lumumba St) Also sells fresh juices and ice cream; diagonally opposite Ally's Restaurant.

Getting There & Away

AIR

Just around the corner from NBC bank, **Precision Air** (☎ 028-280 4720) flies daily between Kigoma and Dar es Salaam (Tsh368,000), stopping in Tabora en route from Dar to Kigoma.

The airport is about 5km southeast of the town centre. A taxi to the airport costs Tsh4000.

BOAT
Ferries

For scheduling and price information for the MV *Liemba* between Kigoma and Mpulungu (Zambia) via Lagosa (also called Mugambo; for Mahale Mountains National Park) and other lake-shore towns, see p358. The *Liemba* departs from the main port area, just south of the old Lake Tanganyika Beach Hotel.

Cargo ferries to Burundi and Democratic Republic of Congo (Zaïre) – many of which also take passengers – depart from the Ami port, reached by following the dirt lane down to the left of the train station. Watch for the sign 'To Kigoma Port, Managed by APO'.

Lake Taxis

Lake taxis are small, wooden motorised boats, piled high with people and produce, that connect villages along the lake shore as far north as the Burundi border, including a stop at Gombe Stream National Park. They are inexpensive, but offer no shade or other creature comforts. The lake taxis don't stop at Kigoma itself, but at Kibirizi village, about 2.5km north of Kigoma. To get here, follow the railway tracks north, or alternatively follow the road uphill past the post office, turn left at the top and continue straight for about 2km (Tsh2000 in a taxi).

BUS

Roads from Kigoma in all directions are rough, although improving. For all long-distance departures, including to Biharamulo, Bukoba, Mwanza and other destinations near Lake Victoria, departures are from the bus stand on the small road turning left off the Ujiji Rd just before Bero petrol station. (Coming from Kigoma, look for the large, white, unmarked petrol station on the left shortly before reaching the Kasulu–Kibondo junction). Buy your tickets here, or at one of the booking offices signposted along the main road in the Mwanga area.

To Mwanza, there are two buses daily, departing from Kigoma at 5am (Tsh15,000, 15 hours), with most going via Lusahunga, Biharamulo and the Busisi ferry crossing. To Bukoba (Tsh15,000, 12 to 15 hours), there are two to three direct buses weekly departing at 5am, though it's often just as fast to take a Mwanza-bound bus as far as Biharamulo and get onward transport from there. Although significantly longer distance wise, it can sometimes be just as fast – especially if you're driving – to travel to Mwanza via Nyakanazi junction, Kahama and Shinyanga, as the stretch from Nyakanazi to Mwanza is paved the whole way, and there's no need to wait for the ferry near Mwanza.

The road via Uvinza to Mpanda is in various stages of repair, ranging from quite decent to very bad, though there's no direct public transport and very little traffic other than sporadic trucks.

TRAIN

For schedule and price information on the ageing and these days unreliable Central Line train from Dodoma, Tabora or Mwanza, see p361.

Getting Around

Dalla-dallas to Bero bus stand, Mwanga and Ujiji run throughout the day, departing from the transport stand just uphill from the train station. Taxis between the town centre and Bero bus stand charge Tsh2000.

UJIJI

Tiny Ujiji, one of Africa's oldest market villages, earned its place in travel lore as the spot where explorer-journalist Henry Morton Stanley uttered his famously casual 'Dr Livingstone, I presume?' The site where Stanley's encounter with Livingstone allegedly occurred is commemorated by a plaque set in a walled compound near a small garden. Nearby are two mango trees, which are said to have been grafted from the original tree that shaded the two men during their encounter. There's also a tiny and rather neglected **museum** (admission free, donation appreciated; 🕑 9am-5.30pm) housing a few pictures by local artists of Livingstone scenes, plus some letters and other Livingstone memorabilia. An information centre, including a restaurant and hostel rooms, is under construction next door. Once finished, the museum will be moved here. The site is about 300m off the main road coming from Kigoma and signposted – just ask for Livingstone and the *dalla-dalla* driver will make sure you get off at the right place.

Prior to Livingstone, Ujiji enjoyed prominence as the main settlement in the region (a status it lost only after the railway terminus was built at Kigoma), and as a major dhow-building centre. Burton and Speke also stopped here in 1858 before setting out to explore Lake Tanganyika. Thanks to its position as a terminus of the old caravan route to the coast, Ujiji still shows various Swahili traits, primarily in local building style.

Despite its distinguished past, little remains today of Ujiji's former significance, and many people find the village underwhelming. But it's easy enough to reach from Kigoma and its long history makes it well worth a stop if you're in the area. From the Livingstone compound, you can continue about 500m further along the same street to Ujiji's beach and small dhow port. No power tools are used in building the boats and construction methods are the same as they were generations ago. Once the rooms at the information centre are built, it would make an ideal base for anyone interested in getting off the main track and gaining insights into local village life.

Sleeping & Eating

There are a couple of very basic guesthouses and eateries along the main road, with bare-bones rooms and bucket baths for about Tsh3000.

Getting There & Away

Ujiji is about 8km south of central Kigoma; *dalla-dallas* run between the two towns throughout the day (Tsh200).

GOMBE STREAM NATIONAL PARK

With an area of only 52 sq km, Gombe Stream is Tanzania's smallest national park. It's also the site of the longest-running study of any wild animal population in the world and, for those interested in primates, it's a fascinating place.

The Gombe Stream area was gazetted as a game reserve in 1943. In 1960 British researcher Jane Goodall arrived to begin a study of wild chimpanzees, and in 1968 Gombe was designated as a national park. Goodall's study is now in its fifth decade.

CHIMPANZEES

The natural habitat of Tanzania's chimpanzees *(Pan troglodytes schweinfurthii)* once extended along much of the western border of the country, throughout the Kigoma and Rukwa regions and into Burundi, Rwanda, Uganda and Democratic Republic of Congo (Zaïre). Deforestation and human population pressures have reduced these areas, and today the chimps are found mainly in Gombe Stream National Park and in and around Mahale Mountains National Park.

In addition to deforestation, the main threat to Tanzania's remaining chimp populations is illegal trafficking. Chimpanzees, which are coveted as pets, sought for medical research and wanted for commercial zoos, command high prices on the black market. Yet, to capture a baby chimpanzee, all nearby adults must be killed. The result is many dead chimps and many orphans. For young chimps that are recaptured from illegal traffickers, there is also the problem of reintegration. With few exceptions, chimps cannot be reintroduced to the wild in an area where there are other chimps living. While there are numerous groups working hard to halt illegal trafficking, the networks are entrenched and it's an uphill battle that requires constant vigilance.

If you're considering visiting either Gombe Stream or Mahale Mountains National Parks, also remember that chimpanzees are susceptible to human diseases, so don't visit if you're ill. (And if park officials get wind of a sniffle or the flu, you won't be allowed to enter.)

Gombe Stream's approximately 100 chimps are well habituated and you can sometimes get to within 5m of them. In addition to observing the chimps, it's possible to swim in the lake or hike in Gombe's forest. Other animals you may see in the park include colobus and vervet monkeys, bushbucks, baboons, bush pigs and a variety of birdlife. If you're really interested in the chimpanzees, allow at least two days at Gombe.

Information

Entry fees per adult/child aged seven to 15 years per 24 hours are US$100/20. They technically apply from when you land on the beach at Kasekela, but in practice, park officials tend to interpret the guidelines generously and only charge you for the time you spend in the forest – which means that for a two-night stay (necessary, assuming you arrive/depart via lake taxi) and one day of chimp tracking, you'll most likely be charged only for one 24-hour entry. Guides cost US$20 per group per day. Children aged under seven are not permitted in the park.

Gombe Stream can be visited year-round. There's a park office in Kibirizi, at the far end of the beach, and about a 10-minute walk from the footbridge at the entrance to the village. It's unsignposted, but anyone should be able to point out the way. Accommodation bookings can be made here. Otherwise, book through Kigoma travel agents (see p263) or directly through the **senior park warden** (☎ 028-280 2586; gonapachimps@yahoo.com). Park headquar-

ters are on the beach at Mitumba Valley at the northern end of the park. All tourism activities are south of here at Kasekela, on the beach near the centre of the park, and this is where you'll need to disembark when you visit.

For photos, bring high-speed film or appropriate equipment for use in the forest; flashes aren't permitted.

Sleeping & Eating

The park hostel is currently being rebuilt, and once finished will also include a restaurant. Meanwhile, there are simple rooms with nets in the park resthouse (per person US$20) at Kasekela, on the beach near the centre of the park. You can also camp (per person US$20) on the beach, although park staff don't recommend it because of the danger from baboons, and it doesn't save you any money anyway. If you do camp, don't underestimate the baboons, and bring a metal container for storing food. There's a small shop at park headquarters selling drinks and a few basics, and it's possible to arrange inexpensive grilled fish or other local meals with staff. Otherwise, until the restaurant is completed or unless you're staying at the luxury tented camp (see below), bring whatever provisions you will need from Kigoma.

Gombe Luxury Tented Camp (☎ 028-280 4437; www .chimpanzeesafaris.com; s/d all-inclusive US$645/1090) On the beach at Mitumba in the northern part of the park, this is Gombe's only upmarket camp, with en suite tents and a shady, waterside location. It's run by Kigoma Hilltop Hotel in Kigoma, which offers transport and accommodation deals.

Getting There & Away

Gombe Stream is about 20km north of Kigoma on the shores of Lake Tanganyika. The only way to reach the park is by boat – either charter or lake taxi. At least one lake taxi to the park departs from Kibirizi (see p264) Monday to Saturday between about noon and 2pm (Tsh2000, three hours). Returning, it passes by Gombe (Kasekela) at about 7am (which means you'll need to spend two nights at the park if travelling by public transport).

Alternatively, you can arrange with local fishermen to charter a boat – and you'll be besieged with offers to do so when you arrive at Kibirizi. Expect to pay from about Tsh80,000 to Tsh100,000 return. You may have to pay an advance for petrol (which should not be more than one-third of the total price), but don't pay the full amount until you have arrived back in Kigoma. It's common practice for local boat owners to try to convince you that there are no lake taxis, in an effort to get business.

Faster boats (taking about 1½ hours) can be organised through **Aqua Lodge** (☎ 028-280 2408) in Kigoma for US$175 return per boat for up to eight passengers, plus a US$82 per night stopover fee, and **Kigoma Hilltop Hotel** (☎ 028-280 4437; kht@raha.com; www.chimpanzeesafaris .com) for US$655 return per boat for up to 20 passengers, plus a US$50 per night stopover fee from the second night onwards.

MAHALE MOUNTAINS NATIONAL PARK

It's difficult to imagine a more idyllic combination: clear, blue waters, white-sand beaches backed by lushly forested mountains, some of the most challenging and intriguing wildlife watching on the continent and a setting of such unrivalled remoteness that you're likely to have it all almost to yourself. Mahale – Tanzania's most isolated national park – stretches along the Lake Tanganyika shoreline about 130km south of Kigoma, with the misty and rugged Mahale range running down its centre. Like Gombe Stream National Park to the north, Mahale is primarily a chimpanzee sanctuary, home to about 700 of our primate relatives, with roan antelopes, buffaloes, zebras and even some

lions keeping them company (although the lions are seldom seen).

Mahale has been the site of an ongoing Japanese-sponsored primate research project since 1965, when the Kyoto University Africa Primatological Expedition initiated research here, and the chimpanzee communities that have been focal points of study are well habituated to people. While Mahale's size and terrain mean that it can take time (and some strenuous, steep and sweaty walking) to find the chimps, almost everyone who spends at least a few days here comes away well rewarded.

Mahale Mountains was gazetted as a national park in 1980 with an area of around 1600 sq km. The park's highest peak is Mt Nkungwe (2462m), first climbed in 1939.

Information

Entry fees are US$80/30 per adult/child aged 10 to 16 years. For camping fees, see p77. Children under seven years aren't permitted in Mahale. Camping and park *bandas* can be booked through **Kigoma Hilltop Hotel** (☎ 028-280 4437; kht@raha.com; www.chimpanzeesafaris .com) in Kigoma, which can also help you contact park headquarters if you'll be arriving independently. Guide fees are US$20 per group.

Park headquarters, where fees are paid, are at Bilenge in the park's northwestern corner. About 10km south of here are Kasiha (site of the park camp site and *bandas*) and Kangwena beach (with two top-end camps). The park's eastern section is currently closed to tourists, although trail development is planned.

The park is open year-round, although during the rains it gets too muddy to do much walking, and the private camps close. There are no roads in Mahale; walking (and boating along the shoreline) are the only ways to get around. Bring high-speed film or appropriate equipment for use in the forest; flashes aren't permitted.

Following an outbreak of human influenza virus among Mahale's chimpanzees in 2006, park officials currently require all visitors to wear surgical-style masks while trekking, and not to get closer than 10m to the chimps. Each group's viewing time is also limited – currently to one hour per day – and the maximum group size is six. No eating or drinking is permitted within sight of the chimps.

LAKE TANGANYIKA

Lake Tanganyika is the world's longest (670km) and second-deepest (over 1400m) fresh-water lake. At somewhere between nine and 12 million years old, it is also one of the oldest lakes on the planet and, thanks to its age and ecological isolation, is home to an exceptional variety of fish. Most notable are its colourful cichlids, many of which are found nowhere else, and which make for some wonderful snorkelling in the lake's clear waters.

During the late 18th and early 19th centuries the lake was a major conduit for slaves and trade along the old caravan routes, while today its shores bustle with cross-border traders and refugees. The best way to get a feel for local life is to set off on the MV *Liemba*, which calls in at a string of small ports as it makes its way down the shoreline. There are few docking jetties, so at each place where the *Liemba* pulls in, it's met by dozens of small boats racing out to the ferry, with boat owners and food vendors all jostling for custom from the passengers. At night the whole scene is lit up by the glow of dozens of tiny kerosene lamps, waving precariously in the wind and waves.

Besides Kigoma (the largest town on the Tanzanian lake shore), Ujiji (one of the oldest lake-shore settlements) and Lagosa (for Mahale Mountains National Park), ports of call include the village of Ikola, the old mission station of Kalema (Karema), about 15km further south, and – further south – the village and mission station of Kipili. In Ikola, there is the simple **Zanzibar Guest House** (r about Tsh3000), with buckets of hot water on request and filling, inexpensive meals. The owners can help you organise a local boat to explore the surrounding lake shore and nearby rivers. At Kalema is an old Catholic mission station, parts of which were originally a Belgian fort before being handed over to the White Fathers in 1889. Kipili is the site of an old Benedictine mission, set on a hill on the edge of town, and of the small St Bernard's Monastery & Guest House, with simple, clean rooms and meals. From both Kalema and (better) Ikola, you can get transport to Mpanda, while from Kipili there is transport – usually 4WDs or trucks – to Sumbawanga (four to six hours), or (in stages) to Katavi and Mpanda.

About 3.5km offshore from Kipili on tiny Lupita Island is the very exclusive **Lupita Island Resort & Spa** (www.firelightexpeditions.com; s/d all-inclusive US$1100/1725), with just a dozen suites, each with its own plunge pool, and a lake cruiser for day and overnight charters.

Also immediately offshore from Kipili is **Ntanga Island Retreat** (www.awesomeafricansafaris.com; candlhorsfall@gmail.com), a lovely and genuinely eco-friendly place which will be opening right about when this book is published. In addition to reasonably priced accommodation, it will offer overnight kayak and dive safaris along the lake, and overland camping trips to Katavi National Park.

Sleeping

Mango Tree Bandas (per person US$20) Basic, but quite decent, park-run double *bandas* at Kasiha – and the most convenient budget option. There are en suite bucket baths, but no meals or canteen, so bring what you need from Kigoma.

Park Resthouse (per person US$20) Near park headquarters at Bilenge, it's possible to stay at this resthouse. It's less convenient for chimp tracking (which starts at Kasiha, 10km to the south), but has the advantage of local-style meals and drinks being available.

Nkungwe Luxury Tented Camp (☎ 028-280 4437; www.chimpanzeesafaris.com; s/d all-inclusive US$635/1070) This place, run by Kigoma Hilltop Hotel, has six comfortable double tents, and makes a good-value alternative to Greystoke Mahale for those on more moderate budgets. It's on the beach north of Kangwena and about 1km north of Greystoke Mahale.

Greystoke Mahale (www.nomad-tanzania.com; per person all-inclusive from US$750; ☿ mid-May–mid-March) An exclusive camp in a stunning setting on Kangwena beach, with six over-the-top tented *bandas* with solar power and bush showers. Children under 12 years are not permitted on chimpanzee-tracking walks. Book through upmarket travel agencies or safari operators.

Getting There & Away

AIR

Flying in to Mahale treats you to some impressive aerial views of the Lake Tanganyika shoreline. The airstrip is just north of the park boundary at Sitolo. Charter flights from Arusha can be arranged through **Chimpanzee Safaris** (☎ 028-280 4437; www.mbalimbali.com) in

Kigoma, **Nomad Safaris** (www.nomad-tanzania.com) and **Flycatcher Safaris** (www.flycat.com), all of whom operate camps in the park and have twice-weekly flights to/from Arusha primarily for their guests, although some are willing to take other passengers on a space-available basis. Foxtreks (p47) also has twice-weekly charters to Mahale from Ruaha and Katavi. Expect to pay from US$1000 per person per seat for Arusha–Mahale–Arusha, and about US$600 one way from Ruaha to Mahale via Katavi. All of these operators fly on twice-weekly rotations (either Monday and Thursday, or Tuesday and Friday), so fly-in guests will generally need to plan on a minimum stay of three nights. All flights also stop at Katavi en route, and the parks are thus frequently visited as a combination package.

BOAT

Despite the lake's temperamental choppiness and the length of the journey, it's hard to beat the satisfyingly adventurous edge – and the impressive lake-shore scenery – of journeying to Mahale via ferry. The MV *Liemba* stops at Lagosa (also called Mugambo), to the north of the park (1st/2nd/economy class US$25/20/15, about 10 hours from Kigoma). From Lagosa, it's possible to continue with small local boats to park headquarters, about two hours further south, but not the best idea as the *Liemba* reaches Lagosa about 2am or 3am on Thursday morning. (If you do decide to try this, there's a basic guesthouse in Lagosa where you can wait until dawn.) It's better to radio park headquarters in advance from Kigoma and arrange a pick-up. **Kigoma Hilltop Hotel** (☎ 028-280 4437; kht@raha.com; www.chimpanzee safaris.com) nd the *Liemba* office in Kigoma can help with the radio call. The park boat costs US$50 per boat (for up to about 15 people, one way), although if the park is sending a boat up anyway, you may be able to negotiate something better. Coming from Mpulungu (Zambia) the *Liemba* passes Lagosa sometime between late Saturday night and early Sunday morning around 3am or 4am.

The other option is to charter a boat through either Kigoma Hilltop Hotel for US$2985 return per boat (about 10 hours) for up to 20 persons, plus US$50 per night stopover charge from the second night onwards, or **Aqua Lodge** (☎ 028-280 2408) in Kigomafor US$900 per boat for up to eight people, including two nights waiting at Mahale, plus US$82 for each ad-

ditional night. Kigoma Hilltop Hotel also has a faster, pricier speedboat, which cuts travel time by more than half.

Guests of Lupita Island Resort & Spa (opposite) can travel on the resort's exclusive boat from Lupita Island to Mahale.

UVINZA

Salt production has kept Uvinza on the map for at least several centuries, and the town is still one of Tanzania's major salt-producing areas. If you find yourself here, a highlight is visiting the local salt factory, which has been running since the 1920s. As so few travellers pass this way, staff will be happy to see you; permits can be arranged at the entry gate. For lodging, there are several no-frills guesthouses in the town centre.

Uvinza is about two hours southeast of Kigoma via the Central Line train. There's no regular public transport to/from the town, but the road towards Kigoma is gradually being upgraded, and is regularly traversed by trucks and at least one vehicle daily (Tsh6000, about three hours). From Uvinza, it's also possible to get a vehicle to Kasulu, from where there are daily minibuses to Kigoma (Tsh1500). Trucks also run sporadically between Uvinza and Mpanda, especially during the dry season (about Tsh7000, one day). However, there is little traffic on this road and few supplies available en route, so stock up before setting off.

MPANDA

☎ 025

This small and somewhat scruffy town is of interest mainly as a starting point for visits to Katavi National Park. It's also the terminus of a branch of the Central Line railway and a useful junction town if you're heading inland from Lake Tanganyika.

Sleeping & Eating

Marangu Guest House & Bar (r Tsh3500) For something inexpensive in the town centre, try this noisy but cheap option, with small rooms and shared bucket baths. It's near the market and behind the Sumry bus line office.

Super City Hotel (☎ 028-282 0459; s/d from Tsh4000/6000) No-frills rooms with mosquito nets and a restaurant about 1.5km from the town centre, near the roundabout (ask for 'Super City Ghorofani'). It's convenient to the train station, and buses to Katavi and

Sumbawanga have their stand out the front. From the train station, follow the tracks to the end, then take the first left and look for the multistorey building.

Highway Guesthouse (☎ 025-282 0001; r Tsh7000) Diagonally opposite Super City on the other side of the roundabout, with reasonable-value en suite rooms with showers.

Getting There & Away

BUS

Dalla-dallas run several times daily between Mpanda and Sitalike (for Katavi National Park; Tsh1500, 45 minutes) from in front of Marangu Guest House & Bar in the town centre. A better option is to head to the main transport stand in front of Super City Hotel and catch one of the daily buses (watch for Sumry bus line) and 4WDs to Sitalike and on to Sumbawanga (about Tsh12,000, seven hours). The best time to find transport is around midday on Tuesday, Thursday and Saturday, just after the train has arrived, when there's always at least one bus heading southwards.

The train is the best option to Kigoma, although trucks ply the route towards Uvinza and Kigoma fairly regularly, especially during the dry season; allow at least 12 hours.

From Mpanda southwest to Kalema and Ikola (the main Lake Tanganyika ports in this area), there are sporadic trucks, which are usually timed to coincide with arrivals of the MV *Liemba* ferry.

TRAIN

There is a branch of the Central Line that connects Mpanda with Tabora via Kaliua. For schedule and fare information, see p361. If you're heading to Kigoma or Mwanza from Mpanda, you will need to spend at least a day in Tabora or Kaliua. You can wait for the connection at Kaliua, but as there are few guesthouses and little to do, most travellers continue on to Tabora and wait there.

KATAVI NATIONAL PARK

Katavi, about 35km southwest of Mpanda, is Tanzania's third-largest national park and one of its most unspoiled wilderness areas. For travellers seeking an alternative to more popular destinations elsewhere in the country, it is a high-adventure, rugged safari experience. Katavi's predominant feature is its enormous flood plain, the vast, grassy ex-

panses of which cover much of the northern section of the park. The plains are broken by the Katuma River and several seasonal lakes, which support huge populations of hippos, plus crocodiles and a wealth of birds (over 400 bird species have been identified in Katavi thus far). In the west and centre of the park, the floodplains yield to vast tracts of brush and woodland, which are the best areas for sighting roan and sable antelopes; together with Ruaha National Park, Katavi is one of the few places where you have a decent chance of spotting both.

The park comes to life in the dry season, when the river and lakes dry up and huge herds of buffaloes, elephants, lions, zebras, giraffes and many more make their way to the remaining pools and streams. At these times it's hard not to feel that you've reached the heart of Africa, vast, uncontainable and pulsing to the primeval rhythms of the wild.

Katavi was originally gazetted in 1974 with an area of 2253 sq km. In 1997 it was extended to about 4500 sq km and, together with the contiguous Rukwa Game Reserve, encompasses a conservation area covering 12,500 sq km. Because of its remote location and, at least until recently, its completely under-publicised attractions, the park receives relatively few visitors.

Information

Entry fees are US$20/5 per adult/child aged five to 15 years. For information on camping fees, see p77.

Katavi is open year-round, but should only be visited during the dry season, between June and November or December, with the peak months for wildlife watching from late July to October. **Park headquarters** (☎ 025-282 0213; katavinp@yahoo.com), for hut bookings, entry-fee payments and other information, is just off the main road, about 1.5km south of Sitalike, on the park's northern edge. The Celtel network includes Sitalike and Vodacom works from a point about 2km from town.

Wildlife viewing is permitted in open vehicles, and park vehicles can be hired if they aren't being used by staff. Rates are US$1 per kilometre with a minimum charge of US$100, plus guide fees. It's also possible to drive in the park with your own vehicle. While it's not required to bring a guide along in the original (western) section of the park, it's highly recommended. In the newer (eastern) section there are only rough bush tracks and you'll need an armed ranger.

Walking safaris are permitted with an armed ranger. For any safaris in Katavi, bring along thick, long-sleeved shirts and trousers, preferably in khaki or other drab shades (avoid anything bright, very contrasting or very dark), as protection against tsetse fly bites.

Sleeping

There are several public camp sites in the park, including the well-situated Chada Campsite near Lake Chada; Ikuu Campsite at Ikuu ranger post northwest of Lake Chada; and Lake Katavi Campsite near Lake Katavi, just west of the Sumbawanga–Mpanda road. About 2km from park headquarters there is also a public camp site, as well as double-bedded *bandas* (per person US$30). For camp sites and *bandas*, bring all food and drink with you.

Katavi Hippo Garden Hotel (☎ 025-282 0393, 023-262 0461, 0784-120498; camping per person US$5, r per person US$30) In Sitalike village just outside the park gate, this is a good budget choice, and under the same management as Genesis Motel in Mikumi (p280). It has self-contained *bandas* – some with double bed and others with twins – along the river about 1km from park headquarters and an easy walk from the Sitalike bus stand, which is good value, especially considering its location. The river forms the park border here and there's a resident pod of hippos just out the front. You can arrange a rental vehicle here to go into Katavi (US$150 per day). A drop at Mpanda train station costs US$80.

Katavi Wildlife Camp (☎ 0784-237422; www.tanzania safaris.info; s/d full board plus wildlife drives US$450/700) This comfortable, rustic camp in a prime setting near Ikuu ranger post offers great value, with spacious en suite tents overlooking the flood-plains, top-notch guides and excellent cuisine. Owned by Foxes African Safaris (p47), which also runs camps in Ruaha and Mikumi, it offers some excellent combination itineraries.

Palahala Luxury Camp (www.firelightexpeditions.com; per person all-inclusive US$595; ☾ Jun-Feb) The newest of Katavi's upmarket camps, with six spacious tented suites and a riverside setting, and the same management as Lupita Island Resort & Spa (p268).

Chada Katavi Camp (www.nomad-tanzania.com; s/d all-inclusive US$730/960; ☾ Jun-Oct & mid-Dec–mid-Mar) Set in a prime location overlooking the Chada floodplains, this place mixes a classic safari ambience with the bare minimum of amenities. The camp has just seven double tents, each with bush shower and solar-powered lighting, can only be booked through upmarket travel agencies.

Other recommendations:

Katume Katavi Camp (☎ 022-213 0501; www .chimpanzeesafaris.com; s/d all-inclusive US$585/970; ☾ mid-May–mid-Feb) Under the same ownership as Kigoma Hilltop Hotel (p264), with six fairly spacious and well-appointed tents on low stilts.

Flycatcher Safaris (www.flycat.com) This long-established Swiss-run outfit offers Katavi itineraries based out of its own temporary camp, and can arrange combination itineraries taking in Katavi, Mahale Mountains and Rubondo Island National Parks, as well as other destinations in Tanzania. Prices are midrange to top end.

Riverside Guesthouse (per person US$20) Just a short walk away from Katavi Hippo Garden Hotel and a good budget alternative in this area.

Bateleur Tented Camp (www.awsomeafricansafaris. com; candlhorsfall@gmail.com; ☾ May-Feb) This six-tent place is scheduled to open near Lake Katavi by the time this book is published. Balloon safaris and combination Katavi-Lake Tanganyika itineraries are planned.

Getting There & Away

AIR

There are airstrips for charter flights in Mpanda, Sitalike and at Ikuu ranger post near Lake Chada.

BUS

Any bus running between Mpanda and Sumbawanga can drop you at the park gate, where you can hire a vehicle to visit the park. Alternatively, it's an easy (about 1km) walk between the gate and the Sitalike bus stand, from where there is daily transport to/from Mpanda. Alternatively, it's sometimes possible to find a lift with one of the park vehicles that come frequently to Mpanda for supplies. If you're driving, the closest petrol stations are in Mpanda and Sumbawanga.

SUMBAWANGA

☎ 025

The peppy and surprisingly pleasant capital of the Rukwa region is set on the fertile Ufipa plateau at about 1800m altitude in the far southwestern corner of the country. While there's little reason to make the town a destination in itself, Sumbawanga is a useful stopping point if you're travelling between Zambia or Mbeya and Katavi National Park.

The market is a good place for stocking up (there's nothing to rival it until you get to Mpanda or Mbeya), and the climate can be refreshingly cool, especially in the evenings. The surrounding Ufipa plateau, which lies at around 2000m, cradled between the eastern and western branches of the Great Rift Valley, is home to an ecologically important mixture of forests and montane grasslands.

East of Sumbawanga, below the escarpment, is the vast, shallow Lake Rukwa, and to the east, the seldom-visited Mbizi mountains, both of which make potential excursions if you find yourself in Sumbawanga with extra time on your hands. The most straightforward access to Lake Rukwa is via the small village of Zimba, down the eastern slopes of the Mbizi escarpment and served by relatively regular public transport from Sumbawanga. Zimba is also a possible starting point for hiking in the Mbizi range, though you'll need to make your way back up the escarpment. Accommodation can usually be arranged with the Catholic mission in Zimba. Guides for excursions towards the Mbizi Forest Reserve can be arranged at Mbizi Forest Hotel.

Sleeping & Eating

Zanzibar Guest House (☎ 025-280 0010; d Tsh7000, r without bathroom Tsh4000) The en suite rooms are worth the splurge. It's just a few minute's walk from the bus stand, off Kiwelu Rd and south of Upendo View Hotel. There's no food.

Moravian Conference Centre (☎ 025-280 2853/4; Nyerere Rd; standard s/d Tsh7000/14,000, executive s/d Tsh12,000/20,000) A good place with spare but clean rooms and inexpensive meals. Breakfast costs extra. It's fairly centrally located in a quiet compound along the road to the Regional Block area.

Upendo View Hotel (☎ 025-280 2242; Kiwelu Rd; r Tsh10,000) Reasonably large and clean rooms, inexpensive meals and a central location just southeast of the bus stand. On Friday and Saturday nights it has a loud disco.

Mbizi Forest Hotel (☎ 025-280 2746; s/d Tsh15,000/20,000) Simple but good-value en suite rooms, and meals available. It's about 3km from town off Nyerere Rd and signposted.

Forestway Country Club (☎ 028-280 2800/2412; Nyerere Rd; r Tsh20,000) Large, clean rooms and a good restaurant. It's about 2km from town

along Nyerere Rd in the Regional Block area, past the Moravian Conference Centre (Tsh2000 in a taxi from the bus stand).

Getting There & Away

Sumry has two buses daily between Mbeya and Sumbawanga via Tunduma (for Zambia), departing in each direction between 5.30am and 7am (Tsh10,000 to Tsh13,000, seven hours, book in advance). To Mpanda, Sumry buses depart from Sumbawanga daily at 10am, and during the dry season again at 1pm (Tsh12,000, six to seven hours). There are also daily 4WDs departing from the petrol station on the main road from about 7am (Tsh13,000). The road passes through Katavi National Park, although it is not necessary to pay the park fees if you are just in transit. To Zimba (for Lake Rukwa), there's at least one pick-up daily leaving from near the market; coming back, the last vehicle usually leaves by about 4.30pm.

KASANGA & KALAMBO FALLS

Plunging about 212m down the Rift Valley escarpment into Zambia are the Kalambo Falls. In addition to being Africa's second-highest single-drop waterfall, the area is also important archaeologically, as the site of some major Stone Age finds.

The main access route to the falls is from Zambia, via Mbala. It's also possible to reach the falls from Kasanga, which is about 120km southwest of Sumbawanga on Lake Tanganyika and the last (or first) stop in Tanzania on the MV *Liemba* (see p358). From Kasanga, you'll need to get a lift towards the falls and then walk for about four hours in each direction.

There is a basic guesthouse in the Muzei section of Kasanga, where you can also arrange a guide.

Trucks journey sporadically between Sumbawanga and Kasanga, and a bus meets the MV *Liemba* arrivals (Tsh4000, up to nine hours). These arrivals can be anywhere between midnight and 6am, although the boat often remains at the dock until dawn. You're allowed to stay on board during this time, but the boat pulls out without much warning, so best to ask staff to wake you in time to disembark.

Southern Highlands

Green hills rolling to the horizon, lively markets overflowing with produce, jacaranda-lined streets and wildlife are among the attractions that await you in Tanzania's scenic and often overlooked Southern Highlands.

Officially, the Highlands begin at the Makambako Gap, about halfway between Iringa and Mbeya, and extend southwards into Malawi. In this guide, the term is used to designate the entire region along the mountainous chain running between Morogoro in the east and Lake Nyasa and the Zambian border in the west. In addition to being beautiful, the Highlands are also one of Tanzania's most important agricultural areas, producing a large proportion of the country's maize, as well as coffee, tea and other crops.

On the region's eastern edge, near Morogoro, are the Uluguru Mountains – home to the matrilineal Luguru people and many unique plant and bird species. Just southwest of here is the easily accessed Mikumi National Park, as well as Udzungwa Mountains National Park, an offbeat destination for hikers. Further west, past Iringa, is the sublime and unspoiled Ruaha National Park, with striking riverine scenery and one of Africa's largest elephant populations. The heart of the Southern Highlands is in the far southwest, with secluded valleys, rolling hills and verdant mountains that cascade down to the tranquil and seldom-trodden shores of Lake Nyasa, where there is almost no tourist infrastructure.

While many travellers pass through the Southern Highlands en route to or from Malawi or Zambia, few stop along the way, even though there is much of interest. Main roads are in generally good condition and there is a reasonable selection of accommodation.

SOUTHERN HIGHLANDS

HIGHLIGHTS

- Sitting by the river in **Ruaha National Park** (p286), taking in the magnificence of the wild

- Watching lions, wildebeest and buffaloes in **Mikumi National Park** (p278)

- Getting away from it all on the shores of **Lake Nyasa** (p298)

- Exploring off the beaten track around **Iringa** (p282), **Njombe** (p289) or **Songea** (p301)

- Enjoying the green, rolling panoramas around **Tukuyu** (p297) and **Mbeya** (p295)

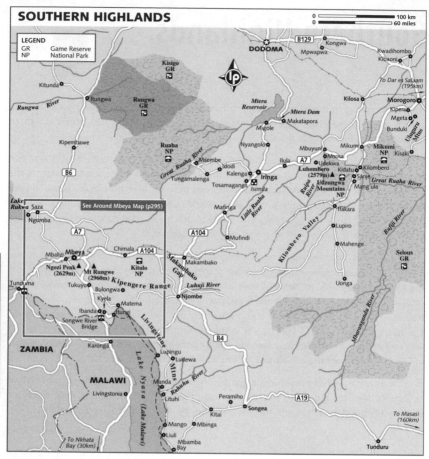

SOUTHERN HIGHLANDS

LEGEND
GR   Game Reserve
NP   National Park

National Parks & Reserves

The region's parks include Mikumi (p278) and Ruaha (p286) for wildlife-watching, Udzungwa Mountains (p280) for hiking and Kitulo (p290) for taking in the beautiful panoramas and wildflowers.

Getting There & Around

Scheduled and charter flights, operated primarily by Coastal Aviation and Safari Airlink (p356), serve Mikumi, Ruaha, Iringa, Mufindi and Mbeya during the dry season. An international airport is being built at Mbeya.

Road travel is straightforward, thanks to the good tarmac highway (the southwestern part of which is a section of the Great North Road on the Cape to Cairo route) from Dar es

Salaam southwest into Zambia, with tarmac branch routes leading to Songea and to Kyela. Otherwise, everything is unsealed.

Several ferries run on Lake Nyasa, with sporadic connections between towns on the Tanzanian side and between Tanzania and Malawi; see p357.

MOROGORO

☎ 023 / pop 250,000

Bustling, sprawling Morogoro would be a fairly scruffy town were it not for its verdant setting at the foot of the Uluguru Mountains, which brood over the landscape from southeast. The surrounding area is one of the country's breadbaskets, home to the prestigious Sokoine University (Tanzania's national agricultural institute) and a major educational and mission station. While there are few tourist attractions in Morogoro itself, it's an unpretentious place, a good introduction to Tanzanian life outside Dar es Salaam and the best base for hiking in the Ulugurus.

Information

IMMIGRATION OFFICE
The immigration office is signposted about 200m south of the main road, though visa extensions generally must be handled in Dar es Salaam.

INTERNET ACCESS
Daus Internet Café (off Lumumba St; per hr Tsh1000; ☼ 8am-10pm Sun-Fri, 7-10pm Sat) Around the corner from Pira's Supermarket, with a good connection.
Matanda Internet Café (Mahenge St; per hr Tsh500; ☼ 8am-8pm) Next to Princess Lodge.

MEDICAL SERVICES
Bede Pharmacy (Mahenge St)
Morogoro Medical Stores Pharmacy (Old Dar es Salaam Rd)

MONEY
Exim Bank (Lumumba St) Opposite Pira's Supermarket; ATM (MasterCard, Visa, Cirrus and Maestro).
NBC (Old Dar es Salaam Rd) Changes cash; ATM (Visa only).

POST & TELEPHONE
Main post office (Old Dar es Salaam Rd; ☼ 8am-5pm) With card phones nearby.

TOURIST INFORMATION
Chilunga Cultural Tourism (☎ 0754-477582, 0713-663993; YWCA Compound, Rwegasore Rd) Organises hikes in the Uluguru Mountains, village visits and other excursions – stop by the office for a sampling of the possibilities. Prices average about Tsh20,000 per day for a guide, plus village and administration fees (these vary, depending on the hike, but average Tsh3000 to Tsh7000 per person per hike).

Sights & Activities
The **market** has good deals on textiles. With your own clubs, you could try the **golf course** opposite Morogoro Hotel.

Morogoro is a logical base for excursions to Mikumi National Park (p278) and Selous Game Reserve (p311), although you'll need to have your own vehicle or rent one in Dar es Salaam, as they're difficult to find in Morogoro.

Sleeping
BUDGET
Princess Lodge (☎ 0754-319159; Mahenge St; r without bathroom Tsh7000) This lodge has clean, small no-frills rooms, all with double bed, fan and net, plus helpful management and a good, cheap restaurant downstairs. It's one block in from the main road in the town centre.

Mama Pierina's (☎ 0713-786913; Station St; d Tsh9000) The ageing Mama Pierina's is in an agreeable location off the main road, but rooms – all with nets and fan, and set around a tiny garden – are long past their prime, with decaying facilities and paper-thin walls. The attached restaurant serves up large portions of unexciting food.

Sofia Hotel (☎ 023-260 4848; Mahenge St; s/d Tsh15,000/24,000, d without bathroom Tsh9000) A long-standing place with small, dark rooms and a restaurant. It's diagonally opposite Princess Lodge.

Mt Uluguru Hotel (☎ 023-260 3489; s/d Tsh15,000/20,000, d with air-con Tsh30,000; 🖭) A nondescript multistorey hotel worth a look for its central location. Rooms are reasonable (ask for one with a view) and there's an inexpensive restaurant and a large outdoor bar. It's south of the main road, off Mahenge St.

MIDRANGE & TOP END
Kola Hill Hotel (☎ 023-260 3707; r with fan/air-con from Tsh16,500/22,800; 🖭) Rooms here – all doubles or twins, some with TV – are faded and nothing special, but the setting is tranquil, in a green and quiet area about 3km east of the centre. It's a reasonable choice if you have your own transport. Meals are available. It's about 300m off Old Dar es Salaam Rd along the Bigwa *dalla-dalla* (minibus) route (Tsh200 from town), and signposted opposite the Teachers' College Morogoro. Taxis charge Tsh2000 to Tsh3000.

Morogoro Hotel (☎ 023 261 3270/1/2; morogorohtl@morogoro.net; Rwegasore Rd; s/d/tr from US$30/45/65) Once a Morogoro institution, this is another place that has seen better days, although it's been spruced up recently. Accommodation is in detached bungalows set in green grounds about 1.5km off the main road and opposite the golf course. It's popular for weddings and other functions on weekends, which can mean loud music until late.

Hotel Oasis (☎ 023-261 4178, 0754-377602; hotel oasistz@morogoro.net; Station St; s/d/tr incl breakfast US$35/40/50; 🖭 🖭) Faded but good-value

SOUTHERN HIGHLANDS

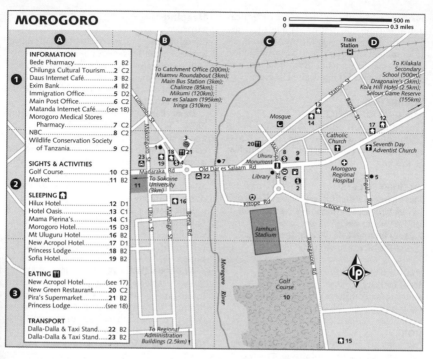

MOROGORO

0 — 500 m
0 — 0.3 miles

INFORMATION	
Bede Pharmacy.....................1	B2
Chilunga Cultural Tourism.....2	C2
Daus Internet Café...............3	B2
Exim Bank...........................4	B2
Immigration Office...............5	D2
Main Post Office...................6	C2
Matanda Internet Café......(see 18)	
Morogoro Medical Stores	
Pharmacy........................7	C2
NBC...................................8	C2
Wildlife Conservation Society	
of Tanzania.....................9	C2

SIGHTS & ACTIVITIES	
Golf Course........................10	C3
Market..............................11	B2

SLEEPING	
Hilux Hotel........................12	D1
Hotel Oasis........................13	C1
Mama Pierina's...................14	C1
Morogoro Hotel..................15	D3
Mt Uluguru Hotel................16	B2
New Acropol Hotel..............17	D1
Princess Lodge....................18	B2
Sofia Hotel.........................19	B2

EATING	
New Acropol Hotel..........(see 17)	
New Green Restaurant........20	C2
Pira's Supermarket..............21	B2
Princess Lodge................(see 18)	

TRANSPORT	
Dalla-Dalla & Taxi Stand.....22	B2
Dalla-Dalla & Taxi Stand.....23	B2

To Catchment Office (200m);
Msamvu Roundabout (3km);
Main Bus Station (3km);
Chalinze (85km);
Mikumi (120km);
Dar es Salaam (195km);
Iringa (310km)

To Kilakala Secondary
School (500m);
Dragonaire's (2km);
Kola Hill Hotel (2.5km);
Selous Game Reserve
(155km)

To Sokoine University (3km)

To Regional Administration Buildings (2.5km)

rooms – all with fan, air-con, TV and small fridge – plus grassy grounds and a popular restaurant serving good Indian cuisine, plus Chinese and continental dishes.

New Acropol Hotel (☎ 023-261 3403, 0754-309410; www.newacropolhotel.biz; Old Dar es Salaam Rd; s/d from Tsh45,000/55,000, ste Tsh80,000; ⬛ 🖥) This B&B-style hotel has spacious, well-decorated rooms (all with TV, fridge and large double bed), a classy restaurant, a cosy bar and a porch overlooking the small gardens – ideal for sipping an afternoon drink.

Dragonaire's (☎ 0787-117368; r incl breakfast Tsh50,000; ⬛) This restaurant has four new, modern rooms overlooking an expansive lawn. Located upstairs is a family suite with two attached doubles and a kitchenette, while downstairs are two doubles. All come with TV. It's signposted about 2.5km east of town, about 700m off the Old Dar es Salaam Rd.

Also recommended:

Hilux Hotel (☎ 023-261 3946; Old Dar es Salaam Rd; r Tsh45,000) Small, albeit clean and well-equipped, rooms and a restaurant; next door to New Acropol Hotel.

Eating & Drinking

Princess Lodge (☎ 0754-319159; Mahenge St; meals from Tsh1500; ☽ breakfast, lunch & dinner) A good bet for inexpensive local dishes, with meals promised in '30 minutes or less'.

Dragonaire's (☎ 0787-117368; pizza Tsh3000-6000, meals from Tsh5000; ☽ 3-11pm Mon-Fri, 11am-midnight Sat & Sun) Expansive, green grounds, a small children's playground and tasty pizzas on weekends. The rest of the menu is mainly Chinese dishes, plus steak, lasagne and other continental fare – all good, though waits for food can be very long. Friday and Saturday are karaoke nights. It's signposted about 2.5km east of town, about 700m off the Old Dar es Salaam Rd.

New Green Restaurant (☎ 023-261 4021; Station St; meals Tsh5000-8000; ☽ lunch & dinner, closed dinner Sun) A long-standing place with Indian dishes, including vegetarian meals, plus grilled chicken or fish and chips. The quality of cuisine and service tends to vary, but if you're lucky enough to stop by on an up day, it's a good choice.

New Acropol Hotel (☎ 023-261 3403, 0754-309410; www.newacropolhotel.biz; Old Dar es Salaam Rd; meals from Tsh10,000; ☽ Tue-Sun) Morogoro's classiest restaurant, the New Acropol has *nouvelle cuisine*-style meals, a well-stocked bar and excellent local coffee (you can also buy some to take home).

For self-catering try **Pira's Supermarket** (Lumumba Rd).

Getting There & Away

BUS
The main bus station is about 3km north of town on the main Dar es Salaam road, about 300m east of Msamvu roundabout (Tsh2000 in a taxi and Tsh200 in a *dalla-dalla*). It's chaotic, with no real order to things – you'll need to ask where to find buses to your destination. The Scandinavian Express office is on the other side of the roundabout in its own compound, and much quieter.

Scandinavian Express buses go daily to Dodoma, Mikumi, Iringa, Mbeya and Dar es Salaam, but none originate in Morogoro, so you'll need to book in advance at the Scandinavian office. Smaller buses to Dar es Salaam leave throughout the day, from 5.45am

---

HIKING IN THE ULUGURU MOUNTAINS

The Uluguru Mountains rise up from the plains just southeast of Morogoro, dominating vistas from town. Part of the Eastern Arc chain, the mountains contain some of Africa's oldest original forest plus a wealth of birds, plants and insects. These include many unique species, such as the Uluguru bush shrike. The only comparable mountain-forest area in East Africa, as far as age and endemism are concerned, is the Usambara Mountains (p168).

The main tribal group in the Ulugurus are the matrilineal Luguru, who earn their living primarily through subsistence agriculture. Due to the high population density in the Ulugurus, most of the original forest cover has been depleted – you'll see this immediately on the hillsides – with only a few small protected patches remaining on the upper slopes. This deforestation has led to severe erosion.

The best contact for organising hiking guides is Chilunga Cultural Tourism (p275) in Morogoro. Come prepared with a jacket, as it can rain at any time of year. The shortest route from Morogoro is to **Morningside**, an old German mountain hut to the south of town at about 1000m. The path, which can easily be done in half a day return, starts at the regional administration buildings about 3km south of Morogoro at the end of Boma Rd. From here, a track leads uphill and then curves to the right through small farm plots and degraded forest before reaching the Morningside hut. It's possible to camp at Morningside with your own tent and supplies; there's a small waterfall nearby. Once at Morningside, it takes another 40 minutes or so to reach the border of the Uluguru North Forest Reserve. It's generally not permitted to continue beyond here because of sensitivities about the Bondwe Peak communications tower higher up the slopes. There has been a spate of muggings on this route recently, including attacks on hikers who were accompanied by guides. Don't bring any valuables, be wary of strangers who arrive wanting to join your group and think twice before you consider camping.

Another possibility from town is the hike to **Lupanga Peak** (2147m), the highest point in the immediate vicinity, although views from the top are obscured by the forest. The starting point is at Kilakala Secondary School, 1km east of town off Old Dar es Salaam Rd. The trek is detailed in the Uluguru tourist-information booklet mentioned below; it takes about five hours return. Since part of the hike is in the forest reserve, you'll need to first get a permit (Tsh5000) from the **Catchment Office** (7.30am-3.30pm Mon-Fri) in Morogoro. It's 1.5km north of the town centre on the road to Msamvu junction, in an unmarked building on the left just after crossing the second set of railway tracks. There are also various cultural walks from **Bunduki**, about 2½ to three hours drive south of Morogoro, and best accessed with your own 4WD. Transport can also be arranged with Chilunga (about Tsh50,000 per vehicle).

The **Wildlife Conservation Society of Tanzania** (WCST; ☎ 023-261 3122; uluguru@morogoro.net; 1st fl, Bodi ya Pamba Bldg, Old Dar es Salaam Rd, Morogoro), in collaboration with the Uluguru Mountains Biodiversity Conservation Project, has published *Tourist Information for the Uluguru Mountains*, with detailed route descriptions and information on places to stay. It's for sale at the WCST office in Morogoro or can be downloaded for free at www.africanconservation.com/uluguru (click on Contents, then on Section 4).

until about 4pm (Tsh2500, 3½ hours). Buses from Dar es Salaam going southwest towards Mikumi and Iringa begin passing Morogoro about 9am.

To Arusha, several direct buses daily do the route (nine hours), including Shabiby, originating in Dodoma.

To Tanga, there is a direct bus daily (Tsh5000, five hours), departing by 8am.

The main *dalla-dalla* stand is in front of the market, where there is also a taxi rank. There's another *dalla-dalla* stop and taxi rank further east along Old Dar es Salaam Rd before the post office.

TRAIN

Morogoro is on the Central Line (p361), but this section of track is currently closed. Even when open, it's much faster to travel via bus.

MIKUMI NATIONAL PARK

Lovely, but often-underrated, Mikumi – part of the vast Selous ecosystem – is Tanzania's fourth-largest national park. It's also the most accessible from Dar es Salaam and, with al-most guaranteed sightings of wildlife, makes an ideal destination for a safari for those who don't have much time. Within its 3230 sq km, set between the Uluguru Mountains to the northeast, the Rubeho Mountains to the northwest and the Lumango Mountains to the southeast, Mikumi hosts buffaloes, wildebeests, giraffes, elephants, lions, zebras, leopards, crocodiles and more, and chances are high that you'll see a respectable sam-pling of these within a short time of entering the park.

The best and most reliable viewing is around the Mkata floodplain, to the north-west of the main road, with the Millennium ('Little Serengeti') area particularly rewarding. Another attraction is the Hippo Pools area, just northwest of the main entry gate, where you can watch these lumbering behemoths at close range, plus do some fine birding.

To the south, Mikumi is contiguous with Selous Game Reserve, although there's cur-rently no all-weather road linking the two (most operators go via Morogoro) and only minimal track development. More feasible is a combination of Mikumi with Udzungwa Mountains National Park, which is about a two-hour drive southwest.

Mikumi is an important educational and research centre. Among the various projects

being carried out is an ongoing field study of yellow baboons, which is one of just a handful of such long-term primate studies on the continent.

Information

Entry fees are US$20/5 per adult/child aged five to 15 years. For camping fees see p77. Mikumi can be visited year-round, though it's best in the dry season – during the rainy season (from about December to May) some areas become inaccessible and the animals are more widely scattered. For booking camp sites and park *bandas* (thatched-roof huts or shelters), contact the **senior park war-den** (☎ 023-262 0487). Hours for driving within the park (off the main highway) are 6.30am to 6.30pm. Foxes African Safaris, which runs two lodges in the park, has safari vehicles for its guests (US$120 for half a day, unless you've booked an all-inclusive package). Otherwise, you'll need to either have your own vehicle to visit the park or arrange an organised tour. Two-hour guided walking safaris can be ar-ranged at the park entrance, but these are cur-rently being done almost exclusively in the more heavily vegetated area of the park, just south of the main highway, and may leave you disappointed.

Sleeping & Eating

The park has four ordinary camp sites, for which you'll need to be self-sufficient. The two closest to the park headquarters have toilet facilities and one has a shower. There is a special camp site near Choga Wale in the north of the park; permission to camp else-where can be requested from park headquar-ters and is charged at special camp-site rates. There is also a hostel for students, which must be reserved in advance through park head-quarters; bring your own food and other sup-plies. Better are the new **park bandas** (s/d US$30/50) just behind the main park office complex. The rooms – in attached brick bungalows with shared and clean hot-water bathrooms – are spare but spotless and have nets. Meals can be arranged and there's a shared kitchen for cooking your own meals.

Mikumi Wildlife Camp (Kikoboga; ☎ 022-260 0352/4; obh@bol.co.tz; s/d full board US$160/280; ☒) Kikoboga, about 500m northeast of the park gate and within easy access of the main wildlife cir-cuits, has attractive stone cottages spread along a grassy field frequented by grazing zebras and gazelles and is good overall value. Given its proximity to the highway, it's not a wilderness experience, but the animals don't seem to mind and you'll probably see plenty from your front porch. A good family choice. Wildlife drives cost US$130/200 per vehicle per half/full day.

Vuma Hills Tented Camp (☎ 0784-237422; www.tan zaniasafaris.info; s/d full board plus wildlife drives US$305/490; 🔊) This easily accessed and popular camp is set on a rise about 7km south of the main road, with views over the plains in the distance. The 16 tented en-suite cottages each have a double and a single bed, the mood is relaxed and the cuisine is good. A recommended family choice. The turn-off is diagonally opposite the park entry gate.

Foxes Safari Camp (☎ 0784-237422; www.tanzania safaris.info; s/d full board plus wildlife drives US$305/490; 🔊) Under the same management as Vuma Hills camp, this 12-tent upmarket camp is set on a rocky outcrop with good access to the rewarding wildlife-viewing circuits around Chamgore and Mwanambogo dam in Mikumi's northeastern section, with wide views over the surrounding Mkata plains. It's 6km off the tarmac road and accessed via a signposted turn-off about 29km northeast of the main park gate.

Also see the accommodation options in Mikumi town (right), 23km west.

Getting There & Around

BUS
Although getting to the gate of Mikumi is easy via public transport (take any of the buses running along the Morogoro–Iringa highway and ask the driver to drop you off there), there is no vehicle rental at the park, so you'll need to have your own car or arrange a rental in advance with one of the lodges. It's often possible to see animals along the roadside if you're passing through on a bus, especially if you travel in the early morning or evening, but the buses move too fast for decent viewing. Good budget options for visiting the park include one of the frequent special deals offered by Dar es Salaam–based tour operators (see p88), or alternatively, to take the bus to Mikumi town and organise transport to the park through Genesis Motel or Tan-Swiss Hotel (see the Mikumi town section, following). If you're planning to continue from the park by bus, purchase your onward ticket in advance with the bus company (Scandinavian is best for

this) and get their telephone number to confirm with them so they will remember to stop and pick you up at the park gate.

CAR
The park gate is about a four-hour drive from Dar es Salaam; speed limits on the section of main highway inside the park are controlled (70km per hour during the day and 50km per hour at night). A limited network of roads in Mikumi's northern section are accessible with a 2WD during most of the year; the south is strictly 4WD, except the road to Vuma Hills Tented Camp. For combining Mikumi with Selous, the best route is via Morogoro. The rough tracks that directly link the two areas are steep in part and passable only in the dry season with a well-equipped vehicle and a driver who knows the area.

MIKUMI
☎ 023

Mikumi is the last of the lowland towns along the Dar es Salaam–Mbeya highway before it starts its beautiful climb through the Ruaha River gorge up into the hills and mountains of the Southern Highlands. The town itself is stretched out along a few kilometres of highway and has an unmistakable truck-stop feel. It's of interest almost exclusively as a transit point for visits to the Mikumi or Udzungwa Mountains National Parks, although it's quite possible to visit both without staying overnight here.

Sleeping & Eating

Kilimanjaro Village Inn (☎ 023-262 0429; bill_willynm 2003@yahoo.co.uk; Main Highway; s/d Tsh6000/8000, without bathroom Tsh3000/4000) A good shoestring choice, with clean, no-frills rooms with nets and most with fan, and meals for about Tsh3500. It's a bit away from the main truck park area, set back from the road about 1km east of the Ifakara junction and just west of the railway tracks.

Mikumi Health Centre Guest House St Kizito (☎ 023-262 0421, 0784-402765; mikumi@raha.com; camping per person Tsh4000, r per adult/child Tsh3500/7000) Several simple rooms in small guesthouses set on the quiet grounds of the Mikumi Health Centre. There is mosquito netting, hot water and a simple kitchen, and meals can be arranged if you bring your own food. Watch for the small signpost on the south side of the road, just east of the Ifakara junction.

Genesis Motel (☎ 023-262 0461; camping per person US$5, r per person US$20, with half board US$35) This efficient hotel is located on the edge of Mikumi town, directly on the main highway and about 2.5km east of the Ifakara junction. Rooms are clean and fine for the price (ask for one of the newer ones, which are lined up in a closely spaced row along flower-fringed walkways), staff are helpful and there's a restaurant and an attached snake park (adult/child US$5/2). For campers, there are hot-water showers and a kitchen. Genesis is also a good place to organise visits to Mikumi and Udzungwa Mountains National Parks (each US$100 per vehicle per day), and can help with bus bookings for onward travel. The same management also runs a hotel near Katavi National Park and can arrange overland excursions there from Mikumi.

Tan-Swiss Hotel & Restaurant (☎ 0755-191827, 0784-246322; zillern@vtxmail.ch; Main Rd; camping per person Tsh3000, d/tr Tsh40,000/55,000) This newly reopened Swiss- and Tanzanian-run establishment has four comfortable en-suite rooms with nets, fans, small porches and wooden floors, and a good restaurant-bar with meals for about Tsh8000. Staff can help you organise visits to Mikumi and Udzungwa Mountains National Parks, car rentals and other excursions.

Getting There & Away

Minibuses heading towards Udzungwa Mountains National Park (Tsh5500, two hours) and on to Ifakara (Tsh7000, 3½ hours) leave throughout the day from the Ifakara junction just south of the highway. The Dar es Salaam to Ifakara bus passes the junction at about noon.

Going west, Scandinavian Express and other lines from Dar es Salaam begin passing Mikumi en route to Iringa (Tsh6000, three hours), Mbeya and Songea, beginning about 9.30am and stopping along the main highway just east of the Ifakara junction. Few buses originate in Mikumi, so you'll need to stand on the roadside and wait until one comes by with space. Smaller buses from Mikumi to Iringa go throughout the day from the stand at the Ifakara junction (Tsh6000, three to four hours), from about 9am. There is also a direct bus from Kilombero to Iringa, passing Mikumi about 5.30am. Going east, buses to Dar es Salaam (Tsh8000 to Tsh12,000, 4½ hours) start to pass Mikumi from 8.30am.

If you're staying at Genesis or Tan-Swiss, staff will help you arrange things so that the bus stops in front of the hotel and you don't need to go to the junction.

UDZUNGWA MOUNTAINS NATIONAL PARK

Towering steeply over the Kilombero Plains about 350km southwest of Dar es Salaam are the wild, lushly forested slopes of the Udzungwa Mountains, portions of which are protected as part of Udzungwa Mountains National Park. In addition to an abundance of unique plants, the park is home to an important population of primates (10 species – more than in any of Tanzania's other parks) as well as the grey-faced sengi (*Rhynchocyon udzungwensis*) – a newly discovered species of elephant shrew, and makes an intriguing offbeat destination for anyone botanically inclined or interested in hiking well away from the crowds.

The going can be tough in parts: the trail network is limited and those trails that do exist are often muddy, steep, humid and densely overgrown. Infrastructure is rudimentary and you'll need to have your own tent and do your hiking accompanied by a guide. But the night-time symphony of forest insects, the rushing of streams and waterfalls and the views down over the plains compensate. Plus, because the Udzungwas aren't on the way to anywhere, relatively few travellers come this way and you'll often have most trails to yourself.

The park was gazetted in 1992 with an area of 1900 sq km. Among its residents are the rare Iringa red colobus, the Sanje crested mangabey and the Udzungwa forest partridge, which has been sighted near the park's boundaries. While there are also elephants, buffaloes, leopards, hippos and crocodiles, these – particularly hippos and crocodiles – are primarily in the park's southwest and are seldom seen along the main hiking routes.

There are no roads in Udzungwa; instead, there are about eight major and several lesser hiking trails winding through various sections of the park. Most trails are on the eastern side of the park, although development has started in the west and there are now several trails open there as well. The most popular route is a short (three to five hours), but steep, circuit from Sanje village through the forest to **Sanje Falls**, where swimming and camping are possible. More satisfying is the two-night, three-day (or two long days if you're fit) hike up to

---

> ### THE UDZUNGWA MOUNTAINS
> The Udzungwas' high degree of endemism and biodiversity is due, in large part, to the area's constant climate over millions of years, which has given species a chance to evolve. Another factor is the Udzungwas' altitudinal range. From the low-lying Kilombero Valley south of the park (at approximately 200m) to Luhombero Peak (the park's highest point at 2579m), there is continuous forest, making this one of the few places in Africa with continuous rainforest over such a great span.

Mwanihana Peak (2080m), the park's second-highest point. The challenging four- to five-day trail from Mang'ula to **Luhombero Peak** (2579m) is currently not cleared, although it's worth checking with park headquarters for an update on this, as well as about the six-day **Lumemo Trail** (about to reopen). There are also some day trails in the baobab-studded northwestern corner of the park around Mbatwa Ranger Post and a multiday trail from Udekwa up to Luhombero Peak.

Information
Entry fees are US$20/5 per adult/child aged five to 15 years. For camping fees, see p77. Porter fees range between Tsh5000 and Tsh9000 per day, depending on the trail.

The park is best visited between June and October. For all hikes, you'll need to be accompanied by a guide (US$15 per day or US$25 for an armed ranger, necessary for longer hikes). For birding, bring your own field guidebook along, as they are not generally available at the park. For overnight hikes, allow an extra day at Mang'ula to organise things and time to get from park headquarters to the trailheads.

The main entrance gate, the **park headquarters** (☎ 023-262 0224; www.udzungwa.org) and the senior park warden's office are located in Mang'ula, 60km south of Mikumi town along the Ifakara road. Entry posts are planned to open at Msosa, about 10km off the main highway just south of Mbuyuni, and at Udekwa, on the western side of the park and accessed via a turn-off from the main highway at Ilula (from where it's 60km further). Both will be useful if you are coming from Iringa or want to climb Luhombero Peak from the west.

There's a tiny market in Mang'ula near the train station, and another small one in town to the north of the station, both with only limited selections. It's a good idea to stock up on major items in Dar es Salaam or Morogoro and, if you'll be staying in the park for a while, to bring a supply of dried fruit and nuts to supplement the bland locally available offerings. You can usually find bottled water near the markets.

Sleeping & Eating
There are three rudimentary camp sites near park headquarters, one with a shower and the others near a stream, though visitors rarely stay at them as they cost US$30/5 per adult/child for the most basic facilities, versus US$5 per person for camping at Udzungwa Mountain View Hotel. Bring a tent and all supplies. The main site is signposted about 100m south of the park gate. There are also several camp sites along the longer trails.

Twiga Hotel (☎ 023-262 0239; r with/without bathroom Tsh12,000) Twiga has no-frills rooms that are quite reasonable shoestring value, and meals available on order. It's just outside the park gate, about 200m off the road and signposted.

Udzungwa Mountain View Hotel (☎ 023-262 0218; camping per person US$5, r per person US$20) This recently expanded hotel, under the same management as Genesis Motel in Mikumi, has simple but clean rooms in a forested setting and a restaurant (set menu Tsh7500). It's about 500m south of the park entrance, along the main road.

Getting There & Away
BUS
Minibuses and pick-ups run daily between Mikumi town (from the *dalla-dalla* stand on the Ifakara road just south of the main highway) and Kilombero, where you'll need to wait for onward transport towards Mang'ula. However, it's faster to wait for one of the larger direct buses coming from either Dar es Salaam or Morogoro to Ifakara and Mahenge via Mang'ula. These depart both Morogoro and Dar between 6.30am and 10am, and pass Mikumi any time from about 8.30am to 2pm. Going in the other direction, there are several departures each morning from Ifakara, passing Mang'ula between about 7am and noon; park staff can help you with the connections. The fare between Mang'ula and Mikumi (two hours) is Tsh3500; between Ifakara and Mang'ula (two hours) it's Tsh3000.

From Iringa to Kilombero (Tsh6000, five hours), there are one or two buses daily in each direction, departing by around midday from Iringa and between 5am and 7am from Kilombero.

Allow plenty of time to get from the park gate (where you pay your entry fee) to Sanje village, 10km to the north, which is the trailhead for a few of the hikes. There are sporadic minibuses between Mang'ula and Sanje (Tsh500) and the occasional lorry. With luck, you may be able to arrange a lift on a park vehicle (Tsh10,000 one way). If you decide to walk, the only route is along the main road. Allow a day to get from Mang'ula to the western side of the park by road; you'll need your own transport or else take your chances on being able to arrange something with park staff. Entering the park from the west, there's no reliable public transport to the Msosa or Udekwa entry gates, apart from very sporadic pick-ups, so you'll either need to walk (feasible for Msosa, as it's only 10km off the highway) or have your own transport. Riverside Campsite in Iringa (opposite) is the best contact for arranging excursions to the western part of the park.

TRAIN
Tazara ordinary trains stop at Mang'ula (Tsh10,000/6700/4900 for 1st/2nd/economy class from Dar es Salaam). The station is about a 30-minute walk from park headquarters; if you make advance arrangements, staff from the hotels will meet you. Express trains stop only at Ifakara, about 50km further south.

IRINGA
☎ 026 / pop 110,000
With its attractive bluff-top setting, streets lined with jacarandas, healthy climate and highland feel, Iringa is a likeable place – one of the nicest towns along the Dar es Salaam to Mbeya highway, a slow-paced introduction to local life and well worth a stop. Perched at a cool 1600m on a cliff overlooking the valley of the Little Ruaha River, Iringa was initially built up by the Germans at the turn of the century as a bastion against the local Hehe people. Now it's a district capital, an important agricultural centre and the gateway for visiting Ruaha National Park.

Information
INTERNET ACCESS
MR Hotel (Mkwawa Rd; per hr Tsh1000; ☽ 8am-9pm)
Skynet (Uhuru Ave; per hr Tsh1000; ☽ 8am-8pm Mon-Fri, 8.30am-3pm Sat & Sun) Next to Iringa Info; also good for uploading digital photos.

MEDICAL SERVICES
Aga Khan Health Centre (☎ 026-270 2277; Jamat St; ☽ 8am-6pm Mon-Fri, 8am-2pm Sat & Sun) Next to the Lutheran cathedral and near the market.
Myomboni Pharmacy (☎ 026-270 2277/2617; ☽ 7.30am-7.30pm) Just downhill from the Aga Khan Health Centre.

MONEY
CRDB (Uhuru Ave) ATM (Visa only).
NBC (Uhuru Ave) Opposite the Catholic cathedral at the western end of town. Changes cash and has an ATM (Visa only).

POST & TELEPHONE
Post office (☽ 8am-4.30pm Mon-Fri, 9am-noon Sat) Just off Uhuru Ave.
Telecom Shop (☽ 8am-7.30pm) For calling booths, try this private shop diagonally opposite TTCL (look for the yellow sign), where calls cost Tsh2000 per minute to anywhere.
TTCL Next to the post office; sells phone cards.

TOURIST INFORMATION
Iringa Info (☎ 026-270 1988; riversidecampsitetz@hotmail.com; Uhuru Ave; ☽ 9am-5pm Mon-Fri, 9am-3pm Sat) A recommended first stop and a good place to organise Ruaha safaris (sometimes including favourably priced walk-in rates at some of the lodges during the low season), as well as reliable car rentals and excursions. Opposite Hasty Tasty Too.
Tatanca Safaris & Tours (☎ 026-270 0601, 0787-338335; tatancatours@iringanet.com; Uhuru Ave) An efficient operator offering Ruaha safaris, as well as excursions elsewhere in the country; around the corner from Neema Crafts.

Sights & Activities
Iringa's colourful **market** is piled high with fruits and vegetables, plus countless other wares, including large, locally made Iringa baskets, and is well worth a stroll. Nearby, in front of the police station, is a **monument** to the Africans who fell during the Maji Maji uprising between 1905 and 1907. West along this same street is Iringa's main trading area, dominated by the impressive German-built **Ismaili Mosque** with its distinctive clock tower.

IRINGA

0 — 600 m
0 — 0.4 miles

INFORMATION		
Aga Khan Health Centre	1	C3
CRDB Bank	2	C2
Iringa Info	3	C2
MR Hotel	4	C3
Myomboni Pharmacy	5	C3
NBC Bank	6	A3
Post Office	..........................(see 9)
Skynet	................................(see 3)
Tatanca Safaris & Tours	7	D2
Telecom Shop	8	C3
TTCL	9	C3

SIGHTS & ACTIVITIES		
Commonwealth War Graves		
Cemetery	10	D3
Ismaili Mosque	11	C3
Maji Maji Uprising Monument	...12	C3
Market	13	C3

SLEEPING 🏠 🏡		
Annex of Staff Inn	14	B3
Central Lodge	15	C2
Dr AJ Nsekela Executive Lodge...16	D2
Iringa Lutheran Centre	17	D2
Isimila Hotel	18	D1
MR Hotel	...........................(see 4)
Staff Inn White House Lodge	...19	B3

EATING 🍴		
Best Snacks & Take Away	20	D2
Hasty Tasty Too	21	C2
Lulu's	22	D2
Mama Miho's	23	C3
Premji's Cash & Carry	24	B3
Saju's Home Cooking	25	D2

SHOPPING 🛍		
Neema Crafts	26	D2

TRANSPORT		
Bus Station	27	B3
Myomboni Dalla-Dalla Stand	28	C3
Scandinavian Booking Office	29	C3
Taxi Stand	30	C3
Taxi Stand	31	C2

To Dodoma (275km)

Hospital

NMB Bank

To Gangilonga Rock (1km)

Tanganyika Arms Building

Uhuru Monument Roundabout

Mosque

To Kalenga Historical Museum (15km); Ruaha National Park (115km)

Catholic Cathedral

Uhuru Ave

Mkwawa Rd

Miseban St

Miomboni St

Jamat St

Lutheran Cathedral

Uhuru Park

Iringa District Hospital

Bendera St

Kawawa Rd

Market (Sokoni) St

To Main Highway to Mbeya & Morogoro (2km); Ipogoro Bus Station (2.5km); Riverside Campsite (13km); Isimila & Tosamaganga (15km); Kisolanza – The Old Farm House (50km)

Some Minor Roads Not Depicted

Rising up to the northeast is **Gangilonga Rock** (*'gangilonga'* means 'talking stone' in Hehe), which is where Chief Mkwawa (p286) often meditated and where he learned that the Germans were after him. It's an easy climb to the top, and there are wide views over town.

Southeast of town is a **Commonwealth War Graves Cemetery** with graves of the deceased from both world wars.

Sleeping

BUDGET

Iringa Lutheran Centre (☎ 026-270 2489; Kawawa Rd; dm Tsh2500, s Tsh7000, s/d without bathroom Tsh3000,4000) This long-standing place has reasonably clean dorm-style rooms with nets, including one en-suite single, and hot-water buckets on request. Breakfast is available with advance order. It's on the northeastern edge of town, about 700m southeast of Neema Crafts and the main road.

Riverside Campsite (☎ 0755-033024, 0787-111663; www.riversidecampsite-tanzania.com; camping adult/child Tsh5000/2500, tented/stone bandas per person Tsh7500/15,000) Riverside Campsite, 13km northeast of Iringa and signposted from the main road, has a lovely, tranquil setting on the banks of the Little Ruaha River and is a great stop for families and budget travellers. In addition to a shaded, green and expansive riverside camping area, it offers pleasant twin-bedded tented *bandas,* a rustic six-person stone *banda,* hot-water showers, good meals (breakfast/lunch/dinner Tsh3000/5000/5000) and a small campsite shop with charcoal and other basics. It's excellent overall value, with children's discounts of 50% for accommodation and meals. Tents are available to rent (Tsh5000 per day), including for Ruaha safaris, as are bicycles. The surrounding area is ideal for walking. There are also on-site Swahili language and culture courses ranging from one day up to four months and including full-board accommodation. To get here, take a *dalla-dalla* heading towards Ilula and ask the driver to drop you off at the turn-off (Tsh800), from where it's 1.5km further on foot. Taxis charge Tsh10,000 to Tsh15,000 from town. Staff can also help you arrange car rentals and Ruaha safaris.

Annex of Staff Inn (☎ 026-270 1344/0165; Uhuru Ave; r Tsh10,000-25,000) Small and crowded but reliable, with clean, no-frills rooms with hot water, nets and some with TV, plus a restaurant with inexpensive meals. It's along the main road, about five minutes' walk from the bus station.

Central Lodge (☎ 0786-126888; Uhuru Ave; d Tsh15,000-20,000, tr Tsh30,000) Simple, quiet rooms with bathrooms in a convenient central location around a small garden. The front rooms facing the garden are spacious; smaller rooms are in the row behind. It's just behind Iringa Info – look for the signpost.

There are many nondescript, noisy guesthouses in the small valley behind the bus station, including **Staff Inn White House Lodge** (☎ 026-270 0161; s Tsh7000-15,000), where rooms have nets and most have a small double bed. Hot buckets of water can be organised on request.

MIDRANGE

Isimila Hotel (☎ 026-270 1194; Uhuru Ave; s/d Tsh12,000/14,000) Some things never change and this hotel is one of them, looking almost the same as it did nearly a decade ago and offering about the same prices. Rooms – all en suite and with nets – are good value, and there's a restaurant. It's past the Bankers' Academy (see next listing) at the northern end of town.

Dr AJ Nsekela Executive Lodge (Bankers' Academy; ☎ 026-270 2407; Uhuru Ave; s/d Tsh12,000/14,000) Set in a former school, and as staid as its name would suggest, this place has clean but soulless rooms and an institutional ambience. It's on the main road at the northern end of town. There's no food.

MR Hotel (☎ 026-270 2006/2779; www.mrhotel .co.tz; Mkwawa Rd; s/d/ste US$30/35/40; 🍴 🖳) This multistorey business travellers' hotel in a convenient but noisy location next to the bus station has declined considerably since its opening, with faded rooms (no nets) and a restaurant (meals Tsh4000).

Eating

Hasty Tasty Too (☎ 026-270 2061; Uhuru Ave; snacks & meals from Tsh500; 🕑 7.30am-8pm Mon-Sat, 10am-2pm Sun) Good breakfasts, yogurt, shakes and reasonably priced main dishes, plus an amenable mix of local and expat clientele. You can get toasted sandwiches packed to go and arrange food for Ruaha camping safaris.

Saju's Home Cooking (Haile Selassie St; snacks & meals from Tsh500; 🕑 7am-11pm) This family-run eatery makes an amenable stop for cheap local food. It's at the northern end of town, on a small lane running parallel to the main road.

Best Snacks & Take Away (☎ 0784-356894; meals Tsh3000-4500; 🕑 7am-10pm) Tasty snacks and meals, including pizza, stir-fry and the usual standards. It's on a side lane just around the corner from the Tanganyika Arms building.

Lulu's (☎ 027-270 2122; Titi St; meals Tsh3500-8000; 🕑 8.30am-3pm & 6.30-9pm Mon-Sat) A quiet place with mostly Chinese and Asian dishes, plus softserve ice cream, milkshakes and an umbrella-shaded outdoor seating area. It's one block southeast of the main road, just off Kawawa Rd. Next door is Iringa Bakery, with a limited supply of fresh rolls and bread.

For self-catering try the small but well-stocked **Mama Miho's** (Jamat St), opposite the police and fire stations, or the pricier **Premji's Cash & Carry** (Jamat St).

Getting There & Away

To catch any bus not originating in Iringa, you'll need to go to the main bus station at Ipogoro, about 3km southeast of town below the escarpment (Tsh2000 in a taxi from town), where the Morogoro–Mbeya highway bypasses Iringa. This is also where you'll get dropped off if you're arriving on a bus continuing towards Morogoro or Mbeya. *Dalla-dallas* to Ipogoro leave from the Myomboni *dalla-dalla* stand at the edge of Uhuru Park in town. All buses originating in Iringa start at the bus station in town and stop also at Ipogoro to pick up additional passengers.

Scandinavian Express (☎ 026-270 2308) goes daily to Dar es Salaam, leaving at 10.30am (Tsh15,000, 7½ hours); book in advance at the Scandinavian booking office, opposite the bus station in town.

To Mbeya, there's a bus departing daily at 8am (Tsh9000, four to five hours). Otherwise, you can book a seat on the Scandinavian bus from Dar es Salaam that passes Iringa (Ipogoro bus station) about 1pm, or just show up at the station and take your chances that there will be space.

To Njombe (Tsh7000, 3½ hours) and Songea (Tsh12,000, eight hours), Super Feo departs at 6am from the town bus station, with a second bus to Njombe only departing at 10am. Alternatively, you can wait for the Scandinavian bus from Dar es Salaam (best booked in advance).

To Dodoma, Kings Cross – an old relic of a vehicle stuffed with chickens, baskets and produce – and Urafiki depart on alternate days at 8am (Tsh10,000, nine to 10 hours), going via Nyangolo and Makatapora. Otherwise, all transport is via Morogoro, which is the route most travellers take; if you leave Iringa early, you can reach Dodoma in one day. If you're driving to Dodoma via Makatapora in a private car, allow five to six hours.

Getting Around
The main *dalla-dalla* stand ('Myomboni') is just down from the market and near the bus station. *Dalla-dallas* also stop along the edge of Uhuru Park. Taxi ranks are along the small road between the bus station and the market, in front of MR Hotel, and at the Ipogoro bus station.

AROUND IRINGA
Isimila Stone Age Site
About 20km from Iringa, off the Mbeya road, is **Isimila** (admission Tsh3000; ☉ 8am-5.30pm), where, in the late 1950s, archaeologists unearthed one of the most significant Stone Age finds ever identified. The tools found at the site are estimated to be between 60,000 and 100,000 years old. Although the display itself is not particularly exciting, the surrounding area is intriguing, with small canyons and eroded sandstone pillars. The main pillar area is accessed via a walk down into a steep valley (about one hour round-trip), for which you'll

need a guide (small tip expected). Visits are best in the morning or late afternoon, before the sun gets too high. A small museum in which all the Stone Age finds are to be gathered is being built (entry is included in the admission price). There's also a covered picnic area (bring your own food and drink).

Isimila is signposted off the main road to the left, and with a bit of endurance for heat and traffic, is straightforward to reach via bicycle from Iringa. Via public transport, take an Ifunda *dalla-dalla* from the bus station and ask the driver to drop you at the Isimila junction, from where it's a 20-minute walk to the site. Alternatively, if you're in a group, you can catch a 'Njia Panda ya Tosa' *dalla-dalla* from the Myomboni *dalla-dalla* stand and ask the driver to take you all the way in to Isimila. The charge is about Tsh1000 per person, but most drivers are only willing to do this if there are enough people wanting to go. Taxis charge about Tsh10,000 for the return trip.

A possible detour on bicycle is to nearby **Tosamaganga**, a pretty hilltop town about 7km southwest with a hospital and a mission station.

Kalenga
About 15km from Iringa on the road to Ruaha National Park is the famed former Hehe capital of Kalenga. It was here that Chief Mkwawa (p286) had his headquarters until Kalenga fell to the Germans in the 1890s, and it was here that he committed suicide rather than succumb to the German forces. The small **Kalenga Historical Museum** (admission Tsh2000) contains Mkwawa's skull and a few other relics from the era. It's just off the park road and signposted.

Mtera Dam
This dam, about 120km north of Iringa off the Dodoma road, forms a huge reservoir for the waters of the Great Ruaha River as it flows out of the Southern Highlands and through Ruaha National Park on its way to join the Rufiji in Selous Game Reserve. Nearby is one of Tanzania's major hydroelectric power stations. There's also fine angling at the dam, notably for tiger fish, though you'll need your own gear. It's beautiful in the rains, and the brush and reed landscapes along the shoreline attract many water birds. There's currently no accommodation.

SOUTHERN HIGHLANDS

SOUTHERN HIGHLANDS

CHIEF MKWAWA

Mtwa (Chief) Mkwawa, chief of the Hehe and one of German colonialism's most vociferous resisters, is a legendary figure in Tanzanian history. He is particularly revered in Iringa, near which he had his headquarters. Under Mkwawa's leadership during the second half of the 19th century, the Hehe became one of the most powerful tribes in central Tanzania. They overpowered one group after another until, by the late 1880s, they were threatening trade traffic along the caravan route from western Tanzania to Bagamoyo. In 1891, after several attempts by Mkwawa to negotiate with the Germans were rejected, his men trounced the colonial troops in the infamous battle of Lugalo, just outside Iringa on the Mikumi road. The next year, Mkwawa's troops launched a damaging attack on a German fort at Kilosa, further to the east.

The Germans placed a bounty on Mkwawa's head and, once they had regrouped, initiated a counterattack in which Mkwawa's headquarters at Kalenga were taken. Mkwawa escaped, but later, in 1898, committed suicide rather than surrender to a contingent that had been sent after him. His head was cut off and the skull sent to Germany, where it sat almost forgotten (though not by the Hehe) until it was returned to Kalenga in 1954. The return of Mkwawa's remains was due, in large part, to the efforts of Sir Edward Twining, then the British governor of Tanganyika. Today, the skull of Mkwawa and some old weapons are on display at the Kalenga Historical Museum (p285).

The grave of Chief Mkwawa is about 40km outside Iringa and signposted about 11km off the main road to Ruaha National Park.

RUAHA NATIONAL PARK

Ruaha National Park, together with neighbouring Rungwa and Kisigo Game Reserves and several smaller conservation areas, forms the core of a wild and extended ecosystem covering about 40,000 sq km and providing home to one of Tanzania's largest elephant populations. In addition to the elephants, which are estimated to number about 12,000, the park (Tanzania's second-largest and soon to be extended) hosts large herds of buffaloes, as well as greater and lesser kudus, Grant's gazelles, wild dogs, ostriches, cheetahs, roan and sable antelopes, and more than 400 different types of birds. Bird life is especially prolific along the Great Ruaha River, which winds through the eastern side of the park, as are hippos and crocodiles.

Ruaha is notable for its wild and – around the Great Ruaha River – striking topography. Much of it is undulating plateau averaging about 900m in height with occasional rocky outcrops and stands of baobabs, and mountains in the south and west reaching to about 1600m and 1900m, respectively. Running through the park are several 'sand' rivers, most of which dry up during the dry season, when they are used by wildlife as corridors to reach areas where water remains. The overall combination of rugged riverine scenery, large numbers of readily sighted wildlife (during the dry season) and good selection of camps is unbeatable.

Although the area around the camps on the eastern side of the park fills up during the high season, Ruaha receives relatively few visitors in comparison with the northern parks. Large sections are unexplored, and, apart from the August to October high season, you'll likely have things to yourself. Whenever you visit, set aside as much time as you can spare; it's not a place to be discovered on a quick in-and-out trip.

Information

Entry fees are US$20/5 per adult/child aged five to 15 per 24-hour period; multiple entries are permitted. For accommodation fees, see p77.

There are two official entry points to the park, one at the main gate about 8km inside the park boundary on its eastern side, and the other at Msembe airstrip, about 6km northeast of the main gate, where visitors arriving by plane can pay their entry fees. Park headquarters are at Msembe. The main entry gate is open from 7am to 6pm. Driving is permitted within the park from 6am to 6.30pm.

The road network in Ruaha is reasonably good and the park can be visited at any time of year. The driest season is between June and November, and this is when it's easiest to spot wildlife along the river beds. During the rainy season, some areas become impassable and wildlife is widely dispersed and difficult to locate in the impressive numbers possible during the dry months (August through October are peak). However, especially for repeat visitors, the green panoramas, lavender-coloured fields and rewarding birding compensate.

From June to January, it's possible to organise short (two- to three-hour walks) with park staff (or through your lodge). Park rates are US$25 per group (up to six people); book in advance.

Sleeping & Eating
INSIDE THE PARK

There are two ordinary camp sites about 9km northwest of park headquarters, and about 1.5km apart. Neither has water; the only facilities are pit toilets. There are also about five special camp sites, all well away from the Msembe area. Near the river and close to park headquarters are several park *bandas*, including some doubles and two larger family *bandas*, accommodating four to five people each. Water is available for showers and the park sells soft drinks and a few basics, but otherwise you'll need your own supplies. There is also a hostel for students and a resthouse, which is usually reserved for staff, but is open to the public space permitting. All park accommodation should be booked either through Iringa Info (p282) or directly with park headquarters.

Ruaha River Lodge (☎ 0784-237422; www.tanzania safaris.info; s/d full board incl wildlife drives US$330/540) This unpretentious 28-room lodge about 15km inside the gate was the first in the park and is the only place on the river. Run by the Fox family, who have several decades of experience in Ruaha, it's centred on two separate sections, each with its own dining area, giving the feel of a smaller lodge. The recently remodelled stone cottages – all with one double and one single bed – are directly on the river, and there's a treetop-level bar-terrace with stunning riverine panoramas. Vehicle safaris cost from US$120 per vehicle unless you've booked a fly-in package. Discounted drive-in accommodation rates are offered.

Mdonya Old River Camp (☎ 022-245 2005; www .adventurecamps.co.tz; s/d all-inclusive US$345/580; ☒ Jun-Mar) The rustic and relaxed Mdonya Old River Camp, about 1½ hours drive from Msembe, has eight tents set in the shade on the bank of the Mdonya Sand River, with the occasional

elephant or other animal wandering through camp. It's run by Coastal Travels in Dar es Salaam (p127). While not as luxurious as the other Ruaha camps, it's quite comfortable and very natural in ambience, and if you take advantage of Coastal's specials – including a 'last minute' deal that offers a 50% discount on combined accommodation-flight packages for bookings less than 72 hours before departure – Mdonya Old River offers fine value for a Ruaha safari.

Mwagusi Safari Camp (☎ in the UK 020-8846 9363; www.ruaha.org; s/d all-inclusive from US$530/940; ☒ Jun-Mar; ☒ Jun-Mar) This highly regarded 16-bed luxury tented camp is set in a prime location for wildlife-viewing – favoured by elephants, among other visitors – on the Mwagusi Sand River about 20km inside the park gate. The atmosphere is intimate, there are superb views from the tents and the quality of guiding is top-notch. Walks and other excursions can be arranged.

Jongomero Camp (www.jongomero.com; per person full board, airstrip transfers & activities US$550; ☒ Jun-Mar; ☒) This exclusive camp is set off on its own in the remote southwestern part of the park, about 60km from Msembe on the banks of the Jongomero Sand River. Its eight spacious tents have large verandas and furnishings made from recycled wood. Wildlife-watching from the camp itself is arguably not as good as at some of the other Ruaha camps, however, the wilderness ambience is excellent. One of the nicest aspects of this camp is the privacy of each tent and the fact that you're unlikely to see other visitors. Almost all visits are part of fly-in safaris to the nearby airstrip.

OUTSIDE THE PARK

There are several good places just outside the park boundaries along the Tungamalenga village road (take the left fork at the junction when coming from Iringa).

Chogela Camp (camping per person US$5) A simple place with well-maintained, spacious, shaded grounds, a large, clean cooking-dining area and spotless hot-water showers. Come with your own transport and bring your own tent or hire one through Riverside Campsite in Iringa. Also bring your own food and drink. Book through Iringa Info (p282).

Tungamalenga Camp (☎ 026-278 2196, 0754-983519; www.ruahatungacamp.com; camping per person US$10, r per person with breakfast/full board US$20/40) This long-standing place in Tungamalenga village, about

35km from the park gate and close to the bus stand, was the first of the Tungamalenga road options to open. In addition to a small garden for camping, there are small, clean en-suite rooms and a restaurant (meals Tsh7000). Cultural tours in the area can be arranged, and (soon – check with them first) also Ruaha safaris (US$150 per vehicle per day).

Ruaha Hilltop Lodge (☎ 026-270 1806, 0784-726709; www.ruahahilltoplodge.com; s/d US$80/160) This newish lodge has a hilltop perch about 1.5km off the Tungamalenga road, with wide views over the plains below from the raised restaurant-bar area. Behind this are simple two-person cement *bandas* with nets. Water can be a problem sometimes, but overall the lodge is an amenable choice, especially during the dry season when it's common to see elephants and other wildlife passing by down below. Cultural walks in the surrounding area can also be arranged. If you don't have your own vehicle, you'll need to organise one in Iringa town for Ruaha safaris.

Tandala Tented Camp (www.tandalatentedcamp .com; per person full board US$120; ☙ Jun-Mar) A lovely place just outside the park boundary about 12km from the park gate and shortly before the Tungamalenga road rejoins the main park access road. Accommodation is in raised tents scattered around shaded grounds with a bush feel (elephants and other animals are frequent visitors). The camp can help you arrange vehicle rental to Ruaha (US$60 per person), as well as guided walks in park border areas.

Getting There & Away

AIR
There are airstrips at Msembe and Jongomero.

Coastal Aviation flies from Dar es Salaam and Zanzibar to Ruaha via Selous Game Reserve (US$300 one way from Dar es Salaam or Zanzibar, US$270 from Selous Game Reserve), and between Ruaha and Arusha (US$300). Foxes African Safaris (p47) has a plane based in Ruaha for flights to Katavi (US$450), Dar es Salaam (US$300), Selous (US$270), Mikumi (US$240) and other destinations on request.

BUS
A bus (Upendo and Shanila lines alternate on the route) goes daily between Iringa and Tungamalenga village, departing Iringa at 1pm and Tungamalenga (from the village bus stand, just before Tungamalenga Camp) at 5am (Tsh3000, five to six hours). From Tungamalenga, there is no onward transport to the park, other than rental vehicles arranged in advance through the camps along the Tungamalenga road, and there is no vehicle rental once at Ruaha, unless you've arranged for a vehicle safari in advance with one of the lodges.

Iringa Info (p282) offers day safaris for US$200 per vehicle per day plus park fees and overnight safaris for US$180 per day, and is a good contact for finding other travellers interested in joining a group. Tatanca Safaris & Tours (p282) in Iringa also arranges Ruaha safaris that are pricey for day trips (US$300), but work out at roughly the same price for multi-night stays in the park (US$100 for each additional day).

CAR
Ruaha is 115km from Iringa along an unsealed road, which is decent except during the rains when it can be rough. About 58km before the park, the road forks; both sides go to Ruaha and the distance is about the same each way. To access Tungamalenga and accommodation outside the park, take the left fork. The right fork ('never-ending road') is maintained by the park and is generally in marginally better condition.

Roads within the park are in reasonable condition, though 4WD is necessary. The closest petrol station is in Iringa.

IRINGA TO MAKAMBAKO
From Iringa, the Tanzam highway continues southwest, winding its way gradually up, past dense stands of pine, before reaching the junction town of Makambako.

Kisolanza – The Old Farm House (www.kisolanza.com; camping per person with hot showers US$4, tw stables/chalets US$20/25, d/f cottages US$45/55, luxury cottage per person with half board US$75) is a gracious 1930s farm homestead fringed by stands of pine and rolling hill country about 50km southwest of Iringa and just off the highway. It comes highly recommended, both for its accommodation and for its cuisine. There are two camping grounds, one for overlanders and one for private vehicles, plus spotless twin-bedded rooms with common bathroom in the nearby 'stables'; wooden two-person chalets; lovely en-suite camp-site cottages with a double bed below and a sleeper loft above; and two new luxury cottages built entirely with locally sourced materials and set amid beautiful gardens. One of the luxury cottages – the honeymoon farm cottage suite – is set off on its own with a private breakfast area in the surrounding gardens and a fireplace. There is also a bar and a shop selling home-grown vegetables and fruit, meat, fish, eggs and bread. The entire set-up is lovely, with fresh flowers in the rooms and no detail overlooked, and the cuisine is excellent. In addition to being a convenient stopover, Kisolanza also makes a good base for exploring the area, with fine walking and birding in the surrounding countryside. Buses will drop you at the Kisolanza turn-off, from where it's about a 1.5km walk in to the lodge. Advance bookings are advisable for accommodation, but there is always room for campers.

Continuing southwestwards, about 45km further on is **Mafinga**, the turn-off point to reach the forested highlands around **Mufindi**, which are laced with small streams and known for their tea estates and trout-fishing. The family-run **Southern Highlands Lodge** (☎ 0784-237422; www.tanzaniasafaris.info; s/d full board US$200/280) – set amid the hills and tea plantations around Mufindi – is another highly recommended place for anyone looking for cool highland air and the chance to hike or recharge. Accommodation is in cosy wooden cabins with large pane-glass windows and sunset views over the hills, and the cuisine – all prepared fresh with produce from the farm – is delicious. There's also a larger two-family chalet with an upper balcony and a private honeymooners cabin with a stone fireplace. Surrounding these are beautifully landscaped gardens, expansive grounds with walking trails, small lakes for fishing, cycling (bikes are available) and horse riding. Fantastic! The same family also runs safari camps in Ruaha, Mikumi and Katavi parks, and the lodge makes a fine mid-safari break. The lodge is about 45km inland from Mafinga. Pick-ups can be arranged, and there are scheduled flights during the dry season from Ruaha, Dar es Salaam and other points to a nearby airstrip.

In Mafinga itself, try **Hilton Guest House** (r Tsh10,000-12,000), within walking distance of the Mafinga town bus stand just off the main highway and signposted.

For reliable vehicle hire with driver in the Iringa-Mafinga area and beyond, contact **Conrad Msekwa** (☎ 0753-026744, 0754-559230; msekwaconrad@yahoo.com).

MAKAMBAKO
☎ 026

Makambako is a dry, windy highland town at the junction where the road from Songea and Njombe meets the Dar es Salaam–Mbeya highway, and a stop on the Tazara railway line. Geographically, the area marks the end of the Eastern Arc mountain range and the start of the Southern Highlands. Makambako is also notable for its large market, which includes an extensive used-clothes section.

There's an **internet café** (per hr Tsh1500) adjoining Midtown Lodge.

Sleeping & Eating

Makambako Lutheran Centre (☎ 026-273 0047; Tanzam Highway; r Tsh3000-4000) Basic and rather faded rooms, including one with bathroom and some with a large bed. It's just east of the junction and opposite the train station. Food can be arranged with lots of advance notice.

Midtown Lodge (r Tsh7000-10,000) Clean en-suite rooms in varying sizes and a restaurant. The rooms for Tsh10,000 have beds big enough for two people. It's about 1½ blocks in from both the Mbeya and Songea roads, and signposted from both.

Jay Jay Highlands Hotel (☎ 026-273 0475, 0784-310177; s/d Tsh15,000/20,000) Another good place, with small, clean and somewhat overly furnished rooms and a restaurant serving great-value four-course meals for about Tsh4500. It's about 1km south of the main junction along the Njombe road, and signposted.

Getting There & Away

The bus stand is about 1.5km south of the main junction along the Njombe road. The first bus to Mbeya (Tsh5000, three hours) leaves at 6am, with another bus at 7am. Otherwise, you can wait at the main junction for passing transport (Tsh4000). The first buses (all smaller Coastals) to Njombe (Tsh2000, one hour) and Songea (Tsh7000, five hours) depart about 6.30am, and there's a larger bus departing at 6.30am for Iringa and Dar es Salaam.

NJOMBE
☎ 026

The peppy town of Njombe, about 60km south of Makambako and 235km north of Songea, is a district capital, regional agricultural centre and home of the Bena people. It would be unmemorable but for its highly scenic setting on the eastern edge of the Kipengere mountain range at almost 2000m. In addition to giving it the reputation of being Tanzania's coldest town, this perch provides wide vistas over hills that seem to roll endlessly into the horizon. The surrounding area – dotted with tea plantations and fields of wildflowers – is ideal for walking and cycling, although there is no tourism infrastructure so anything you undertake will need to be under your own steam and with a GPS. At the northern edge of town – visible from the main road and an easy walk – are the Luhuji Falls. It's also possible to go from Njombe along beautiful highland backroads to the Kitulo Plateau area, and down to the shores of Lake Nyasa. For more details, and other suggestions for walking and driving routes, see p298 and the excellent *A Guide to the Southern Highlands of Tanzania* (see the boxed text, p293).

There's a good internet connection and you can upload photos at **Altek Computing Centre** (per hr Tsh1000; ☽ 8am-8pm), behind the TFA building along the main road. There are no ATMs yet.

Sleeping & Eating

Lutheran Centre Guest House (☎ 026-278 2118; r without bathroom Tsh3000, s Tsh5000) No-frills rooms in a small compound one block off the main street and diagonally behind (and south of) the Lutheran church. It's about a 10-minute walk from the bus stand. Meals can be arranged with advance order.

Milimani Hotel (Songea Rd; s/d Tsh6000/8000) Bare and drab, but things are reasonably clean and the price isn't bad. It's at the southern end of town, near the Lutheran church.

Chani Motel (☎ 026-278 2357, 0748-324644; s/d Tsh8500/10,500) This cosy place has modest but clean good-value rooms with hot running water, small gardens and a restaurant with TV and what are arguably Njombe's best meals (Tsh2000 to Tsh4000). Just down a few steps is the Cliff Look bar. It's signposted at the northern end of town and about 600m west off the main road.

Mwambasa Lodge (☎ 026-278 2301; Main Rd; r Tsh10,000-12,000) Clean en-suite rooms with hot water, TV, small double beds and continental breakfast. It's centrally located, about 500m north of the bus stand and on the opposite side of the street.

Mexons Cliff Hotel (☎ 026-278 2282, 0787-282725; mexonscliffhotelltd@yahoo.com; s/d/ste Tsh20,000/25,000

/35,000) Njombe's newest hotel has a prime setting on the escarpment overlooking the surrounding countryside, although most of the rooms are rather small and somewhat cramped, with windows looking out on the back parking lot. There's a restaurant and parking. It's at the northern end of town and signposted just off the main road.

Duka la Maziwa (Cefa Njombe Milk Factory; ☎ 026-278 2851; ☽ noon-6pm Mon, 8.30am-1pm & 3-6pm Tue-Fri, 8.30am-6pm Sat) This little place sells fresh milk and yogurt and excellent cheeses. It's two blocks off the main road – turn in by the TFA building.

Getting There & Away

The bus stand is on the west side of the main road, about 600m south of the large grey-water tank.

Super Feo goes daily to Songea (Tsh7000, four hours), Makambako (Tsh2000, one hour) and Mbeya (Tsh7000, four hours), with the first departures at 6.30am.

For hikers, there are daily pick-ups to both Bulongwa (departing Njombe about 10am) and Ludewa (departing by 8am), from where you can walk down to Matema and Lupingu, respectively, both on the Lake Nyasa shoreline.

KITULO NATIONAL PARK

Tanzania's newest national park protects the flower-clad Kitulo Plateau, together with sections of the former Livingstone Forest Reserve, which runs south from the plateau paralleling the Lake Nyasa shoreline. The area (see Map p295) – much of which lies between 2600m and 3000m in the highlands northeast of Tukuyu – is stunningly beautiful and a paradise for hikers. The park reaches its prime during the rainy season from about December until April, when it explodes in a profusion of colour, with orchids (over 40 species have been identified so far), irises, aloes, geraniums and many more flowers carpeting its grassy expanses. Rising up from the plateau, the park's other attraction is Mt Mtorwi (2961m), one metre higher than Mt Rungwe and southern Tanzania's highest peak. The park is the centrepiece of one of Tanzania's most scenic and undiscovered corners, and is an essential place to visit if you are in the area and enjoy walking or things botanical. The best months for seeing the flowers are December to March, which is also when hiking is at its muddiest. Orchids

– the plateau's most renowned residents – are at their peak in February.

Information

Park infrastructure is still in the early stages. Entry fees (US$20/5 per adult/child) should be paid at Tanapa's temporary headquarters at Matamba village, where guides can also be arranged, if desired. For any hiking, you'll need to be self-sufficient with food and water (there are plenty of sources within the park area), and carry a GPS. The best source of route descriptions is *A Guide to the Southern Highlands of Tanzania* (see the boxed text, p293).

Sleeping & Eating

Apart from very basic rooms (Tsh2000) at Kitulo Farm (ask at Tanapa's temporary headquarters for directions), the only accommodation option inside the park is camping. Sites are currently being established, so you'll need to enquire at park headquarters.

Otherwise, there are several inexpensive guesthouses in Matamba village:

Zebra Park Guest House (s Tsh3000, without bathroom Tsh2000) One block in from the main road and signposted just beyond the turn-off for Edeni Guest House, this place has clean, basic rooms and bucket baths.

Fema (r per person Tsh5000) No-frills, clean rooms sharing a bathroom in a large house behind the Tanapa office (just a few minutes on foot across the field). It has hot water (usually) and good meals (breakfast/lunch/dinner about Tsh2500/4000/4000), including packed picnic lunches.

For meals, try **Green Garden Restaurant** (meals Tsh1000) at the junction of the roads from Mfumbi and Chimala, near the Tanapa office.

At the southern edge of town, and just off the Kitulo road, is the soon-to-be-opened Kipunji Hotel. En-suite rooms in detached cement *bandas*, camping and a restaurant are planned.

Getting There & Away

The best access to Kitulo is via Mfumbi village, about 90km east of Mbeya along the main highway, from where a small, currently unsignposted and unpaved but good (all-weather) road winds its way 32km up to Matamba village and the park's temporary base. From Matamba, it's about an hour further via 4WD with high clearance (or a

couple of hours on foot) along a rough road (sometimes impassable in the rains) up onto the plateau itself and the official park area, marked by a sign board and the yet-to-be-built Mwakipembo Gate.

It's also possible to reach Kitulo via the signposted park turn-off 2km west of Chimala town, about 80km east of Mbeya along the main highway. From here, a rough (4WD essential) and rocky but beautiful road (slated for rehabilitation) winds its way for 9km up the escarpment via a series of 50-plus hairpin turns, offering wide vistas over the Usangi plains below. From the top, it's a further 12km or so to Matamba, along a wonderfully scenic route across the Chimala River, past fields of sunflowers and the occasional small house.

In the dry season, in a good vehicle with high clearance, it's also possible to reach Kitulo via Isyonje village, along the Tukuyu road. Once on the plateau, a reasonable road leads to Kitulo Farm, which is the planned site for park headquarters.

The only public transport to Kitulo is via Mfumbi village, from where one or two pick-ups daily go as far as Matamba (Tsh3000, one hour) from Mfumbi's Standi ya Uwanje. Once at Matamba, it's sometimes possible to hire a park vehicle to take you on up to the plateau. Otherwise, it's about two to three hours on foot up to the plateau, and about seven hours to Kitulo Farm.

In Mbeya, Gazelle Safaris (p292) and Utengule Country Hotel (p293) can both help organise transport up to the park.

MBEYA
☎ 025 / pop 270,000

The thriving town of Mbeya sprawls at about 1700m in the shadow of Loleza Peak (2656m), in a gap between the verdant Mbeya mountain range to the north and the Poroto mountains to the southeast. It was founded in 1927 as a supply centre for the gold rush at Lupa, to the north, but today owes its existence to its position on the Tazara railway line and the Tanzam highway, and its status as a major trade and transit junction between Tanzania, Zambia and Malawi. The surrounding area, in addition to being lush, mountainous and highly scenic, is also a major farming region, with coffee, tea, bananas and cocoa all grown here. While the town centre is on the scruffy side (especially around the bus station), the cool climate, jacaranda trees and views of the hills compensate, and there are dozens of excursions nearby.

Information
INTERNET ACCESS
BIC Internet Café (per hr Tsh1000; 🕑 7am-7pm Mon-Fri, 7.30am-6pm Sat) At the back of the Maktaba Complex and near the post office.

Gazelle Safaris Internet Café (Jacaranda Rd; per hr Tsh1000; 🕑 8.30am-5.30pm, sometimes later) At Gazelle Safaris.

Nane Information Centre (Market Sq; per hr Tsh1000; 🕑 8am-6.30pm Mon-Sat)

MEDICAL SERVICES
Aga Khan Medical Centre (☎ 025-250 2043; cnr North & Post Sts; 🕑 8am-8pm Mon-Sat, 9am-2pm Sun) Just north of the market.

MONEY
CRDB (Karume Ave) ATM (Visa only).
NBC (cnr Karume & Kaunda Aves) Changes cash; ATM (Visa only).
Stanbic (Karume Ave) ATM (Visa, MasterCard, Maestro Cirrus); just up from CRDB.

POST & TELEPHONE
Post Office (Post St; 🕑 8am-6pm)
Telephone office (🕑 8am-6.30pm Mon-Fri, Sat 8am-3pm) At the post office; Tsh2000 per minute to anywhere.

TOURIST INFORMATION
Gazelle Safaris (☎ 025-250 2482, 0713-069179; www.gazellesafaris.com; Jacaranda Rd) A new and helpful operator that can help you arrange guides and transport for excursions around Mbeya, excursions to Kitulo National Park, reliable car rental and safaris further afield, especially in the southern circuit.

Sisi Kwa Sisi (Station Rd) Near the rhino statue between the market and the bus station, this sometimes-on, sometimes-off place can occasionally be useful for arranging guides to local attractions.

Dangers & Annoyances
As a major transport junction, Mbeya attracts many transients, particularly in the area around the bus station. Watch your luggage here, don't change money with anyone, only buy bus tickets in the bus company offices and avoid walking alone through the small valley behind the station. Also be very wary of anyone presenting themselves as a tourist

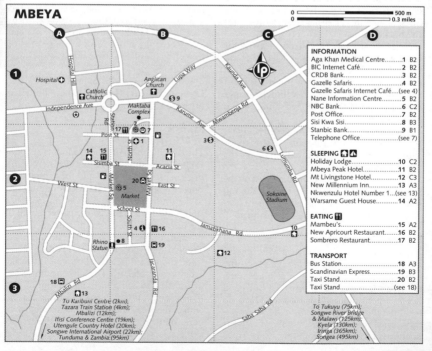

MBEYA

0 _____ 500 m
0 _____ 0.3 miles

INFORMATION
Aga Khan Medical Centre.........**1** B2
BIC Internet Café......................**2** B2
CRDB Bank..............................**3** B2
Gazelle Safaris.........................**4** B2
Gazelle Safaris Internet Café....(see 4)
Nane Information Centre..........**5** B2
NBC Bank................................**6** C2
Post Office...............................**7** B2
Sisi Kwa Sisi............................**8** B3
Stanbic Bank...........................**9** B1
Telephone Office..................(see 7)

SLEEPING 🏠🏯
Holiday Lodge.........................**10** C2
Mbeya Peak Hotel...................**11** B2
Mt Livingstone Hotel...............**12** C3
New Millennium Inn................**13** A3
Nkwenzulu Hotel Number 1...(see 13)
Warsame Guest House.............**14** A2

EATING 🍴
Mambeu's................................**15** A2
New Apricourt Restaurant.......**16** B2
Sombrero Restaurant...............**17** B2

TRANSPORT
Bus Station.............................**18** A3
Scandinavian Express..............**19** B3
Taxi Stand...............................**20** B2
Taxi Stand..........................(see 18)

To Kariboni Centre (2km);
Tazara Train Station (4km);
Mbalizi (12km);
Ifisi Conference Centre (19km);
Utengule Country Hotel (20km);
Songwe International Airport (22km);
Tunduma & Zambia (95km)

To Tukuyu (75km);
Songwe River Bridge
& Malawi (125km);
Kyela (130km);
Iringa (365km);
Songea (495km)

THE SOUTHERN HIGHLANDS

For more about the Southern Highlands region, see www.southernhighlandstz.org or get a copy of Liz de Leyser's excellent *A Guide to the Southern Highlands of Tanzania*, available at many bookstores and hotels in the region for Tsh5000. The booklet is an essential companion if you'll be visiting Kitulo National Park (p290).

---

guide and don't make tourist arrangements with anyone outside of an office.

Sleeping
BUDGET
Karibuni Centre (☎ 025-250 3035/4178; mec@maf.or.tz; camping per person Tsh3000, d/tr Tsh15,000/19,000) This clean and quiet mission-run place is in an enclosed compound where you can also pitch a tent, and has long been popular with campers and budget travellers. Rooms, most of which are en suite, are solid value, and there's a good restaurant (meals cost about Tsh4000 and it's open from 7.30am to 8pm Monday to Friday and 3pm Saturday; on Sunday it's open for breakfast only). Karibuni is 3km southwest of the town centre and about 10 minutes on foot from the *dalla-dalla* stop for transport into town. Watch for the signpost along the north side of the main highway and about 500m west of the first junction coming from Dar es Salaam. From the turn-off, head through what looks like an empty lot for about 300m to reach the gate.

Warsame Guest House (Sisimba St; s/d without bathroom Tsh3000/4000) This is one of Mbeya's cheapest options, with surprisingly decent rooms (no mosquito nets), grubby shared facilities and a central location just northwest of the market.

Holiday Lodge (☎ 025-250 2821; Jamatikhana Rd; d Tsh10,000-12,000, without bathroom Tsh3500) A somewhat faded, whitewashed local guesthouse with clean-ish rooms – some with bathroom – and meals with advance order. It's just off the main road behind the large Rift Valley Hotel, about 10 minutes' walk from the market area and about 15 minutes on foot from the bus stand.

Other recommendations:

New Millennium Inn (☎ 025-250 0599; Mbalizi Rd; s Tsh 7000-10,000, without bathroom Tsh6000) Located directly opposite the bus station and convenient if you have an early bus. Rooms are small, noisy and reasonably clean;

there's no food. The more expensive rooms have beds big enough for two, but there's no same-gender sharing.

Nkwenzulu Hotel Number 1 (☎ 025-250 2225; Mbalizi Rd; s/d Tsh15,000/20,000) Next to New Millennium Inn and of a similar standard, this hotel is not to be confused with the grubbier Nkwenzulu Hotel Number 3, which is at the base of the small hill and is the closest place to get a meal.

MIDRANGE & TOP END
Utengule Country Hotel (☎ 025-256 0100, 0753-020901; www.riftvalley-zanzibar.com; camping per site US$10, cottages per person US$30, s/tw/ste/f from US$55/80/135/120; 🏊) This lovely lodge is set on a working coffee plantation in the hills about 20km west of Mbeya with beautiful sunset views over the surrounding hills. There's a range of accommodation for all budgets, including spacious standard rooms and two-storey king-size suites with an upper balcony. There's also a family room set off on its own, plus large, self-catering cottages in separate grounds well away from the main hotel. Surrounding are expansive grounds with squash and tennis courts and a pool. The hotel makes a comfortable base for exploring the surrounding region, and guides, including for climbs up Mbeya Peak, and pricey car rentals can be arranged. Take the Tunduma road west from Mbeya for about 12km to Mbalizi, where there's a signposted turn-off to the right. Follow this road for 8.5km, keeping left at the first fork. The lodge is signposted to the right. Via public transport, take any Tunduma-bound *dalla-dalla* to Mbalizi, from where sporadic pick-ups en route to Chunya will take you within about 2km of the lodge. Credit cards are accepted up to US$450 maximum. Free pick-ups from Mbeya can be arranged if you're staying more than one night.

Mbeya Peak Hotel (☎ 025-250 3473; Acacia St; s/d/ste Tsh17,500/20,000/50,000) With a central, sunny setting and decent rooms, some with views over the hills, this is one of the better-value choices. It's on a small side street about 300m east of the market. There's also a restaurant with garden seating (meals from Tsh4000).

Mt Livingstone Hotel (☎ 025-250 3334, 0713-350484; Jamatikhana Rd; s/d from Tsh35,000/55,000) Once the *grande dame* of Mbeya's hotels, this place is past its prime, although after recent renovations it once again offers quite decent value. There are a variety of rooms, including the nicer deluxe ones on the ground floor, and a restaurant. It's in a quiet area about 200m off Jamatikhana Rd.

Another recommendation:

Ifisi Conference Centre (☎ 025-250 4178, 0753-011622; mec@maf.or.tz; Tanzam Hwy; r Tsh30,000-40,000) A church-run centre about 20km from Mbeya and 7km past Mbalizi junction, with spacious rooms and a restaurant. There's also a guesthouse (r Tsh15,000) in the compound, with no-frills, good-value rooms with bathrooms.

Eating & Drinking

Mambeu (cnr Sisimba St & Market Sq; meals Tsh1000; ☯ lunch & dinner) A local favourite, with inexpensive *ugali* (a staple made from maize or cassava flour, or both), chips, chicken and the like.

New Apricourt Restaurant (Jacaranda Rd; meals from Tsh2000; ☯ lunch & dinner) Good, inexpensive meals, just opposite Gazelle Safaris.

Sombrero Restaurant (Post St; meals Tsh5000-7500; ☯ breakfast, lunch & dinner) A limited menu, including vegetarian curry, spaghetti bolognaise and a few other standards.

Utengule Country Hotel (☎ 025-256 0100, 0753-020901; www.riftvalley-zanzibar.com; meals about Tsh12,500; ☯ breakfast, lunch & dinner) The place to go for fine dining, with a daily set menu and à la carte, and a bar. On Sunday afternoons there's a pizza and barbecue lunch on the lawn. Speciality coffees (including to take home) are a feature. See p293 for details on how to get there.

For self-catering, try the small shops around the market area, most of which have reasonable selections of boxed juices, tinned cheese and the like.

Getting There & Away

AIR

Songwe international airport is being constructed about 22km outside Mbeya near Mbalizi, but its opening has been indefinitely postponed. Meanwhile, the Mbeya airfield, about 5km south of town, handles occasional charter flights.

BUS

Scandinavian Express departs daily to Dar es Salaam at 7am (Tsh25,000, 12 hours), going via Iringa (Tsh13,000) and Morogoro. Departures are currently from the bus station, but are scheduled to be moved to the Scandinavian office on Jacaranda St, just down from Gazelle Safaris. It's also possible to take Scandinavian's Lusaka-Dar 'luxury' line from Mbeya to Dar (Tsh31,000, 12 hours), departing Mbeya about 11am. Sumry line is the next best bet, with a daily departure at 6.30am (Tsh22,000).

To Njombe (Tsh7000, four hours) and Songea (Tsh12,000, eight hours), Super Feo departs daily at 6am, sometimes with a later departure as well.

To Tukuyu (Tsh1500, one to 1½ hours), Kyela (Tsh3000, two to 2½ hours) and the Malawi border (Tsh3000, two to 2½ hours; take the Kyela bus – see p351), there are two or three smaller Coastal buses daily. It's also possible to get to the Malawi border via *dalla-dallas* that run throughout the day, but you'll probably need to change vehicles in Tukuyu. For Itungi port, you'll need to change vehicles in Kyela.

To Lilongwe (Malawi), there's a bus several times weekly departing Dar es Salaam at 5am, reaching Mbeya between 3pm and 4pm, and then continuing to Lilongwe. Coming from the other direction, expect long delays. For more on connections between Mbeya and Malawi, see p351.

To Tunduma, on the Zambian border, there are daily minibuses (Tsh2500, two hours). Once over the border, you can change to Zambian transport. Scandinavian Express has a Dar es Salaam-Mbeya-Tunduma-Lusaka service (Tsh46,000 between Mbeya and Lusaka, departing Mbeya four times weekly at 5pm and Lusaka at about the same time); also see p353.

To Sumbawanga, the best bet is Sumry, which goes daily at 6am and 8am (Tsh10,000 to Tsh12,000, seven hours). For Mpanda, you'll need to change vehicles in Sumbawanga. Plan on spending the night there, since most vehicles to Mpanda depart Sumbawanga in the morning, although sometimes in the dry season it's possible to get a direct connection without staying overnight in Sumbawanga.

To Tabora, there are a few vehicles weekly during the dry season, going via Rungwa. Some, which you can pick up at Mbalizi junction, take the western route via Saza and Makongolosi, while others – catch them along the main Tanzam highway just east of central Mbeya – go via Chunya.

TRAIN

Tickets for all classes should be booked at least several days in advance at the **Tazara train station** (☯ 8am-noon & 2-5pm Mon-Fri, 10am-1pm Sat). See p361 for schedules and fares between Mbeya and Dar es Salaam, and p353 for information about connections with Zambia.

Getting Around

Taxis park at the bus station and near the market. The Tazara train station is 4km out of town on the Tanzania–Zambia highway (Tsh2000 in a taxi). *Dalla-dallas* from the road in front of Nkwenzulu Hotel Number 1 run to the station and to Mbalizi, but the ones to the station often don't have room for luggage.

AROUND MBEYA
Loleza & Mbeya Peaks

Rising up over Mbeya from the north is **Loleza Peak** (2656m; also known as Mt Kaluwe), which can be climbed as an easy half-day hike. There's an antenna at the top, so you can't go to the summit, but you can still get high enough for views. The walk begins on the road running north from town past the hospital.

Just west of Loleza is **Mbeya Peak** (2820m), the highest point in the Mbeya range and an enjoyable day hike. There are several possible routes. One goes from Mbalizi junction, about 12km west of town on the Tunduma road. Take a *dalla-dalla* to Mbalizi, get out at the sign for Utengule Country Hotel, head right and follow the dirt road for about 1km to a sign for St Mary's Seminary. Turn right here and follow the road up past the seminary to Lunji Farm and then up to the peak. With a vehicle, you can park at Lunji Farm and go the remaining way on foot. For an alternative route, proceed as above, but ignore the turn-off to the seminary and keep walking along the road from Mbalizi

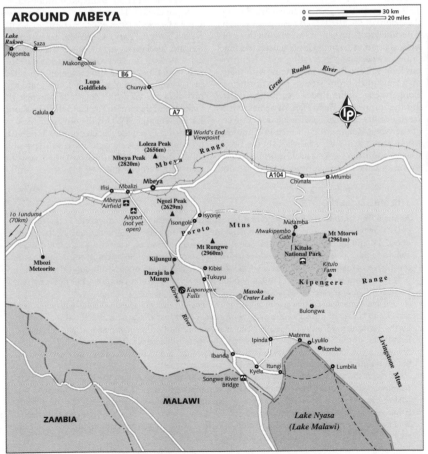

AROUND MBEYA

towards Utengule Country Hotel. Just after the seminary turn-off you'll see a tiny bridge. Continue past two more small bridges to an unmarked dirt path heading off to the right, 2.7km from Mbalizi junction. This path winds its way towards the peak, though you'll probably need to ask locals to point out the way as it forks several times. Allow five to six hours for the return trip, a bit less for the slightly shorter Lunji Farm route. There's also another, longer route from Mbeya, beginning near Lolozi Secondary School to the west of town.

Both Loleza and Mbeya Peak should only be climbed accompanied by a guide, which you can arrange at Gazelle Safaris (p292) or Sisi Kwa Sisi (p292) in Mbeya.

Chunya

This old gold-mining town came to life during the height of the 1920s gold rush, after which it declined to its present status as something of a ghost town. Although Chunya itself has few draws, it's part of an interesting and adventurous loop to Lake Rukwa for anyone with their own transport. From Mbeya, head northeast along the edge of the Mbeya escarpment, passing the impressive **World's End Viewpoint**, with views over the Usangu catchment area (source of the Great Ruaha River). Once in Chunya, where there is a basic guesthouse, it's possible to continue via Saza and Ngomba to the shores of Lake Rukwa, although there are no

facilities en route. You can return the same way, or alternatively, at Saza, head south via Galula and Utengule Country Hotel towards Mbeya on a somewhat rougher road.

Pick-ups go daily between Mbeya and Chunya (three hours), but you'll probably need to stay overnight in Chunya as return transport departs in the mornings. Departures are from just outside of Mbeya before the Sae area for the northern loop, and from Mbalizi junction for the road going via Galula. The rough route from Chunya north to Rungwa and on to Tabora is traversed by several buses weekly during the dry season.

Lake Rukwa

Remote Lake Rukwa is a large salt lake notable for its many water birds and its enormous crocodile population. The northern section is part of Rukwa Game Reserve, which is contiguous with Katavi National Park. As the lake has no outlet, its water level varies greatly between the wet and dry seasons. It rarely exceeds about 3m in depth, and sometimes splits into two lakes separated by swamplands. From Mbeya, the main approaches are via Chunya or alternatively via Galula, and then on to Saza and the lake shore. For either route, 4WD is the only realistic way to visit, and even then, access to the shoreline is difficult. There are no facilities. It's also possible (and easier via public transport) to access the lake from Sumbawanga; see p271.

THE MBOZI METEORITE

About 65km southwest of Mbeya is the Mbozi (also known as Mbosi) meteorite – the fourth-largest meteorite in the world, with an estimated weight of about 25 metric tons, a length of about 3m and a height of about 1m. Scientists are unsure of when it hit the earth, but it is assumed to have been many thousands of years ago, since there are no traces of the crater that it must have made when it fell, nor any local legends regarding its origins. Although the site was only discovered by outsiders in 1930, it had been known to locals for centuries, but not reported because of various associated taboos.

Like most meteorites, the one at Mbozi is composed primarily of iron (90%), with about 8% nickel and traces of phosphorous and other elements. It was declared a protected monument by the Tanzanian government in 1967 and is now mounted on a small pedestal and under the jurisdiction of the Department of Antiquities. The meteorite's dark colour is due to its high iron content, while its burnished look comes from the melting and other heating that occurred as the meteorite hurtled through the atmosphere towards Earth.

To reach the site you will need your own vehicle. From Mbeya, follow the main road towards Tunduma. About 50km from Mbeya there is a signposted turn-off to the left. From here, it's 13km further down a dirt road (no public transport). During the wet season, you'll need a 4WD. Otherwise, a 2WD can get through without difficulty, except perhaps for a tiny stream about 2km before the meteorite. There is a caretaker. There is no charge for visiting, but you can buy an informative leaflet with details on the meteorite.

TUKUYU

☎ 025

The small town of Tukuyu is set in the heart of a beautiful area of hills and orchards near Lake Nyasa. There are many hikes and natural attractions nearby, but only a basic tourist infrastructure (though this is slowly changing), so be prepared to rough things.

NBC in the centre of town changes cash and travellers cheques and has an ATM (Visa only), and you can get online at **Syaka Internet Café** (per hr Tsh1000), diagonally opposite the bank, and **Hope Internet Café** (per hr Tsh1000), in the Lutheran compound next to the bank.

Rungwe Tea & Tours (www.rungweteatours.com), a small, locally run place next to the post office and just off the main road leading up to Landmark Hotel, can help you organise guides for hikes and excursions in the surrounding area. Prices start about Tsh15,000 per day including a guide and local community fee. Another contact for arranging guides is Bongo Camping (p298).

Hiking

Hiking is possible throughout most of the year, although during the wet season paths get very muddy. The best months are from July to October. Below are brief descriptions of a few routes. Topographical maps of the area are available from the Surveys & Mapping Division in Dar es Salaam (p85); the booklet *A Guide to the Southern Highlands of Tanzania* has detailed descriptions (see the boxed text, p293).

MT RUNGWE

This 2960m dormant volcano, much of which is protected as the Rungwe Forest Reserve, rises up to the east of the main road north of Tukuyu, adjoining Kitulo National Park. It marks the point where the eastern and western arms of the Rift Valley meet, and is an important centre of endemism. If you start early, you can hike up and down in a day – passing through lovely patches of tropical forest; you'll need to allow about 10 hours. There are several routes, including one starting from near Rungwe Secondary School, signposted off the Mbeya road about 15km north of Tukuyu. A guide can be arranged at Rungwe or in Tukuyu. Mt Rungwe can also be reached as a day hike from Isongole village between Tukuyu and Mbeya.

NGOZI PEAK & CRATER LAKE

This lushly vegetated 2629m-high volcanic peak, with its beautiful, deep-blue lake – the subject of local legends – lying 200m below the crater rim, is about 7km west of the main road north of Tukuyu. To get here via public transport, take any *dalla-dalla* travelling between Mbeya and Tukuyu and ask to be dropped off; there's a small sign for Ngozi at the turn-off. Once at the turn-off, if you haven't come with a guide you'll be approached by locals offering their services; the going rate is about Tsh2000. If you're short on time, you can go about half the distance from the main road to Ngozi by vehicle and then walk the remainder of the way. Once at the base, it's about another steep hour or so on foot up to the crater rim.

DARAJA LA MUNGU

This 'Bridge of God', south of Ngozi Peak and west of the main road, is a natural bridge estimated to have been formed around 1800 million years ago by water flowing through cooling lava that spewed out from the nearby Rungwe volcano. The bridge spans a small waterfall. Further south along the Kiriwa River are the pretty **Kaporogwe Falls.** Also nearby is **Kijungu** (Cooking Pot), where the river tumbles through a rocky gorge.

Sleeping & Eating

Lutengano Moravian Centre (☎ 0784-592633; camping Tsh5000, s without bathroom Tsh4000, tr Tsh6000) This no-frills place has a handful of simple rooms with nets, plus large grounds where you can pitch a tent, and is sometimes used by overland trucks. Meals can be arranged or you can use the kitchen. Head north from Tukuyu for about 3km to the signposted turn-off on the western side of the road, from where it's 7km down a dirt road. There's a pick-up from Tukuyu (Tsh1000) daily except Sunday, departing from the minibus station near the market about 2pm and returning the next morning.

Langiboss Lodge (☎ 025-255 2080; r without bathroom Tsh4000, d Tsh8000) The Langiboss was long Tukuyu's only accommodation, and is still one of the better shoestring options, with no-frills clean rooms around a tiny courtyard and meals with lots of advance notice. Hot-water buckets can be arranged. It's about 1km east of the town centre; from the small roundabout at the top of town, head straight and then right. If you have trouble contacting them, book through Rungwe Tea & Tours (left).

**COMMUNITY TOURISM SPOTLIGHT:
BONGO CAMPING**

Bongo Camping (www.bongocamping.com; camping per person Tsh5000) This community-integrated place has a pleasant camping area with clean showers and toilets, cooking facilities for campers, plus a simple restaurant and secure parking. Profits go to support local educational initiatives, and there's also a small local theatre group that gives performances on Sunday afternoons. It's at Kibisi village just off the main road – coming from Mbeya, it's signposted to the left shortly before reaching Tukuyu.

DM Motel (☎ 025-255 2332; r Tsh10,000) Clean en-suite rooms with a large bed (no same-gender sharing permitted) and meals on request. It's just off the main road at the turn-off into Tukuyu town, and signposted.

Landmark Hotel (☎ 025-255 2400, 022-245 0510; landmahotel@yahoo.co.uk; camping per site Tsh8000, s/d/tw from Tsh20,000/25,000/30,000) This hotel has modern rooms, all with TV and hot water, green grounds where you can pitch a tent (showers can be arranged) and a restaurant. It's the large multistorey building at the main junction just up from NBC bank.

Ima's Kitchen (Main Rd; meals from Tsh1000) Just downhill from NBC bank, with inexpensive meals and snacks.

Getting There & Away

Minibuses run several times daily between Tukuyu and both Mbeya (Tsh1000, one to 1½ hours along a scenic, tarmac road) and Kyela (Tsh1500, one hour).

Two roads connect Tukuyu with the northern end of Lake Nyasa. The main tarmac road heads southwest and splits at Ibanda, with the western fork going to Songwe River Bridge and into Malawi, and the eastern fork to Kyela and Itungi port. A secondary dirt road, which was being rehabilitated as we passed through, heads southeast from Tukuyu to Ipinda and then east towards Matema.

LAKE NYASA

Lake Nyasa (also known as Lake Malawi) is Africa's third-largest lake after Lake Victoria and Lake Tanganyika. It's more than 550km long, up to 75km wide and as deep as 700m in parts. It also has a high level of biodiversity, containing close to one-third of the world's known cichlid species. The lake is bordered by Tanzania, Malawi and Mozambique. The Tanzanian side is rimmed to the east by the Livingstone Mountains, whose green, misty slopes form a stunning backdrop that cascades down to the sandy shoreline. Few roads reach the towns strung out between the mountains and the shore along the lake's eastern side. To the north and east, the mountains lead on to the Kitulo Plateau.

While the mountains are beckoning to hikers, you'll need to be completely self-sufficient (including with tent and water filter) and carry a GPS. One possibile fun a route is from the mission station of Bulongwa (reached via *dalla-dalla* from Njombe) to Matema, which offers some superb views as you make your way down to the lake shore. Allow about 14 hours for the trip and start out at daybreak. There are inexpensive guesthouses in Bulongwa where you can spend the night before. A longer version of this hike is also possible, starting near the Kitulo Park gate. Another possibility is to take a *dalla-dalla* from Njombe to Ludewa, from where you could make your way down to Lupingu and wait for the MV *Iringa*. Once at the shoreline, note that both crocociles and malaria-carrying *falciparum* mosquitoes are real hazards, so take the appropriate precautions by the water.

Other places of interest around the Tanzanian side of the lake include the following (from north to south).

Kyela
☎ 025

There's no reason to linger in this scruffy, nondescript transit town unless your boat arrives late at Itungi and you need somewhere to spend the night. Photography is prohibited in most areas. The surrounding area – much of which is wetlands dotted with rice paddies – is more appealing, and if you do find yourself here with some extra time, it's possible to organise cultural visits with the enterprising Newton Mwakabambo; contact **Kyela Envirocare** (☎ 025-254 0280, 0787-630814; kyelaenvirocare@yahoo .com), based at the CCM building in Kyela.

There's **internet access** (per hr Tsh1000; ⏰ 7am-9pm) in the large container shop just next to the entrance to Matema Beach Hotel. For updated information on the sailing schedules for MV *Iringa* and MV *Songea*, ask at

Kyela Commercial, situated just around the corner from Steak Inn Restaurant. There are no ATMs; the best bet for changing money is with one of the hotel proprietors or shop owners.

SLEEPING & EATING
Makete Half London Guest House (☎ 025-254 0459; s Tsh6500) Rooms here are basic but clean, with mosquito nets, one small-ish bed and bathrooms. There are no doubles. It's in the centre of town, opposite the former Scandinavian Express bus office.

Pattaya Hotel (☎ 025-254 0015; s/d from Tsh7000/ 15,000) A step up from the Makete, with rooms with either one or two large beds, nets and bathrooms. It's on the same road as the Makete and the old Scandinavian bus office, and about 300m in from the corner (heading northwest).

Matema Beach Hotel (☎ 025-254 0158, 0786-565117; matemabeach2002@yahoo.com; Tukuyu Rd; s/d from Tsh12,000/20,000; 🏊) This incongruous place, with its massive entrance area about 500m before town, seems rather out of place in sleepy Kyela. Rooms are fine for the price – all with TV – and most have computers (though no internet facilities yet), and there's a restaurant. Staff can help arrange guides if you're interested in exploring the surrounding area. A pool is in the works.

Kyela Resort (☎ 025-254 0152, 0784-232650; kyelaresort @yahoo.com; s/d Tsh25,000/35,000; 🏊) If you have your own transport, this is a good bet, with simple but pleasant, well-ventilated rooms (windows on both walls) and a restaurant. It's about 1.5km from town, just off the Tukuyu road.

Steak Inn Restaurant (meals Tsh1500) One block north from the Pattaya Hotel, this restaurant has inexpensive meals (though no steaks).

GETTING THERE & AWAY
Minibuses go several times daily from Kyela to Tukuyu (Tsh1500, one hour) and Mbeya (Tsh3000, two to 2½ hours) from the minibus stand about two blocks north of Pattaya Hotel. Pick-ups run daily between Kyela and Itungi port (Tsh200), in rough coordination with boat arrivals and departures.

Itungi
Itungi, about 11km southeast of Kyela, is the main port for the Tanzanian Lake Nyasa ferry service. There is no accommodation,

and photography is forbidden. Pick-ups run sporadically, in rough coordination with boat arrivals and departures, to and from Kyela (Tsh200). For ferry schedules and fares, see p358.

Matema
☎ 025
This quiet lakeside settlement is the only spot on northern Lake Nyasa that has any sort of tourist infrastructure, and with its stunning beachside setting backed by lush mountains it makes an ideal spot to relax for a few days. You can arrange walks and dugout canoe rides or lounge on the beach. On Saturdays, there's a **pottery market** at Lyulilo village, about 1.5km east of the Lutheran Guest House along the lake shore, where Kisi pots from Ikombe are sold. There's nowhere in Matema to change money, so bring enough shillings with you.

SLEEPING & EATING
On the beach about 300m past the Lutheran Guest House, the Swiss-built **Matema Lake Shore Resort** (☎ 025-250 4178, 0754-487267; mec@maf .or.tz; camping per person with shower Tsh3000, d without bathroom Tsh10,000, 3-, 4- & 5-bed r Tsh20,000-30,000) has two en-suite chalets, each of which can accommodate up to five people, plus two smaller en-suite cottages, with some triples and a quad, and a simple meals available. There's also a grill, with a nominal charge for charcoal use. Bookings can also be arranged through the Karibuni Centre in Mbeya (p293).

Rooms at the no-frills beachside **Lutheran Guest House** (☎ 0787-275164; d/q without bathroom Tsh15,000/25,000) are rather dilapidated these days, although the local ambience and cuisine are amenable. Before heading down, check in with the **Lutheran mission** (☎ 025-255 2597/8) in Tukuyu, just downhill from the NBC bank, who will radio to be sure space is available.

GETTING THERE & AWAY
Boat
The MV *Iringa* (p358) stops at Matema on its way from Itungi port down the eastern lake shore. Note that the MV *Songea* (p354) doesn't stop here, which means you'll need to head back to Itungi port if you're going to Malawi.

Bus

From Tukuyu, pick-ups to Ipinda leave around 8am most mornings from the roundabout by NBC bank (Tsh1500, two hours). Although drivers sometimes say they are going all the way to Matema, generally they go only as far as Ipinda. About 20km out of Tukuyu en route to Ipinda is the scenic Masoko Crater Lake, into which fleeing Germans allegedly dumped a small fortune of gold pieces and coins during WWI. From Ipinda, pick-ups run sporadically to Matema (Tsh1500, 35km), departing around 2pm, which means you'll need to wait around in Ipinda for a while. Departures from Matema back to Ipinda are in the morning. Chances are better on weekends for finding a lift between Matema and Ipinda with a private vehicle. If you get stuck in Ipinda, there are several basic guesthouses.

There's also at least one pick-up daily from Kyela to Ipinda (Tsh1500), a few of which then continue on to Matema. From Kyela, it's also fairly easy to hire a vehicle to drop you off.

Car & Motorcycle

If you are heading to Matema in your own vehicle, the usual route from Tukuyu is via Ipinda (not via Kyela). During the dry season and with a 4WD, it's also possible to take the main road from Tukuyu to Kyela and then head east along a signposted, bad road to Ipinda and on to Matema. The Lutheran Mission in Tukuyu can sometimes arrange transport between Tukuyu and Matema from about US$70 per vehicle one way (about US$120 return, including waiting time).

Ikombe

The tiny village of Ikombe is notable for its clay pots, which are made by the local Kisi women and sold at markets in Mbeya and elsewhere in the region. It's reached via dugout canoe from Matema. There are no tourist facilities.

Liuli

Liuli is the site of an old and still-active Anglican mission and the small St Anne's mission hospital, the major health facility on the eastern lake shore. It's also notable for a (with some imagination) sphinxlike rock lying just offshore, which earned the settlement the name of Sphinxhafen during the German era. There's no accommodation.

Mbamba Bay

The relaxing outpost of Mbamba Bay is the southernmost Tanzanian port on Lake Nyasa. With its low-key ambience and attractive beach fringed by palm, banana and mango trees, it makes a good spot to spend a few days waiting for the ferry or as a change of pace if you have been travelling inland around Songea or Tunduma.

SLEEPING & EATING

Neema Lodge (Mama Simba's; r without bathroom Tsh7000) Decent value, with very basic but adequate rooms, meals and a pleasant waterside setting. To get here, turn left just before the bridge as you enter town.

Nyasa View (d without bathroom Tsh7500) Also not bad, though the rooms aren't really worth the marginal price difference compared with those at the Neema. Meals can be arranged. To get here, continue straight through town after the bridge, towards the beach.

Both places can help organise boat hire for exploring the nearby shoreline.

GETTING THERE & AWAY

There's one direct vehicle daily from Songea (see p303), but otherwise you will need to change vehicles at Mbinga.

For details of ferry services between Mbamba Bay and Itungi port, see p358. For ferry connections with Nkhata Bay, see p354.

From Mbamba Bay northbound, there are occasional 4WDs to Liuli mission station. Between Liuli and Lituhi there is no public transport and little traffic, and from Lituhi northwards, there is no road along the lake, only a footpath. There's also a rough track leading from Lituhi southeast towards Kitai and Songea, which opens the possibility for an interesting loop.

Entering or leaving Tanzania via Mbamba Bay, you will need to stop at the immigration post office/police station near the boat landing to take care of passport formalities.

MBINGA
☎ 026

This small but prosperous town lies en route between Songea and Mbamba Bay in the heart of one of Tanzania's major coffee-producing areas. If you're travelling via public transport, you'll probably need to change vehicles here. The main points of interest are the large Catholic cathedral and the panoramic road leading down to Mbamba Bay and Lake Nyasa.

For accommodation and meals, try **Mbicu Hotel** (☎ 026-264 0168; r Tsh12,000), which also has a restaurant. It's on the edge of town along the Songea road.

SONGEA
☎ 025

The sprawling town of Songea, just over 1000m in altitude, is capital of the surrounding Ruvuma region and will probably seem like a major metropolis if you've just come from Tunduru or Mbamba Bay. Away from the scruffy and crowded central market and bus station area, it's a pleasant, attractive place, with shaded leafy streets, surrounded by beautiful rolling hill-country dotted with yellow sunflowers and grazing cattle. The main ethnic group here is the Ngoni, who migrated into the area from South Africa during the 19th century, subduing many smaller tribes along the way. Songea takes its name from one of their greatest chiefs, who was killed following the Maji Maji rebellion (see p302) and is buried about 1km from town near the Maji Maji museum.

Information

NBC, on the street behind the market, changes cash, and both NBC and CRDB (at the beginning of the Njombe road) have ATMs (Visa cards only). There's an internet connection at **Valongo Computer Centre** (Songea Network Centre; per hr Tsh1000; ⏰ 7.30am-9pm), on a side street directly opposite the main market entrance. The immigration office (where you'll need to get your passport stamped if you are travelling to or from Mozambique), is at the beginning of the Tunduru Rd, about 400m up and opposite Angoni Arms Hotel.

Sights & Activities

Songea's colourful **market** (Soko Kuu) along the main road is worth a visit. The impressive carved wooden doors on the **cathedral** diagonally opposite the bus stand are also worth a look, as are the beautiful wall paintings inside.

About 1km from the centre of town, off the Njombe road, is the small **Maji Maji museum** (admission free but donation appreciated; ⏰ 8am-4pm Mon-Fri), which is quite run down but nevertheless interesting. Behind the museum is the tomb of Chief Songea. The museum is

kept locked; ask for the caretaker, who lives nearby. To get to the museum from town, take the first tarmac road to the right after passing CRDB bank and continue about 200m. The museum entrance is on the left; look for the large, pale-blue archway.

About 30km west of town, in Peramiho, is a large Benedictine **monastery**.

Sleeping
BUDGET

Anglican Church Hostel (☎ 026-260 0693; s/d Tsh3000/3500, without bathroom Tsh2000/2500) This long-standing place has no-frills rooms with mosquito nets, set around a courtyard in a quiet area just northwest of the main road. Food is available with advance order. Nearby, on the road leading into the hostel grounds, are ovens where you can buy fresh bread on weekday afternoons. To get to the hostel, head uphill from the bus stand, past the market to the Tanesco building. Go left and wind your way back about 400m to the Anglican church compound. The hostel is also signposted from the Njombe road.

Don Bosco Hostel (dm Tsh3000, s Tsh5000) Reasonably clean basic rooms and a central location are the attractions at this church-run hostel. Food can be arranged. It's two blocks off the main road, diagonally behind the Catholic church and a five-minute walk from the bus stand.

Annex of Yapender Lodge (☎ 026-260 2855, 0787-126414; s/d Tsh7000/8000) The slickest budget option in the town centre, with small, clean, no-frills rooms with bathroom, and buckets of hot water on request. From the bus stand, head uphill 400m past the market, take the first right (watch for the sign for the Lutheran church) and continue about 300m to the end of the dirt lane. It's diagonally opposite and just past the Lutheran church.

White House Inn (☎ 025-260 0892; r Tsh15,000) If you have your own transport, this is one of the better-value budget choices. Rooms are small and clean, and there's a restaurant with terrace seating serving tasty chicken and chips and other meals (from Tsh1500). It's about 2.5km north of the centre of town in the Bomba Mbili neighbourhood, set back about 200m from the Njombe road and signposted.

Angoni Arms Hotel (r Tsh22,000) This once-nice place has seen better days, but is still worth a look. Accommodation is in quiet

SOUTHERN HIGHLANDS

THE MAJI MAJI REBELLION

The Maji Maji rebellion, which was the strongest local revolt against the colonial government in German East Africa, is considered to contain some of the earliest seeds of Tanzanian nationalism. It began around the turn of the 20th century when colonial administrators set about establishing enormous cotton plantations in the southeast and along the railway line running from Dar es Salaam towards Morogoro. These plantations required large numbers of workers, most of whom were recruited as forced labour and required to work under miserable salary and living conditions. Anger at this harsh treatment and long-simmering resentment of the colonial government combined to ignite a powerful rebellion. The first outbreak was in 1905 in the area around Kilwa, on the coast. Soon all of southern Tanzania was involved, from Kilwa and Lindi in the southeast to Songea in the southwest. In addition to deaths on the battlefield, thousands died of hunger brought about by the Germans' scorched-earth policy, in which fields and grain silos in many villages were set on fire. Fatalities were undoubtedly exacerbated by a widespread belief among the Africans that enemy bullets would turn to water before reaching them, and so their warriors would not be harmed – hence the name Maji Maji (*maji* means 'water' in Swahili).

By 1907, when the rebellion was finally suppressed, close to 100,000 people had lost their lives. In addition, large areas of the south were left devastated and barren, and malnutrition was widespread. The Ngoni, a tribe of warriors much feared by their neighbours, put up the strongest resistance to the Germans. Following the end of the rebellion, they continued to wage guerrilla-style war until 1908, when the last shreds of their military-based society were destroyed. In order to quell Ngoni resistance once and for all, German troops hanged about 100 of their leaders and beheaded their most famous chief, Songea.

Among the effects of the Maji Maji uprising were a temporary liberalisation of colonial rule and replacement of the military administration with a civilian government. More significantly, the uprising promoted development of a national identity among many ethnic groups and intensified anti-colonial sentiment, kindling the movement for independence.

doubles in detached bungalows set in green grounds(there are a few larger, regular rooms as well for the same price). The water supply has long since been cut off, but staff bring you hot-water buckets for washing, and there's a restaurant with garden seating. It's about 1.5km from the market area, along the Tunduru road.

Also recommended:

Lika Guest House (Mwasiti St; s/d Tsh10,000/15,000) Small, clean rooms with TV, fan and parking. It's a six-minute walk downhill from the bus stand in the Mfaranyaki area, and signposted just off the main road.

MIDRANGE

Heritage Cottage (☎ 025-260 0888; Njombe Rd; r/ste Tsh30,000/40,000) This large, busy place has modern, clean rooms with TV, a popular and large bar-restaurant (rooms near the bar can get noisy on weekends), a lawn area behind and a small playground for children. It's about 3km north of town along the Njombe Rd.

Seed Farm Villa (☎ 025-260 2500, 0752-842086; seedfarmvilla@yahoo.co.uk; s/d from Tsh40,000/45,000) Just opened, this eight-room place is argu-

ably the most comfortable hotel in Songea, with modern, spacious and quiet rooms with TV and nets, set in tranquil garden surroundings away from the town centre in the Seed Farm area. There's a sitting room with TV and a restaurant (with advance order), and an internet connection is planned. Head out of town along the Tundumu Rd for 2.5km to the signposted turn-off, from where it's 200m further. Sometimes camping can be arranged in the grounds.

Eating

Agape Café (Main Rd; snacks & meals from Tsh1000; ✆ 8am-5.30pm) Just uphill from the Catholic church, with pastries and inexpensive meals.

Heritage Annex (Main Rd; meals about Tsh4000; ✆ lunch & dinner) At the upper end of the main road near the Tundumu–Njombe road junction and the post office, with snacks, chicken and chips and other standards, and slow service.

Of the hotel restaurants, those at White House Inn and Angoni Arms Hotel (allow plenty of time at the latter) are both worth a try.

Getting There & Away

To Dar es Salaam, Scandinavian Express departs daily at 6am (Tsh27,000, 12 to 13 hours). Super Feo also does this route (Tsh26,000); going with them as far as Iringa costs Tsh12,000.

To Mbeya, Super Feo departs daily at 6am in each direction (Tsh12,000, eight hours) via Njombe (Tsh7000, four hours). There are also departures to Njombe at 9.30am and 3pm.

For Mbamba Bay, there's one direct vehicle departing daily at 7am (Tsh8000, six to eight hours). Otherwise, you'll need to get transport to Mbinga (Tsh3500, four hours) and from there on to Mbamba Bay (Tsh5000). During the wet season, when the trip often needs to be done with 4WDs, prices rise.

Transport to Mozambique departs from the Majengo C area, southwest of the bus stand and about 600m in from the main road – ask locals to point out the way through the back streets. See p351 for more information.

TUNDURU

Dusty, remote Tunduru, halfway between Masasi and Songea, is in the centre of an important gemstone-mining region, with a bit of a Wild West feel. The town is also a truck and transit stop, and you'll need to spend at least one night here if travelling between Masasi and Songea. The better guesthouses are at the western end of town. There are plenty to choose from with rooms from about Tsh3000 to Tsh10,000; all are around the same standard.

Four-wheel drives to Songea also congregate at the western end of town. Reserve a seat for onward travel when you arrive in Tunduru, as the vehicles fill up quickly.

The road from Tunduru in either direction is in rough condition, especially during the rains, although thanks to recent rehabilitation work it's better than it was. There's at least one bus (and sometimes also a 4WD) daily between Tunduru and Masasi, departing by 6am (Tsh8000, five hours). Between Tunduru and Songea, the main options are 4WDs, which go daily (Tsh17,000, seven to eight hours, departing Tunduru between 3am and 7am and Songea by 6am), as well as usually one bus in the dry season. If you are staying at a guesthouse near the 4WD 'station' you can arrange for the driver to come and wake you before departure. There is little en route, so bring food and water with you.

Southeastern Tanzania

Time seems to have stood still in Tanzania's remote and sparsely populated southeast. It lacks the development and bustle of the north, tourists numbers are a relative trickle and Arusha's crush of Land Cruisers and safari companies is so far removed that it might as well be in another country. During the Mozambican war the southeast was considered to be a sensitive border zone and many areas were off limits to tourists. As a result – although travel restrictions have long since been lifted and the welcome here is as warm as it is elsewhere in the country – the region remains in many ways traditional and reserved. It makes an ideal destination for getting to know local life that has been relatively insulated from outside influences.

Among the southeast's major attractions are the untrammelled expanses of the Selous Game Reserve, with a clutch of intimate lodges, boat safaris and top-notch wildlife watching. Another draw is the long coastline. Here, deserted white-sand beaches shimmer under an unrelenting sun, shoals of colourful fish flit past amazing coral formations in Tanzania's two marine parks at Mafia island and Mnazi Bay, and the ruins on Kilwa Kisiwani and in other old Swahili towns testify to days when this part of the continent was the centre of trading networks stretching to the Far East.

Mafia and the Selous both offer a full range of accommodation and Western amenities. Elsewhere, while there are good air connections to major destinations, infrastructure is undeveloped, and road journeys can be long and rugged.

HIGHLIGHTS

- Taking a boat safari along the Rufiji River in **Selous Game Reserve** (p311)
- Diving amidst colourful fish or relaxing on white sands in the **Mafia archipelago** (p306)
- Exploring traces of bygone days at the old Swahili trading towns of **Mikindani** (p326) and **Kilwa Kivinje** (p319)
- Visiting the ruins of the famed medieval city-state of **Kilwa Kisiwani** (p318)
- Relaxing on the beaches around **Mtwara** (p322) and the **Mnazi Bay-Ruvuma Estuary Marine Park** (p327)

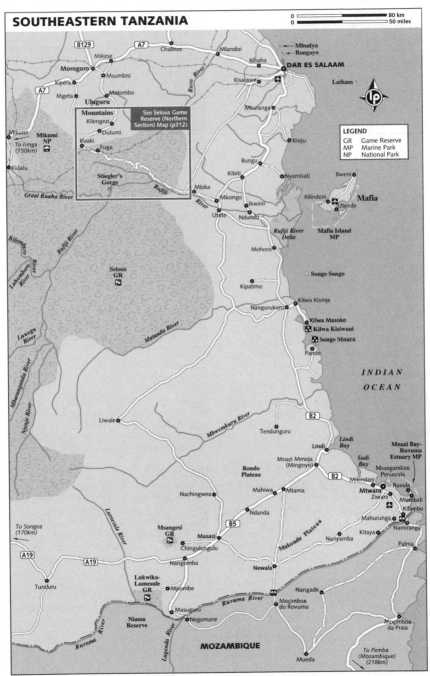

SOUTHEASTERN TANZANIA

SOUTHEASTERN TANZANIA

National Parks & Reserves

Selous Game Reserve (p311) covers much of southeastern Tanzania, although only the northern sector is open for tourism. Along the Ruvuma River are Lukwika-Lumesule and Msangesi Game Reserves (p330) – offbeat destinations outside of the hunting season for intrepid travellers with time – while along the coast are Mafia Island (p309) and Mnazi Bay-Ruvuma Estuary (p327) Marine Parks for diving and snorkelling.

Getting There & Around

Mafia, Selous Game Reserve, Kilwa Masoko, Lindi and Mtwara are easily reached by scheduled flights. Mafia and the Selous are also well-linked via air to Zanzibar, to the northern circuit parks, to other coastal destinations and to Ruaha National Park.

The road from Dar es Salaam south is tarmac to the Rufiji (where there's now a bridge), under rehabilitation from the Rufiji River to Lindi, and mostly tarmac from Lindi to Mtwara. Buses run year-round, and – barring breakdowns – it's possible to make the journey in a long day. Dhows ply the waters between other coastal towns; see p357. Inland, apart from the tarmac road between Mtwara and Masasi, there are only dirt roads, and minibuses and old Land Rovers are the only public transport.

The Tazara train passes along the Selous' northern border, and is a good option, especially for the northernmost camps.

MAFIA

☎ 023

Secluded and seductive Mafia – a green wedge of land surrounded by turquoise waters, pristine islets and glinting white sandbanks – remained off the beaten track for years, undiscovered by all except deep-sea fishing aficionados and a trickle of visitors. That's changing fast – the island's tourist accommodation has grown from one hotel to over half a dozen in just a few years. For now, though, Mafia remains free of the mass tourism that threatens to overwhelm Zanzibar. It makes an amenable post-safari respite and is a rewarding destination in its own right.

Among Mafia's attractions are its tranquil pace, stunning underwater life, upmarket lodges, a strong traditional culture and a long and fascinating history. Green and hawksbill turtles have breeding sites along the island's

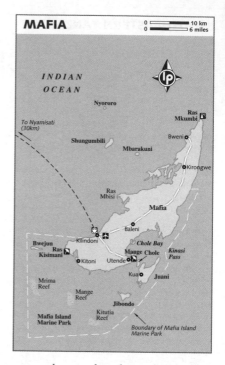

eastern shores and on the nearby islands of Juani and Jibondo. To protect these and other local ecosystems, the southeastern part of the island, together with offshore islets and waters, has been gazetted as a national marine park. Whale sharks (*potwe* in Swahili) visit Mafia between about November and February and are best seen offshore near Kilindoni.

History

In addition to Mafia island, the Mafia Archipelago includes Juani (southeast of Mafia), Chole (between Mafia and Juani), Jibondo (south of Juani) and at least a dozen other islets and sandbars. The archipelago first rose to prominence between the 11th and 13th centuries in the days when the Shirazis controlled much of the East African shoreline. Thanks to its central buffer position between the Rufiji River delta and the high seas of the Indian Ocean, it made an amenable trading base, and the local economy soon began to thrive. One of the first settlements was built during this era at Ras Kisimani, on Mafia's southwestern corner, followed by another at Kua on Juani.

By the time the Portuguese arrived in the early 16th century, Mafia had lost much of its significance and had come under the sway of the Sultan of Kilwa. In the early 18th century, the island's fortunes revived, and by the mid-19th century it had come within the domain of the powerful Omani sultanate, under which it flourished as a trade centre linking Kilwa to the south and Zanzibar to the north. It was during this era that the coconut palm and cashew plantations that now cover much of the island were established.

Following an attack by the Sakalava people from Madagascar, Mafia's capital was moved from Kua to the nearby tiny island of Chole. Chole's star ascended to the point where it became known as Chole Mjini (Chole City), while the now main island of Mafia was referred to as Chole Shamba (the Chole hinterlands). Mafia's administrative seat continued on Chole throughout the German colonial era until it was moved to Kilindoni on the main island by the British, who used Mafia as a naval and air base.

Today, farming and fishing are the main sources of livelihood for Mafia's approximately 45,000 residents, most of whom live on the main island. As a result, while shopping in the markets, you'll find cassavas, cashews and coconuts in abundance.

Orientation

Kilindoni – where all boats and planes arrive – is Mafia's hub, with the bank, port, market, small shops and several budget guesthouses. The only other settlement of any size is Utende, 15km southeast of Kilindoni on Chole Bay, where most of Mafia's upmarket lodges are located. The Utende-Chole Bay area is also the best divers' base. Mafia's western side is dotted with small villages, offshore islands and sandbanks, and stands of mangrove interspersed with patches of beach, including at Ras Mbisi, where there's a hotel.

Information

INTERNET ACCESS
Internet Café (Kilindoni; per hr Tsh2000) At New Lizu Hotel.

MEDICAL SERVICES & EMERGENCIES
For malaria tests, there's a village clinic on Chole Island. For treatment or for other serious ailments, go to Dar es Salaam.

MONEY
National Microfinance Bank Just off the airport road, and near the main junction in Kilindoni; changes cash only (dollars, euros and pounds). There are no ATMs.

TELEPHONE
Calls can be made at New Lizu Hotel in Kilindoni. Mobile networks now reach Mafia.

Sights

It doesn't take too much imagination to step back in time on Mafia's coconut plantations, with village life here going on much as it did during the island's Shirazi-era heyday. **Chole island** (day visitors per person US$5) is a good place to start exploring, especially around its crumbling but atmospheric ruins, which date from the 19th century. Also on Chole, thanks to the efforts of a local women's group who bought the area where an important nesting tree is located, is what is probably East Africa's only **fruit bat sanctuary** (Comoros lesser fruit bat). Chole Mjini (see boxed text on p310) has recently opened a restaurant at the ruins for day visitors.

The much larger and heavily vegetated **Juani** island, just southeast of Chole, has overgrown but evocative ruins at Kua, including the remains of several mosques dating from a Shirazi settlement during the 18th and 19th centuries, and crumbling palace walls. Also note the main ablutions area just to the right of the main entrance to the settlement. Access to the ruins is only possible at high tide. South of here is a channel and nearby lagoon for birding and swimming.

Sparsely vegetated **Jibondo**, while less aesthetically appealing than the other islands, and with inhabitants who are traditionally somewhat unwelcoming towards visitors, is intriguing in that it supports a population of about 3000 people although it has no natural water sources. Except for during the peak rainy season (when rain water is collected on the island from run-off), boats ply daily between Jibondo and Mafia island transporting large yellow containers filled with water. The best time to watch all the activity is just after sunrise, at the beach near Kinasi Lodge. Jibondo is also renowned as a boat-building centre, with much of the wood coming from the forests around Kilwa. In Jibondo's village centre, look for the giant, non-functional dhow (now in the process of being disassembled) and for the carved doorframe on the mosque, said to come from the old settlement at Kua.

On Mafia itself, there are good beaches at the three main Chole Bay lodges (the beach at Mafia Island Lodge is the best), and some idyllic nearby sandbanks; all the lodges arrange excursions. One of the closest is **Mange**, with beautiful white sand populated only by sand crabs and sea birds and surrounded by crystal-clear aqua waters. With more time, you can make your way through the coconut groves to the beach at **Ras Kisimani** in the southwestern corner of the island.

At **Ras Mkumbi**, Mafia's windswept northern-most point, there's a **lighthouse** dating to 1892, as well as **Kanga beach** and a forest that's home to monkeys, blue duikers and many birds.

Activities
DIVING & SNORKELLING
Mafia offers divers excellent corals, an impressive variety of fish, including numerous pelagics, and relaxing, uncrowded diving, often done from motorised dhows. There are various sites in Chole Bay, which is diveable year-round, plus seasonal diving outside the bay. The best month is generally October, and the least favourable are April, May and sometimes into June, when everything shuts down. The main dive operators (all of whom also arrange dive certification courses and snorkelling) include:

Big Blu (☎ 0784-918069; www.bigblumafia.org; Chole Bay; Single/double dives US$35/60 including equipment, snorkelling US$10 per person) A flexible, reasonably priced operator catering to budget and midrange travellers, and the only one on the island with a RIB (rubber inflatable boat) for accessing all dive sites fast. Also organises other water-based activities, including fishing and island excursions. . It's on the beach just north of Mafia Island Lodge.

Mafia Island Lodge Watersports Centre (☎ 022-260 1530; www.mafialodge.com; Mafia Island Lodge, Chole Bay; Single/double dives US$40/70 including equipment, snorkelling US$19 per person) A well-equipped place under the direction of Moez, a veteran diver with long experience on Mafia. Also offers a full range of watersports and excursions, and has a refurbished dhow for island sails.

Prices are similar to those in the Zanzibar Archipelago (see p118). Kinasi Lodge also offers diving and instruction for its guests, and Chole Mjini has a well-equipped dive centre for its guests where you can also arrange coral reef ecology courses (US$400, advance bookings only).

FISHING
Long popular in deep-sea fishing circles, Mafia is known especially for its marlin, sailfish, tuna and other big-game fish. Conditions are best between September and March, with June and July the least-appealing months due to strong winds. Contact the dive operators listed above, or Kinasi Lodge, which offers light sport fishing, and big game fishing from Mafia's northern tip.

Within the marine park, fishing is prohibited in much of Chole Bay, in Kinasi Pass, along the eastern edge of the island to the north of Chole Bay, along the eastern and southern edges of Juani, along the eastern edge of Jibondo, and around the Mange and Kitutia reefs. Sport fishing is permitted elsewhere, although there's a maximum weight limit for most species. Spear-gun and harpoon fishing are prohibited. Licences are organised by the hotels for those booking through them. Otherwise, they can be arranged through marine park headquarters, next to Pole Pole Bungalow Resort.

Sleeping & Eating
For all Chole Bay accommodation, you'll need to pay marine park entry fees, whether you go diving or not. It is generally not included in accommodation rates. In addition to the places listed here, there are also several new budget and midrange places being built at Chole Bay, that should open within the lifetime of this book, including Shamba Kilolo near the park gate just before reaching Utende, and away from the water.

BUDGET
Whale Shark Lodge (Sunset Camp; ☎ /fax 023-201 0201, 0755-696067; carpho2003@yahoo.co.uk; Kilindoni; camping per person US$7, bandas per person without bathroom & with breakfast US$14) This backpacker-friendly place, in a quiet, cliff-top setting overlooking a prime whale-shark viewing area, is a good all-around budget choice, with pleasant camping, plus simple but clean *bandas* (thatched-roof hut or shelter) with mosquito nets, screens and fans, and spotless communal ablutions. There's also a gazebo for watching the sunset, and local-style meals on order. Just a short walk down the cliffside is a beach with high-tide swimming, and the owner is helpful with arranging excursions to outlying islands and elsewhere. It's about 1.5km from the town centre, behind the hospital (Tsh2000 in a taxi).

MAFIA ISLAND MARINE PARK

Mafia Island Marine Park – at c. 822 sq km the largest marine protected area in the Indian Ocean – shelters a unique complex of estuarine, mangrove, coral reef and marine channel ecosystems. These include the only natural forest on the island and almost 400 fish species. There are also about 10 villages within the park's boundaries with an estimated 15,000 to 17,000 inhabitants – all of whom depend on its natural resources for their livelihoods. Accordingly, the park has been classified as a multi-use area to assist local communities in developing sustainable practices that allow conservation and resource use to coexist. The main way to visit is on a diving excursion with one of the Chole Bay dive operators.

Entry fees (payable by everyone, whether you dive or not) are US$10/5 per adult/child per day. They are collected at a barrier gate across the main road about 1km before Utende, and can be paid in any major currency. Save your receipt, as it will be checked again when you leave. The **park office** (☎ 023-240 2690; wwfmafia@bushlink.co.tz; www.marineparktz.com) is in Utende, just north of Pole Pole Bungalow Resort.

New Lizu Hotel (☎ 023-201 0180, 240 2683, 0754-273722; Kilindoni; s/d Tsh6000/10,000; 🖳) The long-standing and reliable 'Mama Lizu's' has clean, spartan rooms with basic bathrooms, nets and fan, good cheap food and a central location at Kilindoni's main junction, less than a 10-minute walk from both the airfield and the harbour.

Harbour View Resort (Kilindoni; d with fan/air-con Tsh15,000/20,000, s without bathroom & with fan Tsh10,000) No-frills rooms in a small house in the harbour area, with several less appealing box-like rooms out back. Most rooms have mosquito nets; food can be arranged with advance notice. It's about a 10 minute walk from town. Head down the hill in Kilindoni and go into the port area; turn left, and follow the waterside road for about 500m to the unsignposted house to your left.

Big Blu Diving College (☎ 0784-918069; www .bigblumafia.org; Chole Bay; d US$40; ⊙ Jul–mid-April; 🖳) This dive outfitter on the beach next to Mafia Island Lodge has soon-to-open en suite rooms with mosquito nets, open to divers and those organising other excursions with Big Blu. Breakfast is included, and evening barbecues can be arranged with advance notice. Otherwise, there's no food.

MIDRANGE & TOP END

All of the following are closed in April and May.

Mafia Island Lodge (☎ 022-260 1530; www.mafia lodge.com; Chole Bay; s/d US$52/75, s/d club US$70/95; 🐾🖳) The former government hotel, this lodge is set on a long lawn sloping down to a palm-studded beach, and is a recommended choice if your budget or tastes don't stretch

to a stay at one of its more upmarket neighbours. There's a mix of renovated ('club') and standard rooms, all lined up at the top of the lawn about 300m in from the water, and all pleasant and relaxing despite the 1970s architectural backdrop. The main restaurant overlooks Chole Bay and serves up tasty meals featuring seafood and Italian cuisine. There's a beachside bar and a well-equipped diving and watersports centre, where you can also arrange excursions.

Ras Mbisi Lodge (☎ 0754-663739; www.mafiaislandtz .com; per person full board US$140; 🔄) This new place, in a stunning setting on Mafia's western coast, was just getting its finishing touches as this book went to print. Accommodation is in nine lovely tented *bandas*, which overlook the beach. There's also a beachside restaurant and a rooftop sundowner bar. Emphasis is put on the cuisine, with homemade jams and preserves at breakfast, salads and fresh pastries, and meals featuring home-grown vegetables and fruits. It's a fine, good value and off-the-beaten track alternative. Excursions include dhow trips to Ras Kisimani and nearby islands, dugout canoe trips, village walks and whale shark outings. Accommodation prices include transfers from Kilindoni.

Kinasi Lodge (☎ 022-284 2525; www.mafiaisland .com; Chole Bay; s/d garden view with full board US$165/300, s/d sea view with full board US$205/360; 🔄 🖳) This is another fine choice, with 14 stone-and-thatch cottages set around a long, manicured hillside sloping down to Chole Bay, Moroccan-influenced décor – at its most attractive in the evening, when the grounds are lit by small lanterns – a genteel ambience, and an imposing spa with masseuses from Thailand. There's

---

COMMUNITY TOURISM SPOTLIGHT: CHOLE MJINI

If your idea of the ultimate getaway is sleeping in the treetops in a rustic but comfortable ambience, while at the same time supporting local community development initiatives, **Chole Mjini** (☎ 0787-712427; 2chole@bushmail.net; Chole Island; s/d full board US$282/420; ☿ Jul-Easter; ☲), on Chole Island, is the place to stay. Accommodation is in six beautifully designed tree houses (a couple of which are actually lower stilt houses), each nestled away amidst the surrounding vegetation, and with views over the bay, the mangroves or the Chole ruins, and each accommodating up to three people. Although there's no electricity, the tree houses have a range of amenities. Dining focuses around simple seafood-based meals, and diving can be arranged (both owners are certified instructors and the lodge has two new boats) as can excursions to view the whale sharks (in season). Chole Mjini also has its own dhow, which can be chartered for day, overnight or multinight safaris – a superb opportunity if you want to experience local coastal culture. Destinations range from nearby deserted islands to Kilwa Kisiwani and the Rufiji River delta.

The concept of Chole Mjini grew out of the owners' commitment to the local community, and community development is still at the heart of the undertaking. A portion of earnings are channelled back into health and education projects, and over the decade or so of the project's life, a reputable health clinic, a kindergarten and a primary school have been established, as well as vocational training and small lending schemes. In contrast to the all-too-common scenario where tourism destroys an island paradise, Chole Mjini is an example of the huge positive benefits that can result when there is genuine integration of tourism with community development and environmental and cultural conservation initiatives.

Children under two cannot be accommodated. Accommodation rates include some shared excursions, plus marine park fees and a daily per person community fee that goes directly to the local villagers.

---

an open lounge area with satellite TV, a small beach and windsurfing rentals, plus a dive centre. Kinasi offers a full range of excursions, including an upscale camping trip to Mafia's northern tip (where the lodge is building a bush camp), as well as packages combining visits to Mafia with Zanzibar, the Selous and boating along the Rufiji.

Pole Pole Bungalow Resort (☎ 022-260 1530; www.polepole.com; Chole Bay; s/d full board US$260/400; ☲) This understated, classy place is set amidst the palm trees and tropical vegetation on a long hillside overlooking Chole Bay. Except for the excellent restaurant and the beautiful, open-sided *duara* (gazebo), which has stunning views over the water, it can be visually underwhelming at first glance. But its quiet style, impeccable service, cuisine, the premium placed on privacy, the lack of TVs and other distractions and the simple elegance of its bungalows – all made completely out of natural materials and with large private verandas – make it a fantastic getaway. The overall ambience is an ideal balance between luxury and lack of pretension. A full range of excursions is offered, including to the Rufiji River delta, and there's a resident masseuse.

Getting There & Away

AIR

Coastal Aviation flies daily between Dar es Salaam and Mafia (US$100), and between Mafia and Kilwa Masoko (US$100, minimum two passengers), both routes with connections on to Zanzibar, Selous Game Reserve and Arusha. The other option is Kinasi Lodge, which has its own charter aircraft for its guests, with seats open on a space-available basis to other passengers.

All the Chole Bay hotels arrange airfield transfers for their guests (included in the room price at some, otherwise US$10 to US$30 per person – inquire when booking).

BOAT

The best (albeit adventurous) boat connection to/from the mainland is at Nyamisati, along the coast south of Dar es Salaam. Get a south-bound *dalla-dalla* (minibus) from Mbagala or Rangi Tatu (both along the Kilwa road, and reached via *dalla-dalla* from Dar es Salaam's Posta) no later than about 11am to Nyamisati (Tsh3000), from where the motorised MV *Potwe* departs daily at 4pm (Tsh5000; three hours) to Kilindoni. You'll arrive after dusk on Mafia and, unless you've made arrangements with the Chole Bay lodges, will need to sleep in Kilindoni. To get to the centre of town, head straight up the hill for about 300m. Departures from Kilindoni are daily at 6am. Once at Nyamisati, it's easy to find *dalla-dallas* north to Mbagala and central Dar es Salaam. On Mafia, purchase boat tickets the afternoon before at the MV *Potwe* office at the Yamaha shop along the main road, on the right side around 20m downhill as you head towards the harbour.

Getting Around

Dalla-dallas connect Kilindoni with Utende (Tsh1000, 45 minutes) and Bweni (Tsh1000, four to five hours), with at least one vehicle daily in each direction. On the Kilindoni-Utende route, vehicles depart Kilindoni at about 1pm and Utende at about 7am, with sporadic vehicles later in the day – the last departure from Utende is about 4.30pm. Departures from Kilindoni to Bweni are at about 1pm, and from Bweni at about 7am. In Kilindoni, the *dalla-dalla* stop is along the road leading down to the port.

It's also possible to hire pick-ups in Kilindoni to take you around the island. Bargain hard, and expect to pay at least Tsh15,000 return between Kilindoni and Utende.

The other option is bicycle – either your own (bring a mountain bike) or a rental (about Tsh500 per hour for a heavy single-speed – ask around at the Kilindoni market).

Between Utende and Chole Island, most of the Chole Bay hotels provide boat transport for their guests. Otherwise, local boats sail throughout the day from the beach in front of Mafia Island Lodge (Tsh100). Boats also leave from here to Juani, and from Chole it's possible to walk to Juani at low tide. To Jibondo, you can usually catch a free lift on one of the water transport boats leaving from the beach near Pole Pole Resort.

SELOUS GAME RESERVE

At the heart of southern Tanzania is the Selous – a vast 48,000 sq km wilderness area stretching over more than 5% of the mainland. It is Africa's largest wildlife reserve, and Tanzania's most extensive protected area, although the extended ecosystems of Ruaha National Park and the Serengeti come close. It's also home to large herds of elephants, plus buffaloes, crocodiles, hippos, wild dogs, an impressive diversity of birds and some of Tanzania's last remaining black rhinos. Bisecting it is

the Rufiji River, which winds its way more than 250km from its source in the highlands through the Selous to the sea, and boasts one of the largest water-catchment areas in East Africa. En route, it cuts a path past woodlands and grasslands and stands of borassus palm, and provides the chance for some unparalleled water-based wildlife watching. In the river's delta area, which lies outside the reserve opposite Mafia island, the reddish-brown freshwater of the river mixes with the blue salt water of the sea, forming striking patterns and providing habitats for many dozens of bird species, passing dolphins and more.

In the northwestern part of the reserve is **Stiegler's Gorge**, which averages 100m in depth, and is named after a Swiss explorer who was killed here by an elephant in 1907.

Although the number of tourists visiting the Selous has increased markedly over the past decade, it remains low in comparison with Tanzania's northern parks, and the congestion of the north is refreshingly absent. While wildlife concentration and diversity are also generally considered to be lower in the Selous than in some of the northern parks, there is still plenty to be seen. Other advantages of the Selous include its wonderful and still very intact wilderness backdrop, its fine collection of small, atmospheric safari camps and an absence of the mass tourism that threatens to overwhelm parts of the north. From the moment you arrive – whether by plane, flying low over the hippo-filled Rufiji, by train, watching giraffes, zebras and more silhouetted against the setting sun, or by vehicle over bumpy roads lined by small villages – to your introduction to camp (most are notably scenic) and to boat and foot safaris, the Selous' wealth of wildlife and its stunning riverine scenery rarely fails to impress. Boat safaris down the Rufiji or on the reserve's lakes are offered by most of the camps and lodges. Most also organise walking safaris, usually three-hour hikes near the camps, or further afield, with the night spent at a fly camp. Both the boat and foot safaris, as well as the chance to explore in open safari vehicles come as a welcome change of pace if you've been cooped up in minivans or closed 4WDs on dusty roads during other parts of your travels.

Only the section of the reserve north from the Rufiji River is open for tourism; large areas of the south have been zoned as hunting concessions.

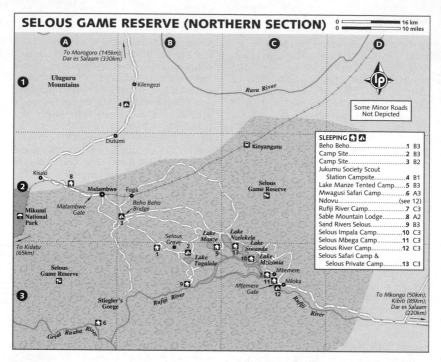

SELOUS GAME RESERVE (NORTHERN SECTION)

SLEEPING
Beho Beho...........................1 B3
Camp Site..........................2 B3
Camp Site..........................3 B2
Jukumu Society Scout
    Station Campsite.............4 B1
Lake Manze Tented Camp......5 B3
Mwagusi Safari Camp...........6 A3
Ndovu.............................(see 12)
Rufiji River Camp..................7 C3
Sable Mountain Lodge...........8 A2
Sand Rivers Selous...............9 B3
Selous Impala Camp............10 C3
Selous Mbega Camp............11 C3
Selous River Camp..............12 C3
Selous Safari Camp &
    Selous Private Camp........13 C3

History

Parts of the reserve were set aside as early as 1896, although it was not until 1922 that it was expanded and given its present name (after Frederick Courteney Selous, the British explorer who was killed in the reserve during WWI). The area continued to be extended over the next several decades until 1975 when it assumed its current boundaries. In more recent years, there has been ongoing work to link Selous Game Reserve with the Niassa Reserve in Mozambique, with the first stages of the project – including establishment of a wildlife corridor – already underway.

Information

The best times to visit the reserve are during the cool, dry season from June to October, with August peak for both boat and land safaris, and in January and February when the rains break and the landscape is green and in flower. Much of the reserve is inaccessible between March and May as a result of the heavy rains, and some of the tourist camps close for at least part of this time,

usually during April and May. If you do visit in the wet season, the main challenge will be getting yourself to the reserve, as roads are sometimes impassable and airstrips too soft for landing. You'll also need to keep your itinerary and expectations flexible, and be prepared for mud.

Both the Mtemere and Matambwe Gates are open from 6am to 6pm daily. The booklet *Selous Game Reserve: The Travel Guide* by Drs Rolf Baldus & Ludwig Siege is an excellent source of background information, including information and tips on wildlife viewing. It's available at bookshops, and at the Selous' Mtemere Gate. An earlier edition, *Selous: Africa's Largest & Wildest Game Reserve*, is similar.

Reserve headquarters are at Matambwe on the Selous' northwestern edge.

Serengeti Balloon Safaris (☎ 027-250 8578, 254 8967; www.balloonsafaris.com; US$499; ☸ 6.30am) offers daily balloon safaris, as the name implies; with easy pick ups from all Selous lodges. The safaris are similar to those in the Serengeti – see p218 for a description of what to expect.

Sleeping

All of the reserve's upmarket lodges and camps offer boat safaris (some on the Rufiji River, others on Lake Tagalala), wildlife drives and guided walks. Several new lodges are planned for the near future, especially near the reserve's northern border around Kinyanguru, so watch for changes here.

BUDGET

There are two **ordinary camp sites**, one at Beho Beho bridge, about 12km southeast of Matambwe, and one at Lake Tagalala, roughly midway between Mtemere and Matambwe. Each has a pit toilet, but otherwise there are no facilities. For both, you will need to be self-sufficient, including with drinking water. **Special camp sites** can be arranged in the area between Mtemere Gate and Lake Manze (northeast of Lake Tagalala). Contact the Wildlife Division (p77) in advance for bookings and information on permitted locations. You'll need to be self-sufficient at these camps as well. See the boxed text, below for camping fees.

About 60km north of Matambwe between Kilengezi and Dutumi is the **Jukumu Society Scout Station Campsite** (camping per person Tsh7000). It's run by an association of game scouts from villages surrounding the reserve and the money earned is used to support local development projects, anti-poaching efforts and similar work. There is a pit toilet and bathing area, and water is available from a small nearby waterfall.

In Mloka village, just east of Mtemere Gate, there's the basic **Mloka Best** (s/d Tsh3000/4500) local guesthouse, which is a potential shoestring option if you have your own transport to get around inside the reserve. Also in the area near Mtemere Gate and away from the river are several budget tented camps, although for these, too, you'll need to have your own transport to explore the reserve, and be self-sufficient with food. Two to try are **Selous River Camp** (www.selousriver camp.com; camping per person US$10, mud hut per person US$35), which has a few tents for rent plus a 'mud hut' bungalow with bathroom, boat safaris and a vehicle available for wildlife drives, and **Ndovu** (☎ 0754-782378; camping/tent per person US$10/35), just behind, with camping, plus several no-frills permanent tents sharing bath and boat safaris. Bring all your own food.

Selous Mbega Camp (☎ 022-265 0250; www .selous-mbega-camp.com; camping per person US$10, s/d full board US$135/190, s/d 'backpackers' special US$85/120 for those arriving by public bus at Mloka, excursions extra) This laid-back, family-friendly camp, located about 500m outside the eastern boundary of the Selous near Mtemere Gate and about 3km from Mloka village, provides good value for money. It has eight no-frills tents set in the foliage somewhat back from the riverbank, each with three beds, a bathroom and veranda, and a small camping ground (for which you'll need to be self-sufficient with food). Excursions – including boat safaris, wildlife drives and walks – can be arranged (US$35 per person, plus reserve fees where applicable). The camp is open year-round. Pick-ups and drop-offs to and from Mloka are free. Payments are cash only. Road transfers to/from Dar es Salaam, and Kilwa Masoko (where the same management has another hotel) cost US$250 per vehicle, one-way.

SELOUS GAME RESERVE FEES

All fees are per 24-hour period.

- **Admission** US$50/30/free per adult/child six to 16 years/child five and under
- **Conservation fee** US$25 per person (payable only by those staying at camps within the Selous' boundaries)
- **Vehicle fee** US$30
- **Camping at ordinary camp site** US$20/5/free per adult/child six to 15 years/child five and under
- **Camping at special camp site** US$40/10/free per adult/child six to 15 years/child five and under
- **Wildlife guard (mandatory in camping areas)** US$20
- **Guide** US$10 (US$15 outside normal working hours and US$20 on walking safaris)

MIDRANGE

The Selous' wonderful lodges come at a high price, with the Midrange listings here equivalent to Top End in many other parts of the country, and many of the Top End listings at the uppermost end of the spectrum.

Sable Mountain Lodge (☎ 022-211 0507; www .saadani.com; s/d full board US$200/290, all-inclusive US$310/510; 🏊) Friendly, relaxed and good value, Sable Mountain is about halfway between Matambwe Gate and Kisaki village on the northwestern boundary of the reserve, in an area known for its elephants. The cosy and comfortable en suite stone cottages all have views. There are also five tented *bandas*, including two luxurious honeymoon *bandas*, plus a tree house overlooking a water hole, a spring-water swimming pool and a snug for stargazing. In addition to walking safaris and wildlife drives, the lodge offers a combined wildlife drive and boat safari on Lake Tagalala, and night drives outside the reserve. Free pick-ups and drop-offs are provided to the Kisaki train station (watch for fly-rail specials) and staff are very helpful if you're travelling independently. It's open year-round, and recommended.

Rufiji River Camp (☎ 022-212 8663; www.rufijiriver camp.com; per person all-inclusive US$310; 🏊) This long-standing and unpretentious camp is larger than most of its neighbours, but with a fine location on a wide bend in the Rufiji River about 1km inside Mtemere Gate. The 20 en suite tents all have river views, there's a sunset terrace and a small library. Activities include boat safaris, and half-day walking safaris with the possibility of staying overnight at a fly camp. Open year-round (advance notice required during the rainy season).

Lake Manze Tented Camp (☎ 022-245 2005; www .adventurecamps.co.tz; s/d all-inclusive US$345/580; 🌙 Jun-Mar) Run by the same management that oversees the Selous Impala Camp, this place is more rustic than its sister camp but quite comfortable and favourably situated, with 12 well-outfitted tents in a good location along an arm of Lake Manze.

Selous Impala Camp (☎ 022-245 2005; www.adven turecamps.co.tz; s/d all-inclusive US$515/890; 🌙 Jun-Mar; 🏊) The intimate and well-located Impala is one of the smallest of the Selous camps, and excellent value if you take advantage of some of Coastal Travel's flight-accommodation deals. It has eight well-spaced, comfortable tents, each nestled away on its own directly on the river near the beautiful Lake Mzizimia, with its stands of borassus palms and surrounding panorama of green vistas. Each tent has its own terrace and river views, and all are beautifully appointed, with polished-wood floors and 270-degree open screening for optimal views and ventilation. The restaurant overlooks the river and has an adjoining bar area on a deck jutting out towards the water. The surrounding area is rich in wildlife, although Maasai guards ensure peace of mind while you're at the camp. Favourably priced packages including flights and accommodation are offered in combination with Ruaha National Park. Fly camping can be arranged.

TOP END

Selous Safari Camp (www.selous.com; per person full board plus airstrip transfers & activities US$625; 🌙 Jun-mid Mar; 🏊) This luxurious camp is set on a side arm of the Rufiji in a particularly beautiful and lush setting overlooking Lake Nzelekela, with 12 spacious, widely spaced tents, a lofty, raised dining and lounge area, impeccable service and the chance for fly-camping and walking safaris (minimum two nights), as well as wildlife drives and walks and boat safaris. The same management also runs the exclusive **Selous Private Camp** (per full four-tent camp US$3800; 🏊), which consists of just four tented suites and a private pool, and is generally rented only in its entirety. No children under six years of age.

The Retreat (www.retreatsafaris.co.tz; per person all-inclusive from US$770; 🏊) The newest camp in the Selous (at the moment), this 12-tent retreat is set well southwest of the other lodges along the Great Ruaha River. It's the only lodge in the Selous with a spa, and emphasis throughout the camp is very much on a holistic experience of the surrounding nature. It also offers the possibility of a night's fly camping and walking safari at no additional cost if you've made a four-night booking.

Sand Rivers Selous (www.sand-rivers-selous.com; s/d all-inclusive US$870/1450; 🏊) Beautiful Sand Rivers Selous, set splendidly on its own on the Rufiji River south of Lake Tagalala, is arguably the Selous' most exclusive option, in ambience, if not in price, and boasts some of Tanzania's most renowned wildlife guides. Its eight luxurious stone cottages are all open in front with full river views. Bookings can only be made through upmarket travel agents. Nomad, who run the camp, also offer superlative walking safaris of up to six days based out of mobile fly camps.

Beho Beho (www.behobeho.com; per person all-inclusive US$900; 🔊) Beho Beho, set on a rise northwest of Lake Tagalala and well away from the river, is one of the most upmarket camps in the Selous, with spacious stone and thatch *bandas* with large verandas and commanding views over the plains. Boat safaris are done on Lake Tagalala, which is notable for its birdlife, as well as its populations of hippos and crocodiles.

Getting There & Away

AIR
Coastal Aviation and ZanAir have daily flights linking Selous Game Reserve with Dar es Salaam (US$140 one-way), Zanzibar (US$160) and (via Dar) Arusha, with connections to other northern circuit airstrips. Coastal also flies between the Selous and Mafia, and the Selous and Ruaha National Park (US$270). Flights into the Selous are generally suspended during the March to May wet season. All lodges provide airfield transfers.

BUS
Akida (the better option) and Mwera/Mloka bus lines have daily buses between Dar es Salaam's Temeke bus stand (departing from the Sudan Market area) and Mloka village, about 10km east of Mtemere Gate (Tsh4500, seven to nine hours). Departures in both directions are at 5am. From Mloka, you'll need to arrange a pick-up in advance with one of the camps. Note that hitching within the Selous isn't permitted, and there are no vehicles to rent in Mloka.

CAR & MOTORCYCLE
You'll need 4WD in the Selous. There's no vehicle rental at the reserve and motorcycles aren't permitted.

To get here via road, there are two options. The first: take the Dar es Salaam to Mkongo road, via Kibiti, and on to Mtemere (250km). The road is in reasonable to good shape as far as Mkongo. From Mkongo to Mtemere (75km) is sometimes impassable during heavy rains. Allow about eight hours from Dar es Salaam.

Alternatively, you can go from Dar es Salaam to Kisaki via Morogoro and then on to Matambwe via a scenic, but longer, 350km route through the Uluguru Mountains. Allow

at least nine hours for the journey. This route has improved in recent times, but is still sometimes impassable during heavy rains and a 4WD is required at any time of the year. From Dar es Salaam, the road is good tarmac as far as Morogoro. Once in Morogoro, take the Old Dar es Salaam road east towards Bigwa. About 3km or 4km from the centre of town, past the Teachers' College Morogoro and before reaching Bigwa, you will come to a fork in the road, where you bear right. From here, the road becomes steep and rough as it winds its way through the Uluguru Mountains onto a flat plain, which is usually the most difficult section to pass during the rains due to poor drainage. Shortly before Kisaki there is – except for at the height of the dry season – a small river to cross, which isn't usually too much of a problem, apart from the steep bank on the far side. Allow between five to eight hours for the stretch from Morogoro to Matambwe, depending on the season. If you are coming from Dar es Salaam and want to bypass Morogoro, take the an unsignposted left-hand turn-off via Mikese, about 25km east of town on the main Dar es Salaam road that meets up with the Kisaki road at Msumbisi.

Coming from Dar es Salaam, the last petrol station is at Kibiti (about 100km northeast of Mtemere Gate), although supplies aren't reliable (otherwise try Ikwiriri). Coming from the other direction, the last reliable petrol station is at Morogoro (about 160km from the Matambwe ranger post). Occasionally you may find diesel sold on the roadside at Matombo, 50km south of Morogoro. If you plan to drive around the Selous, bring sufficient petrol supplies with you as there is none available at any of the lodges, nor anywhere close to the reserve.

TRAIN
The train is a good option for the adventurous, especially if you're staying on the northwestern side of the reserve, and with luck, you may even get a sneak preview of some of the wildlife from the train window. All Tazara trains stop at Kisaki, which is about five to six hours from Dar es Salaam and the first stop for the express train, and ordinary trains stop at Kinyanguru and Fuga stations (both of which are closer to the central camps) and at Matambwe (near Matambwe Gate). All the lodges do pick-ups (usually combined with a wildlife drive) at varying prices. For schedules, see p361.

It works best to take the train from Dar es Salaam to Selous Game Reserve. If you decide to do it the other way around, be prepared for delays of up to 20 hours going back to Dar es Salaam. The lodges can help you monitor its progress with their radios.

KILWA MASOKO
☎ 023

Kilwa Masoko (Kilwa of the Market) is a sleepy coastal town nestled amidst dense coastal vegetation and several fine stretches of beach about halfway between Dar es Salaam and Mtwara. It's the springboard for visiting the impressive ruins of the 15th-century Arab settlements at Kilwa Kisiwani and Songo Mnara, and as such, is the gateway into one of the most significant eras in East African coastal history, although the town itself is a relatively modern creation, with minimal historical appeal.

Thanks to an archaeological/tourism initiative by the French and Japanese governments, plus the rehabilitation of the coastal road from Dar es Salaam and the arrival of several new hotels, visitor numbers to Kilwa are slowly starting to increase.

The **National Microfinance Bank** (Main Rd) changes cash. There's no internet connection or ATM.

Sights & Activities
On the eastern edge of town is **Jimbizi Beach**, an attractive stretch of sand dotted with the occasional baobab tree; it's reached via a path that heads downhill by the Masoko Urban Health Centre. Much better is the long, idyllic palm-fringed beach at **Masoko Pwani**, about 5km northeast of town, and best reached by bicycle or taxi (Tsh5000 one-way). This is also where Kilwa Masoko gets its fish, and the colourful harbour area is worth a look, especially in the late afternoon. Dhow excursions through some of the mangrove swamps on the outskirts of Kilwa – interesting for their birdlife and resident hippos – can be arranged with Kilwa Seaview Resort. About 85km northwest of Kilwa at Kipatimo are extensive limestone **caves**.

Sleeping
BUDGET

Hilton Guest House (r Tsh4000, without bathroom Tsh3000) Strictly shoestring, with basic rooms, fans, nets and squat toilets. It's 300m east of the main road, near the market.

KILWA MASOKO

INFORMATION	
District Commissioner's Office............................1 A3	
National Microfinance Bank.............................2 A2	

SLEEPING 🏠	
Hilton Guest House...3 B2	
Kilwa Ruins Lodge..4 B3	
New Mjaka Guest House....................................5 A2	

EATING & DRINKING 🍴🍷	
Kilwa Ruins Lodge..(see 4)	
Night Market...6 B2	
Roadside Classic Park..7 A2	

TRANSPORT	
Buses to Dar es Salaam......................................8 B2	
Jetty & Boats to Kilwa Kisiwani, Songo Mnara &	
Pande..9 A3	
Sudi Travel Agency & Coastal Aviation Booking	
Office...10 A1	
Taxi Stand...(see 11)	
Transport to Kilwa Kivinje & Nangurukuru.....11 A1	

New Mjaka Guest House (☎ 023-201 3071; Main Rd; s without bathroom Tsh3000, s/d banda Tsh10,000/20,000) This otherwise undistinguished place holds the honour of being the best of Kilwa's clutch of local guesthouses, with a few basic rooms in the main building sharing facilities and somewhat nicer *bandas* next door. Some *bandas* have two rooms sharing a bathroom and common area while others are standard doubles. All have fan and nets. There's no food.

MIDRANGE

Kilwa Dreams (☎ 0784-585330; www.kilwadreams.com; Masoko Pwani; camping per person US$10, d/f bungalow US$50/75) A handful of bright blue, spartan bungalows with nets, cold water and no electricity in an idyllic setting on the beach at Masoko Pwani, and a beachside bar-restaurant.

Kilwa Seaview Resort (☎ 022-265 0250; www .kilwa.net; Jimbizi Beach; camping per person US$5; s/d/tr/q US$60/70/80/90, full board per person US$15 extra; airport transfers per vehicle Tsh5000; 🖳) Straightforward, pleasant and good-value A-frame cottages perched along a small escarpment at the eastern end of Jimbizi beach, including six breezy waterfront cottages and a row of double-story bungalows, just behind, with balconies on the upper level. There's a restaurant built around a huge baobab tree with local-style fixed menus, and the beach is just a short walk away. Staff are helpful with arranging excursions, including to Kilwa Kisiwani, and to see the hippos in the nearby mangroves. Driving, the access turnoff is signposted from the main road. By foot, the quickest way to get here from the bus stand is to head south along the main road (towards the port), then turn left near the police station, making your way past the police barracks and health clinic down the hill by Kilwa Ruins to Jimbizi Beach. At the northeastern end of the beach is a small path leading up to the cottages. Pick-ups can be arranged from the bus stand in town. Transfers to/from Dar es Salaam or to Selous Mbega Camp (under the same management, see p313) cost US$250 per vehicle one-way.

Kilwa Ruins Lodge (☎ 023-240 2397, 0784-637026; www.kilwaruinslodge.com; Jimbizi Beach; per person full board US$80-120; 🍴🖳) This upmarket angling camp is well-located in the centre of Jimbizi beach, with a popular waterside bar-restaurant area. Accommodation is in a choice of rustic 'chalets', nicer, more modern 'beach *bandas*' and a few spiffy 'fisherman *bandas*'. All are on the bland side, but spotless and well-equipped (although the chalets don't have hot water). There's a full array of fishing equipment – big game fishing costs from US$350 to US$800 per boat per day, depending on boat and location – and the resident manager is a renowned angler. The camp also has its own plane for charters, a vehicle for hire and sea kayaks, and can organise overnight diving/fishing 'island

cruises' for US$1600 per boat (4-person) per day, all-inclusive, plus local excursions in the Kilwa area. The big game fishing season runs from late July to early April. Book well in advance if you plan on visiting during the late October peak season.

Eating & Drinking

Kilwa Seaview Resort (Jimbizi Beach; breakfast Tsh3000, lunch/dinner Tsh8000) and **Kilwa Ruins Lodge** (☎ 023-240 2397, 0784-637026; Jimbizi Beach; meals from Tsh9000; advance bookings required) have good restaurants. For inexpensive fish/chicken and chips, try **Roadside Classic Park** (Main Rd; meals from Tsh1000), diagonally opposite New Mjaka Guest House, with local food and a bar, or the lively **night market**, between the main street and the market, with inexpensive fish and other street snacks from dusk onwards.

Getting There & Away

AIR

Coastal Aviation has daily flights between Dar es Salaam and Kilwa (US$120 one-way) and between Kilwa and Mafia (US$100, minimum two passengers). Book through their Dar es Salaam office (p88), or in Kilwa through **Sudi Travel Agency** (☎ 023-201 3004; Main Rd), north of the petrol station. The airstrip is about 2km north of town along the main road.

BUS

To Nangurukuru (the junction with the Dar-Mtwara road, Tsh2000, one hour) and Kilwa Kivinje (Tsh1800, 45 minutes), pick-ups depart several times daily from the transport stand on the main road just north of the market. This is also the place to hire taxis for local excursions.

To Dar es Salaam, there is at least one bus daily (stopping also in Kilwa Kivinje, departing in each direction at about 5am (Tsh7000, six hours). Buses from Kilwa depart from the market, and should be booked the day before. Departures in Dar es Salaam are from the Temeke bus stand (Sudan Market area), with smaller buses also departing from Mbagala (take a *dalla-dalla* to 'Mbagala Mwisho'), along the Kilwa road. Coming from Dar es Salaam it's also possible to get a bus heading to Lindi or Mtwara and get out at Nangurukuru junction, from where you can get local transport to Kilwa Kivinje (Tsh500, 11km) or Kilwa Masoko (35km), although you'll often need to pay the full Lindi or Mtwara fare. This doesn't work as well leaving Kilwa, as buses are often full when they pass Nangurukuru (from about 11am).

To Lindi, there's at least one direct bus daily (Tsh7000, four hours), departing from the market and continuing on to Mtwara; book a day in advance.

BOAT

There are no scheduled passenger-boat services to/from Kilwa. Dhows are best arranged in Kilwa Kivinje. Boats to Kilwa Kisiwani, Songo Mnara and Pande leave from the jetty at the southern end of town.

AROUND KILWA MASOKO
Kilwa Kisiwani

Today, Kilwa Kisiwani (Kilwa on the Island) is a quiet fishing village baking in the sun just off-shore from Kilwa Masoko, but in its heyday it was the seat of sultans and centre of a vast trading network linking the old Shona kingdoms and the gold fields of Zimbabwe with Persia, India and China. Ibn Battuta, the famed traveller and chronicler of the ancient world, visited Kilwa in the early 14th century and described the town as being exceptionally beautiful and well constructed. At its height, Kilwa's influence extended north past the Zanzibar Archipelago and south as far as Sofala on the central Mozambican coast.

While these glory days are now well in the past, the ruins of the settlement – together with the ruins on nearby Songo Mnara – are among the most significant groups of Swahili buildings on the East African coast and a Unesco World Heritage site. Thanks to funding from the French and Japanese governments, significant sections of the ruins have been restored, and are now easily accessible, with informative signboards in English and Swahili.

HISTORY

The coast near Kilwa Kisiwani has been inhabited for several thousand years, and artefacts from the late and middle Stone Age have been found on the island. Although the first settlements in the area date to around AD 800, Kilwa remained a relatively undistinguished place until the early 13th century. At this time, trade links developed with Sofala, 1500km to the south in present-day Mozambique. Kilwa came to control Sofala and to dominate its

lucrative gold trade, and before long it had become the most powerful trade centre along the Swahili coast.

In the late 15th century, Kilwa's fortunes began to turn. Sofala freed itself from the island's dominance, and in the early 16th century Kilwa came under the control of the Portuguese. It wasn't until more than 200 years later that Kilwa regained its independence and once again became a significant trading centre, this time as an entrepôt for slaves being shipped from the mainland to the islands of Mauritius, Réunion and Comoros. In the 1780s, Kilwa came under the control of the Sultan of Oman. By the mid-19th century, the local ruler had succumbed to the sultan of Zanzibar, the focus of regional trade shifted to Kilwa Kivinje on the mainland, and the island town entered a decline from which it never recovered.

INFORMATION

To visit the ruins, you will need to get a permit (per person Tsh1500) from the **District Commissioner's office** (Halmashauri ya Wilaya ya Kilwa; ⏱ 7.30am-3.30pm Mon-Fri) in Kilwa Masoko, diagonally opposite the post office. Ask for the Ofisi ya Utamaduni (Antiquities Office); the permit is issued without fuss while you wait. To maximise your chances of finding the Antiquities Officer in, it's best to go in the morning. On weekends, Kilwa Seaview Hotel can help you track down the permit officer, who is usually quite gracious about issuing permits outside of working hours. You'll also need to be accompanied by a guide to visit the island, arranged through the Antiquities Office or Kilwa Seaview Hotel.

For detailed information in English about the ruins, look on the web or in libraries at home for a copy of HN Chittick's informative manuscript. The National Museum in Dar es Salaam has a small but worthwhile display on the ruins at Kilwa Kisiwani.

There are no tourist facilities on the island.

THE RUINS

The ruins at Kilwa Kisiwani are in two groups. When approaching Kilwa Kisiwani, the first building you'll find is the Arabic **fort** (*gereza*). It was built in the early 19th century by the Omani Arabs, on the site of a Portuguese fort dating from the early 16th century. To the southwest of the fort are the ruins of the beautiful **Great Mosque**, with its columns and graceful vaulted roofing, much of which has been impressively restored. Some sections of the mosque date to the late 13th century, although most are from additions made to the building in the 15th century. In its day, this was the largest mosque on the East African coast. Further southwest and behind the Great Mosque is a smaller **mosque** dating from the early 15th century. This is considered to be the best preserved of the buildings at Kilwa and has also been impressively restored. To the west of the small mosque, with large, green lawns and placid views over the water, are the crumbling remains of the **Makutani**, a large, walled enclosure in the centre of which lived some of the sultans of Kilwa. It is estimated to date from the mid18th century.

Almost 1.5km from the fort along the coast is **Husuni Kubwa**, once a massive complex of buildings covering almost a hectare and, together with nearby **Husuni Ndogo**, the oldest of Kilwa's ruins. The complex, which is estimated to date from the 12th century or earlier, is set on a hill and must have once commanded great views over the bay. Watch in particular for the octagonal bathing pool. Husuni Ndogo is smaller than Husuni Kubwa and is thought to date from about the same time, although archaeologists are not yet sure of its original function. To reach these ruins, you can walk along the beach at low tide or follow the slightly longer inland route.

GETTING THERE & AWAY

Local boats go from the port at Kilwa Masoko to Kilwa Kisiwani (Tsh200) whenever there are enough passengers – usually only in the early morning, about 7am, which means you'll need to arrange your permit the day before. To charter your own boat costs Tsh1000 one way (Tsh10,000 return for a boat with a motor). There is a Tsh300 port fee for tourists, payable in the small office just right of the entry gate. With a good wind, the trip takes about 20 minutes. Kilwa Seaview Hotel arranges excursions for US$20 per person (minimum two people), including guide, permit and boat costs.

Songo Mnara

Tiny Songo Mnara, about 8km south of Kilwa Kisiwani, contains ruins at its northern end – including of a palace, several mosques and numerous houses – that are believed to date from the 14th and 15th centuries. They are considered in some respects to be more significant architecturally than those at Kilwa Kisiwani – with one of the most complete town layouts along the coast, although they're less visually impressive. Just off the island's western side is **Sanje Majoma**, with additional ruins dating from the same period. The small island of **Sanje ya Kati**, between Songo Mnara and Kilwa Masoko, has some lesser ruins of a third settlement in the area, also believed to date from the same era.

The Kilwa Kisiwani permit includes Songo Mnara. There's no accommodation on the island.

The best way to get to Songo Mnara is via motorboat from Kilwa Masoko, arranged through the District Commissioner's office or with Kilwa Seaview Hotel (US$80 per dhow, maximum five people). Alternatively, there's a much cheaper motorised local dhow that departs Kilwa Masoko between about 6am and 8am most mornings to Pande, and will stop on request at Songo Mnara. With luck, the boat returns to Kilwa Masoko the same day, departing Pande about 1pm. Dhows between Kilwa Masoko and Songo Mnara take about two to three hours with a decent wind.

After landing at Songo Mnara, be prepared to wade through mangrove swamps before reaching the island proper.

Kilwa Kivinje

Kilwa Kivinje (Kilwa of the Casuarina Trees) owes its existence to Omani Arabs from Kilwa Kisiwani who set up a base here in the early 19th century following the fall of the Kilwa sultanate. By the mid19th century the settlement had become the hub of the regional slave trading network, and by the late 19th century, a German administrative centre. With the abolition of the slave trade, and German wartime defeats, Kilwa Kivinje's brief period in the spotlight came to an end. Today, it's a crumbling, moss-covered and atmospheric relic of the past with a Swahili small-town feel and an intriguing mixture of German colonial and Omani Arab architecture.

The most interesting section of town is around the old German **Boma**. The boma itself is completely dilapidated, but it's worth picking your way through the rubble and climbing the stairs to the first floor for the view towards the water. The street behind the boma is lined with small houses, many with carved Zanzibar-style doorways. Nearby is a **mosque**, which locals claim has been in continuous use since the 14th century, and a warren of back streets where you can get an excellent slice of coastal life, with children playing on the streets and women sorting huge trays of *dagga* (tiny sardines) for drying in the sun. Just in from here on the water is the bustling **dhow port**, where brightly painted vessels set off for Songo Songo, Mafia and other coastal ports.

The best way to visit Kilwa Kivinje is as an easy half-day or day trip from Kilwa Masoko. Overnight options are limited to a clutch of non-descript guesthouses near the market, all with rooms for about Tsh3500, and each rivalling the others in grubbiness.

GETTING THERE & AWAY

Kilwa Kivinje is reached by heading about 25km north of Kilwa Masoko along a sealed road and then turning in at Nangurukuru for about 5km further. Pick-ups travel several times daily to/from Kilwa Masoko, and the bus between Dar es Salaam and Kilwa Masoko also stops at Kilwa Kivinje.

Dhows sail regularly from Kilwa Kivinje to both Dar es Salaam and Mtwara, although the journey to both destinations is long and not recommended; every year several boats capsize. Expect to pay about Tsh6000 for trips in either direction. There are also dhows to Songo Songo (about Tsh1000) and to Mafia (about Tsh5000), although for Mafia, it's much better to take a bus up the coast towards Dar es Salaam and get a boat at Nyamisati. See p310 for more details.

Songo Songo

Coconut palms, low shrub vegetation, about 3500 locals, lots of birds, a good beach and a major natural-gas field that is being exploited as part of the Songo Songo Gas to Electricity Project (see www.tpdc-tz.com/songo_songo.htm for more) are the main attractions on this 4 sq km island. Together with several surrounding islets, it forms the Songo Songo Archipelago, an ecologically important area for nesting sea turtles and marine birds. The surrounding waters also host an impressive collection of hard and soft corals. The archipelago, together with the nearby Rufiji River delta, the Mafia Archipelago and the coastline around Kilwa Masoko have been declared a Wetland of International Importance under the Ramsar Convention. The best beach is in

Songo Songo's southeastern corner, reached through a coconut plantation. There are no tourist facilities on the island.

Songo Songo lies about 30km northeast of Kilwa Kivinje, from where it can be reached by dhow in about 3½ hours with favourable winds. There are also frequent charter flights in connection with the gas project; check with Dar es Salaam–based air charter operators, or Coastal Aviation, which occasionally stops here on its Kilwa-Mafia run.

LINDI

☎ 023 / pop 42,000

In its early days, Lindi was part of the Sultan of Zanzibar's domain, a terminus of the slave caravan route from Lake Nyasa, regional colonial capital, and the main town in southeastern Tanzania. The abolishment of the slave trade and the rise of Mtwara as a local hub sent Lindi into a slow decline, from which it has yet to recover, although it again moved briefly into the limelight in the early 20th century when dinosaur bones were discovered nearby (see boxed text, p322).

Today, Lindi is a lively, pleasant place and worth wandering around for a day or so to get a taste of life on the coast. Although it's not nearly as atmospheric as Kilwa Kivinje, further north, its small dhow port still bustles with local coastal traffic, a smattering of carved doorways and crumbling ruins line the dusty streets, and a Hindu temple and Indian merchants serve as a reminder of once-prosperous trade routes to the east.

Salt production is the main local industry, announced by the salt flats lining the road into town. There's also a sisal plantation in Kikwetu, near the airfield. The coral reef running from south of Lindi to Sudi Bay hosts abundant marine life, and the site has been proposed as a possible protected marine area.

Information

INTERNET ACCESS

Malaga Internet Café (Uhuru St; per hr Tsh2000; ✆ 9am-6pm) Near the Shi'a mosque and Precision Air, and a few blocks up from the harbour.

MEDICAL SERVICES

Brigita Dispensary (☎ 023-220 26/9; Makonde St) An efficient, Western-run clinic, and the best place for medical emergencies; it's just around the corner from Gift Guest House.

SOUTHEASTERN TANZANIA

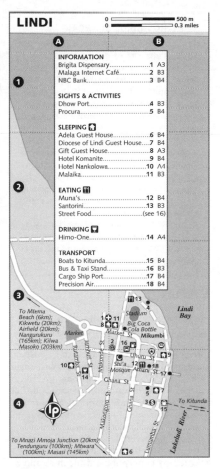

LINDI

0 ——————— 500 m
0 ——————— 0.3 miles

MONEY

NBC (Lumumba St) On the waterfront; changes cash and has an ATM.

Sights & Activities

The old, historical part of town is the section along the waterfront, though you'll have to really hunt for the few still-standing remnants of the town's more glorious past. Watch for the remains of the old German boma, ruins of an Arab tower and the occasional carved doorway. The small **dhow port** on palm-fringed Lindi Bay is lively and colourful and worth a stroll. From some of the hills on the edge of town there are good views over large stands of palm trees and Lindi Bay, and across the Lukeludi River to **Kitunda peninsula** – ask locals

to point you in the direction of Mtanda, Wailes ('Wire-less') or Mtuleni neighbourhoods. On Kitunda itself, which was formerly a sisal estate, there's nothing much now other than a sleepy village, but it's a pleasant destination for walking and offers a glimpse of traditional local life. At the end of the peninsula behind the hill is a good beach (hire a local boat to get there).

About 6km north of town off the airfield road is **Mtema beach**, which is usually empty except for weekends and holidays. Take care with your valuables.

Sleeping

Gift Guest House (☎ 023-220 2462; cnr Market & Makonde Sts; s/d without bathroom Tsh3000/4000) Just down Market St from Malaika, and a decent, albeit considerably more basic, alternative. Rooms have mosquito nets and fans; there's no food.

Hotel Nankolowa (☎ 023-220 2727; Rutamba St; s/d Tsh5000/10,000, r without bathroom Tsh3500) Basic, tiny rooms with fan, net and continental breakfast. It's about 400m southwest of the market.

Adela Guest House (☎ 023-220 2310; Ghana St; r Tsh10,000) Not to be confused with the eponymous but grubbier Adela Guest House I several blocks closer to the town centre, this place – sometimes referred to as 'Adela II' – has arguably the best rooms in town (at least until Hotel Komanite opens, see later in this section). All have net, fan, TV and private bathroom, and there's a restaurant and a small plant-filled terrace. It's inside a walled compound – look for the large, unmarked grey metal gate.

Malaika (☎ 023-220 2880; Market St; s/d Tsh10,000/12,000, ste Tsh15,000) Malaika, one block east of the market, is another good budget bet. Rooms are clean, no-frills and fine, with net and fan, and meals can be arranged.

Diocese of Lindi Guest House (☎ 023-220 2288; Ghana St; r Tsh12,000) This place has two spacious, breezy rooms near the waterfront, but church and aid workers have priority. It's best booked in advance (at the main diocesan offices ('Procura'), just inland from the guesthouse compound).

The new three-star **Hotel Komanite** (Waterfront road) was being built on the waterfront just down from the harbour and should be open, with Lindi's best rooms, by the time this book is published.

Eating & Drinking

Lindi isn't distinguished for its dining options, but you can get some delicious grilled fish. Otherwise, the menu is usually chicken with rice or *ugali* (a staple made from maize or cassava flour, or both). Places to try include **Himo-One** (Jamhuri St; meals Tsh3000), with a good menu selection, reasonably fast service and no alcohol; **Muna's** (Amani St; meals Tsh2000), a few blocks up from the harbour; and **Santorini** (Waterfront road; meals from Tsh1500), which is behind the stadium in the Mikumbi area near the water, and a good place for a drink. The cheapest and best street food is at the bus stand, where there's a row of stalls dishing up grilled chicken and chips each evening, plus a few stools to sit and watch the passing scene.

Getting There & Away

AIR

Precision Air (☎ 023-220 2366; Amani St) flies twice weekly between Dar es Salaam, Lindi and Mtwara, with a connection twice weekly on to Pemba (Mozambique). The airfield is about 20km north of town.

BUS

All transport departs from the main bus and taxi stand on Uhuru St. Minibuses to Mtwara depart daily between about 5.30am and 11am. Otherwise, there are minibuses throughout the day to Mingoyo junction (Mnazi Mmoja; Tsh1000), where you can wait for the Masasi–Mtwara bus.

To Masasi, there are two or three direct buses daily, departing between about 5am and noon. Alternatively, go to Mingoyo and wait for onward transport there. The last Mtwara–Masasi bus passes Mingoyo about 2pm.

To Dar es Salaam, there are direct buses daily, departing Lindi at about 5am (Tsh17,000, eight to 10 hours).

To Kilwa Masoko, there's a direct bus leaving Lindi daily around 5am (Tsh7000, four hours).

BOAT

Cargo boats along the coast, including to Dar es Salaam, call at the port near the NBC bank, although they generally don't take passengers. The dhow port is about 800m further up the coast.

Boats across the Lukeludi River to Kitunda sail throughout day from in front of NBC.

BRACHIOSAURUS BRANCAI

Tendunguru, about 100km northwest of Lindi, is the site of one of the most significant palaeontological finds in history. From 1909 to 1912, a team of German palaeontologists unearthed the remains of more than a dozen different dinosaur species, including the skeleton of *Brachiosaurus brancai*, the largest known dinosaur in the world. The Brachiosaurus skeleton is now on display at the Museum of Natural History in Berlin. Scientists are unsure why so many dinosaur fossils were discovered in the region, although it is thought that flooding or some other natural catastrophe was the cause of their demise.

Today, Tendunguru is of interest mainly to hardcore palaeontologists. For visitors, there is little to see and access to the site is difficult, even with your own vehicle.

MTWARA

☎ 023 / pop 93,000

Sprawling Mtwara is southeastern Tanzania's major town. It was first developed after WWII by the British as part of the failed East African Groundnut Scheme to alleviate a postwar shortage of plant oils. Grand plans were made to expand Mtwara, then an obscure fishing village, into an urban centre of about 200,000 inhabitants. An international airport and Tanzania's first deep-water harbour were built and the regional colonial administration was relocated here from Lindi. Yet, no sooner had this been done than the groundnut scheme – plagued by conceptional difficulties and an uncooperative local climate – collapsed and everything came to an abrupt halt. While Mtwara's port continued to play a significant role in the region over the next few decades as an export channel for cashews, sisal and other products, development of the town came to a standstill and for years it resembled little more than an oversized shell.

In recent times Mtwara has got something of a second wind, with a revival of interest in the tourism potential of the southeast. While it lacks the historical appeal of nearby Mikindani and other places along the coast, it has decent infrastructure, easy access and a relaxed pace, and is a convenient entry/exit point for travelling between Tanzania and Mozambique.

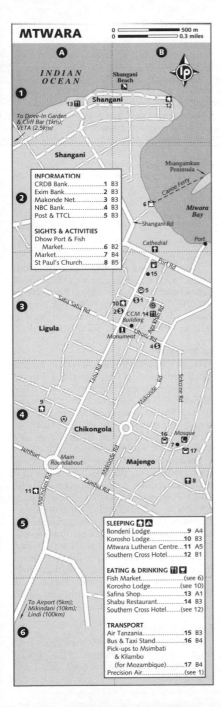

MTWARA

0 — 500 m
0 — 0.3 miles

INDIAN
OCEAN

Shangani
Beach

To Drive-In Garden
& Cliff Bar (1km);
VETA (2.5km)

Shangani

Shangani

Msangamkuu
Peninsula

Canoe Ferry

Mtwara
Bay

Shangani Rd

Cathedral

Port

Saba Saba Rd

Port Rd

CCM
Building

Ligula

Uhuru Rd

Tanu Rd

Sokoine Rd

Makonde Rd

Chikongola

Mosque

Jamhuri

Main
Roundabout

Majengo

Zambia Rd

Mikindani Rd

To Airport (5km);
Mikindani (10km);
Lindi (100km)

INFORMATION
CRDB Bank.................1 B3
Exim Bank..................2 B3
Makonde Net.............3 B3
NBC Bank...................4 B3
Post & TTCL...............5 B3

SIGHTS & ACTIVITIES
Dhow Port & Fish
 Market.....................6 B2
Market........................7 B4
St Paul's Church........8 B5

SLEEPING
Bondeni Lodge......................9 A4
Korosho Lodge....................10 B3
Mtwara Lutheran Centre.....11 A5
Southern Cross Hotel.........12 B1

EATING & DRINKING
Fish Market.......................(see 6)
Korosho Lodge................(see 10)
Safina Shop........................13 A1
Shabu Restaurant..............14 B3
Southern Cross Hotel........(see 12)

TRANSPORT
Air Tanzania......................15 B3
Bus & Taxi Stand..............16 B4
Pick-ups to Msimbati
 & Kilambo
 (for Mozambique).........17 B4
Precision Air......................(see 1)

Orientation

Mtwara is loosely located between a business and banking area to the northwest, near Uhuru and Aga Khan Rds, and the market and bus stand about 1.5km away to the southeast. The main north–south street is Tanu Rd. In the far northwest on the sea, and 30 to 40 minutes on foot from the bus stand, is the Shangani quarter, with a small beach. In Mtwara's far southeastern corner, just past the market, are the lively areas of Majengo and Chikongola.

Information

Tide tables are available at the port: after entering the port area, but before reaching the gate, turn right and go behind the buildings to the harbour master's office.

INTERNET ACCESS
Makonde Net (per hr Tsh1000; 8am-6pm Mon-Sat, 9am-2pm Sun) Just off Aga Khan Rd in the town centre.

MONEY
CRDB (Tanu Rd) ATM (Visa).
Exim Bank (Tanu Rd) ATM (MasterCard; Cirrus).
NBC (Uhuru Rd) Changes cash and travellers cheques; ATM (Visa).

POST
Main Post Office (Tanu Rd)

TELEPHONE
TTCL (Tanu Rd; 8am-12.45pm & 1.30pm-4.30pm Mon-Fri, 9am-12.30pm Sat) Operator-assisted domestic and international calls, and a card phone.

Sights & Activities

In town there's a lively **market** with a small traditional-medicine section next to the main building. North of here, and just east of the NBC bank, watch for used clothing auctions most afternoons. Aga Khan St is lined with old Indian trading houses dating from the late 1950s and 1960s. Much of Mtwara's fish comes from Msangamkuu on the other side of Mtwara Bay, and the small **dhow port** and adjoining **fish market** are particularly colourful in the early morning and late afternoon. The **beach** in Shangani is popular for swimming (high tide only); its gentle currents and general absence of sea urchins and other hazards make it ideal for children. For views over the bay and the white sands of Msangamkuu peninsula, look for the tiny footpath leading to

ST PAUL'S CHURCH

If you happen to be in the Majengo area of Mtwara, it's worth stopping in at St Paul's church to view its remarkable artwork. The entire front and side walls are covered with richly coloured biblical scenes painted by a German Benedictine priest, Polycarp Uehlein. The paintings, which took about two years to complete, are part of a series by the same artist decorating churches throughout southern Tanzania and in a few other areas of the country, including churches in Nyangao, Lindi, Malolo, Ngapa and Dar es Salaam. In addition to their style and distinctive use of colour, the paintings are notable for their universalised portrayal of common biblical themes. The themes were chosen to assist churchgoers to understand the sermons and to relate the biblical lessons to their everyday lives.

During the years he has worked in Tanzania, Father Polycarp has taught several African students. The best known of these is Henry Likonde from Mtwara, who has taken biblical scenes and 'Africanised' them. You can see examples of Likonde's work in the small church at the top of the hill in Mahurunga, south of Mtwara near the Mozambican border, and in the cathedral in Songea.

a viewpoint near the Southern Cross Hotel. Mikindani (p326) is an easy half-day excursion from Mtwara.

Sleeping
BUDGET
Drive-In Garden & Cliff Bar (☎ 023-233 3911/3146, 0784-503007; Shangani; camping per person Tsh5000, r per person Tsh10,000) This is a shady, secure spot for camping, with clean bucket baths and a small bar-restaurant serving tasty grilled chicken, fish and other meals with advance notice, plus cold drinks. Also available are several simple, spotless rooms in a six-bed house that has a refrigerator and small cooker. The room price includes breakfast, and this place is overall good value. Go left at the main Shangani junction and follow the road paralleling the beach for about 1.2km to the small signpost on your left. If you have trouble finding it, ask at the Safina (Container shop) at the main Shangani junction, just after the Shangani Dispensary.

Mtwara Lutheran Centre (☎ 023-233 3294; Mikindani Rd; dm Tsh3000, s/d Tsh12,000/15,000, d without bathroom Tsh6000) Another good budget choice, with reasonable no-frills rooms with nets and meals with advance notice. The rooms vary, so check a few, and try to book in advance, as it's often full. It's on the southern edge of town, just off the main roundabout along the road heading to Mikindani. Arriving by bus, ask the driver to drop you at the roundabout.

Korosho Lodge (☎ 023-233 4093; Tanu Rd; r with fan/ air-con Tsh25,000/30,000, ste Tsh35,000) Spartan and rather soulless but spiffy rooms with cold water and clean bathrooms, and a restaurant.

It's in a walled compound diagonally opposite the taxi stand. Breakfast is included.

If none of these suit, there's a clutch of low-budget local guesthouses on the back roads just west of Tanu Rd, including **Bondeni Lodge** (☎ 023-233 3669; s/d Tsh9000/14,000), with no-frills block-style rooms, all with fan and net, lined up next to a tiny courtyard, and a pub next door.

MIDRANGE
VETA (☎ 023-233 4094; Shangani; s Tsh15,000, ste Tsh35,000; ⬛) Clean rooms, all with a large bed, TV and views over the water, plus a restaurant. It's in Shangani, about 200m back from the water (though there's no swimming beach here). From the T-junction in Shangani, go left and continue for about 3km. There's no public transport; taxis charge Tsh3000- to Tsh000 from town.

Southern Cross Hotel (Msemo; ☎ 023-233 3206; www .msemo.com; Shangani; s/d US$35/55) A recommended place with spotless, good-value rooms, all with fan, TV, nice tiled bathrooms, a sea-facing window and a Scandinavian touch to the furnishings. There's also a relaxing seaside restaurant that's a popular spot for sundowners. It's on a small outcrop directly overlooking the water in Shangani, with Shangani beach just a few minutes walk away. Staff can help arrange excursions in the area. Profits from the hotel are channelled into primary health-care services in the Mtwara region.

Eating & Drinking
The **fish market** at the Msangamkuu boat dock is good for street food, selling grilled *pweza* (octopus), *vitambua* (rice cakes) and other delicacies.

For sundowners and tasty meals, try the restaurant at the **Southern Cross Hotel** (Msemo; Shangani; meals from Tsh5000). Drive-In Garden & Cliff Bar is another amenable spot for a drink or meal. Other options include **Shabu Restaurant** (Aga Khan Rd; meals Tsh2000; 8am-10pm Mon-Sat, Sun 8am-1pm) in the town centre, serving local dishes, Indian snacks and sometimes fresh yogurt, and the restaurant at **Korosho Lodge** (Tanu Rd; meals Tsh5000-6000; lunch & dinner) near the bus stand, with a selection of Indian and standard fare.

For self-caterers: there are several reasonably useful shops along Uhuru Rd, including the first one on the left after passing the taxi stand. **Safina** ('Container Shop'; Shangani; 8am-7pm), at the main junction in Shangani, has a good selection of basic supermarket items, frozen meat and sausages and cold drinks.

Shopping

Mtwara and around are good places to buy Makonde carvings, although many carvers only work on commission. A good place to start is the family of carvers under the second tree after the airport turn-off. For high-quality, commissioned carvings, contact **Paulo Hokororo** (0784-260727), or through the Safina (see above).

Getting There & Away

AIR

There are daily flights between Mtwara and Dar es Salaam (Tsh150,000 one-way) on **Air Tanzania** (023-233 3147; Bodi ya Korosho Bldg, Tanu Rd; closed during flight arrivals & departures), and **Precision Air** (023-233 4116; Tanu Rd), which also sometimes stops in Lindi. Twice weekly, the Precision Air flight continues on to Pemba (Mozambique).

BUS

All long-distance buses depart between about 5am and 8am from the main bus stand just off Sokoine Rd near the market.

To Masasi, there are roughly hourly departures between about 6am and 2pm (Tsh4500, five hours); once in Masasi you'll need to change vehicles for Tunduru and Songea.

To Lindi (three hours), there are several direct minibuses daily, departing in both directions in the morning. Otherwise, take any Masasi bus to Mingoyo junction and wait for onward transport from there.

There's at least one direct bus daily to Kilwa Masoko (Tsh7000, five hours), departing between 5am and 6am in each direction.

Direct buses to Newala (Tsh4500, six to eight hours) use the southern route via Nanyamba. Departures from Mtwara are between 6am and 8am daily, except during the wet season when services are more sporadic. It's also possible to reach Newala via Masasi, although this may entail an overnight stay in Masasi.

To Dar es Salaam, there are daily buses (Tsh18,000 to Tsh20,000, 10 to 12 hours), departing in each direction by about 6am. Lines to watch for include Wifi and Sollo's. Book in advance. In Dar es Salaam, departures are from Ubungo, or – better – from Temeke's Sudan Market area, where all the southbound bus lines also have booking offices.

To Mozambique, there are several pickups daily to Mahurunga and the Tanzanian immigration post at Kilambo (Tsh2500), departing Mtwara between about 8am and 11am. Departures are from the eastern side of the market near the mosque. For information on crossing the Ruvuma River, see p351. The best places for updated information on the vehicle ferry are The Old Boma and Ten Degrees South, both in Mikindani (p326). Note that Mozambican visas are *not* issued at this border and there is no Mozambique consulate in Mtwara (the closest one is in Dar es Salaam).

CAR & MOTORCYCLE

If you're driving to/from Dar es Salaam, there are petrol stations in Kibiti, Ikwiriri, Nangurukuru, Kilwa Masoko, Lindi and Mtwara.

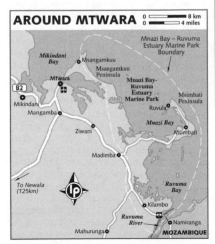

Getting Around

Taxis to and from the airport (6km south-east of the main roundabout) cost Tsh6000. There are taxi ranks at the bus stand and near the CCM building; the cost for a town trip is Tsh2000 (Tsh2500 from the centre to Shangani). Tuk-tuks (*majaji*) are slightly cheaper.

There are a few *dalla-dallas* running along Tanu Rd to and from the bus stand, although none to Shangani. To arrange bicycle rental, ask at the market or at one of the nearby bicycle shops.

MIKINDANI

☎ 023

Mikindani – set on a picturesque bay surrounded by coconut groves – is a quiet, charming Swahili town with a long history. Although easily visited as a day trip from Mtwara, many travellers prefer it to its larger neighbour as a base for exploring the surrounding area.

History

Mikindani gained prominence early on as a major dhow port and terminus for trade caravans from Lake Nyasa. By the late 15th century, these networks extended across southern Tanzania as far as Zambia and present-day Democratic Republic of Congo (Zaïre). Following a brief downturn in fortunes, trade – primarily in slaves, ivory and copper – again increased in the mid16th century as Mikindani came under the domain of the Sultan of Zanzibar. In the 19th century, following the ban on the slave trade, Mikindani fell into decline until the late 1880s when the German colonial government made the town its regional headquarters and began large-scale sisal, coconut, rubber and oilseed production in the area. However, the boom was not to last. With the arrival of the British and the advent of larger ocean-going vessels, Mikindani was abandoned in favour of Mtwara's superior harbour, and now, almost a century later, seems not to have advanced much beyond this era. Much of the town has been designated as a conservation zone, and life today centres on the small dhow port, which is still a hub for local coastal traffic.

For David Livingstone fans, the famous explorer spent a few weeks in the area in 1866 before setting out on his last journey.

Information

The closest banking facilities are in Mtwara.

The Old Boma has a tourist information office and an internet connection. Walking tours of towns and local excursions can be organised here and at Ten Degrees South.

Sights & Activities

The imposing German **boma**, built in 1895 as a fort and administrative centre, has been beautifully renovated as a hotel (see below). Even if you're not staying here, it's worth taking a look, and climbing the tower for **views** over the town.

Downhill from the boma is the old **slave market**, which now houses several craft shops. Unfortunately, it was much less accurately restored than the boma and lost much of its architectural interest when its open arches were filled in. The original design is now preserved only on one of Tanzania's postage stamps, and in a photo in an earlier edition of this guidebook.

The **prison ruins** are opposite the jetty, and nearby is a large, hollow baobab tree that was once used to keep unruly prisoners in solitary confinement.

Apart from the various historical buildings, it's well worth just strolling through town to soak up the atmosphere and see the numerous carved Zanzibar-style doors. With more time, make your way up Bismarck Hill, rising up behind the Old Boma, for some views.

Sleeping & Eating

Ten Degrees South Lodge (ECO2; ☎ 0784-855833; www.eco2.com; r without bathroom Tsh20,000) A good budget travellers' base, all with refurbished rooms – all with large beds and nets, plus bay views and deck chairs up on the roof. Self-contained chalets are planned (about US$50 per double), and there's a restaurant-bar (meals from Tsh5000) under a shady, thatched *banda* with a TV and a good vibe in season. **ECO2** (www.eco2.com) is based here, and is the best contact for arranging diving in Mnazi Bay-Ruvuma Estuary Marine Park. They also have a dhow that can be chartered for excursions. Check their website for information on volunteer marine research opportunities.

The Old Boma at Mikindani (☎ 023-233 3875, 0756-455978; www.mikindani.com; r without/with balcony from US$90/120, triple ste US$200; ▣) This beautifully restored building, on a breezy hilltop overlooking town and Mikindani Bay, offers spacious, atmospheric, high-ceilinged doubles and the closest to top-end standards that you'll find in these parts. There's a sunset terrace overlooking the bay, a pool surrounded by bougainvillea bushes and lush gardens, and a restaurant. Rooms vary, so check out a few before choosing. It's run by Trade Aid (www.tradeaiduk.org), a non-profit group committed to improving employment and educational opportunities for the local community. A stay at the Old Boma supports their work; check out their website if you want to get more involved.

Mikindani Yacht Club (contact through ECO2; admission Tsh2500, snacks from Tsh1500) Temporarily closed when we passed through, but when open, this waterside place is a good spot for snacks and light meals. Boat hire is also sometimes possible.

Ismaili's Corner Bar (snacks & light meals from Tsh2000; buffet per person Tsh3500, minimum four persons) At the old Slave Market, and just below the Old Boma, with snacks and light meals, and a Friday seafood buffet with advance notice.

Getting There & Away

Mikindani is 10km from Mtwara along a sealed road. Minibuses (Tsh200) run between the two towns throughout the day. Taxis from Mtwara charge Tsh5000 to Tsh10,000, depending on your bargaining abilities.

MNAZI BAY-RUVUMA ESTUARY MARINE PARK

Tanzania's newest marine park encompasses a narrow sliver of coastline extending from Msangamkuu peninsula (just north and east of Mtwara) in the north to the Mozambique border in the south. In addition to about 5000 people, it provides home to over 400 marine species and an impressive array of delicate coastal ecosystems. Although still very much in its initial stages, it's ultimately hoped that the park will be the core of a conservation area extending as far south as Pemba in Mozambique.

The heart of the conservation area is **Msimbati Peninsula**, together with the bordering Mnazi Bay. Among its attractions: a lovely palm-lined beach, a string of offshore reefs and a lack of crowds. Most visitors head straight to the tiny village of **Ruvula**, which is about 7km beyond Msimbati village along a sandy track (or along the beach at low tide), and which boasts a fine stretch of sand, although

the views have been marred in recent times by the rigs set up at one end in connection with exploitation of offshore gas fields found in Mnazi Bay. In addition to its beach – one of the few on the mainland offering sunset views – Ruvula is notable as the spot where British eccentric Latham Leslie-Moore built his house and lived until 1967 when he was deported after agitating for independence for the Msimbati Peninsula. Deportation seemed a better option to Leslie-Moore than being subjected to the government of the newly independent Tanzania. His story is chronicled in John Heminway's *No Man's Land*, and in *Africa Passion*, a documentary film. Today, Leslie-Moore's house stands in ruins; the property is privately owned.

Msangamkuu Peninsula, at the northern edge of the marine park and best visited from Mtwara, boasts a fishing village, an attractive beach and snorkelling (bring your own equipment).

Marine park entry fees are US$10 (US$5/ free for children from five to 16 years/under five) per day for adults, and are collected at the marine park gate at the entrance to Msimbati village. To arrange diving, contact **ECO2** (www.eco2.com), based at Ten Degrees South Lodge in Mikindani, which is also the best source of updated information on the park.

Ruvula Sea Safari (☎ 0784-367439, 0784-484184; camping per person Tsh10,000, s/d bandas with full board Tsh85,000/150,000) The only place to stay, with rustic *bandas* sharing facilities (prices are currently set disproportionately high in comparison with what's on offer so as to tap into the coffers of the gas company staff based nearby), delicious grilled fish meals (Tsh10,000 per person) and the beach at your doorstep. A few basic supplies are available in Msimbati village, but if you're camping, stock up in Mtwara and bring a torch. Staff can help you sort out excursions to Bird Island, directly opposite, and boating through nearby mangrove channels. Watch for the tiny sign marking the turnoff from the Msimbati–Ruvula road. Day visitors are charged Tsh5000 per person for beach use (the fee is waived if you eat a meal).

GETTING THERE & AWAY

There is at least one pick-up daily in each direction between Mtwara and Msimbati (Tsh1800, two hours), departing Mtwara about 11am from the eastern side of the market near the mosque. Departures from Msimbati are around 5.30am from the police post near the park gate. On weekends, many of Mtwara's foreign residents head towards Msimbati and it's usually easy to find a lift.

Driving from Mtwara, take the main road from the roundabout south for 4km to the village of Mangamba, branch left at the signpost onto the Mahurunga road and continue about 18km to Madimba. At Madimba, turn left again and continue for 20km to Msimbati; the road is unpaved, but in good condition. If you are cycling, the major village en route is Ziwani, which has a decent market.

There is no public transport between Msimbati and Ruvula. On weekends, it's sometimes possible to hitch a lift. Otherwise, arrange a lift on a motorbike (about Tsh5000) with one of the locals or walk along the beach at low tide (one-hour-plus). Although sandy, the road is in reasonably good condition thanks to maintenance work by the gas company and Ruvula Sea Safari can generally be reached in a regular 2WD taxi from Mtwara (Tsh45,000 to Tsh60,000 round-trip).

Dhows and canoes travel between the Shangani dhow port dock in Mtwara and Msangamkuu peninsula throughout the day (Tsh100; about 15 minutes with favourable winds).

MAKONDE PLATEAU & AROUND

This cool and scenic plateau, much of which lies between 700m and 900m above sea level, is home to the Makonde people, famed throughout East Africa for their exotic wood carvings (see opposite). With its comparative isolation, scattered settlements and seeming oblivion to developments elsewhere in the country, it in many ways epitomises inland areas of southeastern Tanzania, and is worth a detour if you're in the area.

Newala
☎ 023

Dusty, bustling Newala is the major settlement on the plateau. Thanks to its perch at 780m altitude, it offers a pleasantly brisk climate, and views over the Ruvuma River valley and into Mozambique. At the edge of the escarpment on the southwestern side of town is the old German boma (now the police station) and, nearby, the Shimo la Mungu (Hole of God) viewpoint. There are numerous paths from the edge of town leading down to the river. If

you plan to do this it's not a bad idea to carry your passport (which you should carry around anyway in Newala, given its proximity to the border) and arrange a local guide. Bicycles can be rented near the market.

SLEEPING & EATING
Country Lodge Bed & Breakfast ('Sollo's'; ☎ 023-241 0355; Masasi road; s/d Tsh22,000/30,000; ⓢ) This long-standing place is the best choice in town. Rooms have nets and a bathroom, the doubles have two large beds, and there's a small pool. There's also a decent restaurant, with the usual array of standard dishes, plus better fare with an advance order. It's about 600m from the bus stand, on the road to Masasi.

For something cheaper, there are several less-expensive guesthouses in the area around the market and bus stand, with no-frills rooms sharing a bathroom from about Tsh4000, and cheap eateries nearby.

GETTING THERE & AWAY
Daily buses run from Newala to Mtwara and to Masasi (Tsh3000, three hours). There is usually also at least one vehicle daily between Newala and Mtama, east of Masasi on the road to Mtwara. All roads from Newala are unpaved. The journeys to Masasi and Mtama offer beautiful views as you wind down the side of the plateau.

Masasi
☎ 023

Masasi, a bustling district centre and birthplace of former Tanzanian President Benjamin Mkapa, stretches out along the main road off the edge of the Makonde Plateau against a backdrop of granite hills. The history of the modern settlement dates to the late 19th century, when the Anglican Universities' Mission to Central Africa (UMCA) came from Zanzibar to establish a settlement of former slaves here. Today, it's notable primarily as a transport hub for onward travel along the wild road west towards Tunduru, or north to Nachingwea and Liwale. About 70km east of Masasi along the Mtwara road is **Mahiwa**, the site of one of WWI's bloodiest battles in Africa, in which more than 2000 people lost their lives.

Many Makonde woodcarvers are based in the area. The group of carvers along the Nachingwea road, on the left side and about 500m from the bus stand, generally have reasonable prices.

THE MAKONDE

The Makonde, known throughout East Africa for their woodcarvings, are one of Tanzania's largest ethnic groups. They originated in northern Mozambique, where many still live, and began to make their way northwards during the 18th and 19th centuries. The Mozambican war sparked another large influx into Tanzania, with up to 15,000 Makonde crossing the border during the 1970s and 1980s in search of a safe haven and employment. Today, although the Makonde on both sides of the Ruvuma River are considered to be a single ethnic entity, there are numerous cultural and linguistic differences between the two groups.

Like many tribes in this part of Tanzania, the Makonde are matrilineal. Children and inheritances normally belong to the woman, and it's common for husbands to move to the village of their wives after marriage. Settlements are widely scattered – possibly a remnant of the days when the Makonde sought to evade slave raids – and there is no tradition of a unified political system. Each village is governed by a hereditary chief and a council of elders.

Due to their isolated location, the Makonde have remained insulated from colonial and postcolonial influences, and are considered to be one of Tanzania's most traditional groups. Even today, most Makonde still adhere to traditional religions, with the complex spirit world given its fullest expression in their carvings.

Traditionally, the Makonde practised body scarring and while it's seldom done today, you may see older people with markings on their face and bodies. It's also fairly common to see elderly Makonde women wearing a wooden plug in their upper lip, or to see this depicted in Makonde artwork.

Most Makonde are subsistence farmers, and there is speculation as to why they chose to establish themselves on a waterless plateau. Possible factors include the relative safety that the area offered from outside intervention (especially during slave trading days), and the absence of the tsetse fly.

If you're planning to visit Lukwika-Lumesule and Msangesi Game Reserves (see p330), it's essential to first stop in Masasi at the **reserve warden's office** (☎ 023-251 0364, 0784-634972, 0713-311129). It's on the Newala road, a few hundred metres southeast of the Mtwara road on the right, near the immigration office. Ask for *Mali Asili* (Natural Resources).

SLEEPING & EATING

In town, there's a clutch of inexpensive and noisy guesthouses, including **Holiday Guest House** (d Tsh7000) at the western end of town near the petrol station, and **Sayari Hotel** (☎ 023-251 0095; r Tsh11,000), at the eastern end of town near the post office.

Kilema Kyaro (d Tsh15,000) About 2km out of town on the Newala road, with quieter rooms than you'll find in town, and a restaurant. It's signposted on your left when leaving Masasi.

For meals – the offerings are limited to chicken, chips and ugali – try the restaurant at **Sayari Hotel** (meals Tsh2500), or **Mummy's** (meals Tsh2000), behind the bus stand, and near the district council building. Street food is available near the market.

GETTING THERE & AWAY

The bus stand is at the far western end of Masasi on the Tunduru road. If you're arriving from Mtwara, ask the driver to drop you off at your hotel or at the petrol station to avoid having to walk back into town.

The road between Masasi and Mtwara is mostly paved and in generally good condition. Buses travel between the two towns approximately hourly between 6am and 2pm daily (Tsh4500, five hours).

To Tunduru, the road is in rough but reasonable shape – allow up to five hours to cover the 200km stretch. Land Rovers and the occasional bus travel this stretch daily during the dry season. During the wet season, departures are more sporadic and prices higher.

Ndanda

Ndanda is a small town about 40km northeast of Masasi off the edge of the Makonde plateau. It's dominated by a large Benedictine monastery, which was founded by German missionaries in 1906. Adjoining the monastery is a hospital, which serves as the major health clinic for the entire surrounding region. About a 45-minute walk south (uphill) from the monastery is a small dam with clean water for swimming, although you'll need permission from the abbey before taking a dip.

Apart from the monastery guesthouse (reserved for monastery guests only), the only accommodation is in a few unappealing budget guesthouses along the main road at the bus stand, and diagonally opposite the hospital.

Buses run daily between Masasi and Ndanda, and any vehicle along the main road will drop you.

LUKWIKA-LUMESULE & MSANGESI GAME RESERVES

These tiny game reserves are hidden away in the remote hinterlands southwest and west of Masasi. They're officially off-limits during the July to December hunting season (thanks to local hunting concessions), and unofficially off-limits during much of the rest of the year due to the rains. If you're keen on heading down this way, late June is the best time to come.

Lukwika-Lumesule is the more interesting of the two. It's separated from Mozambique's Niassa Reserve by the Ruvuma River, and animals frequently wade across the border. With luck you may see elephants, sable antelopes, elands, greater kudus, crocodiles and hippos. The main challenge, apart from getting around the reserve, is spotting the animals through the often dense vegetation.

Because Msangesi Game Reserve has no permanent water source, wildlife concentrations are often low. It's rumoured to have buffaloes, elands, zebras, sable antelopes and duikers, though it's unlikely you'll spot many of these.

Before visiting, it's essential to stop by the **reserve warden's office** (☎ 023-251 0364, 0784-634972, 0713-311129) in Masasi to get a letter of permission, and to confirm that the reserves are open for tourism during the time you wish to visit. In Mtwara you can sometimes get information on the reserve from the Office of Natural Resources in the Regional Block complex (go to the small white building at the back). There's a US$30 per person per day entry fee for each reserve.

SLEEPING & EATING

Camping is permitted with your own tent; there's currently no charge. Bring everything with you, including food and drinking water. Water for bathing is normally available at Lukwika-Lumesule, but not at Msangesi.

GETTING THERE & AWAY

The entry point into Lukwika-Lumesule is about 2.5km southwest of Mpombe village on the northeastern edge of the reserve, and reached via Nangomba village, 40km west of Masasi.

To reach Msangesi from Masasi, follow the Tunduru road west to the Masasi airfield. Turn right, and continue to Chingulungulu, the last village before the reserve.

There is no regular public transport to either reserve, although you may occasionally be able to get a lift with a vehicle from the reserve warden's office in Masasi. Otherwise, you'll need your own 4WD transport. During the dry season, it's possible to drive around Lukwika-Lumesule, following a road running along its periphery. Getting around in Msangesi is more difficult. The road is not maintained and is sometimes impassable.

Directory

CONTENTS

ACCOMMODATION

Accommodation in Tanzania ranges from humble cinderblock rooms with communal bucket baths to some of Africa's most luxurious safari lodges. Choice is good in tourist areas and limited off the beaten track. Most upmarket hotels consider July, August and the Christmas and New Year holidays to be peak season, and sometimes levy a peak-season surcharge on top of regular high-season rates. During the March to early June low season, it's often possible to negotiate significant discounts – up to 50% – on room rates. A residents' permit entitles you to discounts at some hotels.

Sleeping listings in this book are divided into budget, midrange and top-end categories (see inside front cover).

Camping

It's worth carrying a tent for saving money, for flexibility, especially off the beaten track, and when visiting parks (though camping in most national parks costs at least US$30 per person per night – more than sleeping in most park *bandas* (thatched-roof huts or shelters) and huts, where these are available.

NATIONAL PARKS

All parks have camp sites, designated as either 'public' ('ordinary') or 'special'. Public camp sites have toilets (usually pit latrines), and sometimes have a water source. Most sites are in reasonable condition and some are quite pleasant. Special camp sites are smaller and more remote than public sites, with no facilities at all. The idea is that the area remains as close to pristine as possible. Unlike public camp sites, which don't require bookings, special camp sites must be booked in advance. They are also more expensive. Usually, once you make a booking, the special camp site is reserved exclusively for your group. For either type of site, plan on being self-sufficient, including with drinking water.

PRACTICALITIES

- Tanzania uses the metric system for weights and measures.
- Access electricity (220-250V AC, 50Hz) with British-style three-square-pin or two-round-pin plug adaptors.
- English-language newspapers include: *Guardian* and *Daily News* (dailies); *Business Times, Financial Times* and *East African* (weeklies).
- English-language radio stations include: Radio Tanzania (government-aligned); Radio One; Radio Free Africa; BBC World Service; Deutsche Welle

Most parks also have simple huts or *bandas*, several have basic resthouses and many northern circuit parks have hostels (for student groups). For park camping and resthouse prices, see p77.

ELSEWHERE

There are camp sites situated in or near most major towns, near many of the national parks and in some scenic locations along a few of the main highways (ie Dar es Salaam–Mbeya, and Tanga–Moshi); prices average from US$5 per person per night to more than double this for camp sites near national parks. Camping away from established sites is generally not advisable. In rural areas, seek permission first from the village head or elders before pitching your tent. Camping is not permitted on Zanzibar. Camping prices quoted in this book are per person per night except as noted. For more on fly camps and permanent and luxury tented camps, see right.

Guesthouses

Almost every Tanzanian town has at least one basic guesthouse. At the bottom end of the scale, expect a cement-block room – often small and poorly ventilated, and not always very clean – with a foam mattress, shared bathroom facilities (often long-drop toilets and bucket showers), and sometimes a fan and/or mosquito net. Rates average Tsh3000 to Tsh6000 per room per night. The next level up gets you a cleaner, decent room, often with a bathroom (although not always with running or hot water). Prices for a single/double room with bathroom average from about Tsh10,000/15,000.

For peace and quiet, guesthouses without bars are the best choice. In many towns, water is a problem during the dry season, so don't be surprised if your only choice at budget places is a bucket bath. Also, many of the cheaper places don't have hot water. This is a consideration in cooler areas, especially during winter, although most places will arrange a hot bucket if you ask. In Swahili, the word *hotel* or *hoteli* does not mean accommodation, but rather a place for food and drink. The more common term used for accommodation is *guesti* (guesthouse), or, more formally, *nyumba ya kulala wageni*.

There are many mission hostels and guesthouses, primarily for missionaries and aid-organisation staff, though some are willing to accommodate travellers, space permitting.

In coastal areas, you'll find *bandas* or bungalows – small thatched-roof structures with wooden or earthen walls – ranging from simple huts on the sand to luxurious en suite affairs.

Hotels & Lodges

Larger towns offer from one to several mid-range hotels with en suite rooms (widely referred to in Tanzania as 'self-contained' or 'self-containers'), hot water, and a fan or an air conditioner. Facilities range from not so great to quite good value, with prices ranging from US$30 to US$40 per person.

At the top end of the spectrum, there's an array of fine hotels and lodges with all the amenities you would expect at this price level – from US$100 or more per person per night. Especially on the safari circuits there are some wonderful and very luxurious lodges costing from US$150 to US$500 or more per person per night, although at the high end of the spectrum, prices are usually all-inclusive.

In many park areas, you'll find 'permanent tented camps' or 'luxury tented camps'. These offer comfortable beds in spacious canvas tents, with screened windows and most of the comforts of a hotel room, but with a wilderness feel. Most such tents also have private bathrooms with hot running water, as well as generator-provided electricity for at least part of the evening. In contrast to permanent tented camps, which are designed to stay in the same place from season to season, 'mobile' or 'fly' camps are temporary camps set up for one or several nights, or perhaps just for one season. In the Tanzanian context, fly camps are used for walking safaris away from the main tented camp or lodge, or to offer the chance for a closer, more intimate bush experience. Although fly camps are more rugged than permanent luxury tented camps (ie they may not have running water or similar features), they fully cater to their guests, including with bush-style showers (where an elevated bag or drum is filled with solar-heated water). They are also usually more expensive than regular tented camps or lodges, since provisions must be carried to the site.

ACTIVITIES
Bird-Watching
Tanzania is an outstanding birding destination, with well over 1000 species identified thus far, including numerous endemics. In addition to the national parks and reserves, top birding spots include the eastern Usambara Mountains (p168) and Lake Victoria (p240). Useful websites include the **Tanzania Bird Atlas** (www.tanzaniabirdatlas.com), the Tanzania Hotspots page on www.camacdonald.com/birding/africatanzania.htm and http://birds.intanzania.com.

Boating, Sailing & Kayaking
Local dhow trips are easily arranged along the coast. They are generally best booked for short sails – a sunset or afternoon sail, for example – rather than longer journeys. Ask your hotel for recommendations of a reliable captain; for more on the realities of dhow travel, see the boxed text, p357. Another option is to contact one of the coastal or island hotels, many of which have private dhows that can be chartered for cruises. For some suggestions, see p357. Catamarans and sailboats can be chartered on Zanzibar, Pemba and Kilwa, and

Dar es Salaam, Tanga and Mikindani have yacht clubs.

Trips down the Rufiji River and across the channel to Mafia island can be arranged by several upmarket Chole Bay hotels (Mafia).

Chimpanzee Tracking
Gombe Stream National Park (p265) and Mahale Mountains National Park (p267) have both hosted international research teams for decades, and are the places to go if you're interested in observing our primate cousins at close range. It's also possible to see chimpanzees at Rubondo Island National Park (p252).

Cycling
For information on cycling in Tanzania, see p356.

Diving
Although pricier than places such as the Red Sea, Tanzania is a popular and rewarding destination for diving and for diving certification courses. The main hubs (all with at least one, and often several, certified dive operators) include Zanzibar, Pemba and Mafia islands; the southeast around Msimbati and Mtwara (Mikindani is the base) and the coast north of Dar es Salaam. In addition to extensive coral reef systems and rich marine life, there's the chance for wreck dives and a favourable mix of conditions, although in many areas dives involve at least a 30 minute boat ride to the sites. For more, see p118. Dive operator contacts are listed in the destination chapters.

Fishing
Mafia, the Pemba channel and the waters around Zanzibar have long been insider tips in deep-sea fishing circles, and upmarket hotels in these areas are the best places to arrange charters. Other contacts include Kilwa Ruins Lodge (p317) in Kilwa Masoko, Game Fish Lodge in Nungwi on Zanzibar (p131) and upper end hotels in most coastal destinations. In Dar es Salaam, anglers can inquire at Msasani Slipway and at the Dar es Salaam Yacht Club. Also see www.fishingtanzania.20m.com/sud.html for an overview.

Inland, Lake Victoria is renowned for its fishing, particularly for Nile perch. The best contacts here are Lukuba Island Lodge (p243), Rubondo Island Camp (p252) and Wag Hill Lodge (p247).

Hiking & Trekking

For an overview of hiking and trekking areas, see the Trekking chapter (p49). Many Cultural Tourism Programs (see p205) also involve walking and light hiking. For most hiking, and for all hiking in national parks, you'll need to be accompanied by a guide. For any extended hiking, get a copy of Lonely Planet's *Trekking in East Africa*.

Horse Riding

Riding safaris are possible in the West Kilimanjaro and Lake Natron areas. Contacts include **Equestrian Safaris** (www.safaririding.com) and Makoa Farm (see p187).

Wildlife Watching

Tanzania is one of Africa's premier wildlife watching destinations, and it is famed for its exceptional variety and concentrations of large animals and a stellar array of national parks and reserves covering almost one-third of the country. See the Safaris chapter (p36), and the Wildlife and Habitat special section (p57).

BUSINESS HOURS

Business hours are listed inside the front cover, with exceptions noted in the individual listings. In addition to regular banking hours, most forex bureaus remain open until 5pm Monday to Friday, and until noon on Saturday. Many shops and offices close for one to two hours between noon and 2pm, and – especially in coastal areas – on Friday afternoons for mosque services. Supermarkets in major cities are often open on Saturday afternoon and Sunday for a few hours around midday.

CHILDREN

Tanzanians tend to be very friendly towards children, and travelling here with young ones is unlikely to present any major problems. The main concerns are likely be the presence of malaria, the scarcity of decent medical facilities outside major towns, the length and safety risks involved in many road journeys, and the difficulty of finding clean, decent bathrooms outside midrange and top-end hotels.

It's a good idea to travel with a blanket to spread out and use as a make-shift nappy changing area. Processed baby foods, powdered infant milk, disposable nappies and similar items are available in major towns, but otherwise carry your own wipes, as well as food (avoid feeding your children street food). Informal childcare is easy to arrange; the best bet is to ask at your hotel. Child seats for hire cars and safari vehicles are generally not available unless arranged in advance.

Many wildlife lodges have restrictions on accommodating children under 12; otherwise, most hotels are family friendly. Most places, including all national parks, offer significant discounts for children on entry fees and accommodation or camping rates although you'll need to specifically request these, especially when booking through tour operators. Children under two years of age often stay free, and for those up to 12 years old sharing their parents' room you'll pay about 50% of the adult rate. In hotels without special rates, triple rooms are commonly available for not too much more than a double room. Midrange and top-end places often have pools, or grassy areas where children can play, and any of the coastal beach areas are likely to win points with young travellers.

In beach areas, keep in mind the risks of hookworm infestation in populated areas, and watch out for sea urchins. Other things to watch out for are bilharzia infection in lakes, and thorns and the like in the brush.

For protection against malaria, it's essential to bring along mosquito nets for your children and ensure that they sleep under them, and to check with your doctor regarding the use of malarial prophylactics. Bring long-sleeved shirts, trousers and socks for dawn and dusk, and ensure that your children wear them – and use mosquito repellent.

Wildlife watching is suitable for older children who have the patience to sit for long periods in a car, but less suitable for younger ones, unless it's kept to manageable doses. Good destinations include anywhere along the coast, Saadani National Park, with its clean beach and generally calm waters, the area around Lushoto (for children old enough to enjoy walking), and the water amusement parks north of Dar es Salaam (p102).

Lonely Planet's *Travel with Children* by Cathy Lanigan has more tips for keeping children and parents happy while on the road.

CLIMATE CHARTS

Tanzania has a generally comfortable, tropical climate year-round, although there are significant regional variations. Along the warmer and humid coast, the climate is determined in large part by the monsoon winds, which bring rains in two major periods. During the *masika* (long rains), from mid-March to May, it rains heavily almost every day, although seldom for the whole day, and the air can get unpleasantly sticky. The lighter *mvuli* (short rains) fall during November, December and sometimes into January. Inland, altitude is a major determinant of conditions. The central plateau is somewhat cooler and arid, while in the mountainous areas of the northeast and southwest, temperatures occasionally drop below 15°C at night during June and July, and it can rain at any time of year. The coolest months countrywide are from June to October and the warmest from December to March.

COURSES
Language

Tanzania is the best place in East Africa to learn Swahili. Schools (many of which can arrange home stays) are listed below. Also see the **Kiswahili Home Page** (www.glcom.com/cyberswahili/swahili.htm) and the **Kiswahili Resource Page** (www.unb.ca/web/civil/dccchair/dmm/swahili.html). Another contact is Riverside Campsite (p283) in Iringa.

ELCT Language & Orientation School (www.study swahili.com; Lutheran Junior Seminary, Morogoro)

Institute of Swahili & Foreign Languages (Map p113; ☎ 024-223 0724, 223 3337; takiluki@zanlink.com; PO Box 882, Zanzibar, attn: Department of Swahili for Foreigners; Vuga Rd, Zanzibar Town) Also see www.glcom.com/hassan/takiluki.html

KIU Ltd (☎ 022-285 1509; www.swahilicourses.com) At various locations in Dar es Salaam, plus branches in Iringa and Zanzibar.

Makoko Language School (☎ 028-264 2518; swahili musoma@juasun.net) In Makoko neighbourhood, on the

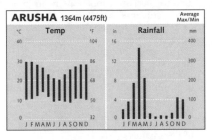

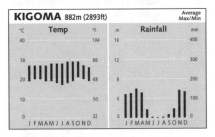

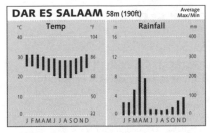

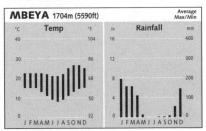

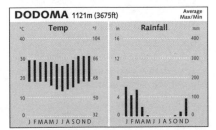

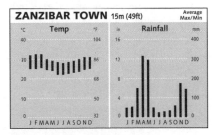

DIRECTORY

outskirts of Musoma; also see www.stgertrude
.org/frben/makoko/makoko.htm
MS Training Centre for Development Cooperation
(☎ 027-255 3837/8; www.mstcdc.or.tz) About 15km
outside Arusha, near Usa River.
University of Dar es Salaam (☎ 022-241 0757;
www.udsm.ac.tz/kiswahilicourses.html)

CUSTOMS

Exporting seashells, coral, ivory and turtle
shells is illegal. You can export a maximum
of Tsh2000 without declaration. There's no
limit on the importation of foreign currency;
amounts over US$10,000 must be declared.

DANGERS & ANNOYANCES

Tanzania is in general a safe, hassle-free country and can be a relief if you've recently been
somewhere like Nairobi. That said, you do need
to take the usual precautions. Avoid isolated
areas, especially stretches of beach, and in cities and tourist areas take a taxi at night. When
using public transport, don't accept drinks or
food from someone you don't know, and be
sceptical of anyone who comes up to you on
the street asking whether you remember them
from the airport, your hotel or wherever.

In tourist areas – especially Arusha, Moshi
and Zanzibar – touts and flycatchers can be
extremely aggressive, especially around bus
stations and budget tourist hotels. Do everything you can to minimise the impression that
you're a newly arrived tourist. Duck into a
shop if you need to get your bearings or look
at a map and don't walk around any more
than necessary with your luggage. While looking for a room, leave your bag with a friend
or reliable hotel rather than walking around
town with it. Buy your bus tickets a day in
advance (without your luggage) and, when
arriving in a new city, take a taxi from the bus
station to your hotel. Be very wary of anyone
who approaches you on the street, at the bus
station or in your hotel offering safari deals,
and never pay any money for a safari or trek
in advance until you've thoroughly checked
out the company.

In western Tanzania, along the Burundi
border, there are sporadic outbursts of ban-
ditry and political unrest. Things are currently
quiet, but it's worth getting an update from
your embassy before travelling there.

A few more tips:

- Avoid external money pouches, dangling
  backpacks and camera bags, and leave
  jewellery, fancy watches, personal stereos
  and the like at home. Carry your passport, money and other documents in a
  pouch against your skin, hidden under
  loose-fitting clothing. Or, better, store
  valuables in a hotel safe, if there's a reliable one, ideally inside a pouch with a
  lockable zip to prevent tampering.
- Arriving for the first time at major bus stations, especially in Arusha, can be a fairly
  traumatic experience, as you'll probably
  be besieged by touts as you get off the bus,
  all reaching to help you with your pack
  and trying to sell you a safari. Have your
  luggage as consolidated as possible, with
  your valuables well hidden under your
  clothes. Try to spot the taxi area before
  disembarking and make a beeline for it.
  It's well worth a few extra dollars for the
  fare, rather than attempting to walk to
  your hotel with your luggage.
- Take requests for donations from 'refugees', 'students' or others with a grain
  of salt. Contributions to humanitarian
  causes are best done through an established agency or project.
- Keep the side windows up in vehicles
  when stopped in traffic and keep your
  bags out of sight (eg on the floor behind
  your legs).
- When bargaining or discussing prices,
  don't do so with your money or wallet
  in your hand.

DISCOUNT CARDS

A student ID gets you a 50% discount on train
fares, and sometimes on museum entry fees.

EMBASSIES & CONSULATES
Tanzanian Embassies & Consulates

Australia Melbourne (☎ 03-9667 0243; www.tanza
niaconsul.com; Level 2, 222 La Trobe St, Melbourne, VIC
3000); Perth (☎ 08-9221 0033; legal@murcia.com.au; 3rd
fl, MPH Bldg, 23 Barrack St, Perth WA 6000)

TRAVEL ADVISORIES

Government travel advisories are good
sources of updated security information:

- Australia – www.smarttraveller.gov.au
- Canada – www.dfait-maeci.gc.ca
- UK – www.fco.gov.uk
- US – www.travel.state.gov/travel

Burundi (tzrepbj@sina.com; 4 United Nations Rd, Plot 382, Bujumbura)
Canada (☎ 0613-232 1500; tzottawa@synapse.net; 50 Range Rd, Ottawa, Ontario KIN 8J4)
France (☎ 01-53 70 63 66; www.amb-tanzanie.fr; 13 Ave Raymond Poincaré, 75116 Paris)
Germany (☎ 030-303 0800; www.tanzania-gov.de; Eschenallee 11, 14050 Berlin-Charlottenburg)
Italy (☎ 06-334 85801; Viale Cortina d'Ampezzo 185, Rome)
Japan (☎ 03-3425 4531; www.tanzaniaembassy.or.jp; 4-21-9, Kamiyoga, Chome Setagaya-Ku, Tokyo 158-0098)
Kenya (☎ 020-311948; Reinsurance Plaza, 9th fl, btwn Tarifa Rd & Aga Khan Walk, Nairobi)
Malawi (☎ 01-775038, 01-770148; Plaza House, Capital City, Lilongwe 3)
Mozambique (☎ 21-490110; ujamaa@zebra.ume.mz; Ujamaa House, 852 Ave Mártires de Machava, Maputo)
The Netherlands (☎ 0180-312 644; Parallelweg Zuid 215, 2914 LE Nieuwerkerk aan den Ijssel)
Rwanda (☎ 756 567; tanzarep@tanzarep.gov.rw; 15 Ave Paul VI, Kigali)
South Africa (☎ 012-342 4371; www.tanzania.org.za; 822 George Ave, Arcadia 0007, Pretoria)
Uganda (☎ 041-256272; tzrepkla@imul.com; 6 Kagera Rd, Kampala)
UK (☎ 020-7569 1470; www.tanzania-online.gov.uk; 3 Stratford Place, London W1C 1AS)
USA Washington (☎ 1-202-939 6125; www.tanzania embassy-us.org; 2139 R St, NW, Washington DC 20008); New York (☎ 1-212-972 9160; 201 East 42nd St, Ste 1700, New York, NY 10017)
Zambia (☎ 01-227698; tzreplsk@zamnet.zm; Ujamaa House, 5200 United Nations Ave, Lusaka)

Tanzania also has diplomatic representation in Belgium (Brussels), China (Beijing), Democratic Republic of Congo (Zaïre); (Kinshasa), Egypt (Cairo), Ethiopia (Addis Ababa), India (New Delhi), Nigeria (Lagos), Russia (Moscow), Saudi Arabia (Riyadh), Sweden (Stockholm), Switzerland (Geneva) and Zimbabwe (Harare).

Embassies & Consulates in Tanzania

Embassies and consulates in Dar es Salaam include the following. Except as noted, most are open from about 8.30am to 3pm, often with a midday break. Visa applications for all countries neighbouring Tanzania should be made in the morning. Australians can contact the Canadian embassy (www.embassy.gov.au/).
Belgium (Map p86; ☎ 022-211 2688; daressalaam @diplobel.org; 5 Ocean Rd, Upanga)
Burundi (Map p86; ☎ 022-212 7008; Lugalo St, Upanga;

☑ 8am-3.30pm) Just up from the Italian embassy, and opposite the army compound. Three-month single-entry visas cost US$50 plus two photos, and are issued in 24 hours. The consulate in Kigoma (p262) issues one-month single entry visas for US$40 plus two photos within 24 hours.
Canada (Map p90; ☎ 022-216 3300; www.dfait-maeci .gc.ca/tanzania; Umoja House, cnr Mirambo St & Garden Ave)
Congo (Zaïre) (Map p86; 435 Maliki Rd, Upanga; ☑ 10am-1pm & 2pm-3.30pm) Three-month single-entry visas cost US$150 plus two photos and a letter of invitation from someone in Congo. Allow plenty of time for issuing. The consulate in Kigoma (p262) is much easier, issuing single-entry visas for US$50 (US$30 for Tanzania residents) plus two photos within two days or less.
France (Map p86; ☎ 022-219 8800; www.ambafrance -tz.org; Ali Hassan Mwinyi Rd)
Germany (Map p90; ☎ 022-211 7409 to 7415; www .daressalam.diplo.de/en/Startseite.html; Umoja House, cnr Mirambo St & Garden Ave)
India (Map p86; ☎ 022-266 9040; www.hcindiatz.org; 82 Kinondoni Rd)
Ireland (Map p86; ☎ 022-260 2355/6; iremb@raha .com; Toure Rd) Opposite Golden Tulip Hotel
Italy (Map p86; ☎ 022-211 5935; www.ambdares salaam.esteri.it; 316 Lugalo Rd, Upanga)
Kenya (Map p86; ☎ 022-266 8285; 127 Mafinga St, Kinondoni)
Malawi (Map p90; ☎ 022-213 6951; 1st fl, Zambia House, cnr Ohio St & Sokoine Dr; ☑ 8am-3pm) Many nationalities, including USA, UK and various European countries, do not require visas.
Mozambique (Map p90; ☎ 022-211 6502; 25 Garden Ave; ☑ 8.30am-3pm) One-month single-entry visas cost US$40 (US$55 for express service) plus two photos and are issued within three days.
Netherlands (Map p90; ☎ 022-211 0000; www .netherlands-embassy.go.tz; Umoja House, cnr Mirambo St & Garden Ave)
Rwanda (Map p86; ☎ 022-211 5889, 213 0119; 32 Ali Hassan Mwinyi Rd, Upanga; ☑ 8am-noon & 2-4pm) Three-month single entry visas cost US$60 plus two photos, and are issued within 48 hours. Citizens of the USA, Germany, South Africa, Canada and various other countries do not require visas.
Uganda (Map p86; ☎ 022-266 7009; 25 Msasani Rd, near Oyster Bay Primary School; ☑ 8.30am-3pm) Three-month single-entry visas cost US$30 plus two photos and are issued the same day.
UK (Map p90; ☎ 022-211 0101; www.britishhighcom mission.gov.uk/tanzania; Umoja House, cnr Mirambo St & Garden Ave)
USA (Map p86; ☎ 266 8001; http://usembassy.state .gov/tanzania; Old Bagamoyo & Kawawa Rds)
Zambia (Map p90; ☎ 022-212 5529; Ground fl, Zambia House, cnr Ohio St & Sokoine Dr; ☑ 9am-2pm Mon, Wed

& Fri for visa applications, 2-3.30pm Tue, Thu & Mon for pick-up) One-month single-entry visas cost from Tsh25,000 to Tsh125,000, depending on nationality, plus two photos, and are issued the next day.

FESTIVALS & EVENTS

The best festivals and celebrations in Tanzania are the small-scale ones that aren't announced anywhere, such as being invited to a wedding in a small town or to a rite of passage celebration. Getting away from the tourist haunts and into the villages and mingling with Tanzanians is the best way to find out about these.

FEBRUARY/MARCH

Sauti za Busara (www.busaramusic.com) A three-day music and dance festival centred around all things Swahili, traditional and modern; dates and location vary. See www.busaralive.com for live coverage of the current festival.

Kilimanjaro Marathon (www.kilimanjaromarathon .com) Something to do around the foothills, in case climbing to the top of the mountain isn't enough; it's held in February or March, starting and finishing in Moshi.

MAY

Bagamoyo Arts Festival (www.sanaabagamoyo.com) A week of traditional music, dance, acrobatics, poetry reading and more, featuring local and regional ensembles. Dates vary.

Music Crossroads Southern Africa (www.jmi.net /activities/crossroads/) A showcase for young musical talent from southern and East Africa; host country and dates vary.

JULY

Festival of the Dhow Countries (www.ziff.or.tz) A two-week extravaganza of dance, music, film and literature from Tanzania and other Indian Ocean countries, with the **Zanzibar International Film Festival** as its centrepiece; it's held in early July.

Mwaka Kogwa A four-day festival in late July to mark Nairuzim (the Shirazi New Year); festivities are best in Makunduchi (p138) on Zanzibar.

FOOD

For more on Tanzanian cuisine, see Food & Drink (p79).

Eating listings in this book are ordered by price (see inside front cover).

In addition to what you'll find in restaurants there is an abundance of fresh tropical fruits and a reasonably good selection of vegetables at markets countrywide.

GAY & LESBIAN TRAVELLERS

Homosexuality is illegal in Tanzania, incurring penalties of up to 14 years imprisonment. While prosecutions rarely occur, discretion is advised as gay sexual relationships are culturally taboo, and public displays of affection, whether between people of the same or opposite sex, are frowned upon. Traditionally, gay travellers have experienced few particular difficulties. However, in early 2003, a demonstration was staged in Dar es Salaam by an influential Muslim organisation protesting the anticipated arrival of a large group of gay tourists from the USA. The group's visit was ultimately postponed due to other factors and there have been no further incidents on the mainland. Zanzibar has tended to be more tolerant of gay relationships. However, in 2004, the Zanzibari parliament passed a law banning homosexuality and lesbianism, with penalties of up to 25 years in prison for those in gay relationships and seven years for those in lesbian relationships, and in 2006, a protest movement was staged against celebration of Freddie Mercury's 60th birthday on the island, resulting in the cancellation of the event.

The website www.purpleroofs.com/africa /tanzaniata.html lists gay and gay-friendly tour companies in the region that may be able to help you plan your trip. For all-inclusive packages, try **Atlantis Events** (www.atlantisevents .com), **David Tours** (www.davidtours.com), **Karibu Mgeni** (☎ in the Netherlands 061-449 3841) and **Gay2Afrika** (www.gay2afrika.com). Also check the Tanzania link on www.mask.org.za.

HOLIDAYS

Government holidays tend to be quiet affairs, with all businesses closed, but if you're in the right place at the right time, you might catch parades and other events. Christian religious feasts invariably centre on long, beautiful church services and singing. Eid al-Fitr and the other Muslim holidays are colourful anywhere, but particularly on Zanzibar, where you'll be treated to the sight of entire families dressed up and celebrating, processions in the streets and other festivities.

New Year's Day 1 January
Zanzibar Revolution Day 12 January
Easter March/April – Good Friday, Holy Saturday and Easter Monday
Union Day 26 April
Labour Day 1 May

Saba Saba (Peasants' Day) 7 July
Nane Nane (Farmers' Day) 8 August
Independence Day 9 December
Christmas Day 25 December
Boxing Day 26 December

The dates of Islamic holidays depend on the moon and are known for certain only a few days in advance. They fall about 11 days earlier each year and include the following:

Eid al-Kebir (Eid al-Haji) Commemorates the moment when Abraham was about to sacrifice his son in obedience to God's command, only to have God intercede at the last moment and substitute a ram. It coincides with the end of the pilgrimage (*hajj*) to Mecca.
Eid al-Fitr The end of Ramadan, and East Africa's most important Islamic celebration; celebrated as a two-day holiday in many areas.
Eid al-Moulid (Maulidi) The birthday of the Prophet Mohammed.
Ramadan The annual 30-day fast when adherents do not eat or drink from sunrise to sunset.

Approximate dates for these events are shown below. Although Ramadan is not a public holiday, restaurants are often closed during this time on Zanzibar and in other coastal areas.

Event	2008	2009	2010
Ramadan begins	2 Sep	22 Aug	11 Aug
Eid al-Fitr (end of Ramadan, two day holiday)	2 Oct	21 Sep	10 Sep
Eid al-Kebir (Eid al-Haji)	8 Dec	27 Nov	16 Nov
Eid al-Moulid	20 Mar	9 Mar	26 Feb

INSURANCE

Travel insurance covering theft, loss and medical problems is highly recommended. Before choosing a policy, shop around, as those designed for short package tours in Europe may not be suitable for the wilds of Tanzania. Be sure to read the fine print, as some policies specifically exclude 'dangerous activities', which can mean scuba diving, motorcycling and even trekking. A locally acquired motorcycle licence isn't valid under some policies. Some policies pay doctors or hospitals directly, while others require you to pay on the spot and claim later. If you have to claim later, keep all documentation. Most importantly, check that the policy covers an emergency flight home.

Before heading to Tanzania, consider taking out a membership with one of the following:
African Medical & Research Foundation (Amref; www.amref.org) Dar es Salaam branch office (Map p90; ☎ 022-211 6610, 211 3673; 1019 Ali Hassan Mwinyi Rd just north of Bibi Titi Mohammed Rd) Nairobi emergency lines (☎ 254-20-315454, 254-20-600090, 254-733-628422, 254-722-314239, satellite 000-873 762 315580) Nairobi head office (☎ 254-20-699 3000) . Membership entitles you to emergency regional evacuation by the Flying Doctors' Society of Africa, which operates a 24-hour air ambulance service based out of Nairobi's Wilson airport. A two month membership costs US$25/50 for evacuations within a 500km/1000km radius of Nairobi. The 1000km membership encompasses the entire East African region, except for southernmost Tanzania around Songea, Tunduru and Mtwara.
First Air Responder (☎ 0754-777073; www.knightsupport.com) Tanzania-based, with air evacuation units in Dar es Salaam and in Arusha, and offering air evacuation within Tanzania to Dar es Salaam or Nairobi with purchase of a 30-day Tourist Card membership.

INTERNET ACCESS

There are many internet cafés in Dar es Salaam, Arusha and Zanzibar, and at least one in major towns, except in parts of southern and western Tanzania. Prices range from less than Tsh500 per hour in Dar es Salaam to about Tsh2000 per hour in outlying areas. Speed is not necessarily related to price, and varies greatly, though truly fast connections are rare. Reliable and reasonably priced internet cafés tend to fill up and you'll often need to wait for a terminal. A small but increasing number of business-class hotels have wireless access points. Some upmarket safari camps have satellite connections, but it's generally not possible to connect while on safari.

A recommended computer shop in Dar es Salaam is **Imagination Computer Centre** (Map p90; ☎ 022-211 7598; sales@imagination.co.tz; Ground fl; Sukari House; cnr Sokoine Dr & Ohio Sts).

LEGAL MATTERS

Apart from traffic offences such as speeding and driving without a seatbelt (mandatory for driver and front-seat passengers), the main area to watch out for is drug use and possession. Marijuana (*bangi* or *ganja*) is readily available in some areas and is frequently offered to tourists on the street in places like Zanzibar and Dar es Salaam – almost always as part of a setup involving the police or fake police. If you're caught, expect to pay a large bribe to avoid arrest or imprisonment. In Dar es Salaam, the typical scam is that you'll be approached by a couple of men who walk along with you, strike up a conversation and try to sell you drugs. Before you've had a chance to shake them loose, policemen (sometimes legitimate, sometimes not) suddenly appear and insist that you pay a huge fine for being involved in the purchase of illegal drugs. Protestations to the contrary are generally futile and there's often little you can do other than instantly hightailing it in the opposite direction if you smell this scam coming. If you are caught, insist on going to the nearest police station before paying anything and whittle the bribe down as far as you can. Initial demands may be as high as US$300, but savvy travellers should be able to get away with under US$50.

MAPS

Good country maps include those published by Nelles (1:1,500,000) and Harms-ic, both available in Tanzania and elsewhere, and both also including Rwanda and Burundi. Harms-ic also publishes maps for Lake Manyara National Park, the Ngorongoro Conservation Area and Zanzibar.

The **Surveys and Mapping Division's Map Sales Office** (Map p86; cnr Kivukoni Front & Luthuli St, Dar es Salaam; 8am-2pm Mon-Fri), sells dated topographical maps (1:50,000) for mainland Tanzania, although individual sheets covering popular areas are often out of stock. Topographical maps for Zanzibar and Pemba are available in Stone Town.

An excellent series of attractive, colourful maps, hand-drawn by Giovanni Tombazzi and marketed under the name **MaCo** (www.gtmaps .com), cover Zanzibar, Arusha and the northern parks. They're sold in bookshops in Dar es Salaam, Arusha and Zanzibar Town, and are also available online and internationally.

MONEY

Tanzania's currency is the Tanzanian shilling (Tsh). There are bills of Tsh10,000, 5000, 1000 and 500, and coins of Tsh200, 100, 50, 20, 10, five and one shilling(s). For exchange rates, see the inside front cover. For information on costs, see p12.

Prices can be high in Tanzania, but credit cards are frequently not accepted, even at many upmarket hotels. Where they are ac-cepted, it's often only with steep commissions, which means that you will need to rely here more heavily on cash, ATMs and (in major centres) travellers cheques.

The best currency to bring is US dollars in a mixture of large and small denomina-tions, plus some travellers cheques as an emergency standby and a Visa card for with-drawing money from ATMs. Euros are also easily changed.

ATMs

ATMs are widespread in major towns, al-though they are out of service with enough frequency that you should always have some sort of back-up funds. Standard Chartered (with branches in Dar es Salaam, Arusha, Moshi and Mwanza), Barclays (Dar es Salaam, Arusha and Zanzibar), National Bank of Commerce (NBC; major towns coun-trywide), Stanbic (Dar es Salaam, Arusha, Mbeya, major towns) and TanPay/SpeedCash (Dar es Salaam, Arusha, Zanzibar) all have ATMs that allow you to withdraw shillings with a Visa or MasterCard to a maximum of Tsh300,000 to Tsh400,000 per transac-tion. (Formerly the limit was per day, but now most machines seem to have no daily limits, other than what your own bank might place.) Visa is by far the most useful card for ATM cash withdrawals (and still the only one possible in many towns – NBC and CRDB machines take only Visa). However, Barclays and Stanbic ATMs also accept MasterCard and cards tied in with the Cirrus/Maestro network, and there are a few machines that only work with MasterCard. All ATMs are open 24 hours, although it's not uncom-mon to find them temporarily out of service or out of cash. In Arusha especially, lines at ATM machines on Friday afternoons are notoriously long so take care of your banking before then. Also, throughout the country if your withdrawal request is rejected (no mat-ter what reason the machine gives), it could be for something as simple as requesting above the allowed transaction amount for that particular machine, so it's always worth trying again.

Black Market

There's essentially no black market for foreign currency. You can assume that the frequent offers you'll receive on the street to change at high rates are a set-up.

WAYS TO SAVE

- Travel in the low season, and ask about discounted room and safari prices.
- Families: ask about children's discounts at parks and hotels.
- Travel in a group (four is ideal) for organised treks and safaris.
- Watch for last-minute deals.
- Stay outside park boundaries, especially at those parks and reserves where you can do wildlife excursions in border areas, or where the entry fee is valid for multiple admissions within a 24-hour period.
- Enter parks around mid-day: as fees are calculated on a 24-hour basis, you'll be able to enjoy prime evening and morning wildlife viewing hours for just one day's payment.
- Camp whenever possible.
- Focus on easily accessed parks and reserves to minimise transportation costs.
- Use public transport where possible.
- Do Cultural Tourism Programs rather than wildlife safaris.
- Eat local food.
- Stock up on food and drink in major towns to avoid expensive hotel fare and pricey tourist-area shops.
- Offer to pay in cash – sometimes this may result in a discount.
- Focus on off-the-beaten-track areas, where prices are usually considerably lower.

Cash

US dollars, followed by euros, are the most convenient foreign currencies and get the best rates, although other major currencies are readily accepted in major centres. Note that US$50 and US$100 note bills get better rates of exchange than smaller denominations. Old-style US bills are not accepted anywhere.

Credit Cards

Several top-end hotels and tour operators, and some midrange establishments accept credit cards – generally with a commission averaging from 5% to 10%. However many don't, including at the upper end of the price spectrum, so always verify in advance that you can pay with a card or carry back-up cash or travellers cheques. Otherwise, credit cards (primarily Visa) are useful for withdrawing money at ATMs.

With the proliferation of ATMs, most banks no longer give cash advances against credit cards.

Exchanging Money

Cash can be changed with a minimum of hassle at banks or foreign exchange (forex) bureaus in major towns and cities; rates and commissions vary, so shop around. Forex bureaus are usually quicker, less bureaucratic and offer higher rates, although most smaller towns don't have them. The most useful bank for foreign exchange is NBC, with branches throughout the country. Countrywide, banks and forex bureaus are closed from noon on Saturday until Monday morning.

In order to reconvert Tanzanian shillings to hard currency, it's a good idea to save at least some of your exchange receipts, although they are seldom checked. The easiest places to reconvert currency are at the airports in Dar es Salaam and Kilimanjaro. Otherwise, try at forex shops or banks in major towns.

In theory, it's required for foreigners to pay for accommodation, park fees, organised tours, upscale hotels and the Zanzibar ferries in US dollars, though shillings are accepted almost everywhere at the going rate

Taxes

Tanzania has a 20% value-added tax (VAT) that's usually included in quoted prices.

Tipping

Tipping is generally not practised in small, local establishments, especially in rural areas. However, in major towns and in places frequented by tourists, tips are expected. Some top-end places include a service charge in the bill. Otherwise, depending on the situation, either rounding out the bill, or adding about 10% is standard practice, assuming that the service warrants it. On treks and safaris, it's common practice to tip drivers, guides, porters and other staff. For guidelines on amounts, see p38 for safaris and p193 and p209 for treks.

Travellers Cheques

Travellers cheques can be reasonably easily cashed in Dar es Salaam, Arusha, Zanzibar and Mwanza, but not at all or only with difficulty elsewhere. Exchange rates are slightly lower than for cash, and most hotels and safari operators won't accept them as direct payment. Almost all banks and forex bureaus that accept travellers cheques require you to show the original purchase receipt before exchanging the cheques. Most banks (but not forex bureaus) charge commissions ranging from 0.5% of the transaction amount (at NBC) to more than US$40 per transaction (Standard Chartered) for exchanging travellers cheques.

PHOTOGRAPHY & VIDEO
Tips & Restrictions

Always ask permission first before photographing people and always respect their wishes. In many places, locals will ask for a fee (usually from Tsh1000 to Tsh5000 and up) before allowing you to photograph them, which is fair enough – if you don't want to pay up, then don't snap a picture.

Don't take photos of anything connected with the government and the military, including army barracks, and landscapes and people anywhere close to army barracks. Government offices, post offices, banks, ports, train stations and airports are also off limits.

For detailed tips and information about photographing your Tanzania travels, get a copy of the highly recommended *Travel Photography* by Richard I'Anson.

POST

Postage via airmail to the USA/Australia/ Europe costs from about Tsh800/1000/600 and is reasonably reliable, but don't send valuables.

Major towns have poste restante, with a charge of Tsh200 per received letter. Mail is held for at least one month.

SHOPPING

Tanzania has a wide selection of crafts, ranging from basketry and woodcarvings to textiles and paintings, *shukas* (blankets) and jewellery. Craft centres and artist cooperatives in major towns have good variety and reasonable prices. Watch for Makonde carvings (Dar es Salaam and Mtwara); Tingatinga paintings (the best buys are in Dar es Salaam); Singida baskets (in the villages around Singida and at craft shops in Dar es Salaam and Arusha); and *vibuyu* (carved gourds) and Gogo woodcarvings (Dodoma). There are also some wonderful textiles, primarily the *kanga* – the traditional cloth garment worn by many Tanzanian women, with Swahili sayings printed along the edge – and the heavier *kitenge* (Zanzibar Town has some great buys). Dar es Salaam is a good place to shop for textiles, especially batiks. For more unusual choices, look for some of the crafts made by children from recycled wires, soft-drink cans and the like.

When buying woodcarvings, remember most of the pieces marketed as ebony are really *mpingo* (African blackwood), while others are simply lighter wood that has been blackened with dye or shoe polish. Rubbing the piece with a wet finger, or smelling it, should tip you off. When assessing quality, look at the attention given to detail and the craftsmanship. With textiles, spread them out to check for flaws or uneven cuts.

Bargaining

Bargaining is expected by vendors in tourist areas, particularly souvenir vendors, except in a limited number of fixed-price shops. However, at markets and non-tourist venues, the price quoted to you will often be the 'real' price – so in these situations don't immediately assume that the quote you've been given is too high.

There are no set rules for bargaining, other than that it should always be conducted in a friendly and spirited manner. Before starting, it's worth shopping around to get a feel for the 'value' of the item you want. Asking others what they have paid can be helpful. Once you start negotiating, if things become exasperating, or seem like a waste of time, politely take your leave. Sometimes sellers will call you back if they think their stubbornness has been counterproductive. Very few will pass up the chance of making a sale, however thin the profit. If the vendor won't come down to a price you feel is fair, it means that they aren't making a profit, or that too many high-rolling foreigners have passed through already.

SOLO TRAVELLERS

While solo travellers may be a minor curiosity in rural areas, especially solo women travellers, there are no particular problems with travelling solo in Tanzania, whether you're male or female. The times when it's advantageous to join a group are for safaris and treks – when going in a group can be a significant cost-saver – and when going out at night. If you go out alone at night, take taxis and use extra caution, especially in urban and tourist areas. Whatever the time of day, avoid isolating situations, including lonely stretches of beach.

TELEPHONE

Tanzania Telecom (TTCL) no longer provides a call-and-pay service in many towns (Mwanza and Arusha are notable exceptions). Instead, you'll need to look for a private telecom shop – almost always located at or near the post office/TTCL compound – where you can make your domest or international calls. International calls are billed at a flat rate of US$2 per minute. It's slightly cheaper to dial internationally by buying a pre-paid card from TTCL (open business hours only) and using it in the card phones found outside TTCL offices in major towns. Local calls are cheap – about Tsh100 per minute. Costs for domestic long-distance calls vary depending on distance, but average about Tsh1000 for the first three minutes plus Tsh500 per minute thereafter. Calls to mobile phones cost about Tsh500 per minute.

Mobile Phones

Mobile (cell) phones are everywhere. The ever-expanding network covers major towns throughout the country, plus a wide arc encompassing most of the north and northeast. In the south, west and centre, you may not get a signal away from larger towns. Celtel is your best bet for these areas, with a wider network range outside town centres than the other companies. Mobile phone numbers are six digits, preceded by 07XX; the major companies are currently Celtel, Vodacom, Tigo and (on Zanzibar) Zantel. To reach a mobile telephone number from outside Tanzania,

dial the country code, then the mobile phone code without the initial 0, and then the six-digit number. From within Tanzania, keep the initial 0 and don't use any other area code.

All the companies sell pre-paid starter packages for about US$2, and top-up cards are on sale at shops throughout the country. Watch for frequent specials (Vodacom is currently offering SIM cards for free).

All mobile companies in Tanzania have changed their prefixes since publication of the last edition of this book. If you come across old numbers, the prefixes should be changed as follows: 0741 is now 0713; 0748 (now 0784); 0745 (now 0755); 0747 (now 0777 or 0774). For a full list of prefix changes not listed, see http://www.tcra.go.tz/press/change in mndcs.pdf.

Phone Codes

Tanzania's country code is ☎ 255. To make an international call, dial ☎ 000, followed by the country code, local area code (without the initial '0') and telephone number.

All land-line telephone numbers are seven digits. Area codes (included with all numbers in this book) must be used whenever you dial long-distance.

TIME

Tanzania time is GMT/UTC plus three hours. There is no daylight saving. See pp391-1.

Tanzanians use the Swahili system of telling time, in which the first hour is *saa moja* (*asubuhi*), corresponding with 7am. Counting begins again with *saa moja (jioni)* (the first hour, evening, corresponding with 7pm). Although most will switch to the international clock when speaking English with foreigners, confusion sometimes occurs, so ask people to confirm whether they are using *saa za kizungu* (international time) or *saa za kiswahili* (Swahili time). Signboards with opening hours are often posted in Swahili time.

TOILETS

Toilets vary from standard long-drops to full-flush luxury conveniences that spring up in the most unlikely places. Almost all midrange and top-end hotels sport flushable sit-down types, although at the lower end of the price range, toilet seats are a rare commodity. Budget guesthouses often have squat-style toilets – sometimes equipped with a flush mechanism, otherwise with a scoop and a bucket of water for flushing things down.

Toilets with running water are a rarity outside major hotels. If you see a bucket with water nearby, use it for flushing. Paper (you'll invariably need to supply your own) should be deposited in the can that's usually in the corner.

Many upmarket bush camps have 'dry' toilets – a fancy version of the long drop with a Western-style seat perched on top – though it's all generally quite hygienic.

TOURIST INFORMATION

The **Tanzania Tourist Board** (TTB; www.tanzaniatourist board.com) has offices in Dar es Salaam (p88) and Arusha (p197). In the UK, the Tanzania Tourist Board is represented by the **Tanzania Trade Centre** (www.tanzatrade.co.uk).

TRAVELLERS WITH DISABILITIES

While there are few facilities for the disabled, Tanzanians are generally quite accommodating and willing to offer whatever assistance they can as long as they understand what you need. Disabled travel is becoming increasingly common on the northern safari circuit, and Abercrombie & Kent and several other operators listed on p355 cater to disabled travellers. Some considerations:

- While newer lodges often have wheelchair accessible rooms (noted in individual listings), few hotels have lifts (elevators) and many have narrow stairwells. This is particularly true of Stone Town on Zanzibar, where stairwells are often steep and narrow. Grips or railings in the bathrooms are rare.
- Many park lodges and camps are built on ground level. However, access paths – in an attempt to maintain a natural environment – are sometimes rough or rocky and rooms or tents raised, so it's best to inquire about access before booking.
- As far as we know, there are no Braille signboards at any parks or museums, nor any facilities for deaf travellers.
- Minibuses are widely available on Zanzibar and on the mainland and can be chartered for transport and for customised safaris. Large or wide-door vehicles can also be arranged through car-rental agencies in Dar es Salaam and with Arusha-based tour operators. Taxis countrywide are usually small sedans and buses are not wheelchair equipped.

One helpful starting point is **Accessible Journeys** (www.disabilitytravel.com), with a northern circuit safari itinerary for disabled travellers. Other entities – all of which disseminate travel information for the mobility impaired – include **Access-Able Travel Source** (www.accessable.com); **Mobility International** (www.miusa.org); **National Information Communication Awareness Network** (www.nican.com.au); and **Holiday Care** (www.holidaycare.org.uk). For information on the **Tanzania Association for the Physically Disabled** (Chawata; ☎ 0744-587376; chawatahq@hotmail.com) and other organisations in Tanzania, see www.tanzania.disabilityafrica.org and click on Organisations. Another local contact to check out is the **Zanzibar Association of the Disabled** (☎ 024-223 3719; uwz@zanzinet.com) in Zanzibar Town.

VISAS

Almost everyone needs a visa, which costs between US$20 and US$50, depending on nationality, for a single-entry visa valid for up to three months. It's best to get the visa in advance (and necessary if you want multiple entry), though visas are currently readily issued at Dar es Salaam and Kilimanjaro airports and at most border crossings (all nationalities US$50, US dollars cash only, single-entry only). Some embassies require you to show proof of an onward ticket before they'll issue a visa, though a flight itinerary will usually suffice.

Visa Extensions

One month is the normal visa validity and three months the maximum. For extensions within the three-month limit, there are immigration offices in all major towns; the process is free and straightforward. Extensions after three months are difficult – you'll usually need to leave the country and apply for a new visa.

VOLUNTEERING

There are various opportunities for volunteering, generally teaching, or in environmental or health work, and almost always best arranged prior to arriving in Tanzania. Some places to start your search: **Voluntary Service Overseas** (VSO; www.vso.org.uk), which provides placements for young professionals, or the similar US-based **Peace Corps** (www.peacecorps.gov); **Volunteer Abroad** (www.volunteerabroad.com), with a long list of Tanzania opportunities; **Trade Aid** (www.tradeaiduk.org/volunteer.html); **Frontier** (www.frontier.ac.uk); **School of St Jude** (www.schoolofstjude

.co.tz); **Livingstone Tanzania Trust** (www.livingstonetan
zaniatrust.com); **Village Africa** (www.villageafrica.org
.uk); and **Foot 2 Afrika** (www.foot2afrika.com). There
are also various volunteer holiday opportunities included in the Tanzania listings of
ResponsibleTravel.com (www.responsibletravel.com).
Also check out www.volunteerafrica.org. If
you're looking for a way to help out closer to
home, see www.books4tanzania.org.uk.

WOMEN TRAVELLERS

Tanzania is a relatively easy place to travel,
either solo or with other women, especially
when compared with parts of North Africa,
South America and certain Western countries.
You're not likely to encounter many specifically gender-related problems and, more often
than not, you'll meet only warmth, hospitality
and sisterly regard, and find that you receive
special treatment that you probably wouldn't
be shown if you were a male traveller. That
said, you'll inevitably attract some attention,
especially if you're travelling alone, and there
are some areas where caution is essential.
Following are a few tips:

- Dress modestly: trousers or a long skirt,
  and a conservative top with a sleeve.
  Tucking your hair under a cap or scarf,
  or tying it back, also helps.
- Use common sense, trust your instincts
  and take the usual precautions when out
  and about. Avoid walking alone at night.
  Avoid isolated areas at any time and be
  particularly cautious on beaches, many
  of which can become quickly deserted.
- If you find yourself with an unwanted
  suitor, creative approaches are usually
  effective. For example, explain that your
  husband (real or fictitious) or a large
  group of friends will be arriving imminently at that very place. Similar tactics
  are also usually effective in dealing with

the inevitable curiosity that you'll meet
as to why you might not have children
and a husband, or if you do have them,
why they aren't with you. The easiest response to the question of why you aren't
married is to explain that you are still
young (*bado kijana*), which whether you
are or not will at least have some humour
value. Just saying *bado* ('not yet') to ques-
tions about marriage or children should
also do the trick. As for why your family
isn't with you, you can always explain
that you'll be meeting them later.

- Seek out local women, as this can en-
  rich your trip tremendously. Places to
  try include tourist offices, government
  departments or even your hotel, where
  at least some of the staff are likely to be
  formally educated young to middle-aged
  women. In rural areas, starting points
  include women teachers at a local school,
  or staff at a health centre.

WORK

Unemployment is high, and unless you have
unique skills, the chances of lining up something are small. The most likely areas for employment are the safari industry, tourism, dive
masters and teaching, but, in all areas, competition is stiff and the pay is low. The best way
to land something is to get to know someone
already working in the business. Also check
safari operator and lodge websites, some of
which advertise vacant positions.

Work and residency permits should be
arranged through the potential employer or
sponsoring organisation; residency permits
normally need to be applied for from outside
Tanzania. Be prepared for lots of bureaucracy.
Most teaching positions are voluntary and
best arranged through voluntary agencies or
mission organisations at home.

Transport

CONTENTS

GETTING THERE & AWAY

ENTERING THE COUNTRY

Provided you have a visa (p344), Tanzania is straightforward to enter. There are no vaccination requirements, although there are several worth considering (p362).

Passport

There are no entry restrictions for any nationalities.

AIR
Airports & Airlines

Tanzania's air hub is **Julius Nyerere International Airport** (DAR; ☎ 022-284 2461/2402; www.tanzaniaairports .com) in Dar es Salaam, with a modest array of services, including an internet connection, souvenir shops and forex bureaus. **Kilimanjaro International Airport** (JRO; ☎ 027-255 4252/4707; www .kilimanjaroairport.co.tz), between Arusha and Moshi, also handles international flights, and is the best option for itineraries in Arusha and the northern safari circuit. It has a forex bureau and an internet connection, and shouldn't be confused with the smaller Arusha Airport (ARK), 8km west of Arusha, which handles some domestic flights. There are also international flights to/from Zanzibar International

---

THINGS CHANGE

The information in this chapter is particularly vulnerable to change. Shop carefully, and check directly with the airline or travel agent to understand how a fare works. Details given in this chapter should be regarded as pointers and aren't a substitute for your own careful research.

Airport (ZNZ), Mwanza Airport (MWZ) and Mtwara Airport (MYW). Kigoma Airport occasionally handles regional flights.

Air Tanzania (TC; ☎ 022-211 8411, 022-284 4239, www .airtanzania.com; hub Julius Nyerere International Airport) is the national airline, with a limited but generally reliable network. Current regional destinations are Moroni (Comoros), Entebbe (Uganda) and Johannesburg (South Africa).

Regional and international carriers include the following (all servicing Dar es Salaam, except as noted):

Air Burundi (8Y; airbdi@cbinf.com; hub Bujumbura)

Air India (AI; ☎ 022-215 2642; www.airindia.com; hub Mumbai)

Air Kenya (REG; ☎ 027-250 2541; www.airkenya.com; hub Nairobi) Affiliated with Regional Air in Arusha (p202).

British Airways (BA; ☎ 022-211 3820; www.britishair ways.com; hub Heathrow Airport, London)

Emirates Airlines (EK; ☎ 022-211 6100; www.emir ates.com; hub Dubai International Airport)

Ethiopian Airlines (ET; ☎ 022-211 7063; www.fly ethiopian.com; hub Addis Ababa). Also serves Kilimanjaro International Airport (KIA).

Kenya Airways (KQ; ☎ 022-211 9376/7; www.kenya-airways.com; hub Jomo Kenyatta International Airport, Nairobi)

KLM (KL; ☎ 022-213 9790/1; www.klm.com; hub Schiphol Airport, Amsterdam) Also serves Kilimanjaro International Airport.

Linhas Aéreas de Moçambique (TM; ☎ 022-213 4600; www.lam.co.mz; hub Mavalane International Airport, Maputo)

Precision Air (PW; ☎ 022-216 8000; www.precision airtz.com; hub Dar es Salaam) In partnership with Kenya Airways.

South African Airways (SA; ☎ 022-211 7044; www.flysaa.com; hub OR Tambo International Airport, Johannesburg)

Swiss International Airlines (LX; ☎ 022-211 8870; www.swiss.com; hub Kloten Airport, Zurich)
Yemenia Yemen Airways (IY; ☎ 022-212 6036; www .yemenairways.net; hub Sana'a International Airport)
Zambian Airways (Q3; ☎ 022-212 8885/6; www .zambianairways.com; hub Lusaka International Airport)

Tickets

Fares from Europe and North America are highest in December/January, and in July/ August, but lowest from March to May, except around Easter. London is the main discount hub. You can find discounted fares into Nairobi (Kenya), and then make your way to Tanzania. Recommended online ticket sellers.

Cheapflights (www.cheapflights.co.uk)
Cheap Tickets (www.cheaptickets.com)
Expedia (www.expedia.com)
Flight Centre (www.flightcentre.com)
LowestFare.com (www.lowestfare.com)
OneTravel.com (www.onetravel.com)
Orbitz (www.orbitz.com)
STA Travel (www.statravel.com)
Travelocity (www.travelocity.com)

Africa & The Middle East

Useful airlines and connections:
Air Burundi (airbdi@cbinf.com) Bujumbura (Burundi) to Kigoma.

Air Madagascar (www.airmadagascar.mg) Antananarivo (Madagascar) to Nairobi, with connections to Tanzania.
Air Tanzania (www.airtanzania.com) Moroni (Comoros), Johannesburg and Entebbe to Dar es Salaam.
Emirates (www.emirates.com) Cairo to Dar es Salaam via Dubai.
Ethiopian Airlines (www.flyethiopian.com) Abidjan (Côte d'Ivoire), Lagos (Nigeria), Cairo, Entebbe and Kigali (Rwanda) to Addis Ababa (Ethiopia), and on to Dar es Salaam or Kilimanjaro.
Kenya Airways (www.kenya-airways.com) Abidjan, Bujumbura (Burundi), Cairo, Douala (Cameroon), Harare (Zimbabwe), Johannesburg, Khartoum (Sudan), Kigali, Lilongwe (Malawi), Maputo (Mozambique) and many other African cities to Nairobi, then on to Dar es Salaam or Kilimanjaro.
Linhas Aéreas de Moçambique (www.lam.co.mz) Maputo to Dar es Salaam via Pemba (Mozambique).
Precision Air (www.precisionairtz.com) Mombasa (Kenya) and Nairobi to Dar es Salaam, Zanzibar, Kili-manjaro and elsewhere in Tanzania. The airline also flies between Dar es Salaam, Lindi, Mtwara and Pemba (Mozambique), and between Kilimanjaro, Mwanza and Entebbe.
Rwandair Express (www.rwandair.com) Kigali to Kilimanjaro.
SAA (www.flysaa.com) Johannesburg to Dar es Salaam.
Zambian Airways (www.zambianairways.com) Lusaka (Zambia) to Dar es Salaam.

CLIMATE CHANGE & TRAVEL

Climate change is a serious threat to the ecosystems that humans rely upon, and air travel is the fastest-growing contributor to the problem. Lonely Planet regards travel, overall, as a global benefit, but believes we all have a responsibility to limit our personal impact on global warming.

Flying & climate change

Pretty much every form of motorised travel generates CO2 (the main cause of human-induced climate change), but planes are far and away the worst offenders, not just because of the sheer distances they allow us to travel, but because they release greenhouse gases high into the at-mosphere. The statistics are frightening: two people taking a return flight between Europe and the US will contribute as much to climate change as an average household's gas and electricity consumption over a whole year.

Carbon offset schemes

Climatecare.org and other websites use 'carbon calculators' that allow travellers to offset the level of greenhouse gases they are responsible for with financial contributions to sustainable travel schemes that reduce global warming – including projects in India, Honduras, Kazakhstan and Uganda.

Lonely Planet, together with Rough Guides and other concerned partners in the travel in-dustry, support the carbon offset scheme run by climatecare.org. Lonely Planet offsets all of its staff and author travel.

For more information check out our website: www.lonelyplanet.com.

> **DEPARTURE TAX**
>
> The departure tax for regional and interna-
> tional flights (US$30) is included in ticket
> prices for mainland departures. On Zanzibar
> it's levied separately at the airport (payable
> in US dollars or Tanzanian shillings).

Return excursion fares for intra-African
flights are frequently significantly cheaper
than standard return fares.

Ticket discounters include **Rennies Travel**
(www.renniestravel.com) and **STA Travel** (www.statravel
.co.za), with offices throughout southern Africa.
Flight Centre (☎ 0860 400 727, 011-778 1720; www.flight
centre.co.za) has offices in Johannesburg, Cape
Town and several other cities. In the Middle
East: **Al-Rais Travels** (www.alrais.com) in Dubai;
Egypt Panorama Tours (☎ 2-359 0200; www.eptours
.com) in Cairo; **Israel Student Travel Association**
(ISTA; ☎ 02-625 7257) in Jerusalem; and **Orion-Tour**
(www.oriontour.com) in Istanbul.

Asia
Popular connections are via Singapore and the
United Arab Emirates, or via Mumbai (India),
from where there are connections to Dar es
Salaam on Kenya Airways and Air India (one
way about US$600). Ethiopian Airlines (via
Addis Ababa) also flies this route, and Kenya
Airways flies from Hong Kong, Bangkok and
Guangzhou to Nairobi. A longer but competitively priced option is from Singapore or Hong
Kong to Johannesburg, connecting to Dar es
Salaam. Discounters include **STA Travel** Bangkok
(☎ 02-236 0262; www.statravel.co.th); Singapore (☎ 6737
7188; www.statravel.com.sg); Hong Kong (☎ 2736 1618; www
.statravel.com.hk); Japan (☎ 03 5391 2922; www.statravel
.co.jp), with branches throughout Asia. In Japan,
also try **No 1 Travel** (☎ 03 3205 6073; www.no1-travel
.com); in Hong Kong try **Four Seas Tours** (☎ 2200
7760; www.fourseastravel.com/english). **STIC Travels** (www
.stictravel.com) Delhi (☎ 11-233 57 468) Mumbai (☎ 22-221
81 431) has offices in many Indian cities.

Australia & New Zealand
There are no direct flights from Australia
or New Zealand to East Africa. However,
Qantas (from Sydney and Perth) and South
African Airways (from Perth) have several
flights weekly to Johannesburg, with connections to Dar es Salaam. Other options include: Emirates via Dubai to Dar es Salaam;
Qantas or Air India via Mumbai; and Air

Mauritius via Mauritius and Nairobi. **STA Travel**
(☎ 1300 733 035; statravel.com.au) and **Flight Centre**
(☎ 133 133; www.flightcentre.com.au) have offices
throughout Australia. For online bookings,
try www.travel.com.au.

From New Zealand, try Emirates via Dubai,
or Qantas or South African Airways via
Sydney and Johannesburg. Both **Flight Centre**
(☎ 0800 243 544; www.flightcentre.co.nz) and **STA Travel**
(☎ 0508 782 872; www.statravel.co.nz) have branches
throughout the country. Try www.travel.co.nz
for online bookings.

UK & Continental Europe
Return tickets between London and Dar es
Salaam cost from about £400 return. From
Continental Europe, low-season return fares
start from about €600. Prices are often better
to Nairobi. Charter flights, especially from
London, are also worth investigating.

European airlines to check include Swiss,
KLM and British Airways – all fly to Dar es
Salaam, and KLM also services Kilimanjaro.
Non-European carriers include Kenya
Airways (via Nairobi), Ethiopian Airlines
(via Addis Ababa), Emirates (via Dubai) and
Yemen Airways (via Sana'a).

In the UK, travel agency ads appear in the
travel pages of the weekend broadsheet newspapers, in *Time Out*, the *Evening Standard*
and in the free online magazine *TNT* (www
.tntmagazine.com). Discount ticket agencies
in the UK:
Bridge the World (☎ 0870 444 7474; www.b-t-w.co.uk)
Flightbookers (☎ 0870 814 4001; www.ebookers.com)
Flight Centre (☎ 0870 890 8099; flightcentre.co.uk)
North-South Travel (☎ 01245 608 291; www
.northsouthtravel.co.uk)
Quest Travel (☎ 0870 442 3542; www.questtravel.com)
STA Travel (☎ 0870 160 0599; www.statravel.co.uk) For
travellers under the age of 26.
Trailfinders (www.trailfinders.co.uk)
Travel Bag (☎ 0870 890 1456; www.travelbag.co.uk)

For discounted fares from Continental
Europe:
Airfair (☎ 020 620 5121; www.airfair.nl) Netherlands
Barcelo Viajes (☎ 902 116 226; www.barceloviajes
.com) Spain
CTS Viaggi (☎ 06 462 0431; www.cts.it) Italy
Expedia (www.expedia.de) Germany
Just Travel (☎ 089 747 3330; www.justtravel.de)
Germany
Lastminute (☎ 01805 284 366; www.lastminute.de)
Germany

Nouvelles Frontières (☎ 90 217 09 79; www
.nouvelles-frontieres.es) Spain
Nouvelles Frontières (☎ 0825 000 747; www
.nouvelles-frontieres.fr) France
OTU Voyages (www.otu.fr) France
STA Travel (☎ 01805 456 422; www.statravel.de)
Germany; for travellers under the age of 26.
Voyageurs du Monde (☎ 01 40 15 11 15; www.vdm
.com) France

USA & Canada

Most flights from North America are via
Europe; there are few bargain deals. Expect
to pay from US$1300 (for tickets through
consolidators or discount agencies) to over
US$2500 return, depending on the season and
your starting point. Fares offered by Canadian
discounters tend to be around 10% more
expensive than those sold in the USA.

The cheapest routing is generally to London
on a discounted transatlantic ticket, where
you can then purchase a separate ticket on
to Tanzania. Most airlines listed for the UK
& Continental Europe (opposite) also offer
direct fares from North America.

A roundabout, but occasionally cheaper, alternative is South African Airways from New
York or Washington DC to Johannesburg,
from where you can connect to Dar es Salaam
(from about US$1100 return for the transcon-
tinental portion of the trip). Other options
include Ethiopian Airways between New York
and Dar es Salaam or Zanzibar via Rome and
Addis Ababa, and Kenya Airways together
with **Virgin Atlantic** (www.virgin-atlantic.com) from
New York to Dar es Salaam via London and
Nairobi. For online bookings, see the agencies
listed under Tickets (p347). In Canada, also
try **Travel Cuts** (☎ 800-667-2887; www.travelcuts.com),
Canada's national student travel agency.

LAND
Bus

Buses cross the borders between Tanzania and
Kenya, Malawi, Uganda and Zambia. Apart
from sometimes lengthy waits for passport
checks, there are usually no hassles. At the
border, you'll need to disembark on each side
to take care of visa formalities, then reboard
and continue on. Visa fees aren't included in
bus ticket prices for trans-border routes. It's
also possible to travel to/from all of Tanzania's
neighbours by minibus. Most main routes go
direct; otherwise you'll need to walk across the
border and change vehicles on the other side.

Car & Motorcycle

Entry requirements include the vehicle's
registration papers and your driving licence
(p359), as well as a temporary import permit
(Tsh20,000 for one month, purchased at the
border), third-party insurance (Tsh50,000 for
one year – purchased at the border or in the
nearest large town) and a one-time fuel levy
(Tsh5000). You'll also need a *carnet de passage en douane*, which acts as a temporary
waiver of import duty. The carnet – arranged
in advance through your local automobile association – should also specify any expensive
spare parts that you are carrying.

Most rental companies don't permit their
vehicles to cross international borders; if you
find one that does, arrange the necessary
paperwork with it in advance.

Most border posts don't have petrol stations or repair shops; you'll need to head to
the nearest large town.

Burundi

The main crossing is at Kobero Bridge between Ngara (Tanzania) and Muyinga
(Burundi), with other crossings at Manyovu,
north of Kigoma, and at Kagunga (south
of Nyanza-Lac).

For Kobero Bridge: the trip is done in
stages via Nyakanazi (the junction village
where the unpaved road southwest to Kigoma
branches off from the tarmac road southeast
to Kahama and Nzega) and Lusahunga (from
where there's regular transport north towards
Biharamulo and Lake Victoria and southeast
via Kahama towards Nzega or Shinyanga).
There are several direct buses weekly between Mwanza and the border. Otherwise,
take a Kigoma-bound bus, disembark at
Lusahunga and get onward transport from
there. The road from Nzega to the Burundi
border via Ngara is mostly tarmac and in
good condition.

For the Manyovu crossing, *dalla-dallas*
(minibuses) leave Kigoma from behind Bero
petrol station (Tsh5000, three hours). Once
through the Tanzanian side of the border, you
can sometimes find cars going to Bujumbura
(Tsh5000, three to four hours). Otherwise,
you'll need to take one of the many waiting
vehicles across the border and on to Makamba
(about 70km from Manyovu), where the
Burundian immigration post is located,
and then from there get another vehicle on
to Bujumbura.

TRANSPORT

TRANSPORT

Kenya

With the exception of the Serengeti–Masai Mara crossing, there is public transport across all Tanzania–Kenya border posts.

BORDER CROSSINGS

The main route to/from Kenya is the sealed road connecting Arusha (Tanzania) and Nairobi (Kenya) via the popular Namanga border post (open 24 hours). There are also border crossings at Horohoro (Tanzania), north of Tanga; at Holili (Tanzania), east of Moshi; at Illassit (Tanzania), northeast of Moshi; at Bologonya in the northern Serengeti; and at Sirari (Tanzania), northeast of Musoma.

TO/FROM MOMBASA

Buses between Tanga and Mombasa depart daily in the morning in each direction (Tsh6500, four to five hours).

The road is well sealed between Dar es Salaam and Tanga, potholed between Tanga and the border at Horohoro, and in good condition from the border to Mombasa. There's nowhere official to change money at the border. Touts here charge extortionate rates, and it's difficult to get rid of Kenyan shillings once in Tanga, so plan accordingly.

TO/FROM NAIROBI
Bus

Scandinavia Express goes daily between Dar es Salaam and Nairobi via Arusha (Tsh39,000, 14 hours from Dar, Tsh15,000 from Arusha, departing Dar at 6am and Arusha at 4pm), as does Akamba (Tsh35,000). Both bus lines also have daily services between Mwanza and Nairobi (Tsh20,000, 12 to 14 hours), departing from Mwanza about 2pm and Nairobi at about 10pm.

Between Arusha and Nairobi, a good option is one of the daily shuttle buses, departing daily at 8am and 2pm in each direction (five hours). Following are the main companies – both of which also have one bus daily to/from Moshi:

Impala Arusha (☎ 027-250 7197; www.impalashuttle .com; Impala Hotel, cnr Moshi & Old Moshi Rds, Arusha); Nairobi (☎ 020-273 0953; Silver Springs Hotel)

Riverside Arusha (☎ 027-250 2639, 027-250 3916; www .riverside-shuttle.com; Sokoine Rd, Arusha); Nairobi (☎ 020-229618, 020-241032; riverside_shuttle@hotmail.com; Pan African Insurance House, 3rd fl, Room 1, Kenyatta Ave)

Both charge about US$25 one way, and with a little prodding, it's easy enough to get the resi-

BORDER HASSLES

At the Namanga border post watch out for touts – often claiming they work for the bus company – who tell you that it's necessary to change money, pay a fee or come over to 'another building' to arrange the necessary payments to enter Tanzania–Kenya. Apart from your visa, there are no border fees, payments or exchange requirements for crossing, and the rates being offered for forex are sub-standard.

dents' price (US$10). In Arusha, drop offs are at the bus company offices. In Nairobi, drop offs are at centrally located hotels and at Jomo Kenyatta International Airport. For Nairobi pick-ups, if you book in advance, they'll meet your flight. Otherwise, contact the shuttles through the tourist information desk in the international arrivals area. Confirm the drop-off point when booking, and insist on being dropped off as agreed. Also watch out for touts who board the bus at the New Stanley Hotel (Nairobi) and say that it's the end of the line to drum up business for waiting taxis.

Regular buses also link Arusha and Nairobi daily (Tsh11,000, six to seven hours), departing between 6.30am and 8am. Departures in Arusha are from the bus station; in Nairobi most leave from Accra Rd.

Taxi

Not recommended, but shared taxis go between the Arusha bus station and the Namanga border throughout the day, from 6am. Most are nine-seater sedans that do the journey at hair-raising speeds. At Namanga, you'll have to walk a few hundred metres across the border and then catch one of the frequent *matatus* (Kenyan minibuses) or share taxis to Nairobi (about US$7). From Nairobi, the *matatu* and share-taxi depots are on Ronald Ngala St, near the River Rd junction.

TO/FROM VOI

Dalla-dallas go daily between Moshi and the border town of Holili via Himo junction (Tsh1000, one hour). At the **border** (☒ 6am-8pm), you'll need to hire a *piki-piki* (motorbike; Tsh500) or bicycle to cross 3km of no-man's land before arriving at the Kenyan immigration post at Taveta. From Taveta, sporadic minibuses go to Voi along a rough road (KSh300), where you can then find onward transport to Nairobi and Mombasa. If you're arriving/departing with a foreign-registered vehicle, the necessary paperwork is only done during working hours (8am to 1pm and 2pm to 5pm daily).

TO/FROM MASAI MARA

There's no public transport between the northern Serengeti and Kenya's Masai Mara Game Reserve, and only East African residents and citizens can cross here. If you're a resident and are exiting Tanzania here, take care of immigration formalities in Seronera, to the south. Entering Tanzania from Masai Mara, park fees should be paid at the Lobo ranger post, between the border and Seronera.

TO/FROM KISII
Bus

Minibuses go daily between Musoma and the Sirari–Isebania border post, where you can get Kenyan transport to Kisii, and then on to Kisumu or Nairobi. Scandinavian Express and Akamba also pass Kisii on their daily runs between Mwanza and Nairobi (Tsh20,000, 12 to 14 hours between Mwanza and Nairobi), with some buses continuing on to Arusha and Dar es Salaam.

Car

The road is good tarmac from Mwanza to the border, and into Kenya.

Malawi
BORDER CROSSINGS

The only crossing is at **Songwe River bridge** (7am-7pm Tanzanian time, 6am-6pm Malawi time), southeast of Mbeya (Tanzania).

BUS

Buses go several times weekly between Dar es Salaam and Lilongwe (27 hours), though they are overcrowded (even if you have a ticket, it's often not possible to board midroute in Mbeya) and often greatly delayed. It's better to travel from Dar es Salaam to Mbeya and get onward transport there. From Mbeya, buses depart in the afternoons several times weekly, arriving in Lilongwe the next day (Tsh28,000). Coming from Malawi, the best option is to take a minibus from the border to Mbeya, and then get an express bus from there towards Dar es Salaam. This entails staying overnight in Mbeya, as buses to Dar es Salaam depart from Mbeya between 6am and 7am.

There are also daily minibuses and 30-seater buses (known as 'Coastals' or *thelathini*) connecting both Mbeya (Tsh3000, two hours) and Kyela with the border. In Mbeya, look for buses going to Kyela (these detour to the border) and verify that your vehicle is really going all the way to the border, as some that say they are atually stopping at Tukuyu (40km north) or at Ibanda (7km before the border). Asking several passengers (rather than the minibus company touts) should get you the straight answer. Your chances of getting a direct vehicle are better in the larger *thelathini*, which depart from Mbeya two or three times daily and usually go where they say they are going. The buses stop at the transport stand, about a seven-minute walk from the actual border, so there's no real need for the bicycle taxis that will approach you. If you get stuck at the border, try **Mala Green** (☎ 0752-029010; camping per person Tsh5000, r Tsh7000), with clean rooms and food on order. Coming from Mbeya, it's on the left (south) side of the main road, before the small Kiriwa River bridge and about 2km before the border. It's poorly signposted – watch instead for the Celtel sign.

Once across the Tanzanian border, there's a 300m walk to the Malawian side, and minibuses to Karonga. There's also one bus daily between the border and Mzuzu (Malawi), departing the border by mid-afternoon and arriving by evening. Many vehicles and trucks ply between Mbeya and Karonga, so it's easy to find a lift.

CAR

The road from Mbeya to Karonga is good tarmac, and rough from Karonga south towards Chiweta. There's a petrol station at the Ibanda junction.

Mozambique
BORDER CROSSINGS

There are no bridges over the Ruvuma River border (yet). The main crossing is at Kilambo (south of Mtwara, Tanzania), where there is a ferry. It's also possible to get your passport stamped between Newala (Tanzania) and Moçimboa do Rovuma (Mozambique). Travelling by boat, there are immigration officials at Msimbati (Tanzania) and at Palma and Moçimboa da Praia (Mozambique). You can also use the crossing between Songea (Tanzania) and Nova Madeira (Mozambique), although there's no immigration office on the

TRANSPORT

Tanzanian side, so you'll need to get stamped in/out in Songea. Mozambique visas are not issued anywhere along the Tanzania border, so arrange one in advance.

BUS

Buses depart daily from Mtwara between 7am and 9am to the Kilambo border post (Tsh2500, one hour) and on to the Ruvuma, which is crossed via dugout canoe (Tsh2000, 10 minutes to over an hour, depending on water levels, and dangerous during heavy rains). If you happen to be at the river when the vehicle ferry is departing, this is a better alternative. On the Mozambique side, there are usually two pick-ups daily to the Mozambique border post (4km further) and on to Moçimboa da Praia (US$9, four hours), with the last one departing by about noon. If you get stuck, there's a makeshift and bedbug-ridden guesthouse on a sandbank in the middle of the river; camping on the Mozambique side is a better option.

The Ruvuma crossing is notorious for pick-pockets. Watch your belongings, especially when getting into and out of the boats, and keep up with the crowd when walking to/from the river bank.

The rarely used border crossing south of Newala entails long walks on both sides (up to 25km in Tanzania, and at least 10km in Mozambique). The main Mozambique town is Moçimboa do Rovuma, from where there's a daily vehicle to Mueda.

Further west, one or two 4WDs or trucks depart daily from Songea's Majengo C area by around midday, reaching the Ruvuma in the evening (Tsh10,000, six hours plus). Try to get a seat in the cab, rather than with the cargo load. Cross the river via dugout canoe (Tsh2000) and spend the night on the river banks before continuing the next morning to Lichinga (Tsh24,000, eight to 10 hours) via Segundo Congresso (where you'll need to change vehicles) to Macalogue. There's no accommodation on the Tanzanian side of the border, nor any official immigration post (take care of formalities in Songea). On the Mozambique side there are basic rooms near the immigration post, a short walk from the river. The whole journey is rugged and hardcore. It's best to pay in stages, rather than paying the entire Tsh34,000 Songea–Lichinga fare in Songea, as is sometimes requested.

CAR

The road from Mtwara to the border is in reasonably good condition. There's a vehicle ferry at Kilambo, operating at high tide (per person/vehicle Tsh200/25,000). Especially during the August to November dry months, the boat can only cross at high spring tides, so you'll need to coordinate your trip accordingly. To avoid long waits at the river, get an update first at the Old Boma or Ten Degrees South Lodge (both in Mikindani, p326), or at **Russell's Place** (Cashew Camp; ☎ in Mozambique 82-686 2730; www.pembamagic.com) in Pemba, or try contacting the **ferryman** (☎ 0754-869357).

In Mozambique, the road is unsealed, but in reasonable condition from the border to Palma, a mix of tarmac and good dirt from Palma to Moçimboa da Praia, and tarmac from there to Pemba.

Work has started on the Unity Bridge over the Ruvuma, well southwest of Kilambo, near the confluence of the Lugenda River.

Rwanda

BORDER CROSSINGS

The main crossing is at Rusumu Falls, southwest of Bukoba (Tanzania).

BUS

Daily minibuses go from Kigali to Rusumu (Rwanda; US$6.50, three hours), where you'll need to walk across the Kagera river bridge. Once across, there are pick-up taxis to the tiny town (and former refugee camp) of Benako (marked as Kasulo on some maps; Tsh2500, 25 minutes), about 20km southeast. In Benako, there's **Silent Night Guest House** (d Tsh5000), with a helpful proprietor who is a good source of information on travel onwards to Kigoma and points east. Daily buses go from Benako to Mwanza (Tsh17,000, eight hours), though it's often easier to go in stages via Kahama and Shinyanga along the tarmac road. There are also daily connections from Benako to Nyakanazi junction, where you can try hitching a lift or squeezing into a bus on to Kibondo, Kasulu and Kigoma (Tsh4500 and two hours from Benako to Nyakanazi, plus Tsh9000 and about seven hours from there to Kigoma).

Uganda

BORDER CROSSINGS

The main post is at Mutukula (Tanzania), northwest of Bukoba (although you actually get stamped in and out of Tanzania at Kyaka,

30km south of the Mutukula border), with good tarmac on both sides. There's another crossing further west at Nkurungu (Tanzania), but the road is bad and sparsely travelled.

BUS
Scandinavian Express goes daily between Dar es Salaam and Kampala via Nairobi (Kenya) (Tsh62,000, 27 hours) and Arusha (Tsh38,000 from Arusha to Kampala), departing from Dar in the morning, Arusha at 4pm and Kampala at midday. Dolphin and Jaguar lines go daily between Bukoba and Kampala, departing from Bukoba about 7am (Tsh11,000, five to six hours). Departures from Kampala are at 7am and usually again at about 11am. Tawfiq/Falcon goes several times weekly along this route, continuing on to Nairobi (Tsh27,000) and Dar es Salaam, though if you're headed to Nairobi, it's better to sleep in Kampala and continue the next day.

From Mwanza, Akamba goes Wednesday, Friday and Sunday to/from Kampala (Tsh25,000, 19 hours), departing from Mwanza at 2pm.

Zambia
BORDER CROSSINGS
The main border **crossing** (☺ 7.30am-6pm Tanzania time, 6.30am-5pm Zambia time) is at Tunduma (Tanzania), southwest of Mbeya. There's also a crossing at Kasesya (Kasesha, Tanzania), between Sumbawanga (Tanzania) and Mbala (Zambia).

BUS
Scandinavian Express is planning to imminently resume its Dar es Salaam–Mbeya–Lusaka routing, departing from Dar es Salaam four times weekly at 5am (Tsh70,000, 30 hours to Lusaka). Departures from Lusaka are at 5pm. Otherwise, minibuses ply between Mbeya and Tunduma (Tsh3000, two hours), where you walk across the border for Zambian transport to Lusaka (US$20, 18 hours). The road from Dar es Salaam into Zambia is good tarmac.

For the Kasesya crossing, there are pick-ups from Sumbawanga to the border, where you'll need to change to Zambian transport.

TRAIN
The Tanzania–Zambia (Tazara) train line links Dar es Salaam with Kapiri Mposhi in Zambia (1st/2nd/economy class Tsh55,000 /40,000/33,000, about 40 hours) twice weekly via Mbeya and Tunduma. Prices between Mbeya and Kapiri Mposhi are Tsh28,900/21,600/17,100 for 1st/2nd/economy class. Departures from Dar es Salaam are at 3.50pm Tuesday and 3pm Friday, and from Kapiri Mposhi at about 3pm on the same days. Departures from Mbeya to Zambia are at 2.30pm Wednesday and Saturday. Students with ID get a 50% discount. From Kapiri Mposhi to Lusaka, you'll need to continue by bus.

Tazara also has one slower ordinary train weekly between Dar es Salaam and Mbeya (p361).

CAR
If driving from Zambia into Tanzania, note that vehicle insurance isn't available at the Kasesya border, but must be purchased 120km further on in Sumbawanga.

SEA & LAKE
There's a US$5 port tax for travel on all boats and ferries from Tanzanian ports.

Burundi
The regular passenger ferry service between Kigoma and Bujumbura is currently suspended. Previously, there had been a weekly service on the MV *Liemba* (1st/2nd/economy class US$30/20/15, 11 hours) and on the MV *Mwongozo*. Inquire at the port in Kigoma for an update. However, it's possible to take a lake taxi from Kibirizi (just north of Kigoma) or from Gombe Stream National Park to Kagunga (the Tanzanian border post). Once there, look for passage in one of the frequent small cargo boats going on to Nyanza-Lac, from where there is regular transport on to Bujumbura.

It's also sometimes possible to arrange passage on one of the regular cargo ferries between Kigoma's Ami port and Bujumbura; ask at the port for the Alnorak office.

Congo (Zaïre)
Cargo boats go two to three times weekly from Kigoma's Ami port, departing from Kigoma about 5pm and reaching Kalemie before dawn (US$20, deck class only, seven hours). Check with the Congolese embassy in Kigoma about sailing days and times. Bring food and drink with you, and something to spread on the deck for sleeping.

TRANSPORT

TRANSPORT

Kenya
DHOW

Dhows sail sporadically between Pemba, Tanga and Mombasa; the journey can be long and rough. Ask at the ports in Tanga, or in Mkoani or Wete on Pemba for information on sailings. In Kenya, ask at the port in Mombasa, or better, at Shimoni.

FERRY

There's no passenger ferry service on Lake Victoria between Tanzania and Kenya. Occasionally cargo boats depart from Mwanza for Kenya and are sometimes willing to take passengers. Inquire at the Mwanza South port about sailings.

Malawi

The MV *Songea* sails between Mbamba Bay and Nkhata Bay, in theory departing from Mbamba Bay on Friday morning and Nkhata Bay on Friday evening (1st/economy class US$10/4, four to five hours). The schedule is highly variable and sometimes cancelled completely.

Mozambique
DHOW

Dhows between Mozambique and Tanzania (12 to 30 or more hours) are best arranged at Msimbati and Moçimboa da Praia (Mozambique).

FERRY

The official route between southwestern Tanzania and Mozambique is via Malawi on the MV *Songea* between Mbamba Bay and Nkhata Bay, and then from Nkhata Bay on to Likoma Island (Malawi), Cóbuè and Metangula (both in Mozambique) on the MV *Ilala*. Unofficially, there are small boats that sail along the eastern shore of Lake Nyasa between Tanzania and Mozambique. However, Lake Nyasa is notorious for its severe and sudden squalls, and going this way is risky and not recommended.

See the Malawi section (above) for schedule information for the MV *Songea*. The MV *Ilala* departs from Monkey Bay (Malawi) at 10am Friday, arriving in Metangula (via Chipoka and Nkhotakota in Malawi) at 6am Saturday, reaching Cóbuè around midday, Likoma Island at 1.30pm and Nkhata Bay at 1am Sunday morning. Southbound, departures are at 8pm Monday from Nkhata Bay and at

6.30am Tuesday from Likoma Island, reaching Cóbuè at 7am and Metangula at midday. The schedule changes frequently; get an update from **Malawi Lake Services** (☎ in Malawi 01-587311; ilala@malawi.net). Fares are about US$40/20 for 1st-class cabin/economy class between Nkhata Bay and Cóbuè. There's an immigration officer at Mbamba Bay, Mozambique immigration posts in Metangula and Cóbuè, and immigration officers on Likoma Island and in Nkhata Bay for Malawi. You can get a Mozambique visa at Cóbuè, but not at Metangula.

Uganda

There's no passenger-ferry service, but it's relatively easy to arrange passage between Mwanza and Kampala's Port Bell on cargo ships (about 16 hours). On the Ugandan side, you'll need a letter of permission from the train station director (free). Ask for the managing director's office, on the 2nd floor of the building next to Kampala's train station. In Mwanza, a letter isn't required, but check in with the immigration officer at the South Port. Expect to pay about US$20, including port fees. Crew are often willing to rent out their cabins for a negotiable extra fee.

Zambia

The venerable MV *Liemba* has been plying the waters of Lake Tanganyika for the better part of a century on one of Africa's classic adventure journeys. It connects Kigoma with Mpulungu in Zambia weekly (1st/2nd/economy class US$55/45/40, US dollars cash only, at least 40 hours), stopping en route at various lake shore villages, including Lagosa (for Mahale Mountains National Park), Kalema (southwest of Mpanda), Kipili and Kasanga (southwest of Sumbawanga). Departures from Kigoma are on Wednesday at 4pm, reaching Mpulungu Friday morning. Departures from Mpulungu are on Friday afternoon at about 2pm, arriving back in Kigoma on Sunday afternoon. Food is available, but bring supplements and drinking water. First class is surprisingly comfortable, with two reasonably clean bunks, a window and a fan. Second-class cabins (four bunks) and economy-class seating are poorly ventilated and uncomfortable – it's better to find deck space than pay for economy-class seating. Keep watch over your luggage, and book early for a cabin – Monday morning is your best bet.

There are docks at Kigoma and Kasanga, but at many smaller stops you'll need to disembark in the middle of the lake, exiting from a door in the side of the boat into small boats that take you to shore. While it sounds adventurous, it can be rather nerve-wracking at night, if the lake is rough or you have a heavy pack.

The smaller MV *Mwongozo,* which used to ply between Kigoma and Mpulungu, is currently being used to transport refugees to Democratic Republic of Congo (Zaïre) and Burundi.

Elsewhere in the World
FREIGHTERS & CRUISES
Several cargo shipping companies sailing between Europe and East Africa have passenger cabins. Contacts include **Strand Voyages** (www .strandtravel.co.uk) and **Freighter World Cruises** (www .freighterworld.com), which is currently not servicing East African ports, though may resume doing so in the future. **Cruise Lines International Association** (www.cruising.org) is a good contact for cruise ships that stop at Zanzibar. For route and shipping-line information, check the quarterly **Reed Travel Group** (☎ in the UK 01582-600111) *OAG Cruise & Ferry Guide.* Durban (South Africa) is a good place to look for a lift on private yachts sailing up the East African coast, including to Tanzanian ports.

TOURS
For Tanzania-based operators, see p44 and p54.

Australia & New Zealand
African Wildlife Safaris (☎ 03-9249 3777, 1300-363302; www.africanwildlifesafaris.com.au) Customised trips to the northern circuit parks and Zanzibar.
Classic Safari Company (☎ 1300-130218, 02-9327 0666; www.classicsafaricompany.com.au) Upmarket customised itineraries, including to the south and west.
Peregrine Travel (☎ 03-8601 4444, 1300-854444; www.peregrine.net.au) Northern circuit treks and safaris for all budgets; also family itineraries.

South Africa
Wildlife Adventures (☎ 021-702 0643; www.wildlife adventures.co.za) Northern circuit and southern/East Africa combination itineraries.
Wild Frontiers (☎ 011-702 2035; www.wildfrontiers .com) A range of itineraries, including to Kilwa and elsewhere in the south and west.

UK
Abercrombie & Kent (☎ 0845-070 0611; www.aber crombiekent.co.uk) Customised tours and safaris, including to the southern and western parks.

Africa-in-Focus (☎ 01803-770956; www.africa-in -focus.com) Overland tours.
African Initiatives (☎ 0117-915 0001; www.african -initiatives.org.uk) Fair-traded safaris in northern Tanzania.
Baobab Travel (☎ 0870-382 5003; www.baobabtravel .com) A culturally responsible operator with itineraries countrywide.
Camps International (☎ 0870-240 1843; www.camps internatinal.com) Community-focused budget itineraries in the northern circuit and on Zanzibar.
Discover Tanzania (☎ 01908-221114; www.discover tanzania.org) Small-group itineraries focusing on the southern parks and Zanzibar.
Dragoman (☎ 01728-861133; www.dragoman.com) Overland tours.
Expert Africa (☎ 020-8232 9777; www.expertafrica .com) A long-standing operator with itineraries countrywide.
Explore Worldwide (☎ 0870-3334001; www.explore worldwide.com) Small-group tours, treks and safaris.
Gane & Marshall (☎ 020-8445 6000; www.ganean dmarshall.co.uk) Customised itineraries, including to the west and south.
Guerba (☎ 01373-826611; www.guerba.com) Overland tours and Kilimanjaro treks.
Responsible Travel.com (☎ 01273-600030; www.res ponsibletravel.com) Matches you up with ecologically and culturally responsible tour operators to plan an itinerary
Safari Drive (☎ 01488-71140; www.safaridrive.com) Self-drive safaris, primarily in northern Tanzania.
Simply Tanzania (☎ 020-8986 0615; www.simplytan zania.co.uk) Offbeat community-oriented cultural tours run by a former VSO director.
Tribes Travel (☎ 01728-685971; www.tribes.co.uk) Fair-traded safaris and treks, including in the south and west.

USA & Canada
Abercrombie & Kent (☎ 630-954 2944, 800-554 7016; www.abercrombiekent.com) Customised tours and safaris.
Africa Adventure Company (☎ 954-491 8877; www .africa-adventure.com) Upscale specialist safaris, including in southern and western Tanzania, and Kilimanjaro treks.
African Environments (www.africanenvironments. com) Top-end treks organised by one of the pioneering companies on Mt Kilimanjaro. Also luxury northern circuit vehicle safaris, and walking safaris in Ngorongoro Conservation Area and in Serengeti border areas.
African Horizons (☎ 877-256 1074, 847-256 1075; www.africanhorizons.com) A small operator offering various packages, including in the south and west.
Big Five Tours & Expeditions (☎ 800-244 3483, 772-287 7995; www.bigfive.com) Upmarket tours and safaris in the north and south.
Born Free Safaris (☎ 800-372 3274, 818-981 7185; www.bornfreesafaris.com) Northern circuit itineraries, including a women's-only tour.

Deeper Africa (☎ 888-658 7102; www.deeperafrica .com) Socially responsible, upmarket northern circuit safaris & treks.

Explorateur Voyages (☎ 514-847 1177; www.explor ateur.qc.ca in French) Northern circuit treks and safaris.

Good Earth (☎ 813-929 7232; www.goodearthtours .com) Northern circuit safaris.

International Expeditions (☎ 800-633 4734, 205-428 1700; www.ietravel.com) Naturalist-oriented northern circuit safaris.

Mountain Madness (☎ 206-937 8389; www.mountain madness.com) Upmarket Kilimanjaro treks.

Naipenda Safaris (☎ 888-404-4499; www.naipenda safaris.com) Northern circuit safaris, including for families.

Thomson Family Aventures (☎ 800-262 6255, 617-923 2004; www.familyadventures.com) A range of itineraries, and especially recommended for family safaris.

GETTING AROUND

AIR
Airlines in Tanzania

The national airline, **Air Tanzania** (www.airtanzania .com) Arusha (☎ 027-250 3201/3); Dar es Salaam (Map p90; ☎ 022-211 8411, 022-284 42930); Zanzibar (☎ 024-223 0213) has flights connecting Dar es Salaam with Mwanza, Mtwara and Kilimanjaro. Following is a list of other airlines flying domestically, all of which also do charters:

Air Excel (☎ 027-254 8429, 027-250 1597; reservation @airexcelonline.com) Arusha, Serengeti, Lake Manyara, Dar es Salaam, Zanzibar.

Chimpanzee Safaris (☎ 022-213 0553; www.chimpan zeesafaris.com) Shared twice-weekly charter between Arusha, Katavi and Mahale Mountains National Parks

Coastal Aviation (☎ 022-284 3293, 022-211 7959; www.coastal.cc) A recommended contact for travellers, with flights to many parks and major towns, including Arusha, Dar es Salaam, Dodoma, Kilwa Masoko, Lake Manyara NP, Mafia, Mwanza, Pemba, Ruaha NP, Rubondo Island NP, Saadani GR, Selous GR, Serengeti NP, Tanga, Tarangire NP and Zanzibar.

Precision Air (☎ 022-216 8000; www.precisionairtz. com) Flights to most major towns, including Bukoba, Dar es Salaam, Kigoma, Kilimanjaro, Lindi, Mtwara, Musoma, Mwanza, Shinyanga, Tabora and Zanzibar.

Regional Air Services (☎ 027-250 4477/2541; www .regional.co.tz) Arusha, Dar es Salaam, Kilimanjaro, Lake Manyara NP, Ndutu, Serengeti NP (Seronera, Sasakwa, Grumeti and Klein's Camp) and Zanzibar.

Safari Airlink (☎ 0773-723274; www.safariaviation .info) Affiliated with Foxes African Safaris (see p47), with flights linking the coast with the southern and western parks in a network, including Bagamoyo, Dar es Salaam, Iringa, Katavi NP, Kipili, Mahale Mountains NP, Mbeya,

---

> **DEPARTURE TAX**
>
> Airport departure tax for domestic flights is Tsh5000. It's sometimes included in the ticket price on the mainland (though not for smaller flights leaving from Terminal 1). On Zanzibar, it's payable separately at the airport.

Mikumi, Mufindi, Pangani, Ruaha NP, Saadani, Selous GR and Zanzibar. Also flights linking Ruaha with Arusha and the northern parks.

ZanAir (☎ 024-223 3670/8; www.zanair.com) Reliable connections between Arusha, Dar es Salaam, Lake Manyara NP, Mafia, Pangani, Pemba, Saadani NP, Selous GR, Serengeti NP, Tarangire NP and Zanzibar.

BICYCLE

Main sealed roads aren't good for cycling, as there's often no shoulder and traffic moves dangerously fast. Secondary roads are ideal, and a small but steady trickle of cyclists are exploring the country – either on longer point-to-point rides, generally part of longer transregional journeys, or from a fixed base (eg the western Usambaras around Lushoto, anywhere on Pemba etc). For point-to-point journeys, carry basic supplies, including water (at least 4L), food, a water filter, at least four spare inner tubes, a spare tyre and plenty of tube patches.

Throughout the country, cycling is best in the early morning and late afternoon, and in the drier winter season (June to August/ September). Plan on taking a break from the midday heat, and don't count on covering as much territory as you might in a northern European climate.

Mountain bikes should be brought from home, although it's possible to rent them from several operators; see the following listings. Local rental bicycles (about Tsh500 per hour, check at hotels and markets) are usually heavy single speeds or beat-up mountain bikes.

Other considerations include rampaging motorists (a small rear-view mirror is worthwhile), sleeping (bring a tent) and punctures (thorn trees are a problem). Cycling isn't permitted in national parks or wildlife reserves.

In theory, bicycles can be transported on minibuses and buses, though many drivers are unwilling. For express buses, make advance arrangements to stow your bike in the hold. Bicycles can be transported on the Zanzibar ferries and any of the lake ferries for no additional cost. The highly recommended **International Bicycle Fund** (www.ibike.org /bikeafrica) organises cycling tours in Tanzania and provides information. Another recommended contact is **AfriRoots** (www.afriroots.co.tz), which organises cycling trips in various areas of the country, including in the Usambara Mountains and in the southern highlands. Hoopoe Safaris (p44) and Summits Africa (p55) are both highly recommended for upmarket adventure cycling in the northern circuit. **Green Footprint Adventures** (www.green footprint.co.tz) organises upmarket rides around Lake Manyara. Also try **Tanzanian Bike Safaris** (www.tanzaniabiking.com).

BOAT
Dhow

Main routes connect Zanzibar and Pemba with Dar es Salaam, Tanga, Bagamoyo and Mombasa; Kilwa Kivinje, Lindi, Mikindani, Mtwara and Msimbati with other coastal towns; and Mafia and the mainland.

However, foreigners are officially prohibited on non-motorised dhows, and on any dhows between Zanzibar and Dar es Salaam; captains are subject to fines if they're caught, and may be unwilling to take you. Coastal hotels that arrange charters (many with their own dhows) include The Tides (p163), Peponi Holiday Resort (p162), Kilwa Seaview Resort (p317), Ten Degrees South Lodge (p326), The Old Boma (p326), Fundu Lagoon (p148) and any of the Chole Bay lodges on Mafia (p308). Safari Blue (p119) and **SwahiliSail** (www.swahilisail .com) are other good contacts.

Ferry

Ferries operate on Lake Victoria, Lake Tanganyika and Lake Nyasa, and between Dar es Salaam, Zanzibar and Pemba. There's a US$5 port tax per trip. While all of the lake ferries are slow and crowded, travelling with them offers an authentic glimpse into local

---

DHOW TRAVEL

With their billowing sails and graceful forms, these ancient sailing vessels have become a symbol of East Africa for adventure travellers. Yet, despite their romantic reputation, the realities can be quite different.

If winds are favourable and the water calm, dhow travel can be enjoyable, and will give you a better sense of the centuries of trade that shaped East Africa's coastal communities. If you're becalmed miles from your destination, or in a leaky, overloaded boat on rough seas, if it's raining, or if the sun is very strong, the experience will be considerably less pleasant.

Before undertaking a longer journey, test things out with a short sunset or afternoon sail. Coastal hotels are also generally good contacts for arranging reliable dhow travel. If you do decide to give a local dhow a try:

- Be prepared for rough conditions. There are no facilities on board, except possibly a toilet hanging off the stern. As sailings are wind and tide dependent, departures are often during predawn hours.
- Journeys can take much longer than anticipated; bring plenty of extra water and sufficient food.
- Sun block, a hat and a covering are essential, as is waterproofing for your luggage and a rain jacket.
- Boats capsize and people are killed each year. Avoid overloaded boats and don't set sail in bad weather.
- Travel with the winds, which blow from south to north from approximately July to September and north to south from approximately November to late February.

Note that what Westerners refer to as dhows are called either *jahazi* or *mashua* by Tanzanians. *Jahazi* are large, lateen-sailed boats. *Mashua* are smaller, and often with proportionately wider hulls and a motor. The *dau* has a sloped stem and stern. On lakes and inland waterways, the *mtumbwi* (dugout canoe) is in common use. Coastal areas, especially Zanzibar's east-coast beaches, are good places to see *ngalawa* (outrigger canoes).

TRANSPORT

life. The Lake Tanganyika and Lake Nyasa routes are also very scenic, sliding slowly past mountains and lake-shore villages. For details of ferries between Dar es Salaam and Zanzibar, see p99.

LAKE VICTORIA

The MV *Victoria* departs from Mwanza at 10pm on Tuesday, Thursday and Sunday (1st class/2nd-class sleeping/2nd-class sitting/3rd class Tsh20,500/16,500/13,500/12,500 plus port tax, nine hours). Departures from Bukoba are at 9.30pm Monday, Wednesday and Friday. First class has two-bed cabins and 2nd-class sleeping has six-bed cabins. Second-class sitting isn't comfortable, so if you can't get a spot in 1st class or 2nd-class sleeping, the best bet is to buy a 3rd-class ticket. With luck, you may then be able to find a comfortable spot in the 1st-class lounge. First- and 2nd-class cabins fill up quickly in both directions, so book as soon as you know your plans. Food is available on board. Sailing in both directions, the ferry stops also at Kemondo Bay (just south of Bukoba).

Weekly connections on the MV *Butiama* between Mwanza and Nkome, and between Mwanza and Nyamirembe via Maisome island, are currently suspended.

For information on connections to/from Ukerewe island, see p251.

LAKE TANGANYIKA

For the MV *Liemba* schedule between Kigoma and Mpulungu (Zambia), see p354. See p353 for boat connections between Kigoma and Bujumbura.

LAKE NYASA

In theory, the MV *Songea* departs from Itungi port about noon on Thursday and makes its way down the coast via Lupingu, Manda, Lundu, Mango and Liuli (but not via Matema) to Mbamba Bay (1st/economy class Tsh15,000/8500, 18 to 24 hours). It continues to Nkhata Bay in Malawi, before turning around and doing the return trip.

The smaller MV *Iringa* services lake-side villages between Itungi and Manda (about halfway down the Tanzanian lake shore), departing from Itungi by about midday on Monday and stopping at Matema, Lupingu and several other ports before turning back again on Tuesday for the return trip. Schedules for both boats are highly unreli-able and change frequently. For an update, ask in Kyela (p298), or at one of the Matema hotels (p299).

BUS

Bus travel is an inevitable part of the Tanzania experience for many travellers. Prices are reasonable for the distances covered, and there's often no other way to reach many destinations.

On major long-distance routes, there's a choice of express and ordinary buses. Express buses make fewer stops, are less crowded and depart on schedule. Some have toilets and air-conditioning, and the nicest ones are called 'luxury' buses. On secondary routes, the only option is ordinary buses, which are often packed to overflowing, stop often and run to a less rigorous schedule (and often not to any recognisable schedule at all).

For popular routes, book in advance. You can sometimes get a place by arriving at the bus station an hour prior to departure. Scandinavian Express and Royal Coach bus lines fill up quickly on all routes: book at least one day in advance. Each bus line has its own booking office, at or near the bus station.

Express buses have a compartment below for luggage. Otherwise, stow your pack under your seat or at the front of the bus near the driver.

Prices are basically fixed, although over-charging happens. Most bus stations are chaotic, and at the ones in Arusha and other tourist areas you'll be incessantly hounded by touts. Buy your tickets at the office and not from the touts, and don't believe anyone who tries to tell you there's a luggage fee, unless you are carrying an excessively large pack.

For short stretches along main routes, express buses will drop you on request, though you'll often need to pay the full fare to the next major destination.

Major lines along the Dar–Arusha route include Dar Express, Royal Coach and Scandinavian Express. Scandinavian Express is also good for destinations between Dar and Mbeya, and to Njombe and Songea. Although Scandinavian is still generally regarded as the best company in the south, its fleet is ageing, and you'll generally need to pay for its luxury buses for a reasonably comfortable ride.

Minibus & Shared Taxi

For shorter trips away from the main routes, the choice is often between 30-seater buses

PERILS OF THE ROAD

Road accidents are probably your biggest safety risk while travelling in Tanzania, with speeding buses being among the worst offenders. Road conditions are poor and driving standards leave much to be desired. Overtaking blind is a problem, as are high speeds. Your bus driver may, in fact, be at the wheel of an ageing, rickety vehicle with a cracked windshield and marginal brakes on a winding, potholed road. However, he'll invariably be driving as if he were piloting a sleek racing machine coming down the straight – nerve-wracking to say the least. Impassioned pleas from passengers to slow down usually have little effect, and pretending you're sick is often counterproductive. Many vehicles have painted slogans such as *Mungu Atubariki* (God Bless Us) or 'In God we Trust' in the hope that a bit of extra help from above will see them safely through the day's runs.

To maximise your chances of uneventful travels, stick with more reputable companies such as Scandinavian Express and Royal Coach. Also, if you have a choice, it's usually better to go with a full-sized bus than a minibus or 30-seater bus.

Buses aren't permitted to drive at night and, on most routes, the last departure is generally timed so that the bus should reach its destination by evening (assuming that all goes well). For cross-border routes, departures are usually timed so that night driving will be done once outside Tanzania.

('Coastals' or *thelathini*) and *dalla-dallas*. Both options come complete with chickens on the roof, bags of produce under the seats, no leg room and schedules only in the most general sense of the word. *Dalla-dallas*, especially, are invariably filled to overflowing. Shared taxis are rare, except in northern Tanzania near Arusha and several other locations. Like ordinary buses, *dalla-dallas* and shared taxis leave when full, and are the least safe transport option.

CAR & MOTORCYCLE

Unless you have your own vehicle and are familiar with driving in East Africa, it's relatively unusual for travellers to tour mainland Tanzania by car. More common is to focus on a region and arrange local transport through a tour or safari operator. On Zanzibar, however, it's easy and economical to hire a car or motorcycle for touring, and self-drive is permitted.

Bringing Your Own Vehicle

For requirements on bringing your own vehicle, see p349.

Driving Licence

On the mainland you'll need your home driving licence or (preferable) an International Driving Permit (IDP) together with your home licence. On Zanzibar you'll need an IDP plus your home licence, or a permit from Zanzibar (p127), Kenya, Uganda or South Africa.

Fuel & Spare Parts

Petrol costs about Tsh1400 per litre (Tsh1250 for diesel). Filling and repair stations are found in all major towns, but are scarce elsewhere, so tank up whenever you get the opportunity and carry a range of spares for your vehicle. In remote areas and in national parks, it's essential to carry jerry cans with extra fuel.

Hire

In Dar es Salaam, daily rates for 2WD start at about US$45, excluding fuel, plus US$20 to US$30 for insurance and tax. Prices for 4WD are US$70 to US$200 per day plus insurance (US$30 to US$40 per day), fuel and driver (US$15 to US$35 per day). There's also a 20% value added tax.

Outside the city, most companies require 4WD. Also, most will not permit self-drive outside of Dar es Salaam, and none presently offer unlimited kilometres. Charges per-kilometre are around US$0.50 to US$1. Try to clarify what the company's policy is in the event of a breakdown. See p100 for hire agencies.

Elsewhere in Tanzania, you can hire 4WD vehicles in Arusha, Karatu, Mwanza, Mbeya, Zanzibar Town and other centres through travel agencies, tour operators and hotels. See the individual sections for hire agency listings. Except on Zanzibar, most come with driver. Rates average US$80 to US$150 per day plus fuel, less on Zanzibar.

TRANSPORT

TRANSPORT

Insurance

Unless you're covered from other sources, such as your credit card, it's advisable to take the full coverage offered by hire companies.

Road Conditions & Hazards

Around 20% of Tanzania's road network is sealed (although roadworks are underway at an impressive pace), including the roads from Dar es Salaam to Arusha via Chalinze, and from Dar es Salaam to Mbeya via Iringa. Secondary roads range from good to impassable, depending on the season. For most trips outside major towns you'll need 4WD.

If you aren't used to driving in East Africa, watch out for pedestrians, children and animals on the road or running into the road. Especially in rural areas, many people have not driven themselves and aren't aware of necessary braking distances and similar concepts. Avoid driving at night, and be particularly alert for vehicles overtaking blind on curves. Tree branches on the road are the local version of flares or hazard lights and mean there's a stopped vehicle, crater-sized pothole or similar calamity ahead.

Road Rules

Driving is on the left (in theory), and traffic already on roundabouts has the right of way. Unless otherwise posted, the speed limit is 80km per hour; on some routes, including Dar es Salaam to Arusha, police have radar. Tanzania has a seat-belt law for drivers and front-seat passengers. The traffic-fine penalty is Tsh20,000.

Motorcycles aren't permitted in national parks except for the section of the Dar es Salaam–Mbeya highway passing through Mikumi National Park and on the road between Sumbawanga and Mpanda via Katavi National Park.

HITCHING

Hitching is generally slow going. It's prohibited inside national parks, and is usually fruitless around them. That said, in remote areas, hitching a lift with truck drivers may be your only option. Expect to pay about the same or a bit less than the bus fare for the same route, with a place in the cab costing about twice that for a place on top of the load. To flag down a vehicle, hold out your hand at about waist level, palm to the ground, and wave it up and down.

Expat workers or well-off locals may also offer you a ride. Payment is usually not expected, but still offer some token of thanks, such as a petrol contribution for longer journeys.

As elsewhere in the world, hitching is never entirely safe, and we don't recommend it. Travellers who hitch should understand that they are taking a potentially serious risk. If you do hitch, it's safer doing so in pairs and letting someone know your plans.

LOCAL TRANSPORT
Dalla-Dalla

Local routes are serviced by *dalla-dallas* and, in rural areas, pick-up trucks or old 4WDs. Prices are fixed and inexpensive – Tsh100 to Tsh200 for town runs. The vehicles make many stops and are extremely crowded. Accidents are frequent, particularly in minibuses. Many accidnets are caused when the drivers race each other to an upcoming station in order to collect new passengers. Destinations are either posted on a board in the front window, or called out by the driver's assistant, who also collects fares. If you have a large backpack, think twice about getting on a *dalla-dalla*, especially at rush hour, when it will make the already crowded conditions even more uncomfortable for the other passengers.

Taxi

Taxis, which have white plates on the mainland and a *'gari la abiria'* (passenger vehicle) sign on Zanzibar, can be hired in all major towns. None have meters, so agree on the fare with the driver before getting in. The standard rate for short town trips is Tsh1000 to Tsh2000. In major centres, many drivers have an 'official' price list, although rates shown on it – often calculated on the basis of Tsh1000 per 1km – are generally significantly higher than what is normally paid. If you're unsure of the price, ask locals what it should be and then use this as a base for negotiations. For longer trips away from town, negotiate the fare based on distance, petrol costs and road conditions, plus a fair profit for the driver.

TOURS

For safari and trekking operators, see p44 and p54. For local tour operators, see the regional chapters.

TRAIN

We wish we could say that train travel was a classic Tanzania experience, watching the landscapes roll by and getting a snapshot of local life, but the country's rail lines are so under-maintained these days, and so often beset by delays and breakdowns, that it would be too much of a stretch – but if you get lucky, you're likely to enjoy the ride. Once planned privatisation and upgrading programmes are implemented, the situation is bound to improve.

There are two lines: **Tazara** (☎ 022-286 5137, 022-286 0340/4, 0713-225292; www.tazara.co.tz; cnr Nyerere & Nelson Mandela Rds, Dar es Salaam), linking Dar es Salaam with Kapiri Mposhi in Zambia via Mbeya and Tunduma; and the Tanzanian Railway Corporation's **Central Line** (Map p90; ☎ 022-211 7833; www.trctz.com; cnr Railway St & Sokoine Dr, Dar es Salaam), linking Dodoma with Kigoma and Mwanza via Tabora (service between Dodoma and Dar es Salaam is suspended). Central Line branches also link Tabora with Mpanda, and Dodoma with Singida.

Tazara is more comfortable and efficient, but on both lines, breakdowns and long delays – up to 12 hours or more – are common. If you want to try the train, consider shorter stretches – eg from Dar es Salaam into the Selous, or between Tabora and Kigoma.

Classes

There are three classes: 1st class (two- or four-bed compartments); 2nd-class sleeping (six-bed compartments); and economy class (benches, usually very crowded). Some trains also have a '2nd-class sitting section', with one seat per person. Men and women can only travel together in the sleeping sections by booking the entire compartment. At night, secure your window with a stick, and don't leave your luggage unattended even for a moment.

Reservations

Tickets for 1st and 2nd class should be reserved at least several days in advance, although occasionally you'll be able to get a seat on the day of travel. Economy-class tickets can be bought on the spot.

Schedules & Costs

Both lines are undergoing management changes, so expect schedule and price changes.

TAZARA

Tazara runs three trains weekly: two 'express' trains between Dar es Salaam and Kapiri Mposhi in Zambia via Mbeya; and an 'ordinary' train between Dar es Salaam and Mbeya.

For express train schedule information, see p353. Express train fares between Dar es Salaam and Mbeya are Tsh24,500/18,000/14,800 for 1st/2nd/economy class. Ordinary trains depart from Dar es Salaam at 9am Monday, reaching Mbeya about 10am the next day (1st/2nd/economy class Tsh20,700/14,500/12,000, 24 hours); departures from Mbeya are at 1.30pm Tuesday.

CENTRAL LINE

Central Line trains depart from Dodoma at 7pm Monday, Wednesday, Thursday and Saturday for both Kigoma and Mwanza (splitting at Tabora). Both journeys take about 24 hours, though it's often much longer. Trains to Dar es Salaam depart at 7.30am (from Kigoma) and 8am (from Mwanza) on Monday, Wednesday, Friday and Saturday, arriving at Tabora at about 6pm. Travelling between Mwanza and Kigoma, you'll need to stay overnight in Tabora. Departures from Tabora are at 9pm Monday, Wednesday, Friday and Saturday for Dodoma, and at 7.30am on Sunday, Tuesday, Thursday and Friday for Kigoma.

Trains between Tabora and Mpanda (about 14 hours) depart from Tabora at 9.30pm Monday, Wednesday and Friday, and Mpanda at 1pm Tuesday, Thursday and Saturday.

Trains depart from Dodoma for Singida (about seven hours) at 10am Wednesday, Friday and Sunday. Departures from Singida are at 8am Monday, Thursday and Saturday.

Destination	1st class	2nd-sitting class	Economy class
Dodoma to Tabora	Tsh21,900	Tsh16,700	Tsh7500
Tabora to Kigoma	Tsh22,700	Tsh17,300	Tsh7800
Dodoma to Mwanza	Tsh37,000	Tsh27,400	Tsh12,000
Mwanza to Tabora	Tsh21,200	Tsh16,200	Tsh7300
Tabora to Mpanda	Tsh19,700	Tsh15,100	Tsh6900
Dodoma to Singida	-	-	Tsh4800

Health Dr Caroline Evans

CONTENTS

As long as you stay up-to-date with your vaccinations and take basic preventive measures, you're unlikely to succumb to most of the health hazards covered in this chapter. While Tanzania has an impressive selection of tropical diseases on offer, it's more likely you'll get a bout of diarrhoea or a cold than a more exotic malady. The main exception to this is malaria, which is a real risk throughout the country.

BEFORE YOU GO

A little predeparture planning will save you trouble later. Get a check-up from your dentist and your doctor if you have any regular medication or chronic illness, such as high blood pressure or asthma. You should also organise spare contact lenses and glasses (and take your optical prescription with you), get a first-aid and medical kit together and arrange necessary vaccinations.

Travellers can register with the **International Association for Medical Advice to Travellers** (IAMAT; www.iamat.org), which provides directories of certified doctors. If you'll be spending much time in remote areas (ie anywhere away from Dar es Salaam, Arusha and Zanzibar), consider doing a first-aid course (contact the Red Cross or St John Ambulance) or attending a remote medicine first-aid course, such

as that offered by the **Royal Geographical Society** (www.wildernessmedicaltraining.co.uk).

If you bring medications with you, carry them in their original (labelled) containers. A signed and dated letter from your physician describing all medical conditions and medications, including generic names, is also a good idea. If carrying syringes or needles, be sure to have a physician's letter documenting their medical necessity.

INSURANCE

Find out in advance if your insurance plan will make payments directly to providers or reimburse you later for overseas health expenditures. Most doctors in Tanzania expect payment in cash. It's vital to ensure that your travel insurance will cover any emergency transport required to get you at least as far as Nairobi (Kenya), or – preferably – all the way home, by air and with a medical attendant if necessary. It's worth taking out a temporary membership with the **African Medical & Research Foundation** (Amref; www.amref.org; Nairobi emergency lines ☎ 254-20 315454, 254-20 600090, 254-733 628422, 254-722 314239, satellite ☎ 000-873 762 315580; Nairobi head office ☎ 254-20-699 3000; Dar es Salaam branch office ☎ 022-211 6610, 211 3673; 1019 Ali Hassan Mwinyi Rd just north of Bibi Titi Mohammed Rd). See p339 for further details.

RECOMMENDED VACCINATIONS

The **World Health Organization** (www.who.int/en/) recommends that all travellers be covered for diphtheria, tetanus, measles, mumps, rubella, polio and hepatitis B, regardless of their destination. The consequences of these diseases can be severe and outbreaks do occur.

According to the **Centers for Disease Control and Prevention** (www.cdc.gov), the following vaccinations are recommended for Tanzania: hepatitis A, hepatitis B, rabies and typhoid, and boosters for tetanus, diphtheria and measles. While a yellow-fever vaccination certificate is not officially required to enter the country unless you're coming from an infected area, carrying one is also advised; check with your doctor before travelling, and also see p367.

MEDICAL CHECKLIST

It's a very good idea to carry a medical and first-aid kit with you, to help yourself in the case of minor illness or injury. Following is a list of items to consider packing:

- Acetaminophen (paracetamol) or aspirin
- Acetazolamide (Diamox) for altitude sickness (prescription only)
- Adhesive or paper tape
- Antibacterial ointment (eg Bactroban) for cuts and abrasions (prescription only)
- Antibiotics eg ciprofloxacin (Ciproxin) or norfloxacin (Utinor)
- Antidiarrhoeal drugs (eg loperamide)
- Antihistamines (for hay fever and allergic reactions)
- Anti-inflammatory drugs (eg ibuprofen)
- Antimalaria pills
- Bandages, gauze, gauze rolls and tape
- DEET-containing insect repellent for the skin
- Digital thermometer
- Iodine tablets (for water purification)
- Oral rehydration salts
- Permethrin-containing insect spray for clothing, tents and bed nets
- Pocket knife
- Scissors, safety pins, tweezers
- Self-diagnostic kit that can identify from a finker prick if malaria is in the blood
- Sun block
- Sterile needles, syringes and fluids if travelling to remote areas

INTERNET RESOURCES

A good place to start is the **Lonely Planet website** (www.lonelyplanet.com). The World Health Organization publishes the helpful *International Travel and Health*, available free at www.who.int/ith. Other useful websites include **MD Travel Health** (www.mdtravelhealth.com) and **Fit for Travel** (www.fitfortravel.scot.nhs.uk).

Government travel-health websites:

- Australia: www.smartraveller.gov.au
- Canada: www.phac-aspc.gc.ca/tmp-pmv /index.html
- UK: www.dh.gov.uk/PolicyAndGuidance /HealthAdviceForTravellers/fs/en
- USA: wwwn.cdc.gov/travel

FURTHER READING

- *A Comprehensive Guide to Wilderness and Travel Medicine* by Eric A Weiss (1998)
- *Healthy Travel* by Jane Wilson-Howarth (1999)
- *Healthy Travel Africa* by Isabelle Young (2000)
- *How to Stay Healthy Abroad* by Richard Dawood (2002)
- *Travel in Health* by Graham Fry (1994)
- *Travel with Children* by Cathy Lanigan (2004)

IN TRANSIT

DEEP VEIN THROMBOSIS (DVT)

Deep vein thrombosis (DVT) occurs when blood clots form in the legs during plane flights, chiefly because of prolonged immobility. Although most of these blood clots are reabsorbed uneventfully, some of them may break off and travel through the blood vessels to the lungs, where they may cause life-threatening complications.

The chief symptom of DVT is swelling or pain of the foot, ankle or calf, usually but not always on just one side. When a blood clot travels to the lungs, it may cause chest pain and difficulty in breathing. If you are travelling and have any of these symptoms listed above you should immediately seek medical attention.

In order to help to prevent the development of DVT on long airline flights you should walk about the cabin, perform isometric compressions of the leg muscles (ie contract the leg muscles while sitting), drink plenty of fluids and avoid alcohol and tobacco.

MOTION SICKNESS

Eating lightly before and during a trip will reduce the chances of motion sickness. If you are prone to motion sickness try to find a place that minimises movement – near the wing on aircraft, near the centre on buses and next to a window if possible. Fresh air usually helps; reading and cigarette smoke don't.

Commercial preparations for motion sickness, which can cause drowsiness, have to be taken before the trip commences. Ginger (available in capsule form) and peppermint (including mint-flavoured sweets) are natural preventatives.

IN TANZANIA

AVAILABILITY & COST OF HEALTH CARE

Good, Western-style medical care is available in Dar es Salaam. However, for serious matters, you'll need to go to Nairobi (Kenya), which is the main destination for medical evacuations from Tanzania, or return home. Elsewhere, reasonable-to-good care is available in Arusha, Moshi, Zanzibar and in some mission stations, including Kigoma and Songea. If you have a choice, try to find a private or mission-run clinic, as these are generally better equipped than government ones. If you fall ill in an unfamiliar area, ask staff at a top-end hotel or resident expatriates where the best nearby medical facilities are, and in an emergency contact your embassy. All towns have at least one clinic where you can get an inexpensive malaria test and, if necessary, treatment.

Pharmacies in Dar es Salaam and major towns are generally well stocked for commonly used items, and usually don't require prescriptions; always check expiry dates. In villages, selection is limited, although you can get chloroquine (for malaria) and paracetamol almost everywhere. Antimalarials are also relatively easy to obtain, although antimalarials in general, as well as drugs for chronic diseases, should be brought from home. Some drugs for sale in Tanzania might be ineffective: they might be counterfeit or might not have been stored under the right conditions. The most common examples of counterfeit drugs are antimalaria tablets and expensive antibiotics, such as ciprofloxacin. Also, the availability and efficacy of condoms cannot be relied upon; they might not be of the same quality as in Europe or Australia and might have been incorrectly stored.

There is a high risk of contracting HIV from infected blood transfusions. The **BloodCare Foundation** (www.bloodcare.org.uk) is a good source of safe blood, which can be transported to any part of the world within 24 hours.

INFECTIOUS DISEASES

Following are some of the diseases that are found in Tanzania, though with a few basic preventive measures, it's unlikely that you'll succumb to any of these.

Cholera

Cholera is usually only a problem during natural or artificial disasters, such as war, floods or earthquakes, although small outbreaks can also occur at other times. Travellers are rarely affected. It is caused by a bacteria and spread via contaminated drinking water. The main symptom is profuse watery diarrhoea, which causes debilitation if fluids are not replaced quickly. An oral cholera vaccine is available in the USA, but it is not particularly effective. Most cases of cholera could be avoided by close attention to good drinking water and by avoiding potentially contaminated food. Treatment is by fluid replacement (orally or via a drip), but sometimes antibiotics are needed. Self-treatment is not advised.

Diphtheria

Diphtheria is spread through close respiratory contact. It usually causes a temperature and a severe sore throat. Sometimes a membrane forms across the throat and a tracheotomy is needed to prevent suffocation. Vaccination is recommended for those likely to be in close contact with the local population in infected areas, but is more important for long stays than for short-term trips. The vaccine is given as an injection, alone or with tetanus, and lasts 10 years. Self-treatment: none.

Filariasis

Filariasis is caused by tiny worms migrating in the lymphatic system and is spread by a bite from an infected mosquito. Symptoms include localised itching and swelling of the legs and/or genitalia. Treatment is available. Self-treatment: none.

Hepatitis A

Hepatitis A is spread through contaminated food (particularly shellfish) and water. It causes jaundice and, although it is rarely fatal, it can cause prolonged lethargy and delayed recovery. If you've had hepatitis A, you shouldn't drink alcohol for up to six months afterwards, but once you've recovered, there won't be any long-term problems. The first symptoms include dark urine and a yellow colour to the whites of the eyes. Sometimes a fever and abdominal pain are present. Hepatitis A vaccine (Avaxim, VAQTA, Havrix) is given as an injection: a single dose will give protection for up to a year, and a booster after a year gives 10-year protection. Hepatitis A

ANTIMALARIAL A TO D

▪ **A** – Awareness of the risk. No medication is totally effective, but protection of up to 95% is achievable with most drugs, as long as other measures have been taken.

▪ **B** – Bites: avoid at all costs. Sleep in a screened room, use a mosquito spray or coils and sleep under a permethrin-impregnated net at night. Cover up at night with long trousers and long sleeves, preferably with permethrin-treated clothing. Apply appropriate repellent to all areas of exposed skin in the evenings.

▪ **C** – Chemical prevention (ie antimalarial drugs) is usually needed in malarial areas. Expert advice is needed as resistance patterns can change and new drugs are in development. Not all antimalarial drugs are suitable for everyone. Most antimalarial drugs need to be started at least a week in advance and continued for four weeks after the last possible exposure to malaria.

▪ **D** – Diagnosis. If you have a fever or flu-like illness within a year of travel to a malarial area, malaria is a possibility and immediate medical attention is necessary.

---

and typhoid vaccines can also be given as a single-dose vaccine, hepatyrix or viatim. Self-treatment: none.

Hepatitis B

Hepatitis B is spread through sexual intercourse, infected blood and contaminated needles. It can also be spread from an infected mother to her baby during childbirth. It affects the liver, causing jaundice and sometimes liver failure. Most people recover completely, but some people might be chronic carriers of the virus, which could lead eventually to cirrhosis or liver cancer. Those visiting high-risk areas for long periods, or those with increased social or occupational risk, should be immunised. Many countries now routinely give hepatitis B as part of childhood vaccination. It is given singly or can be given at the same time as hepatitis A.

A course will give protection for at least five years. It can be given over four weeks or six months. Self-treatment: none.

HIV

Human immunodeficiency virus (HIV), the virus that causes acquired immune deficiency syndrome (AIDS), is a major problem in Tanzania, with infection rates averaging about 6.5%, and much higher in some areas. The virus is spread through infected blood and blood products, by sexual intercourse with an infected partner and from an infected mother to her baby during childbirth and breastfeeding. It can be spread through 'blood to blood' contact, such as with contaminated instruments during medical, dental, acupuncture and other body-piercing procedures, and through sharing used intravenous needles. At present there is no cure; medication that might keep the disease under control is available, but these drugs are too expensive, or unavailable, for the overwhelming majority of Tanzanians. If you think you might have been infected with HIV, a blood test is necessary; a three-month gap after exposure and before testing is required to allow antibodies to appear in the blood. Self-treatment: none.

Malaria

Malaria is endemic throughout most of Tanzania and is a major health scourge (except at altitudes higher than 2000m, where the risk of transmission is low). Infection rates are higher during the rainy season, but the risk exists year-round and it is extremely important to take preventive measures, even if you will be in the country for just a short time.

Malaria is caused by a parasite in the bloodstream spread via the bite of the female anopheles mosquito. There are several types, falciparum malaria being the most dangerous and the predominant form in Tanzania. Unlike most other diseases regularly encountered by travellers, there is no vaccination against malaria (yet). However, several different drugs are used to prevent malaria and new ones are in the pipeline. Up-to-date advice from a travel-health clinic is essential, as some medication is more suitable for some travellers than others (see p366). The pattern of drug-resistant malaria is changing rapidly, so what was advised several years ago might no longer be the case.

SYMPTOMS

The early stages of malaria include headaches, fevers, generalised aches and pains, and malaise, which could be mistaken for flu. Other symptoms can include abdominal pain, diarrhoea and a cough. Anyone who develops a fever in Tanzania or within two weeks after departure should assume malarial infection until blood tests prove negative, even if you have been taking antimalarial medication. If not treated, the next stage could develop within 24 hours, particularly if falciparum malaria is the parasite: jaundice, then reduced consciousness and coma (also known as cerebral malaria) followed by death. Treatment in hospital is essential, and the death rate might still be as high as 10% even in the best intensive-care facilities.

SIDE EFFECTS & RISKS

Many travellers are under the impression that malaria is a mild illness, that treatment is always easy and successful and that taking antimalarial drugs causes more illness through side effects than actually getting malaria. Unfortunately, this is not true. Side effects of the medication depend on the drug being taken. Doxycycline can cause heartburn and indigestion; mefloquine (Larium) can cause anxiety attacks, insomnia and nightmares and (rarely) severe psychiatric disorders; chloroquine can cause nausea and hair loss; and proguanil can cause mouth ulcers. These side effects are not universal and can be minimised by taking medication correctly, eg with food. Also, some people should not take a particular antimalarial drug, eg people with epilepsy should avoid mefloquine, and doxycycline should not be taken by pregnant women or children younger than 12.

If you decide that you really don't want to take antimalarial drugs, you must understand the risks and be obsessive about avoiding mosquito bites. Use nets and insect repellent, and report any fever or flu-like symptoms to a doctor as soon as possible. Some people advocate homeopathic preparations against malaria, such as Demal200, but as yet there is no conclusive evidence that this is effective, and many homeopaths do not recommend their use. Malaria in pregnancy frequently results in miscarriage or premature labour and the risks to both mother and foetus during pregnancy are considerable. Travel in Tanzania when pregnant should be carefully considered.

STAND-BY TREATMENT

If you will be away from major towns, carrying emergency stand-by treatment is highly recommended, and essential for travel in remote areas. Seek your doctor's advice before setting off as to recommended medicines and dosages. However, this should be viewed as emergency treatment only and not as routine self-medication, and should only be used if you will be far from medical facilities and have been advised about the symptoms of malaria and how to use the medication. If you do resort to emergency self-treatment, seek medical advice as soon as possible to confirm whether the treatment has been successful. In particular, you want to avoid contracting cerebral malaria, which can be fatal within 24 hours. Self-diagnostic kits, which can identify malaria in the blood from a finger prick, are available in the West and are worth investing in.

Meningococcal Meningitis

Meningococcal infection is spread through close respiratory contact and is more likely in crowded places, such as dormitories, buses and clubs. While the disease is present in Tanzania, infection is uncommon in travellers. Vaccination is recommended for long stays and is especially important towards the end of the dry season. Symptoms include a fever, severe headache, neck stiffness and a red rash. Immediate medical treatment is necessary.

The ACWY vaccine is recommended for all travellers in sub-Saharan Africa. This vaccine is different from the meningococcal meningitis C vaccine given to children and adolescents in some countries; it is safe to be given both types of vaccine. Self-treatment: none.

Onchocerciasis (River Blindness)

This disease is caused by the larvae of a tiny worm, which is spread by the bite of a small fly. The earliest sign of infection is intensely itchy, red, sore eyes. It's rare for travellers to be severely affected. Treatment undertaken in a specialised clinic is curative. Self-treatment: none.

Poliomyelitis

This disease is generally spread through contaminated food and water. It is one of the vaccines given in childhood and should be boosted every 10 years, either orally (a drop on the tongue) or else as an injection. Polio can be carried asymptomatically (ie showing no symptoms) and could cause a transient fever. In rare cases it causes weakness or paralysis of one or more muscles, which might be permanent. Self-treatment: none.

Rabies

Rabies is spread via the bite or lick of an infected animal on broken skin. It is always fatal once the clinical symptoms start (which might be up to several months after an infected bite), so post-bite vaccination should be given as soon as possible. Post-bite vaccination (whether or not you've been vaccinated before the bite) prevents the virus from spreading to the central nervous system. Consider vaccination if you'll be travelling away from major centres (ie anywhere where a reliable source of post-bite vaccine is not available within 24 hours). Three preventive injections are needed over a month. If you have not been vaccinated you'll need a course of five injections starting 24 hours, or as soon as possible, after the injury. If you have been vaccinated, you'll need fewer post-bite injections, and have more time to seek medical help. Self-treatment: none.

Schistosomiasis (Bilharzia)

This disease is a risk throughout Tanzania. It's spread by flukes (parasitic flatworm) that are carried by a species of freshwater snail, which then sheds them into slow-moving or still water. The parasites penetrate human skin during swimming and then migrate to the bladder or bowel. They are excreted via stool or urine and could contaminate fresh water, where the cycle starts again. Swimming in suspect freshwater lakes (including Lake Victoria) or slow-running rivers should be avoided. Symptoms range from none to transient fever and rash, and advanced cases might have blood in the stool or in the urine. A blood test can detect antibodies if you might have been exposed, and treatment is readily available. If not treated, the infection can cause kidney failure or permanent bowel damage. It's not possible for you to infect others. Self-treatment: none.

Trypanosomiasis (Sleeping Sickness)

This disease is spread via the bite of the tsetse fly. It causes headache, fever and eventually coma. If you have these symptoms and have negative malaria tests, have yourself evaluated by a reputable clinic in Dar es Salaam, where you should also be able to obtain treatment for trypanosomiasis. There is an effective treatment. Self-treatment: none.

Tuberculosis (TB)

TB is spread through close respiratory contact and occasionally through infected milk or milk products. BCG vaccination is recommended if you'll be mixing closely with the local population, especially on long-term stays, although it gives only moderate protection against TB. TB can be asymptomatic, only being picked up on a routine chest X-ray. Alternatively, it can cause a cough, weight loss or fever, sometimes months or even years after exposure. Self-treatment: none.

Typhoid

This is spread through food or water contaminated by infected human faeces. The first symptom is usually a fever or a pink rash on the abdomen. Septicaemia (blood poisoning) can sometimes occur. A typhoid vaccine (typhim Vi, typherix) will give protection for three years. In some countries, the oral vaccine Vivotif is also available. Antibiotics are usually given as treatment, and death is rare unless septicaemia occurs. Self-treatment: none.

Yellow Fever

Although Tanzania (including Zanzibar) no longer officially requires you to carry a certificate of yellow-fever vaccination unless you're arriving from an infected area (which includes Kenya), it's still sometimes asked for at some borders and is a requirement in some neighbouring countries. When trying to decide whether to get jabbed or not, remember that yellow fever exists in Tanzania, and the vaccine is recommended for almost all visitors by the **Centers for Disease Control and Prevention** (wwwn.cdc.gov/travel/contentYellowBook.aspx).

Yellow fever is spread by infected mosquitoes. Symptoms range from a flu-like illness to severe hepatitis (liver inflammation), jaundice and death. The yellow-fever vaccination must be given at a designated clinic and is valid for 10 years. It is a live vaccine and must not be given to immunocompromised or pregnant travellers. Self-treatment: none.

TRAVELLERS' DIARRHOEA

It's not inevitable that you'll get diarrhoea while travelling in Tanzania, but it's certainly likely. Diarrhoea is the most common travel-related illness, and sometimes can be triggered

HEALTH

simply by dietary changes. To help prevent diarrhoea, avoid tap water, only eat fresh fruits or vegetables if cooked or peeled and be wary of dairy products that might contain unpasteurised milk. Although freshly cooked food can often be a safe option, plates or serving utensils might be dirty, so be selective when eating food from street vendors (make sure that cooked food is piping hot all the way through). If you develop diarrhoea, be sure to drink plenty of fluids, preferably an oral rehydration solution. A few loose stools don't require treatment, but if you start having more than four or five stools a day you should start taking an antibiotic (usually a quinoline drug, such as ciprofloxacin or norfloxacin) and an antidiarrhoeal agent (such as loperamide) if you are not within easy reach of a toilet. If diarrhoea is bloody, persists for more than 72 hours or is accompanied by fever, shaking chills or severe abdominal pain, seek medical attention.

Amoebic Dysentery

Contracted by eating contaminated food and water, amoebic dysentery causes blood and mucus in the faeces. It can be relatively mild and tends to come on gradually, but seek medical advice if you think you have the illness as it won't clear up without treatment (which is with specific antibiotics).

Giardiasis

This, like amoebic dysentery, is caused by ingesting contaminated food or water. The illness usually appears a week or more after you have been exposed to the offending parasite. Giardiasis might cause only a short-lived bout of typical travellers' diarrhoea, but it can also cause persistent diarrhoea. Seek medical advice if you suspect you have giardiasis. If you are in a remote area you could start a course of antibiotics, with medical follow-up when feasible.

ENVIRONMENTAL HAZARDS
Altitude Sickness

Reduced oxygen levels at altitudes above 2500m affects most people. The effect may be mild or severe and occurs because less oxygen reaches the muscles and the brain at high altitudes, requiring the heart and lungs to compensate by working harder. Symptoms of Acute Mountain Sickness (AMS) usually develop during the first 24 hours at altitude but may be delayed for up to three weeks. Mild

symptoms include headache, lethargy, dizziness, sleeping difficulties and loss of appetite. AMS may become more severe without warning and can be fatal. It is a significant risk for anyone – no matter what their fitness level – who tries to ascend Mt Kilimanjaro or Mt Meru too rapidly. Severe symptoms include breathlessness; a dry, irritative cough (which may progress to the production of pink, frothy sputum); severe headache; lack of coordination and balance; confusion; irrational behaviour; vomiting; drowsiness; and unconsciousness. There is no hard-and-fast rule as to what is too high: AMS has been fatal at 3000m, although 3500m to 4500m is the usual range.

Treat mild symptoms of AMS by resting at the same altitude until recovery, which usually takes a day or two. Paracetamol or aspirin can be taken for headaches. If symptoms persist or become worse, however, immediate descent is necessary; even descending just 500m can help. Drug treatments should never be used to avoid descent or to enable further ascent.

The drugs acetazolamide and dexamethasone are recommended by some doctors for the prevention of AMS; however, their use is controversial. They can reduce the symptoms, but they may also mask warning signs and cause severe dehydration; severe and fatal AMS has occurred in people taking these drugs. In general we do not recommend them for travellers.

To prevent AMS, try the following:

- Ascend slowly – have frequent rest days, spending two to three nights at each rise of 1000m. If you reach a high altitude by trekking, acclimatisation takes place gradually and you are less likely to be affected than if you fly or drive directly to an area of high altitude.

- It is always wise to sleep at a lower altitude than the greatest height reached during the day, if possible ('climb high, sleep low'). Also, once above 3000m, care should be taken not to increase the sleeping altitude by more than 300m per day.

- Drink lots of fluids. Mountain air is dry and cold and moisture is lost as you breathe. Evaporation of sweat may occur unnoticed and result in dehydration.

- Eat light, high-carbohydrate meals for more energy.

- Avoid alcohol as it increases the risk of dehydration.

- Avoid sedatives.

Heat Exhaustion

This condition occurs after heavy sweating and excessive fluid loss with inadequate replacement of fluids and salt, and is primarily a risk in hot climates when taking unaccustomed exercise before full acclimatisation. Symptoms include headache, dizziness and tiredness. Dehydration is already happening by the time you feel thirsty – aim to drink sufficient water to produce pale, diluted urine. Self-treatment: fluid replacement with water and/or fruit juice, and cooling the body with cold water and fans. The treatment of the salt-loss component consists of consuming salty fluids (as in soup) and adding a little more table salt to foods than usual.

Heatstroke

Heat exhaustion is a precursor to the much more serious condition of heatstroke. In this case there is damage to the sweating mechanism, with an excessive rise in body temperature; irrational and hyperactive behaviour; and, eventually, loss of consciousness and death. Rapid cooling by spraying the body with water and fanning is ideal. Emergency fluid and electrolyte replacement is usually also required by intravenous drip.

Hypothermia

Too much cold can be just as dangerous as too much heat. If you are trekking at high altitudes, such as on Mt Kilimanjaro or Mt Meru, you'll need to have appropriate clothing and be prepared for cold, wet conditions. Even in lower areas, such as the Usambara Mountains, the rim of Ngorongoro Crater or the Ulugurus, conditions can be wet and quite chilly.

Hypothermia occurs when the body loses heat faster than it can produce it and the core temperature of the body falls. It is surprisingly easy to progress from being very cold to being dangerously cold due to a combination of wind, wet clothing, fatigue and hunger, even if the air temperature is above freezing. It is best to dress in layers: silk, wool and some of the new artificial fibres are all good insulating materials. A hat is important, as a lot of heat is lost through the head. A strong, waterproof outer layer (and a 'space' blanket for emergencies) is essential. Carry basic supplies, including food that contains simple sugars to generate heat quickly, and fluid to drink.

Symptoms of hypothermia are exhaustion, numb skin (particularly of the toes and fingers), shivering, slurred speech, irrational or violent behaviour, lethargy, stumbling, dizzy spells, muscle cramps and violent bursts of energy. Irrationality may take the form of sufferers claiming they are warm and trying to take off their clothes.

To treat mild hypothermia, first get the person out of the wind and/or rain, remove their clothing if it's wet and replace it with dry, warm clothing. Give them hot liquids – not alcohol – and high-kilojoule, easily digestible food. Do not rub victims: allow them to slowly warm themselves instead. This should be enough to treat the early stages of hypothermia. The early recognition and treatment of mild hypothermia is the only way to prevent severe hypothermia, which is a critical condition.

Insect Bites & Stings

Mosquitoes might not always carry malaria or dengue fever, but they (and other insects) can cause irritation and infected bites. To avoid these, take the same precautions as you would for avoiding malaria (see boxed text, p365). Bee and wasp stings cause real problems only to those who have a severe allergy to the stings (anaphylaxis), in which case, carry an adrenaline (epinephrine) injection.

Scorpions are found in arid areas. They can cause a painful bite that is sometimes life-threatening. If bitten by a scorpion, seek immediate medical assistance.

Bed bugs are often found in hostels and cheap hotels. They lead to very itchy, lumpy bites. Spraying the mattress with crawling insect killer after changing the bedding will get rid of them.

Scabies is also frequently found in cheap accommodation. These tiny mites live in the skin, particularly between the fingers. They cause an intensely itchy rash. The itch is easily treated with Malathion and permethrin lotion from a pharmacy; other members of the household also need to be treated to avoid spreading scabies, even if they do not show any symptoms.

Snake Bites

Basically, avoid getting bitten! Don't walk barefoot or stick your hand into holes or cracks. However, 50% of those bitten by

HEALTH

TRADITIONAL MEDICINE MARY FITZPATRICK

According to some estimates, at least 80% of Tanzanians rely in part or in whole on traditional medicine, and close to two thirds of the population have traditional healers as their first point of contact in the case of illness. The *mganga* (traditional healer) holds a revered position in many communities, and traditional medicinal products are widely available in local markets. In part, the heavy reliance on traditional medicine is because of the comparatively high costs of conventional Western-style medicine, and because of prevailing cultural attitudes and beliefs, but also because it sometimes works. Often, though, it's because there is no other choice. In northeastern Tanzania, for example, it is estimated that while there is only one medical doctor to over 30,000 people, there is a traditional healer for approximately every 150 people. While the ratio is somewhat better countrywide (one medical doctor to about 20,000 people), hospitals and health clinics are concentrated in urban areas, and most are limited in their effectiveness because of insufficient resources and chronic shortages of equipment and medicines.

While some traditional remedies seem to work on malaria, sickle-cell anaemia, high blood pressure and some AIDS symptoms, most traditional healers learn their art by apprenticeship, so education (and consequently application of knowledge) is often inconsistent and unregulated. At the centre of efforts to address problems arising from this is the **Institute of Traditional Medicine** (www.muchs.ac.tz; Muhimbili Medical Centre, Dar es Salaam). Among other things, the institute is studying the efficacy of various traditional cures, and promoting those that are found to be successful. There are also local efforts to create healers' associations, and to train traditional practitioners in sanitation and various other topics. On a broader scale, the Organisation of African Unity has declared 2001 to 2010 the Decade of Traditional Medicine in Tanzania and across the continent.

venomous snakes are not actually injected with poison (envenomed). If bitten by a snake, do not panic. Immobilise the bitten limb with a splint (such as a stick) and apply a bandage over the site, with firm pressure – similar to bandaging a sprain. Do not apply a tourniquet, or cut or suck the bite. Get medical help as soon as possible so an antivenin can be given if needed. Try to note the snake's appearance to help in treatment.

Water

Unless your intestines are well accustomed to Tanzania, don't drink tap water that hasn't been boiled, filtered or chemically disinfected (such as with iodine tablets). Also avoid drinking from streams, rivers and lakes unless you've purified the water first. The same goes for drinking from pumps and wells – some do bring pure water to the surface, but the presence of animals can still contaminate supplies.

Language

CONTENTS

Along with English, Swahili is the official language of Tanzania. Standard Swahili is based on the variety of the language spoken in Zanzibar Town, although there are several other dialects. Written Swahili – the language of newspapers, textbooks and literature – usually conforms to that spoken on the East African coast.

Although Swahili may seem a bit daunting at first, its structure is fairly regular and pronunciation uncomplicated. You'll soon discover that just a handful of basic words will go a long way, and will rapidly break down barriers between you and the many people you meet on your travels in Tanzania.

If your time is limited, concentrate first on the greetings (of critical importance in Tanzanian society), and then on numbers (very useful when negotiating with market vendors, taxi drivers etc). The words and phrases included in this chapter will help you get started. For a more comprehensive guide to the language, get hold of Lonely Planet's *Swahili Phrasebook*. Good luck and *Safari njema!* (happy travels).

PRONUNCIATION

Perhaps the easiest part of learning Swahili is the pronunciation. Every letter is pronounced, unless it's part of the consonant combinations discussed in the 'Consonants' section below. If a letter is written twice, it is pronounced twice – *mzee* (respected elder) has three syllables: *m-ZE-e*. Note that the 'm' is a separate syllable, and that the double 'e' indicates a lengthened vowel sound.

Word stress in Swahili almost always falls on the second-to-last syllable.

Vowels

Correct pronunciation of vowels is the key to making yourself understood in Swahili. If the following guidelines don't work for you, listen closely to how Swahili speakers pronounce their words and spend some time practising. There's also a useful audio pronunciation guide available on the Kamusi website: www.kamusiproject.org/.

Remember that if two vowels appear next to each other, each must be pronounced in turn. For example, *kawaida* (usual) is pronounced *ka-wa-EE-da*.

a	as in 'calm'
e	as the 'ey' in 'they'
i	as the 'ee' in 'keep'
o	as in 'go'
u	as the 'oo' in 'moon'

Consonants

Most consonants in Swahili have equivalents in English. The only one that might be a bit unusual for an English speaker is the sound **ng**. It can be a bit tricky at first, but with a little practice it should come easily – say 'sing along' a few times and then drop the 'si', and that's how it sounds at the beginning of a word. The sounds **th** and **dh** occur only in words borrowed from Arabic.

r	Swahili speakers make only a slight distinction between **r** and **l**; use a light 'd' for 'r' and you'll be pretty close.
dh	as 'th' in 'this'
th	as 'th' in 'thing'
ny	as the 'ni' in 'onion'
ng	as in 'singer'
gh	like the 'ch' in Scottish *loch*
g	as in 'get'
ch	as in 'church'

LANGUAGE

ACCOMMODATION

Where's a ...?	... iko wapi?
camping ground	uwanja wa kambi
guesthouse	gesti
hotel	hoteli
youth hostel	hosteli ya vijana

Can you recommend cheap lodging?
Unaweza kunipendekezea malazi rahisi?
What's the address?
Anwani ni nini?

Do you have a ... room?	Kuna chumba kwa ...?
single	mtu mmoja
double	watu wawili, kitanda kimoja
twin	watu wawili, vitanda viwili
triple	watu watatu

How much is it per day/person?
Ni bei gani kwa siku/mtu?
Can I see the room?
Naomba nione chumba?
Where's the bathroom?
Choo iko wapi?
Where are the toilets?
Vyoo viko wapi?
I'll take it.
Nataka.
I'm leaving now.
Naondoka sasa.

CONVERSATION & ESSENTIALS

Greetings are probably the most important vocabulary for a traveller to Tanzania. It's worth taking the time to familiarise yourself with the few we include here.

Jambo is a pidgin Swahili word, used to greet tourists who are presumed not to understand the language. There are two possible responses: *Jambo* (meaning 'Hello, now please speak to me in English'), and *Sijambo* (or 'Things aren't bad with me, and I'm willing to try a little Swahili').

If people assume you can speak a little Swahili, greetings may involve one or a number of the following exchanges:

How are you? (to one person)	Hujambo?
I'm fine.	Sijambo.
How are you all?	Hamjambo?
We're fine.	Hatujambo.

The word *habari* (meaning 'news') can also be used for general greetings. You may hear the word *salama* substituted for *habari*, or the *habari* may be dropped altogether.

How are you?	Habari?
How are you all?	Habari zenu?
What's the news?	Habari gani?
Good morning.	Habari za asubuhi?
Good day.	Habari za leo?
Good afternoon.	Habari za mchana?
Good evening/night.	Habari za jioni?
What's happening with you?	Habari yako?

By memorising these three simple words, you can reply to almost anything:

Good.	Nzuri.
Fine.	Salama.
Clean.	Safi.

There is also a respectful greeting for elders:

Greetings.	Shikamoo.
(response)	Marahaba.

Once you've dealt with all the appropriate greetings, you can move onto other topics:

What's your name?	Jina lako nani?
My name is ...	Jina langu ni ...
Where are you from?	Unatoka wapi?
I'm from ...	Natoka ...
I like ...	Ninapenda ...
I don't like ...	Sipendi ...

Farewells are generally short and sweet:

Goodbye.	Kwa heri.
Until tomorrow.	Kesho.
Later on.	Baadaye.
Good night.	Usiku mwema.

And a few basics never hurt ...

Yes.	Ndiyo.
No.	Hapana.
Please.	Tafadhali.
Thank you (very much).	Asante (sana).
You're welcome.	Karibu.
Excuse me.	Samahani.
Sorry.	Pole.
Just a minute.	Subiri kidogo.

SIGNS

Mahali Pa Kuingia	Entrance
Mahali Pa Kutoka	Exit
Maelezo	Information
Imefunguliwa	Open
Imefungwa	Closed
Ni Marufuku	Prohibited
Polisi	Police
Choo/Msalani	Toilets/WC
Wanaume	Men
Wanawake	Women

DIRECTIONS

Where's ...?	*... iko wapi?*
It's straight ahead.	*Iko moja kwa moja.*

Turn ...	*Geuza ...*
at the corner	*kwenye kona*
at the traffic lights	*kwenye taa za barabarani*
left	*kushoto*
right	*kulia*

behind	*nyuma ya*
in front of	*mbele ya*
near	*karibu na*
next to	*jirani ya*
opposite	*ng'ambo ya*

EMERGENCIES

Help!	*Saidia!*
There's been an accident!	*Ajali imetokea!*
Call the police!	*Waite polisi!*
Call a doctor!	*Mwite daktari!*
I'm lost.	*Nimejipotea.*
Leave me alone!	*Niache!*

HEALTH

I'm sick.	*Mimi ni mgonjwa.*
It hurts here.	*Inauma hapa.*

I'm allergic to ...	*Nina mzio wa ...*
antibiotics	*viuavijasumu*
aspirin	*aspirini*
bees	*nyuki*
nuts	*kokwa*
peanuts	*karanga*

antiseptic	*dawa ya kusafisha jeraha*
condoms	*kondom*
contraceptives	*kingamimba*

insect repellent	*dawa la kufukuza wadudu*
iodine	*iodini*
painkillers	*viondoa maumivu*
thermometer	*pimajoto*
water purification tablets	*vidonge vya kusafisha maji*

LANGUAGE DIFFICULTIES

Do you speak (English)?
Unasema (Kiingereza)?
Does anyone speak (English)?
Kuna mtu yeyote kusema (Kiingereza)?
What does (asante) mean?
Neno (asante) lina maana gani?
Yes, I understand.
Ndiyo, naelewa.
No, I don't understand.
Hapana, sielewi.
Could you please write ... down?
Tafadhali ... andika?
Can you show me (on the map)?
Unaweza kunionyesha (katika ramani)?

NUMBERS

0	*sifuri*
1	*moja*
2	*mbili*
3	*tatu*
4	*nne*
5	*tano*
6	*sita*
7	*saba*
8	*nane*
9	*tisa*
10	*kumi*
11	*kumi na moja*
12	*kumi na mbili*
13	*kumi na tatu*
14	*kumi na nne*
15	*kumi na tano*
16	*kumi na sita*
17	*kumi na saba*
18	*kumi na nane*
19	*kumi na tisa*
20	*ishirini*
21	*ishirini na moja*
22	*ishirini na mbili*
30	*thelathini*
40	*arobaini*
50	*hamsini*
60	*sitini*
70	*sabini*
80	*themanini*
90	*tisini*
100	*mia moja*
1000	*elfu*

PAPERWORK

name	*jina*
nationality	*raia*
date of birth	*tarehe ya kuzaliwa*
place of birth	*mahali pa kuzaliwa*
sex/gender	*jinsia*
passport	*pasipoti*
visa	*viza*

QUESTION WORDS

Who?	*Nani?*
What?	*Nini?*
When?	*Lini?*
Where?	*Wapi?*
Which?	*Gani?*
Why?	*Kwa nini?*
How?	*Namna?*

SHOPPING & SERVICES

department store	*duka lenye vitu vingi*
general store	*duka lenye vitu mbalimbali*

I'd like to buy ...	*Nataka kununua ...*
I'm just looking.	*Naangalia tu.*
How much is it?	*Ni bei gani?*
Can I look at it?	*Naomba nione.*
I don't like it.	*Sipendi.*
That's too expensive.	*Ni ghali mno.*
Please lower the price.	*Punguza bei, tafadhali.*
I'll take it.	*Nataka.*

Do you accept ...?	*Mnakubali ...?*
credit cards	*kadi ya benki*
travellers cheques	*hundi ya msafiri*

more	*zaidi*
less	*chache zaidi*

Where's (a/the) ...?	*... iko wapi?*
bank	*benki*
market	*soko*
tourist office	*maarifa kwa watalii*
... embassy	*ubalozi ...*
hospital	*hospitali*
post office	*posta*
public phone	*simu ya mtaani*
public toilet	*choo cha hadhara*
telecom centre	*telekom*

TIME & DATES

What time is it?	*Ni saa ngapi?*
It's (ten) o'clock.	*Ni saa (nne).*
morning	*asubuhi*
afternoon	*mchana*

evening	*jioni*
today	*leo*
tomorrow	*kesho*
yesterday	*jana*

Monday	*Jumatatu*
Tuesday	*Jumanne*
Wednesday	*Jumatano*
Thursday	*Alhamisi*
Friday	*Ijumaa*
Saturday	*Jumamosi*
Sunday	*Jumapili*

January	*mwezi wa kwanza*
February	*mwezi wa pili*
March	*mwezi wa tatu*
April	*mwezi wa nne*
May	*mwezi wa tano*
June	*mwezi wa sita*
July	*mwezi wa saba*
August	*mwezi wa nane*
September	*mwezi wa tisa*
October	*mwezi wa kumi*
November	*mwezi wa kumi na moja*
December	*mwezi wa kumi na mbili*

TRANSPORT
Public Transport

What time is the ... leaving?
... inaondoka saa ngapi?

Which ... goes to (Mbeya)?
... ipi huenda (Mbeya)?

bus	*basi*
minibus	*daladala*
plane	*ndege*
train	*treni*

When's the ... (bus)?
(Basi) ... itaondoka lini?

first	*ya kwanza*
last	*ya mwisho*
next	*ijayo*

A ... ticket to (Iringa).
Tiketi moja ya ... kwenda (Iringa).

1st-class	*daraja la kwanza*
2nd-class	*daraja la pili*
one-way	*kwenda tu*
return	*kwenda na kurudi*

cancelled	*imefutwa*
delayed	*imeche leweshwa*
platform	*stendi*
ticket window	*dirisha la tiketi*
timetable	*ratiba*

Private Transport

I'd like to hire a/an ...   *Nataka kukodi ...*
  bicycle   *baisikeli*
  car   *gar i*
  4WD   *forbaifor*
  motorbike   *pikipiki*

Are you willing to hire out your car/motorbike?
  Unaweza kunikodisha gari/pikipiki yako?
(How long) Can I park here?
  Naweza kuegesha hapa (kwa muda gani)?
Is this the road to (Embu)?
  Hii ni barabara kwenda (Embu)?
Where's a petrol station?
  Kituo cha mafuta kiko wapi?
Please fill it up.
  Jaza tangi/tanki.
I'd like ... litres.
  Nataka lita ...

diesel   *dizeli*
leaded/unleaded   *risasi/isiyo na risasi*
I need a mechanic.   *Nahitaji fundi.*
I've had an accident.   *Nimepata ajali.*
I have a flat tyre.   *Nina pancha.*
I've run out of petrol.   *Mafuta yamekwisha.*

The car/motorbike has broken down (at Chalinze).
  Gari/pikipiki ime haribika (Chalinze).
The car/motorbike won't start.
  Gari/pikipiki haiwaki.
Could I pay for a ride in your truck?
  Naweza kulipa kwa lifti katika lori lako?
Could I contribute to the petrol cost?
  Naweza kuchangia sehemu ya bei ya mafuta?
Thanks for the ride.
  Asante kwa lifti.

TRAVEL WITH CHILDREN

I need a/an ...   *Nahitaji ...*
Is there a/an ...?   *Kuna ...?*
  baby change room   *chumba cha kuvalia mtoto*
  baby seat   *kiti cha kitoto*
  child-minding   *anayeweza kumlea mtoto*
    service
  children's menu   *menyu kwa watoto*
  disposable nappies/   *nepi*
    diapers
  (English-speaking)   *yaya (anayesema Kiingereza)*
    babysitter
  highchair   *kiti juu cha mtoto*
  potty   *choo cha mtoto*
  stroller   *kigari cha mtoto*

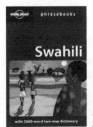

Also available from Lonely Planet:
Swahili Phrasebook

Glossary

ASP – Afro-Shirazi Party

banda – thatched-roof hut with wooden or earthen walls
bangi – marijuana
bao – a board game widely played in East Africa, especially on Zanzibar
baraza – the stone seats seen along the outside walls of houses in Zanzibar's Stone Town, used for chatting and relaxing
boma – a fortified living compound; in colonial times, an administrative office
bui-bui – black cover-all worn by some Islamic women outside the home
Bunge – Tanzanian Parliament

chai – tea
chakula – food
Chama Cha Mapinduzi (CCM) – Party of the Revolution (governing party)
choo – toilet
Cites – UN Convention on International Trade in Endangered Species
Civic United Front (CUF) – main opposition party

dada – sister; often used as a form of address
dalla-dalla – minibus
Deutsch-Ostafrikanische Gesellschaft (DOAG) – German East Africa Company
dhow – ancient Arabic sailing vessel
duka – small shop or kiosk

fly camp – a camp away from the main tented camps or lodges, to enjoy a more authentic bush experience
flycatcher – used mainly in Arusha and Moshi to mean a tout working to get you to go on safari with 'his' particular operator, from whom he knows he can get a commission. The name may come from a comparison with the sticky-sweet paper used to lure flies to land (and then get irretrievably stuck) – similar to the plight of a hapless traveller who succumbs to a flycatcher's promises and then is 'stuck' (ie with their money and time lost in a fraudulent safari deal. If any readers have a better explanation, let us know.)
forex – foreign exchange (bureau)

ganja – see *bangi*
gongo – distilled cashew drink

hodi – called out prior to entering someone's house; roughly meaning 'may I enter?'
hotel/hoteli – basic local eatery

jamaa – clan, community

kahawa – coffee
kaka – brother; used as a form of address, and to call the waiter in restaurants
kanga – printed cotton wrap-around worn by many Tanzanian women; Swahili proverbs are printed along the edge of the cloth
kanzu – white robe-like outer garment worn by men, often for prayer, on the Zanzibar Archipelago and in other Swahili areas
karanga – peanuts
karibu – Swahili 'welcome'; heard throughout Tanzania
kidumbak – an offshoot of *taarab* music, distinguished by its defined rhythms and drumming, and hard-hitting lyrics
kikoi – cotton linen wraparound traditionally worn by men in coastal areas
kitenge – similar to a *kanga,* but larger, heavier and without a Swahili proverb
kofia – a cap, usually of embroidered white linen, worn by men on the Zanzibar Archipelago and in other Swahili areas
kopjes – rocky outcrop or hill
kwaya – church choir music

maandazi – doughnut
majaji – tuk-tuk
makuti – thatch
marimba – musical instrument played with the thumb
mashua – motorised dhow
masika – long rains
matatu – Kenyan minivan
matoke – cooked plantains
mbege – banana beer
mgando – see *mtindi*
mihrab – the prayer niche in a mosque showing the direction to Mecca
mishikaki – meat kebabs
mnada – auction or market
moran – Maasai warrior
mpingo – African blackwood
mtepe – a traditional Swahili sailing vessel made without nails, the planks held together with only coconut fibres and wooden pegs
mtindi – cultured milk product similar to yogurt
mvuli – short rains
Mwalimu – teacher; used to refer to Julius Nyerere
mzungu – white person, foreigner (pl *wazungu*)

nazi – fermented coconut wine
NCA – Ngorongoro Conservation Area
NCAA – Ngorongoro Conservation Area Authority
ndugu – brother, comrade
ngoma – dance and drumming
northern circuit – the northern safari route, including Serengeti, Tarangire and Lake Manyara National Parks and the Ngorongoro Conservation Area

papasi – literally 'tick'; used on Zanzibar to refer to street touts
piki-piki – motorbikes
potwe – whale shark
public (ordinary) camp site – type of national park camp site, with basic facilities, generally including latrines and a water source
pweza – octopus, usually served grilled, at night markets and street stalls

shamba – small farm plot
shehe – village chief
shetani – literally, demon or something supernatural; in art, a style of carving embodying images from the spirit world
shikamoo – Swahili greeting of respect, used for elders or anyone in a position of authority; the response is '*marahaba*'
shuka – blanket
special camp site – type of national park camp site, more remote than *public camp sites,* and without facilities

TAA – Tanganyika Africa Association, successor of the African Association and predecessor of *TANU*

taarab – Zanzibari music combining African, Arabic and Indian influences
Tamofa – Tanzania-Mozambique Friendship Association
Tanapa – Tanzania National Parks Authority
TANU – Tanganyika (later, Tanzania) African National Union
TATO – Tanzanian Association of Tour Operators
Tazara – Tanzania-Zambia Railway
tilapia – Nile perch
Tingatinga – Tanzania's best-known style of painting, developed in the 1960s by Edward Saidi Tingatinga; traditionally in a square format with colourful animal motifs against a monochrome background
TTB – Tanzania Tourist Board

ugali – maize and/or cassava meal pap
uhuru – freedom; also the name of Mt Kilimanjaro's highest peak
ujamaa – familyhood, togetherness
umoja – unity
Unguja – Swahili name for Zanzibar island

vibuyu – carved gourds
vitambua – rice cakes

wali – cooked rice

zeze – one-stringed violin
ZIFF – Zanzibar International Film Festival
ZNP – Zanzibar Nationalist Party
ZPPP – Zanzibar & Pemba People's Party
ZTC – Zanzibar Tourist Corporation

Behind the Scenes

THIS BOOK

This is the 4th edition of Lonely Planet's *Tanzania*. The 1st edition of this book (entitled *Tanzania, Zanzibar & Pemba*) was researched and written by Mary Fitzpatrick, with contributing author David Else. Mary also wrote the 2nd and 3rd editions, with Sean Pywell updating the wildlife guide. Mary undertook the research and writing yet again in this 4th edition, with contributions from Natalie Folster (History) and David Lukas (Wildlife & Habitat). This guidebook was commissioned in Lonely Planet's Melbourne office, and produced by the following:

Commissioning Editor Lucy Monie
Coordinating Editor Jeanette Wall
Coordinating Cartographers Ross Butler, Csanad Csutoros
Coordinating Layout Designer Paul Iacono
Managing Editors Geoff Howard, Katie Lynch
Managing Cartographer Shahara Ahmed
Managing Layout Designers Celia Wood, Adam McCrow
Assisting Editors Judith Bamber, Michelle Bennett, Gabrielle Stefanos, Kristin Odjik
Assisting Cartographers Valeska Canas, Tony Fanhkauser
Cover Designer Pepi Bluck
Language Content Coordinator Quentin Frayne
Project Manager Chris Love

Thanks to Sasha Baskett, Melanie Dankel, Sin Choo, Helen Christinis, Rebecca Davey, Justin Flynn, Jennifer Garrett, Laura Jane, Lisa Knights, Rebecca Lalor, John Mazzocchi, Raphael Richards, Sarah Sloane

THANKS
MARY FITZPATRICK

Many people helped me with researching this edition. In particular, I'd like to thank Pascali M. Lubuva in Kolo; Lucy Fitzjohn; Hildegard Vogt and family in Lindi; Daniela Scheubeck and Stefan Summerer; Mr Bukagire Sospeter of Benaco for his helpful letter; Zabron 'Solloo' Tweve at Kitulo National Park; Tim Davenport; 'Masasi Chris'; and, Karen and Nathan Rasmussen in Kigoma. A huge thanks to Rick for his unceasing support, encouragement and enthusiasm. The biggest thanks of all goes to Christopher, who walked the streets of Kigoma with me, carrying a stick just in case we met any lions, who helped me find new hiking routes around Lushoto and discerningly cast his vote for Tanzania's best beach (Matemwe on Zanzibar), who in countless towns suggested streets to check out 'just in case there's a new hotel' (which there often was....), who rarely complained, and who with his wonderful sense of humour and patience was the best travel companion ever.

THE LONELY PLANET STORY

Fresh from an epic journey across Europe, Asia and Australia in 1972, Tony and Maureen Wheeler sat at their kitchen table stapling together notes. The first Lonely Planet guidebook, *Across Asia on the Cheap,* was born.

Travellers snapped up the guides. Inspired by their success, the Wheelers began publishing books to Southeast Asia, India and beyond. Demand was prodigious, and the Wheelers expanded the business rapidly to keep up. Over the years, Lonely Planet extended its coverage to every country and into the virtual world via lonelyplanet.com and the Thorn Tree message board.

As Lonely Planet became a globally loved brand, Tony and Maureen received several offers for the company. But it wasn't until 2007 that they found a partner whom they trusted to remain true to the company's principles of travelling widely, treading lightly and giving sustainably. In October of that year, BBC Worldwide acquired a 75% share in the company, pledging to uphold Lonely Planet's commitment to independent travel, trustworthy advice and editorial independence.

Today, Lonely Planet has offices in Melbourne, London and Oakland, with over 500 staff members and 300 authors. Tony and Maureen are still actively involved with Lonely Planet. They're travelling more often than ever, and they're devoting their spare time to charitable projects. And the company is still driven by the philosophy of *Across Asia on the Cheap*: 'All you've got to do is decide to go and the hardest part is over. So go!'

OUR READERS

Many thanks to the travellers who used the last edition and wrote to us with helpful hints, useful advice and interesting anecdotes:

A Isis Amitirigala, Michael Andersen, Siena Anstis, Andy Art, Kristen Austin, Alessandro Azzoni **B** Tanja Baar, Fritz Balletshofer, Oliver Balmer, Penny Barten, Tracy E Bartley, Sylvia Basten, Paulo Bastos, Melissa Bates, Jackie Beare, Abbey Beck, Farzaneh Behroozi, Claudia Bell, Ellinor Bengtsson, Wihelmine Bennett, Björn Bergman, Rik Blondeel, Marije Boot, Alex Bowles, Mark Boyd, Joan Bressendorff, Tim Briggs, Barbara Brighouse, Louise Brorstrom, Caroline Brown, Hans De Bruijn, Anna Bryant, Sussy Bullock, Kim Burgon, Josh Busby, Elke Busch **C** Burel Camille, Francis Carlisle-Kitz, Linda Chambers, Samantha Chande, Matt Chessum, Francesca Chiellini, Lisa Christensen, Jm Le Clement, Donna Corcoran, Oliver Craig, Tracy Crawford, Riva Cristina, Ee & Erwin Crovetto **D** Tara Daley, Boris Delaine, Caroline Dessing, Tammy Dong, Melinda Downey, Brid Doyle, Rosalía Díaz **E** Ben Edwards **F** Candida Fawcett, Christian Fleck, Aaron Flint, Nynke Fortuin, Zoe Fox, Theresa Foy, Rob Franklin, Göran Frisk, Christl Fuchslechner **G** R J Gardner, Yannick Gareau, Bronwen Gill, Joerg Glaser, Rachel Godley, Sharira Gonzalez, Jan Goossens, Rosalind Gordon, Walter Gostner, Matthew Greene, Tanja Gyldengren **H** Ines Hackbusch, Andreas Jacob Hansen, Mette Hansen, Claudia Hauser, Harold Hedin, Oliver Henke, Marybeth Holleman, Roelof Horn, Pascalle Hovingh, Gethin Howells, Chris Hughes **J** Hemmy Jackson, Hilde Jakobsen, Anders Jeppsson, Andy Jonston **K** Michiel Kamma, Jennifer Kerkhoff, Glynny Kieser, Eliane Kingswood, Richard Knight, Maarten Kockelkoren, Niels Kramer, Mateja Krivec, Dietmar Krumpl, Peter Kuis, Daniel Kunzler, Ibrahim Kyaruzi **L** Tom Laing, Birthe Larisch, Dyveke Larsen, Marjolein Leguijt, Leina Lemomo, Lisa Linpower **M** Margarita Mahindi, Christine Mannetta, Chris Manuel, Dona Mariano, Colin Martin, Joanna Martin, Marian Martin, George Mcdonald, Judi Mcdonald, Valerie Mcgivern, Monica Meling, Christina Mermiga, Olivia Mirodone, Doto Mkanzabi, Sheedeh Moayery, Jesper Mogensen, Annette Mollel, Cara Moody **N** Guus Nellen, Trang Nguyen, Jan Nicholas, Mads Nielsen, Jennifer Nikerle **O** Frank O'Brien, Kevin O'Connor, Helena Olsson, Jasper Oostland, Stefanie Opper, Norm Orava, Alvaro Orrantia, Heather Osborn **P** Sue Pacey, Patrycja Pajak, Mari & Frank Passoudis, Inge Tornbjerg Pedersen, Bookey Peek, Simone Pereira, David Peterka, Mary Wickler Peterson, Cesar Piotlo, Cornelis Potgieter, Anna Ptaszynska, Helen Pugh, Beatrice Puyo **R** John Ragatz, Mary Ralston, Sanjay Ranchod, Wolfgang Renner, Paul Richards, Raphael Richards, Martin Rievers, Monica Rosati, Nicolas Rouquette, Kristen Rupp **S** Gabbriela Sabados, Chris Sanders, Gail Sasse, Hanno Schaefer, Peter Schuppli, Mark Schwabacher, Rejean Sevigny, Anna Shah, M T Shea, Chiaki Shiga, Kerry Shilling, Tony Shilling, Gwen Spencer, Rick Steiner, Margrethe Stensland, Ros Stow, Alison Stretton, Peter Susan, Therese Svensson, Carol Swift **T** David Taylor, Susie Thomas, Richard Thompson, V Thorburn, Tabitha Tuckett **V** Vanessa van Bongarcon, Monique Der van Mey, Willemijn Der van Stouw, Zyl De van Villiers, Joane Vincent, Katrine Vinther, Roland De Vlam, Inge Vreeke, Paul De Vries, Wendy De Vries **W** Rebecca Walser, Katie Walsh, Carolyn Waltenberg, Sheldon & Gudrun Weeks, Gary Wertheimer, Marijke Wevers, Denise Wielgosz, Hannah Williams, Kathleen & Terry Williams, Terence Wong **Z** Josh Zuker

ACKNOWLEDGMENTS

Many thanks to the following for the use of their content:

Globe on title page ©Mountain High Maps 1993 Digital Wisdom, Inc.

Internal photographs p69 by David Boag/Alamy; p61, p67 Danita Delimont/Alamy; p61 Arco Images/Alamy; p68 Martin Harvey/NHPA, p71 Mike Lane/Alamy; p72 AfriPics.com/Alamy; p60 Adam Seward/Alamy; p67 Ariadne Van Zandbergen/Alamy. All other photographs by Lonely Planet Images, and by Judy Bellah p72 (#2); Tom Cockrem p58 (#2); Alex Dissanayake p58 (#1); Jason Edwards p58 (#4), p69 (#3); Dave Hamman p66 (#1); AB Images p62 (#1); Mitch Reardon p63 (#3); Oliver Strewe p63 (#2); David Wall p71 (#2); Ariadne Van Zandbergen p57, p59 (#3), p60 (#1), p62 (#4), p64 (#3), p65 (#2), p66 (#4), p68 (#4), p69 (#1), p70 (#1).

All images are the copyright of the photographers unless otherwise indicated. Many of the images in this guide are available for licensing from Lonely Planet Images: www.lonelyplanetimages.com.

SEND US YOUR FEEDBACK

We love to hear from travellers – your comments keep us on our toes and help make our books better. Our well-travelled team reads every word on what you loved or loathed about this book. Although we cannot reply individually to postal submissions, we always guarantee that your feedback goes straight to the appropriate authors, in time for the next edition. Each person who sends us information is thanked in the next edition – and the most useful submissions are rewarded with a free book.

To send us your updates – and find out about Lonely Planet events, newsletters and travelnews–visitouraward-winningwebsite: **www.lonelyplanet.com/contact.**

Note: we may edit, reproduce and incorporate your comments in Lonely Planet products such as guidebooks, websites and digital products, so let us know if you don't want your comments reproduced or your name acknowledged. For a copy of our privacy policy visit www.lonelyplanet.com/privacy.

Index

INDEX

INDEX

GreenDex

It seems like everyone's going green these days, but how can you know which businesses are actually eco-friendly and which are simply jumping on the sustainable-travel bandwagon?

The following attractions, tours and accommodation choices have been selected by the author because they demonstrate an active sustainable-tourism policy. Some are involved in environmental or wildlife protection, and many are community-owned or make a point of employing local people, thereby maintaining and preserving local identity and culture, and alleviating poverty.

We want to keep developing our sustainable-tourism content. If you think we've omitted someone who should be listed here, or if you disagree with our choices, email us at talk2us@lonelyplanet.com.au and set us straight for next time. For more information about sustainable tourism and Lonely Planet, see www.lonelyplanet.com/responsibletravel.

MAP LEGEND

ROUTES

Primary		Mall/Steps	
Secondary		Tunnel	
Tertiary		Walking Tour	
Lane		Walking Tour Detour	
Under Construction		Walking Trail	
Unsealed Road		Walking Path	
One-Way Street		Track	

TRANSPORT

Ferry		Rail	
Bus Route			

HYDROGRAPHY

River, Creek		Water	
Intermittent River		Lake (Dry)	
Swamp		Lake (Salt)	
Reef		Mudflats	

BOUNDARIES

International		Regional, Suburb	
State, Provincial		Ancient Wall	
Marine Park		Cliff	

AREA FEATURES

Airport		Land	
Area of Interest		Mall	
Beach, Desert		Market	
Building		Park	
Campus		Rocks	
Cemetery, Christian		Sports	
Cemetery, Other		Urban	
Forest			

POPULATION

CAPITAL (NATIONAL)		CAPITAL (STATE)
Large City		Medium City
Small City		Town, Village

SYMBOLS

Sights/Activities
Beach
Christian
Hindu
Islamic
Monument
Museum, Gallery
Point of Interest
Pool
Ruin
Trail Head
Zoo, Bird Sanctuary

Eating
Eating

Drinking
Drinking
Café

Entertainment
Entertainment

Shopping
Shopping

Sleeping
Sleeping
Camping

Transport
Airport, Airfield
Border Crossing
Bus Station
General Transport
Parking Area
Petrol Station
Taxi Rank

Information
Bank, ATM
Embassy/Consulate
Hospital, Medical
Information
Internet Facilities
Police Station
Post Office, GPO
Telephone
Toilets

Geographic
Lighthouse
Lookout
Mountain, Volcano
National Park
Oasis
Pass, Canyon
Picnic Area
River Flow
Shelter, Hut
Waterfall

LONELY PLANET OFFICES

Australia
Head Office
Locked Bag 1, Footscray, Victoria 3011
☎ 03 8379 8000, fax 03 8379 8111
talk2us@lonelyplanet.com.au

USA
150 Linden St, Oakland, CA 94607
☎ 510 893 8555, toll free 800 275 8555
fax 510 893 8572
info@lonelyplanet.com

UK
2nd Floor, 186 City Rd,
London EC1V 2NT
☎ 020 7106 2100, fax 020 7106 2101
go@lonelyplanet.co.uk

Published by Lonely Planet Publications Pty Ltd
ABN 36 005 607 983

© Lonely Planet Publications Pty Ltd 2008

© photographers as indicated 2008

Cover photograph: African elephants with trunks entwined, Serengeti National Park, Tanzania, Anup Shah/Nature PL.

Many of the images in this guide are available for licensing from Lonely Planet Images: www.lonelyplanetimages.com.

Printed by Hang Tai Printing Company.
Printed in China.